Producing

VEGETABLE CROPS

George W. Ware

U.S. Department of Agriculture, Retired;
Formerly, in Charge,
Fruit and Truck Branch Experiment Station,
University of Arkansas

Producing

J. P. McCollum

Professor of Plant Physiology, Emeritus,
College of Agriculture,
University of Illinois

VEGETABLE CROPS ———

**The Interstate
Printers & Publishers, Inc.**

Danville, Illinois

Library of Congress Catalog Card No. 79-87467

ISBN 0-8134-2083-0

FOREWORD

The continuous supply of fresh and processed vegetables on the markets of the United States indicates the tremendous economic importance of the vegetable industry and the contribution of vegetables to the dietary requirements of the people. With expected increases in population, it is safe to predict that vegetable crops will continue to comprise a major segment of the agricultural economy.

Producing Vegetable Crops deals with the principles, economics, and production practices of vegetable growing. It is a practical and down-to-earth guide for the operating vegetable grower and is also widely used as a text in horticulture and vegetable courses. This revised edition will be helpful to anyone seeking guidance in developing and conducting profitable vegetable-growing enterprises.

In preparing this book, the authors have made use of information obtained through studies and research carried on by agricultural colleges and experiment stations, processors, and merchants, as well as practices followed by successful growers. The presentation is made by combining the text with supporting charts, maps, tables, and illustrations in a unique and interesting fashion. As a result, the book contains reliable, current information which has general application to all vegetable-growing regions of the United States.

The authors of *Producing Vegetable Crops* are well qualified through years of extensive studies, research, and production experience to write on the subject. They are also familiar with the "action" method of teaching and have presented the contents in a manner which will have the greatest impact upon those who use the book.

George W. Ware, an agricultural graduate of the University of Arkansas, has spent his professional years in agricultural teaching, extension, research, and administration. For sixteen years he was in charge of the University of Arkansas Fruit and Truck Branch Experiment Station, specializing in fruit and vegetable research. With a master's degree in vegetable crops from Cornell University, he wrote the popular textbook *Southern Vegetable Crops* and co-authored *Raising Vegetables*, both of which were used extensively. Mr. Ware has also served the U.S. Government in Europe, South America, Africa, and the Far East as an agriculturist in several important posts. With these experiences, he has had an unusual opportunity to study and observe the domestic and international importance of vegetables.

J. P. McCollum is one of the nation's recognized authorities in the field of vegetable crops. He has had extensive experience and training in this field. Professor McCollum holds a B.S. degree in horticulture from the Oklahoma State University and a Ph.D. degree with a major in vegetable crops from Cornell University. For many years he was engaged in teaching and research in the Division of Vegetable Crops at the University of Illinois. In addition, he has worked with vegetables in some of the intensive vegetable-growing regions of New York, Florida, and Illinois. His research experience includes investigations of factors affecting fruit development, ascorbic acid, carotenoids, and other constituents of quality. He co-authored *Raising Vegetables* and has also conducted research on seed problems, asparagus production, and soil fertility. Professor McCollum is indeed well qualified to play an important role in the production of this book.

Contacts with students, colleges and experiment stations, professional workers, seed breeders, growers, food processors, and handlers of fresh produce throughout the country reveal the need for a convenient up-to-date manual on the production, handling, and marketing of vegetable crops. It is believed that this book, *Producing Vegetable Crops*, will fill that need.

Gene Bottoms

Executive Director
American Vocational Association
Washington, D.C.

David W. Davis

Professor
Department of Horticultural Science
and Landscaping
University of Minnesota
St. Paul

Floyd F. Hedlund

Director
Fruit and Vegetable Division, AMS
U.S. Department of Agriculture
Washington, D.C.

Charles E. Magoon

Director of Research
United Fresh Fruit and
Vegetable Association
Alexandria, Virginia

Joe McFerran

Professor
Department of Horticulture and Forestry
University of Arkansas
Fayetteville

Joseph S Vandemark

Professor of Vegetable Crops
Department of Horticulture
University of Illinois
Urbana

George W. Ware, Jr.

Professor and Head
Department of Entomology
University of Arizona
Tucson

Orvin L. Wilhite

Chief
Agricultural Division
Bureau of the Census
Suitland, Maryland

PREFACE

The principles of vegetable growing are generally applicable, but production practices may vary materially in different sections of the country, depending upon economic, environmental, and edaphic factors.

Section One, containing Chapters 1 through 13, deals with basic information and fundamental "principles." The information presented is generally applicable to all sections of the country. Section Two, embracing Chapters 14 through 34, discusses special crop production "practices" in the regions where the respective crops are grown.

The production practices are discussed in order of seasonal sequence in the vegetable chapters. The action idea prevails in spirit, arrangement, and content. The latest results of the agricultural experiment stations are incorporated and interpreted in the light of experience. The student or grower may adapt the general information to his own needs.

The purpose of this book is to give reliable, complete, coordinated, up-to-date information on the various phases of vegetable growing in the most systematic and convenient manner.

The chapters are complete in themselves, but cross references are made to avoid repetition and to supply additional information. A brief glossary, including the most difficult words, precedes the index.

It is suggested that the reader, when using this book, study the chapters dealing with principles in connection with each production job as it is discussed. Teachers will find it helpful to assign pertinent parts of the general chapters on principles along with corresponding production practices in the crop chapters. Questions and problems have been omitted, as no set list will satisfy a large number of instructors or students under the existing widely different conditions.

The authors wish to express their appreciation to the many research workers, teachers, students, growers, and handlers for their valuable information and suggestions which were used generously in the contents and arrangement of this book.

Credit is due the U.S. Department of Agriculture, state experiment stations, and private establishments for photographs, charts, and related materials. Their aid made it possible to present a comprehensive view of the vegetable industry, and the text is abundantly documented with the latest tabular and graphic information on the different vegetables. Data on the harvest seasons, acreages, yields, unit prices, and values of the principal vegetable crops were taken from official reports of the Statistical Reporting Service of the U.S. Department of Agriculture, and these are gratefully acknowledged.

The authors are especially indebted for contributions by Dr. A. E. Thompson to Chapters 4, 5, 20, 21, 23, 27, 28, and 32; by Dr. George W. Ware, Jr., to Chapter 11; and by Dr. M. R. Fontes to Chapter 33. Appreciation is also expressed to Dorothy Ware and Vashti McCollum for proofreading and editing.

George W. Ware   *J. P. McCollum*

Cover design by
WILLIAM SILHAN

CONTENTS

SECTION TWO: PRACTICES

Section One

PRINCIPLES

INTRODUCTION TO SECTION ONE

The first thirteen chapters in Section One deal with the "principles" of plant growth and general information on vegetable production, handling, and marketing. The object of this section is to provide scientific information as a foundation for studying subsequent Chapters 14 through 34 of Section Two, which discuss the various production "practices" required in growing and marketing individual vegetable crops.

Some of the chapters, such as "Vegetable Breeding and Improvement," "Classification of Vegetables," and "Plant Growth and Development," may not appeal to the practical person, but they give a more thorough understanding of vegetables, and help one to see and meet production problems in the most scientific manner.

Chapters 5 through 13 discuss general principles of the various operations involved in vegetable production. The purpose of these discussions is not to give specific instructions in the production of any particular vegetable but to present general information which will help one to understand and carry out the specific practices contained in the crop chapters, 14 through 34, of Section Two.

A list of "Selected References" appears at the end of each chapter for the convenience of the reader in obtaining additional information on specific subjects.

CHAPTER 1

The Vegetable Industry

Although vegetables occupy less than 1.5 percent of all cropland in the United States, they account for 8.6 percent of the value of all fruit, vegetable, and field crops (Table 1.1). Commercial vegetable production has developed into a highly mechanized-computerized industry requiring special managerial and technical skills to meet the competition of other foods. Never before have people been so well fed by so few farmers as in this country today.

Vegetable production is a dynamic $4.7 billion industry which contributes substantially to the nation's economy and general welfare of its 225 million inhabitants. It is a part of the United States' unmatched, flexible food production system which has the potential to meet changing food demands at home and abroad.

American farmers are now producing two-thirds more per man-hour than in 1960, and six times more than in 1930—on considerably less acreage. In 1930, only 10 persons were supplied farm products by one farm worker. With improved management, technology, machines, and materials, 21 consumers were supplied farm products per farm worker in 1960. This number increased astronomically to more than 57 in 1977, and more and more persons are expected to be fed by one farm worker in the future. Correspondingly, vegetable output, per man-hour, has shown spectacular gains in recent years (see Table 1.6).

Although vegetable growing may appear dynamic, glamorous, and lucrative in some respects, it is a highly competitive, speculative endeavor. Hard work, skillful management, expensive machines, and special skills and aptitudes are required for success. The readers of this book deserve a broad view of this important segment of our national life—both its technical and economic aspects. The authors, thereby, endeavor to present herein a comprehensive picture of the history, development, and magnitude of the vegetable industry.

Historical

The growing of vegetables has been practiced for centuries in the civilized countries. Some kinds of vegetables were used for medicinal purposes long before they became important food crops after many years of plant improvement.

The American colonial families were largely self-supporting, growing vegetables for a part of their food supply. With the industrial expansion which began about 1865, a marked change in vegetable growing took place. Concentrated populations became largely dependent upon special producers for their food supply, and as a result, commercial production of vegetables developed near population centers. This practice persisted from Civil War days until about 1910. Since then, vegetables have been produced commercially to a large extent in distant, specially adapted areas having favorable climate and the advantages of labor supply and season.

For a period following 1920, vegetable production increased more rapidly than any other type of crop production. This was due to improved facilities for production, processing, and distribution; educational and promotional programs dealing with the importance of vegetables in the diet; and rising purchasing power and changing food habits. In response to consumer demand, a large variety of fresh vegetables became available throughout the year. In recent years, vegetable production has increased at about the same rate as population expansion. This trend may be expected to continue in the future.

Types of Vegetable Growing

The several types of vegetable growing, some of which have been developed as a result of changing economic and social conditions, are briefly discussed here.

HOME GARDENING. In colonial days, the home garden was the principal source of the fresh food supply for a large part of the population. Today, the importance of the city, suburban, and farm home gardens as a factor in the total production of vegetables cannot be overemphasized. This type of vegetable production is discussed fully in Chapter 34.

MARKET GARDENING. As the cities became larger and more congested, residents of the outskirts increased their production and peddled the surplus to those living in the more fully occupied areas. This gave rise to the market-gardening industry, which has for its objective the production of an assortment of vegetables for home market. Most markets, particularly the large ones, are no longer local. The market gardeners, who originally grew a large variety of vegetables under intensive and very expensive conditions, have been forced to change their types of farming to meet competition from specially adapted distant areas. These gardeners no longer grow many kinds of vegetables, but are necessarily confined to producing those which can be most profitably grown to supply or supplement the demand in their respective localities.

COMMERCIAL PRODUCTION. Increased demand for vegetables throughout the year, rapid transportation, and uniform refrigeration facilities led to the production of special crops in relatively large quantities for distant markets. Commercial vegetable growing is more extensive and specialized than market gardening, and the location of producing regions is determined primarily by climatic factors and soils favoring the culture of special crops. Since 1910, large areas for vegetable production in the West, South, and Southwest have been developed, as shown in Figure 1.2 and Table 1.2.

PRODUCTION FOR PROCESSING. Although California, Wisconsin, Minnesota, Oregon, and Washington lead in the production of canned and frozen vegetables, this industry is scattered over a large part of the United States. Vegetables for processing are usually produced on a more extensive scale than those grown for market, and are frequently grown in rotation with farm crops. Because of the necessity of low-cost production, the industry has sought areas of favorable climate and lower costs. As a rule, processors contract for tonnage, with certain limitations on quality, at a figure lower than the market price for fresh vegetables. Primarily because of the convenience and economy of processed vegetables, the market demand for them has increased much faster than the demand for fresh vegetables. (See Fig. 1.4 and Table 1.5).

VEGETABLE FORCING. Vegetable forcing, the production of vegetables out of their normal season, is accomplished by heat or protection from cold. Greenhouses are largely employed in the North, while cold frames are used to a considerable extent in the South.

CONTROLLED-ENVIRONMENT AGRICULTURE. Controlled-environment agriculture is a total concept of modifying the natural environment for
optimum plant growth. Control of air, light, temperature, humidity,
composition of atmosphere, and nutrients make it possible to grow some
vegetables at any time anywhere. This method of production is gaining
in importance throughout the world. By 1974, more than 850 acres of
greenhouses or other protective coverage were utilized in the United
States alone. These facilities were used primarily for producing tomatoes,
lettuce, and cucumbers. This process of culture is discussed fully in
Chapter 33, and acreage and value are shown in Table 33.1.

VEGETABLE SEED PRODUCTION. The production of vegetable seed is a
rather specialized industry carried on in regions where climatic conditions
are favorable to seed production and curing (Fig. 5.2). While most
vegetable growers should not attempt to grow seed, they should know
something of the problems involved in seed production and handling.
These subjects are discussed in Chapters 4 and 5.

PHYSICAL FACTORS AND REQUIREMENTS

Climatic Requirements

Climate is the most important limiting factor in the commercial production of vegetables at long distances from the market. The principal
vegetable-growing regions of the country have developed as a result of
climatic conditions favorable to certain crops during the season in which
they are grown. Now that transportation is generally available to all
regions of the country, it is possible to grow any particular vegetable in
any area which is best suited to it.

Of the climatic factors, temperature is generally the most important
in determining the localization of vegetable-growing areas. Atmospheric
humidity is also very important for some crops. For example, muskmelons
are grown extensively in those areas where temperatures are high and
humidity is low. Rainfall is very important for the production of all vegetable crops except where irrigation is used.

Thompson and Kelley, in *Vegetable Crops,* state as follows: "Nearly
all the important vegetable-growing regions of the South and parts of
California, and the Southwest are important because the climate of those
regions permits production during winter and spring when other regions
cannot produce vegetables. In fact, these regions have become important

in spite of transportation handicaps in the form of long hauls and high cost of transportation. While good refrigerator car service and good railroads make it possible for the Imperial Valley of California to be an important lettuce and muskmelon center, no one would produce these crops there because of these factors alone, for regions nearer the important markets have as good transportation facilities with shorter hauls and lower costs. All vegetable regions located at long distances from market are important primarily because of suitable climatic conditions for the production of the crop or crops at the time they are grown. For example, the Imperial Valley produces lettuce during the winter when the climate is satisfactory for the crop and muskmelons in the spring and summer when the hot, dry weather is favorable for the growth and ripening of this crop. The area around Salinas, California, is the most important summer lettuce-producing region of the United States primarily because of the relatively low summer temperatures. In spite of high transportation costs, these regions and a few others in the West now control the lettuce market in the large cities of the Middlewest and East."

Soil Requirements

While climate largely determines the vegetable-growing regions, soil character is an important factor in selecting specific locations. Since soil requirements vary somewhat for different kinds of vegetables, the selection of the type of soil which is best suited to the crop or crops is important. Soil preference for different crops is discussed generally in Chapter 6, and in the chapters on specific crops.

Transportation Requirements

The earliest development of commercial vegetable production in the South and some other areas was confined to places which provided waterways for boat transportation to the major markets. This naturally restricted the kinds of vegetables and the flexibility of supply. Railroads delivered the bulk of the produce for many years. With the introduction of commercial refrigeration in 1886 and the subsequent development of the refrigerator car, vegetable production spread to distant areas providing the most suitable climatic conditions.

Improved farm-to-market roads and the subsequent development of superhighways introduced the motor truck as the major means of transportation. With the improvement of the size, speed, and refrigeration of trucks, this means of transporting vegetables to market has continued to

Fig. 1.1—Fresh sweet corn shipped in refrigerator truck.

USDA Photograph

increase with resulting economy and promptness of delivery. Further improvement of roads, fast refrigerator trucks, improved rail transportation, refrigerated boats, and the development of more economical air transportation will continue to stimulate vegetable growing in the areas with the most favorable growing conditions. The transportation of vegetables is discussed fully in Chapter 13.

OTHER FACTORS AND REQUIREMENTS

The Personal Factor

Successful vegetable farming depends to a considerable extent on the aptitude of the individual producer. Some farmers adapt themselves easily to vegetable growing, while others are slow to adjust themselves to such a type of farming. For example, many farmers do not like to produce vegetables, and they have little patience with the exacting requirements of intensive vegetable production, preferring to grow a crop that has a wider planting and harvesting range. Where the farms are large enough, many growers prefer to raise crops that can be handled entirely by machinery instead of growing vegetables which give higher returns per acre but require more hand labor.

Economic Difference Between Vegetable and Fruit Growing

Observers generally appreciate the fact that the requirements of horticultural crops are considerably different from those of field crops or livestock farming. There are also several essential differences between the vegetable and fruit industries which should be called to the attention of the reader.

1. Vegetable production does not ordinarily involve a long-time investment as does an orchard, and the vegetable grower is not bound to produce the same crop each year.
2. Many vegetable areas, particularly those in the process of development and exploitation, lack the stability of the orchard district which was methodically developed over a period of years. Getting into fruit growing is a slow process, and getting out may be even slower.
3. Since the problem of financing a vegetable crop is largely an annual one, tenants can be used, whereas few orchardists are willing to turn over their growing or bearing trees to temporary operators.
4. Co-operative effort and organization are somewhat more difficult among vegetable producers than fruit growers. Orchardists have

years for making permanent plans and perfecting an organization, whereas vegetable "deals" come and go, and growers are
often disappointed.

5. Vegetable farming may be promoted and financed by dealers or
commission men, and production is determined accordingly. Fruit
growers are usually more independent and are more able to secure
long-term credit.

6. The acreage and resulting production of vegetable crops are
flexible, responding easily to promotion, enthusiasm, or price outlook, whereas the fruit industry is slowly adjustable.

7. Vegetable crops may be grown by farmers with limited experience, and as a result, frequent failures occur. If the fruit grower
develops his own orchard, he is likely to be generally acquainted
with the industry by the time his trees start bearing.

From the contrasts mentioned, one may infer that the vegetable industry is generally unstable and comparatively undesirable. This is not
necessarily the case, as many permanent, well organized, vegetable-
producing areas have been established throughout the country.

SCOPE AND IMPORTANCE

An Extensive Major Industry

The vegetable industry contributes heavily to the national economy.
In addition to the farmer's role, many businesses and millions of people
are involved in processing, transporting, and marketing; and in manufacturing and supplying machines, seeds, fertilizers, pesticides, herbicides,
packages, and related materials. Extensive educational, supply, and maintenance services are necessarily associated with the physical requirements
of this dynamic industry.

The present outlook indicates that the vegetable industry should
continue to be an important and comparatively profitable branch of agriculture. With increasing competition, the industry will profit by reducing
the cost of production and marketing. This can be accomplished by growing improved varieties, using fertilizers judiciously, practicing effective
pest control, supplementing cultivation with herbicides, managing labor
more efficiently, utilizing mechanical harvesters and other labor-saving
devices where possible, and by adopting improved marketing methods.

Acreage and Value

Vegetables as a group constitute an important segment of American agriculture, accounting for approximately 9 percent in value of all crops in 1977. The annual farm value of the principal vegetable crops, including potatoes and sweet potatoes, has averaged above $1.5 billion since 1945 and attained a level of $4,614,000 in 1977. Table 1.1 shows the relative acreage and value of vegetables in comparison with the other principal crops. The commercial values presented in this table do not include the products from gardens and the minor vegetable crops, the value of which is estimated to approximate a billion dollars.

Table 1.1—Area Harvested and Value of Principal Crops Grown in the United States 1957, 1967, and 1977.

Major Crops	1957		1967		1977	
	Acres, 1,000	Value, $ Million	Acres, 1,000	Value, $ Million	Acres, 1,000	Value, $ Million
Total vegetables, melons, and potatoes	5,311	1,679	5,165	2,309	4,673	4,674
Vegetables and melons	3,678	1,136	3,565	1,681	3,202	3,290
Potatoes	1,359	467	1,460	568	1,359	1,254
Sweet potatoes	274	76	140	60	112	130
Fruits, nuts, and berries	2,995	1,230	3,032	1,756	3,467	4,145
Corn for grain	63,065	3,806	60,694	5,044	70,006	12,887
Wheat	43,754	1,848	58,353	2,090	66,216	4,677
Soybeans for beans	20,857	1,003	39,805	2,434	57,911	9,945
Cotton	13,558	1,625	7,997	954	13,259	3,569
Tobacco	1,122	936	960	1,316	966	2,236
Rice	1,340	220	1,970	444	2,249	936
Other major crops*	151,499	4,542	111,366	5,449	106,873	11,322
Total all crops	303,501	16,889	289,342	21,796	325,620	54,391

*Sorghum grain, oats, barley, rye, flaxseed, sunflower seed, peanuts, all hay, dry peas, suger beets, sugarcane, popcorn, and dry edible beans.

Tables showing acreage, yield, production, unit price, and value of principal vegetable crops by important states are provided in individual vegetable chapters in Section Two.

Data in this table are from USDA, ESCS–Statistics, Crop Reporting Board.

Principal Areas of Production; Values and Trends

Due primarily to the increase in out-of-season vegetables, production has shifted to and expanded particularly in the West, South, and Southwest. Figure 1.2 shows the approximate acreage distribution and corresponding farm value of commercial vegetables, excluding potatoes and sweet potatoes. Figure 1.4 shows the production trends of fresh and processed vegetables between 1965 and 1977.

Fig. 1.2—Acreage, distribution, production, and value of the 22 principal commercial vegetables (excluding potatoes and sweet potatoes).

UNITED STATES TOTAL

Year	Acreage	Production in Tons	Value, $1,000
1949	3,852,770	297,438	874,674
1959	3,433,840	345,147	1,084,052
1969	3,333,050	409,744	1,695,655
1977	3,202,800	438,150	3,290,000

Table 1.2 ranks the relative importance of the leading states in the production of the 22 principal fresh and processed vegetables in 1977 and shows the corresponding value of each crop. California accounts for 46.5 percent of the estimated $3,290,000 total value of these vegetables which exclude potatoes, sweet potatoes, and some minor vegetables. Florida ranks second with 12.9 percent of the total value, followed by Texas with 7.2 percent, New York with 3.6 percent, Michigan with 3.3 percent, and Arizona with 3.0 percent. Because of the relatively high- or low-unit values of different vegetables, some states have large acreages with comparatively low value.

Relative Importance of Commercial Vegetables

The acreage and value of vegetable crops change primarily according to the increasing population, changing food habits, and corresponding demand. Table 1.3 shows some of these fluctuations and trends since 1957.

Table 1.2—Principal Vegetables for Fresh Market and Processing:
Estimated Harvested Acreage, Production, and Value by
Leading States, 1977.* (Ranked according to total
acreage by states.)

| State | Harvested Acreage, 1,000 Acres | | | Production | | Value, $1,000,000 | | |
	Fresh Market	Processed	Total	Fresh Market, 1,000 Cwt.	Processed, 1,000 Tons	Fresh Market	Processed	Total
California	526.7	330.3	857.0	108.6	6,899.8	1,069.7	461.5	1,531.2
Wisconsin	7.6	331.2	338.8	2.9	1,164.1	14.3	93.6	107.9
Florida	246.5	19.4	265.9	35.5	71.3	414.0	9.6	423.6
Texas	169.8	16.9	186.7	22.9	96.9	228.2	10.0	238.2
Washington	32.5	108.1	140.6	4.9	343.6	39.0	37.5	76.5
New York	64.3	75.6	139.9	11.4	373.8	90.1	27.4	117.5
Oregon	15.8	104.3	120.1	5.5	527.2	26.2	44.5	70.7
Michigan	62.8	50.9	113.7	7.2	237.5	68.4	23.4	91.8
Illinois	10.2	91.8	102.0	0.8	331.4	5.1	29.6	34.7
N. Carolina	41.3	29.6	70.9	2.8	75.3	24.0	9.9	33.9
New Jersey	47.9	14.8	62.7	4.5	147.7	54.5	11.9	66.4
Arizona	58.9	0.6	59.5	11.4	2.1	97.6	0.2	97.8
Ohio	22.1	29.4	51.5	2.4	514.0	22.8	37.9	60.7
S. Carolina	38.5	8.8	47.3	2.7	25.0	19.5	3.5	23.0
Georgia	43.4	3.9	47.3	3.1	8.5	15.4	1.2	16.6
Indiana	11.4	23.4	34.8	1.5	213.2	11.5	14.7	26.2
Pennsylvania	16.6	17.8	34.4	1.5	144.7	11.8	10.2	22.0
Delaware	3.3	30.1	33.4	0.3	48.8	1.3	7.9	9.2
Alabama	25.4	6.9	32.3	1.6	13.0	19.7	2.0	21.7
Virginia	16.5	12.8	29.3	1.2	49.8	13.3	4.7	18.0
Tennessee	5.2	14.9	20.1	0.5	33.9	10.7	4.7	15.4
Mississippi	12.0	3.6	15.6	0.8	8.7	1.7	1.2	2.9
Arkansas	7.4	8.5	15.9	0.6	21.6	7.1	2.2	9.3
New Mexico	7.0	0.9	7.9	1.8	9.9	14.2	0.7	14.9
Other States	74.4	300.2	374.6	12.0	1,225.7	71.3	89.5	160.8
United States	1,567.5	1,634.7	3,202.2	248.4	12,587.5	2,351.4	939.5	3,290.9

*Excludes potatoes, sweet potatoes, and some of the less important vegetables.

Above data from the "Annual Summary of Acreage, Production, and Value of Principal Vegetables" USDA, ESCS–Statistics, Crop Reporting Board, 1978.

Detailed data on acreage, yield, production, unit price, and value of principal vegetable crops are presented by states in the vegetable chapters of Section Two.

The 22 principal vegetables, nine of which are also processed in large quantities, are ranked in descending order by total acreage in the 1977 column while comparative values are shown in the right-hand column of the table.

Potatoes continue to be the leading vegetable in acreage and value, accounting for about 34 percent of the total farm value of all commercial

Table 1.3—Principal Commercial Vegetables for Fresh Market and Processing: Estimated Harvested Acreage and Value in 1957, 1967, and 1977. (Ranked according to total acreage in 1977.)

Principal Crops	Harvested Acreage, 1,000 Acreas			Value, $1,000		
	1957	1967	1977	1957	1967	1977
Potatoes	1,359	1,460	1,359	467,865	567,557	1,253,616
Corn, sweet	194	190	170	49,756	63,852	107,052
Corn, sweet*	442	471	449	30,358	52,541	114,286
Total Corn	636	661	619	80,114	116,393	221,338
Tomatoes	218	148	124	155,723	195,553	407,011
Tomatoes*	304	327	346	83,558	222,061	497,976
Total tomatoes	522	475	470	239,281	417,614	904,987
Peas, green	8	2	NR	2,898	854	NR
Peas, green*	455	458	352	49,918	64,296	100,842
Total Peas	463	460	352	52,816	65,150	100,842
Beans, green	126	98	78	43,177	43,580	60,965
Beans, green*	153	274	258	42,260	64,621	96,128
Total beans	279	372	336	85,437	108,201	157,093
Lettuce	234	221	231	139,271	214,564	424,496
Watermelons	393	273	227	46,418	58,279	89,414
Cucumbers	57	50	52	22,763	31,787	55,402
Cucumbers*	129	156	124	19,981	54,662	79,244
Total cucumbers	186	206	176	42,744	86,449	134,646
Sweet potatoes	274	140	112	75,964	60,412	129,592
Onions	110	103	108	71,688	104,113	203,053
Cabbage	110	100	81	43,438	54,357	165,801
Cabbage*	11	14	10	2,556	4,653	7,065
Total cabbage	121	114	91	45,994	59,010	172,866
Asparagus	156	126	86	38,678	54,336	80,249
Cantaloupes	120	107	80	56,954	78,504	113,991
Broccoli	40	43	71	13,666	24,696	92,748
Carrots	79	81	70	61,069	72,873	141,432
Lima beans	13	11	NR	2,963	3,373	NR
Lima beans*	91	97	60	13,137	20,552	25,426
Total limas	104	108	60	16,100	23,925	25,426
Peppers, green	45	47	56	28,938	45,892	87,294
Cauliflower	33	26	37	16,167	21,447	76,663
Celery	35	33	34	58,413	69,719	140,576
Spinach	29	16	10	9,832	8,651	13,746
Spinach*	33	27	21	5,300	6,337	10,600
Total spinach	62	43	31	15,132	14,988	24,346
Honeydew	9	11	15	6,523	9,186	25,561
Beets	4	3	NR	2,178	1,202	NR
Beets*	17	18	14	3,127	4,226	7,981
Total beets	21	21	14	5,305	5,428	7,981
All vegetables**	5,311	5,165	4,673	1,679,346	2,308,794	4,674,112

*Crops for processing

**Includes the 22 principal vegetables listed above, artichokes, eggplants, escarole-endive, Brussels sprouts, and garlic.

N.R. = Not Reported.

Data from USDA, ESCS–Statistics, Crop Reporting Board.

vegetables in 1977. Tomatoes ranked second in value, accounting for 16 percent, followed by lettuce at 9 percent, and onions at about 4 percent. Consumer preference will no doubt continue to change the relative importance of vegetables and vegetable products.

Principal Vegetable-Producing States

A great majority of the commercial vegetables are grown in a few states. The five leading states in the 1977 production of fresh vegetables and melons in order of total output were California, Florida, Texas, New York, and Michigan. These states accounted for 68 percent of the harvested acreage, 76 percent of the production, and 80 percent of the value of fresh vegetables and melons produced in the nation (Table 1.4).

Table 1.4—Leading Fresh Market Vegetable States in 1977.

	Harvested Acreage		Production		Value	
Rank	State	Percent of Total	State	Percent of Total	State	Percent of Total
1	California	32.7	California	43.0	California	43.8
2	Florida	15.9	Florida	14.6	Florida	18.1
3	Texas	11.0	Texas	9.4	Texas	9.8
4	New York	4.2	Arizona	4.6	Arizona	4.3
5	Michigan	4.1	New York	4.5	New York	4.1
Percent of total		67.9		76.1		80.1

The five leading states for processed vegetables are Wisconsin, California, Minnesota, Washington, and Oregon. These states harvested 61 percent of the acreage with 78 percent of the production and 73 percent of the total value in the United States in 1977. (Table 1.5.)

The information in Tables 1.4 and 1.5, with that presented in Tables 1.1, 1.2, and 1.3, provides a broad overview of the relative importance of vegetables with other crops. Comparisons are also made of the production and value of different vegetables by states.

Trends in Vegetable Consumption

The per capita consumption of commercially produced fresh and processed vegetables combined has increased slowly, with annual fluctuations, from 200 pounds in 1947 to 227 pounds in 1977. During this 30-year

Table 1.5—Leading Processing Vegetable States in 1977.*

	Area Harvested		Production		Value	
Rank	State	Percent of Total	State	Percent of Total	State	Percent of Total
1	Wisconsin	20.3	California	54.8	California	49.1
2	California	20.2	Wisconsin	9.2	Wisconsin	10.0
3	Minnesota	11.7	Minnesota	6.1	Minnesota	5.6
4	Washington	6.6	Oregon	4.2	Oregon	4.7
5	Oregon	6.4	Ohio	4.1	Ohio	4.0
Percent of total		65.2		78.4		73.4

*Lima and snap beans, beets, cabbage, corn, cucumbers, peas, spinach, and tomatoes.

period, fresh vegetable consumption declined from 121 to 101 pounds, while the consumption of processed vegetables (canned and frozen) increased from 79 pounds in 1947 to 126 pounds in 1977. (See Fig. 1.3.)

Of the processed vegetables (canned and frozen), the per capita consumption of canned increased from 73 pounds in 1947 to 105 pounds in 1977. Concurrently, during this 30-year period, frozen vegetable consumption increased from 7 to 21 pounds per capita. Obviously the trend has been to consume more processed and less fresh vegetables. Also the recent tendency has been for consumers of fresh vegetables to eat more in the raw state with less cooking. (See last two paragraphs of page 28.)

THE CHANGING VEGETABLE INDUSTRY

Vegetable production is a dynamic, ever-changing major segment of the American economy. In spite of the great competition among food items and the whims of consumers, the present per capita consumption of vegetables is expected to be maintained at approximately the current level.

Trends in Labor Efficiency

While some labor efficiencies have been achieved, the vegetable industry still has uneven labor requirements throughout the year. From the standpoint of labor, vegetable production is perhaps the most unstable and critical of all farm industries in the United States. The seasonality of growing and harvesting precludes the year-round employment of workers for vegetables only, and critical periods of growing and

VEGETABLE CONSUMPTION PER CAPITA

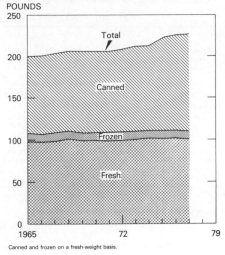

POUNDS

Canned and frozen on a fresh-weight basis.

Vegetable Consumption Per Capita

	1970	1971	1972	1973
	Pounds			
Total consumption	213.4	212.3	216.0	224.1
Fresh[1]	98.8	98.5	99.3	100.6
Frozen[2]	20.6	20.2	20.4	21.9
Canned[2]	94.0	93.6	96.3	101.6

	1974	1975	1976	1977
	Pounds			
Total consumption	224.6	223.8	226.2	227.3
Fresh[1]	102.8	102.1	102.7	101.2
Frozen[2]	20.9	19.8	20.5	21.0
Canned[2]	100.9	101.9	103.0	105.1

[1] Includes dehydrated onions; excludes melons. [2] Fresh-weight basis.

Fig. 1.3—Per capita consumption of fresh and processed vegetables.

USDA, ESCS

harvesting tax the ingenuity of vegetable growers and others involved in this important industry.

In 1956, as many as 445,197 Mexican nationals, commonly known as "Braceros," supplemented the domestic work force. The program was terminated in December 1964, cutting off this source of labor. Since large numbers of domestic laborers were not available, the industry was further spurred in its efforts to mechanize. Also, in a short time, rapid development of the vegetable industry took place in Mexico, especially in the state of Sinaloa. Generally, increasing quantities of winter and spring supplies of tomatoes, peppers, cucumbers, and onions have been coming from this area—in many cases, the result of American capital and management, teamed with Mexican ownership.

The Economics, Statistics, and Cooperatives Service (ESCS) of the U.S. Department of Agriculture points out that areas of vegetable production are scattered from the Gulf Coast and Mexican border northward to Canada. Seasonal progression of production has these areas overlapping in need for workers, and the demand for labor in an area frequently exceeds the supply. Unlike most of the field crops, many vegetables mature unevenly and require frequent repetitive pickings. Many crops are being

PRODUCTION OF FRESH
AND PROCESSED VEGETABLES

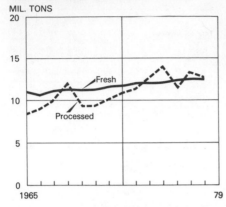

Production of Fresh and Processed Vegetables

	1971	1972	1973	1974
	Million tons			
Total	21.4	22.5	23.3	24.5
Fresh[1]	11.4	11.6	11.9	12.0
Processed	10.0	10.9	11.4	12.5
	1975	1976	1977	1978[2]
	Million tons			
Total	25.9	23.9	25.7	25.1
Fresh[1]	11.9	12.3	12.4	12.5
Processed	14.0	11.6	13.3	12.6

[1] Includes melons. The processing portion of broccoli, carrots, and cauliflower are included with the processing crops beginning in 1972. [2] Estimated.

Fig. 1.4—Relative production of fresh and processed vegetables.

USDA, ESCS

harvested mechanically, but for some vegetables, mechanization of harvesting appears remote, and labor used per acre remains extremely high. In most vegetable areas, there are too few local workers to meet the demand. Producers depend upon the migration of great numbers of workers from one area to another to take care of peak labor requirements during critical production and harvest periods. These are only some of the reasons why vegetable production presents a baffling picture to farmers, economists, labor-placement officials, and others interested in terminating stoop-labor and eliminating the necessity for farm workers to leave home and migrate from one area to another in quest of work.

The application of mechanization to some crops and not to others has produced gaps in the northward sequence of the vegetable harvest requiring additional farm labor. Workers from Texas, for example, now wait for August to harvest pickles in Michigan and Wisconsin, as there is no longer sufficient work after the fresh vegetable harvest is over in the spring and early summer season in Texas. Furthermore, there is a different mix of crops requiring harvest labor now. Most processing vegetables are now mechanically picked. Fresh or processing vegetables which cannot be harvested mechanically may gradually disappear from the market or be produced in outside areas where hand labor is more plentiful and less expensive.

The task of producing vegetables for a growing population with changing food habits is not small. Within this dynamic industry which has experienced increases in acre yields of most vegetables and expanded overall production considerably, what has happened to labor requirements? Has the stoop-labor involved in thinning, weeding, and harvesting continued at the comparatively high level of man-hours required for such operations? Are vegetable crops still produced by hand predominantly; and with increasing yields, are these crops using more labor per acre? The information provided in Table 1.6 reveals that most vegetables enjoyed a remarkable increase in output per man-hour between 1939 and 1959, and considerably more up to 1977.

Comparison of Labor Requirements, by Crops and Years

The overall average labor requirements of growing and harvesting an acre of commercial vegetable crops dropped from approximately 119 man-hours (53 preharvest and 66 harvest) in 1939 to 90 man-hours (31 preharvest and 59 harvest) in 1959. During this 20-year period, labor requirements for fresh market vegetables declined from 147 man-hours (66 preharvest and 81 harvest) in 1939 to 112 man-hours (43 preharvest and 69 harvest) in 1959. Vegetables grown for processing required an average of 73 man-hours per acre (31 preharvest and 42 harvest) in 1939, and this figure decreased to 63 man-hours (16 preharvest and 47 harvest) in 1959. More dramatic increases in man-hour output were made between 1959 and 1977 as shown in Table 1.6.

The Economics, Statistics, and Cooperatives Service (ESCS) of the U.S. Department of Agriculture reported that up to 1964, the fresh market vegetables registering the greatest gains in efficiency of labor were spinach, carrots, onions, beets, and garlic. For each of these crops, output per man-hour more than doubled from 1939 to 1959 and increased substantially thereafter. Spinach experienced the greatest increase in labor efficiency during that period. Operations performed in growing most vegetables have changed materially in the past 38 years as shown in the 1939-1977 man-hour output increases (Table 1.6). Preharvest labor has dropped sharply, largely as a result of precision planting and the application of selective herbicides. The former has eliminated the need for hand thinning, and the latter has eliminated the need for hand hoeing and weeding. Harvest labor declined dramatically, while yields have increased substantially. Spinach harvesting in 1939 was performed entirely by hand, with workers cutting and packing leaves into baskets. Virtually the entire fresh market crop was mechanically harvested as early as 1959.

Beans, potatoes, corn, carrots, and sweet potatoes experienced tremendous declines in preharvest labor per acre. Selective herbicides are providing effective weed control and eliminating the costly, repetitive hand weeding and hoeing operations which were commonly performed in 1939. Precision planters are especially helpful in reducing the labor required in thinning carrots and onions, for example; and most growers no longer thin these crops.

Considerable mechanization is also employed in the production and harvesting of vegetables for processing. The output per man-hour of vegetables for processing increased 71 percent from 1939 to 1959, while that for fresh market crops increased 94 percent during the same period. The percent increase in man-hour production rose even more dramatically between 1959 and 1977.

Factors Responsible for Increased Labor Efficiency

Motor power and several other factors are responsible for increasing output per man-hour. Prior to 1939, the shift from horse to tractor power had not been so rapid in vegetable production as in other crop enterprises, because many vegetable operations were too small to justify the purchase of a tractor. Also, a small row-crop tractor having good maneuverability and good operator visibility was not available to vegetable growers until about 1940. Thus, the 1939 man-hours reflect, to a considerable extent, horse-powered operations—particularly in the preharvest operations. Since that time, the shift from horse to tractor power has been virtually completed.

Besides tractor power, crop dusting, spraying, and fertilizing operations are now being performed by airplane in many areas. This source of power and the improvement of machinery in general have further reduced labor input per acre. Additional factors contributing to labor efficiency include the shifting of vegetable crops, particularly those for processing, to more suitable areas of production; the increase in size of vegetable farms; and improved farm and market transportation.

Vegetable yields per acre have been increasing as a result of many factors. Plant breeders have developed new and better producing cultivars; more fertilizers and better methods of placement are used; chemical controls for weeds, insects, and diseases have been developed and adopted; improved machines and equipment have been developed which enable growers to perform tasks at the optimum time with a minimum of plant damage; and irrigation of vegetable acreage has increased even in the

Table 1.6—Estimated Yield, Output per Man-hour, and Percent Increase in Output per Man-hour of Commercially Produced Vegetables in 1939, 1959, and 1977.

Crops	Yield per Acre, Cwt.			Man-hours per Acre			Output per Man-hour, Cwt.			Percent Increase in Output per Man-hour	
	1939	1959	1977	1939	1959	1977	1939	1959	1977	1959–1977	1939–1977
Asparagus	22	23	25	190	173	71	.12	.13	.35	269	292
Beans, snap	29	36	37	132	133	15	.22	.27	2.47	915	1,123
Cabbage	124	167	259	108	104	63	1.15	1.61	4.11	255	357
Carrots	154	190	276	284	105	77	.54	1.81	3.58	198	663
Celery	251	415	491	371	335	143	.68	1.24	3.43	277	504
Corn, sweet	32	60	78	49	48	15	.65	1.25	5.20	416	800
Cucumbers	54	77	107	127	114	73	.43	.68	1.47	216	342
Lettuce	101	159	243	141	115	78	.72	1.38	3.12	226	433
Onions	135	226	319	271	139	86	.50	1.63	3.71	728	742
Peas (processing)	16	27	28	25	11	9	.64	2.40	3.11	130	486
Peppers (green)	62	71	94	180	200	160	.34	.36	.59	164	174
Potatoes	73	184	261	69	50	26	1.05	3.67	10.04	274	956
Spinach	46	58	82	124	32	18	.37	1.81	4.56	252	1,232
Sweet potatoes	47	74	111	118	96	55	.39	.76	2.02	266	518
Tomatoes	66	102	159	189	186	86	.35	.55	1.85	236	529
Watermelons	59	82	116	60	44	35	.98	1.86	3.31	178	338

The estimated output per man-hour for each reported year is figured by dividing man-hours per acre into yield per acre in corresponding year. The percentage increase in output per man-hour from 1959 to 1977 is derived by dividing the 1977 output per man-hour per cwt. by the 1959 output per man-hour per cwt. Likewise, the percentage increase in man-hour output from 1939 to 1977 is obtained by dividing the 1939 man-hour output by that of 1977.

The above 1939 and 1959 data are from "Labor Used to Produce Vegetables," USDA Statistical Bulletin 341, by E. E. Gavett, 1964. The figures in the 1977 "Man-hours per Acre" column are relative projections based on the result of research from 1974-77 trends. The cooperative U.S. Department of Labor—U.S. Department of Agriculture Study "Fruit and Vegetable Harvest Mechanization Manpower Implications," edited by B. F. Cargill and G. E. Rossmiller of Michigan State University, 1969, was also involved in this study.

humid areas of the East. These are some of the factors responsible for the 76 percent increase in yield per acre of all vegetables from 1949 to 1977.

The cost of producing vegetables and the trends in labor efficiency are discussed under the "Trends in Production Efficiency" sections of the respective vegetable chapters of Section Two.

Increasing Importance of Processed Vegetables

In addition to the rising population and per capita income, the development of new and improved products by recent technologies should increase the demand for processed vegetables. The increased number of employed women; a growing aversion of the average housewife to products which have to be peeled, shucked, scraped, chopped, or washed; and the general desire of the average American to spend more time in activities outside of the home will have a continuing impact on the demand for "convenience foods," including vegetables.

The big increase in frozen vegetables has been due not only to technological improvements in freezing and packaging but also to the development of refrigerated facilities in retail stores for handling the products. The difficulty in maintaining quality in very perishable vegetables is greatly reduced by freezing. It is easy to understand why a vegetable like peas, frozen and attractively packaged, has replaced the more expensive fresh product that has to be shelled before use.

The range and versatility of vegetable products are also increasing due to new methods of processing. Dehydrofreezing of vegetables, by which some of the water is removed before freezing, reduces bulk and weight. The process is expensive, but the cost of packaging and handling is reduced. Freeze-drying, a process whereby moisture is removed from a product in the frozen state, produces a lightweight, dried product that can be shipped and stored without refrigeration. New products suitable for special uses and improvements in quality due to methods of processing will increase the demand for processed vegetables.

Trends in the Number and Size of Farms

The 1969 Census of Agriculture reported that the 3,352,000 acres of vegetables, excluding potatoes and sweet potatoes, harvested for sale represented 1.2 percent of the acreage of land from which crops were harvested in 1969. Of all types of farms, 3.7 percent were classified as vegetable farms. In 1974, only 3.4 percent of all farms were so classified.

From 1949 to 1974, harvested vegetable acreage decreased about 15 percent overall, but substantial declines were registered in New England and the East and West South Central regions. The greatest increase in acreage developed in the Pacific and some parts of the West North Central areas (Table 1.7). Concurrently, the number of vegetable farms decreased from about 348,000 to 79,000 during the 25-year period. The average size of vegetable farms rose from 11 acres in 1949 to 19 acres in 1959, on to 33 acres in 1969, and up to 42 acres in 1974. This trend points out the competitive pattern of mechanized-commercial production now required by growers to stay in business. The size and type of vegetable farms and the shifting of production varied considerably on a regional, state, and local basis.

The Census of Agriculture reveals that the number of farms growing vegetables declined from 347,850 in 1949, to 182,327 in 1959, down to 101,760 in 1969, and then to 78,566 in 1974. However, the acreages remained fairly steady during the 1949-1974 period, which accounts for the substantial increase in the average size of farms. (Table 1.7.)

Table 1.7—Number and Percent of All Farms Reporting Vegetable Sales and Total Acreage and Percent of Cropland Harvested in Vegetables (Other than Potatoes and Sweet Potatoes) by Geographical Divisions.

Geographical Divisions	Number of Farms, 1,000				Percent of All Farms in 1974	Harvested Acreage, 1,000				Percent of Cropland Harvested in 1974
	1949	1959	1969	1974		1949	1959	1969	1974	
New England	11	5	3	3	11.6	63	50	43	41	2.8
Middle Atlantic	37	20	11	9	9.1	452	374	315	293	3.4
E. North Central	73	36	20	17	3.8	639	616	658	692	1.2
W. North Central	19	12	7	6	1.0	195	197	214	207	0.2
South Atlantic	93	45	23	17	5.6	835	671	567	502	2.9
E. South Central	35	23	15	10	3.2	161	123	101	75	0.5
W. South Central	51	22	10	7	2.0	614	402	289	198	0.5
Mountain	12	6	4	3	2.8	187	177	190	156	0.6
Pacific	18	12	9	8	6.2	723	881	975	1,150	6.9
U.S. totals*	348	182	102	79	3.4	3,869	3,491	3,352	3,314	1.1

*U.S. totals may not add because of rounding.

Data from U.S. Census of Agriculture.

Shifting Marketing Requirements

A knowledge of supply and consumption is essential to an understanding of the changes in marketing in the vegetable industry. Supply, consumption, and markets interact constantly in our dynamic economy. The introduction of a technological change such as quick-freezing started a chain of events in the vegetable industry which affected almost every part of it. New areas increased production, while others stood still or declined. New marketing channels, embodying new firms with different buying, selling, and handling practices, took a share of the market from established firms handling fresh and canned vegetables.

When consumers increase their demand for one product, or for one form of a product at the expense of the other products, the market structure is influenced, and the demand for the services of some firms increases while the demand for others decreases. Such a change in consumer demand for the products of different areas affects not only the growers in those areas but marketing firms and transportation agencies as well.

The tendency for more vegetables to be merchandised by large retailers has increased the demand for large supplies of vegetables, graded and packed uniformly. This has placed the small grower at a disadvantage as compared to the large grower in a specialized region of production.

CONTRACT PRODUCTION OF COMMERCIAL VEGETABLES

Contracting activities in vegetable production is more important for processing vegetables than those for fresh market. Fresh market vegetables are now primarily in the hands of trained production and marketing specialists. Contracting activities in vegetable processing increased from 67 percent in 1960 to 89 percent of the production in 1970 and to 97 percent in 1977.

By contrast, vertical integration (when processors or dealers are also growers) in production is more common in vegetables grown for fresh market than in vegetables produced for processing. Growers handled the dealer and processor services for 20 percent of the acreage for fresh vegetables in 1960, and this increased to 30 percent by 1970. During the same 10-year period, fresh market production contracts increased from 20 to 21 percent. Concurrently, processing vegetable growers, who increased their contracted production from 67 to 85 percent, held down their vertical-integration production to 8 and 10 percent for 1960 and 1970 respectively.

Processing vegetable growers generally depend on contracts with canners and freezers and no longer rely on open market outlets. This serves the processor's interest as well, because he may want to specify the variety to be grown, certain cultural practices, and usually the planting and harvest dates. Furthermore, varieties best suited for processing are often not the best for fresh market sales. Therefore, opportunities for dual marketing are limited or nonexistent. Vegetable growers are more specialized than ever and generally consider themselves as either fresh market or processing vegetable producers.

Specifications set forth in contracts vary widely among crops and areas. Price arrangements are indicated in nearly all contracts, either as a specific price commitment, or in terms of how the price is calculated. Many different specifications for variety, grade, seed, fertilizers, and cultural practices may be involved in contracts. Many contracts provide some labor, equipment, materials, or financing for such items. Nearly all contracts call attention to the processor's field man for advice, counsel, and inspection—as a key link in the decision-making process.

Processing vegetable growers have shown increasing interest in bargaining activities. In some instances they have banded together to form bargaining groups. For example, the Potato Growers of Idaho, Inc., bargains annually on an industry-wide basis with about a dozen French fry packers and dehydrators in the state. Generally, for the California cannery tomato crops, the California Tomato Growers Association, Inc., handled the pricing part of contracts signed with canners in the Central Valley. In other states, the American Agricultural Marketing Association, a National Farm Bureau affiliate, has helped organized growers establish bargaining groups.

SOURCES OF INFORMATION

During the formative period of the vegetable-growing industry, producers relied largely on commercial agencies for information on varieties and production methods. As vegetable growing became more stabilized in specially adapted areas, trial and error resulted in improved varieties and cultural practices. Vegetable growers, seed companies, and handling agencies have been alert to make improvements as problems and competition increased. As the industry expanded, more complex problems of production and marketing arose. Producers did not have the time, money, patience, facilities, or training to solve many of them.

The experiment stations and commercial organizations have worked out many of the vegetable growers' problems of pest control, nutrition, processing, marketing, and other economic factors. With restricted resources, it has been impossible for the experiment stations to answer specific questions as they arose in a fast-developing, ever-changing industry. Realizing that production problems vary considerably from section to section, most of the states and the U.S. Department of Agriculture have established branch stations and outlying test fields in the areas of production. With the improvement of research personnel and working facilities during recent years, the experiment stations have made many valuable findings on varieties, fertilizers, pest control, and general cultural and marketing practices for the different crops.

Producers, processors, distributors, and consumers of agricultural products need a great deal of information on changes in production and on markets. The U.S. Department of Agriculture publishes a vast array of information on many aspects of the production, marketing, and consumption of foods. Likewise, the state experiment stations (a list of which is provided in the Appendix) and many commercial industries and organizations have published general and specific information on practically all aspects of producing, handling, and marketing vegetables. Many of these publications are free upon request.

A Change in Vegetable Usage

Early in 1970 a changing pattern of vegetable use began to emerge. From the end of World War II to about 1970, the vegetable industry adjusted to consumers' demand for convenience with canned and frozen vegetables making substantial gains at the expense of fresh produce. The cooking vegetables requiring extensive preparation, such as peas, lima beans, snap beans, and beets, continued to be processed, but their use decreased relative to that of vegetables eaten raw. These include those normally eaten raw as well as those of dual usage such as carrots, cabbage, tomatoes, and onions. This trend largely reflected the increased cost of processing and of containers.

Thus far in the decade of the 70's, total vegetable use in all forms has increased from 213 pounds to 227 pounds, a gain of 7 percent. This includes fresh, canned, and frozen vegetables, plus 2 pounds of dehydrated onions. Excluded from these data are potatoes, sweet potatoes, and home garden vegetables.

RELEVANT PERIODICALS WITH INFORMATION ON VEGETABLES

Agricultural Research, U.S. Department of Agriculture, Washington, D.C. 20250 (by volume and no. monthly).

American Vegetable Grower, Meister Publishing Company, Willoughby, Ohio 44094 (monthly).

California Agriculture, Calif. Agr. Exp. Sta. and Ext. Ser., Davis, Calif. 95616 (quarterly).

Canadian Food Processors Association (periodical reports and publications), 130 Albert St., Ottawa, Ont., Can. KIP-5G4.

Chain Store Age, 2 Park Ave., New York, N.Y. 10016 (periodical).

Citrus and Vegetable Magazine, P.O. Box 2349, Tampa, Fla. 33601 (periodically).

Food Marketing Institute (annual and special reports), 1750 K St. N.W., Washington, D.C. 20006.

Great Lakes Vegetable Growers News, 343 S. Union St., Sparta, Mich. 49345 (monthly).

Outlook, Published by the United States Fresh Fruit and Veg. Assoc., 727 N. Washington St., Alexandria, Va. 22314 (monthly except in summer).

Progressive Grocer, 708 3rd Ave., New York, N.Y. 10017 (monthly).

The Packer, One Gateway Center, Kansas City, Kan. 66101 (weekly).

The Produce News, 333 Sylvan Ave., Englewood Cliffs, N.J. 07632 (weekly).

Seedmen's Digest, 1910 W. Olmos Drive, San Antonio, Tex. 78201 (monthly).

Voc. Ed, American Vocational Association, Inc. 2020 N. 14th St., Arlington, Va. 22201 (monthly).

Western Grower and Shipper, 3001 Red Hill Ave., Costa Mesa, Calif. 92626 (monthly).

SELECTED REFERENCES

Anonymous, "Annual Summary of Vegetables—Fresh Market," USDA, ESCS, 1979 (issued annually).

Anonymous, "Annual Summary of Vegetables—Processing," USDA, ESCS, 1979 (issued annually).

Anonymous, "Cropland for Today and Tomorrow," USDA, AER 291, 1975.

Anonymous, "Per Capita Consumption of Fresh and Processed Vegetables," USDA, ERS, 1973.

Anonymous, "The World Food Situation and Prospects to 1985," USDA, FAS, ERS, 1974.

Banks, Vera J., "Farm Population Estimates for 1976," USDA, AER Rep. 383, 1977.

Cargill, B. F., and Rossmiller, G. E., "Fruit and Vegetable Harvest Implications," Mich. State Univ. Rural Manpower Center, 1969.

Dean, G. W., *et al.,* "Projections of California Agriculture to 1980 and 2000," Calif. Exp. Bull. B847, 1970.

Durost, Donald D., and Black, Evelyn T., "Changes in Farm Production and Efficiency," USDA, ESCS Bull. 612, 1978.

Gavett, E. E., "Labor Used to Produce Vegetables—Estimates by Years," USDA Stat. Bull. 341, 1964.

Kelsey, M. P., and Motes, J. E., "Computing Production Costs of Fruits and Vegetables," Mich. Ext. Ser. Bull. E-941, 1976.

Metzger, H. B., and Flanders, N. E., "Improving the Incomes of Small Farm Families," Univ. of Me. Exp. Sta. Bull. 742, 1977.

Mighell, R. L., and Hoofnagle, W. S., "Contract Production and Vertical Integration in Farming, 1960 and 1970," USDA, ERS–479, 1972.

Pollack, B. L., "Commercial Vegetable Production Recommendations," N.J. State Univ. Agr. Ext. Bull. 406E.

Porter, C. W., "The American Vegetable Industry in the 1970's," USDA, ERS, 1975.

Porter, C. W., "The Size of the Market for Fresh and Processed Vegetables to 1980 and Beyond," USDA, ERS Art., Dec., 1973.

Porter, C. W., "Where Is Vegetable Use Headed?" "Outlook," Magazine of the United Fresh Fruit and Veg. Assoc., Alexandria, Va., Sept., 1978.

Porter, C. W., and Podany, J. C., "The Vegetable Situation," USDA, ESCS, 1979 (issued quarterly).

Rowe, Gene, and Smith, L. W., "The Hired Farm Working Force of 1975," USDA, ERS, Ag. Econ. Rep. 355, 1976.

CHAPTER 2

Classifying Vegetables

Vegetable crops may be classified according to: botanical relationship, use as human food, or climatic and cultural requirements. Growth requirements and susceptibility to injury by insects and diseases are likely to be similar for plants closely related botanically. Time of planting in a given area may be dictated by climatic requirements. The reader should be familiar with the various relationships between vegetables because in later chapters the crops will be discussed individually rather than as closely related groups.

All vegetables belong to the division of plants known as *Angiospermae,* having ovules in a carpel or ovary. They may be grouped into either Class I, *Monocotyledonae* or Class II, *Dicotyledonae,* having one or two seed leaves, respectively. The plants may be further classified into family, genus, species, and sometimes botanical variety.

The members of the same botanical family may be grown for different plant parts. For example, some members of the *Umbelliferae* are grown for their foliage, others for their fruits, and still others for their fleshy root parts. The following classification is based upon the use made of the vegetable. By comparing the three lists, the student may see at a glance which crops belong to the same botanical family. Even though some of the vegetable crops in these lists are uncommon, they have been included in order to acquaint the student with the general relationships and the uses for which these little-known vegetables may be grown.

BOTANICAL FAMILIES AND CROP USE

1. Vegetables of which the leaves, flower parts, or stems are used.

Liliaceae. Lily family.
Asparagus, *Asparagus officinalis* var. *altilis.*
Chive, chives, *Allium schoenoprasum.*
Chenopodiaceae. Goosefoot family.
Beet, *Beta vulgaris.*
Chard, *Beta vulgaris* var. *cicla.*
Orach, *Atriplex hortensis.*
Spinach (prickly-seeded), *Spinacia oleracea.*
Spinach (round-seeded), *Spinacia oleracea* var. *inermis.*
Umbelliferae. Parsley family.
Celery, *Apium graveolens* var. *dulce.*
Chervil, *Anthriscus cerefolium.*
Fennel, *Foeniculum vulgare.*
Parsley, *Petroselinum crispum.*
Valerianaceae. Valerian family.
Corn salad, fetticus, *Valerianella oliteria.*
Compositae. Composite or Sunflower family.
Artichoke, *Cynara scolymus.*
Cardoon, *Cynara cardunculus.*
Chicory, witloof, *Cichorium intybus.*
Dandelion, *Taraxacum officinale.*
Endive, *Cichorium endivia.*
Lettuce, *Lactuca sativa.*
Polygonaceae. Buckwheat family.
Rhubarb, *Rheum rhaponticum.*
Sorrel, *Rumex acetosa.*
Spinach dock, *Rumex patientia.*
Aizoaceae. Carpetweed family.
New Zealand spinach, *Tetragonia expansa.*

Araliaceae. Ginseng family.
Udo, *Aralia cordata.*
Cruciferae. Mustard family.
Brussels sprouts, *Brassica oleracea* var. *gemmifera.*
Cabbage, *Brassica oleracea* var. *capitata.*
Cauliflower, *Brassica oleracea* var. *botrytis.*
Collard, *Brassica oleracea* var. *viridis.*
Cress, *Lepidium sativum.*
Kale, Borecole, *Brassical oleracea* var. *viridis.*
Kohlrabi, *Brassica oleraceae* var. *gongylodes.*
Mustard, leaf, *Brassica juncea.*
Mustard, Southern Curled, *Brassica juncea* var. *crispifolia.*
Pak-choe. Chinese cabbage, *Brassica chinensis.*
Pe-tsai, Chinese cabbage, *Brassica pekinensis.*
Seakale, *Crambe maritima.*
Sprouting broccoli, *Brassica oleracea* var. *italica.*
Turnip, Seven Top, *Brassica rapa* var. *septiceps.*
Upland cress, *Barbarea verna (praecox).*
Watercress, *Rorippa nasturtiumaquaticum.*

2. Vegetables of which the underground parts are used.

Liliaceae. Lily family.
Garlic, *Allium sativum.*
Leek, *Allium porrum.*
Onion, *Allium cepa.*
Shallot, *Allium ascalonicum.*
Welsh onion, *Allium fistulosum.*
Dioscoreaceae. Yam family.
Yam (true), *Dioscorea batatas.*
Chenopodiaceae. Goosefoot family.
Beet, *Beta vulguris.*
Cruciferae. Mustard family.
Horseradish, *Armoracia rusticana.*
Radish, *Raphanus sativus.*
Rutabaga. *Brassica campestris* var. *napobrassica.*
Turnip, *Brassica rapa.*
Convolvulaceae. Morning-glory family.
Sweet potato, *Ipomoea batatas.*

Umbelliferae. Parsley family.
Carrot, *Daucus carota* var. *sativa.*
Celeriac, *Apium graveolens* var. *rapaceum.*
Hamburg parsley, *Petroselinum crispum* var. *radicosum.*
Parsnip, *Pastinaca sativa.*
Solanaceae. Nightshade family.
Potato, *Solanum tuberosum.*
Compositae. Composite or Sunflower family.
Black salsify, *Scorzonera hispanica.*
Chicory, *Cichorium intybus.*
Jerusalem artichoke, *Helianthus tuberosus.*
Salsify, *Tragopogon porrifolius.*
Spanish salsify, *Scolymus hispanicus.*

3. Vegetables of which the fruits or seeds are used.

Gramineae. Grass family.
Sweet corn, *Zea mays* var. *saccharata.*
Malvaceae. Mallow family.
Okra (gumbo), *Hibiscus esculentus.*
Leguminosae. Pulse or Pea family.
Asparagus or Yardlong bean, *Vigna sesquipedalis.*
Broad bean, *Vicia faba.*
Bush bean, *Phaseolus vulgaris* var. *humilis.*
Bush Lima bean, *Phaseolus limensis* var. *limenanus.*
Cowpea, *Vigna sinensis.*
Edible podded pea, *Pisum sativum* var. *macrocarpon.*
Kidney bean, *Phaseolus vulgaris.*
Lima bean, *Phaseolus limensis.*
Pea (English pea), *Pisum sativum.*
Peanut (underground fruits), *Arachis hypogaea.*
Scarlet runner bean, *Phaseolus coccineus.*
Sieva bean, *Phaseolus lunatus.*
Soybean, *Glycine max.*
White Dutch runner bean, *Phaseolus coccineus* var. *albus.*

Umbelliferae. Parsley family.
Caraway, *Carum carvi.*
Dill, *Anethum graveolens.*
Martyniaceae. Martynia family.
Martynia, *Proboscidea louisiana.*
Solanaceae. Nightshade family.
Eggplant, *Solanum melongena.*
Groundcherry (husk tomato), *Physalis pubescens.*
Pepper (bell or sweet), *Capsicum frutescens* var. *grossum.*
Tomato, *Lycopersicon esculentum.*
Cucurbitaceae. Gourd or Melon family.
Bush pumpkin, (summer squash). *Cucurbita pepo* var. *melopepo.*
Chayote, *Sechium edule.*
Cucumber, *Cucumis sativus.*
Cushaw, *Cucurbita moschata.*
Gherkin, *Cucumis anguria.*
Muskmelon (cantaloupe), *Cucumis melo.*
Pumpkin, *Cucurbita pepo.*
Squash, *Cucurbita maxima.*
Watermelon, *Citrullus lunatus.*
Winter melon (cassaba), *Cucumis melo* var. *inodorus.*

A botanical classification alone, however, does not completely satisfy the needs of the student interested in the production of vegetables. He needs to have some orderly arrangement in mind which will help him relate one crop to another in respect to their cultural requirements and uses as human food.

ADAPTATION TO HEAT AND COLD

Vegetables vary considerably in their temperature requirements; some need relatively cool temperatures while others need warm temperatures for best development. There are also wide differences in resistance to freezing; some withstand heavy freezing, some light freezing, some no freezing, and others are injured by exposure to low, nonfreezing temperatures. Even resistant plants may be injured by freezing if they are not hardened or adapted to freezing temperatures. A classification on the basis of hardiness (Table 2.1) is valuable in determining when crops may be planted in a given region.

The cool-season crops can withstand light frosts. Some of them can

Table 2.1—General Classification by Resistance to Spring Frosts.

| Cool-Season Crops | | Warm-Season Crops | |
Hardy	Half Hardy	Tender	Very Tender
Asparagus	Beet	Cowpea	Cucumber
Broccoli	Carrot	New Zealand	Eggplant
Brussels sprouts	Cauliflower	spinach	Lima bean
Cabbage	Celery	Snap bean	Muskmelon
Chives	Chard	Soybean	Okra
Collards	Chinese cabbage	Sweet corn	Pepper
Dasheen	Globe artichoke	Tomato	Pumpkin
Garlic	Endive		Squash
Horseradish	Lettuce		Sweet potato
Kale	Parsnip		Watermelon
Kohlrabi	Potato		
Leek	Salsify		
Mustard			
Onion			
Parsley			
Peas			
Radish			
Rhubarb			
Rutabaga			
Spinach			
Turnip			

even endure winter freezing, notably asparagus and rhubarb. Thus, it is this group of crops that one plants earliest in the spring and late in the season for fall and winter harvest. These are the hardy and half-hardy vegetables listed in Table 2.1. The separation into hardy and half-hardy crops is based primarily on the ability of the seed to germinate at low soil temperatures and of the young plants to withstand frosts. This grouping does not necessarily apply to the full-grown plants. Carrots, beets, parsnips, and salsify can remain in the ground late in the fall because of the protection given the root by the soil. In this sense they are more hardy than some of the so-called hardy crops.

The plants that will grow successfully in warm weather are so tender that their growth is checked when the air is cool and death results quickly if they are frosted. The tender crops are a little less susceptible to injury from cool weather than are the very tender crops. There is considerable variation in the soil temperature necessary for seed germination within the tender and very tender groups.

While the cool-season crops are unable to withstand the higher summer temperatures of the South, some of them are affected also by prolonged exposure to relatively cool temperatures. The biennials—celery, beet, cabbage, and carrot—may produce seedstalks instead of edible growth the first year if, during the winter months, growing plants are subjected to an average temperature of 50° F. or lower for several weeks. The spring and fall planting dates of different vegetables are given by zones in Tables 8.2 and 8.3 respectively.

SEASON OF GROWTH OF VEGETABLES

The season of the year in which a vegetable may be grown most successfully depends upon the region of production. In southern Florida and in the lower Rio Grande Valley some of the warm-season crops can be grown during winter. In the spring, plantings must be made progressively later from south to north, with every hundred miles making about a week's difference in planting time. This rule-of-thumb may be modified, however, where climate is affected by large bodies of water.

A system of listing vegetables according to the time of year in which they may be grown is an advantage in planning rotations and making cropping plans. The following classification is based on season of growth and use.

Cool-Season Crops

1. Crops quickly reaching edible maturity (spring and fall):
   Leaf lettuce, spinach, mustard, radishes, turnips, kohlrabi, and peas.
2. Crops usually transplanted:
   a. Springs crops
      Head lettuce, Cos lettuce, cabbage, cauliflower, broccoli, and celery.
   b. Fall crops
      Cabbage, cauliflower, broccoli, Brussels sprouts, and celery.
3. Crops that endure summer heat:
   Swiss chard, kale, collards, New Zealand spinach, parsley, endive, onions, leeks, garlic, shallots, chives, potatoes, beets, carrots, parsnips, salsify, and horseradish (the last three withstand winter freezing).
4. Perennial crops:
   Asparagus, rhubarb, and globe artichoke.

Warm-Season Crops

1. Crops usually not transplanted:

   Snap beans, Lima beans, southern peas, sweet corn, popcorn, okra, muskmelon, watermelon, cucumber, squashes, and pumpkin.

2. Crops usually transplanted:

   Tomatoes, eggplants, peppers, and sweet potatoes.

SELECTED REFERENCES

Bailey, L. H., *Manual of Cultivated Plants,* New York: The Macmillan Company, 1949.

Benson, L., *Plant Classification,* Boston: D. C. Heath & Company, 1957.

Candolle, A., *Origin of Cultivated Plants,* New York: Hafner Publishing Co., Inc., 1964.

Fernald, M. L., *Gray's Manual of Botany,* New York: American Book Company, 1950.

Magness, J. R., Markle, G. M., and Compton, C. C., "Food and Feed Crops of the United States," N. J. Agr. Exp. Sta. Bull. 828, 1971.

Smith, Paul G., and Welch, J. E., "Nomenclature of Vegetables and Condiment Herbs Grown in the United States," *Proc. Amer. Soc. Hort. Sci.* 84, 535, 1964.

CHAPTER 3

Plant Growth and Development

The production of a crop is usually more successful if the grower understands the nature of the plant and its development. Most vegetables are propagated from seed which contains the embryonic plant supplied with stored food. These are surrounded by a seed coat which protects them before and during germination. Until rapid vital activity resumes, the embryo and reserve food are very susceptible to decay organisms. The seed coats of some seeds do not provide enough protection during germination, while others provide too much, thus restricting water absorption and penetration by the embryo.

The plant embryo is a bipolar axis containing a growing point for shoots and one for roots. The cotyledons are attached laterally and may expand into photosynthetic organs. In other instances they function as storage organs, having absorbed the endosperm before maturation of the seed. The cotyledons may remain below ground during germination as in the pea, or emerge as in the bean. In the latter case, difficulties may be encountered with soil penetration. Although the emerging cotyledons have problems penetrating the soil, they are less susceptible to decaying organisms than hypogeous or nonemerging cotyledons.

GERMINATION

Germination of a seed begins with the imbibition of water. The embryo is stimulated to activity with the radicle beginning to elongate. It pushes through the seed coat weakened by enzymes. Cell division in the apex produces new cells for the developing root and also for the root cap, which prevents injury to the young root as it penetrates the soil. Growth activity in the shoot growing point follows that in the root, the shoot of each kind of seed having its particular method of penetrating the soil. The embryonic leaves of corn are surrounded by a sheaf (coleoptile) which pushes up through the soil. The coleoptile restricts the growth of the leaves inside until it reaches the surface and is exposed to light. At this time, elongation of the coleoptile ceases, the leaves rapidly push through the sheaf, and secondary roots already initiated begin development. During germination of the bean, the hypocotyl, the stem below the cotyledons, elongates, pushing a bow or hook through the soil. When the stem is exposed to light, it straightens, pulling the cotyledons to the surface. Meanwhile, stored food in the cotyledons is being digested and translocated to the emerging plant, causing the cotyledons to shrink and facilitate removal from the old seed coat. The onion seedling reaches the surface by elongation of the seed leaf, the terminal end of which remains in the old seed coat absorbing nutrients of the endosperm. If the seed is planted too deeply, the seedling may be incapable of reaching the surface or, if planted too shallow, the seed will emerge and dry out before the endosperm is absorbed, resulting in a weakened seedling. The food reserves in the seed should be sufficient to last until photosynthesis is established.

PHOTOSYNTHESIS

The process of photosynthesis takes place in two separate steps. The first includes the absorption and conversion of light to chemical energy. It may be limited by the amount of chlorophyll or light intensity. The second step involves a series of chemical and enzymatic reactions. This step may be limited by CO_2, temperature, water, mineral nutrients, or the accumulation of photosynthetic products.

The amount of chlorophyll is not likely to limit photosynthesis in a leaf unless it is chlorotic, a condition where chlorophyll fails to develop normally. Light intensity, on the other hand, may be an important factor, especially during some seasons, where there is shading, or in thick plantings. A single leaf may be saturated with a light intensity of 1,000 foot-candles (ft.-c.) or less, but the entire plant may require several thousand due to mutual shading of leaves. Light requirement also varies with the kind of plant. In general, plants that develop storage organs, seeds, or fruits require wider spacing and more light than those grown for foliage only.

The normal CO_2 content of the air (0.03%) is far below the optimum for photosynthesis. It would be difficult to increase the carbon dioxide of the ambient air of plants in the field, but it might be done economically in a closed greenhouse. Carbon dioxide may be restricted to plants by closure of stomates due to a deficiency of water in the leaves. This often happens during the day when transpiration is high and soil moisture is deficient.

While the light reaction for photosynthesis increases very little with temperature, the chemical-enzymatic reactions are highly temperature-dependent. The Q_{10} for photosynthesis may therefore be quite variable, depending upon what reactions are limiting. Photosynthesis may be restricted by a deficiency of mineral elements such as magnesium, a constituent of chlorophyll, or phosphorus necessary for the transfer of energy. In order to have maximum photosynthesis the products produced during the light period must be removed from the leaf by the end of the following dark period. This is facilitated by providing proper temperature, moisture, nutrients, and other optimum conditions for plant growth.

MINERAL REQUIREMENTS

A plant grown in a well aerated quartz sand watered with a mineral solution may make optimum growth without organic additives. However, the nutrient solution would have to be changed or adjusted continually to keep it balanced and to prevent a deficiency of some of the nutrients. A soil containing organic matter would retain moisture, provide buffer action, and supply the soil solution with nutrients, especially nitrogen, as the organic matter decomposes. If a plant is grown in a medium deficient in some essential element, it will become unhealthy and develop deficiency symptoms, some of which are readily recognized. Although the deficiency may be corrected, it can seldom be done in time to prevent a reduction in the yield of a crop after symptoms become apparent.

Of the elements essential to plants, C, H, O, and N are derived ultimately from the atmosphere, while K, Ca, Mg, P, S, Fe, Cu, Mn, Zn, Mo, B, and Cl are constituents of the parent rock from which soil is formed. The elements constituting the major building blocks of the plant are: C, H, O, N, and P. The cell wall, carbohydrates, and fats are composed almost exclusively of C, H, and O. Proteins, the major organic constituents of cytoplasm, are composed mainly of C, H, O, and

N. The nucleic acids of the nucleus and cytoplasm are made of C, H, O, N, and P.

Potassium is known to activate several important enzymes, though it has not been isolated as a constituent of an enzyme system. *Calcium* forms insoluble salts with the acidic pectins to form calcium pectate which binds cells together and gives rigidity to plants. The element also plays a role in the permeability of cell membranes. *Magnesium* is an essential part of the chlorophyll molecule and is a specific cofactor for several enzymes.

Phosphorus is a component of nucleic acids (DNA and RNA), the principal genetic material of the cell, and is critically involved in all energy transfer, including that in photosynthesis. *Sulfur* is a constituent of several amino acids and such compounds as glutathione and thioctic acid, believed to play a role in oxidation-reduction reactions. *Fe, Cu, Mn, Zn,* and *Mo* function as coenzymes. *Boron* is essential for the development of meristematic cells, and *chlorine* is known to stimulate photosynthetic phosphorylation, but the mechanisms of these reactions are still obscure.

Most mineral absorption by plants occurs near the apexes of young roots. The older roots develop layers impervious to water and are relatively ineffective in the absorption of ions. The absorbing areas of roots have to be in contact with the immobile or absorbed ions such as K^+ or $H_2PO_4^-$ to absorb them from the soil. Young plants with limited root systems are inefficient absorbers of these ions and usually require high fertility to make optimum growth.

Mineral elements in the soil must pass through the differentially permeable membrane of a cell to enter a plant. Elements may accumulate in a cell against an electro-chemical gradient. The expenditure of energy is required and aerobic respiration is essential. Roots may excrete ions to the outside medium in exchange for ions absorbed. For example, H^+ is frequently exchanged for K^+ or an organic acid ion for NO_3^-. After entering a cell, an ion usually moves across the cortex to the xylem and is carried to transpiring leaves in the water stream. Ions may also move up the plant stem in the phloem, but at a slower rate. The mineral elements move out of the leaves with the products of photosynthesis through the phloem to the actively developing parts of the plant.

WATER ECONOMY

Succulent vegetables are very high in water content, lettuce having about 95 percent. To maintain succulence and tenderness, the plant usually requires a continuous supply of water throughout its development. Large losses of water occur from plants because of the structure of leaves. They consist essentially of layers of wet photosynthetically active cells, well supplied with vascular elements and encased in a fairly waterproof but performated layer, the epidermis. The wet surfaces of the mesophyll cells evaporate large quantities of water into the intercellular spaces. Since the open stomates occupy from 1 to 3 percent of the surface of a leaf, they offer but little resistance to the diffusion of water to the atmosphere. Under conditions of high humidity and still air, net loss from the leaf is greatly diminished, but with low humidity and turbulent air, water vapor is quickly removed from the leaf surface, greatly increasing the rate of transpiration.

Even with the soil well supplied with moisture, a plant may become deficient during the middle of a bright, warm day. As a result, guard cells of leaves become flaccid and stomates close, restricting CO_2 uptake as well as loss of water and thus decreased photosynthesis. As plants become more deficient in moisture, stomates may remain closed for longer periods during the day. Cell division and enlargement are dependent upon plant turgidity. If a plant loses water, even though not wilted, the rate of growth is reduced, and the products of photosynthesis may accumulate even with reduced photosynthesis.

Water is absorbed by young roots primarily by osmotic forces. The soil forms a reservoir which alternately is filled and depleted. When the soil is filled and the free water removed by percolation, it is said to be at *field capacity*. Then water is easily removed by roots. But as the soil becomes progressively desiccated, absorption by roots becomes more difficult. The *wilting percentage* is reached when plants will not recover from wilting. Soils vary widely in wilting percentage. It is low in coarse, sandy soils and relatively high in fine, clay soils. Plants cannot absorb water from soil particles if a pressure of more than 15 atmospheres is required for release. As compared with sandy soils, clay soils hold more water, but it is held more tenaciously, and a smaller percent is available to plants.

TEMPERATURE REQUIREMENTS

Vegetable crops differ in their temperature requirements. Some crops, such as melons, cucumbers, and eggplants, thrive best under relatively high temperatures, while others, such as lettuce, cabbage, celery, and peas, thrive best under relatively cool temperatures. However, the best temperature is not necessarily the one at which the plant makes the most rapid growth. At low temperatures the rate of cell division and growth is slow. Also, sugars tend to accumulate, and plants develop less fiber and strong flavors, such as pungency in onions and crucifers. Low temperatures stimulate some plants to change from the vegetative to the reproductive phase. Among these are the biennials and some perennials. At relatively high temperatures, growth is rapid, and sugars, instead of accumulating, are used in respiration and growth. The pea, at high temperatures, flowers at a lower node when the plant is smaller and consequently produces a smaller yield. Most plants make best growth when night temperatures are several degrees lower than day temperatures.

The time required for a nonphotoperiodic plant to mature is closely related to temperatures during its development. A heat-unit system can therefore be used to make rather precise predictions of crop maturity. Plantings can also be spaced for a desired succession of harvests. Precision is gained when temperature records are taken near the plantings in a limited area. Commercial growers and processors find the heat-unit system very valuable in handling their crops.

GROWTH SUBSTANCES

Growth hormones are known to be involved in many plant responses. They may be classified roughly as auxins, gibberellins, cytokinins, and inhibitors.

The auxin, indole-3-acetic acid, is generally distributed in plants. It is known as the growth hormone and is vitally involved with cell elongation, proliferation, and differentiation. Many plant responses, such as apical dominance, phototropism, geotropism, and root initiation can be traced to auxin. Its content in plants is controlled by the enzyme indole acetic acid oxidase. Some of the synthetic auxins such as 2,4-D are much more active than the plant auxin primarily because they are not readily metabolized by plant enzymes.

Applied gibberellins have been dramatic responses in stem elongation of plants. These growth substances are natural constituents of plants and are known to participate in the endogenous control of growth activities and a variety of developmental activities including dormancy, flowering, and responses to light and temperature. Dwarfness in some plants has been shown to be due to a deficiency of gibberellin.

Fig. 3.1—Sweet potato roots treated with ethephon to increase sprouting. (Top) control; (bottom) treated.

Photograph by Dan Tomkins

The cytokinins include a diverse group of growth substances. Unlike auxins and gibberellins, they are nonacidic and relatively immobile. Cytokinins are apparently necessary for cell growth and differentiation, but also have other interesting physiological roles. Detached leaves treated with cytokinins stay green longer and retain their proteins. Constituents tend to accumulate in areas where cytokinins are applied, indicating a mobilizing effect.

In addition to growth promoting substances, plants also contain inhibitors. These are associated with such plant responses as restricted growth, dormancy, abscission, and senescence. The inhibition of growth during fruiting is an important factor in reproduction. Dormancy is important during periods unfavorable for growth and for storage. Dormant buds of the potato have been found to be high in inhibitors which decrease when dormancy is broken. Abscission seems to be a protective mechanism of plants and is enhanced by abscisic acid and ethylene, both of which are associated with senescence.

The use of chemicals to control certain phases of growth has be-

Fig. 3.2—Brussels sprouts treated with SADH to concentrate set of sprouts for mechanical harvesting. (Left) control; (right) treated.

Photograph by Dan Tomkins

come important in the production of many crops. The control of fruit setting, sex ratios, sprouting in storage, dormancy, and weeds are a few of the many uses.

SELECTED REFERENCES

Benjamin, L. R., and Wren, M. J., "Root Development and Source—Sink Relations in Carrot *(Daucus carota* L.)," *J. Exp. Bot.* 29 (109): 425-433, 1978.

Black, Michael, and Edelman, Jack, *Plant Growth*, London: Heineman Educational Books, Ltd., 1971.

Borthwick, H. A., and Hendricks, S., "Effects of Radiation on Growth and Development," *Encyl. Plant Physiol.* XVI, 299, 1961.

Carolus, R. L., *et al.*, "The Interaction of Climate and Soil Moisture on Water Use, Growth, and Development of Tomato," Mich. Agr. Exp. Sta. Quart. Bull. 47 (4), 1968.

Crookston, R. K., *et al.*, "Photosynthetic Depression in Beans After Exposure to Cold for One Night," *Crop Sci.* 14: 457-464, 1974.

Ewing, E. E., "Critical Photoperiod for Tuberization: A Screening Technique with Potato Cuttings," *Amer. Potato J.* 55 (2) 43-53, 1978.

Fig. 3.3—Rhubarb treated with gibberellic acid to break dormancy. (Left) control; (right) treated.

Photograph by Dan Tomkins

Ewing, E. E., and Wareing, P. F., "Shoot, Stolon, and Tuber Formation on Potato (*Solanum tuberosum* L.) Cuttings in Response to Photoperiod," *Plant Physiol.* 6: 348-353, 1978.

Galston, A. W., *The Life of the Green Plant*, Englewood Cliffs, N.J.: Prentice-Hall, Inc., 1964.

Kretchmer, P. J., *et al.*, "Morphological Instability in *Phaseolus vulgaris* L. as Influenced by Red and Far-Red Light Interruption," *Crop Sci.* 17: 797-799, 1977.

Lasley, S. E., and Garber, M. P., "Photosynthetic Contribution of Cotyledons to Early Development of Cucumber," *HortSci.* 13 (2): 191-193, 1978.

Lauer, F. I., "Tubers from Leaf Bud Cuttings: A Tool for Potato Seed Certification and Breeding Programs," *Amer. Potato J.* 54 (10): 457-464, 1977.

Leopold, A. C., and Kriede, P. E., *Plant Growth and Development*, New York: McGraw-Hill Book Company, 1975.

Liu, Phyllis, Wallace, D. H., and Ozbun, J. L., "Influence of Translocation on Photosynthetic Efficiency of *Phaseolus vulgaris* L.," *Plant Physiol.* 52: 412-415, 1973.

Loewy, A. G., and Siekevitz, P., *Cell Structure and Function*, New York: Holt, Rinehart & Winston, Inc., 1963.

Makmur, A., *et al.*, "Physiology and Inheritance of Efficiency in Potassium Utilization in Tomatoes Grown Under Potassium Stress," *J. Amer. Soc. Hort. Sci.* 103 (4): 545-549, 1978.

Martin, F. A., Ozbun, J. L., and Wallace, D. H., "Intraspecific Measurements of Photorespiration," *Plant Physiol.* 49: 764-768, 1972.

McElroy, W. P., and Swanson, E. P., *Modern Cell Biology* 2nd Ed., Englewood Cliffs, N.J.: Prentice-Hall, 1976.

Pierpont, R. A., and Minotti, P. L., "Effects of Calcium Carbonate on Ammonium Assimilation by Tomato Seedlings," *J. Amer. Soc. Hort. Sci.* 102: 20-23, 1977.

Rosenberg, J. L., *Photosynthesis*, New York: Holt, Rinehart & Winston, Inc., 1965.

Rudich, J., Zamski, E., and Regev, Y., "Genotypic Variation for Sensitivity to High Temperature in the Tomato: Pollination and Fruit Set," *Bot. Gaz.* 138 (4): 448-452, 1977.

"Symposium: Chemical Regulation of Plant Processes," *HortSci.* 4 (2), 1969.

"Symposium: Environmental Factors Affecting Vegetable Production," *HortSci.* 6 (1), 1971.

"Symposium: Potassium in Horticulture," *HortSci.* 4 (1), 1969.

"Symposium: The Role of Phosphorus in Plant Growth," *HortSci.* 4 (4), 1969.

Van Overbeek, J., "Plant Hormones and Regulators," *Science* 152: 721, 1966.

Wein, H. C., *et al.*, "The Influence of Flower Removal on Growth and Seed Yield *Phaseolus vulgaris* L., *HortSci.* 98: 45-59, 1973.

CHAPTER 4

Breeding and Improving Vegetables

While many good vegetable cultivars are now available, there is a continuous demand for improvement. The trend toward mechanical harvesting has created the need for cultivars with concentrated fruit set, multiple-disease resistance, different maturities, and adaptation to high-plant populations. In the attempt to get as many desirable characteristics as possible combined in a cultivar, the problem of breeding becomes very complicated. If sufficient genetic variability cannot be found among existing cultivars, crosses may have to be made with related species. Interspecific crosses usually result in problems of sterility. Also, crosses introduce many undesirable characteristics which must be eliminated, after which the desirable characteristics may be selected by elaborate screening. As progress in improving cultivars is made, the task of further improvement becomes more difficult. On the other hand, with advanced techniques such as gene transplanting, future possibilities of plant improvement seem almost unlimited. The vegetable breeder will find it increasingly important to understand how the genes that control plant development are passed from parents to progenies.

CELLS, CHROMOSOMES, AND GENES

An organism, plant or animal, consists of cells, each of which contains a nucleus and other organelles embedded in cytoplasm. Within the nucleus is a number of rod-shaped bodies, the chromosomes. They contain the basic genetic information of the cell, deoxyribonucleic acid or

DNA. The molecules of DNA occur in the form of double strands of intertwined helixes. The individual molecules are long linear aggregates of four basic building blocks called nucleotides. The order in which the nucleotides occur in the chain determines the genetic information carried. On the template of DNA is produced the nucleotide RNA, which migrates from the nucleus to the cytoplasm and determines the many kinds of proteins produced. Proteins with specific catalytic properties are called enzymes. Each controls one chemical reaction or a group of related chemical reactions and thereby regulates the development of the organism. The chromosomes are distinguishable only when the cells are undergoing division. All cells of the same species have the same number of chromosomes, occurring in pairs. In other words, every chromosome within a cell has its exact duplicate in size, shape, and composition. Each body cell of the onion *(Allium cepa)* contains eight pairs of chromosomes, one set of eight having been derived from the male parent and the other set of eight from the female parent. At each cell division, during growth of the plant, these 16 chromosomes divide longitudinally, each daughter cell receiving chromosomes of the same number and composition as the mother cell. These chromosomes carry the factors or "genes" that determine whether a fertilized egg will develop into an animal or plant and whether the individual will possess desirable or undesirable characters. Each character is the expression of one or more genes as modified by the environment. Characters are the attributes which identify an individual.

The genes are distributed along the chromosome like beads on a string, each in its definite location. During cell division, when the chromosomes divide lengthwise, all genes also divide, so that the two daughter cells have the same genic complex as the parent cell.

In most chromosomes there are probably several hundred genes, all tending to remain together as a unit. Genes belonging in the same chromosome are said to be linked; collectively they are known as a linkage group. A plant has as many linkage groups as it has pairs of chromosomes. When certain genes are linked, the characters they express will also be linked. In other words, linked characters tend to remain together more often than they tend to be separated.

Not only are the chromosomes in pairs but also the genes on them are in pairs, arranged in the same lineal order. The two members of a pair of genes are called *allelomorphs*. If both members of a pair of genes are alike, the plant is homozygous (pure) at that point; that is, it will breed true for the character that depends upon this pair of genes for its expression.

SEGREGATION AND RECOMBINATION

In plant growth, when the body cells divide, the daughter cells receive the same number of chromosomes that were in the mother cell. In the flower, however, another type of division known as reduction division occurs in cells preceding the formation of the sperms and eggs. Instead of each chromosome dividing, the pairs meet at the middle of the cell; then the members of each pair move to opposite ends, and two cells are formed in which the number of chromosomes is reduced to one-half that of the body cells (Fig. 4.1).

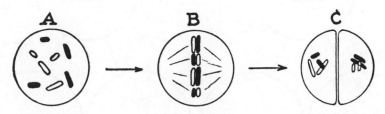

Fig. 4.1—The mother cell (A) contains four pairs of chromosomes. Those colored black have been derived from the male parent, the white from the female parent. Preparatory to reduction division (B) members of a pair meet at the center of the cell. And (C), members of a pair have moved away from each other, and a wall has formed between. Note that the chromosomes derived from the male or female parent do not remain together.

The set of chromosomes derived from the one parent or the other do not remain together; they segregate in all possible combinations. For example, two cultivars of tomatoes differ in the color of the mature fruit, one being red and the other yellow. This difference is determined by a single pair of genes. The genes for red color are represented by the symbols *R R;* the genes for yellow by *r r.* In the formation of the germ cells the red-fruited tomato will produce sperms and eggs with the gene for red, and the yellow-fruited tomato, sperms and eggs with the gene for yellow (Fig. 4.2). When a cross is made, the chromosome number is doubled, and the pair of chromosomes containing *R* and *r* are present in the fertilized egg and in all the body cells of the hybrid. This hybrid will produce eggs and sperms of which one-half will have the chromosome with the gene for red *(R)* and the other half will have the chromosome with the gene for yellow *(r).*

When this hybrid (F_1) is self-fertilized, there will be three possible combinations between eggs and sperm—*RR, Rr,* and *rr,* as shown in the checkerboard (Fig. 4.4). Fertilized eggs will be produced in the ratio of one *RR* pure for red, two *Rr* hybrid for red, and one *rr* pure for yellow.

The *Rr* plant will have red fruit because in this instance red is dominant to yellow. The yellow gene, though present, does not express itself and is therefore said to be recessive. The fertilized egg containing *rr* will produce a plant that will breed true for yellow, and the *RR* plant will breed true for red. The *Rr* plant, however, is hybrid for fruit color, and when

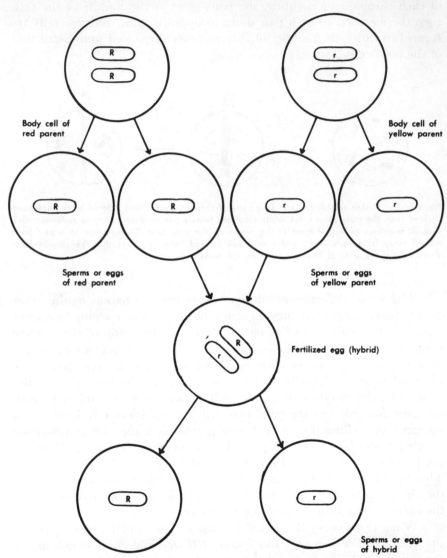

Fig. 4.2—This diagram shows only the pair of chromosomes carrying the genes "R" and "r."

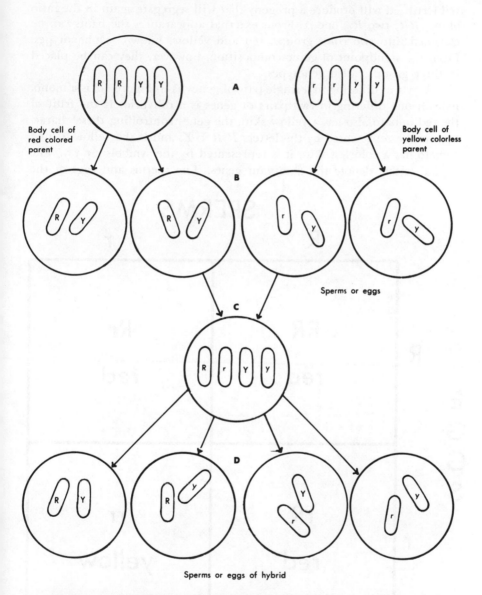

Fig. 4.3—A: Genic composition of two tomato plants, one being pure for red fruit and yellow skin, and the other for yellow fruit and colorless skin. B: Sperms or eggs, only one member of each pair present. C: Fertilized egg (hybrid). D: Four kinds of sperms and eggs formed. Only those chromosomes and genes are represented with which we are concerned here.

self-fertilized will produce a progeny that will segregate again in the ratio of one *RR:* two *Rr:* one *rr.* From external appearances the fruits can be classified into two color groups, red and yellow, known as phenotypes. From the standpoint of genic composition, however, they can be placed in three groups called genotypes.

A hybrid differing in a single pair of genes as in Figure 4.2 is a mono-hybrid; one differing in two pairs of genes is a dihybrid. If the fruit of the red tomato also has a yellow skin, the genes controlling these charac-ters can be represented by the letters *R R Y Y;* and if the yellow-fruited tomato has a colorless skin, it is represented by the symbols *r r y y.* The capital letters denote the dominant genes. The sperms and eggs of the

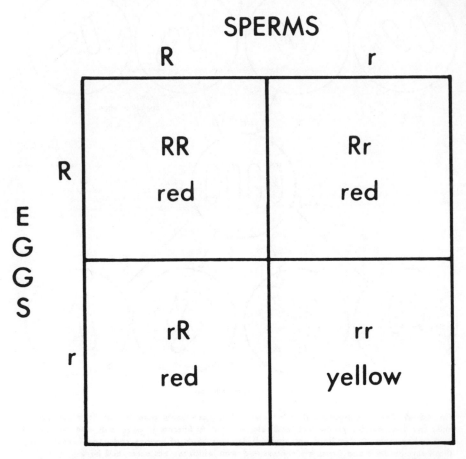

Fig. 4.4—Checkerboard to demonstrate all possible combinations between eggs and sperms when the "F₁" hybrid for genes "Rr" is self-fertilized.

red, yellow-skinned tomato will all contain genes *R Y*, and those of the yellow, colorless-skinned tomato, genes *r y* (Fig. 4.3). The fertilized egg and all body cells of the hybrid (F₁) will contain *Rr Yy*; and will have red fruit with yellow skins. At reduction division four kinds of eggs and sperms will be formed: *RY Ry, rY,* and *ry*. When this hybrid plant is self-fertilized, eggs and sperms will unit in all possible combinations, best illustrated with a checkerboard (Fig. 4.5).

In the resulting progeny (F₂) there are four phenotypic classes in the following ratio: nine of the plants will have red fruit with yellow skin; three will have red fruit with colorless skin and will be pink in appear-

SPERMS

		RY	Ry	rY	ry
	RY	RRYY red colored	RRYy red colored	RrYY red colored	RrYy red colored
E G G S	Ry	RRyY red colored	RRyy red colorless	RryY red colored	Rryy red colorless
	rY	rRYY red colored	rRYy red colored	rrYY yellow colored	rrYy yellow colored
	ry	rRyY red colored	rRyy red colorless	rryY yellow colored	rryy yellow colorless

Fig. 4.5—Checkerboard to demonstrate all possible combinations between eggs and sperms when the "F₁" hybrid for the genes "RrYy" is self-fertilized.

ance because of the lack of yellow pigment in the skin; three will have
yellow fruit with yellow skin; and one will have yellow fruit with colorless skin, appearing pale yellow. Of the two new combinations—red fruit-
colorless skin and yellow fruit-colored skin—one plant out of three will
breed true for the new combination. Phenotypic dihybrid ratios other
than the 9:3:3:1 occur frequently, but lack of space prevents their consideration.

If, in a certain case, the genes A and B occurred in the same chromosome, and their allelomorphs a and b occurred in the other member of
the pair (Fig. 4.6), then, more of the eggs and sperms would contain
the AB and ab combination than Ab and aB, and segregation in the

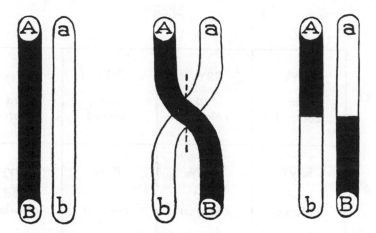

Fig. 4.6—In this figure, on the left, are shown two genes, "A" and "B," and their allelomorphs
in opposite ends of a pair of chromosomes. A break causing an exchange in similar parts of a
pair of chromosomes would have "A" and "b" in one member and "aB" in the other member
of the pair. This phenomenon is known as crossing-over.

F_2 would not correspond to the 9:3:3:1 ratio. Fortunately for the breeder,
even two genes in the same chromosome do not always remain together.
At some stage in the early reduction division, when the members of a
pair of chromosomes lie close together, a break occasionally occurs, and
there is an exchange of homologous parts, known as crossing-over. More
breaks occur between two genes located far apart on a chromosome than
between two that are close together. Where genes are closely linked, one
must usually grow a large number of plants in order to secure the desired
crossover.

FLOWERS, POLLINATION, AND FERTILIZATION

People do not, as a rule, think of plants in terms of sex, mainly because the two sexes are not always separated as they usually are in animals. In only a few vegetables (spinach and asparagus, for example) are the sexes in different plants. Sex is expressed primarily in the flower parts; and when making crosses one must distinguish male from female whether they be in the same flower (perfect), in different flowers of the same plant (monoecious), or in different plants (dioecious).

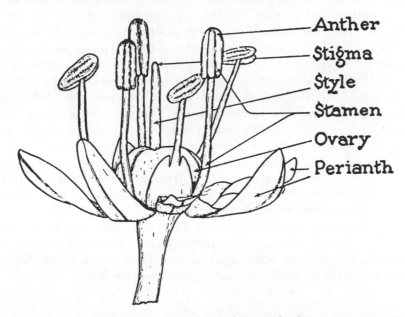

Anther
Stigma
Style
Stamen
Ovary
Perianth

Fig. 4.7—Onion flower. Inner whorl of stamens has burst open.

Truck-Crop Plants, McGraw-Hill Book Co.

Most species of vegetables have four whorls of floral organs—sepals, petals, stamens, and pistils; some lack one or more whorls. From the standpoint of reproduction only the stamens and pistils are important. The stamen, or male part of the flower, contains within its mature anther a yellowish powder called pollen that produces the sperms. The pistil, or female part, has within its ovary one or more small, white, kidney-shaped objects, the ovules, which contain the eggs.

The transfer of pollen from the anther to the stigma of the pistil is called pollination. Self-pollination occurs when pollen is transferred from the anther to the stigma of the same flower or from one flower to another of the same plant; cross-pollination occurs when the transfer is from one plant to another. Plants that depend upon insects and wind are mainly cross-pollinated. Asparagus, onions, and cabbage are pollinated chiefly by insects; spinach, beets, and corn by the wind. In peas, beans, lettuce, and tomatoes, self-pollination is the rule.

The technique one uses to make a pollination will vary with the structure and the normal mode of pollination of the flower and whether self- or cross-pollinations are being made. To develop a technique the flower structure must be studied to determine the size, shape, and position of the anthers and stigmas, and the blooming habit. It is important to know the time of opening of the flower and the time of shedding pollen in relation to the opening of the flower and receptivity of the stigma. As a general rule the stigma is receptive shortly before the flower naturally opens. However, with certain vegetables such as onions and celery the pollen of an individual flower may shed two to four days before the stigma is receptive. The reverse may be true with other species. The length of time a stigma may remain receptive varies considerably and may be affected markedly by environmental factors such as temperature and humidity. The stigmas of most species remain receptive from one to two days on the average, but as a general rule the best results are obtained when one pollinates immediately. The longevity and viability of the pollen varies considerably with different species. Pollen of certain species, such as the tomato, has been successfully stored for relatively long periods of time under proper conditions of temperature and humidity. Greenhouses, where growing conditions can be controlled, are commonly used for self- and cross-pollinations (Fig. 4.8).

VARIATION

It is rare that two plants are exactly alike, no matter how uniform the cultivar to which they belong appears en masse. The variations between plants may be of two types: those caused by the environment and those caused by the difference in genic make-up of the chromosomes. Variations caused by a difference in environmental factors such as moisture, temperature, and light are not inherited. The principal effect of these factors is upon the size of the plant or its parts.

Variations originating in the genic material of the chromosomes are heritable. They may arise in several ways—as a recombination of characters; change of a single gene; change of several genes; or a loss

Fig. 4.8—Carrots grown in the greenhouse for controlled pollination.

USDA Photograph

or gain of a portion of a chromosome, an entire chromosome, or whole sets of chromosomes.

Methods have been recently devised to increase variability within plants. One method is to change the number of chromosomes. A chemical called colchicine has been found that will double the number of chromosomes. Besides colchicine, other chemicals, applications of heat, and wounding the stems have also done the same. Plants with more sets of chromosomes than the two normally found are called polyploids. Tomato plants which normally have 12 pairs or 24 chromosomes before treatment with colchicine have been shown to have 48 chromosomes after treatments. These plants with four sets of chromosomes are called tetraploids. The normal tomatoes are called diploids. Plants with three sets of chromosomes, called triploids, have been obtained by crossing a tetraploid with a diploid. The hybrid seedless watermelon, which is a triploid, is obtained in this way. The triploid is highly sterile and seedless, and is grown commercially by interplanting it with a normal diploid line that serves as a pollinator necessary for fruit set.

Polyploids can sometimes be recognized by their increased size and more luxuriant growth, but this is not always true. Artificially induced tetraploids generally are less fertile than their diploid parents. As a general rule tetraploids have not proved directly useful for most vegetable crops. They have, however, proved directly useful in some flowers such as snapdragons and marigolds where the increased size of the flower is of importance.

Changes in genes and sections of chromosomes have been induced by various means. Mutations can be brought about by the use of X rays, gamma rays, thermal neutrons, ultraviolet rays, and certain chemicals such as the nitrogen mustards. Many of the mutations or changes that result are detrimental to the plant, but sources of disease resistance and higher yields have been found recently with these methods.

Crop improvement is possible because plants do differ in their heritable characteristics. However, it is often impossible to tell by looking at a superior-appearing plant whether the desirable characters are heritable or nonheritable. The plant breeder has to spend much of his time distinguishing between these two kinds of variation. The real proof of a selection's superiority is to grow progenies from the plant. If the characteristic is passed down from parent to progeny then we know it is inherited and can be successfully selected.

METHODS OF IMPROVEMENT

Crop improvement through plant breeding is chiefly accomplished by selection and hybridization and the combination of the two. Selection is effective only when differences are heritable. Variation is not created by selection, but existing, desirable variation may be collected and concentrated by selection. Hybridization or crossing two or more sources may result in new and superior combinations of characters.

Hybrids are valuable for a number of reasons. A combination of uniformity and vigor can be obtained that is difficult to get in any other way; early and total yields can be increased. Certain characteristics such as the seedless condition in watermelons are possible only in hybrids. However, indiscriminate crossing of plants should be avoided. One should always have a definite reason or clear-cut objective in mind before starting to make crosses between plants. If not, much effort can be lost and no worthwhile results obtained.

The natural sources of variation should be adequately explored before hybridizing. When progress is no longer possible or economical through continued use of natural variation, then it is time to resort to controlled hybridization. On the other hand, hybridization may be needed early in a breeding program if the cultivars in use do not contain a specific character which is needed. Early hybridization may be necessary, for example, to obtain disease resistance, since many otherwise good varieties are limited in production because they are susceptible to one disease or another.

Selection usually follows hybridization to isolate the superior combinations that may arise. Frequently selections may be back-crossed to one of the parents for several generations. This is done to incorporate some desirable feature such as disease resistance into an otherwise desirable cultivar lacking only in this one character.

Commercial use may sometimes be made of F_1 hybrids, or the first generation following a cross. Many combinations are usually made and tested to find the one that is best suited to the conditions under which it is to be used.

Certain situations make the production of hybrid seed economical. Any condition which aids in the separation of the male and female elements of a flower or plant will help provide a method for making economical crosses between plants. The monoecious flowering habit in corn separates the female ear from the male tassel. An inbred line can be made essentially female by removing the tassel before it has shed its pollen. Allowing another line to shed pollen in the presence of the detasseled line will make the desired cross, provided the two lines are isolated from other corn plantings. Another means is provided by conditions of male sterility. Certain inherited factors bring about sterility within the male parts of the flowers that effectively make the flower and plant female. If some means are provided to transfer fertile pollen from another line, hybrid seed can be easily and economically produced. Male sterility has been found in nearly every kind of vegetable. The production of hybrid seed in onions is entirely based upon the use of male sterility. Methods of using male sterility are being worked out to produce hybrids with such crops as beets, carrots, squash, sweet corn, tomatoes, eggplant, and peppers.

The actual method of breeding used depends upon the crop and the objectives sought. For our purposes here, we divide crops into four groups: (1) those naturally self-pollinated, (2) those naturally cross-pollinated, (3) those often or partially cross-pollinated, and (4) those vegetatively propagated. Space does not permit an extensive discussion of breeding methods and objectives for all the crops in each group.

PLANTS NATURALLY SELF-POLLINATED

Important vegetable crops that are naturally self-pollinated include peas, snap and field beans, tomatoes, and lettuce. Self-pollination is not absolute, as some crossing usually occurs in all. Within this group of plants little if any loss in vigor is caused by inbreeding that results from self-pollination. Essentially homozygous or pure lines are developed in a few generations because self-pollination is the most intensive form of inbreeding. Selection within a pure line is therefore likely to be ineffective. In old or unselected cultivars an opportunity exists for increased variability arising from mixtures, mutations, and natural crossing. Therefore, the chances for obtaining improvement by selection are much greater from old than from new cultivars.

The two general methods of selection are mass selection and pedigree selection. With mass selection a fairly large number of desirable plants with relatively similar characteristics are selected and the seed is bulked and planted. The selected lot is usually compared with the original cultivar. Mass selection is most useful in dealing with characters that are not modified greatly by environment. Under certain conditions it is possible to obtain quicker results from mass selection than from pedigree selection since uniformity for one character may be obtained with less danger of altering other varietal characteristics. Rapid changes in varietal type are not usually made with mass selection. Mass selection is less useful than pedigree selection for characters which are modified greatly by environment because the effects of heredity and environment are not separated. A form of mass selection is commonly used by seedsmen to maintain a stock or cultivar by eliminating undesirable or inferior plants. This practice is commonly called roguing. As a general rule, seed stocks of self-pollinated crops are relatively easy to maintain true to type by isolation and selection.

The pedigree system of selection may be superior to mass selection as more rapid progress may usually be expected. It is, however, more expensive to operate and requires more record-taking. In practice, the single-plant selections are kept separate and the progenies are grown out for evaluation. The original selections from a variable population will isolate many pure lines, within which further selection is not likely to be effective. The main problem is to find out which pure lines are the best. Further selection of lines is usually based upon the performance of the whole row. Many of the lines are discarded for one reason or another, leaving a relatively small number to be tested in the following years. Final selection should be based on tests in several seasons and in different locations throughout the area in which the cultivar is expected to be used.

When controlled hybridizations are made between plants to produce new sources of variation and obtain new combinations, some form of selection is begun as soon as segregation of the characters occurs. Pedigree selection is most commonly used and mass selection is seldom used following hybridization.

Within self-pollinated crops, hybrid vigor is commonly found when different pure lines are crossed. Since self-pollination is the general rule, inbreeding is unnecessary to obtain pure lines in this group of plants.

Whether or not it is economically feasible to use hybrid vigor depends upon the cost of producing the hybrid seed in relation to the value of the increased yields. Since most self-pollinated crops produce a relatively small amount of pollen, which is not transferred by the wind or by insects to any significant degree, hand-pollination is most likely necessary to bring about a transfer of pollen between plants. If many seeds are produced by each hand-pollination and if few seeds are needed per acre, it may be feasible to use hybrids. With tomatoes, for example, a relatively large number of seeds may be obtained in each fruit by each hand-pollination, and the increased yields justify hybridization for greenhouse and early-market use. With crops like peas and beans, it is very unlikely that hybrids will ever be used because of the difficulty in making hand-pollinations and the small number of seeds per pollination.

PLANTS NATURALLY CROSS-POLLINATED

Important vegetable crops that are naturally cross-pollinated include plants of the cabbage family such as cabbage, cauliflower, rutabagas, turnips, and radishes; root crops including carrots, beets, parsnips; and other crops such as onions, sweet corn, asparagus, spinach, and rhubarb. Most of these crops have perfect flowers (both sexes in the same flower). The pollen of the perfect-flowered species is largely transferred by the wind or insects. Sweet corn is monoecious (male and female flowers separate but on the same plant), and asparagus and spinach are dioecious (separate male and female plants). The monoecious and dioecious conditions are responsible for a very high degree of cross-pollination. Most crops that are highly cross-pollinated lose vigor with inbreeding.

The development of true breeding cultivars may be accomplished by selecting naturally occurring plants with desirable characteristics. Mass selection is usually preferable to pedigree selection because cultivars can be obtained that are relatively uniform for observable characters but still retain vigor. The Danish type of cabbage used in New York and other Eastern states was originally developed by this method. If pedigree selection is used with controlled pollination, these crops ordinarily lose so much vigor by inbreeding that the strains developed are seldom directly useful. Pedigree selection is occasionally practiced without control of the pollen parent and is commonly referred to as ear-to-row breeding in corn. The results from this method have not been completely satisfactory. It has proved successful in changing specific characters, but the yield is often reduced at the same time because of the close breeding.

Combinations of pedigree and mass selection are sometimes used. This method is useful in dealing with characters that are modified greatly by environment. After a generation or two of pedigree selection, a fairly large number of selected lines should be massed to regain vigor. This method has been used successfully with both onions and carrots.

Variation may be produced by controlled hybridization in much the same manner as with self-pollinated crops. Frequently natural crossing will provide abundant recombinations of characters within existing cultivars. If specific characters are missing in a cultivar, they may be incorporated by making appropriate controlled crosses.

It is with cross-pollinated crops that the commercial use of first-generation F_1 hybrids has gained the most favor. F_1 hybrids make up a very high percentage of the sweet corn grown both for marketing and for processing. Hybrids of cabbage and spinach are in commercial production. Experimental hybrids of asparagus, carrots, and beets have been produced and should soon join the commercial ranks. Hybrid vigor is commonly found when two inbred lines are crossed.

Yields of hybrid onions were compared with that of the leading cultivar, Early Yellow Globe. In summarizing the data recorded for three years at four locations in New York State the following was found: 12 percent of the hybrids yielded significantly more and 14 percent significantly less, while 74 percent were not significantly different from Early Yellow Globe. The hybrids that outyielded this cultivar produced an average yield of 213 fifty-pound bushels per acre more than the check cultivar. Some of the hybrids that yielded the most were not acceptable commercially because of such things as poor storage quality, poor color, and thin skins. Some of the hybrids which yielded no more than Early Yellow Globe were actually superior because of earlier maturity, better color, and the ability to keep longer in storage (Fig. 4.9).

Breeding methods for improvement of dioecious crops have not received much study. Mass selection has been the most common method.

Since the sexes are separated into separate plants they cannot be closely inbred. Brother-sister or sib mating is the closest form of inbreeding. Dioecious plants usually lose vigor on sibbing. Occasionally plants can be found in crops such as spinach and asparagus that have both sexes on the same plant. These plants can then be inbred. As already mentioned, F_1 hybrids are now in use with spinach and have been experimentally produced in asparagus. Increased yields of from 20 to 50 percent have been reported for spinach hybrids over that obtained by commercial cultivars.

Fig. 4.9—Comparative yields of the hybrid Granex (center) and parents, TEG 951, left and YB 936, right.

USDA Photograph

PLANTS PARTIALLY CROSS-POLLINATED

Lima beans, eggplants, peppers, celery, potatoes, and .those in the cucurbit family such as cucumbers, squash, pumpkins, muskmelons, and watermelons are usually classified as being partially cross-pollinated. The amount of crossing will vary for these crops depending upon the environment. The breeding methods employed will vary depending upon the amount of crossing and the loss in vigor resulting from self-pollination. In general most of these crops do not lose as much vigor with inbreeding as one might expect. Care must be taken in producing seed of these plants in order to maintain purity of stocks and cultivars. Hybrids of summer squash, winter squash, cucumbers, muskmelons, watermelons, and eggplants are in production. Pepper hybrids are appearing on the market. Male sterility has been found and is the basis for the economical production of hybrid seed within most of the vegetables in the group.

An experiment with eggplant in Pennsylvania illustrates the extent of hybrid vigor one may obtain in this group of plants. Seven cultivars of eggplant representing a range of types were crossed in all possible combinations. Sixteen of the possible 21 hybrids were compared with the parents for yields. Table 4.1 shows the ranges in yield in tons per acre and the average yields of the parents and hybrids. The hybrids clearly outyielded the parent varieties in both early and total yield.

Table 4.1—A Comparison of Early and Total Yields of Parental Varieties of Eggplants and Their F₁ Hybrids.

	Parental Varieties		F₁ Hybrids	
	Range in Tons/Acre	Average Yield, Tons/Acre	Range in Tons/Acre	Average Yield, Tons/Acre
Early yield	1.5-6.6	4.1	3.6-11.8	8.0
Total yield	11.0-19.9	15.2	19.3-37.1	24.9

PLANTS VEGETATIVELY PROPAGATED

Vegetable crops propagated chiefly by vegetative means are: potatoes, sweet potatoes, globe artichokes, rhubarb, garlic, and horseradish. In breeding vegetatively propagated crops, if one plant is found with desirable characteristics, an indefinite number of plants can be obtained that are identical to the selected plant. Selection among plants produced by vegetative propagation will not be effective.

In some crops favorable mutations may occur quite frequently. These may accumulate in old or unselected cultivars. Some mutations or changes are easily recognized, such as red skins on white potato tubers.

Much of the improvement in the sweet potato has been made by the selection of favorable mutations. In the Puerto Rican cultivar of sweet potato, the mutation rate is fairly high, one in about every 7,000 plants. Most cultivars of sweet potatoes do not bloom readily in the United States, but in the West Indies, conditions are favorable for flowering of some cultivars. The sweet potato flower closely resembles that of the morning glory, to which it is closely related. The nonflowering varieties of sweet potatoes have been induced to flower by grafting a small portion of the growing point on certain species of morning glory. It is now possible to make crosses among any of the varieties of sweet potatoes. As with the potato, desirable seedlings can be maintained indefinitely by vegetative propagation.

In spite of the great effort to produce new cultivars, many old ones with obvious shortcomings are still being used. A well known cultivar may still be in demand and must be supplied by seedsmen even though others are superior. The seedsman has a problem handling a large number of cultivars, especially when they have to be grown in isolation to maintain purity. One cultivar with limited demand is seldom profitable. Unless a new one has received special publicity, such as receiving an All-American Award or has some exceptional character such as disease resistance, it is difficult to get a seedsman to produce it. He cannot afford to advertise a particular cultivar because the competition would have it the following year—unless the cultivar happened to be an F_1 hybrid where the inbreds are controlled. To introduce a new cultivar and have it accepted, the plant breeder must combine in it as many desirable characters as possible. It must have wide adaptability and be significantly better in some aspect than others that are already available.

SELECTED REFERENCES

Allard, R. W., *Principles of Plant Breeding*, New York: John Wiley & Sons, Inc., 1960.

Anonymous, "Commercial Muskmelon Breeding in Texas," USDA Tech. Bull. 1405, 1969.

Bohn, G. W., and Andrus, C. F., "Cantaloupe Breeding," USDA Tech. Bull. 1403, 1969.

Bourdette, V. R., "Somatic Hybridization—Removing Sex from Plant Breeding: Eggplant," U.S. Agr. Res. Ser., Agr. Res. 26 (5): 3-4, 1977.

Cullinan, F. P., "Breeding for Harvesting," USDA *Agriculture Yearbook,* 1965.

Gentile, A. G., and Stoner, A. K., "Resistance in *Lycopersicon* and *Solanum* Species to the Potato Aphid," *Jour. Econ. Ent.* 61: 1152-1154, 1968.

McCreight, J. D., Lower, R. L., and Moll, R. H., "Heritability of Reducing Sugar Concentration in Pickling Cucumber Fruit and Its Implications on Selection," *J. Amer. Soc. Hort. Sci.* 103 (2): 271-274, 1978.

Nelson, R. R., *Breeding Plants for Disease Resistance*, Pa. State Univ. Press, 1973.

O'Brien, M. J., and Winters, H. F., "Evaluation of Selected Spinach Accessions for Resistance to *Fusarium oxysporum* F.," Plant Dis. Rep. 62 (5): 427-429, 1978.

Quisumbing, A. R., and Lower, R. L., "Influence of Plot Size and Seedling Rate in Field Screening Studies for Cucumber Cultivars, Resistance to Cucumber Beetles," *J. Amer. Soc. Hort. Sci.* 103 (4): 523-527, 1978.

Robinson, R. W., *et al.*, "Genes of Cucurbitaceae," *HortSci.* 11: 554-568, 1976.

Stevens, M. A., *et al.*, "Genotypic Variation for Flavor and Composition in Fresh Market Tomatoes," *J. Amer. HortSci.* 102 (5): 680-689, 1977.

Stoner, A. K., "Breeding for Insect Resistance in Vegetables," *HortSci.* 5 (2), 1970.

"Symposium: Horticultural Plant Breeding," *HortSci.* 3 (4), 1968.

Tarn, T. R., and Tai, G. C. C., "Heterosis and Variation of Yield Components in F. Hybrids Between Group *Tuberosum* and group *Indigena* Potatoes," *Crop Sci.* 17 (4): 517-521, 1977.

Wallace, D. H., *et al.*, "Physiological Genetics of Crop Yield," *Advan. Agron.* 24: 97-146, 1972.

Wann, E. V., and Hills, W. A., "Earworm Resistance in Sweet Corn," *Proc. Amer. Soc. Hort. Sci.* 89, 491-496, 1966.

CHAPTER 5

Seeds and Seed Growing

The trend toward mechanization in vegetable production has greatly increased the need for high-quality seed. Precision planters, electronic thinners, and mechanical harvesters are not successful unless high-quality seed is used. In the days of thick seeding, hand thinning, and hand harvesting, a high premium was not placed upon high-percent germination and uniformity.

The product as harvested by the planter may be much worse than the seed from which it has sprung, but it can be no better. The hereditary content of the seed sets the upper limit of both performance and quality. We can do much with fertilizer, water, and care to get out of a plant the best that it has, but we can get no more than it has received from its parents.

The price of seed for most vegetable crops is a small fraction of the total cost, and merit in seed may greatly increase yield or selling value or both. Hence, the utmost care is called for in buying seed, and one may well afford to pay increased prices for seed, provided he is satisfied value is delivered.

THE CHARACTERS OF GOOD SEED

Good seed is (1) clean, (2) disease-free, (3) viable, (4) well developed, and (5) of good heritage.

To be clean, seed must be free of foreign matter, such as other kinds of seeds, dirt, or plant fragments. Vegetable seeds seldom cause serious trouble in this respect.

Freedom from Diseases

Seed should not carry disease to infect the new crop. To insure that it doesn't, the seed should be grown without contamination. This may be accomplished by its production in disease-free areas and by the use of rigid control methods. Sometimes diseases on the outside of the seed can be destroyed by poison treatments. Thiram and captan, for example, can be used for damping-off fungi. In other cases, such as blackleg of cabbage, heat (hot-water treatment) will kill fungi within the seed. Great care must be used, however, not to injure the germinating seed.

Viability of Seed

Seed must have enough vitality to complete the process of germination. The little plant must be able to break the soil and bring its leaves above ground so that it may grow independently of its stored food. Growth prior to that stage may be described merely as sprouting.

A correct stand of plants in the field is very important. It costs nearly as much to cultivate half a stand as a full stand, and overseeding results in either costly thinning or harmful crowding. So the planter should know what his seed will do under his own conditions of soil, temperature, and moisture. Many kinds of seed, a year or more old, are usable, but one must know their viability to use them safely.

Most good seedsmen test their seeds and sell only seed of high viability (Fig. 5.1). Minimum germination requirements for most vegetables have been set by the Federal government. If germination is below these minimums for seed moving in interstate commerce, the package must be labeled "Below Standard" and the percentage of germination must be stated. Many states have similar laws applying to seed raised and sold within the state.

Probably the best test for casual use is to plant counted seeds in rows in a flat of the soil to be used or in a greenhouse bed, covering as usual. The temperature and moisture are kept constantly favorable, and the seedlings counted after they appear. From these data the percentage of germination can be calculated.

Another way is to count out the seeds, placing them between folds of blotters or cotton flannel in a dish with water enough to keep them moist but not enough to exclude air. The dish is kept at a temperature of about 70° F., and the sprouts are counted. Weak or slow sprouts should not be counted, as they may not be able to get through the soil under field conditions. The "rag-doll" test is good for coarse seeds such as

Fig. 5.1—Seed should not only germinate but also produce vigorous seedlings.

Associated Seed Growers, Inc.

peas, beans, and sweet corn. Seeds are counted out on long strips of cotton flannel or other cloth and properly marked. The cloth is then rolled up, moistened, and kept at about 65° to 70° F. The sprouted seeds are later counted, and the percentage is calculated.

The viability of seeds may be determined by a cold test. The seeds are usually planted in flats of unsterilized soil and held at a temperature of about 45° F. for one week. They are then germinated at normal temperatures. Weak and injured seeds become infected with microorganisms and fail to germinate. This test simulates field conditions early in the season, but is difficult to standardize.

Seed testing has become a highly technical enterprise, and good laboratories do not always entirely agree. Nevertheless, both professional and home testing are of great value. Tests must be made carefully and, in case of doubt, they should be rechecked, checked with seedsmen, or with the state seed laboratories.

Different kinds of seed require different conditions of temperature, aeration, and even light. For example, spinach will not germinate well in very warm weather, even though there is moisture in the soil. Also, some seeds, such as lettuce, undergo a period of dormancy just after harvest when viability is very low. Light is effective in breaking this dormancy. Some seeds such as beans may not germinate well if taken from dry storage and planted immediately. They should be conditioned for one or two weeks at relative humidity between 60 and 70 percent.

Longevity of Seed

A sample of celery seed 15 years old gave a 50 percent stand in a trial some years ago, and other kinds occasionally perform similarly. Onions, sweet corn, and parsnips, on the other hand, are known to be unreliable the second season and should be used only after satisfactory tests. When it is desirable to use old seed, a careful test should be made and the rate of sowing increased as necessary.

Changes in temperature alone seem to have little influence on the vitality of seed. If seed is dry, freezing is harmless, as is heating to any ordinary atmospheric temperature. Let the climate be humid or the seed moist and the seed is soon worthless. Onion seed stored eight months in Michigan lost nothing in vitality, while a similar lot in Alabama declined to zero. Tomatoes, watermelons, and radishes suffered less. Seeds generally keep well in cool northern climates and in the dry climate of the Southwest, but in the humid South and Southeast seeds lose their viability very rapidly. Conditions favoring longevity of seeds are low temperature, low humidity, and low seed moisture content.

Table 5.1 gives a general idea of the length of time seeds may be expected to retain their vitality under normal conditions. Information on the different kinds of seed appears in the special crop chapters.

Size of Seed

If one sifts the seed and plants the larger ones, will he harvest a better crop? Much study has been focused on this problem with considerable confusion of results, but it seems to resolve itself into the following: larger seeds give a slightly earlier and more uniform maturity. Medium-sized seeds will also mature evenly. Sizing the seed makes it possible to sow more accurately with seeders or drills and get more uniform stands. These advantages make it profitable in some cases to separate the seeds into three sizes, planting the two larger sizes separately,

Table 5.1—Length of Time Seeds May Be Expected to Retain Their Vitality.*

Kind of Vegetable	Years	Kind of Vegetable	Years
Asparagus	3	Onion	1
Beans	3	Parsley	2
Beet	4	Parsnip	1
Brussels sprouts	4	Peas	3
Cabbage	4	Pepper	3
Carrot	3	Pumpkin	4
Cauliflower	4	Radish	4
Celery	5	Rutabaga	4
Cucumber	5	Spinach	4
Eggplant	5	Squash	4
Endive	5	Sweet corn	1
Kale	4	Tomato	3
Lettuce	5	Turnip	4
Muskmelon	5	Watermelon	5
Okra	2		

*When stored under favorable conditions, seed of the age indicated (from harvest not from time of purchase) should be viable. Seed is often good much longer, but specific lots may not survive so long.

but discarding the small seeds, many of which are weak or improperly matured.

Trueness to a Good Name

After all, the important point about seed is what kind of plant and product it will bring forth, and how it will perform. So far as the seed is concerned, this is mainly a matter of heredity. The seed must truly represent a good cultivar and a strain suitable for the conditions and markets contemplated. These matters are not so easily measured as count per ounce or percentage of viability, but they are just as important.

CLASSIFICATION OF VEGETABLES

To buy seed satisfactorily, one needs to understand the classification of the various forms of vegetable plants. The different vegetables are classified botanically in Chapter 2.

A horticultural classification of the vegetables includes the following gradations: (1) the kind, (2) the cultivar, (3) the strain, and (4) the stock.

Kind

A kind includes all the plants which in general usage are accepted as a single vegetable, as, for example, tomato, cabbage, bean. This is not the same as the genus or the species of botanical classification. The species *Brassica oleracea* includes several kinds (cabbage, cauliflower, and others). The beans come from more than one species (*Phaseolus vulgaris, P. lunatus,* etc.).

Cultivar (Variety)

A cultivar includes those plants of a given kind which are practically alike in important characteristics. Each cultivar should be distinct from all others in one or more prominent and significant features. Named cultivars that are not distinct should be classified as strains of a recognized cultivar or as mere synonyms.

The line between cultivars is not always sharply drawn and is at present a matter of informal consensus, which results in great confusion. The only prospect for making cultivars definite lies in the establishment of some generally accepted authority, such as the U.S. Department of Agriculture or a national board of vegetable nomenclature. Well conducted studies of cultivar characters have much weight in establishing types and should be conducted on a continuing basis from year to year at representative locations throughout the country.

Strain

A strain includes those plants which possess the general characteristics of a given cultivar but which differ from others of the cultivar in one important respect, or two or three minor respects, the differences not being great enough to justify a new cultivar name. Thus Cherokee is a standard cultivar of bean and Resistant Cherokee is a mosaic-resistant strain of this cultivar. Golden Self-Blanching is a standard celery, while Tall Golden Self-Blanching is a strain that is more vigorous, earlier, and more spreading, and has broader and thinner leafstalks. The distinction between cultivar and strain is based simply on degrees of difference.

Stock

A stock represents all plants of the same parentage or pedigree. Differences between various stocks of a cultivar or strain should be very slight. A seed grower may maintain more than one stock of a strain, each representing a single pedigree line. Two seed growers may have stocks so nearly alike as to be indistinguishable, but as long as they are separately maintained, they are distinct stocks.

The distinctions of the definitions of strain and stock are not hard and fast; in fact, the seed trade is anything but consistent in its use of terms. The idea of a stock as distinct from a strain is based on the concept of parentage or pedigree lines. While some seed houses practically ignore the pedigree idea, many keep careful records and are able to trace parentage through several generations. At the same time, stocks of presumably nearly equal excellence are often used interchangeably.

As the buying public becomes more discriminating and willing to pay for greater care in seed production, the pedigree idea is finding fuller application in trade practice.

VEGETABLE TRIALS

The term "trial" usually refers to growing, observing, and recording the characteristics of plant and product of a given sample of seed, while the term "testing" is usually used in connection with purity and germination. Trials are the means of knowing the character of the stocks which are planted. They may be very simple, mere observations of a planted sample in comparison with another, or only in comparison with a memory-picture or an idea of what is wanted. Trials may be elaborate and exhaustive involving great care in procuring samples, in repeating the plantings, in seeing that growing conditions are uniform, and in making careful observations dealing with these many characters. Such elaborate trials are carried on by the U.S. Department of Agriculture, the state experiment stations, and by many progressive breeders and seedsmen. Results appear in public bulletins, in catalogues, and in a variety of manuals for seedsmen.

The grower may well depend on other observers for the main points about a new offering, but he must himself make the final selection for his own situation. This means simple but careful trials and comparisons on a small scale before large plantings are made. Novelties are often alluring and every advance comes first as a novelty. While one is not wise to ignore the new things, neither should he make sudden shifts from the old to the new.

Anyone interested in the careful trial of samples of vegetable seeds may make his own list of points to be observed. He may find schedules of points in many variety bulletins, and he may write for suggestions to experienced workers, who are usually glad to help. The tabular system of recording observations enters characters across the top of the sheet and names or numbers of samples at the side, or vice versa. Thus, one character may be studied at a time in all samples, and notations may be made in harmony with one another. Otherwise, if all characters of small, early sorts are described first and the characters of large, late sorts are taken up later, a "drift" of one's impressions is bound to occur. Measurements by the tabular system are accurate, easily read, easily compared, and easily handled statistically. Brevity and ease of reading are served by using numerical ratings instead of words, one representing a very low degree of a character, five medium, and nine high. Intermediate steps may be used as needed. Mechanical methods should not, however, crowd out the general estimate of merit and informal comparisons that may be less scientific but none the less enlightening.

The grower may learn much from his own short trial rows, but the final verdict will depend upon field performance. Matters of evenness of maturity, small differences in earliness (often important in marketing), yield, ease of harvesting and handling, holding up in marketing, and table quality may be revealed only in very elaborate, formal trials, with many replications and carefully measured observations. After all, a crop or perhaps several crops must be grown to tell the whole story.

THE SEED BUSINESS

Most planters buy their seed in preference to saving it or growing it themselves. The seed trade has become a specialized and highly technical business, having many different branches and offering services of many degrees of merit. In general, breeding and service about keep up to what planters demand and are willing to pay for. Seed houses have constantly advanced in breeding, production, and service. There are enough good houses that one need not take undue risk in buying from unreliable sources. This is especially important, as the merit or demerit of a sample of seed is not evident on inspection. Like insurance or banking, the seed business represents a trust relationship and is dependent upon the character of men, their ideals, integrity, and practices. Even good seed from an unreliable house is of only temporary value, for the buyer does not know that he can get the same value again.

Seed houses may engage in any or all of the following services: (1) breeding, (2) growing, (3) wholesale dealing, (4) importing, and (5) distributing (serving commercial or home planters or both). They may handle but one kind of seed or they may handle all kinds and other merchandise besides. There is some confusion in use of the term "wholesale," as it may be applied to transactions between seed growers and merchants, or between seed growers and planters who grow vegetables to sell.

Improving and Maintaining Stocks

New cultivars and strains arise by discovery of a plant of distinct type among others, by mass selection for better type, or by crossing and selection. For a general understanding of breeding vegetable plants, refer to Chapter 4. In recent years, an increasing number of improvements have come through definite efforts toward a preconceived type, crossing and selecting until the desired result is attained, and fixing the type through pure-line breeding. Many experiment stations and seed houses employ highly trained scientists for this work (Fig. 5.2).

Intensive breeding work yields stock seed in small quantities. A good house treasures its stock seed, reproducing it with great care under selection (choosing the best plants) and roguing (discarding off-type plants) from year to year. Good market seed is faithfully rogued, but if stock

Fig. 5.2—Isolation cages used in a commercial plant breeding operation by the Crookham Company, Caldwell, Idaho.

USDA Photograph

seed has been well bred, only a few plants need to be discarded. From this stock seed, market seed is grown in especially suitable regions. Cheap seed may represent simple crop growing with little attention to keeping the stock true, to say nothing of improving it.

Seed producers must not only improve their stocks, but also be thoroughly acquainted with the merits of these stocks. Dealers also should know the qualities of the stocks they handle. To this end, special trial grounds are often maintained. Some houses depend upon observation in the fields of their customers. A combination of both methods is best, each making its own contributions.

Non-warranty Clause

The non-warranty clause as adopted by the American Seed Trade Association, is as follows: "We give no warranty, expressed or implied, as to description, purity, productiveness, or any other matter of any seeds or bulbs we send out, and we will not be in any way responsible for the crop. If the purchaser does not accept the goods on these terms, they are at once to be returned."

Most seedsmen use this clause, or words to the same effect. While this seems harsh toward the buyer, a moment's thought reveals the fact that a crop failure may be due to many causes other than poor seed, and that it is usually impossible to tell what cause is responsible. If the seedsman were to assume all these risks in addition to the risks of error on his own part or on the part of those upon whom he depends, the cost would be excessive. Furthermore, the clause protects the seedsman against imposition. At the same time, the seedsman should not take advantage of the clause to dodge responsibility that is rightfully his. Good seed houses are careful, and when they are at fault often make substantial adjustments. There are plenty of such houses, where the buyer can obtain good seed and good service on the usual non-warranty terms.

Where Seed Comes From

Vegetable seed may be bred in many climates. Market crops produced by multiplying well-bred stock seeds are grown where soil, climate, and economic conditions are favorable. Pea- and bean-seed production moved from East to West largely because of disease and poor conditions for curing in the East. A large part of the muskmelon and cucumber seed comes from Colorado and California, while production of hybrid sweet-corn seed is centered in Idaho. Before World War II, a large amount of seed was imported from such countries as Denmark and the Netherlands. During the war this supply was cut off and seed was produced in the United States and Canada. Since the war, various quantities of some vegetable seeds have been imported from Mexico, Japan, Canada, Holland, Great Britain, France, and other countries, including Israel, which exports onion seed. Although tomato seed imports have increased five-fold during the last 10 years, some other kinds are imported in lesser quantities. Japan provides some kinds of seed requiring hand pollination. The use of male-sterile plants eliminates expensive hand pollination (Fig. 5.3). Seed growers in the United States are maintaining high quality production, and the nation is becoming more self-sufficient. The skill and care of seedsmen are far more important for seed quality than is the place of production.

BUYING SEED

Judicious buying of seed calls for utmost care, and emphasis should be placed on the ultimate value of the crop rather than on the initial cost of the seed. In general, one should buy from seedsmen of estab-

Fig. 5.3—Roguing male-sterile seed rows in hybrid onion seed production.

USDA Photograph

lished reputation who cater to commercial planters; that is, from houses accustomed to serving critical trade. One may well inquire among neighbors and at meetings to learn what houses hold reputations for quality of seed, dependability, and good service. Then one's own experience becomes a valuable guide.

Catalogues

The seed catalogue is a fascinating book, and no one would care for a drab and colorless offering of goods. A good merchant is enthusiastic after he has expended cash and care to get the best. We need, however, to learn which houses are given to extravagant claims and which keep praise and merit fairly abreast. One may readily distinguish between statements of opinion, "The best we have ever seen," and statements of fact, "A week earlier than Rutgers." Catalogues of the more dependable houses are nowadays giving a larger measure of actual facts, telling what a cultivar is like. Pictures are less extravagant and more informative, though it is the cataloguers' business to show fine specimens of true type. Unfortunately, there are too many catalogues that are less than candid in their statements.

Known Origin

The planter has as much right to assurance about his seed as to know the name of the car he buys. Many seedsmen are not yet ready to tell where they get their seed, but, even in these cases, the buyer should insist on definite stock numbers and assurance that will enable him to buy seed of the same parentage next year or be told it is not available. In the meantime, wholesale producers and breeders are advertising more widely, retailers are realizing it is well to feature the name of a good seed grower, and the idea of known origin is gradually spreading. Some houses now stamp stock numbers on all packages and most good houses keep records of stock numbers of lots delivered.

The planter may profitably learn who are breeders and producers of good seed and ask for their products. If the salesman mentions some other source, the planter should find out if it ranks with the best. Thus knowledge of buying is built up.

Buying in Advance

Many growers buy seed a year ahead and plant a sample for careful trial. Even though the lot proves bad and is discarded, the loss is but a fraction of the value of a crop. This practice is feasible only with suitable climate and storage facilities and only for certain kinds of seed. Onions, parsnips, and sweet corn are likely to decline in germination too rapidly for this plan, and the cost of bean and pea seeds is too great. Growers of celery and cabbage follow the scheme with great satisfaction. As better knowledge of seed storage is developed, the practice may be more widely adopted in areas where it is normally difficult to store seed.

Cost of Good Seed

As already pointed out, the cost of seed for an acre of most crops is but a small fraction of expected returns. Cheap seed, if poor, may cost many dollars per acre. At the same time, a high price does not necessarily mean good seed, and often very good seed is to be had at moderate, though seldom at very low, prices. Buying on bids alone and seeking the cheapest are to be utterly condemned, unless the bidder meets definite specifications regarding purity, vitality, and trueness to the desired type.

GROWING SEED

Growing seed to sell is an alluring business and offers satisfying rewards to the man who likes it and can give it the exacting care it requires.

It is now a common practice for vegetable growers to buy seed produced by specialists. Seed production is big business, geared to the requirements of growers whose needs vary considerably from year to year—according to market demand, weather, and other variables.

The Crop Reporting Board of the U.S. Department of Agriculture makes annual nationwide surveys to determine acreage intentions and expected production of seed. Sixty-three major seed companies, dealers, and growers, representing a cross section of their business, provided the 1976–1978 seed acreage and production information in Table 5.2.

Since most seed can be stored for two or more years (Table 5.1), seed growers are in a position to anticipate and adjust production to a considerable degree. This accounts, in part, for the variable annual acreage and production estimates presented in Table 5.2.

Table 5.2—Annual Acreage and Production of Vegetable Seeds, 1976, 1977, and 1978.

	Acreage			Production, 1,000 pounds		
Seeds	1976	1977	1978*	1976	1977	1978*
Beans, bush green pod	13,844	28,100	35,813	20,108	45,901	58,543
Beans, bush wax pod	1,915	3,098	3,011	2,679	4,347	4,365
Beans, pole	2,271	3,566	3,724	3,009	5,044	6,443
Beans, bush lima	3,889	5,148	5,295	7,852	10,261	10,191
Beans, pole lima	286	565	431	430	868	730
Beets, garden	1,394	1,123	725	1,511	1,450	1,098
Broccoli	174	124	215	66	63	128
Cabbage	1,242	930	1,005	772	710	707
Carrot	4,580	1,639	4,092	3,056	910	2,840
Cauliflower	409	392	443	156	162	203
Celery	60	49	52	46	19	29
Chard, Swiss	157	125	102	183	192	159
Corn, sweet, hybrid	11,296	8,831	11,045	20,276	14,636	17,939
Corn, sweet, open-pollinated	495	205	207	1,116	416	434
Corn, non-sweet	251	213	210	608	536	528
Cucumber	2,542	3,050	3,437	1,163	1,209	1,259
Eggplant	93	5	19	12	1	6
Endive	155	50	77	93	28	52
Kale & collards	492	635	413	543	612	429
Kohlrabi	76	107	130	49	82	118
Lettuce, heading	876	1,427	1,642	250	610	791
Lettuce, loose-leaf	830	663	521	241	270	249
Lettuce, romaine	72	154	102	20	61	47
Muskmelon & cantaloupe	2,039	2,056	2,114	649	633	701
Watermelon	8,635	8,832	5,764	2,152	2,232	1,352
Mustard	248	181	203	284	213	251
Okra	158	214	309	178	277	511
Onion Seed	4,215	4,403	3,532	1,275	1,468	1,304
Parsley	433	302	184	250	192	100
Parsnip	111	80	28	66	64	14
Peas	65,366	61,206	78,365	120,146	94,893	151,641
Pepper	1,827	1,090	2,147	229	139	284
Pumpkin	169	143	150	93	74	74
Radish	2,580	1,594	1,575	2,690	1,470	1,492
Spinach	844	1,403	1,451	1,075	2,592	2,462
Squash, summer	1,702	1,222	1,281	1,100	778	764
Squash, winter	909	422	350	321	192	160
Tomato	3,900	3,891	3,742	480	466	510
Turnip	1,017	193	262	1,772	196	478
Rutabaga	55	10	64	122	8	84
Total, all Vegetables	141,627	147,441	174,232	197,121	194,227	269,477

*Growers intentions.

Source: Crop Reporting Board, ESCS, USDA.

PARTIAL LIST OF SEEDSMEN

Abbott and Cobb, Inc.
4744 Frankford Avenue
Philadelphia, Pa. 19124

Agway, Inc.
P.O. Box 1333
Syracuse, N.Y. 13201

Asgrow Seed Company
San Antonio, Tex. 78211

George J. Ball, Inc.
P.O. Box 335
West Chicago, Ill. 60185

Brawley Seed Company
1010 North Main Street
Mooresville, N.C. 28115

Burgess Seed & Plant Company
P.O. Box 218
Galesburg, Mich. 49053

W. Atlee Burpee Company
Clinton, Ia. 52732

D. V. Burrell Seed Growers Co.
Rocky Ford, Colo. 81067

Farmers Seed and Nursery
Faribault, Me. 55021

Ferry-Morse Seed Company
755 Royal Street
P.O. Box 7321, North Station
Memphis, Tenn. 38107

Henry Field Seed & Nursery Co.
Shenandoah, Ia. 51602

Germains, Inc.
Los Angeles, Calif. 90058

Gurney Seed & Nursery Co.
Yankton, S. Dak. 57078

Joseph Harris Co., Inc.
Rochester, N.Y. 14600

H. G. Hastings Company
P.O. Box 44088
Atlanta, Ga. 30302

Herbst Brothers Seedsmen, Inc.
1000 N. Main Street
Brewster, N.Y. 10509

J. W. Jung Seed Company
Randolph, Wisc. 53956

Keystone Seed Company
P.O. Box 1438
Hollister, Calif. 95023

Earl May Seed & Nursery Co.
Shenandoah, Ia. 51603

Midwest Seed Growers
505 Walnut Street
Kansas City, Mo. 64106

Northrup, King and Company
P.O. Box 959
Minneapolis, Minn. 55440

George W. Park Seed Co., Inc.
Greenwood, S.C. 29647

Petoseed Company, Inc.
P.O. Box 4206
Saticoy, Calif. 93003

Reuter Seed Company, Inc.
320 N. Carrollton Avenue
New Orleans, La. 70119

Seedway, Inc.
Hall, N.Y. 14463

Stokes Seeds, Inc.
P.O. Box 548
Buffalo, N.Y. 14240

Otis S. Twilley Seed Co.
Salisbury, Md. 21801

Vaughan's Seed Co.
Downers Grove, Ill. 60515

The information given herein is supplied with the understanding that no discrimination is intended and no endorsement is implied.

SELECTED REFERENCES

Anonymous "Acreage and Production of Vegetable Seeds," USDA, SRS, 1979 (issued annually).

Anonymous, "High Quality Seed Cost You Less," Ore. State Univ. Ext. Pub. FS 65 (current).

Anonymous, "Relationship Between the Size and Performance of Snap Bean Seeds," Cornell Univ. Agr. Exp. Sta. Circ. G819 (current).

Anonymous, "Seeds," USDA *Agriculture Yearbook*, 1961.

Anonymous, "Seed Starting and Transplanting," Univ. of Alas. Agr. Ext. Ser. P-32, 1978.

Anonymous, "Starting Plants from Seeds," USDA, AFS 8-9-1 (current).

Anonymous, "Truth in Seed Labeling," USDA, AMS, PA-917, 1974.

Anonymous, "Why Grow Certified Seed?" Ore. State Univ. Ext. Pub. FS 66 (current).

Duncan, A. A., "Brussels Sprouts, Cabbage, Cauliflower, Chinese Cabbage and Kale Seed Production," Ore. Exp. Sta. FS-89, 1965.

Duncan, A. A., "Cucurbits: Cucumbers, Squash, Pumpkin, Muskmelon and Watermelon Seed Production," Ore. Exp. Sta. FS-104, 1965.

Ells, J. E., "Saving Seed from the Home Garden," Colo. State Univ. Ext. Circ. 7.602, 1977.

Harrington, J. F., "The Value of Moisture-Resistant Containers for Vegetable Seed Packaging," Calif. Exp. Sta. Bull. 792, 1963.

James, E., Base, L. N., and Clark, D. C., "Varietal Differences in Longevity of Vegetable Seeds and Their Response to Various Storage Conditions," *Proc. Amer. Soc. Hort. Sci.* 91, 521, 1967.

Justice, O. L., and Kulik, M. M., "Some Effects of Gamma Radiation on Germination and Storage Life of Seeds," USDA, ARS Reprint 70, 1970.

Sandsted, R. F., "Pounds of Bean Seed Required per Acre," Cornell Veg. Crops Dept. Mimeo. 153, 1970.

Sandsted, R. F., and Warner, J., "Number of Seeds per Ounce of Dry Beans," Cornell Veg. Crops Dept. U. C. Mimeo. 180, 1975.

Tompkins, D. R., "Broccoli Maturity and Production as Influenced by Seed Size," *Proc. Amer. Soc. Hort. Sci.* 88, 400, 1966.

CHAPTER 6

Managing Soils and Fertilizing

Quality in many vegetables depends primarily on tender, succulent growth, which requires soils with a continuous supply of available nutrients and moisture. Many of the vegetable crops have limited root systems and grow during a very short season. Since the ability of a plant to absorb nutrients such as phosphorus and potassium from a soil depends on the extent of it's root system, these vegetables require a high level of fertility. This is also true of a crop such as the pea that must develop before summer's unfavorable weather. Most seed and fruit producing plants cease growing at the time of fruit set, and subsequent yields are dependent upon the amount of growth before fruiting. Again, high fertility is required for rapid early growth and is necessary for good yields.

CHOOSING SOILS FOR VEGETABLES

Physical Requirements

When earliness is of more importance than total yield, sandy soils and sandy loams are best. These soils are well aerated, drying out and warming up rapidly in the spring. They are often low in nutrients and moisture retention, but moisture is usually excessive in the spring anyway.

When large yields are more important than earliness and moisture is likely to become limited, silt loams, clay loams, and muck soils are best. They usually contain considerable reserve food material and retain moisture well. By proper soil management, the food reserves may be made available. If not worked while wet, these soils are fairly loose and friable, qualities necessary for vegetable crops. Clays and heavy soils are not usually well adapted to vegetable crops, because of poor aeration and consequent poor nutrient liberation and root growth. They may, however, be used advantageously for late crops started during warm, dry weather.

Chemical Requirements

Silt and clay loams have high base exchange capacities and will adsorb and hold large quantities of elements such as phosphorus and potassium. These soils can usually be fertilized sufficiently with P and K before planting to supply the crop during its development. These soils are relatively free from leaching, so the application of nutrients depends primarily on the requirements of a particular crop. A sandy soil, on the other hand, has low base exchange capacity, high watering requirement, and susceptibility to leaching. Such a soil may require frequent light applications of fertilizer during the development of a crop. The total amount of nutrients added may be far in excess of those actually needed by the crop.

CONSERVING SOIL AND MOISTURE

Soils with only a slight grade are desired for growing vegetables. When soils of moderate to steep grades are used, measures should be adopted to conserve soil and moisture. These include terracing, contour cultivation, and strip cropping.

Flat land may have no erosion problem, but it does have drainage and leaching problems. If the subsoil is loose and permits ready drainage, no provision for drainage need be made, but, if the subsoil is tight, and water tends to stand on the land, a drainage system pays big dividends. Tile properly installed is best because it permits free use of the land, although open ditch drainage is better than none. Care must be taken to prevent overdrainage because excessive leaching and lack of moisture may result.

Leaching is greatest during periods when the land is not in use, especially in the winter, and during these periods some sort of cover crop may be used to absorb nutrients as they are liberated, and to hold them for use by the next crop.

PREPARING THE SOIL

Breaking

Land should be loosened 6 to 8 inches for vegetables. If the soil has never been plowed more than 6 inches, care should be taken to bring up only about an inch of subsoil at a time, especially if the subsoil is fine textured.

Fall plowing has advantages in regions of winter freezing, but in the South its value is questionable, because of leaching and erosion of sloping soils, which do not freeze much in the winter. However, if level, loamy soils are plowed deeply, and especially if a covering of coarse organic matter is turned under, the losses from leaching and erosion are not so great, and probably will be more than offset by the following advantages: (1) improved physical conditions, resulting from alternate wetting and drying and light freezing; (2) reduction in insects, because of exposure to the weather; (3) rotting of organic materials in contact with the soil, thereby increasing the humus and liberating nutrients; and (4) relieving the pressure of spring work by making it possible to work the soil earlier in the spring.

Spring plowing should not be done too far in advance of planting unless heavy cover crops are turned under. Special care must be used to avoid working the soil when it is too wet. If the soil crumbles readily after being pressed in the hand, it is dry enough to plow; but if it retains its form, the land is too wet for breaking. Cultipackers and rollers also break up clods and smooth the surface for planting.

Finishing

Vegetables with small seeds require a fine seedbed free of trash for even seeding and uniform germination. Plowed land must be disced well, usually in both directions, before planting. A harrow and float or a bed former are commonly used to follow the discings.

CHOOSING THE SOIL REACTION

The proper soil reaction depends more on the nature of the soil than it does on the peculiar reaction requirements of the crop to be grown. If the proper amounts and ratios of nutrients for the crop are maintained and no compounds are allowed to be present in toxic concentrations, it makes little difference to the crop what the reaction is as long as it is in the growth range of pH 5 to pH 8 (Table 6.1). The reaction, however, greatly varies the nutrient balance and toxic conditions in each soil type, and it is very difficult to maintain the balance in an alkaline soil.

Table 6.1—pH and Corresponding Soil Reaction.*

pH	Soil Reaction	pH	Soil Reaction
4.5	Very acid	7.0	Neutral
5.0	Acid	7.25	Slightly alkaline**
5.5	Medium acid	7.5	Medium alkaline
6.0	Slightly acid	7.75	Strongly alkaline
6.5	Very slightly acid	8.0	Very strongly alkaline

*pH represents the degree of active acidity and alkalinity (not total acidity and alkalinity) in a soil. The scale used to indicate the degree sets the value 7.07 as the neutral point, or the pH of pure water (the active acidity or alkalinity of water). With this as the starting point, the value for alkalinity is anything greater—up to 14.14. The reason for this scale and these limits requires an understanding of logarithms, normal solutions, and ionization.

**Graduation is less on the alkaline side than on the acid side as there are 2.5 units on the acid side and only one unit on the alkaline side, which are within the limits of plant growth.

When the average of many soil types is taken, vegetable crops seem to fall into certain classes as to the pH preference, because of certain nutrient preferences and toxic tolerances. The vegetable crops vary in their responses to soil reaction (pH), some growing best on acid soils while others require soils of neutral reaction. The vegetable crops are grouped according to pH requirements (Fig. 6.1). As may be seen, all thrive at a pH range of 6.0 to 6.5. Sometimes potatoes may be grown in soil with a pH of about 5.0 to avoid serious damage from scab. Also, cabbage may be grown in a slightly alkaline soil to reduce damage from club root.

CONTROLLING SOIL REACTION

Determining the Need for Lime

Use should be made of soil reaction kits which indicate the approximate pH of soils. Too much confidence, however, should not be placed in the various lime-requirement tests, as they are usually adapted to legume crop rotations in general farming, and may not be indicative of vegetable crop needs.

If reaction tests indicate rather strong acidity, it is advisable to apply several rates of lime on a few small sections of land before liming the entire farm, as liming is not universally beneficial to vegetables, even on acid soils. If lime is found to pay on the particular crops which are to be grown on these sections, it may be used more freely (Table 6.2).

Applying Lime

If lime is needed for quick action, a finely ground agricultural limestone is recommended. Lime should be mixed well in the top 3 to 4 inches of soil. A commercial lime spreader is best for making application, although a shovel may be used for small areas. A grain drill can be used, when light applications are to be made.

The rate of application depends on the type of soil, degree of reaction present, reaction desired, and the form of lime. Less lime is needed to cause change at high acidity than at low acidity.

Table 6.2—Agricultural Ground Limestone Requirement.

| pH Test | Tons per Acre | | | |
	Sandy Soils	Silt Loam Soils	Clay Loam Soils	Muck Soils
6.5 and above	0	0	0	0
6.2-6.4	1	2	2	0
5.8-6.1	2	3	3	0
5.4-5.7	3	4	5	0
4.8-5.3	4	6	7	2
4.2-4.7	5	8	–	3

Sources

Dolomitic limestone contains magnesium as well as calcium, and it is usually best to use limestone that has some magnesium; but too much magnesium is much more likely to cause harmful effects than too much calcium. Marls are a good source of limestone in areas where they are available.

MAINTAINING ORGANIC MATTER

Values of Organic Matter

Organic matter increases the porosity of heavy soils, which, in turn,

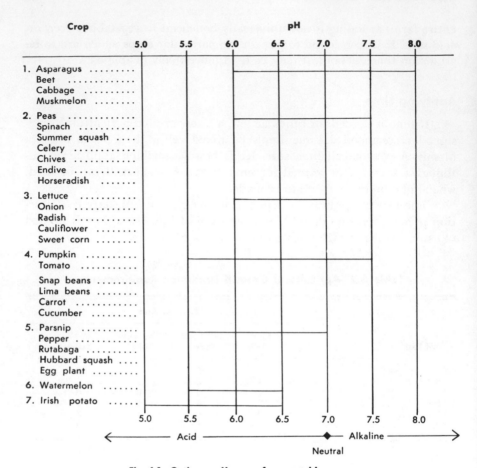

Fig. 6.1—Optimum pH range for vegetable crops.

increases water absorption and lessens water run-off, leaching, and erosion. The increased porosity also causes greater aeration, which favors the
right kind of bacteria for nutrient liberation and direct chemical oxidation processes. On the other hand, organic matter will help to keep sandy
soils from becoming too porous. The black color imparted by organic
matter causes heat absorption, aiding the soil to warm up quickly, provided that the amount of water present is not excessive. The use of fresh
organic matter too close to planting time of vegetables may cause (1)
burning from rapid decomposition; (2) formation of excessively aerated
layers and pockets, which interfere in water movement; (3) locking of

available nitrogen by decomposition bacteria; (4) mechanical interference to plowing and cultivation; and (5) formation of toxic organic compounds, under certain anaerobic and non-colloidal conditions. If air and moisture are favorable and sufficient time is allowed, these difficulties will be overcome. Addition of lime, if needed, and nitrate will aid in cases of nitrogen deficiency.

Maintaining Organic Matter by Animal Manures

If animal manure can be secured cheaply, it is the best material for maintaining the organic content of the soil as well as a good source of nitrogen. When used, however, it is necessary to watch and maintain the phosphorous supply, since animal manure is usually low in phosphorus. Although fresh and strawy manures may cause damage if used too near planting time, they have the following advantage over rotted manure if applied far enough in advance of the crop: (1) less nutrients are lost through decomposition and leaching; (2) more bacteria are added to the soil; (3) more energy is provided for bacteria, resulting in a much greater liberation of nutrients through solvent action; and (4) buffer effects are greater. Decomposed manure which has been well cared for, however, is very valuable because it (1) can be applied just ahead of the crop; (2) is higher in percentage of total nutrients, if excessive leaching has been stopped; (3) is much higher in readily available nutrients; (4) has no burning effects; (5) produces more uniform action throughout the soil mass; (6) usually contains more phosphorus in relation to the nitrogen, thus furnishing a more balanced nutrient supply; (7) destroys or reduces weed seed germination; and (8) offers less mechanical interference. Usually, it is advantageous to use fresh manure in the fall and well-rotted manure in the spring.

In many cases, natural manures are rather expensive and difficult to secure, especially for a market gardener who keeps no livestock. However, with tractors replacing animals on the farm, more crop residues are available for maintaining soil organic matter.

The rate of manurial application varies greatly with the land, the crop, the cost of manure, and the kind of manure. Often 30 to 40 tons, especially of the strawy type of cow manure, are not excessive. Many experiment stations have shown that light applications supplemented by commercial fertilizers, especially phosphate, are more economical than manure alone. Chicken manure should be put on very lightly, and far enough from the plants to avoid burning. Broadcasting of manure is best, except in the case of widely spaced hills of cucurbits or melons.

Maintaining Organic Matter by Green Manures

For the vegetable gardener with plenty of relatively inexpensive land, one of the cheapest and most efficient ways to secure nitrogen and organic matter is through the use of legumes. However, for a gardener located on a limited area of expensive land, the use of legumes may not be advisable, and he would likely profit by the use of manure, crop residues, winter cover crops, and commercial fertilizers.

Green vegetation incorporated into the soil rots much more quickly than dry material. When vegetation is allowed to dry out before it is turned under, the nutrients are transformed to less available forms. Long exposure to oxidation in the weather may result in a loss of nitrogen.

Besides increasing the organic content and adding nitrogen to the soil, legumes (1) conserve soluble nutrients, (2) improve the subsoil by penetrating it and incorporating organic materials into it, (3) make mineral nutrients available, (4) transfer them to the topsoil, (5) favor bacterial growth, and (6) reduce erosion.

The first consideration in choosing a legume is its adaptation to soil and climate. After this, the amount of readily incorporated vegetation produced in the time available should determine the choice.

If the legume is to be grown on land that does not contain inoculating organisms, the seed must be inoculated. This may be done naturally, using soil known to contain the organism, or artificially, with material purchased from a seed firm or other source.

Nonlegumes have all the values of legumes with the exception that they do not actually add atmospheric nitrogen to the soil. The grasses are used as cover crops because they are easily started and form a nonerosive surface which quickly prevents leaching. Rye is almost universally used as a winter cover by general farmers, but there is some question as to its value for the southern vegetable gardener, because it is difficult to kill and hinders early gardening. In many cases in the southern states, vegetables are grown in the late fall and early spring, and cool-season crops are grown during January and February so that rye would be of little value. Oats make a good cover if sown in the fall, but this crop is subject to winter injury.

Various methods are employed in planting cover crops. A seed drill has the advantage of planting at uniform depth and rate and saves unnecessary operations. The hand-broadcast method is uncertain and requires more seed for satisfactory coverage.

USING COMMERCIAL FERTILIZERS

Importance of Commercial Fertilizers

Commercial fertilizers are added to a soil with the particular purpose of directly increasing the amounts of nutrients available to plants. They are not added to improve physical conditions nor to make soil reserves available. Manures and lime do more than simply add nutrients and, for this reason, often produce better results than commercial fertilizers alone. However, stable manure, organic matter, or lime cannot be depended on to produce enough available nutrients in many soils with low reserves; and even in fertile soils, organic materials and lime may cause improper nutrient ratios. No soil without additives can provide the right fertility for all types of vegetables. Commercial fertilizers are necessary to furnish

Fig. 6.2—Celery grown on sandy soil in Florida. Plants on the left received well balanced fertilizer, while those on the right were unfertilized.

limiting elements in the most economical manner and to maintain proper ratios of the nutrients for the particular crop being grown (Fig. 6.2). Both organic and inorganic fertilizers are given in Table 6.3.

NITROGEN. Nitrogen builds up the vegetative portions of the plant, producing large green leaves, and is also necessary for filling out fruits. If it is present in large amounts in relation to other elements, it will cause excessive vegetative growth and succulence.

Nitrogen fertilizers that leave an acid residue are ammonium sulfate, ammonium nitrate, and ammonium phosphate. Nitrogen fertilizers that leave an alkaline residue are sodium nitrate, calcium nitrate, potassium nitrate, and cyanamide.

Cottonseed meal, linseed meal, castor-oil meal, blood, tankage, fish tankage, guano, and urea are all organic and are neutral in their effect on soil reaction. The high cost of organic carriers of nitrogen and their slow availability (except urea) would make them impractical, in most circumstances.

Nitrogen fertilizers should be used cautiously since there is danger of damaging the seeds or plants. The acid fertilizers should be used on nearly neutral to aklaline soils; the alkaline fertilizers, on nearly neutral to acid soils. The neutral organic fertilizers can be used on either acid or alkaline soils, but only when slow availability is desired. Nitrates are immediately available and the ammonia salts are fairly rapidly available.

PHOSPHORUS. Phosphorus is necessary for cellular metabolism and is especially essential in fruit and seed production. The plant will be stunted and the fruit will fail to set if phosphate is inadequate, especially if nitrogen is high. Phosphate also stimulates root production and seed development.

Natural phosphate rocks and animal bones are the chief source of phosphorus fertilizers. Both have to be treated with acid (usually sulfuric) to make the phosphorus readily available to vegetable plants. Superphosphate fertilizers have been standardized to contain 8.8 percent phosphorus. Phosphatic fertilizers with higher analyses (20.7 percent treble superphosphate) are now in general use.

Phosphorus is known as an immobile element. Soon after application it becomes adsorbed on the clay particles and does not remain in solution. The roots of the plant must come in contact with these particles to get phosphorus, and for this reason a crop can absorb only a small amount of the phosphorus available in the soil. In contrast with nitrogen, phosphorus must be present in the soil in large amounts. Phosphorus is often ap-

Table 6.3—The Composition of Fertilizers.

Fertilizer	Nitrogen (N) Percent	Phosphorus (P) Percent	Potassium (K) Percent
Organic Fertilizers			
Bat guano	10.0	1.8	1.7
Blood	13.0	0.9	0.8
Blood and bone	6.5	3.1	...
Bone, black	1.3	6.6	...
Bone meal, raw	3.0	6.6	...
Steamed	2.0	6.6	...
Castor bean meal	5.5	0.9	0.8
Cottonseed meal	6.0	1.3	0.8
Fish meal	10.0	1.8	...
Garbage tankage	1.5	0.9	0.6
Horn and hoof meal	12.0	0.9	...
Sewerage sludge	1.5	0.6	0.3
Activated	6.0	1.3	0.1
Tankage	9.0	2.6	...
Inorganic Fertilizers			
Ammoniated superphosphate	3.0	7.0	...
Ammonium nitrate	33.0 to 33.5	...	...
Ammonium nitrate—lime (A-N-L, Cal-Nitro)	20.5	...	...
Ammonium phosphate	11.0	21.0	...
Ammonium phosphate—sulfate	16.0	8.8	...
Ammonium sulfate	20.5	...	...
Anhydrous ammonia	82.0	...	...
Aqua ammonium phosphate	8.0	10.3	...
Aqueous ammonia	20.0	...	...
Calcium cyanamide	21.0	...	...
Calcium nitrate	15.5	...	...
Calurea	34.0	...	...
Diammonium phosphate	21.0	23.3	...
Nitrate of potash	13.0	...	36.5
Nitrate of soda	16.0	...	...
Nitrate of soda—potash	15.0	...	11.6
Nitrogen solutions	18.0 to 41.0	...	...
Urea	42.0 to 46.0	...	...
Ureaform	35.0 to 38.0	...	...
Basic phosphate slag	...	4.4	...
Calcium metaphosphate	...	27.7	...
Phosphoric acid solution	...	22.3	...
Potassium metaphosphate	...	24.2	31.5
Rock phosphate*	...	14.51	...
Superphosphate	...	7.0 to 8.8	...
Treble (double) superphosphate	...	18.5 to 20.7	...
Kainite	...	...	10.0 to 13.3
Manure salts	...	...	16.6 to 24.9
Muriate of potash	...	...	39.8 to 51.5
Potassium ammonium nitrate	16.0	...	27.0
Sulfate of potash	...	...	39.8 to 43.2
Sulfate of potash—magnesia	...	...	17.4 to 18.3

*Total phosphorus, not the available.

plied in bands at the time of planting to provide a high concentration near the roots of the young plants.

POTASSIUM. Potassium is important in the formation and translocation of carbohydrates and, hence, is important to root and tuber crops and in the formation of large rigid stems as in celery and rhubarb. It is also important in disease resistance, protein formation, and cell division. It does not, however, form part of the cell tissue and is not a bulk nutrient as are nitrogen and phosphorus.

Muriate and sulfate of potash and wood ashes are the main sources of potassium. Some mineral soils contain enough potassium for all crops except those mentioned above, although most muck and sandy soils are deficient. Excess does little harm unless it becomes concentrated enough to cause exosmosis, but the cost of the excess results in financial loss to the grower.

CALCIUM. The main function of calcium seems to be corrective in nature. It combines with toxic acids developed in the life processes of the plant, and helps overcome the effects of too large amounts of other elements, such as magnesium. Calcium seems to be necessary in the normal absorption of all nutrients. It is rarely limiting for plant use, but it is needed in soil reaction control. Rather large amounts do no direct injury to the plant, but indirectly the hydroxide or carbonate in the soil may be injurious by making certain elements unavailable.

OTHER ELEMENTS. Space will not permit discussion of other elements and therefore a few of the more important ones with their main function are merely listed as follows: (1) magnesium, link in chlorophyll-molecule, fat, and oil formation; (2) sulfur, essential to certain proteins in crucifers and onions; (3) iron, catalytic agent in chlorophyll action; and (4) manganese, needed for oxidation and reduction reactions. Boron, copper, and zinc have also been found to be essential, although their exact functions are unknown.

DETERMINING FERTILIZER ANALYSIS, FORMULA, AND RATIO

Analysis

Commercial fertilizers should always bear a tag which gives the analysis, such as 3-8-6. The first figure means 3 percent nitrogen; the second, 8 percent available phosphorus; and the third, 6 percent water-soluble potassium.

This example is a low-analysis fertilizer, but there are now available high-analysis fertilizers, such as 6-16-12, which contain exactly twice the quantity of nutrients as 3-8-6. In buying fertilizer, attention should be paid to the price per fertilizer unit[1] instead of the price per ton. Thirty-three percent ammonium nitrate at $120 per ton makes each pound of nitrogen cost about 18 cents; 20.2 percent treble superphosphate at $123 per ton makes each pound of phosphorus cost 30 cents; and 41.5 percent muriate of potash at $75 per ton makes each pound of potassium cost 9 cents. This would mean that a 3-5-6 should cost $51.60 per ton. One could then afford to pay $103.20 per ton for a 6-10-12 fertilizer, or $154.80 for a 9-20-18. In fact, somewhat more than this could be paid because transportation and application costs are less per unit of nutrients in high-analysis fertilizers. The high-analysis fertilizers are a little more difficult to distribute evenly, and are more likely to burn on contact with seeds or plants; but, other than this, they are as good as the low-analysis fertilizers. Laws in some of the states require that at least 20 units of fertilizer be present; hence a 3-8-6 could no longer be sold in such a state, since it totals only 17 units.

Formula

The formula tells what kinds of materials are used to make the units of available fertilizers. For example, a standard vegetable fertilizer may have an analysis of 5-10-5. This tells how much of each element is available, but does not give the source of the elements. The formula should be given, reading as follows: $2\frac{1}{2}$ percent nitrogen as 20 percent ammonium sulfate; $2\frac{1}{2}$ percent nitrogen as 15 percent sodium nitrate; 10 percent phosphorus as 20 percent treble superphosphate; and 5 percent potassium as 40 percent potassium chloride. A buyer of fertilizers should demand the formula and note the rate of availability of the nitrogen, and the effect the compounds may have on soil reaction. Such physical factors as freedom from caking and ease of drilling are also important.

---

1. A fertilizer unit equals 1 pound of the actual element. For example, 100 pounds of 15 percent nitrate of soda contains 15 units of nitrogen (N), 100 pounds of 20 percent treble superphosphate contains 20 units of phosphorus (P), and 100 pounds of 41 percent muriate of potash contains 41 units of potassium (K). In the past, phosphorus has been listed as P_2O_5 and potassium as K_2O. To convert to the elemental basis multiply the former by 0.437 and the latter by 0.83.

Ratio

Fertilizer ratio differs from analysis in that it expresses the fertilizer in the ratio of one element to another, usually in terms of nitrogen. For instance, 5-10-5 is the analysis, but 1-2-1 is the ratio. Therefore, ratio does not tell how much of each element there is but, in this case, it simply says

Table 6.4—Guide to the Nitrogen Fertilizer Requirements of Vegetable Crops.

Crop	Estimated Total Nitrogen Requirement	
	Dark-colored Soils Lbs. per A.	Light-colored Soils Lbs. per A.
Asparagus	80	100
Beans	30	45
Beet	50	65
Cabbage, late	60	75
Carrot	60	75
Cauliflower	65	80
Corn, late	40	55
Cucumber	20	45
Eggplant	30	45
Horseradish	45	60
Lettuce	45	60
Muskmelon	20	35
Onion	45	60
Parsnip	60	75
Peas	20	35
Pepper	30	45
Potato, late	60	75
Pumpkin and squash		
Summer squash	30	45
Winter pumpkin	60	75
Spinach	50	60
Sweet potato	30	40
Tomato	60	75
Turnip	50	50
Watermelon	20	35

there is twice as much phosphorus as nitrogen and the same amount of potassium as nitrogen. The proportion which the elements bear to each other in a fertilizer is very important. A desirable ratio depends on the time of application, the soil nutrients available to the plant, and the particular demands of the crop being grown.

DETERMINING FERTILIZER REQUIREMENTS

If other soil and climatic factors are favorable, it is desirable to fertilize vegetable crops so as to maintain a high level of production. Rapid soil tests may be used to determine requirements for phosphorus and potassium, but due to the sudden changes in availability of nitrogen, frequent tests are necessary for this element. Plant tissue tests will reveal the nutrient needs of a plant, although a deficiency may be due to an impaired root system and not to the supply of nutrients in the soil. Information from tissue tests can be used for making applications of readily available nitrogen. Phosphorus and potassium should be applied in the soil before the root system of the plant is established and before tissue tests can be made.

A guide for nitrogen requirements is shown in Table 6.4. Previous cropping, the presence of decomposable residues, and leaching should be considered in determining the amounts of nitrogen to be applied.

The vegetable crops are divided into four groups according to their

Table 6.5—Phosphorus (P) and Potassium (K) Recommended for the Vegetable Crops Grouped According to Requirements.*

		Requirement per Group (in Pounds per Acre)			
	Soil Test	I	II	III	IV
P	Very low	132	105	62	26
	Low	105	62	26	9
	Medium	70	18	18	9
	High	35	9	18	9
	Very high	18	9	18	9
K	Very low	200	200	152	56
	Low	160	160	112	16
	Medium	112	112	96	16
	High	64	64	80	16
	Very high	64	16	80	16
Crops:		Tomato	Asparagus	Carrot	Beans
		Potato	Onion	Parsnip	Peas
		Pepper	Sweet corn	Beet	
		Eggplant	Spinach	Radish	
		Cabbage	Lettuce	Turnip	
		Cauliflower	Sweet potato	Horseradish	
		Broccoli			
		Cucumber			
		Melon			
		Squash			
		Pumpkin			

*Phosphorus and potassium are given as elements instead of oxides; 20 percent phosphorus (P) equals 45.5 percent phosphorus pentoxide (P_2O_5), and 40 percent potassium (K) equals 48 percent potassium oxide (K_2O).

phosphorus and potassium requirements. These are shown in Table 6.5 along with amounts to apply for given soil tests. Some fertilizer is recommended even for soils giving very high tests, in order to maintain a high level of fertility. A home garden may be treated as if all crops were in Group 1. The recommendations are based upon soils not subject to serious leaching.

SELECTED REFERENCES

Anonymous, "Fertilizer Recommendations for Louisiana," L.S.U. Agr. Exp. Sta. Circ. 84, Jan., 1967.

Courter, J. W., Vandemark, J. S, and Arnold, C. Y., "Fertilizing Greenhouse Vegetables," Ill. Agr. Ext. Circ. 922, 1966.

Fletcher, Robert F., "Garden Soil and Its Care," Pa. State Univ. Coop. Ext. Ser. Circ., 560.

Hohlt, H. E., and O'Dell, C. R., "Fertilizing Vegetable Crops in Virginia," Va. Poly. Inst. and State Univ. Pub. 148, Jan., 1974.

Jones, L. G., "Soil Analysis: An Aid in the Fertilization of Vegetable Crops," L.S.U. Agr. Exp. Sta. Bull. 671, Feb., 1973.

Minotti, P. L., "Effective and Efficient Use of Nitrogen for Vegetable Production on Organic Soils," Cornell Veg. Crops Bull. 122, Mar., 1977.

Minotti, P. L., "Plant Nutrition and Vegetable Crop Quality," HortSci. 10: 54-56, 1975.

Montelaro, James, "Commercial Vegetable Fertilization Guide," Univ. of Fla. Ext. Ser. Circ. 225-B, Mar., 1978.

Montelaro, James, "Fertilization and General Sequence of Operations Under Full-Bed Plastic Mulch," Univ. of Fla. Veg. Crops Ext. Rpt. VC 9, 1976.

Olsen, R. A., and Robbins, J. E., Fertilizer Technology and Use, Soil Sci. Soc. of Amer., Inc., Madison, Wisc., 1971.

Peck, N. H., "Vegetable Crop Fertilization," N. Y. State Agr. Exp. Sta. Food and Life Sciences Bull. 52, Jan., 1975.

Robertson, L. S., Christenson, D. R., and Warncke, D. D., "Essential Secondary Elements: Calcium," Mich. State Univ. Ext. Bull. E-996, Aug., 1976.

Shickluna, John C., "Sampling Soils for Fertilizer and Lime Recommendations," Mich. State Univ. Ext. Ser. Bull. E-498, Jul., 1975.

Taber, H. G., Davison, A. D., and Telford, H. S., "Organic Gardening," Wash. State Univ. Ext. Ser. Bull. 648, May, 1978.

Vitosh, M. L., "Fertilizers: Types, Uses and Characteristics," Mich. State Univ. Ext. Ser. Bull. E-896, Sept., 1975.

Walsh, L. M., and Benton, J. D., Soil Testing and Plant Analysis, 491 pp. Soil Sci. Soc. of Amer., Inc., Madison, Wisc., Rev., 1973.

Warncke, D. D., Christenson, D. R., and Lucas, R. E., "For Michigan Fertilizer Recommendations for Vegetable and Field Crops," Mich. State Univ. Ext. Ser. Bull. E-550, Farm Sci. Series, Jun., 1976.

White, J. M., "Soil Preparation Effects on Compaction, Carrot Yield, and Root Characteristics in Organic Soil," J. Amer. Soc. Hort. Sci. 103 (4): 433-435, 1978.

CHAPTER 7

Growing Plants, Hardening, and Transplanting

If plants with small seeds are seeded directly in the field, germination is often poor, and the young plants grow very slowly and require a long time for maturity. Also, the season may be too short for full development in the field. To overcome these disadvantages, many vegetable crops are grown from transplants. These are either started in special plant-growing structures or grown in the open in regions where weather is favorable.

Cabbage, cauliflower, Brussels sprouts, celery, tomatoes, eggplant, peppers, sweet potatoes, and others are generally started in special beds so that the grower can give them good care with a minimum of labor during the early stages of growth.

PLANT-GROWING STRUCTURES

There are many advantages in starting plants in greenhouses, hotbeds, or cold frames, including (1) lengthening of the growing season; (2) producing an earlier crop, thereby getting the advantage of early market; and (3) protecting the young plants against unfavorable weather conditions.

Greenhouses

Greenhouse construction and management are specialized subjects and are discussed here only from the standpoint of use by the market gardener and vegetable grower as an adjunct to outdoor gardening.

In the colder regions, greenhouses are superior to hotbeds or cold frames for starting plants. Some of the advantages of greenhouses over other forcing structures are (1) better temperature control, (2) better regulation of ventilation and less danger of chilling the plants, and (3) more convenient arrangement for work in caring for the plants.

When a greenhouse is to be used only for growing plants for transplanting, one cannot afford an expensive structure. For this reason there is demand for small, inexpensive houses. One of the new glazing films seems to be the answer to low-cost greenhouse construction, especially in the milder regions of the country. Such a greenhouse is shown in Figure 7.1. Greenhouses for growing crops are discussed in Chapter 33.

Glazing films in use include polyethylene, polyvinyl chloride (PVC or vinyl), and polyester (Mylar). These are compared in Table 7.1. The cost of plastic-covered greenhouses in terms of square footage of ground covered may be roughly estimated by multiplying 2.4 or 2.0 times the film cost for a 1,000- or 4,000-square-foot house, respectively. Types of construction and comparative costs are discussed in University of Illinois Circular 905. When properly constructed, double-layered houses are more satisfactory than those with a single layer. They require 40 percent less heat, reduce moisture condensation, and provide added insurance in case one layer should rip.

Fig. 7.1—Inexpensive plant-growing house covered with glazing film.

Photograph by E. C. Wittmeyer

Table 7.1—Light and Heat Transmission Characteristics of Some Plastic Films, Glass, and Water.

	Thickness	Transmission of Visible Light	Transparent to	
			Ultraviolet	Infrared
	mils	percent		
Polyethylene*	2	87	Yes	Yes
Polyvinyl chloride* ..	13	87	Slight	No
Polyvinyl chloride* ..	3	88	Yes	Slight
Polyester*	4	88	No	Slight
Fiberglass (clear)	125	80-90	Slight	Intermediate
Glass*	125	90	No	No
Water*	2	96	Yes	No

*Data taken from Trickett, E. S., and Goulden, J. D. S., "The Radiation Transmission and Heat Conserving Properties of Some Plastic Films," **Jour. Agr. Eng. Res.**, 3 (4): 281-287, 1958.

Many growers have built inexpensive frame structures and covered them with hotbed sash. Some of these are low with the eaves only a few inches above the ground level, while others have walls entirely above ground. In the low houses, the walls between the beds are excavated to the depth of 2 or 3 feet and the beds or benches are near the ground level. This type is more easily heated than the high type, but less convenient. The low type of structure is not satisfactory on poorly drained soil.

The high type of sash house has walls extending 2 to 4 or more feet above the surface of the ground. The walls may be of concrete, hollow tile, or wood up to the eaves plate, or they may be part wood or concrete with glass above. The only advantage of a sash house is its low cost; therefore, where considerable labor and money are expended on walls, framework, and heating system, it would seem wise to build a standard greenhouse rather than a sash house.

Hotbeds

A hotbed is a specially prepared bed to which artificial heat is supplied by hot air, hot water, steam, or electricity.

The frame of the hotbed may be made of wood or other building materials. If it is made of wood, 2- by 4-inch lumber is used for posts at the corners and at intervals of 4 to 6 feet along the sides of the bed. Boards or planks are nailed to the posts on the inner side. When 16-inch boards are used, it is desirable to use a double layer. The frame usually extends to the bottom of the bed and it should extend 12 to 18 inches above the ground at the back and 6 to 12 inches at the front. The slope of the sash should be to the south or southeast, if possible. The standard hotbed sash is 3 by 6 feet. Every 3 feet there should be a crossbar or slide placed across the bed for the edges of the sash to rest upon. For these crossbars, 2- by 3-inch pieces are satisfactory, and they should be mortised into the sides of the frames flush with the top of the sides. A ½-inch strip, nailed in the center of these bars to prevent binding of the sash, is an advantage. When this is used the crossbars need to be at least 3 feet and ½ inch apart. Durable wood, such as cedar, locust, or chestnut for posts and cypress for the frame, is desirable (Fig. 7.2).

Fig. 7.2—Sash removed from hotbed to show construction.

Hot water or steam may be used for heating the hotbed, but neither of these methods is practicable in a small bed, unless the system is used for other purposes. For either of these methods, the heating pipes may be placed in a pit beneath the floor of the bed, or the flow pipe may be placed in the bed above the soil. If placed above the soil, the flow pipe may be located under the center of the ridge in double-width beds or near the top of the high side of single-width beds. In either case the returns are placed on the sides at a lower level than the flow pipe. The temperature can be regulated better in steam- or hot-water-heated beds than in flue-heated beds.

Beds heated by hot air are known as flue-heated beds, since the heated air is conducted from a fire box through tile flues placed beneath the bed. These are cheaper to construct than hot-water or steam-heated beds, but they are not as satisfactory. The fire box is built in a pit at one end of the bed, and the heated air and fumes are conducted through tile flues which slope gently upward to the farther end of the bed where they come to the surface. The fumes and air circulate under the floor of the bed and finally pass out through a chimney at one end.

The size of the tile to be used is determined by the size of the bed. A bed 12 by 60 feet should have two lines of 6-inch tiles, while one 12 by 30 feet may be heated satisfactorily with one line of 8-inch tiles.

Electric Hotbeds

When electricity is used for heating hotbeds, a special heating cable is placed in a pit below the ground level. Some authorities recommend placing the cable on a layer of cinders to reduce loss of heat to the soil below. A layer of 4 to 6 inches of soil is placed over the cable. A thermostat is used to control the temperature of the bed. The initial cost of the construction is relatively high, but the cost of labor in caring for beds heated by electricity is less than for beds heated by steam or hot water.

Cold Frames

The main difference between hotbeds and cold frames is that hotbeds have some form of artificial heat while cold frames have not. Cold frames are used for (1) starting plants when some protection is needed; (2) hardening plants that have been started in greenhouses or hotbeds; and (3) growing crops such as lettuce, beets, parsley, and radishes to maturity. If only a little protection is necessary, cold frames are satisfactory. In some sections of the South, as in the vicinity of Norfolk, Virginia, such crops as cucumbers, melons, beets, and others, are started in cold frames; then, when the weather permits, the frames are removed and the crops receive field culture.

Cold frames are constructed in very much the same way as hotbeds except that no provision for heat is necessary for the former (Fig. 7.3). Permanent cold frames commonly are made of concrete, while temporary ones are built of boards or planks.

Cold frames are covered with glass sash, with plastic film, with canvas, or with other kinds of cloth. In the colder regions, glass sash is desirable, but in mild regions, where the temperature permits removing the cover during most of the day, canvas or other cloth covering is satisfactory.

GROWING PLANTS

Good plants are essential for successful vegetable growing. In order to have good plants for setting in the field, the grower must use good seed of the stock and cultivar suited to the conditions under which the crop is to be grown. He must use good soil for the plant bed and use care and judgment in sowing the seed and managing the bed.

Fig. 7.3—Cold frames are quite similar to hotbeds in construction, but they are usually less permanent. These frames are cheap and movable.

USDA Photograph

Preparing the Soil

A loose, friable soil should be used for the plant bed; a sandy loam, well supplied with humus, meets the requirements. It is desirable to prepare a compost pile at least a year before the soil is to be used. The best kind of compost is made by piling soil, containing a good sod, and manure in alternate layers, using one part of manure to two or three parts of soil according to need. If soil is heavy, some sand should be added to the compost pile at the time it is made or at the time the soil is to be used. Two parts of soil, one part of sand, and one part of peat or well decomposed manure make a good mixture for starting plants. Perlite and vermiculite increase water-holding capacity and may improve soil mixes. The pH should be adjusted to 6.0 to 6.8 and any nutrient deficiencies corrected. Before the soil is used for the seedbed, it should be sifted through a coarse screen or run through a soil shredder.

Sowing Seed

Moisture, oxygen, and some degree of heat are necessary for germination. In specially prepared seedbeds, moisture is provided artificially when needed, but to maintain uniform moisture, the soil must be of good texture. Heat is also supplied artificially when the plants are started in greenhouses or hotbeds.

The time of sowing seeds is determined largely by the time it is desired to set the plants in the field and the methods used in growing the plants. If plants are to be set directly from the seedbed to the field, sowing can be done later than if plants are transplanted prior to field setting. Many growers start plants too early, and this results in stunted plants, or else they become too tall and "leggy."

Seeds are planted in flats or directly into the soil of the plant bed. Where greenhouses or hotbeds are used for starting plants, flats are fairly common. They are filled with a good friable soil and well firmed to prevent too much settling. The flat is usually filled and the soil is pressed down with the hands along the edges and in the corners; then more soil is added and a straight edge is used to level off the surface with the top of the flat. A board is then used to compact the soil and to leave it level and slightly below the top of the flat. Cleats may be attached to the board to make the rows (Fig. 7.4).

Most seeds are sown in rows in the flat or in the soil of the bed. In flats, the rows are spaced about 2 inches apart; but when the seeds are sown in the soil of the hotbed, greenhouse bench, or in open beds, the space between the rows is greater, usually 3 to 6 inches.

A simple method of measuring the distance between the rows and making the groove to receive the seed is to use a stick about 2 inches wide, $\frac{1}{4}$ to $\frac{1}{2}$ inch thick, and of a length to fit the flat. The edge of the stick is pressed into the soil to the depth desired. A similar method may also be used when the seed is to be planted in beds up to 6 feet wide, in which case the stick should be about 6 feet long and of the width desired. When this method is used in flats all of the rows are made before sowing any seed. The seed is sown thinly and is covered by sifting fine soil over the rows and firming it lightly (Fig. 7.5 and Fig. 7.6).

A rake-like marker frequently is used for making rows for seed sowing in hotbeds, cold frames, or outdoor beds. For sowing seed in a large scale, a seed drill may be used to advantage. Small seed, such as celery seed, are sometimes sown broadcast and covered very lightly with fine soil or merely covered with burlap.

The depth of covering is governed largely by the size of the seed and the texture of the soil. Very small seed should be covered lightly, if at all. Cabbage seed and others of similar size are covered to the depth of about $\frac{1}{4}$ inch when sown under protection, while beet seed should be covered $\frac{1}{2}$ inch under similar conditions. On heavy soil, the covering should be less than on light soil.

In the milder sections of the South, where winter production of vegetables is important, many plants must be started in the summer or early fall, and some protection against high temperature and intense sunlight is needed. Some method of shading the seedbed usually is employed under these conditions. Lath, cloth of the type of cheesecloth

Fig. 7.4—A board with cleats is used in getting uniform depth and spacing of rows in seeding flats.

Univ. of Ill. Photograph

Fig. 7.5—Vibrator is used to get uniform rate of seeding.

Univ. of Ill. Photograph

or tobacco cloth, sacks, and straw mats are among the materials used for shading the young plants.

Caring for the Seedbed

Good, stocky plants are desired and to get them care must be given to watering and to regulating the temperature and ventilation in greenhouses or other structures.

As soon as the seeds are planted and covered, the seedbed should be carefully watered, preferably with a fine spray from a sprinkling can or with a fine rose on a garden hose. The seedbed should never be allowed to dry out, and it should not be kept soaked. Until the plants are well established, the bed should be kept fairly moist but not wet. After the plants are well established, it is best to water thoroughly, preferably in the forenoon, and then to withhold water until the plants show the

Fig. 7.6—Seeds may be covered with soil, sand, or other materials to improve germination.
Univ. of III. Photograph

need of it. Ordinarily no water should be applied on cloudy, damp days. Before the plants are taken up for planting in the field, the bed should be given a thorough soaking, so that as much soil as possible will adhere to the roots.

The temperature that should be maintained in greenhouses or hotbeds depends on the crops grown. Tomatoes, peppers, eggplants, and melons thrive best at a relatively high temperature, 60° to 70° F., while cabbage, lettuce, cauliflower, celery, and other cool-season crops will make better growth, although not so rapid, at temperatures 10 degrees lower. Slow, steady growth is preferable to rapid growth.

Ventilation aids in the control of temperature and humidity of the air. In greenhouses, ventilation is obtained by opening the ventilators, while in hotbeds and sash-covered cold frames, the sashes may be raised at one end or pulled down a short distance. On warm days the sash may be removed entirely. In ventilating during cool weather, the wind should not be allowed to strike the plants.

Table 7.2—Vegetable Seed Sowing, Growing Temperature and Spacing Guide.

Vegetable	Approx. No. of Seeds per Oz.*	Approx. No. of Plants to Expect per Oz.	Time Needed to Grow Plant, Weeks[†]	Seed Planting Depth, Inches	Temperature Range for Germination, °F	Plant Growing Temperatures, °F Day	Plant Growing Temperatures, °F Night	Minimum Space for Transplants, Inches[a]
Cabbage	7,500	4,000- 5,000	5 to 7	1/2	70-80	60-70	50-60	1 1/2 x 1 1/2[b]
Cauliflower	10,000	3,000- 4,000	5 to 7	1/4 to 1/2	70-80	60-70	55-60	2 x 2[b]
Broccoli	10,000	4,000- 5,000	5 to 7	1/4 to 1/2	70-80	60-70	50-60	2 x 2[b]
Brussels sprouts	8,500	4,000- 5,000	5 to 7	1/4 to 1/2	70-80	60-70	50-60	2 x 2[b]
Head lettuce	20,000	7,000-10,000	5 to 7	1/4 to 1/2	60-75	60-70	50-60	1 1/2 x 1 1/2[b]
Onions	9,500	4,000- 5,000	8 to 10	3/8	65-80	60-70	45-55	
Celery	70,000	10,000-15,000	10 to 12	1/8	60-70	65-75	55-65	1 1/2 x 1 1/2[b]
Tomatoes	10,000	3,000- 4,000	5 to 7	1/4 to 1/2	70-80	70-80	60-65	2 x 2[bc]
Peppers	4,500	1,000- 1,500	6 to 8	1/4 to 1/2	75-85	70-80	60-70	2 x 2[b]
Eggplant	6,000	1,500- 2,500	6 to 8	1/4 to 1/2	75-90	70-80	65-70	2 x 2[b]
Cucumber	1,000	400- 500	3 to 4	3/4 to 1	70-95	70-90	60-70	3 x 3[c]
Muskmelon	1,000	400- 600	3 to 4	3/4 to 1	75-95	70-90	60-70	3 x 3[c]
Watermelon	225-300	150- 175	3 to 4	3/4 to 1	70-95	70-90	60-70	3 x 3[c]
Squash (summer)	225-300	100- 300	3 to 4	3/4 to 1	70-95	70-90	60-70	3 x 3[c]

*Varies with variety and seed sample.

[†]Depends upon type of plant-growing structures used and hearing facilities available.

[‡]Reduce day temperatures 5° to 10° F. during cloudy weather.

[a]Depends on size of plant desired, type of container, and the length of time plants are to remain in the flat or container.

[b]For growing in flats.

[c]Seeded directly into individual containers.

Pennsylvania Cooperative Extension Service Circular 562.

TRANSPLANTING

Plants that are started in greenhouses, hotbeds, or cold frames frequently are transplanted or pricked out before they are set out. Some may be transplanted more than once before being set in the field. Plants grown in the field, as in the South, are not transplanted until removed for shipment.

Fig. 7.7—Transplanting pepper seedlings before they become crowded.

Univ. of Ill. Photograph

Methods Used

A common practice is to sow the seed rather thickly; then, when the first true leaves are fairly well developed, to transplant the seedlings into flats or into the soil of the plant bed (Fig. 7.7). For best results, the soil must be moist but not sticky. After the soil has been compacted with a board, holes to receive the plants are made with the finger, with a small dibble, or with a spotting board. The spotting board saves time and insures that the plants will be evenly spaced in straight rows.

The spacing of the seedlings in the transplanting bed varies with the kind of plant and the time they are to remain in the bed. For celery, spacing varies from 1 by 1 inch to 2 by 2 inches, while larger-growing plants are spaced from 1½ by 1½ to 4 by 4 inches, depending on the time they are to be grown before setting in the field. Some plants, such as tomatoes, peppers, and eggplants, are frequently transplanted more than once before field setting. At the first transplanting, they are spaced 1½ by 1½ or 2 by 2 inches, and, as soon as the plants begin to crowd, they are transplanted again, giving them more space. Unless saving space is of importance, it is better to transplant seedlings only once to give them the desired spacing at this time (Fig. 7.8).

In transplanting, the soil should be pressed down around the roots, taking care to fill the hole at the bottom. Pressure should not be exerted against the stems of soft, succulent plants, as this might injure or kill them. After each transplanting, the soil should be watered to settle it

Fig. 7.8—Well spaced tomato plants in flat.

Univ. of Ill. Photograph

around the roots. Shading the plants for a day after transplanting usually is an advantage.

Plants are frequently grown in individual containers, such as clay, paper, or peat pots; paper or wood veneer bands; or tin cans. The seed may be sown in the soil in the container, or the seedlings may be grown in flats or beds and transplanted into the containers later. The main advantage in using pots and plant bands is that the roots are not disturbed when the plants are set in the field.

Clay pots are considered best, but are expensive, New clay pots absorb nitrates from the soil solution, and for this reason, old pots often give better results than new ones. However, new pots can be soaked in a nitrate of soda to make up the deficiency.

Containers made of carbonaceous material, such as wood, paper, and raw peat, have sometimes given unsatisfactory results. These materials supply energy food for bacteria that cause the decomposition of the carbonaceous material. These bacteria consume nitrates and thus compete with the plants for the nitrate supply in the soil. The remedy is to supply enough nitrates for both the plants and the bacteria. The nitrates used by the bacteria are built up into complex compounds which, on the death and decomposition of the organisms, return the nitrogen to the soil.

Most of the commercial transplanting is done by machine. The plants are usually placed by hand, and the other operations, including watering, are done by the transplanter. A starter is usually included with the water to stimulate rapid recovery. The starter solution is made by dissolving 3 pounds of a high-analysis water-soluble fertilizer in 50 gallons of water.

Advantages and Disadvantages of Transplanting

The main advantages in transplanting plants before setting them in the field are (1) economy in the use of space in the greenhouse, hotbed, or cold frame; (2) saving of labor in the care of the plant bed; and (3) better spacing of the plants in the bed. When the plants are to be transplanted, much less space is needed for the seedbed than is the case when they are to remain there until field setting. If they are not to be transplanted, sufficient space must be given to allow the plants to grow for several weeks without serious crowding. This would require more labor in caring for the seedbed.

When the seedlings are removed from the seedbed, the ends of the roots are broken off and this results in greater root branching. Transplanted plants have a much greater number of short branch roots, and therefore a greater absorbing surface than do similar plants that have not been transplanted. When these plants are taken up for setting in the field, there is a larger mass of feeding roots in the block of soil around the roots than in a similar block of soil around the roots of nontransplanted plants.

Many growers believe that transplanting results in the development of a more stocky plant with a better root system and that these increase the yield and hasten maturity. Experimental evidence presented by Loomis, however, indicates that transplanting in itself does not increase yield or hasten maturity. The increase in space and better conditions usually given the transplanted plants do have these effects.

The main disadvantages of transplanting are the extra labor required and the check in growth that results from taking up and resetting the plants. The extra labor may be offset by the economy in the use of valuable greenhouse or hotbed space and in the saving of labor in caring for the plants. Although all plants are checked in growth by transplanting, some are checked less than others. With those that are checked but little, this may be offset by the increase in root branching. Transplanting when the plants are large usually results in delayed maturity and, in some cases, in reduced yield. Sweet corn, cucumber, melon, and bean plants are seriously checked in growth by transplanting unless it is done while the plants are small. A second transplanting of these plants is very injurious.

Difference in Response to Transplanting

Any of the common vegetable plants can be transplanted satisfactorily during the early stages of growth. With corn, beans, and the cucurbits, however, there is only a short period when they are not seriously injured by transplanting.

The recovery of the plant after transplanting is determined largely by its ability to obtain water, and this depends on the speed of root replacement (Fig. 7.9). Plants seriously injured by transplanting normally have a rapid rate of top growth and a slow rate of root growth, while those that are not greatly checked in growth by transplanting have a relatively slow rate of top growth and a rapid rate of root replacement.

Figure 7.9 illustrates the difference in rate of root replacement of cabbage and corn plants; cabbage is easy and corn difficult to transplant. Eight days after transplanting, the cabbage plant had a much greater root area than the nontransplanted plant. The nontransplanted corn plant, on the other hand, had a much greater absorbing surface than the transplanted one.

The rate of recovery from transplanting depends not only on the kind and age of the plant, but also on the quantity of stored food, especially carbohydrates. These enable the plant to replace its roots rapidly. There is evidence that the roots of some plants are suberized or cutinized at an early age, and such plants are slow to recover following transplanting. Deposition of suberin or cutin in the endoderm or periderm hinders water absorption and branch-root formation.

HARDENING PLANTS

The term "hardening" is applied to any treatment that results in any firming or hardening of the tissues of plants. Hardening enables plants to better withstand unfavorable environmental conditions, such as low

Fig. 7.9—Root systems of cabbage plants (four on left) and corn plants (four on right) showing effect of transplanting on root branching. The plant on the left of each set of two is the non-transplanted plant and the one on the right is the transplanted one eight days after transplanting.

Cornell Univ. Agr. Exp. Sta.

temperatures, hot drying winds, certain types of insect injury, whipping in the wind, and injury from particles of soil and sand blown by the wind.

Methods Used

Any treatment that results in a check in growth increases hardiness, but plants differ in the degree of resistance to certain conditions following the hardening treatment. For example, cabbage and other cool-season plants can be hardened to such extent that they will withstand temperatures several degrees below freezing and will survive actual ice formation in their tissues. Warm-season plants, such as tomato, cucumber, melon, pepper, eggplant, and others, will not withstand ice formation, regardless of the degree of hardening. Checking growth of these results in only slight resistance to cold.

The usual methods of hardening plants are (1) exposing them to temperatures too low for good growth, (2) allowing the soil of the plant bed to become dry, and (3) a combination of these two. When plants are grown under protection during cool weather, it is easy to subject them to relatively low temperatures by reducing the heat in the greenhouse or hotbed, and by ventilation at the proper time.

If the plants are grown during warm weather, it is not possible to harden by low temperature, hence some other method must be used. Withholding water is the best method in this case, but when the plants are grown in outdoor beds, the success of this method is dependent on the weather. During a rainy period, hardening can be accomplished by lifting the plants slightly with a fork or by cutting the roots on both sides of the rows of plants. In both cases, the water-absorbing surface of the root system is reduced and, if the treatment is severe enough, growth is checked and hardening results.

Hardened plants develop new roots faster than do tender ones. It is better to maintain a moderate rate of growth throughout the plant-growing period than to permit rapid growth up to the last week or two and then check growth suddenly. Overhardening results in delayed growth when the plants are set out. Severe hardening of tomato plants decreases the early yield of fruit in the greenhouse. Overhardening will delay fruiting in the field and under some conditions reduce the total yield.

Changes During Hardening

Hardening is accompanied by (1) slowing up of the rate of growth;

(2) thickening of the cuticle; (3) an increase in the waxy covering on the leaves of certain kinds of plants; (4) the development of a pink color, especially in the stems, petioles, and veins; (5) an increase in the dry matter; (6) an increase in the content of water-holding colloids; and (7) a decrease in the percentage of freezable water and other internal changes. Usually the leaves of hardened plants are deeper green and smaller than those of tender plants.

Hardened plants develop new roots faster than do tender ones, and this is of special importance in plants that are grown in beds and later set in the field. The accumulation of food materials during the hardening treatment is important in new root formation. Hardening also increases the water retaining power of the cells and this is of importance in resistance to water loss incident to freezing and in transpiration. In the hardening of cabbage plants there is a change in the constituents of protoplasm which prevents their precipitation as a result of the physical changes incident to freezing. The proteins are changed to forms which are less easily precipitated.

Commercial Plant Growing

The production of vegetable plants for sale is of considerable importance. In a well equipped plant nursery, soil can be sterilized and reused. The operation can be mechanized by the use of conveyors, fork lifts, pallets, soil mixers, and other labor-saving equipment. With adequate control of temperatures and appropriate use of insecticides and fungicides, good plants can be produced economically for most any specialized market. The demand may range from well grown containerized plants to cheaply grown bare-rooted plants.

Because of the cost of equipment and labor needed in growing good plants from seed, most home gardeners and a large number of commercial vegetable growers find it more economical to buy plants for transplanting. Also, growers of vegetables for processors find the less-expensive southern-grown plants satisfactory.

SELECTED REFERENCES

Cook, W. P., et al., "Commercial Vegetable Transplant Production," Clemson Univ. Coop. Ext. Ser. Veg. Leaflet 17, Rev., 1977.
Courter, J. W., "Plastic Greenhouses," Ill. Agr. Ext. Circ. 905, 1965.
Courter, J. W., Vandemark, J. S, and Arnold, C. Y., "Fertilizing Greenhouse Vegetables," Ill. Agr. Ext. Circ. 922, 1966.

Courter, J. W., et al., "Growing Vegetable Transplants," Univ. of Ill. Coop. Ext. Ser. Circ. 884, Rev., 1977.

Dalrymple, D. C., "A Global Review of Greenhouse Food Production," USDA, FAE Rep. 89, 1973.

Fletcher, R. F., "Growing Vegetable Transplants," Pa. State Univ. Coop. Ext. Ser. Circ. 562, 1978.

Jaworski, C. A., et al., "Research Studies on Field Production of Tomato Transplants in Southern Georgia," USDA Agr. Res. Ser. Res. Rep. 148, 1973.

Lucas, R. E., and Rieke, P. E., "Peats for Soil Improvement and Soil Mixes," Mich. Coop. Ext. Ser. Ext. Bull. E-516, 1965.

Marlowe, G. A., Jr., "Vegetable Transplant Production," Univ. of Fla., Veg. Crops Ext. Rep. VC, 1976.

Neild, R. E., "Growing Vegetable Transplants," Univ. of Neb. Coop. Ext. Ser. EC 72-1226.

New, Leon, and Roberts, R. E., "Automatic Drip Irrigation for Greenhouse Tomato Production," Tex. Agr. Ext. Ser. MP-1082, 1973.

Nicklow, C. W., et al., "Growing Transplants," Mich. State Univ. Coop Ext. Ser. Bull. E-675—A, 1970.

O'Dell, C. R., and Massey, P. H., Jr., "Starting Early Plants," Va. Poly. Inst. Ext. Div. Pub. 226, 1976.

Schales, F. D., and Massey, P. H., "Starting Early Plants," Va. Agr. Ext. Ser. Circ. 764, 1965.

Sheldrake, R., Jr., and Boodley, J. W., "Commercial Production of Vegetable and Flower Plants," N. Y. State Col. Agr. Cornell Univ. Inf. Bull. 82, 1974.

Walker, J. N., and Duncan, G. A., "Air Circulation in Greenhouses," Dept. Agr. Eng., Univ. of Ky., AEN-18, 1973.

Walker, J. N., and Duncan, G. A., "Cooling Greenhouses," Dept. Agr. Eng., Univ. of Ky., AEN-28, 1974.

Walker, J. N., and Duncan, G. A., "Estimating Greenhouse Heating Requirements and Fuel Costs," Dept. Agr. Eng., Univ. of Ky., AEN-8, 1973.

Walker, J. N., and Duncan, G. A., "Estimating Greenhouse Ventilation Requirements," Dept. Agr. Eng., Univ. of Ky., AEN-9, 1973.

Walker, J. N., and Duncan, G. A., "Greenhouse Heating Systems," Dept. Agr. Eng., Univ. of Ky., AEN-31, 1973.

Walker, J. N., and Duncan, G. A., "Greenhouse Humidity Control," Dept. Agr. Eng., Univ. of Ky., AEN-19, 1973.

Walker, J. N., and Duncan, G. A., "Greenhouse Structures," Dept. Agr. Eng., Univ. of Ky., AEN-12, 1973.

Walker, J. N., and Duncan, G. A., "Greenhouse Ventilation Systems," Dept. Agr. Eng., Univ. of Ky., AEN-30, 1974.

Wiebe, John, "Greenhouse Vegetable Production in Ontario," Ont. Dept. of Agr. and Food Pub. 526, 1967.

Woodbury, G. W., "Increasing Vegetable Production with Plastics," Ida. Agr. Exp. Sta. Bull. 474, 1966.

CHAPTER 8

Planting in the Open

The vegetable crops vary in their climatic requirements. Each must be planted at a time when it will have a good season for development or will mature at a good time for marketing. In some cases the seed can be sown directly in the field, but in others transplants have to be used. Along with timeliness, getting a stand of good plants is essential for successful vegetable production.

PLANTING SEED

Spacing the Rows

In the open field, 3 to 3½ feet is the usual width between rows for more than half of the common vegetables, including beans, peppers, eggplants, cabbage, corn, and potatoes. This width allows ample room for the use of equipment in cultivating, spraying, or harvesting, as well as space for top and root development of plants. When space is limited and hand labor is used, the width may be reduced.

Vegetables which have a narrow, spreading root system and small top, such as onions, lettuce, carrots, beets, radishes, and celery, will have ample room in 1½- to 2½-foot rows. These vegetables are usually intensely grown, and it is necessary for economic reasons to produce a heavy yield from the land. Most of these will stand crowding and are not seriously injured by partial shade.

Plants with large leaves, trailing vines, or fruit which require direct sunlight for proper development must have more room. Among these are melons, squash, pumpkins, and cucumbers, which should be planted in rows 4 to 12 feet apart, depending on the kind of crop and local practice. Planting data for vegetable crops are given in Table 8.1.

Preparing the Seedbed

In preparing the soil for planting, anything that will interfere with plowing, spading, or hoeing the soil must be removed. If the soil contains sod or clay, it should be plowed to a depth of 6 inches at least a month before planting. Special care should be taken to remove from the land any portions of diseased plants which might infect the new plants.

About two weeks before planting, the soil should be harrowed, rolled, and dragged until it is smooth and mellow. It is then ready to be laid off in rows properly spaced to accommodate the vegetables to be grown. Preparation of beds will vary for seed of different kinds, specific directions for this being found in the special crop chapters.

Planting Methods

Vegetable seeds are planted as follows: (1) by hand in hills, rows, or broadcast (Table 8.1); (2) with one-row hand seeders; and (3) with single- or multiple-row seeders drawn usually by tractors. The method of seeding depends largely on the quantity of seed to be planted and the rapidity with which the work must be done. Regardless of the method of planting, one should make sure that the seeds are planted at the proper depth and that the soil is left smooth and compact.

Melon, squash, and cucumber seeds may be planted by hand or with drills of various kinds. They may be planted in hills or in continuous rows. Most winter-grown salad greens, including mustard, turnips, rape, tender greens, and spinach, may be drilled or sown by hand and covered with a garden rake. These very small seeds are sown to advantage if mixed with four or five parts of fine soil.

Seeders vary from a simple bean dropper to complicated machines which have several attachments for manipulating the soil, fertilizer, and seed in the process of planting. One well-known planter performs the following operations simultaneously: (1) opens two furrows for placement of fertilizer, (2) deposits any desired quantity of fertilizer, (3) covers the fertilizer in the furrow, (4) makes up seedbed, (5) levels off bed at desired height, (6) opens the furrows for seed, (7) sows any quantity of seed, (8) covers the seeds to the proper depth, and (9) packs the soil

Table 8.1—Vegetable Crops Planting Chart.

Kind	Seeds for 100-Ft. Row	Seed for 1 Acre — Drilled in Field	Seed for 1 Acre — If Transplanted	*Approximate Number of Seeds per Pound	Distance Between Rows — Machine Cultivation	Distance Between Rows — Hand Cultivation	Distance Between Rows — Plants Apart in Rows	Depth of Planting	Time of Planting in Open Ground — South	Time of Planting in Open Ground — North	Ready for Use from Date of Seeding
Asparagus, seed	1 oz.	5 lbs.	1 lb.	22,400	30 to 36 in.	18 to 24 in.	3 in.	1 in.	Autumn or early spring	Early spring	1 or 2 yrs. (plants)
Asparagus, root	66 roots	—	6000	—	5 ft.	4 ft.	18 in.	2 in.	Autumn or early spring	Early spring	2 yrs.
Beans, dwarf	1 lb.	60 lbs.	—	1,200	30 to 36 in.	18 to 24 in.	2 in.	1 in.	Feb., Apr., (Aug., Sept.)	Apr. to July	42 to 75 days
Beans, pole	1/2 lb.	30 lbs.	—	1,200	3 to 4 ft.	3 to 4 ft.	3 to 4 ft.	1 in.	Late spring	May and June	65 to 90 days
Beet (and Swiss chard)	1 oz.	10 lbs.	—	19,200	28 to 36 in.	12 to 18 in.	2 in.	1 in.	Feb., Apr., (Aug., Sept.)	April to Aug.	45 to 60 days
Beet, mangel & sugar	1 oz.	5 lbs.	—	24,000	28 to 36 in.	20 in.	4 in.	1 in.	Feb., Apr., (Aug., Sept.)	April to Aug.	90 to 120 days
Broccoli	1/4 oz.	2 lbs.	4 oz.	160,000	30 to 40 in.	24 to 36 in.	18 to 24 in.	1/2 in.	Jan. to July	Mar. and Apr.	90 to 100 days
Brussels sprouts	1/4 oz.	2 lbs.	4 oz.	136,000	30 to 36 in.	24 to 30 in.	12 to 16 in.	1/2 in.	Jan. to July	May and June	100 to 120 days
Cabbage, Chinese	1/4 oz.	2 lbs.	4 oz.	152,000	30 to 36 in.	18 to 24 in.	10 to 12 in.	1/2 in.	July and Aug.	June and July	75 days
Cabbage, early	1/4 oz.	2 lbs.	4 oz.	120,000	30 to 36 in.	24 to 30 in.	12 to 18 in.	1/2 in.	Oct. to Dec.	Mar. and Apr.	90 to 110 days
Cabbage, late	1/4 oz.	2 lbs.	4 oz.	120,000	30 to 40 in.	24 to 36 in.	16 to 24 in.	1/2 in.	June and July	May and June	110 to 120 days
Cantaloupe, Muskmelon	1/2 oz.	3 lbs.	—	16,000	6 to 8 ft.	6 to 8 ft.	4 every 4 ft.	1 in.	Feb. to Apr.	April to June	85 to 150 days
Carrot	1/2 oz.	3 lbs.	—	320,000	30 to 36 in.	12 to 18 in.	2 in.	1/2 in.	Mar. and Apr., (Sept.)	April to June	55 to 80 days
Cauliflower	1/4 oz.	2 lbs.	4 oz.	160,000	30 to 36 in.	24 to 30 in.	14 to 18 in.	1/2 in.	Jan. and Feb.	April to June	95 to 110 days
Celery	1/4 oz.	1 lb.	4 oz.	1,280,000	3 to 6 ft.	18 to 36 in.	2 in.	1/2 in.	Aug. and Oct. (June)	May and June	120 to 150 days
Chicory, witloof	1 oz.	4 lbs.	1 lb.	256,000	30 in.	18 in.	4 in.	1/8 in.	July and Aug.	Apr. to June	100 days
Chicory, Magdeburg	1 oz.	4 lbs.	4 oz.	256,000	30 in.	24 in.	6 in.	1/2 in.	March to July	Apr. to June	100 days
Collards	1/4 oz.	2 lbs.	—	120,000	30 to 36 in.	24 to 30 in.	14 to 18 in.	1/2 in.	May and June	Late spring	100 to 120 days
Corn salad	1 oz.	8 lbs.	—	480,000	30 to 36 in.	12 to 18 in.	3 in.	1/2 in.	July and Aug.	June and July	60 days
Corn, sweet	1/4 lb.	10 lbs.	—	3,520	36 to 42 in.	30 to 36 in.	4 every 3 ft.	1 in.	Feb. to April	May to July	55 to 90 days
Cress, water	1/2 oz.	—	—	2,400,000	Broadcast	—	—	water	Early spring	Apr. to Sept.	60 to 70 days
Cucumber	1/2 oz.	3 lbs.	—	16,000	4 to 6 ft.	4 to 6 ft.	4 every 3 ft.	1 in.	Feb. and Mar.	Apr. to July	50 to 70 days
Eggplant	1/8 oz.	2 lbs.	4 oz.	96,000	30 to 36 in.	24 to 30 in.	18 in.	1/2 in.	Feb. to Apr.	Apr. and May	125 to 140 days
Endive	1 oz.	4 lbs.	—	240,000	30 in.	18 in.	12 in.	1/2 in.	Feb. to Apr.	Apr. (July)	100 days
Kale or Borecole	1/4 oz.	3 lbs.	1 lb.	144,000	30 to 36 in.	18 to 24 in.	18 in.	1/2 in.	Oct. to Feb.	Aug., Sept., (Mar., Apr.)	55 to 60 days
Kohlrabi	1/4 oz.	4 lbs.	1 lb.	135,000	30 to 36 in.	18 to 24 in.	6 in.	1/2 in.	Sept. to May	March to May	50 to 70 days
Leek	1/2 oz.	4 lbs.	—	176,000	30 to 36 in.	14 to 20 in.	4 in.	1/2 in.	May to Sept.	March to May	120 to 150 days

(Continued)

Table 8.1 (Continued).

Kind	Seeds for 100-Ft. Row	Seed for 1 Acre: Drilled in Field	Seed for 1 Acre: If Trans-planted	*Approxi-mate Number of Seeds per Pound	Distance Between Rows: Machine Cultiva-tion	Distance Between Rows: Hand Cultiva-tion	Plants Apart in Rows	Depth of Plant-ing	Time of Planting in Open Ground: South	Time of Planting in Open Ground: North	Ready for Use from Date of Seeding
Lettuce	¼ oz.	3 lbs.	1 lb.	320,000	30 in.	12 to 18 in.	6 in.	½ in.	Sept. to Mar.	Mar. to Sept.	70 to 90 days
Mustard	¼ oz.	4 lbs.	—	288,000	30 to 36 in.	12 to 18 in.	4 to 5 ft.	¼ in.	Autumn or early spring	Mar. to May (Sept.)	60 to 90 days
Okra	2 oz.	8 lbs.	—	7,200	4 to 5 ft.	3 to 4 ft.	24 in.	1 in.	Feb. to Apr.	May and June	90 to 140 days
Onion, seed	1 oz.	4 lbs.	—	120,000	24 to 36 in.	12 to 18 in.	2 in.	½ in.	Oct. to Mar.	Apr. to May	125 to 150 days
Onion seed for sets	1 lb.	50 lbs.	—	120,000	24 to 36 in.	12 to 18 in.	½ in.	½ in.		Apr.	90 days
Onion sets	1 qt.	12 bu.	—	—	24 to 36 in.	12 to 18 in.	2 in.	1 in.	Early spring or autumn	Feb. to May	100 days
Parsley	¼ oz.	3 lbs.	—	240,000	24 to 36 in.	12 to 18 in.	3 in.	⅛ in.	Sept. to May-Sept.	Early spring	65 to 90 days
Parsnip	½ oz.	3 lbs.	—	112,000	30 to 36 in.	18 to 24 in.	2 in.	½ in.	Feb., Mar.	Mar.-Apr.	130 days
Peas	1 lb.	200 lbs.	—	2,000	3 to 4 ft.	30 to 36 in.	1 in.	1 to 2 in.	Sept. to Apr.	Mar. to June	45 to 75 days
Peas, Crowder	½ lb.	25 lbs.	—	2,800	3 to 4 ft.	3 ft.	4 to 6 in.	1 in.	Mar. to June	May	100 to 110 days
Pepper	⅛ oz.	2 lbs.	4 oz.	72,000	30 to 36 in.	18 to 24 in.	15 in.	½ in.	Early Spring	May and June	130 to 150 days
Pumpkin	½ oz.	4 lbs.	—	3,200	8 to 12 ft.	8 to 12 ft.	4 every 6 ft.	1 in.	Apr. and May	May to July	75 to 90 days
Radish	1 oz.	15 lbs.	—	64,000	24 to 36 in.	12 to 18 in.	1 in.	½ in.	Sept. to Apr.	Mar. to Sept.	20 to 75 days
Rhubarb, roots	40 roots	—	3500	—	5 ft.	4 ft.	30 in.	3 to 4 in.	Autumn or early spring	Early spring	2 or 3 yrs.
Rhubarb, seed	½ oz.	8 lbs.	2 lbs.	32,000	30 to 36 in.	18 to 24 in.	4 in.	½ to 1 in.	Early spring	Early spring	1 or 2 yrs. (plants)
Rutabaga	¼ oz.	2 lbs.	—	64,000	30 to 36 in.	18 to 24 in.	6 in.	½ to 1 in.	Aug. and Sept.	June-July	90 days
Salsify	1 oz.	8 lbs.	—	48,000	30 to 36 in.	18 to 24 in.	2 in.	½ in.	Early spring	Early spring	150 days
Soybeans, Vegetable	½ lb.	30 lbs.	—	1,920	30 to 36 in.	16 to 36 in.	2 in.	1 in.	Apr.-May-June	May-June	90 to 120 days
Spinach	1 oz.	15 lbs.	—	48,000	30 to 36 in.	12 to 18 in.	2 in.	½ in.	Sept. to Mar.	Sept. & early spring	45 days is min.
Squash, summer ...	½ oz.	4 lbs.	—	4,800	3 to 4 ft.	3 to 4 ft.	4 every 4 ft.	1 in.	Spring	Apr. to June	65 to 70 days
Squash, winter	½ oz.	2 lbs.	—	2,000	7 to 10 ft.	7 to 10 ft.	4 every 6 ft.	1 in.	Spring	May to July	125 days
Tomato	⅛ oz.	2 lbs.	2 oz.	160,000	3 to 5 ft.	3 to 4 ft.	3 to 4 ft.	½ in.	Mar.-Apr.	May to June	125 to 150 days
Tomato, pelleted ...	1 oz.	6 lbs.	12 lbs.	12,000	3 to 5 ft.	3 to 4 ft.	3 to 4 ft.	½ in.	Mar.-Apr.	May to June	125 to 150 days
Turnip	½ oz.	2 lbs.	—	208,000	24 to 36 in.	18 to 24 in.	2 in.	¼ in.	Aug. to Oct.	Apr. and Aug.	45 to 90 days
Turnip, for greens ..	1 oz.	5 lbs.	—	208,000	Broadcast	12 to 18 in.	—	¼ in.	Aug. to Oct.	Apr. and Aug.	45 to 50 days
Watermelon	1 oz.	3 lbs.	—	3,600	8 to 12 ft.	8 to 12 ft.	4 every 6 ft.	1 in.	Mar. to May	May and June	100 to 130 days

*The number of seeds per pound varies widely between cultivars and lots of same species, but figures given are approximately average.

Data from Corneli Seed Co.

over them. Seeders should not only space seeds properly but should also plant them without injury.

For most vegetables, seed must be fresh, and even then, a germination test is advisable. Soaking certain slow-germinating seeds, such as beet, okra, celery, and pepper, in water overnight, just before planting, increases the percentage and rapidity of germination. Seeds that have been soaked are more difficult to sow with a seed drill than those that have not been soaked.

Planting Dates

The time of planting vegetable seed is based on locality, hardiness, length of season, and time of maturity. The earliest date for planting winter crops is October or November in the extreme South. Following the advance of the season northward, this day may be approximately June 15 in the extreme northern portion of the country. The grower should know the dates of the last killing frost in the spring (Fig. 8.1) and the first killing frost in the fall (Fig. 8.2) for his particular locality, and

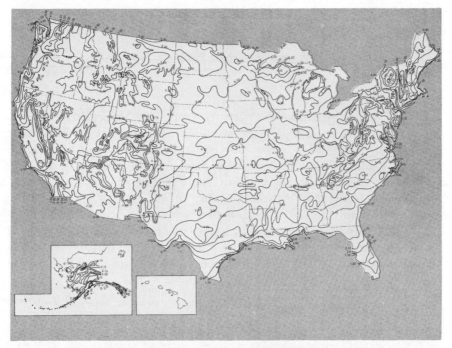

Fig. 8.1—Average dates of the last killing frost in spring.

USDA Farmers' Bull. 934

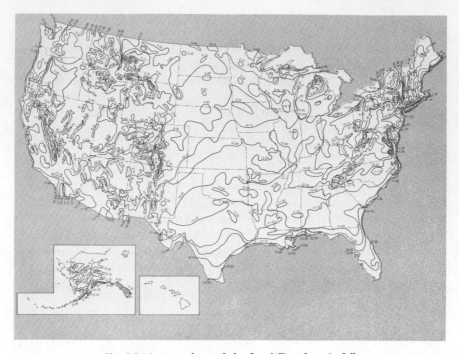

Fig. 8.2—Average dates of the first killing frost in fall.

USDA Farmers' Bull. 934

use these dates as the basis for planting crops that are sensitive to frost. Local experience is usually a safeguard. Figure 8.1 and Table 8.2 show the earliest safe dates for planting vegetables in the spring; while Figure 8.2 and Table 8.3 give the latest safe dates for fall planting.

Hardy vegetables including beets, cabbage, carrots, collards, mustard, onions, peas, rape, shallots, spinach, and turnips may be planted in the fall or winter in the South, because they are not easily injured by freezing. Semi-hardy vegetables, such as lettuce and radishes, must be planted in ice-free seasons, though they will stand frosts. Tender vegetables cannot be safely planted until all danger of frost is past and the ground becomes warm, as is shown in Table 8.1.

The length of season before maturity influences the time of planting different crops. Such vegetables as eggplants, peppers, and sweet potatoes are planted only once each year and continue to grow throughout the season, while other vegetables, such as snap beans, radishes, carrots, and lettuce, may be planted at intervals during the season.

Tender vegetables which require 100 days or more to reach maturity must be planted in the spring, and as a rule, the earlier after the soil becomes warm, the better.

Treating Seed

Vegetable seed for planting should be treated for the control of bacterial and fungus diseases. The organisms are carried either within the seed tissue or on the surface of the seed. The ideal treatment sterilizes the seed without injuring germination or retarding subsequent growth and, unless the seed is recontaminated, also prevents decay after planting and greatly reduces damping-off of seedlings.

Three types of seed treatment in common use are as follows: (1) The hot-water method is used to control disease organisms that reside within seed tissue. Usually, immediately before planting, the seed is immersed for about 10 minutes in water heated to 120° to 125° F. (Some hard seeds germinate more readily after this treatment.) (2) Liquid chemical treatment for the control of disease organisms on seed may be given immediately after harvest or just before planting. If given just after harvest, the seed should be dried, packaged, and stored in such a manner as to avoid recontamination. Chemicals and methods of treatment are discussed in Chapter 11. (3) Chemical dust treatments are similar to the above, with the exception that the materials are applied in the form of a dust rather than in solution. These treatments may be given at any time before planting, and a residue of the chemical should remain on the seed.

The particular type of seed treatment to use depends on the disease or diseases involved and the susceptibility of the seed to injury. It has been found advisable to treat some seeds, such as pepper and tomato, as they are removed from the fruit and before the seeds are dry. Information regarding seed treatment should be obtained from some reliable source, and should be followed carefully. Most commercial compounds carry detailed directions on the packages. Some states have laws requiring and regulating treatment of vegetable seed. In so far as possible, one should purchase only seed that have been properly treated for the control of seed-borne diseases.

Planting Depths

The depth of planting seed depends on a number of conditions, chief among which are the texture of the soil, the availability of mois-

Table 8.2—Earliest Dates, and Range of Dates, for Safe Spring Planting of Vegetables in the Open.

Crop	Planting Dates for Localities in Which Average Date of Last Freeze Is—						
	Jan. 30	Feb. 8	Feb. 18	Feb. 28	Mar. 10	Mar. 20	Mar. 30
Asparagus*	Feb. 1—Apr. 15	Feb. 10—May 1	Mar. 1—May 1	Mar. 15—June 1	Jan. 1—Mar. 1	Feb. 1—Mar. 10	Feb. 15—Mar. 20
Beans, lima	Feb. 1—Apr. 15	Feb. 10—May 1	Mar. 1—May 1	Mar. 10—May 15	Mar. 20—June 15	Apr. 1—June 15	Apr. 15—June 20
Beans, snap	Jan. 1—Mar. 15	Jan. 10—Mar. 15	Jan. 20—Apr. 1	Feb. 1—Apr. 1	Mar. 10—May 15	Mar. 15—May 25	Apr. 1—June 1
Beet	Jan. 1—30	Jan. 1—30	Jan. 15—Feb. 15	Feb. 1—Mar. 1	Feb. 15—June 1	Feb. 15—May 15	Mar. 1—June 1
Broccoli, sprouting*	Jan. 1—30	Jan. 1—30	Jan. 15—Feb. 15	Feb. 1—Mar. 1	Feb. 15—Mar. 15	Feb. 15—Mar. 15	Mar. 1—20
Brussels sprouts*	Jan. 1—30	Jan. 1—30	Jan. 15—Feb. 25	Feb. 1—Mar. 1	Feb. 15—Mar. 15	Feb. 15—Mar. 15	Mar. 1—20
Cabbage*	Jan. 1—Feb. 10	Jan. 1—Feb. 10	Jan. 15—Feb. 25	Jan. 15—Feb. 25	Jan. 25—Mar. 1	Feb. 1—Mar. 1	Feb. 15—Mar. 10
Cabbage, Chinese	(**)	(**)	(**)	(**)	(**)	(**)	(**)
Carrot	Jan. 1—Mar. 1	Jan. 1—Mar. 1	Jan. 15—Mar. 1	Feb. 1—Mar. 1	Feb. 10—Mar. 1	Mar. 1—Apr. 1	Mar. 10—Apr. 10
Cauliflower*	Jan. 1—Feb. 1	Jan. 1—Feb. 1	Jan. 10—Feb. 10	Jan. 20—Feb. 20	Feb. 1—Mar. 1	Feb. 10—Mar. 10	Feb. 20—Mar. 20
Celery and celeriac	Jan. 1—Feb. 1	Jan. 10—Feb. 10	Jan. 20—Feb. 20	Feb. 1—Mar. 1	Feb. 20—Mar. 20	Mar. 1—Apr. 1	Mar. 15—Apr. 15
Chard	Jan. 1—Apr. 1	Jan. 10—Apr. 1	Jan. 20—Apr. 15	Feb. 1—May 1	Feb. 15—May 15	Feb. 20—May 15	Mar. 1—May 25
Chervil and chives	Jan. 1—Feb. 1	Jan. 1—Feb. 1	Jan. 1—Feb. 1	Jan. 15—Feb. 15	Feb. 1—Mar. 1	Feb. 10—Mar. 10	Feb. 15—Mar. 15
Chicory, witloof					June 1—July 1	June 1—July 1	June 1—July 1
Collards*	Jan. 1—Feb. 15	Jan. 1—Feb. 15	Jan. 1—Mar. 15	Jan. 15—Mar. 15	Feb. 1—Apr. 1	Feb. 15—May 1	Mar. 1—June 1
Corn salad	Jan. 1—Feb. 15	Jan. 1—Feb. 15	Jan. 1—Mar. 1	Jan. 1—Mar. 1	Jan. 1—Apr. 1	Jan. 15—Mar. 1	Jan. 15—Mar. 15
Corn, sweet	Feb. 1—Mar. 15	Feb. 10—Apr. 1	Feb. 20—Apr. 15	Mar. 1—Apr. 15	Mar. 10—Apr. 15	Mar. 15—May 1	Mar. 25—May 15
Cress, upland	Jan. 1—Feb. 1	Jan. 1—Feb. 15	Jan. 15—Feb. 15	Feb. 1—Mar. 1	Feb. 10—Mar. 15	Feb. 20—Mar. 15	Mar. 1—Apr. 1
Cucumber	Feb. 15—Mar. 15	Feb. 15—Apr. 1	Feb. 20—Apr. 15	Mar. 1—Apr. 15	Mar. 15—Apr. 15	Apr. 1—May 1	Apr. 10—May 15
Eggplant*	Feb. 1—Mar. 15	Feb. 20—Apr. 15	Feb. 20—May 1	Mar. 10—Apr. 15	Mar. 15—Apr. 15	Apr. 1—May 1	Apr. 15—May 15
Endive	Jan. 1—Mar. 1	Jan. 1—Mar. 1	Jan. 15—Mar. 1	Feb. 1—Mar. 1	Feb. 15—Mar. 15	Mar. 1—Apr. 1	Mar. 10—Apr. 10
Fennel, Florence	Jan. 1—Mar. 1	Jan. 1—Mar. 1	Jan. 15—Mar. 1	Feb. 1—Mar. 1	Feb. 15—Mar. 15	Mar. 1—Apr. 1	Mar. 10—Apr. 10
Garlic	(**)	(**)	(**)	(**)	(**)	Feb. 1—Mar. 1	Feb. 10—Mar. 10
Horseradish*	(**)	(**)	(**)	(**)	(**)	Feb. 1—Mar. 1	Mar. 1—Apr. 1
Kale	Jan. 1—Feb. 1	Jan. 10—Feb. 1	Jan. 20—Feb. 10	Feb. 1—20	Feb. 10—Mar. 1	Feb. 20—Mar. 10	Mar. 1—20
Kohlrabi	Jan. 1—Feb. 1	Jan. 10—Feb. 1	Jan. 20—Feb. 10	Feb. 1—20	Feb. 10—Mar. 1	Feb. 20—Mar. 10	Mar. 1—Apr. 1
Leek	Jan. 1—Feb. 1	Jan. 1—Feb. 1	Jan. 1—Feb. 15	Jan. 15—Feb. 15	Jan. 25—Mar. 1	Feb. 1—Mar. 1	Feb. 15—Mar. 15
Lettuce, head*	Jan. 1—Feb. 1	Jan. 1—Feb. 1	Jan. 1—Mar. 1	Jan. 15—Feb. 15	Feb. 15—Mar. 1	Feb. 15—Mar. 15	Mar. 1—20
Lettuce, leaf	Jan. 1—Feb. 1	Jan. 1—Feb. 1	Jan. 1—Mar. 1	Jan. 1—Mar. 1	Feb. 15—Apr. 1	Feb. 15—Apr. 15	Mar. 1—May 1
Muskmelon	Feb. 15—Apr. 15	Feb. 15—Apr. 1	Feb. 15—Apr. 15	Mar. 1—Apr. 15	Mar. 15—Apr. 15	Apr. 1—May 1	Apr. 10—May 15
Mustard	Jan. 1—Mar. 1	Jan. 1—Feb. 1	Feb. 1—Mar. 1	Feb. 1—Mar. 1	Feb. 10—Mar. 15	Feb. 20—Apr. 1	Mar. 1—Apr. 15
Okra	Feb. 15—Apr. 1	Feb. 15—Apr. 15	Mar. 1—June 1	Mar. 10—June 1	Mar. 20—June 1	Apr. 1—June 15	Apr. 10—June 15
Onion*	Jan. 1—15	Jan. 1—15	Jan. 1—15	Jan. 1—Feb. 1	Jan. 15—Feb. 15	Feb. 10—Mar. 10	Feb. 15—Mar. 15
Onion, seed	Jan. 1—15	Jan. 1—15	Jan. 1—15	Jan. 1—Feb. 1	Jan. 15—Feb. 15	Feb. 10—Mar. 10	Feb. 20—Mar. 15
Onion, sets	Jan. 1—15	Jan. 1—15	Jan. 1—15	Jan. 1—Mar. 1	Jan. 15—Mar. 10	Feb. 1—Mar. 20	Feb. 15—Mar. 20
Parsley	Jan. 1—30	Jan. 1—30	Jan. 1—30	Jan. 1—Mar. 1	Jan. 15—Mar. 1	Feb. 1—Mar. 1	Feb. 15—Mar. 15
Parsnip			Jan. 1—Mar. 1	Jan. 15—Mar. 1	Feb. 1—Mar. 1	Feb. 15—Mar. 15	Mar. 1—Apr. 1
Peas, garden	Jan. 1—Feb. 15	Jan. 1—Feb. 15	Jan. 1—Mar. 1	Jan. 15—Feb. 15	Jan. 15—Mar. 15	Feb. 1—Mar. 15	Feb. 10—Mar. 20
Peas, black-eyed	Feb. 15—May 1	Feb. 15—May 15	Mar. 1—June 15	Mar. 10—June 20	Mar. 15—July 1	Apr. 1—July 1	Apr. 15—July 1

(Continued)

Table 8.2 (Continued).

Planting Dates for Localities in Which Average Date of Last Freeze Is—

Crop	Jan. 30	Feb. 8	Feb. 18	Feb. 28	Mar. 10	Mar. 20	Mar. 30
Pepper*	Feb. 1–Apr. 1	Feb. 15–Apr. 15	Mar. 1–May 1	Mar. 15–May 1	Apr. 1–June 1	Apr. 10–June 1	Apr. 15–June 1
Potato	Jan. 1–Feb. 1	Jan. 1–Feb. 15	Jan. 15–Mar. 1	Jan. 15–Mar. 1	Feb. 1–Mar. 1	Feb. 15–Mar. 1	Feb. 20–Mar. 20
Radish*	Jan. 1–Apr. 1	Jan. 1–Apr. 1	Jan. 1–Apr. 1	Jan. 1–Apr. 1	Jan. 1–Apr. 15	Jan. 20–May 1	Feb. 15–May 1
Rhubarb*							
Rutabaga							
Salsify	Jan. 1–Feb. 1	Jan. 10–Feb. 10	Jan. 15–Feb. 20	Jan. 1–Mar. 1	Jan. 15–Feb. 15	Feb. 15–Mar. 1	Feb. 1–Mar. 1
Shallot	Jan. 1–Feb. 1	Jan. 1–Feb. 10	Jan. 1–Feb. 20	Jan. 15–Mar. 1	Jan. 15–Mar. 1	Feb. 1–Mar. 1	Mar. 1–15
Sorrel	Jan. 1–Mar. 1	Jan. 1–Mar. 1	Jan. 15–Mar. 1	Feb. 1–Mar. 10	Feb. 10–Mar. 15	Feb. 10–Mar. 20	Feb. 15–Apr. 1
Soybean	Mar. 1–June 30	Mar. 1–June 30	Mar. 10–June 30	Mar. 20–June 30	Apr. 10–June 30	Apr. 10–June 30	Apr. 20–June 30
Spinach	Jan. 1–Feb. 15	Jan. 1–Feb. 15	Jan. 1–Mar. 1	Jan. 1–Mar. 1	Jan. 15–Mar. 10	Jan. 15–Mar. 15	Feb. 1–Mar. 20
Spinach, New Zealand	Feb. 1–Apr. 15	Feb. 1–Apr. 15	Mar. 1–Apr. 15	Mar. 15–May 15	Mar. 20–May 15	Apr. 1–May 15	Apr. 10–June 1
Squash, summer	Feb. 15–Apr. 15	Feb. 15–Apr. 15	Feb. 15–Apr. 15	Mar. 15–May 15	Mar. 15–May 1	Apr. 1–May 15	Apr. 20–June 1
Sweet potato	Feb. 15–May 15	Mar. 1–May 15	Mar. 20–June 1	Mar. 20–June 1	Apr. 1–June 1	Apr. 10–June 1	Apr. 20–June 1
Tomato	Feb. 20–Apr. 10	Feb. 20–Apr. 10	Mar. 1–Apr. 20	Mar. 10–May 1	Mar. 20–May 10	Apr. 1–May 20	Apr. 20–June 1
Turnip	Jan. 1–Mar. 1	Jan. 1–Mar. 1	Jan. 10–Mar. 1	Jan. 20–Mar. 1	Feb. 1–Mar. 1	Feb. 1–Mar. 1	Feb. 20–Mar. 20
Watermelon	Feb. 15–Mar. 15	Feb. 15–Apr. 1	Feb. 15–Apr. 15	Mar. 1–Apr. 15	Mar. 15–Apr. 15	Apr. 1–May 1	Apr. 10–May 15

Planting Dates for Localities in Which Average Date of Last Freeze Is—

Crop	Apr. 10	Apr. 20	Apr. 30	May 10	May 20	May 30	June 10
Asparagus*	Mar. 10–Apr. 10	Mar. 15–Apr. 15	Mar. 20–Apr. 15	Apr. 10–Apr. 30	Apr. 20–May 15	May 1–June 1	May 15–June 1
Beans, lima	Apr. 1–June 30	May 1–June 20	May 15–June 15	May 25–June 15	June 1–15	June 1–15	
Beans, snap	Apr. 10–June 30	Apr. 25–June 30	May 10–June 30	May 10–June 30	May 15–June 30	May 25–June 15	June 1–15
Beet	Mar. 20–June 1	Apr. 1–June 15	Apr. 15–June 15	Apr. 15–June 15	Apr. 25–June 15	May 1–June 15	May 15–June 15
Broccoli, sprouting*	Mar. 15–Apr. 15	Mar. 25–Apr. 20	Apr. 1–May 1	Apr. 15–June 1	May 1–June 15	May 10–June 10	May 20–June 10
Brussels sprouts*	Mar. 25–Apr. 20	Mar. 25–Apr. 20	Apr. 1–May 1	Apr. 15–June 1	May 1–June 15	May 10–June 10	May 20–June 10
Cabbage*	Mar. 25–Apr. 20	Mar. 15–Apr. 15	Apr. 1–May 15	Apr. 1–May 15	May 1–June 15	May 10–June 15	May 20–June 10
Cabbage, Chinese	Mar. 1–Apr. 1	Mar. 1–Apr. 1	Apr. 1–May 15	Apr. 1–May 15	May 1–June 15	May 10–June 15	May 20–June 1
Carrot	(**)	(**)	Apr. 10–June 1	Apr. 20–June 15	May 1–June 1	May 20–June 1	May 20–June 1
Cauliflower*	Mar. 10–Apr. 20	Mar. 15–Apr. 20	Apr. 15–May 10	Apr. 15–May 15	May 10–June 15	May 20–June 1	June 1–June 15
Celery and celeriac	Apr. 1–Apr. 20	Mar. 15–Apr. 20	Apr. 10–May 1	Apr. 20–June 1	Apr. 20–June 1	May 20–June 1	June 1–15
Chard	Apr. 15–June 15	Apr. 1–June 15	Apr. 1–June 15	Apr. 20–June 15	May 10–June 15	May 20–June 1	June 1–15
Chervil and chives	Mar. 1–Apr. 1	Mar. 1–Apr. 10	Mar. 20–Apr. 20	Apr. 1–May 1	Apr. 15–May 15	May 1–June 1	May 15–June 1
Chicory, witloof	June 10–July 1	June 15–July 1	June 15–July 1	June 1–20	June 1–20	June 1–15	June 1–15
Collards*	Mar. 1–June 1	Mar. 10–June 1	Apr. 1–June 1	Apr. 15–June 1	May 1–June 1	May 10–June 1	May 20–June 1
Corn salad	Feb. 1–Apr. 1	Feb. 15–Apr. 15	Mar. 1–May 1	May 10–June 1	Apr. 15–June 1	May 1–June 15	May 15–June 15
Corn, sweet	Apr. 10–June 15	Apr. 25–June 15	May 10–June 15	May 10–June 1	May 15–June 1	May 20–June 1	
Cress, upland	Mar. 10–Apr. 15	Mar. 20–May 1	Apr. 10–May 10	Apr. 20–May 20	May 1–June 1	May 15–June 1	May 15–June 15

(Continued)

Table 8.2 (Continued).

Crop	Apr. 10	Apr. 20	Apr. 30	May 10	May 20	May 30	June 10
Cucumber	Apr. 20—June 1	May 1—June 15	May 15—June 15	May 20—June 15	June 1—15		
Eggplant*	May 1—June 1	May 10—June 1	May 15—June 10	May 20—June 15	June 1—15		
Endive	Mar. 15—Apr. 15	Mar. 25—Apr. 15	Apr. 1—May 1	Apr. 15—May 15	May 1—30	May 1—30	May 15—June 1
Fennel, Florence	Mar. 15—Apr. 15	Mar. 25—Apr. 15	Apr. 1—May 1	Apr. 15—May 15	May 1—30	May 1—30	May 15—June 1
Garlic	Feb. 20—Mar. 20	Mar. 10—Apr. 1	Mar. 15—Apr. 15	Apr. 1—May 1	Apr. 15—May 15	May 1—30	May 15—June 1
Horseradish*	Mar. 10—Apr. 10	Mar. 20—Apr. 20	Apr. 1—30	Apr. 15—May 15	Apr. 20—May 20		May 15—June 1
Kale	Mar. 10—Apr. 1	Mar. 20—Apr. 10	Apr. 1—20	Apr. 10—May 1	Apr. 20—May 10	May 1—30	May 15—June 1
Kohlrabi	Mar. 10—Apr. 10	Mar. 20—May 1	Apr. 1—May 10	Apr. 10—May 15	Apr. 20—May 20	May 1—30	May 15—June 1
Leek	Mar. 1—Apr. 1	Mar. 15—Apr. 15	Apr. 1—May 1	Apr. 15—May 15	May 1—May 20	May 1—15	May 1—15
Lettuce, head*	Mar. 20—Apr. 1	Mar. 20—Apr. 15	Apr. 1—May 1	Apr. 15—May 15	May 1—June 20	May 10—June 30	May 20—June 30
Lettuce, leaf	Mar. 15—May 15	Mar. 20—May 15	Apr. 1—June 1	Apr. 15—June 15	May 1—June 30	May 10—June 30	May 20—June 30
Muskmelon	Apr. 20—June 1	May 1—June 15	May 15—June 15	June 1—15			
Mustard	Mar. 10—Apr. 20	Mar. 20—May 1	Apr. 1—May 10	Apr. 15—June 1	May 1—June 30	May 1—30	May 20—June 30
Okra	Apr. 20—June 15	May 1—June 1	May 10—June 1	May 20—June 10	June 1—20	May 1—30	
Onion*	Mar. 1—Apr. 1	Mar. 15—Apr. 10	Apr. 1—May 1	Apr. 10—May 1	Apr. 20—May 15	May 1—30	May 10—June 10
Onion, seed	Mar. 1—Apr. 1	Mar. 1—Apr. 1	Mar. 15—Apr. 15	Apr. 1—May 1	Apr. 20—May 15		May 10—June 10
Onion, sets	Mar. 1—Apr. 1	Mar. 1—Apr. 1	Mar. 10—Apr. 10	Apr. 10—May 1	Apr. 20—May 15	May 10—June 1	May 20—June 10
Parsley	Mar. 10—Apr. 10	Mar. 20—Apr. 20	Apr. 1—May 1	Apr. 15—May 15	May 1—20	May 10—June 1	May 20—June 10
Parsnip	Mar. 10—Apr. 10	Mar. 20—Apr. 20	Apr. 1—May 1	Apr. 15—May 15	May 1—20	May 1—June 15	May 15—June 1
Peas, garden	Feb. 20—Mar. 20	Mar. 10—Apr. 10	Apr. 20—May 1	Apr. 1—May 15	Apr. 15—June 1	June 1—15	May 10—June 15
Peas, black-eyed	May 1—July 1	May 10—June 15	May 15—June 10	May 20—June 10			
Pepper*	May 1—June 1	May 10—June 1	May 15—June 10	June 1—June 15	May 25—June 15	May 15—June 15	May 15—June 1
Potato	Mar. 15—Apr. 1	Mar. 15—Apr. 10	Mar. 20—May 10	Apr. 1—June 1	Apr. 15—June 15	May 1—June 15	May 15—June 1
Radish	Mar. 1—May 1	Mar. 10—May 10	Mar. 20—Apr. 15	Apr. 1—June 1	Apr. 15—June 15	May 1—20	May 15—June 1
Rhubarb*	Mar. 1—Apr. 1	Mar. 10—Apr. 10	Mar. 20—Apr. 15	Apr. 1—May 1	Apr. 15—May 10		May 15—June 1
Rutabaga			May 15—June 15	May 1—June 1	May 1—20	May 10—20	May 20—June 1
Salsify	Mar. 10—Apr. 15	Mar. 20—May 1	Apr. 1—May 15	Apr. 15—June 1	May 1—June 1	May 10—June 1	May 20—June 1
Shallot	Mar. 1—Apr. 15	Mar. 15—May 1	Apr. 1—May 1	Apr. 10—May 1	Apr. 20—May 10	May 1—June 1	
Sorrel	Mar. 1—Apr. 15	Mar. 15—May 1	Apr. 1—May 15	Apr. 1—June 1	May 1—June 1	May 10—June 15	May 10—June 10
Soybean	May 1—June 30	May 10—June 20	May 15—June 15	May 25—June 10			
Spinach	Feb. 15—Apr. 1	Mar. 1—Apr. 15	Mar. 20—Apr. 20	Apr. 1—June 15	Apr. 10—June 15	Apr. 20—June 15	May 1—June 15
Spinach, New Zealand	Apr. 20—June 1	May 1—June 15	May 1—June 15	May 10—June 15	May 20—June 15	June 1—15	
Squash, summer	Apr. 20—June 1	May 1—June 15	May 1—30	May 10—June 10	May 20—June 15	June 1—20	June 10—20
Sweet potato	May 1—June 1	May 10—June 10	May 10—June 10	May 15—June 10			
Tomato	Apr. 1—June 1	May 5—June 10	May 10—June 10	May 1—June 1	May 25—June 15	June 5—20	June 15—30
Turnip	Mar. 1—Apr. 1	Mar. 10—Apr. 1	Mar. 20—May 1	June 1—June 15	Apr. 15—July 1	May 1—June 15	May 15—June 15
Watermelon	Apr. 20—June 1	May 1—June 15	May 15—June 15		June 15—July 1		May 15—June 15

*Plants.
**Generally fall-planted.
Data from USDA H&G Bull. 202.

Table 8.3—Latest Dates, and Range of Dates, for Safe Fall Planting of Vegetables in the Open.

| Crop | Planting Dates for Localities in Which Average Dates of First Freeze Is— | | | | | |
	Aug. 30	Sept. 10	Sept. 20	Sept. 30	Oct. 10	Oct. 20
Asparagus*					Oct. 20–Nov. 15	Nov. 1–Dec. 15
Beans, lima				June 1–15	June 1–15	June 15–30
Beans, snap	May 15–June 15	May 15–June 15	June 1–July 1	June 1–July 10	June 15–July 20	July 1–Aug. 1
Beet	May 1–June 1	May 1–June 1	June 1–July 1	June 1–July 10	June 15–July 25	July 1–Aug. 5
Broccoli, sprouting			May 1–June 15	June 1–30	June 15–July 15	July 1–Aug. 1
Brussels sprouts	May 1–June 1	May 1–June 1	May 1–June 15	June 1–30	June 15–July 15	July 1–Aug. 1
Cabbage*	May 1–June 1	May 1–June 1	May 1–July 1	June 1–July 10	June 1–July 15	July 1–20
Cabbage, Chinese	May 15–June 15	May 15–June 15	June 1–July 1	June 1–July 15	June 15–Aug. 1	July 15–Aug. 15
Carrot	May 15–June 15	May 15–June 15	June 1–July 1	June 1–July 10	June 1–July 20	June 15–Aug. 1
Cauliflower*	May 1–July 1	May 1–July 1	May 1–July 1	May 10–July 15	June 1–July 25	July 1–Aug. 5
Celery* and celeriac	May 1–June 1	May 15–June 15	May 15–July 1	June 1–July 5	June 1–July 15	June 1–Aug. 1
Chard	May 15–June 15	May 15–July 1	June 1–July 1	June 1–July 5	June 1–July 20	June 1–Aug. 1
Chervil and chives	May 10–June 10	May 1–June 15	May 15–June 15	(**)	(**)	(**)
Chicory, witloof	May 15–June 15	May 15–June 15	May 15–June 15	June 1–July 1	June 1–July 1	June 15–July 15
Collards*	May 15–June 15	May 15–June 15	May 15–June 15	June 15–July 15	July 1–Aug. 1	July 15–Aug. 15
Corn salad	May 15–June 15	May 15–July 1	June 15–Aug. 1	July 15–Sept. 1	Aug. 15–Sept. 15	Sept. 1–Oct. 15
Corn, sweet			June 1–July 1	June 1–July 1	June 1–July 10	June 1–July 20
Cress, upland	May 15–June 15	May 15–July 1	June 15–Aug. 1	July 15–Sept. 1	Aug. 15–Sept. 15	Sept. 1–Oct. 15
Cucumber			June 1–15	June 1–July 1	June 1–July 1	June 1–July 15
Eggplant*				May 20–June 10	May 15–June 15	June 1–July 1
Endive	June 1–July 1	June 1–July 1	June 15–July 15	June 15–Aug. 1	July 1–Aug. 15	July 15–Sept. 1
Fennel, Florence	May 15–June 15	May 15–July 15	June 1–July 1	June 1–July 1	June 15–July 15	June 15–Aug. 1
Garlic	(**)	(**)	(**)	(**)	(**)	(**)
Horseradish*	(**)	(**)				
Kale	May 15–June 15	May 15–June 15	June 1–July 1	June 15–July 15	July 1–Aug. 1	July 15–Aug. 15
Kohlrabi	May 15–June 15	June 1–July 1	June 1–July 15	June 15–July 15	July 1–Aug. 1	July 15–Aug. 15
Leek	May 1–June 1	May 1–June 1	(**)	(**)	(**)	(**)
Lettuce, head*	May 15–July 1	May 15–July 1	June 1–July 15	June 15–Aug. 1	July 15–Aug. 15	Aug. 1–30
Lettuce, leaf	May 15–July 15	May 15–July 15	June 1–Aug. 1	June 1–Aug. 1	July 15–Sept. 1	July 15–Sept. 1
Muskmelon			May 1–June 15	May 15–June 15	June 1–June 15	June 15–July 20
Mustard	May 15–July 15	May 15–July 15	June 1–Aug. 1	June 15–Aug. 15	July 15–Aug. 15	Aug. 1–Sept. 1
Okra			June 1–20	June 1–July 1	June 1–July 15	June 1–Aug. 1
Onion*	May 1–June 10	May 1–June 10	(**)	(**)	(**)	(**)
Onion, seed	May 1–June 10	May 1–June 10	(**)	(**)	(**)	(**)
Onion, sets	May 1–June 1	May 1–June 10	(**)	(**)	(**)	(**)

(Continued)

Table 8.3 (Continued).

Crop	Planting Dates for Localities in Which Average Dates of First Freeze Is—					
	Aug. 30	Sept. 10	Sept. 20	Sept. 30	Oct. 10	Oct. 20
Parsley	May 15–June 15	May 1–June 15	June 1–July 1	June 1–July 15	June 15–Aug. 1	July 15–Aug. 15
Parsnip	May 15–June 1	May 1–June 15	May 15–June 15	June 1–July 1	June 1–July 10	(**)
Peas, garden	May 10–June 15	May 1–July 1	June 1–July 15	June 1–Aug. 1	(**)	(**)
Peas, black-eyed					June 1–July 1	June 1–July 1
Pepper*				June 1–July 1	June 1–July 1	June 1–July 10
Potato	May 15–June 1	May 1–June 15	June 1–June 20	June 1–July 1	May 15–June 15	June 15–July 15
Radish	May 1–July 15	May 1–Aug. 1	June 1–Aug. 15	July 1–Sept. 1	July 15–Sept. 15	Aug. 1–Oct. 1
Rhubarb*	Sept. 1–Oct. 1	Sept. 15–Oct. 15	Sept. 15–Nov. 1	Oct. 1–Nov. 1	Oct. 15–Nov. 15	Oct. 15–Dec. 1
Rutabaga	May 15–June 15	May 1–June 15	June 1–July 1	June 1–July 1	June 15–July 15	July 10–20
Salsify	May 15–June 1	May 10–June 10	June 1–July 1	June 1–20	June 1–July 1	June 1–July 1
Shallot	(**)	(**)	May 20–June 20	June 1–20	(**)	(**)
Sorrel	May 15–June 15	May 1–June 15	(**)	(**)	July 1–Aug. 1	July 15–Aug. 15
Soybean			June 1–July 1	June 1–July 15	June 1–25	June 1–July 5
Spinach	May 15–July 1	June 1–July 15		July 1–Aug. 15	Aug. 1–Sept. 1	Aug. 20–Sept. 10
Spinach, New Zealand			June 1–Aug. 1	June 1–Aug. 1	June 1–July 15	June 1–Aug. 1
Squash, summer	June 10–20	June 1–20			June 1–July 1	June 1–July 20
Squash, winter			May 15–July 1	May 15–July 1	June 1–July 1	June 1–July 1
Sweet potato			May 20–June 10		May 20–June 10	June 1–15
Tomato	June 20–30	June 10–20	June 1–20	June 1–20	June 1–20	June 1–15
Turnip	May 15–June 15	June 1–July 1	June 1–July 15	June 1–July 1	July 1–Aug. 1	July 15–Aug. 15
Watermelon			May 1–June 15	May 15–June 1	June 1–June 15	June 15–July 20

Crop	Planting Dates for Localities in Which Average Dates of First Freeze Is—					
	Oct. 30	Nov. 10	Nov. 20	Nov. 30	Dec. 10	Dec. 20
Asparagus*	Nov. 15–Jan. 1	Dec. 1–Jan. 1			Sept. 1	Sept. 1–Oct. 1
Beans, lima	July 1–Aug. 1	July 1–Aug. 15	July 15–Sept. 1	Aug. 15–Sept. 20	Aug. 1–30	Sept. 1–Nov. 1
Beans, snap	July 1–Aug. 15	July 1–Sept. 1	July 1–Sept. 10	Sept. 1–Dec. 1	Sept. 1–Dec. 31	Sept. 1–Dec. 31
Beet	Aug. 1–Sept. 1	Aug. 1–Oct. 1	Sept. 1–Dec. 15	Sept. 1–Dec. 15	Sept. 1–Dec. 1	Sept. 1–Dec. 31
Broccoli, sprouting	July 1–Aug. 15	Aug. 1–Sept. 1	Aug. 1–Sept. 15	Aug. 1–Oct. 1	Aug. 1–Nov. 1	Sept. 1–Dec. 31
Brussels sprouts	July 1–Aug. 1	Aug. 1–Sept. 1	Aug. 1–Sept. 15	Sept. 1–Nov. 1	Aug. 1–Nov. 1	Sept. 1–Dec. 31
Cabbage*	Aug. 1–Sept. 1	Aug. 1–Sept. 15	Sept. 1–Dec. 1	Sept. 1–Dec. 31	Sept. 1–Dec. 31	Sept. 1–Dec. 31
Cabbage, Chinese	Aug. 1–Sept. 15	Aug. 1–Sept. 15	Sept. 1–Oct. 15	Sept. 1–Nov. 1	Sept. 1–Nov. 15	Sept. 1–Dec. 1
Carrot	July 1–Aug. 15	Aug. 1–Sept. 1	Sept. 1–Nov. 1	Sept. 15–Dec. 1	Sept. 15–Dec. 1	Sept. 15–Dec. 1
Cauliflower*	July 15–Aug. 15	Aug. 1–Sept. 1	Aug. 1–Sept. 15	Aug. 15–Oct. 10	Sept. 1–Oct. 20	Sept. 15–Nov. 1
Celery* and celeriac	June 15–Aug. 15	July 1–Aug. 15	July 15–Sept. 15	Aug. 15–Oct. 31	Sept. 15–Dec. 31	Oct. 1–Dec. 31
Chard	June 1–Sept. 10	June 1–Sept. 10	June 1–Oct. 1	June 1–Nov. 1	June 1–Dec. 1	June 1–Dec. 31
Chervil and chives	(**)	July 1–Sept. 15	Nov. 1–Dec. 31	Nov. 1–Dec. 31	Nov. 1–Dec. 1	Nov. 1–Dec. 31
Chicory, witloof	July 1–Aug. 10	July 10–Aug. 20	July 20–Sept. 1	Aug. 15–Sept. 30	Aug. 15–Oct. 15	Aug. 15–Oct. 15
Collards*	Aug. 1–Sept. 15	Aug. 15–Oct. 1	Aug. 25–Nov. 1	Sept. 1–Dec. 1	Sept. 1–Dec. 31	Sept. 1–Dec. 31

(Continued)

Table 8.3 (Continued).

Planting Dates for Localities in Which Average Dates of First Freeze Is—

Crop	Oct. 30	Nov. 10	Nov. 20	Nov. 30	Dec. 10	Dec. 20
Corn salad	Sept. 15–Nov. 1	Oct. 1–Dec. 1	Oct. 1–Dec. 1	Oct. 1–Dec. 31	Oct. 1–Dec. 31	Oct. 1–Dec. 31
Corn, sweet	June 1–Aug. 1	June 1–Aug. 15	June 1–Sept. 1			
Cress, upland	Sept. 15–Nov. 1	Oct. 1–Dec. 1	Oct. 1–Dec. 1			
Cucumber*	June 1–Aug. 1	June 1–Aug. 15	June 1–Aug. 15	July 15–Sept. 15	Aug. 15–Oct. 1	Aug. 15–Oct. 1
Eggplant*	June 1–July 1	June 1–July 15	June 1–Aug. 1	July 1–Sept. 1	Aug. 1–Sept. 30	Aug. 1–Sept. 30
Endive	July 15–Aug. 15	Aug. 1–Sept. 1	Sept. 1–Oct. 1	Sept. 1–Nov. 15	Sept. 1–Dec. 31	Sept. 1–Dec. 31
Fennel, Florence	July 1–Aug. 1	July 15–Aug. 15	Aug. 15–Sept. 15	Sept. 1–Nov. 15	Sept. 1–Dec. 1	Sept. 1–Dec. 1
Garlic	(**)	Aug. 1–Oct. 1	Aug. 15–Oct. 1	Sept. 1–Nov. 15	Sept. 15–Nov. 15	Sept. 15–Nov. 15
Horseradish*	(**)	(**)	(**)	(**)	(**)	(**)
Kale	July 15–Sept. 1	Aug. 1–Sept. 15	Aug. 15–Oct. 15	Sept. 1–Dec. 1	Sept. 1–Dec. 31	Sept. 1–Dec. 31
Kohlrabi	Aug. 1–Sept. 1	Aug. 15–Sept. 15	Sept. 1–Oct. 15	Sept. 1–Dec. 1	Sept. 15–Dec. 31	Sept. 1–Dec. 31
Leek	(**)	(**)	Sept. 1–Nov. 1	Sept. 1–Nov. 1	Sept. 1–Nov. 1	Sept. 1–Nov. 1
Lettuce, head*	Aug. 1–Sept. 15	Aug. 15–Oct. 15	Sept. 1–Nov. 1	Sept. 1–Dec. 1	Sept. 15–Dec. 31	Sept. 15–Dec. 31
Lettuce, leaf	Aug. 15–Oct. 1	Aug. 15–Oct. 1	Sept. 1–Nov. 1	Sept. 1–Dec. 1	Sept. 15–Dec. 31	Sept. 15–Dec. 31
Muskmelon	July 1–July 15	July 15–July 30				
Mustard	Aug. 15–Oct. 15	Aug. 15–Nov. 1	Sept. 1–Dec. 1	Sept. 1–Dec. 1	Sept. 1–Dec. 1	Sept. 15–Dec. 1
Okra	June 1–Aug. 10	June 1–Aug. 20	June 1–Sept. 10	June 1–Sept. 20	Aug. 1–Oct. 1	Aug. 1–Oct. 1
Onion*	(**)	Sept. 1–Oct. 15	Oct. 1–Dec. 31	Oct. 1–Dec. 31	Oct. 1–Dec. 31	Oct. 1–Dec. 31
Onion, seed			Sept. 1–Nov. 1	Sept. 1–Nov. 1	Nov. 1–Dec. 31	Nov. 1–Dec. 31
Onion, sets			Nov. 1–Dec. 31	Nov. 1–Dec. 31	Sept. 1–Dec. 31	Sept. 1–Dec. 31
Parsley	Aug. 1–Sept. 15	Oct. 1–Dec. 1	Nov. 1–Dec. 1	Nov. 1–Dec. 31	Nov. 1–Dec. 31	Nov. 1–Dec. 1
Parsnip		Sept. 1–Nov. 15	Sept. 1–Dec. 31	Sept. 1–Dec. 31	Sept. 1–Dec. 1	Sept. 1–Dec. 1
Peas, garden	Aug. 1–Sept. 15	Sept. 1–Nov. 1	Oct. 1–Dec. 1	Oct. 1–Dec. 31	Oct. 1–Dec. 31	Oct. 1–Dec. 31
Peas, black-eyed	June 1–Aug. 1	June 15–Aug. 15	July 1–Sept. 1	July 1–Sept. 10	July 1–Sept. 20	July 1–Sept. 20
Pepper*	June 1–July 20	June 1–Aug. 1	June 1–Aug. 15	June 15–Sept. 1	Aug. 15–Oct. 1	Aug. 1–Sept. 15
Potato	July 20–Aug. 10	July 25–Aug. 20	Aug. 10–Sept. 15	Aug. 1–Sept. 15	Aug. 15–Oct. 1	July 1–Sept. 20
Radish	Aug. 15–Oct. 15	Aug. 15–Oct. 15	Sept. 1–Dec. 1	Sept. 1–Dec. 31	Aug. 1–Sept. 15	Aug. 1–Sept. 15
Rhubarb*	Nov. 1–Dec. 1	Sept. 1–Nov. 15				
Rutabaga	July 15–Aug. 1	July 15–Aug. 15	Aug. 1–Sept. 1	Sept. 1–Nov. 15	Oct. 15–Nov. 15	Oct. 15–Nov. 15
Salsify	June 1–July 10	June 15–July 20	July 15–Aug. 15	Aug. 15–Sept. 30	Aug. 15–Oct. 15	Sept. 15–Nov. 1
Shallot	(**)	(**)	Aug. 15–Oct. 1	Aug. 15–Oct. 15	Sept. 15–Nov. 1	Sept. 15–Nov. 1
Sorrel	Aug. 1–Sept. 15	Aug. 15–Oct. 1	Aug. 15–Oct. 15	Aug. 15–Oct. 15	Sept. 15–Nov. 1	Sept. 15–Nov. 1
Soybean	June 1–July 15	June 1–July 25	June 1–July 30	June 1–July 30	June 1–July 30	June 1–July 30
Spinach	Sept. 1–Oct. 1	Sept. 15–Nov. 1	Oct. 1–Dec. 1	Oct. 1–Dec. 31	Oct. 1–Dec. 31	Sept. 1–Dec. 31
Spinach, New Zealand	June 1–Aug. 1	June 1–Aug. 15	June 1–Aug. 15	June 1–Sept. 1	June 1–Oct. 1	June 1–July 30
Squash, summer	June 1–Aug. 10	June 1–Aug. 10	June 1–Aug. 20	June 1–Sept. 1	June 1–Sept. 15	June 1–Oct. 1
Squash, winter	June 10–July 10	June 20–July 20	July 1–Aug. 1	July 15–Aug. 15	Aug. 1–Sept. 1	June 1–Sept. 15
Sweet potato	June 1–15	June 1–July 1	June 1–July 1	June 1–July 1	June 1–July 1	June 1–July 1
Tomato	June 1–July 1	June 1–July 15	June 1–Aug. 1	Aug. 1–Sept. 1	Aug. 15–Oct. 1	Aug. 15–Oct. 1
Turnip	Aug. 1–Sept. 15	Sept. 1–Oct. 15	Sept. 1–Nov. 1	Sept. 1–Dec. 1	Oct. 1–Dec. 31	Oct. 1–Dec. 31
Watermelon	July 1–July 15	July 15–July 30	July 15–Aug. 1	Sept. 1–Nov. 15	Oct. 1–Dec. 31	Oct. 1–Dec. 31

*Plants.
**Generally spring-planted.
Data from USDA H&G Bull. 202.

ture, and the length of time required for germination (Table 8.1). When conditions are ideal, seed will germinate best when planted at a depth about four times the diameter of the seed.

A sandy soil, which dries out readily and does not form a crust after each rain, requires that seed be planted about twice as deeply as soil with a clay surface. In time of drought, seed should be planted at about twice the depth as when the surface soil is moist. Seeds which germinate slowly, such as okra, pepper, beet, and carrot, should be planted more deeply than those which germinate readily, such as cabbage, tomato, turnip, and mustard.

Regardless of the depth of planting or kind of seed, the surface of the soil should be leveled and firmly pressed above the seed in such a manner that rain water will neither wash down the bed nor puddle above the seed. While opening a furrow with a hoe and dropping and covering the seed by hand usually gives satisfactory results, a mechanical seeder is desirable because it is more economical of seed and covers them more uniformly.

Planting Rates

Quality of seed is the chief factor that determines rate of seeding. With most vegetables, seed is the cheapest of the five important items which constitute cost of production. The other four items—land, labor, fertilizer, and equipment—are almost the same for a poor stand of plants as for a full stand. It is thus poor economy to limit the quality or quantity of seed.

Table 8.1 shows the rate of seeding for most vegetables, but this is subject to wide variation, based largely on whether the seed is sown in drills, hills, or broadcast. Fully three times as much seed is required to broadcast an area as to plant it in rows. When seed is plentiful and space is limited, much more seed may be used than when seed is scarce and land is plentiful. Time may be the limiting factor and the gardener may use twice the normal amount of seed to make sure there will be no replanting or second planting. Unfavorable weather may make it necessary to greatly increase the quantity of seed.

Attending After Emergence

When properly treated seed is planted in clean soil, the young plants upon emergence will be without diseases and insects. Precautions should be taken to keep them free of pests by spraying at an early date.

Colorado potato beetles attack potato and tomato plants as soon as they are well out of the ground, and Mexican bean beetles begin eating bean plants as soon as the fourth leaf is formed. Leaf-spot and other diseases become active at the same time.

If rain occurs between the time of planting and emergence of the seedlings, a crop of weeds and grass should be destroyed immediately by cultivation, hoeing, or hand pulling. Often, hand weeding can be eliminated by the use of herbicides (Table 9.2). If practiced, irrigation should begin after the rows and middles are weeded. An application of quick-acting fertilizer may be advantageous during the first 10 days to insure early rapid growth of the young plants.

SETTING PLANTS

If plant-growing directions given in Chapter 7 are followed, plants of broccoli, Brussels sprouts, cabbage, cauliflower, celery, collard, eggplant, lettuce, onion, pepper, sweet potato, and tomato will be ready to set in the field at the proper time.

Preparing the Plant Bed

The initial steps in preparing a plant bed are similar to those for a seedbed. Beds for setting long-rooted plants like tomatoes, sweet potatoes, and peppers should be higher (or opened deeper) than beds for short plants such as lettuce. Rows for setting onions or lettuce should be about 1½ or 2 feet apart, while 3 or 3½ feet are required for the other vegetables to be transplanted.

Setting Distances

The distance between plants in the row varies with the scarcity of land, fertility of land, and kind of vegetables. The total yield per acre of most vegetables is increased by close planting, up to the point where the tops receive insufficient sunlight; however, the size of the individual plants or fruits is usually smaller. Greater yields of pepper in Georgia were obtained when the plants were set 12 inches apart as compared with planting of 18, 24, 30, or 36 inches, but the percentage of large specimens was reduced by crowding. Jumbo sweet potatoes can be practically eliminated by setting plants 16 inches or less apart rather than 24 inches or more.

With the exception of sweet potatoes, plants should be set close enough together that the mature specimens will touch without crowding. Very close spacing may be made when a crop such as tomato or cucumber is planted for a single destructive harvest.

Setting Methods

There are three general methods of setting plants—hand setting, hand-machine setting, and riding-machine setting.

Hand setting involves four distinct hand operations: Holes are dug with a hole or dibble, the plants are dropped into the holes, $\frac{1}{2}$ to 1 pint of water is applied, and the plants are set and packed. This is the best method of setting plants because each one can be given individual attention. After the water has soaked well into the soil, the surface around the plant should be covered with dry soil.

In hand-machine setting, holes are made with the point of the plant setter and plants are placed in the holes from the machine. A quantity of water is poured by pressing a lever with the thumb, and the plant roots are covered with dry soil, all in one operation. This method is little used because hand setters are slow and difficult to operate.

In riding-machine setting, a machine opens a furrow into which a riding boy drops a plant. Water is immediately released from a barrel, and two curved slides cover the plant roots by raking soil from either side. This is a rapid method of setting plants and is quite satisfactory when the soil is well prepared and not too dry. With such a machine, one careful driver and two boys may plant as much as 10 acres a day.

Plants do best when set on a cloudy day, late in the afternoon, just after a rain, or just before a rain. Plants moved with the roots intact are less seriously injured than plants whose root systems are largely lost in transplanting; also, young plants whose tissues have not begun to appreciably suberize are less injured by transplanting than older plants.

Size and Quality of Plants

With the exception of lettuce and celery, most plants to be set in the field should be about 6 inches long, equally divided between top and root, and from 6 to 10 weeks old. Larger and older plants are often used to advantage, but those more than 8 inches long are difficult to transplant and the mortality rate is higher.

Freedom from disease, freshness, vigor, and trueness to variety and type are more important than size. In so far as possible, plants should be set in the field on the same day they are pulled from the beds, discarding all that show abnormalities. During the interval that they are out of the ground the roots should be kept moist and the tops relatively dry and in the shade. The roots of plants held overnight should be wrapped in wet sphagnum moss.

Setting Dates

Tomato, eggplant, pepper, and sweet potato plants grow only during the warm season and should be set in the field only when the soil is warm. Lettuce, onion, cabbage, and related plants are semi-hardy and live through the winter in the lower South. Farther north, they are grown as spring or fall crops, not being able to stand either the extreme heat of summer or the cold of winter.

The exact time to set plants depends on (1) the condition of the plants, (2) the condition of the soil, and (3) the prevailing weather. Often it is profitable to postpone planting until a time when conditions are suitable. Only when plants are plentiful and the season is well advanced is it advisable to plant on poorly prepared land or under adverse weather conditions.

Setting Rates and Depths

Plants should be set in the field in about the same manner as they grew in the cold frame, but farther apart and from ½ to 1 inch deeper. Setting should be shallow enough to expose fully the bud and deep enough to prevent the plant from falling over and exposing the stem to the sun. About 4 inches of stem should be left above ground in setting tomato, pepper, cabbage, eggplant, and sweet potato plants, even if the below-ground portion is much more than this.

Attending After Setting

When only a few plants are set, they can be protected from the midday sun by putting a shingle on the south side of each plant. Paper or cardboard protectors are also used to shield newly set plants from drying winds and sun.

Except in arid or semi-arid regions, most vegetables usually need no watering other than at the time of setting. Certain intensely cultivated vegetables such as onions, lettuce, and celery, however, are sometimes grown under irrigation even in humid regions, in which case watering should be started immediately after the plants are set.

With summer vegetables such as tomatoes, pepper, and celery, the soil is sometimes mulched with fine straw, decayed manure, or treated paper. The soil should be thoroughly cultivated just before mulching. Chapter 10, "Irrigating and Mulching," gives full information on these practices.

If a rapid growth is desired early in the spring, as with lettuce, cabbage, celery, and others, a side dressing of readily soluble nitrogenous fertilizer is recommended.

SELECTED REFERENCES

Anonymous, "Know Your Soil," USDA, Inf. Bull. 269, 1970.

Anonymous, "Usual Planting and Harvesting Dates for Fresh Market and Processing Vegetables," USDA, AH 507, 1977.

Cannon, J. M., "Production Pointers for Louisiana Vegetable Growers," LSU Coop. Ext. Ser. Pub., 1978.

Dethier, B. E., and Vittum, M. T., "Growing Degree Days," N.Y. State Exp. Sta. Bull. 801, 1963.

Halsey, L. H., and Kostewicz, S. R., "Seasonal Response of Vegetable Crops for Selected Cultivars in North Florida," Univ. of Fla., Veg. Crops Res. Rep. 1, 1976.

Hayslip, N. C., "Spacing of Vegetable Crop Plants," A. R. Fla. Agr. Exp. Sta., p. 268, 1963-64.

Minges, P. A., "New Vegetable Varieties," Proc. Amer. Soc. Hort. Sci. 86, 1965.

Seaton, H. L., "Scheduling Plantings and Predicting Harvest Maturities for Processing Vegetables," Food Technology 9: 202-209, 1955.

"Symposium: Environmental Factors in Vegetable Production," HortSci. 6(1), 202, 1972.

Vandemark, J. S, and Courter, J. W., "Vegetable Gardening for Illinois," Univ. of Ill. Coop. Ext. Ser. Circ. 1150, 1978.

Webster, R. E., and Kehr, A., "Growing Vegetables in the Home Garden," USDA H & G Bull. 202, 1978.

Wells, O. S., "Planting and Maturity Dates of Vegetables in New Hampshire," Univ. of N. H. Ext. Circ. FFTS 9 (current).

CHAPTER 9

Cultivating and Rotating

The present tendency for the large operator is to do less cultivating and to depend more on herbicides for weed control. The home gardener cannot use herbicides because of the diversity of crops grown and must cultivate to control weeds. Weedy areas formerly not recommended for vegetable crops may be used with the proper application of herbicides. Certain rotations including a vegetable have been avoided because of the weed problem. With effective herbicides this may no longer be necessary.

CULTIVATING

Cultivation, or intertillage of crops, is a very old agricultural practice and its benefits are well recognized. The main benefits derived from cultivation are: (1) weed control, which aids in conserving moisture and nutrients; (2) conservation of moisture through the formation and maintenance of a soil mulch; and (3) increased aeration, which favors nitrification and other chemical changes in the soil. Special cultivation practices employed in producing different vegetables are discussed in the special crop chapters in Section Two, so this chapter deals primarily with basic principles.

Effects of Cultivation on Yield

Under most conditions, cultivation increases the yield of crop plants. This increase in yield results mainly from weed control, but the formation and maintenance of a soil mulch sometimes may be an important factor. Data from experiments carried on at Ithaca, New York, on a sandy loam soil show clearly that weed control is of major importance. They show also that the maintenance of a soil mulch is of value to all crops under some conditions and of no benefit under other conditions. Similar results were obtained with experiments at Riverhead, New York, on a sassafras loam soil. In the experiments at Riverhead, cultivation once a week throughout the season was compared with cultivation once a week until the crops were about half grown, and with scraping the surface of the soil to control weeds. In one set of plots, the weeds were allowed to grow in order to determine their effect on the yield of the various crops. By comparing the yields of the cultivated and the scraped plots, the value of the soil mulch is shown, since weeds were eliminated as a factor in the two treatments. A summary of the results of experiments at Riverhead is given in Table 9.1.

Table 9.1—Effect of Cultivation on Yield.

Kind of Crop	Average Yield of Marketable Portion of Crop in Pounds per Plot			
	Cultivated All Season	Cultivated Half of Season	Scraped	Weeds Allowed to Grow
Carrot	505.3	506.4	519.5	27.9
Beet	240.3	239.7	233.2	45.6
Cabbage	233.6	234.6	207.5	129.1
Onion	67.7	69.6	64.3	3.6
Tomato	164.0	166.6	166.8	23.3
Potato	148.3	150.4	158.8	52.7

Data from Cornell Univ. Exp. Sta. Bull. 521.

A study of the data in Table 9.1 will show only slight differences in yield between the two sets of cultivated plots and between these and the scraped plots. In no case is the difference in average yields between the two sets of cultivated plots significant. The cultivated plots of cabbage produced a higher average yield than did the scraped plots, but the difference is not statistically significant. The scraped plots of potatoes consistently produced a slightly larger yield than the cultivated plots and the difference is statistically significant. Results somewhat similar to these were reported in Pennsylvania with corn, beans, potatoes, mangel beets, and cabbage.

Effects of Cultivation on Soil Moisture

Cultivation nearly always results in moisture conservation through the destruction of weeds. The formation of a soil mulch may also conserve moisture by preventing surface run-off and by slowing up the movement of water to the surface, where it evaporates. However, the benefits derived from the soil mulch have been greatly overemphasized. Results of many experiments have shown much less conservation of moisture than is commonly believed, For example, the study at Ithaca, New York, comparing cultivation with scraping the soil to control weeds shows that cultivation resulted in moisture conservation in about two-thirds of the comparisons, but most of the differences were slight. In the other comparisons, cultivation resulted in no conservation of moisture or even in actual loss.

It is important to know under what conditions stirring the soil is likely to result in loss of moisture and when in conservation. In general, when the soil is cultivated soon after a rain of $\frac{1}{2}$ inch or less, moisture is likely to be lost because evaporation is hastened by exposing more surface to the drying action of the air. In many instances, practically all of the moisture from a light rain is lost by cultivating. Even if the moisture from a light rain were not lost, it would not be available to the plants because the cultivator destroys the roots to the depth cultivated. Moisture is lost also if cultivation is done when a mulch is already present. The mulch is deepened and moist soil from below is brought to the surface, where the moisture is lost by evaporation.

Not only does cultivation sometimes cause loss of moisture at critical periods, but it may also conserve moisture when a lower water content would be an advantage. It should be noted also that cultivation for the purpose of maintaining a mulch does not always increase yields, even if moisture is conserved. Destruction of roots by the cultivator may more than offset the benefits from moisture conservation. Knowledge of these facts enables one to time his cultivating intelligently and to reduce the detrimental effects.

There is no justification for the practice of cultivating at regular intervals regardless of the conditions. When there are no weeds and a soil mulch is present, cultivation is not only an unnecessary expense, but it is usually injurious. When 3 or 4 inches of the surface soil are kept stirred, most of the roots are destroyed so that it is impossible for the plants to get moisture and nutrients in the cultivated zone (Fig. 9.1).

Effects of Cultivation on Soil Temperature

It is often stated that cultivation increases the absorption and retention of heat. This belief is based on the fact that heat is used in the

Fig. 9.1—Roots of beet plants at depth of 2 to 3 inches. Cultivation to depth of 3 inches would have destroyed all of these roots.

Cornell Univ. Agr. Exp. Sta.

evaporation of water. If this were the only factor involved, stirring the soil would raise the temperature whenever it resulted in conserving moisture, and would lower the temperature when cultivation increased the loss of moisture. Many investigators have shown that during the growing season, cultivation reduces the temperature. Usually the reduction is small and probably of little practical significance. The compactness of the surface of the uncultivated soil probably accounts for the higher temperature. A compact soil has been shown to be a better heat conductor than a loose, dry layer of soil.

Effects of Cultivation on Nitrification

Many studies have been made on the effects of cultivation on nitrification, and the results are somewhat conflicting. In some cases, nitrification was increased by stirring the soil, and in other cases, there was no significant difference between cultivated and uncultivated soil. In the studies on a sand loam soil at Ithaca, New York, there was no consistent advantage in favor of cultivation as compared with scraping the soil, as far as nitrification was concerned. Investigations with a Hagerstown silt-loam soil in Pennsylvania show that nitrification proceeded as rapidly on the scraped plots as on plots that were cultivated three to eight times. On the other hand, nitrates have averaged higher on cultivated plots than on comparable scraped plots of Dunkirk silty clay soil at Ithaca, New York.

Any increase in nitrification resulting from cultivation would be brought about by increasing aeration, or by providing better moisture or better temperature conditions for the growth of nitrifying bacteria. Some investigators have shown a positive correlation between soil moisture and nitrates, while others have shown no relation. Since the soil mulch does not always have the same effect on moisture conservation, one might expect that its effect on nitrification would vary with conditions. On heavy soils, cultivation to break the surface crust usually increases aeration and this frequently results in increasing nitrification. On most vegetable soils, cultivation is seldom of much importance from the standpoint of soil aeration.

Cultivating Implements and Tools

Vegetables are cultivated by all types of equipment that are used for cultivating other intertilled crops and, in addition, hand cultivators and special garden tractors are used. Hand cultivators, of the wheel-hoe type, are used mainly for cultivating small growing crops produced intensively and for home gardens. Tractor cultivators range in size from the small garden tractor to the large farm tractors (Fig. 9.2). The heaviest tractors are not well suited to cultivation of most vegetables. Some of the smaller farm tractors are satisfactory for cultivating potatoes, cabbage, tomatoes, and other crops that are grown in rows far enough apart to give ample space for wheels. When garden tractors are used to pull gang seeders, all rows in one operation are equally spaced. The same group of rows can then be carefully cultivated with a tractor pulling a gang cultivator.

Various kinds of attachments are used on all types of cultivators mentioned. The sweep, commonly used in the South, and the blade attachments, such as are employed on hand cultivators, are efficient in controlling weeds and are less destructive to the roots than the shovel and teeth attachments.

Fig. 9.2—Cultivating and fertilizing tomatoes.

USDA Photograph

When and How to Cultivate

Weed control is the most important function of cultivation; therefore, the work should be done at the time most favorable for killing weeds. The best time is before the weeds have become established, since they are more easily killed when they are small. Also, it is important to destroy the weeds before they compete seriously with vegetable plants for moisture, nutrients, light, and air. Cultivation when the weeds are breaking through the surface is most efficient, since at this time they are not well established, and merely breaking the surface of the soil will destroy them.

Cultivation should be done as often as necessary to prevent weeds from injuring the crop. This requires frequent cultivation when conditions are favorable for the germination of weed seeds, as after a rain or after the application of irrigation water. The best time to cultivate after a rain, as after the application of water, is when the soil is dry enough to crumble and not so dry as to break up into lumps. If cultivated when too wet, most classes of soils, except the sands and loose mucks and peats, will bake on drying; and, if allowed to get too dry, the surface will have already become baked and hard and will not crumble when broken up.

Shallow cultivation is preferable to deep cultivation under most conditions. Practically all of the benefits derived from cultivation are obtained through shallow tillage, and such tillage results in a minimum of destruction to the roots. Some vegetable growers practice deep cultivation when the plants are small, with the idea that the breaking of the roots near the surface will result in greater development of roots below the depth cultivated. Experimental evidence with potatoes indicates that this is a mistake and that destroying the surface roots does not make the roots go deeper.

Under most conditions, if sufficient cultivation is given to control weeds, it will be enough to accomplish all other purposes. Cultivation to form a mulch may be desirable when a hard crust forms on the surface and when cracks develop; however, deep cultivation may do more harm than good, even under such conditions. It is certain that no good is accomplished by cultivating when there are no weeds and a mulch is already present. Where high-plant populations are grown for single-harvest cropping, rows may be too close for tillage, and weeds must be controlled by herbicides.

CONTROLLING WEEDS WITH CHEMICALS

In certain cases the cost of controlling weeds can be reduced by the use of chemicals. They may be used advantageously where weed seeds germinate before the crop plants emerge. A particular chemical can be used to kill infesting weeds when the crop plant is tolerant to the herbicide. Perennial weeds, which are difficult to eradicate by cultivation, can often be controlled by spraying or treating the soil. Chemical herbicides can be used along fence rows or irrigation ditches where cultivation is impossible.

The effectiveness of a herbicide often depends upon the care exercised in following the directions for its use. The rate and timeliness of application, soil type, weather conditions, and the kind of crop and weeds on which a herbicide is used should be considered. Practices suggested for the control of weeds are given in Table 9.2. These suggestions were taken from Illinois Extension Circular 907 and were prepared for the commercial grower to be used during the 1979 season. The use of any material and methods of use depend upon registration of the herbicides by Federal and state Environmental and Protection Agencies (EPA). Do not use any herbicide unless the label states that it is cleared for the use on the crop to be treated. Herbicides are not recommended for the home garden because of the wide variety of crops at many stages of development. Always consult the latest information for use of herbicides on vegetables.

ROTATING CROPS

Crop rotation may be defined as the growing of two or more crops in regular sequence on the same land during a period of years. Rotation may cover a period of two, three, or more years. When two or more crops are grown in sequence on the same land in one year, the term "successive cropping" is used. Crop rotation is of importance in disease and insect control and in making the best use of the resources of the soil.

This chapter discusses the principles of rotation primarily, while the chapters on special crops contain specific recommendations concerning this subject.

Rotation as a Factor in Disease and Insect Control

Some diseases can be controlled by a system of rotation in which the host plants are grown on the same land only once in a period of three, four, or more years. Rotation is most effective in disease control when the organisms causing the disease live in the soil only one or two years. Club root of cabbage and other cruciferous plants, for example, can be controlled by rotation, provided no cruciferous crops or cruciferous weeds are allowed to grow for at least three years; a longer rotation is desirable, however, where club root is serious. Some diseases, such as potato scab and onion smut, cannot be controlled by ordinary rotation as the organisms involved live in the soil for many years.

In planning a rotation system, one needs to know what kinds of plants are attacked by a given organism. Some organisms attack only one kind of host plant; others attack all kinds of plants within a genus; and still others are not limited to a given family of plants. Club root affects many kinds of cruciferous plants, and the nematode disease is serious on a large number of crops representing many families.

Rotation helps to control insects, especially those that feed on one kind of crop only and those that are unable to move very far. A short rotation is as good as a long one for controlling most insects, since they die soon after emergence if the food plants are absent.

Table 9.2—Suggestions for Herbicides During 1979 Only.

Crop	Treatment	Active Ingredient Per Acre Actually Covered[1]	Weeds Controlled	Best Time of Application (Based on Crop Stage)	Remarks, Cautions, Limitations
Asparagus (seedlings)	Amiben	3 lb.	Annuals	Immediately after seeding.	Irrigation or rainfall after treatment will give maximum control.
Asparagus (established plantings)	dalapon	5-10 lb.	Perennial grass	End of harvest season following discing.	Apply when grass weeds are 3 to 4 inches tall. Direct spray under fern growth. Use surfactant as directed on label.
	Karmex	1-4 lb.	Annuals	In spring and/or after harvest.	Apply after discing. Do not exceed 6 pounds per growing season. Use a lighter rate on sandy soil. With Karmex and Princep, a spring application may be sufficient after the first year.
	Princep	3-4 lb.	Annuals	In spring and/or after harvest.	Apply after discing. Do not treat during the last year in asparagus because of residue.
	metribuzin	1-2 lb.	Primarily broad-leaf weeds	Early spring before the spears emerge.	Apply after discing. Do not apply within 14 days of harvest. Can help control broadleaf weeds when used with dalapon, Karmex, or Princep.
Beans, dry, lima, and snap	**Preemergence** Treflan	0.5-0.75 lb.	Annuals[2] (primarily grasses)	Preplant soil application. Incorporate with soil immediately.	Plant crop immediately, or within 3 weeks after application. Can be used up to 1 pound per acre on dry beans.
	Tolban	0.5-1 lb.	Primarily annual grasses	Preplant soil incorporation.	
	Premerge-3	6-7.5 lb.	Annuals	Can be used between planting and crop emergence.	Do not use on light, sandy soil. Some stand reduction may result from use. See label for precautions.
	Postemergence Basagran	0.75-1 lb.	Annual broad-leaf weeds, Canada thistle, nutsedge	When weeds are small and are actively growing; after the first trifoliate leaf appears on beans.	Can provide good, broad-spectrum control when combined with a grass-active herbicide. Do not mix with other pesticides. See Basagran entry under corn, postemergence for Canada thistle, and nutgrass control.
Beans, lima and dry	Amiben	2-3 lb.	Broad spectrum of annual weeds	Immediately after seeding.	Field may be rotary-hoed without destroying herbicide action.
Beans, snap	Eptam	3 lb.	Annual grasses and nutgrass[3]	Preplant soil application. Incorporate with soil immediately. Immediately after seeding.	
	Dachal	6-10 lb.	Annuals[4] (primarily grasses)		Do not feed treated plant parts to livestock.
	Vegiben 2E (2E form only)	1.5-3 lb.	Broad spectrum of annual weeds	Immediately after seeding.	This ester form of chloramben may leach less readily from sandy soils. Least effective on sandy soils.

(Continued)

Table 9.2 (Continued).

Crop	Treatment	Active Ingredient per Acre Actually Covered[1]	Weeds Controlled	Best Time of Application (Based on Crop Stage)	Remarks, Cautions, Limitations
Beans, dry	Cobex	0.3-0.6 lb.	Annuals	Preplant soil incorporation.	
Beets, garden	Pyramin	4 lb.	Annuals (primarily broadleaved)	Preemergence or after beets emerge and before weeds have two true leaves.	Rainfall or irrigation needed to activate. Where grasses are a severe problem, use 4 pounds of Pyramin plus 4 pounds of Ro-Neet.
	Ro-Neet	4 lb.	Annual grasses	Preplant soil application. Incorporate with soil immediately.	Use a combination treatment with Pyramin to broaden control spectrum.
Broccoli Brussels sprouts	**Preemergence—direct-seeded or transplanted** Treflan	0.5-0.75 lb.	Annuals[2] (primarily grasses)	Preplant soil application. Incorporate soil immediately.	Stunting or growth reduction may occur at recommended rates under growth stress conditions. Can be used up to 1 pound per acre on transplants.
Cabbage Cauliflower	Dacthal	6-10 lb.	Annuals[4] (primarily grasses)	Immediately after seeding. Can also be incorporated preplant.	
	Postemergence—direct-seeded or transplanted TOK[5]	3-6 lb.	Broadleaved weeds[6]	One to two weeks after crop emergence or transplanting, while weeds are in seedling stage.	Use wettable-powder formulation to reduce injury potential. Use in combination with preplant or preemergence material for annual grass control.
Carrots	**Preemergence** Treflan	0.5-1 lb.	Annuals[2] (primarily grasses)	Preplant soil application. Incorporate with soil immediately.	Seed after application to 3 weeks later.
	Postemergence Lorox	0.75-1.5 lb.	Annuals	Postemergence on carrots only after the crop is 3 inches tall; grasses, less than 2 inches; broadleaves, less than 6 inches.	Do not feed treated foliage to livestock or replant treated area for 4 months. More than one application may be made, but do not exceed a total of 2 pounds per acre. Do not use over 40 PSI. Use no surfactants when temperatures exceed 80° F., or crop injury may result. Can also be used on celery and parsley. Use in combination with preplant or preemergence material for annual grass control.
	TOK	3-6 lb.	Broadleaved weeds[6]	While weeds are in the seedling stage.	
	Stoddard Solvent	60-80 gal.	Annuals	After two true leaves have appeared (do not apply to carrots or parsnips after they are 1/4 inch in diameter, since an oily taste may result).	Most effective when sprayed on cloudy days or during high humidity and when weeds are not more than 2 inches high. May not control ragweed. Do not apply within 40 days of harvest. Can also be used on celery, dill, parsnips, and parsley.

(Continued)

Table 9.2 (Continued).

Crop	Treatment	Active Ingredient per Acre Actually Covered[1]	Weeds Controlled	Best Time of Application (Based on Crop Stage)	Remarks, Cautions, Limitations
Corn, pop	**Preemergence**				
	atrazine	2-3 lb.	See sweet corn	See sweet corn.	See sweet corn, **except the section on preemergence combinations.**
	Princep	2-3 lb.	Annuals	Preemergence.	Plant only crops so specified on the label the following year. Do not graze treated areas. See sweet corn.
	Eradicane	4-6 lb.	Difficult-to-control weeds	Preplant soil application Incorporate with soil.	
	Postemergence				
	2,4-D	0.5 lb.	Broadleaved weeds	Postemergence.	Apply when corn is 3 to 10 inches tall.
	Roundup	2-3 lb.	See remarks	See remarks.	Use for quackgrass or Johnsongrass control. Apply to quackgrass when 6 to 8 inches tall in fall or spring. Apply to Johnsongrass when at least 12 inches tall and actively growing. Do not till until 3 to 7 days after application.
Corn; sweet	**Preemergence**				
	atrazine	2-3 lb.	Annuals, annual and perennial grasses[7]	Preemergence, apply no later than 3 weeks after seeding. Shallow cultivation may improve weed control during dry weather.	Grow corn a second year without atrazine treatment. This chemical has a high soil residue. Do not plant other vegetable crops on a sprayed area until a second year of corn has been grown. Use atrazine where quackgrass is a problem. Residue hazard decreased when banded or in combination with Lasso, propachlor, or Sutan.
	Bladex	See remarks	Annuals	Preemergence only.	Some sweet corn cultivars are sensitive to the application rate. Has been shown to have less soil residual than atrazine. See label for rates and precautions. Do not use postemergence or on sandy or loamy-sandy soils. Can be combined with other herbicides to reduce the rate being used.
	Eradicane	4-6 lb.	Difficult-to-control weeds	Preplant soil application. Incorporate with soil.	Use to control weeds that are difficult to control with other herbicides, such as wild cane, nutsedge, quackgrass, and seedling Johnsongrass. Preplant incorporation may aid control of nutgrass.
	Lasso	2-2.5 lb.	Annuals	Preemergence.	Do **not** use on sandy soils. Is an excellent herbicide on soils with a high organic-matter content.
	propachlor	4-5 lb.	Annuals	Preemergence.	Use on sandy soil and where nutgrass is a problem.
	Sutan +	3-4 lb.	Primarily annual grasses	Preplant soil application. Incorporate with soil.	

(Continued)

Table 9.2 (Continued).

Crop	Treatment	Active Ingredient per Acre Actually Covered[1]	Weeds Controlled	Best Time of Application (Based on Crop Stage)	Remarks, Cautions, Limitations
Corn, sweet (cont.)	**Preemergence combinations**				
	atrazine plus Lasso	1.5 lb. +2 lb.	Annuals and perennial grasses	Preemergence or preplant incorporated.	See label for slightly higher rate of Lasso for preplant incorporation. Use to reduce atrazine residue.
	atrazine plus propachlor	1.5 lb. +3 lb.	Annuals and perennial grasses	Preemergence.	
	atrazine plus Sutan +	1 lb. +3-4 lb.	Annuals and perennial grasses	Preplant soil incorporation. Incorporate with soil immediately.	Use where nutgrass is a problem and to reduce atrazine residue.
	Postemergence				
	2,4-D (amine)	0.5 lb.	Broadleaved weeds	Postemergence.	Preferably, apply before corn is 6 inches tall. If corn is over 12 inches, reduce the rate to 1/4 pound.
	atrazine	2 lb.	Annuals, annual and perennial grasses[7]	Directed spray 3 weeks after emergence.	Can be combined with crop oils for postemergence application as an emergency measure. This may increase residue the following year. Preemergence use preferred. Do not graze or feed treated foliage for 21 days after treatment.
	Basagran	0.75-1 lb.	Broadleaved annual weeds, Canada thistle, and nutsedge	Early postemergence when the weeds are small and actively growing. Delay will result in less control.	For Canada thistle and nutsedge, split applications are preferred. Make the first one when the plants are 6 to 8 inches tall; for nutsedge, 7 to 10 days later; for Canada thistle, 10 to 14 days later (or use one application plus cultivation). Do not mix with other pesticides.
Cucumbers Muskmelons Watermelons	Alanap[8]	3-5 lb. 3-3.5 lb.	Annuals[3]	Immediately after seeding or transplanting. After transplanting or vining.	Do not use on cold soil. Rainfall or irrigation after treatment gives maximum control. Use granular form. Keep away from foliage. Apply to soil after weeds have been removed.
	Prefar	4-6 lb.	Annuals (primarily grasses)	Preplant soil application. Incorporate with soil immediately.	Is primarily a grass killer. Consult label for sensitive crops within 18 months after application. Prefar can be used in rotation with tomatoes, broccoli, cauliflower, lettuce, carrots, onions, and summer squash within 18 months of application.
	Prefar plus Alanap[8]	4 lb. +2-3 lb.	Grasses and broadleaved weeds	Preplant soil incorporation for Prefar; Alanap, as an immediate postseeding application.	Has value for broad-spectrum weed control. Consult label for sensitive crops within 18 months after Prefar application. Has EPA approval as a tank mixture.
	Vegiben 2E (2E form **only**)	1.5-3 lb.	Broad spectrum of annual weeds	Immediately after seeding	This ester form of chloramben may leach less readily in sandy soils. Above 1.5 to 2 pounds per acre, injury chances increase under moist soil conditions. Some muskmelon cultivars may be susceptible to Vegiben injury.

As an alternative to herbicides where earliness is desired, black polyethylene mulch will control annual weeds, conserve moisture, and increase early spring soil temperatures.

(Continued)

Table 9.2 (Continued).

Crop	Treatment	Active Ingredient per Acre Actually Covered[1]	Weeds Controlled	Best Time of Application (Based on Crop Stage)	Remarks, Cautions, Limitations
Eggplant	Dacthal	6-10 lb.	Annuals[4] (primarily grasses)	After plants are established, 4-6 weeks after transplanting.	Cultivate and weed prior to application. Can be applied to plants as part of a uniform soil application.
Greens	Dacthal	6-10 lb.	Annuals[4] (primarily grasses)	Immediately after seeding.	For use on collards, kale, mustard greens, and turnips.
	Treflan	0.5-0.75 lb.	Annuals[2] (primarily grasses)	Preplant soil application. Incorporate with soil immediately.	For use on collards, kale, mustard greens, and turnip greens.
	Furloe	1-2 lb.	Primarily broadleaved annuals	Preemergence.	For spinach only. Use lower rates in cool, wet weather.
Horseradish	Dacthal	6-10 lb.	Annuals[4] (primarily grasses)	Immediately after transplanting.	Use for annual grass control and combine with TOK as an early postemergence treatment for broadleaved weeds.
	TOK[5]	3-6 lb.	Broadleaved weeds[5]	Before weeds are 1 inch high.	Will not consistently control weeds over 1 inch tall. Some emerging annual grass may be controlled by this treatment. Lower rate will control seedling purslane.
Lettuce	Balan	1.5 lb.	Annuals	Preplant soil incorporation. Incorporate with soil immediately.	Is primarily a grass killer. Seed after application to 3 weeks later. Do not plant wheat, barley, rye, grass, onions, oats, beets, or spinach for 12 months after application.
Onions	**Preemergence** Dacthal	6-10 lb.	Annuals[4] (primarily grasses)	Immediately after seeding or transplanting.	May not kill smartweed or common ragweed. Can be used on seeds, sets, or seedlings. Use only on mineral soils. Use lower rates on sandy soils. A double application of Dacthal can be used at seeding, layby, or both. In most situations, the weed spectrum on mineral soils will respond well to a combination of Dacthal preemergence and TOK postemergence.
	Randox	4-6 lb.	Annuals[9] (primarily grasses)	Just before onions emerge.	Use on muck soils. Heavy rainfall may reduce stand. Very effective on purslane and pigweed.
	Postemergence TOK	3-4 lb.	Broadleaved weeds	When weeds are in the seedling stage and not over 1 inch high.	Use a single application of E.C. or W.P. per growing season. Do not apply E.C. until onions are in the two- to three-leaf stage. **Preemergence** use of TOK with heavy rainfall may reduce stand. Use in combination with preplant or preemergence material for annual grass control.

(Continued)

Table 9.2 (Continued).

Crop	Treatment	Active Ingredient per Acre Actually Covered[1]	Weeds Controlled	Best Time of Application (Based on Crop Stage)	Remarks, Cautions, Limitations
Onions (cont.)	Furloe	3-6 lb.	Broadleaved weeds (especially smartweed)	On seeded onions: loop stage or after 3- to 4-leaf stage.	In the later sprays, direct at base of onion plant. If more than one application is applied do not exceed 6 pounds per acre for the season. Use lower rates in cool, wet weather. Use no later than 30 days before harvest.
Peas	**Preemergence** propachlor Treflan	4-4.9 lb. 0.5-0.75 lb.	Annuals Annuals[2]	Preemergence. Preplant soil incorporation. Incorporate with soil immediately.	Do not use on sandy soil. Seed after application to 3 weeks later. Some reduction of growth and stand reduction possible under stress. May suppress some root rot.
	Cobex	0.3-0.5 lb.	Annuals	Preplant soil incorporation.	
	Preemergence or Postemergence Premerge-3	0.3-9 lb.	Annuals (primarily broadleaved weeds)	Preemergence or postemergence.	Preemergence use 6 to 9 pounds; postemergence, use 0.3 pound to 1.1 pounds. Apply prior to bloom when peas are 2 to 8 inches tall. See label for further precautions. Preemergence use may help suppress root rot.
	Postemergence Basagran	0.75-1 lb.	Annual broadleaf weeds, Canada thistle, nutsedge	When weeds are small and are actively growing; after peas have 3 pairs of leaves (or 4 nodes).	Can help control Canada thistle. Can provide good, broad-spectrum control when used with a grass-active herbicide. Do not mix with other pesticides. See Basagran entry under corn, postemergence for Canada thistle and nutgrass control.
	MCPB MCPA	1 lb. 0.25-0.5 lb.	Broadleaved weeds and Canada thistle	When peas are 3-7 inches tall and no later than 4 nodes prior to pea blossom.	May delay maturity 1 to 4 days. Use at least 20 gallons of water per acre. Do not feed vines to livestock. MCPA is more effective on mustard. MCPB is less injurious to peas.
Potatoes, Irish	Eptam	3-6 lb.	Annual grasses and nutgrass[3]	Drag-off treatment at emergence or preplant soil application, incorporate with soil immediately.	Use lower rate on sandy soil.
	Treflan	0.5-1 lb.	Annuals[2] (primarily grasses)	Drag-off treatment at emergence.	Use a light incorporation.
	Lorox	0.75-2 lb.	Annuals	Apply prior to potato emergence.	Plant tubers at least 2 inches deep. Do not re-plant treated area to other crops for 4 months after treatment. May injure crop on light, sandy soil. Do not apply to overexposed tubers.
	chlorbromuron	2-3 lb.	Annuals	At very start of potato emergence.	May injure crop on light, sandy soil. Do not harvest immature potatoes. Do not plant crops other than field corn, potatoes, or soybeans for 6 months after applying.

(Continued)

Table 9.2 (Continued).

Crop	Treatment	Active Ingredient per Acre Actually Covered[1]	Weeds Controlled	Best Time of Application (Based on Crop Stage)	Remarks, Cautions, Limitations
Potatoes Irish (cont.)	dalapon	7 lb.	Quackgrass	Before plowing in spring; wait 4 days before plowing and planting.	Not for fields intended for red-skinned cultivars or White Rose. Do not plant potatoes for 4 weeks. Use surfactant as directed on label.
	metribuzin	0.25-0.5 lb.	Annuals (primarily broadleaved)	Postemergence, following a preemergence grass herbicide.	Can be used preemergence also. Do not exceed 1 pound per acre in a season. Do not apply within 60 days of harvest. Do not use on red-skinned or early maturing white cultivars. Do not apply in cool, wet weather.
	Lasso	2.5-3 lb.	Annuals	Apply at drag-off.	Do not use on sandy soils. Can be used alone or in combination with Lorox or dinoseb.
Potatoes, sweet	Dacthal	6-10 lb.	Annuals[4] (primarily grasses)	Immediately after planting.	Preferred on sandy soil.
	Amiben	3 lb.	Annuals	Immediately after planting.	Preferred on loam soils.
Spinach	Furloe	1-2 lb.	Annuals	Immediately after seeding.	Use 1 pound if the temperature is below 60° F.
Squash Pumpkins	Amiben	3-4 lb.	Annuals	As soon after seeding as possible.	Use on loam soils. In Illinois, Amiben can be applied broadcast or banded over the row in pumpkins.
Squash	Prefar	4-6 lb.	Annuals (primarily grasses)	Preplant soil application. Incorporate with soil immediately.	Is primarily a grass killer. Consult label for sensitive crops within 18 months after application. Prefar can be used in rotation only with tomatoes, broccoli, cauliflower, lettuce, carrots, onions, and summer squash within 18 months of application. Use in combination with Alanap as suggested for cucumbers.
Tomatoes, direct-seeded	Dymid, Enide	4-6 lb.	Annuals	Preemergence.	Do not plant other food crops on treated areas for 6 months. If used under dry soil conditions, a shallow (1 inch) incorporation as a preplant treatment may improve weed control. Can also be used on transplanted tomatoes and peppers.

(Continued)

Table 9.2 (Continued).

Crop	Treatment	Active Ingredient per Acre Actually Covered[1]	Weeds Controlled	Best Time of Application (Based on Crop Stage)	Remarks, Cautions, Limitations
Tomatoes and Peppers, transplanted	Amiben	3-4 lb.	Annuals	Wait 3 days after transplanting to apply.	Use granular formulation only. Apply to dry foliage in order to avoid leaf burn. Do not use on sandy soils.
	Treflan	0.5-1 lb.	Annuals[2] (primarily grasses)	Preplant soil application. Incorporate with soil immediately.	Some reduction of growth may be possible under growth stress conditions, or if rates are higher than suggested for the soil type.
	Sencor	0.25-1 lb. (min.-max.)	Primarily broadleaf. Should be used with a grass-active herbicide.	Preplant incorporated. Post-emergence, can be broadcast or directed.	Apply with ground equipment to seeded and transplanted tomatoes. Do not use air-blast or other high-pressure spray equipment.
		0.25-0.5 lb.		Preplant incorporated, transplant tomatoes.	Use alone or in a tank-mix combination with Treflan.
		0.25-0.5 lb.		Broadcast spray, established tomatoes.	Single or multiple applications. Minimum of 14 days between treatments. Direct-seeded plants should have 5 or 6 leaves; transplants should show new growth.
Asparagus	**Stale seedbed, before crop emergence**				
	Paraquat (Restricted-use herbicide)	0.5-1 lb.	All emerged green foliage	Before crop emergence; allow maximum weed emergence prior to treatment.	Weeds that emerge after treatment will not be controlled. Crop plants that have emerged at application will be injured. Do not apply within 18 months of harvest.

1. Based on active ingredients (actual amount of active herbicide in material or acid equivalent). Use lower rate on sandy soil and higher rate on clay and loam soils. When using a band application over the row, adjust amount of material applied to the part of an acre treated. See Illinois Circular 1047.

2. May not control ragweed and panicum.

3. May not control smartweed.

4. May not control ragweed, smartweed, and velvetleaf.

5. Use of 50% wettable powder is suggested for cabbage and horseradish.

6. May not control ragweed or chickweed. Grass control is sometimes marginal.

7. May not control crabgrass.

8. Do **not** use Alanap Plus, Solo, Whistle, or Amoco Soybean herbicide. These materials all contain Alanap plus another ingredient that may cause injury.

9. May not control smartweed and velvetleaf.

Rotation as a Factor in Soil Management

Rotation is of importance in soil management, since crops differ in their requirements for nutrients, in the extent and distribution of their root systems, and in their effects on soil acidity and on other factors. It is a fairly common belief that certain crops are "hard on land," and it is well known that crops differ in their effects on the yield of those which follow. Experiments conducted under Rhode Island conditions have shown that onions produced a small yield following certain crops such as mangel beets, rutabagas, cabbage, buckwheat, and potatoes, and a relatively large yield following red top, timothy, and a combination of these. Buckwheat, on the other hand, produced a very large yield following rutabagas and a very small yield following corn and millet. In general, the crops which had the most depressing effect on the yield of onions had the opposite effect on buckwheat. The large difference in yield of these two crops is probably due to the varying effects of the preceding crops on soil acidity and the quantity of nutrients removed. It was found that the lowest yield of onions followed those crops which removed the largest quantity of the deficient nutrients and the largest yield followed the crop which removed the smallest quantity of nitrogen and phosphorus. It was not universally true, however, that the crops which removed the largest quantities of the deficient nutrients were the ones which had the greatest depressing effect on the succeeding crop.

Soil acidity is affected differently by different crops and this may account for considerable variation in yield of succeeding crops that are sensitive to acidity or conditions associated with it. It was found in the Rhode Island studies that the yield of onions was highest following those crops giving rise to the least acidity. When the acidity was reduced by liming, the effects of various crops on the yield of onions following was much less divergent. With optimum quantities of nutrients and with favorable soil reaction, a large part of the depressing effects of the crops on the yield of those following largely disappeared. It appears, therefore, that supplying adequate quantities of nutrients and maintaining a favorable soil reaction would eliminate much of the depressing effect of a given crop on the one following.

Order of Crop Rotation

No definite system of rotation can be given that would be satisfactory under a wide range of conditions, but there are a few principles which should be observed. In order to utilize fully the resources of the soil, it is desirable to alternate shallow-rooted plants with deep-rooted ones, and to follow crops that supply organic matter to the soil with those that favor its decomposition. The rotation should be so planned as to give as much time as feasible to the growing of soil-improving crops between the time of harvesting one crop and the planting of the next one on the same land. Where soil erosion is a serious problem, it is important to have a soil-improving crop on the land whenever it is not occupied by a money crop. This is especially important in regions where the land is idle during the winter. In most of the large commercial vegetable-growing regions of the South, the soil-improving crop should be grown in the summer and turned under in preparation for fall or winter crops.

Where vegetables are grown in rotation with general farm crops, it is advisable to follow a hay or pasture crop with corn or cotton rather than with vegetable crops. Small growing crops, such as lettuce, celery, and beets, carrots, and other root crops, should be preceded by a cultivated crop. Weeds are less likely to be serious following a clean-cultivated crop than following a hay or pasture crop.

In planning the order of crop rotation, attention should be given also to disease and insect control as mentioned in a previous paragraph.

SELECTED REFERENCES

Alban, E. K., Brooks, W. M., and Wittmeyer, E. C., "Herbicides for Weed Control in Vegetable Crops," Ohio State Univ. Coop. Ext. Ser. MM 246, 1978.

Anonymous, "Chemical Weed Control Recommendations for Vegetable Crops," Wisc. Ext. Ser. Circ. 55, 1966.

Anonymous, "Effects of Crop Rotation, Soil Fumigation, Variety and Nitrogen on the Yield of Sweet Potatoes," Tex. A & M Univ. MP-938, 1970.

Audus, L. J., *The Physiology and Biochemistry of Herbicides*, London and New York: Academic Press, Inc., 1964.

Bainer, R., *et al.*, "Mechanized Growing and Harvesting of Fruit and Vegetable Crops," *HortSci.* 4(3), 1969.

Hopen, H. J., "Herbicide Guide for Commercial Vegetable Growers," Ill. Agr. Ext. Circ. 907, 1979.

Janes, B. E., "Vegetable Rotation Studies in Connecticut, II," *Proc. Amer. Soc. Hort. Sci.* 57: 252-258, 1951.

Odland, T. E., Bell, R. S., and Smith, J. B., "The Influence of Crop Plants on Those Which Follow, V," R. I. Agr. Exp. Sta. Bull. 309, 1950.

Odland, T. E., and Smith, J. B., "Further Studies on the Effect of Certain Crops on Succeeding Crops," *Jour. Amer. Soc. Agronomy* 40: 99-107, 1948.

Thompson, H. C., Wessels, P. H., and Mills, H. S., "Cultivation Experiments with Certain Vegetable Crops on Long Island," Cornell Univ. Exp. Sta. Bull. 521, 1931.

CHAPTER 10

Irrigating and Mulching

The U.S. Census of Agriculture revealed that approximately half of the vegetable crop land was irrigated in 1974. Of the 3,071,071 acres devoted to vegetables on these farms, 48 percent were wholly irrigated and, in addition, about 10 percent were partly irrigated.

For many years most vegetables in California and other arid and semi-arid regions of the West have been irrigated. For example, 81 percent of the 1,412,677 acres of vegetables in the 17 western states and Louisiana were wholly irrigated in 1969, and an additional 5 percent were partially irrigated. All of the vegetables in California, Arizona, and New Mexico are reported to be irrigated, and a large percentage of those in other western states are fully or partly irrigated.

Irrigation of vegetables in the so-called 30 humid eastern states and Hawaii and Alaska has increased rapidly over the years. Of the 1,847,673 acres in these areas devoted to vegetables in 1969, about 19 percent were wholly irrigated and 14 percent partly irrigated. As the cost of producing vegetables increases, fewer will be grown without irrigation. (All figures apply to Class 1-5 farms which have annual sales of $2,500 or more.)

IRRIGATING

Potentially, irrigation is one of the most important means of increasing yields and quality of vegetable crops. It is not only important in the arid and semi-arid regions, where most of the water for growing crops is supplied by irrigation, but it is also important in the humid regions as well. Rainfall is seldom uniform and adequate enough so that irrigation would not be profitable for high-return, shallow-rooted vegetable crops grown on light soils. With high costs of production, vegetable growers cannot afford crop losses due to drouths. Factors to be considered in irrigation are: method of application, kind of crop, and amount of water to be applied at the different stages of crop development. In general, vegetable crops grown for their foliage require uniform moisture throughout their development, while those grown for fruits and seed require largest amounts during fruit set and development when root systems are least efficient.

During the production of a crop, water is lost from plants, mostly from transpiration, and from evaporation from soil and accumulations on plant surfaces. The sum of these losses is called "evapotranspiration." These losses together with the water retained by the plant tissues—about 1% of the total—are considered the *consumptive use*. The increasing need for irrigation and the limited water usually available demand its efficient use and conservation. A crop covering the surface of the soil will lose about four times as much water as a dry surface and about the same amount as a wet surface of the soil.

Sources of Water

Water for irrigation may be obtained from streams, lakes, wells, springs, and stored storm water. In most states where irrigation is practiced, definite laws and regulations pertaining to the use of water for irrigation purposes have been set up. These regulations should be known and understood before a grower proceeds to spend money on irrigation equipment.

Water may be diverted from streams, lakes, or reservoirs through gravitation or by means of pumps. Some wells are overflowing, while others require pumps to lift the water. A farmer may use one or more sources and systems in obtaining water for irrigation.

Costs obviously vary greatly, and they may be divided into two parts: (1) the costs of initial purchase and installation of equipment and (2) costs connected with actual application of the water to the land. Where water is obtained from flowing wells or springs, or diverted from streams or lakes, the initial expense may be comparatively low. The expense of stream diversion is often borne by a group of people. However, when powerful pumps are required to raise the water, initial expenses become high. The costs of drilling a well and installing a pump and motor, as well as building a reservoir for temporary storage, may easily amount to a substantial investment. The expense of applying water to the land is more or less constant every year.

Applying Water

For determining the amount of water to apply, the soil type, texture, and depth should be checked. From this information, the maximum available water-holding capacity (MAWC) can be determined. The rooting depth of the crop should be considered since the irrigation depth may be limited by it. Available soil moisture may be determined by feel or by instruments such as tensiometers or meters for measuring electrical resistance. The difference between actual available moisture and MAWC would indicate the amount to be applied. Generally, irrigation should begin when 40 percent of the MAWC is removed from fine- and medium-textured soils or when 60 percent is removed from sandy soils. The frequency of application would depend upon effective rainfall and the rate of evapotranspiration. The latter depends upon crop cover, temperature, humidity, and wind. Soils should be wetted to the depth of the crop root systems. Light, frequent irrigations are usually not recommended.

Sprinkler Irrigation

Sprinkler systems are becoming increasingly popular because they can be used satisfactorily under most conditions. Sprinkling is recommended where: (1) the water intake rate is too high for good furrow application, (2) the slope is too steep for the furrow method, (3) the topography or the soil will not permit grading for furrow irrigation, (4) the water supply is barely adequate, and (5) shallow, light irrigations are required. The use of sprinkler irrigation will promote seed germination, maintain moderate temperatures, and aid in the application of fertilizers.

A wide variety of sprinkler equipment is available to the grower. He may choose a solid-set, hand-move, or wheel-move system. The last may be either side-roll (which can be automated), or center-pivot (which is self-propelled). Whether or not an automated or permanent system will pay for the extra cost of installation will depend on the frequency of its use. Water may be distributed by means of rotating sprinklers, fixed sprinkler heads, nozzle heads, or perforated pipeline. The majority of the agricultural sprinklers are of the rotating type. Discharge capacities range from 1 to more than 600 gallons per minute. The rate of application should not be greater than about 75 percent of the soil's capacity to absorb it. At wind speeds above 4 miles per hour, sprinkler patterns become distorted.

A solid-set or permanent system is necessary for frost protection of tender crops. An application rate of about 0.10 inch per hour is adequate to protect against light "radiation" frost, but from 0.3 to 0.5 inches per hour is required to protect against "wind-borne" frost. If the wind velocity exceeds 10 mph, irrigation is not effective for preventing frost injury. Irrigation should continue until ice begins to melt.

Surface (Furrow) Irrigation

Surface irrigation is adapted to soils of medium to low water intake rates and where the surface soil is deep and uniform and the subsoil does not impede drainage. The topography of the land must be gently sloping and uniform for good water distribution. Large quantities of water should be available, but the area to be irrigated at any one time should be restricted to the number of furrows the irrigator can watch closely enough to adjust flow rates satisfactorily. The "cut-back" method is recommended. It consists of allowing the furrow to fill as rapidly as possible and then reducing the flow to match furrow intake (Fig. 10.1).

Correct preparation of the soil surface is most essential in any method of surface irrigation. It saves loss of time during actual irrigation, results in a more even distribution of water, reduces wastes, and leads to the production of larger crops of better quality. Grading after plowing re-

Fig. 10.1—Setting out plastic syphon spiles for surface irrigation.

USDA Photograph

duces the soil to an even plane surface by removing the knolls and filling the depressions, but the entire area is not reduced to the same level. A general slope is desirable, the amount varying with each locality. Manufactured levelers as well as homemade wooden floats or drags are commonly used for this final smoothing process.

When the initial cost for wells, pumps, and accompanying equipment is not so large, surface irrigation requires only a moderate investment. If the supply of water is sufficient, this method is excellently adapted to irrigating immense areas of ground. Among the disadvantages are: (1) the necessity for constant attention, (2) the tendency for soils to crust and bake, and (3) the tremendous losses of water by seepage in supply ditches.

Subirrigation

In subirrigation, water is added to the soil in such a way that it permeates the soil from below. Subirrigation requires an abundance of water, a sandy loam topsoil through which water will move freely by capillary attraction, and an impervious subsoil which will hold the water. At the same time, adequate drainage is necessary. The large amount of water required and the great expense involved in the laying of the tile pipes (although subirrigation does not necessarily involve the laying of any structures) are disadvantages of this system. Advantages include the maintenance of an undisturbed soil mulch and lack of trouble from soil baking. In actual practice, subirrigation is sometimes difficult, justifying considerable investigation of existing soil conditions and the water supply before such a system is installed.

TRICKLE IRRIGATION. In areas where water is scarce, much interest has developed in trickle irrigation. With this method water is applied under low pressure near the plants by seepage through porous hose or through micro-emitters. It is estimated that under desert conditions lettuce can be produced with about 25 percent of the water used by the furrow method. The application of fertilizer may also be reduced. Where the porous hose is placed under the row, salts are leached away from the root zone, enabling crops to grow on soils with harmful salinity. The cost of installing trickle irrigation is high, but the system can be automated, thus saving labor as well as water and fertilizer.

MULCHING

A mulch is created whenever the soil surface is artificially modified. Coverings of straw, leaves, refuse, paper or polyethylene film, and even a

Fig. 10.2—Early peppers showing mulches and trickle irrigation.

Univ. of Ariz. Photograph

loose layer of soil produced by cultivation, are all mulches. The chief purpose of mulches is to conserve moisture, but they are also used to insure clean fruit, control weeds, hasten maturity, and increase yields. Soil temperatures under straw mulch may average several degrees lower than those of unmulched soil. On the other hand, black paper or polyethylene usually increases soil temperatures, which may be beneficial to early crops and especially to those requiring a warm season.

POLYETHYLENE MULCHES. Good results have been reported from the use of black polyethylene for crops such as tomatoes, peppers, and sweet corn on porous soils of very low fertility. Heavy rains and irrigation may leach out as much as 90 percent of the soluble fertilizers. The mulch, by conserving moisture, reduces the requirements for irrigation and fertilizer. Approximately 6,000 acres of tomatoes were mulched in Dade County, Florida, in 1974. Fertilizer is applied, soil fumigated, beds formed, and mulch laid by machine. Planting may be done after about five days using a mixture consisting of moistened sphagnum moss peat, a slow-release fertilizer, and seed. Two ounces of the mix containing about five seeds is plugged into holes cut in the polyethylene by a propane torch and covered with a small amount of vermiculite or perlite to prevent drying. The even germination and uniform growth by this method make it suitable for mechanical harvesting of vine-ripened tomatoes.

PAPER MULCH. Paper mulch can be laid strip by strip as the rows of seeds or plants are set out. It is usually laid first, and then the planting done through the paper (Fig. 10.3 and Fig. 10.4). Special equipment has

Fig. 10.3—Laying paper mulch by machine.

Univ. of Ill. Photograph

been developed to lay the paper and cover the edges with a narrow bank of earth, all in one operation. The cost of paper mulch is very high, especially with complete coverage, and its use is warranted only on crops of high value which are known to respond well. The heavier grades of paper should be used to exclude light, and paper containing volatile or water-soluble materials which are harmful to the plant should be avoided. The paper is usually impregnated with a fungicide to prevent early decay.

Fig. 10.4—Seeding through paper mulch.

Univ. of Ill. Photograph

OTHER MULCHES. Straw, leaves, pine needles, and similar mulches are usually applied after the crop is well established. Such mulches are not commonly used with vegetable crops. However, many growers like to maintain a good soil mulch, which is fully discussed in Chapter 9.

Effect of Mulching

Because of the interest in paper mulch, numerous observations have been made as to its effect on soil moisture, soil temperature, and soil nitrates, as well as its influence on weed growth and the various processes and characteristics of the crop.

EFFECT ON THE SOIL. Most workers have found that the mulch conserves moisture directly by preventing evaporation and indirectly by controlling weeds. In arid and semi-arid regions, where the soil moisture is low to begin with, mulch is no substitute for irrigation and in some cases makes irrigation difficult.

Experiments in three widely separated localities have indicated that there is increased nitrification under mulch paper. Soil temperatures are usually several degrees higher under ordinary black paper mulches than under similar unmulched conditions. With papers of lighter color, and under certain climatic conditions, temperatures under a mulch may be lower.

EFFECT ON THE CROP. Warm-season crops, such as cucumbers, muskmelons, eggplants, and peppers, usually respond to paper mulch by maturing earlier and by yielding more. Quick-maturing spring crops also are often benefited. The response of both these types of crops is probably due to higher soil temperatures. The quality of such crops may be improved by paper mulch, the products being larger and cleaner and containing fewer culls. When growing conditions are already favorable, however, paper mulch rarely improves them, and may indeed affect the crop adversely. Such cool-weather crops as onions, lettuce, beets, cabbage, and cauliflower have been reported as responding rather poorly to paper mulch. Similar results can be expected with polyethylene.

SELECTED REFERENCES

Anonymous, "Irrigation Guide for Illinois," Ill. Coop., Ext. Ser., Ill. Agr. Exp. Sta., and Soil Con. Ser. Agr. Eng. 866, 1965.

Anonymous, "Replenishing Underground Water Supplies on the Farm," USDA Leaflet No. 452, 1976.

Anonymous, *Reynolds Irrigation Digest*, Reynolds Metals Co., 1969.

Anonymous, "Sprinkler Irrigation in the Pacific Northwest," PN.W 63, Pacific Northwest Coop. Ext. Pub., Ore., Wash., and Ida., 1965.

Epstein, E., and Grant, W. T., "Water Stress Relations of the Potato Plant Under Field Conditions," *Agron. J.* 65: 400-404, 1973.

Eris, L. J., French, O. F., and Harris, K., "Consumptive Use of Water by Crops in Arizona," Univ. of Ariz. Agr. Exp. Sta. Tech. Bull. 169, 1968.

Fullilove, W. T., "Self-propelled Tower Irrigation," Univ. of Ga. Agr. Exp. Sta. Res. Rep. 96, 1969.

Hernandez, Teme P., *et al.*, "The Value of Irrigation in Sweet Potato Production in Louisiana," La. State Univ. Agr. Exp. Sta. Bull. 607, 1965.

Hoskyn, J. P., and Bryan, B. B., "Subsurface Irrigation Research in Arkansas," Univ. of Ark. Agr. Exp. Sta. Rep. Ser. 175, 1969.

James, D. W., "The Pros and Cons of Fertigation," *Ut. Sci.*, Sept., 1973.

Jensen, M. C., "Water Consumption by Agricultural Plants," *Water Deficits and Plant Growth*, Vol. 2, New York: Academic Press, Inc., 1968.

Kenworthy, A. L., "Trickle Irrigation: The Concept and Guidelines for Use," Mich. State Univ. Agr. Exp. Sta. Res. Rep. 165, 1972.

Kenworthy, A. L., "Trickle Irrigation: Guidelines for Use in the Home Garden," Mich. State Univ. Agr. Exp. Sta. Res. Rep. 285, 1975.

Kincaid, D. C., Heermann, D. F., and Kruse, E. G., "Application Rates and Runoff in Center-Pivot Sprinkler Irrigation," *Transactions of the ASAE*, Vol. 12, 1969.

Marsh, A. W., *et al.*, "Solid Set Sprinklers for Starting Vegetable Crops," Univ. of Calif. Div. of Agr. Sci. Leaflet 2265, 1977.

Motes, J. E., and Greig, J. K., "Effect of Irrigation on Soil Temperature, Potato Yield and Specific Gravity During Early Summer," *J. Amer. Soc. Hort. Sci.* 94:510-511, 1969.

Oebker, N. F., and Kuykendall, J. R., "Trickle Irrigation in Horticultural Crops in the Desert Southwest," *Proc. Nat. Agr. Plast. Conf.* 11, 1971.

Pair, C. H., "Sprinkler Irrigation," USDA, ARS Leaflet No. 476, 1976.

Pair, C. H., "Water Distribution Under Sprinkler Irrigation," *Transactions of the ASAE*, Vol. II, 1968.

Robinson, A. R., *et al.*, "Distribution, Control and Measurement of Irrigation Water on the Farm," USDA Misc. Pub. 926, 1963.

Salter, P. J., and Goode, J. E., *Crop Responses to Water at Different Stages of Growth*, Commonwealth Agricultural Bureaux, Bucks, Eng., 1967.

Sanders, D. C., and Nylund, R. E., "The Influence of Mist Irrigation on the Potato: II. Growth and Development," *Am. Potato J.* Vol. 49-5, 1972.

Scholz, E. W., and Lana, E. P., "Mulches for Warm Weather Crops," N. Dak. State Univ. Agr. Exp. Sta. 34, 1971.

Shearer, M. N., "Electrical Resistance Blocks for Scheduling Irrigations," Ore. State Univ. Coop. Ext. Ser. Ext. Bull. 810, 1963.

Snyder, W. C., *et al.*, "Overhead Irrigation Encourages Wet-Weather Plant Diseases," *Calif. Agr.*, 1965.

Swan, J. B., *et al.*, "Irrigation—How Much and How Often," Univ. of Minn. Agr. Ext. Ser. Ext. Folder 257, 1971.

Swan, J. B., and Hicks, D. R., "Irrigated Corn Production," Univ. of Minn. Agr. Ext. Ser. Ext. Folder 263, 1972.

Takatori, F. H., Lippert, L. F., and Lyons, J. M., "Petroleum Mulch Studies for Row Crops in California," Univ. of Calif. Agr. Exp. St. Bull. 849, 1971.

Waggoner, P. E., Miller, P. M., and De Roo, H. C., "Plastic Mulching: Principles and Benefits," Conn. Agr. Exp. Sta. Bull. 634, 1960.

CHAPTER 11

Controlling Insects and Diseases

Good pest-control management requires the use of cultural, mechanical, biological, and chemical methods. For best results a combination of these is often necessary. Insecticides and fungicides are effective in the control of most pests, but their use is closely regulated and subject to change. It is imperative that the commercial grower secure the latest recommendations for the control and use of pesticides. Since he is interested in maximum control at minimum cost, it may be necessary for him to consider a wide range of materials. The home gardener generally grows a variety of vegetables and may encounter many pests. A limited number of generally effective pesticides should be used. They should be extremely safe to apply, handle, and store.

IMPORTANCE OF PEST CONTROL

Insect and disease infestations in vegetable crops bring about heavy losses through: (1) reduced yields, (2) lowered quality of produce, (3) increased costs of production and harvesting, and (4) required expenditures for materials and equipment to apply control measures. These losses are important because they reduce the prospective vegetable grower's income and may result in the total loss of a crop.

The insect- and disease-control picture in vegetable production has changed considerably since the advent of more toxic pesticides. Control measures became very effective and the yields of crops such as potatoes increased greatly. With the recognition of the residue problem, strict regulations were instituted, primarily for the protection of the consumer. Further restrictions in the use of pesticides resulted from the fear of environmental pollution. The present tendency is to use a minimum of pesticides, and only those that are readily degradable. Renewed consideration is being given to biological and cultural methods of control and resistant cultivars.

The suggestions made here are summarized from information available in publications of the U.S. Department of Agriculture and state agricultural experiment stations and are presented only as indications of current practices. The reader is reminded that any use made of the control measures suggested are at his own risk, and he is urged to consult his local state experiment station or cooperative extension service for detailed information concerning the proper way to control insect and disease pests in his locality as well as to follow carefully the directions given by the manufacturer on the label of any pesticide to be applied.

GENERAL CONTROL MEASURES

The recommended pesticides are by no means the complete and final answer to insect and disease problems which arise in vegetable production. True, they will solve a large majority of the problems which may be encountered. However, much remains to be learned about the physiological actions of these materials on the plants as well as on the pests being controlled.

Several "common sense" practices, when incorporated into the insecticide-fungicide program, will improve yield, increase produce quality, and in the long run increase profits. These fundamentals can be found in almost any text devoted to the art and science of vegetable production as well as in publications of the U.S. Department of Agriculture and of the state experiment stations and extension services. They are included here for the convenience of the reader.

1. Plant the best quality seed. This means that the seed should be (a) disease-free (b) certified when possible.
2. Select crops which are best suited to the soil and climate. Because a crop isn't grown in an area doesn't mean it cannot be grown there, but it is usually a good indication.
3. Control weeds. Grass and weeds compete strongly with crops for soil moisture and plant nutrients, and they frequently harbor or attract insects which may later attack the crop and may also serve as disease reservoirs.
4. Select plots of land that are fertile and well drained. Substandard land will produce substandard yields while poorly drained areas

will invariably result in sparse stands, damping off, and seed-decay problems.

5. Use only the best quality fertilizers. Soil tests will indicate what fertilizer combination is needed and whether liming is necessary. Bargains in fertilizer are seldom found.

6. Buy plants the same as seed—disease-free and certified—when possible.

7. Use disease-resistant cultivars if they are available. At present these include cultivars that are resistant to only a few diseases of specified crops. The degree of resistance varies considerably through the range of available cultivars.

8. When harvest is completed, destroy the remains of annual crops as soon as practical. Stems, leaves, and roots can serve as disease reservoirs and insect harbors for the following year.

9. Rotate crops. Planting the same crop in a field year after year may eventually result in severe soil-borne diseases and insect or nematode infestations. All of these can be held in check to some degree by crop rotation.

10. Follow recommended planting dates. Some crops can be planted so that they will mature before diseases strike and before or after certain insects begin their attack. Planting dates are usually issued by the state experiment stations or the cooperative extension service.

CONTROLLING INSECTS

A list of insecticides, with restrictions and limitations for use on vegetable crops is given in Table 11.3. This list was taken from Illinois Circular 897 and was prepared for the use of the commercial growers during the 1979 season. The grower is warned that changes may be made without notification, and that he should check with his county extension adviser if there is any doubt about the insecticide he plans to use. Some of the insecticides listed can be poisonous to the applicator. In using them, the commercial gardener is expected to use precautions to protect himself and others from undue or needless exposure. The home gardener should limit his use of the usable insecticides to carbaryl (Sevin) and to malathion and diazinon for soil insects. A list of common garden insects and suggested methods of control are given in Tables 11.1 and 11.2. These tables were taken from Illinois Circular 1091. The latter was revised for the 1979 season.

The label on an insecticide package gives instructions for its use and should be read and followed carefully. Maximum rates suggested should not be exceeded; the insecticide should be applied only to crops for which use has been approved; and the interval between application and harvest should be carefully observed. A record should be made of the product used, the trade name, the percentage content of the insecticide, the dilution, the rate of application per acre, and the dates of application.

OLDER MATERIALS. The older insecticides which have been successfully used for several decades and will undoubtedly be useful for years to come include the two general classifications: (1) botanical insecticides and (2) inorganic insecticides.

Botanical insecticides are derived from plants or plant parts. Those presently accepted for use on vegetables are rotenone, pyrethrum, nicotine sulfate, sabadilla, and ryania.

The inorganic materials acceptable for use are cryolite, sulfur, and calcium arsenate. The latter is applied only to the foliage of plants whose edible parts are underground—for example, potatoes.

BIOLOGICAL CONTROL. Although an old concept, a bacterial culture for the control of certain caterpillars has been made available. The scientific name of this bacteria is *Bacillus thuringiensis,* and it is sold under several trade names, usually in the form of a wettable powder to be sprayed on infested plants. This form of insect control has two advantages: (1) insect predators are not killed and (2) no harmful chemical residues remain on the produce at the time of harvest.

PESTICIDE REGULATIONS. Limits on insecticides and fungicides which can remain in or on raw agricultural commodities are carefully regulated by the U.S. Environmental Protection Agency. The allowable amounts of pesticide *residues* on produce are known as *tolerances*. Tables 11.3 and 11.4 list chemicals and crops on which they may be applied and the times between the last application and harvest. These regulations are subject to change without notice and do not constitute recommendations for pest control. For this information consult the cooperative extension service for the latest suggested measures.

The regulation was designed primarily to protect the consumer, but it also protects the vegetable producer and the pesticide manufacturer. The producer needs only to follow the directions for rate and time of application, which by requirement of law appear on every pesticide container label if the pesticide enters interstate commerce. All states now have laws which require that pesticides be properly labeled for safe use. By adhering to the manufacturer's directions, the grower is assured of placing produce on the market which will meet with tolerances established by the Environmental Protection Agency (EPA). On the other hand, if the grower does not follow label directions, his harvested produce may be confiscated for having pesticide residues higher than the permitted tolerances. Under these conditions the grower must assume complete responsibility for residues in excess of the tolerances. Consequently, it is important to read and follow the directions on the label.

FORMS OF INSECTICIDES. Most of the commonly used insecticides are sold in three forms: (1) dust, (2) emulsible concentrate, and (3) wettable powder. Dusts are used in standard hand and power dusting equipment in the form in which they are purchased. The emulsible concentrates and wettable powders are manufactured to be diluted with water to the desired concentration and sprayed with hand or power equipment. All three forms have their advantage depending on the insect to be controlled, terrain, weather and ground conditions, and equipment available.

The granular material is another form of insecticide which has become popular in recent years. Small clay pellets are evenly impregnated with insecticide and can be distributed by aircraft, fertilizer and seeding equipment, or with equipment made especially for granular application.

Granulars have been used for both soil and foliage applications. One outstanding feature of granular insecticides is their low residues compared to sprays and dusts.

The Critical Period

With few exceptions, vegetable crops represent the highest acre investment of all forms of agricultural endeavor. In the value of the harvested crop they again take the dollar lead. Each year's harvest usually represents an enormous number of man-hours and a tremendous investment in irrigation equipment, fertilizer, and special planting, harvesting, and processing machinery. Considering the expense and effort involved in preparing a crop for market, it would seem unreasonable to permit an insect infestation to lower the market grade or even, as occasionally happens, destroy the crop.

Yet this very tragedy does occur, not because of the producer's failure to apply insecticides, but because of several other factors. These include:

(1) poor timing of insecticide application, (2) improper selection of insecticide, (3) unfavorable weather conditions, (4) low rate of application, (5) equipment failure, and (6) operator negligence. Timing of application is the most important and probably the least attended of these factors.

Every insect pest usually has a time in its development which can be referred to as the "critical period"—that is, a time in which it is most vulnerable to control by chemicals. The term "critical period," could also be applied to some stage in the growth of the plant, or even to the minimum number of days a material can be applied to crops before harvest, according to EPA regulations. All three "critical periods" should be taken into consideration when planning insect control.

Scouting for Insect Pests

Vegetable producers should check or scout their crops every two or three days, carefully examining them for signs of insect infestations, such as eggs, insect frass, and damaged leaves or fruits. In this way, most insect pests can be discovered, and control measures can be applied before the problem becomes serious.

The value of scouting fields to determine the proper time for control applications cannot be overemphasized. A knowledge of the extent of infestation and the stage of insect development will in the long run save the producer time, money, and worry.

CONTROLLING VEGETABLE DISEASES

As with insect control, disease control is an important phase of vegetable production. Disease-control measures must begin BEFORE the disease is observed in the field. In contrast, measures for controlling insects are usually withheld until insects or their damage is observed.

Disease control begins with soil sterilization and seed treatment and continues with applications of fungicides (materials used to kill or control plant diseases) to the growing plant. Even though disease control appears more complicated with the ever-increasing number of new fungicides, the task has actually been simplified. Most vegetable diseases can now be prevented before they strike. Where fungicides have not been applied in time to prevent disease, they may, in some circumstances, be used to decrease the severity of damage after the disease has become established.

Fungicides are included in the new EPA regulations. These regulations limit the amount of chemicals that can remain as residues on or in

Table 11.1—Insects Which Commonly Attack Vegetable Crops.

Vegetable	Insect Pest
Asparagus	Asparagus beetle, cutworm, thrips, wireworm
Beans	Aphid, bean leaf beetle, corn earworm, cutworm, leaf hopper, Mexican bean beetle, root maggot, spider mite, cucumber beetle, western bean cutworm, wireworm, lygus bug, flea beetle
Beet	Beet webworm, blister beetle, cutworm, flea beetle, wireworm, white-fringed beetle grub
Cabbage, Broccoli, Cauliflower, Kale	Aphid, cabbage looper and caterpillars, cutworm, flea beetle, harlequin bug, mole cricket, root maggot, vegetable weevil, white-fringed beetle grub, wireworm
Carrot	Carrot rust fly, leaf hopper, vegetable weevil, wireworm
Celery	Aphid, celery leaf tier, cutworm, lygus bug, spider mite
Cucumber and Melons	Aphid, cucumber beetle, leaf hopper, leaf miner, pickleworm, spider mite, thrips, wireworm
Eggplant	Colorado potato beetle, cutworm, eggplant lace bug, flea beetle, hornworm, spider mite, whitefly, wireworm
Lettuce	Aphid, army worm, cutworm, caterpillars, leaf hopper, mole cricket, wireworm
Onion	Onion maggot, thrips, wireworm, leaf miner
Peas (garden)	Aphid, pea weevil, alfalfa and celery loopers
Pepper	Aphid, cutworm, flea beetle, hornworm, leaf miner, pepper maggot, pepper weevil, spider mite, wireworm
Potato	Aphid, army worm, blister beetle, Colorado potato beetle, cutworm, European corn borer, flea beetle, grasshopper, leaf hopper, mole cricket, plant bug, potato psyllid, potato tuberworm, vegetable weevil, white-fringed beetle grub, white grub, wireworm
Pumpkin and Squash	Aphid, cucumber beetle, cutworm, squash bug, squash vine borer, pickleworm
Spinach	Alfalfa looper, aphid, beet webworm, leaf miner
Sweet corn	Corn earworm, European corn borer, Japanese beetle, wireworm
Sweet potato	Sweet potato weevil, wireworm, white-fringed beetle grub
Tomato	Aphid, army worm, blister beetle, Colorado potato beetle, cutworm, drosophila, flea beetle, hornworm, leaf miner, spider mite, tomato fruitworm, tomato pinworm, tomato psyllid, tomato russet mite
Turnip	Aphid, caterpillars, flea beetle, root maggot, vegetable weevil, wireworm, white fringed beetle grub

crops at the time of harvest. The slogan, READ THE LABEL, cannot be over-emphasized with respect to fungicide and insecticide applications.

Soil Sterilization and Seed Treatment

If possible, the soil should be sterilized to kill fungi, bacterial spores, and weed seeds. This can be done by using a formaldehyde drench, treating with chloropicrin (a tear gas), dipping bagged soil in boiling water

Table 11.2—Common Vegetable Insects and Suggested Control

Insect	Crop	Dust Formula	Spray Formula	Remarks
Aphid	Cabbage Cucumbers Melons Peas Potatoes Tomatoes	5 percent malathion	2 tsp. 50-57 percent emulsifiable malathion	Apply on foliage when aphids appear. Repeat weekly as needed. 1 lb. active ingredient not recommended for some crops.
Blister beetle	Potatoes Corn Tomatoes Beans	5 percent carbaryl	2 tb. wettable carbaryl in 1 gal. water	1½ lbs. per acre on foliage as needed.
Cabbage worms	Broccoli Cabbage Cauliflower Greens		Bacillus thuringiensis; follow label directions	Thorough treatment is necessary. Repeat weekly as needed. Begin treatment when worms are small.
Corn earworm (⅔ nat. size)	Sweet corn Tomatoes	.5 percent carbaryl Bacillus thuringiensis (Thuricide, Dipel, Biotrol) on tomatoes	Inject ½ medicine dropperful of mineral oil into silk channel as silks start to dry or 2 tb. wettable carbaryl in 1 gal. water	Dust or spray silks with carbaryl every other day for 10 days. Dust or spray tomatoes with Sevin 3 to 4 times at 10-day intervals; begin when first fruits are small.
European corn borer	Sweet corn	5 percent carbaryl or 5 percent carbaryl granules	2 tb. wettable carbaryl in 1 gal. water	Apply insecticide four times at 5-day intervals beginning with egg hatching near mid-June. Avoid early spring plantings. On late corn, dust as for corn earworm.

(Continued)

Table 11.2 (Continued).

Insect	Crop	Dust Formula	Spray Formula	Remarks
Striped cucumber beetle	Cucumbers Melons Squash	5 percent carbaryl	2 tb. wettable carbaryl in 1 gal. water	Treat as soon as beetles appear. Repeat when necessary.
Cutworm	Most garden crops	Carbaryl bait		At transplanting, wrap stems of seedling cabbage, pepper, and tomato plants with newspaper or foil to prevent damage by cutworms.
Flea beetle	Most garden crops	5 percent carbaryl	2 tb. wettable carbaryl in 1 gal. water	Apply as soon as injury is first noticed. Thorough application is necessary. 1 lb. active ingredient per acre.
Grasshopper	Most garden crops	5 percent carbaryl	2 tb. wettable carbaryl in 1 gal. water	Treat infested areas while grasshoppers are still small.
Hornworm (½ nat. size)	Tomatoes	5 percent carbaryl **or** **Bacillus thuringiensis** (Thuricide, Dipel, Biotrol)	2 tb. wettable carbaryl in 1 gal. water	Ordinarily hand-picking is more practical in the home garden.

(Continued)

Table 11.2 (Continued).

Insect	Crop	Dust Formula	Spray Formula	Remarks
Leafhopper	Beans Carrots Potatoes Cucumbers Muskmelons	Carbaryl dust	2 tb. wettable carbaryl in 1 gal. water	Spray or dust once a week for 3 to 4 weeks, beginning when plants are small. Apply to underside of foliage.
Mexican bean beetle	Beans	5 percent carbaryl	2 tb. wettable carbaryl in 1 gal. water	Apply insecticide to underside of foliage. Also effective against leaf-hoppers on beans.
Potato beetle	Potatoes Eggplant Tomatoes	5 percent carbaryl	2 tb. wettable carbaryl in 1 gal. water	Apply when beetles or grubs first appear and repeat as necessary.
Squash bug	Squash	Parathion		Adults and brown egg masses can be hand-picked. Trap adults under shingles beneath plants. Kill young bugs soon after they hatch. Certified applicator only.
Squash vine borer	Squash	5 percent carbaryl	2 tb. wettable carbaryl in 1 gal. water	Dust or spray once a week for 3 to 4 weeks beginning in late June when first eggs hatch. Treat crowns of plants and runners thoroughly.

Insects are about natural size except where otherwise indicated. Where two drawings are shown, the smaller one is natural size. One pound of dust or 3 gallons of spray should be sufficient to treat 350 feet of row.
tb. = tablespoon.
tsp. = teaspoon.

Table 11.3—Limitations for Field Vegetables in Days Between Application and Harvest and Other Restrictions on Use of Insecticides in Illinois.

(Blank spaces indicate that the material is not suggested for the specific use in Illinois)

Insecticide	Beans	Peas	Broccoli	Brussels sprouts	Cabbage	Cauliflower	Horse-radish[1]	Radish[1]	Turnip[1]	Onions	Eggplant	Peppers	Tomatoes
acephate (Orthene)	...	...	...	...	...	...	...	...	...	...	...	7	...
azinphosmethyl (Guthion)*[2]	...	...	...	...	...	...	...	...	...	...	...	...	...
Bacillus thuringiensis[3]	...	...	15	7	21	15	...	...	...	...	...	0	0
carbaryl (Sevin)	0	...	0	0	0	0	...	...	...	...	0	0	0
carbofuran (Furadan)	...	...	3	3	3	3	3	3	3, 14A	0	0	21B	...
Dasanit	...	...	...	...	...	...	...	...	...	C, D	...	...	...
demeton (Systox)*	...	...	5	...	7	5	...	...	...	...	...	3	...
diazinon	...	...	...	...	...	...	...	10	10	10	...	...	1
dicofol (Kelthane)	7E	...	...	...	...	...	...	...	...	...	2	2	2
dimethoate (Cygon)	0E	0E	7	...	3	7	...	...	14	...	...	0	7
Dyfonate	...	...	C	...	C	C	...	...	...	...	...	...	...
ethion	...	...	3	...	...	...	7	7	3	C	3	...	...
malathion	1	...	3	7	7	7	7	7	3	3	3	3	1
methomyl (Lannate)*	...	1, 5A	3	3	1	3	...	...	3	...	10	10	2
mevinphos (Phosdrin)[2]	...	...	1	3	1	3	...	...	3	...	...	...	...
Monitor	...	...	21	21	35	28	...	...	4	...	...	...	...
naled (Dibrom)	...	...	1	1	1	1	...	...	...	...	...	...	...
oxydemetonmethyl (Meta-Systox R)	...	...	...	...	...	...	...	...	...	...	7F	0B	...
parathion*[2]	7	...	7	7	10	7	...	15	10	...	15	15	10
phorate (Thimet)[2]	C	...	...	7	...	...	...	10	...	...	...	...	...
rotenone	...	...	...	...	...	...	...	...	...	...	1	1	1
trichlorfon (Dylox)	...	...	21	21	21	21	...	...	28E	...	...	21	21

(Continued)

Table 11.3 (Continued).

Insecticide	Potatoes[1]	Collards	Kale	Lettuce	Spinach	Swiss chard	Sweet corn	Cucumbers[4]	Melons[4]	Pumpkins[4]	Squash[4] Winter	Squash[4] Summer
Bacillus thuringiensis[3]	...	0	0	0	0	...	...	...	...	...	...	...
carbaryl (Sevin)	0	14	14	14	14	14	0	0	0	0	0	0
diazinon	...	10	10	10	10	12	C	7	3	...	3	7
dicofol (Kelthane)	...	...	...	...	...	...	...	2	2	2	2	2
dimethoate (Cygon)	0	14	14	14	14	14	...	...*	3	...	...	...
Dyfonate	...	...	...	...	...	...	C	...	...	...	...	...
malathion	0	7	7	14	7	7	5	1	1	3	1	1
methomyl (Lannate)*	6	...	7	10	7	...	0, 3A	3	3	...	...	3
mevinphos (Phosdrin)*[2]	...	3	3	2	4	...	...	3	3	...	...	3
Mocap	...	...	...	...	...	...	C	...	...	...	...	...
naled (Dibrom)	...	4	4	1	1	1	...	...	...	...	...	...
parathion*[2]	5	10	10	21	14	21	12	15	7	10	15	15
phorate (Thimet)[2]	C	...	...	...	...	...	C	...	...	...	...	...
rotenone	C	1	1	1	1	1	...	...	...	...	...	...
trichlorfon (Dylox)	...	28G	21	28G	...	...	...	...	...	3F	...	...

*Use restricted to certified applicators only.

1. Root crops such as radishes, turnips, carrots, horseradish, potatoes, and sugar beets should not be grown in soil where aldrin, dieldrin, or heptachlor was applied as a soil insecticide the preceding year.

2. Use only by professional applicators or commercial gardeners.

3. Trade names are Bactur, Dipel, and Thuricide.

4. Only apply insecticide late in the day after blossoms have closed to reduce bee kill.

A. If tops or stover are to be used as feed.

B. Not more than twice per season.

C. Soil applications at planting time only.

D. Do not use on green onion crop.

E. Do not use tops for feed or food.

F. Not more than three times per season.

G. Not after edible portions or heads begin to form.

University of Illinois Cooperative Extension Circular 897.

for several minutes, or heating the soil with live steam. Where live steam is available, as in steam-heated greenhouses, steam treatment is the most practical method.

For best results, soil sterilization should be combined with seed treatment. While sterilization of the soil will control many diseases which begin with seed germination, it will not control those which are seed-borne rather than soil-borne. These are controlled by coating the seeds with a good seed protectant, either as a dust or a slurry. Seed treatment is especially important where soil sterilization is not feasible, such as in field seedings.

Seed can be purchased already treated at the packaging house, or it can be treated by the vegetable grower, usually without any special equipment. Some of the materials which are commonly used for seed treatment are captan and thiram.

After seedlings have been transplanted in the field or field seedlings have sprouted and begun to develop, the next stage of disease prevention must be considered. Occasionally some seedlings such as cabbage and pepper can be dipped in a fungicide solution just before transplanting to provide further protection while the plants are adjusting to climatic and soil changes.

"Preventive" Applications of Fungicides

Best results are obtained when the fungicides are applied before there is any evidence of plant damage. Fungicides should be applied to protect the plants during the stage when they are susceptible to pathogens. In some rare instances, applications can be delayed until disease symptoms appear without seriously affecting the crop. However, with crops whose sale value depends strongly on appearance, such as celery and lettuce, this cannot become the practice.

Usually, fungicides can be applied as dusts or sprays, but sprays are generally preferable because the films stick more readily, remain longer, and can be applied during any time of day. Dusts can be applied only when there is little or no wind. In applying a fungicide, one important fact should be kept in mind—only that portion of a plant which has a coating of dust or spray film is protected from disease (Fig. 11.1).

Applications must be repeated whenever the coating or film wears off. In common practice applications are made at 7- to 10-day intervals. In wet weather more frequent applications are necessary for two reasons: (1) the fungicide may be washed off by the rain and (2) some dis-

Fig. 11.1—Spraying potatoes for diseases and insect control.

Firestone Tire and Rubber Co. Photograph

ease pathogens survive better during wet or damp weather than during dry weather.

Failure to obtain good disease control can be due to one or a combination of the factors previously listed as responsible for insect-control failures.

CONTROL OF DISEASES WITH FUNGICIDES

Fungicides approved for use on vegetables are given in Table 11.4. This table was taken from Illinois Circular 999, which suggests control measures for the 1979 season. The commercial grower must follow a disease-control program that will assure the production of vegetables with no excessive fungicide residues. Vegetables marketed with residues exceeding F.D.A. tolerances may be injurious to consumers, may be confiscated, and may cause the grower to be brought to court. Growers have nothing to fear from the law so long as they use fungicides and other pesticides according to the current label only on crops specified, in the amounts specified, and at the times specified. Check with the latest recommendations before using any pesticide.

Table 11.4—Fungicide Uses for Vegetables, Approved by the EPA, October 1, 1978.[a, b]

Crop	Benlate, 0.2-15 ppm	Captan (D) (See ppm Below)	Bravo, 0.1-15 ppm	Difolatan, 0.1-15 ppm	Dyrene, 10 ppm	Maneb, 4-10 ppm; Maneb with Zinc Salt	Mancozeb[c] (See ppm Below)	Zineb, 4-25 ppm
Asparagus	..	root dip	..	..	..		(0.1 ppm), A	A
Beans (dry, lima, snap)	14,[e] B (snap only)	(25 ppm), pp, 0[e]	7,[e] B (snap only)	..	..	A[d] / 0[e]	..	7[e]
lima	28					4 on limas or snap		
Beet, garden		(2 ppm-root, 100 ppm-greens), 0, pp	..				..	7 (tops)
Broccoli		(2 ppm), pp	0[e]			(10 ppm), 3 or trim and wash	..	7
Brussels sprouts	..	(2 ppm), pp	0	..	..		..	..
Cabbage	..	(2 ppm), pp	0	..	..	7	..	7
Cantaloupe (muskmelon)	0	(25 ppm), 0, ph,[d] pp	0	0[e]	0[e]	(10 ppm), 7 / 5	0 ppm in edible parts), 5[e]	5
Carrot	..	(2 ppm), 0	0	..	..	(7 ppm), 0	(2 ppm), 7, B (tops)	7 (tops)
Cauliflower	..	(2 ppm), pp	0	..	0	0	..	7
Celery	(3 ppm), 7	(50 ppm), 0, pb	7	..	0	(5 ppm), strip and wash, 14	(5 ppm), 14	strip and wash, 14
Chinese cabbage			14, B[f]					7
Corn, sweet and pop	..	(2 ppm), 10, B, pp	0	..	..	..	(0.5 ppm-cob and kernel), 7 (5 ppm-fodder and forage, 0.5 ppm-ears)	O, B, C
Cucumber	(1 ppm), 0	(25 ppm), 0, ph, pp	0	0	0	(4 ppm), 5	(4 ppm), 7	5
Eggplant	..	(25 ppm), 0, ph, pb	..	..	..	0	..	0
Endive, escarole	..	..	..	..	..	(10 ppm), 7 and wash	..	10
Fennel	..						7	..
Kale, collard	..	(2 ppm), pp	..	..	..	(10 ppm), 10 and wash	..	10
Kohlrabi	..	(100 ppm), 0	..	..	..	0	..	
Lettuce						(10 ppm), 7 (strip and wash)		(half grown)

(Continued)

Table 11.4 (Continued).

Crop	Benlate, 0.2-15 ppm	Captan (D) (See ppm Below)	Bravo, 0.1-15 ppm	Difolatan, 0.1-15 ppm	Dyrene, 10 ppm	Maneb, 4-10 ppm Maneb with Zinc Salt	Mancozeb[c] (See ppm Below)	Zineb, 4-25 ppm
Mustard greens	..	(2 ppm), pp	..	..	..	(10 ppm), 10 and wash	..	10
Onion	..	(50 ppm green, 25 dry), 0, ph	0	0	0	(7 ppm), 0	(0.5 ppm dry), 7, D	10
Peas	..	(2 ppm), pp	..	..	..	..	..	10, C
Pepper	..	(25 ppm), 0, pb, pp	..	..	..	(7 ppm), 0	E	0
Potato, Irish[d]	..	(25 ppm), 0, ph	0	0	0	(0.1 ppm), 0, C	(1.0 ppm), 0	0 and seed, C, pp
Pumpkin	..	(25 ppm), 0, pp	0	..	0	(7 ppm), 0	..	0
Radish	..	..	..	..	0	..	..	0
Rhubarb (greenhouse)	..	(25 ppm), 0	..	..	..	..	..	..
Spinach	(1 ppm), 0	(100 ppm), 0, pp	..	..	..	(10 ppm), 0	..	10
Squash	..	(25 ppm), 0, pp	0	..	0	7 and wash	(4 ppm), 5	5
Sugar beet[d]	(0.2 ppm-roots, 15 ppm-tops), 21	0	..	..	..	(7 ppm), 5 10, B C, 14, no feeding restrictions	65 ppm-roots, (2 ppm-tops), B, 14	..
Swiss chard	..	0	0	0[g]	0	..	..	10
Tomato	(5 ppm), 0	(25 ppm), 0, pp	0	0	0	(4 ppm), 5, F 10 and wash	(4 ppm), 5	5
Turnip, rutabaga	..	(2 ppm), pp	..	..	..	..	..	(7 ppm), 7-tops
Watermelon	(1 ppm), 0	(25 ppm), 0, pp	0	0	0	5	(0 ppm edible parts), 5[e]	5

a. No tolerances have been set for these fungicides on dill, horseradish, okra, parsley, and parsnip.
b. The following abbreviations are used:
A = Post-harvest application to ferns only or to young plantings that will not be harvested.
B = Do not feed treated tops or forage to livestock.
C = Do not use treated seed or seed pieces for feed or food.
D = Do not apply to exposed bulbs.
E = Do not apply after fruit buds form.
F = To avoid damage, do not use on tender young plants.
pb = Plant bed treatment.
ph = Post-harvest spray or dip.
pp = Preplant soil treatment.
c. Mancozeb is sold as Dithane M-45 and Manzate 200.
d. Tolerances are not needed for pesticides applied only to the foliage and not translocated to the tubers or roots.
e. Number indicates number of days between last application and harvest; 0 = up to harvest.
f. Do not apply if crop is to be used for processing.
g. Machine harvest only.

Antibiotics

Antibiotics are relatively new in plant disease control. Strangely enough they are produced by living fungi. At present streptomycin is used primarily on bacterial diseases such as bacterial spot on peppers and tomatoes, but occasionally it is effective against some fungus diseases. It has been recommended on plant growing beds and potato seed pieces.

Nematodes

Nematodes are neither insects nor fungi, but they do injure all vegetable crops to some degree, depending on the crop, soil type, and the consecutive number of years a crop has been planted on the same field.

Nematodes are small eelworms, usually less than 1/16 inch long, which live in and on the roots and surrounding soil of all vegetable crops. One nematode is probably familiar to the reader—the root knot nematode. It receives its name from the small, distinct galls that it causes on the roots of cabbage and other crucifers. These galls vary from the size of a pinhead to an inch in diameter.

Nematodes usually feed and produce their young on roots of a great number of plants. They live in the soil and in decaying vegetable material from one year to the next. The importance of their damage has just been recognized in the past few years.

These tiny pests can be controlled in two major ways: (1) A nematode-resistant crop can be included in the rotation. (2) The soil can be fumigated. A fumigant (nematocide) applied several inches deep will spread evenly through the soil and kill the nematodes.

Combining Insecticides with Fungicides

Disease and insect problems frequently occur at the same time. Under such circumstances, both insecticide and fungicide may be applied together in one operation—provided they are compatible. Some materials, however, are not compatible with others. Applying incompatible materials together can reduce control of the insect, the disease, or both. This happens through chemical action or breakdown of the compounds in the spray tank.

To be certain that two materials can be mixed in the same spray application, compatibility charts should be consulted. These are charts that show which materials can and which cannot be mixed together. They are usually available on request from your pesticide dealer.

SAFE HANDLING OF INSECTICIDES AND FUNGICIDES

Practically all of the insecticides and fungicides commercially available are toxic to man and animals. The persons most likely to encounter these hazards are the operators and applicators.

They may have insecticides and fungicides enter the body in three ways: by ingestion, or swallowing; by breathing the dusts or vapors; or by absorption through the skin. One form can prove just as fatal as the other, but most cases of poisoning occur through accidental eating or drinking of materials which have lost their labels or have been placed in other containers. Unfortunately children are the most frequent victims of such adult carelessness. Because of this, all materials should be kept in their original containers and locked up or placed out of the reach of children.

There are 12 general rules to follow when handling any of these materials:

1. Read carefully the warning statement and directions for use on the container BEFORE beginning the operation, and use only as recommended.
2. Become familiar with the antidote in case of accidental ingestion.
3. Wear the prescribed clothing, such as rubber gloves, respirator, coveralls, or a rubber suit, with such extremely toxic materials as parathion, phorate, methomyl, and mevinphos.
4. Wash hands before smoking or eating.
5. If clothing becomes saturated with liquid or dust, remove it immediately, take a bath or shower, and change into clean clothes.
6. Keep a special set of old clothes on hand just for handling and applying these materials.
7. At the end of each day's work with these materials take a bath or shower and make a complete change of clothing.
8. Fill tanks and hoppers, treat seeds, make dilutions, etc., in well ventilated places.
9. Do not walk or ride in the downwind trail of dust or spray applications without protective clothing and respirators.
10. Burn or destroy empty containers of highly toxic insecticides and stay out of the smoke.
11. Keep these materials out of reach of children and do not use on warm-blooded animals, in the house, etc.
12. Call a physician if poisoning symptoms occur after handling toxic materials. Such symptoms might be: headaches, dizziness, nausea, and vomiting.

WARNING: Parathion, phorate azinphosmethyl, methomyl, demeton, and mevinphos are extremely effective insecticides, but they are also highly poisonous to human beings if inhaled, absorbed through the skin, or swallowed. They are not, therefore, used in the recommendations of this text. They should be applied only by certified applicators who have the experience, knowledge, and safety equipment necessary to protect all concerned. Danger may be minimized when applying the pesticides recommended here only by rigidly and constantly following the safety precautions listed above.

Sources of Control Recommendations

By the time any publication on insect or disease control reaches the user it has become outdated by more recent results of research. Such is the case with recommendations in this chapter and accounts for the general rather than the specific control measures found here. For a specific insect or a disease on a certain crop, the reader should consult more detailed information from reliable sources.

Insect and disease control recommendations come from many sources, but the most dependable are issued by the U.S. Department of Agriculture, state experiment stations, and the agricultural extension service. The latter is represented by the county agricultural agents and the extension entomologist and plant pathologist. Most control recommendations can be obtained through the county agent's office. U.S. Department of Agriculture publications not available from him can be purchased from the Superintendent of Documents, U.S. Government Printing Office, Washington, D.C. 20402.

Sources of Insect and Disease Identification

Frequently vegetable producers find insects or diseased plants which they cannot identify. These problems should be carried to the local county agricultural agent or sent to the extension specialists concerned who are located at Land Grant Universities and Colleges.

Insect pests, including immature stages if possible, should be carefully wrapped in soft tissue paper (soft-bodied insects such as caterpillars preserved in 70 percent alcohol), packaged in a small can, plastic box, or other strong container, and sent by first class mail to the extension entomologist.

Plant disease specimens should include entire plants, when possible, with the roots wrapped in moist soil, peat moss, or sawdust. They should be carefully packed in a strong container and mailed first class to the extension plant pathologist. *A letter should always be attached to the package describing the crop, area, fungicide or insecticide history, location, and type of damage. The more information given the specialist, the easier it will be for him to identify the specimens.*

SELECTED REFERENCES

Afanasiev, M. M., "Potato Diseases in Montana and Their Control," Mont. State Univ. Coop. Ext. Ser. Bull. 329, 1970.

Anonymous, "Insect Control for Commercial Vegetable Crops and Greenhouse Vegetables," Ill. Coop. Ext. Ser. Circ. 897, 1979.

Banham, T. L., and Arraud, J. C., "Recognition and Life History of the Major Insect and Allied Pests of Vegetables in British Columbia," Victoria, B.C., Dept. of Agr., 1970.

Burgess, E. E., and Mullett, R. P., "How to Control Commercial Vegetable Insects," Univ. of Tenn. Agr. Ext. Ser. EC 817, 1977.

Carruth, L. A., "Home Garden Pests," Univ. of Ariz. Bull., 1974.

Cuthbert, F. P., Jr., "Insects Affecting Sweet Potatoes," USDA *Agriculture Handbook 329*, 1967.

Gentile, A. G., *et al.*, "Insect, Disease and Weed Control for Vegetable Crops in Massachusetts," Univ. of Mass. Coop. Ext. Ser., 1978.

Hadden, C. H., "How to Control Vegetable Diseases," Univ. of Tenn. Agr. Ext. Ser. Pub. 716, 1977.

Miller, R. L., "Home Vegetable Garden Insect Control," Ohio State Univ. Coop. Ext. Ser. Bull. 498, 1978.

Miller, R. L., and Farley, J. D., "Vegetable Insect and Disease Control," Ohio State Univ. Coop. Ext. Ser. Bull. 459, 1978.

Pimentel, D., Shoemaker, C., and Whitman, R. J., "Systems Management Program for Corn Pest Control in New York State," N. Y. State Col. Agr. Cornell Univ. Exp. Sta. Vol. 8, No. 1, 1978.

Rings, R. W., "A Pictorial Field Key to the Armyworms and Cutworms Attacking Vegetables in the North Central States," Ohio Agr. Res. Circ. 231, 1977.

Schultz, O. E., "Foliar Diseases of Corn in New York," N. Y. State Col. Agr. Cornell Univ. Inf. Bull. 70, 1974.

Shurtleff, M. C., and Jacobsen, B., "Fungicide Guide for Commercial Vegetable Growers," Ill. Coop. Ext. Ser. Circ. 999, 1979.

Spackman, E. W., "Vegetable Garden Insect Control," Univ. Wyo. Agr. Ext. Ser. Bull. 539R, 1978.

Turnquist, O. C., *et al.*, "Weed, Insect, and Disease Control Guide for Commercial Vegetable Growers," Univ. of Minn. Agr. Ext. Ser. Spec. Rep. 5, 1978.

Ware, G. W., *The Pesticide Book*, San Francisco: W. H. Freeman & Co., 1978.

Ware, G. W., *Pesticides—An Autotutorial Approach*, San Francisco: W. H. Freeman & Co., 1975.

Watson, T. F., Moore, L., and Ware, G. W., *Practical Insect Pest Management*, San Francisco: W. H. Freeman & Co., 1976.

Wells, A., Potter, H. S., and Bird, G., "Control of Insects, Diseases and Nematodes on Commercial Vegetables," Mich. State Univ. Coop. Ext. Ser. Bull. 312, 1978.

CHAPTER 12

Storing Vegetables

The different vegetables vary widely in perishability. Some can be stored for several months, while others retain quality for only three or four days in storage. For those that store well, storage is essential to prolong the season and facilitate orderly marketing. Many of the very perishable crops are often grown some distance from market. They have to be handled promptly and stored under proper conditions until they reach the consumer. Some of the vegetables grown for home use may be stored so that they can be used over a longer period.

Fresh vegetables intended for storage should be as free as possible from skin breaks, bruises, decay, and other deteriorations. Bruises and other mechanical damage not only detract from the appearance of the product but are the principal avenues for entrance of decay organisms. Mechanical damage also increases moisture loss. Skinned potatoes may lose three or four times as much moisture as ones with unblemished skins.

Maximum storage life of vegetables can be obtained only by storing a high quality product harvested at the right maturity, free from injuries and diseases, and stored promptly. Different lots of the same vegetable may vary greatly in their storage behavior. Keeping quality may be influenced by cultivar, climate, soil, cultural conditions, maturity, and handling practices before storage.

STORAGE REQUIREMENTS

Temperature

Refrigerated storage is recommended because it retards: (1) respi-

ration and other metabolic activity; (2) aging due to ripening, softening, textural, and color changes; (3) moisture loss and wilting; (4) spoilage due to invasion by bacteria, fungi, and yeast; and (5) undesirable
growths, such as potato sprouts. The temperature of storage rooms
should remain fairly constant. Fluctuations may cause condensation of
moisture on stored products, which encourages growth of molds and
decay organisms. Variations in temperature can usually be prevented
if the storage rooms are well insulated throughout and the refrigeration
adequate, with a small spread between the temperature of the refriger-
ant and that of the storage room.

Precooling

The rapid removal of field heat before storage or shipment is essential for the perishable vegetables and is referred to as precooling. The
more quickly field heat is removed after harvest, the longer produce can
be maintained in good condition in storage. Rooms designed for holding
vegetables in storage usually do not have the cooling capacity or the
air movement for rapid cooling. Precooling may be accomplished by
several methods. All involve the rapid transfer of heat from the commodity to the cooling medium, such as water, ice, or air. Precooling
may require from 30 minutes to 24 hours. The rate of cooling is primarily dependent upon four factors: (1) the accessibility of the product
to the refrigerating medium, (2) the difference in temperature between
the produce and the refrigerating medium, (3) the velocity of the refrigerating medium, and (4) the kind of cooling medium.

Hydrocooling is the method by which produce is immersed in
water. It can be one of the most rapid and effective methods of removing heat from produce. The water must be sufficiently cold, and the
produce must be left in long enough to remove the heat. Asparagus,
sweet corn, celery, carrots, and radishes are often hydrocooled. Recir-
culating the water may disseminate decay organisms, which could adversely affect the storage of a product.

Crushed ice placed in containers with produce or on top of the
crates can give effective precooling. This method is often used in the
shipping of leafy vegetables such as spinach. Produce may be cooled
with rapidly moving refrigerated air. The method can be adapted to
storage rooms, rail cars, trucks, or conveyer tunnels.

Vacuum cooling to remove field heat from vegetables was used for
the first time in 1948. Now it is used for most of the lettuce shipped

from California and Arizona. Some celery, cauliflower, green peas, radishes, and sweet corn are vacuum cooled. Lettuce is packed in cartons, which are placed in a large steel chamber that is hermetically sealed and evacuated rapidly. Pressure is reduced to about 4.6 mm. of mercury, at which pressure water will boil at 32° F. Leafy vegetables will lose from 1.5 to 4.7 percent moisture during cooling. About 1 percent is lost for every 10° F. reduction in temperature. Prewetting can supply some of the water required for cooling, and it is particularly important for the rapid cooling of sweet corn. The rate of cooling is dependent largely upon the rate moisture is lost. Prompt refrigeration after cooling is essential.

Moisture

Relative humidity is an important factor affecting the keeping quality of vegetables in storage. If moisture is too low, they wilt or shrivel. If it is too high, the development of decay may be favored. For most vegetables, the relative humidity should be about 90 to 95 percent. Exceptions are noted in Table 12.1. Adequate relative humidity of the air in storage depends on providing good insulation, avoiding leaks, and maintaining the proper spread between the temperature of the cooling surface and that of the commodity in storage. The smaller the spread, the higher the humidity. If the refrigerating surface is not adequate to maintain the desired humidity, atomized water or steam should be added to the air. About 1 gallon of water per hour per ton of refrigeration should be adequate to maintain 95 percent relative humidity. If it is necessary to increase the relative humidity of common storage, the floor can be sprinkled occasionally.

Aeration

Air must be circulated to keep a cold-storage room at an even temperature throughout. Most rapid circulation is needed during the removal of field heat. After produce is cooled, air movement of 50 to 75 linear fpm through the stacks is usually sufficient to remove respiratory heat and that entering through doorways. A temperature difference of more than 1.5° F. between return and delivery air indicates an insufficient volume of cold air. As air follows the path of least resistance, uneven stacking may cause variable storage temperatures. The wide passages get a greater volume of air than the narrow ones.

Table 12.1—Recommended Temperature and Relative Humidity, Approximate Storage Life, Highest Freezing Point, Water Content, and Specific Heat for Fresh Vegetables in Commercial Storage.

Commodity	Tempera-ture	Relative Humidity	Approximate Length of Storage Period	Highest Freezing Point*	Water Content	Specific Heat**
	°F.	Percent		°F.	Percent	B.t.u./lb./°F.
Artichokes, globe	32	90–95	1 month	29.9	83.7	0.87
Artichokes, Jerusalem	31–32	90–95	2–5 months	...	79.8	.84
Asparagus	†32–36	95	2–3 weeks	30.9	93.0	.94
Beans, green or snap	†40–45	90–95	7–10 days	30.7	88.9	.91
Beans, lima	†32–40	90	1–2 weeks†	31.0	66.5	.73
Beets, bunched	32	95	10–14 days	31.3	...	...
Beets, topped	32	95	3–5 months	30.3	87.6	.90
Broccoli, sprouting	32	90–95	10–14 days	30.9	89.9	.92
Brussels sprouts	32	90–95	3–5 weeks	30.5	84.9	.88
Cabbage, early	32	90–95	3–6 weeks	30.4	92.4	.94
Cabbage, late	32	90–95	3–4 months	30.4	92.4	.94
Cabbage, Chinese	32	90–95	1–2 months	...	95.0	.96
Carrots, mature (topped)	32	90–95	4–5 months	29.5	88.2	.91
Carrots, immature (topped)	32	90–95	4–6 weeks	29.5	88.2	.91
Cauliflower	32	90–95	2–4 weeks	30.6	91.7	.93
Celeriac	32	90–95	3–4 months	30.3	88.4	.91
Celery	32	90–95	2–3 months	31.1	93.7	.95
Collards	32	90–95	10–14 days	30.6	86.9	.90
Corn, sweet	32	90–95	4–8 days	30.9	73.9	.79
Cucumbers	45–50	90–95	10–14 days	31.1	96.1	.97

(Continued)

Table 12.1 (Continued).

Commodity	Tempera-ture °F.	Relative Humidity Percent	Approximate Length of Storage Period	Highest Freezing Point* °F.	Water Content Percent	Specific Heat** B.t.u./lb./°F.
Eggplants	45–50	90	1 week	30.6	92.7	.94
Endive and escarole	32	90–95	2–3 weeks	31.9	93.1	.95
Garlic, dry	32	65–70	6–7 months	30.5	61.3	.69
Ginger rhizomes	55	65	6 months	...	87.0	.90
Greens, leafy	32	90–95	10–14 days	...	...	...
Horseradish	30–32	90–95	10–12 months	28.7	74.6	.80
Kale	32	90–95	10–14 days	31.1	86.6	.89
Kohlrabi	32	90–95	2–4 weeks	30.2	90.3	.92
Leeks, green	32	90–95	1–3 months	30.7	85.4	.88
Lettuce	32	95	2–3 weeks	31.7	94.8	.96
Melons:						
Cantaloupe (¾-slip)	36–40	85–90	15 days	29.9	92.0	.94
Cantaloupe (full-slip)	32–35	85–90	5–14 days	29.9	92.0	.94
Casaba	45–50	85–90	4–6 weeks	30.1	92.7	.94
Crenshaw	45–50	85–90	2 weeks	30.1	92.7	.94
Honey Dew	45–50	85–90	3–4 weeks	30.3	92.6	.94
Persian	45–50	85–90	2 weeks	30.5	92.7	.94
Watermelon	†40–50	80–85	2–3 weeks	31.3	92.6	.94
Mushrooms	32	90	3–4 days	30.4	91.1	.93
Okra	45–50	90–95	7–10 days	28.7	89.8	.92
Onions (dry) and onion sets	32	65–70	1–8 months ††	30.6	87.5	.90
Onions, green	32	90–95	...	30.4	89.4	.91
Parsley	32	90–95	1–2 months	30.0	85.1	.88
Parsnips	32	90–95	2–6 months	30.4	78.6	.83
Peas, green	32	90–95	1–3 weeks	30.9	74.3	.79

(Continued)

Table 12.1 (Continued).

Commodity	Temperature	Relative Humidity	Approximate Length of Storage Period	Highest Freezing Point*	Water Content	Specific Heat**
	°F.	Percent		°F.	Percent	B.t.u./lb./°F.
Peppers, chili (dry)	†32–50	60–70	6 months	...	12.0	.30
Peppers, sweet	45–50	90–95	2–3 weeks	30.7	92.4	.94
Potatoes, early-crop	(†)	90	(†)	30.9	81.2	.85
Potatoes, later-crop	(†)	90	(†)	30.9	77.8	.82
Pumpkins	50–55	70–75	2–3 months	30.5	90.5	.92
Radishes, spring	32	90–95	3–4 weeks	30.7	94.5	0.96
Radishes, winter	32	90–95	2–4 months	...	...	...
Rhubarb	32	95	2–4 weeks	30.3	94.9	.96
Rutabagas	32	90–95	2–4 months	30.1	89.1	.91
Salsify	32	90–95	do	30.0	79.1	.83
Spinach	32	90–95	10–14 days	31.5	92.7	.94
Squashes, winter	50–55	††50–75	(†)	30.5	85.1	.88
Squashes, summer	32–50	90	5–14 days†	31.1	94.0	.95
Sweet potatoes	†55–60	85–90	4–6 months	29.7	68.5	.75
Tomatoes, mature-green	†55–70	85–90	1–3 weeks	31.0	93.0	.94
Tomatoes, firm-ripe	45–50	85–90	4–7 days	31.1	94.1	.95
Turnips	32	90–95	4–5 months	30.1	91.5	.93
Turnip greens	32	90–95	10–14 days	31.7	90.3	.92
Watercress	32–35	90–95	3–4 days	31.4	93.3	.95

*Highest freezing points are from Whiteman, (739).

**Specific heat above freezing was calculated from Siebel's formula: S = 0.008 (percent water in food) + 0.20.

†See text.

††See text for cultivar differences.

Respiration and Metabolism

Respiration and other metabolic changes in vegetables are usually lowest just above their freezing points. Sweet corn in one day may lose 60 percent of its sweetness at 86° F., but only 6 percent when stored at 32° F. Some vegetables are injured at low temperatures (32° to 50° F.). At these temperatures they lose ability to carry on normal metabolic processes. Symptoms of chilling include pitting or other skin blemishes, internal discoloration, or failure to ripen. Chilled vegetables may also be more susceptible to decay. Chilling injury is cumulative and may begin in the field before harvest. Recommendations for storage of vegetables susceptible to chilling are given in Table 12.1 from USDA *Agriculture Handbook 66*.

Light

Most vegetables should be stored in the dark or at least in very reduced light; but some light does not seem to harm sweet potatoes, pumpkins, or shallots. Direct sunlight is generally injurious to stored material, but is not often an important factor.

Condition of Crop

The physical condition of stored vegetables does not improve in storage, but usually depreciates to some extent in spite of the best of care. This means that only the best products possible should be stored. They should be handled very carefully, and bruises or other mechanical injuries should be kept at a minimum. No decay or rot should be present, as this is likely to injure the healthy vegetables as well as those that are infected.

Sweet potatoes that are to be stored should be dug before the vines are killed by frost, if successful storage is expected. Before spring- or summer-dug Irish potatoes are placed in cold storage, they should be kept for 10 to 14 days at normal temperatures. The reason for this is that wounds will heal and the skins suberize much more readily at the higher temperatures when the relative humidity is high than they will at cold-storage temperatures. Another advantage of waiting is that the most rapid shrinkage occurs during the first few days and the amount of material on which storage will have to be paid will be reduced.

If Irish potatoes have been exposed to enough sun at digging time to cause injury, there is no use in attempting to store them. It is unwise to take a chance on storing vegetables in questionable condition.

Sanitation

It is very unwise to store excellent produce in places overrun with sources of rot infection. Sanitation is good storage insurance—it does not often entirely prevent rot, but it does help to keep rot at a minimum. The storage room should be kept as clean as possible, and when empty it should be thoroughly disinfected from time to time.

Protection from Rodents

Storage houses should be constructed as nearly rat-proof as possible. If rodents enter the house by coming from the field in storage containers or otherwise, they should be killed the easiest available way. Rats and mice not only directly destroy considerable produce or render it unmarketable, but they also increase loss from decay, since decay organisms find ready entrance to stored vegetables that have been gnawed by rodents.

STORAGE METHODS AND STRUCTURES

Storing in the Field

Vegetables such as cabbage and most of the root crops can be stored in the field in trenches, pits, or mounds. When freezing weather approaches, a well-drained place is selected. The vegetables may be placed in piles surrounded with straw and covered with just enough soil to prevent freezing injury. Ventilation can be provided by placing a flue in the center of the pile and extending it above the cover. In severe weather it can be closed.

Field storage is generally unsatisfactory. Temperature and moisture cannot be controlled, the produce is difficult to remove in disagreeable weather, and a large amount of labor is required.

Storing in Cellars

Where drainage permits, unheated cellars are used to some extent for storing some types of vegetables. Special attention should be given to ventilation, for, at best, cellars will usually have high humidities. Root crops may be successfully stored in them, and potatoes may be kept with fair success.

Storing in Above-Ground Houses

Storage houses can be used advantageously for such crops as onions and sweet potatoes that require a dry atmosphere. The storage can be readily ventilated providing some control of temperature and humidity, and the produce can be conveniently handled. Construction of the house may be varied depending upon the product and the climate.

Cold Storage

In this type of storage, produce is stored at fairly well-controlled low temperatures, and, in some storage houses, the humidity is also controlled. With a few exceptions, this is the ideal type of storage, especially in the South, where even in the winter great fluctuations in temperature and humidity cause considerable variation in most other types of storage. The disadvantages of this type of storage are its high cost and distance from the farm. However, the larger market gardeners may rent or own cold storage units and thus extend the marketing seasons.

Fig. 12.1—Cold storage of Valencia onions in California.

USDA Photograph

Most vegetables will keep for a time in cold storage, and many are easily kept. Cucumbers, however, will soon shrivel badly if kept under ordinary cold storage conditions. Most vegetables are kept in cold storage with temperatures ranging from 32° to 40° F. as shown in Table 12.1. Onions will keep best if stored in a dry atmosphere at a temperature of about 32° F. For root crops and cabbage, 33° to 35° F. is probably low enough, as too low temperatures may be injurious. Sometimes the temperature, even in controlled cold storage rooms, will vary, and if produce is being kept at 32° F., injury may occur if the temperature goes lower. Potatoes, sweet potatoes, pumpkins, squashes, and tomatoes require higher temperatures, as shown in Table 12.1.

SELECTED REFERENCES

Anonymous, "Relative Humidity Determination by the Wet-Dry Psychrometer Method," Hygrodynamics, Inc., Silver Spring, Md., Tech. Bull. 1, 4 pp., 1965.

Apeland, J., "Factors Affecting the Keeping Quality of Cucumbers," Internatl. Inst. Refrig. Bull. Sup. 1:45-58, 1961.

Barger, W. R., "Vacuum-Cooling Lettuce in Commercial Plants," U.S. Agr. Mkt. Serv. AMS-469, 1962.

Barger, W. R., "Vacuum Precooling—A Comparison of the Cooling of Different Vegetables," USDA Mkt. Res. Rep. 600, 1963.

Bennett, A. H., and Kaufman, J., "An Evaluation of Methods for Cooling Potatoes in Long Island Storages," USDA Mkt. Res. Rep. 494, 1961.

Bogardus, R. K., "Wholesale Fruit and Vegetable Warehouses—Guides for Layout and Design," USDA Mkt. Res. Rep. 467, 1961.

Bogardus, R. K., and Lutz, J. M., "Maintaining the Fresh Quality in Produce in Wholesale Warehouses," *Agr. Mkt.* 6(12), 1961.

Buelow, F. H., "Potatoes: Production and Storage," Univ. of Wisc., Coop. Ext. Ser. Pub. A2257, 1978.

Comin, D., "Inhibiting Sprouting of Potatoes and Onions in Storage," Ohio Agr. Exp. Sta. Res. Bull, 874, 1961.

Cook, J. A., "Precooling Fruits and Vegetables for Marketing," Mich. State Univ. Ext. Folder F-285, 1960.

Davis, H. R., Isenberg, F. M. R., and Furry, R. B., "The Control of Natural-Air Cabbage Storage Environment," N. Y. State Col. of Agr., Cornell Univ., Coop. Ext. Ser. Inf. Bull. 137, 1978.

Eaves, C. A., and Lockhart, C. L., "Storage of Tomatoes in Artificial Atmospheres Using the Calcium Hydroxide Absorption System," *HortSci.* 36(2), 1961.

Edgar, A. D., "Shell Ventilation Systems for Potato Storages in the Fall Crop Area," USDA Mkt. Res. Rep. 579, 1963.

Ezell, B. D., and Wilcox, M. S., "Loss of Vitamin C in Fresh Vegetables as Related to Wilting and Temperature," *Jour. Agr. and Food Chem.* 7, 1959.

Fluck, R. C., and Kushman, L. J., "Pallet Boxes and Palletized Containers for Handling and Storing Sweet Potatoes," U.S. Agr. Res. Serv. ARS 52-2, 1965.

Francis, F. J., and Thomson, C. L., "Optimum Storage Conditions for Butternut Squash," *Proc. Amer. Soc. Hort. Sci.* 86, 1965.

Guillow, Rene, and Richardson, H. B., "Humidity's Valuable Role in Keeping Produce Cool," *Produce Market* 8(2), 1965.

Hall, C. B., "The Effect of Low Storage Temperature on the Color, Carotenoid Pigments, Shelf Life and Firmness of Ripened Tomatoes," *Proc. Amer. Soc. Hort. Sci.* 78, 1961.

Harvey, J. M., "Improved Techniques for Vacuum Cooling Vegetables," *ASHRAE Jour.* 5(11), 1963.

Heikal, H. A., and Ismail, M. M., "Cold Storage of Carrots," Agr. Res. Rev. (United Arab Republic) 42(1), 1964.

Hunter, J. H., and Toko, H. V., "Control of Potato-Storage Diseases as Affected by Air Flow, Temperature and Relative Humidity," *Amer. Soc. Agr. Engin. Trans.* 8, 1966.

Isenberg, F. M., and Ang, J. K., "Northern-Grown Onions, Curing, Storing, and Inhibiting Sprouting," N. Y. State Col. Agr., Cornell Ext. Bull. 1116, 1963.

Johnson, E. F., Toko, H. V., and Wilson, J. B., "Pallet Boxes vs. Deep Bins. A Comparison of Potato Quality Control," Me. Agr. Exp. Sta. Bull. 636, 1965.

Kaufman, J., and Ceponis, M. J., "Extended Shelf Life for Green Lima Beans," *Produce Market* 5(7), 1962.

Kushman, L. J., and Wright, F. S., "Overhead Ventilation of Sweet Potato Storage Rooms," N. C. Agr. Exp. Sta. Tech. Bull. 166, 1965.

Lentz, C. P., "Moisture Loss of Carrots Under Refrigerated Storage," *Food Technol.* 20(4), 1966.

Lentz, C. P., "Temperature, Air Movement and Moisture Loss in Fresh Fruit and Vegetable Storages," *Proc. 11th Internatl. Cong. Refrig.* (1963) 2, 1965.

Lipton, W. J., "Effect of Atmosphere Composition on Quality. In California Asparagus: Effect of Transit Environments on Market Quality," USDA Mkt. Res. Rep. 428, 1960.

Lipton, W. J., and Stewart, J. K., "Effect of Hydrocooling on the Market Quality of Cantaloupes," *Proc. Amer. Soc. Hort. Sci.* 78, 1961.

Lipton, W. J., and Stewart, J. K., "Effects of Precooling on the Market Quality of Globe Artichokes," USDA Mkt. Res. Rep. 633, 1963.

Lutz, J. M., and Hardenburg, R. E., "The Commercial Storage of Fruits, Vegetables, and Florist and Nursery Stocks," USDA *Agriculture Handbook 66,* 1968.

McColloch, L. P., "Chilling Injury of Eggplant Fruits," USDA Mkt. Res. Rep. 749, 1966.

McColloch, L. P., and Yeatman, J. N., "Color Changes and Chilling Injury of Pink Tomatoes Held at Various Temperatures," USDA Mkt. Res. Rep. 735, 1966.

McKeown, A. W., Lougheed, E. C., and Murr, D. P., "Compatability of Cabbage,

Carrots, and Apples in Low-Pressure Storage," *J. Amer. Soc. Hort. Sci.* 103 (6): 747-752, 1978.

Parsons, C. S., McColloch, L. P., and Wright, R. C., "Cabbage, Celery, Lettuce, and Tomatoes, Laboratory Tests of Storage Methods," USDA Mkt. Res. Rep. 402, 1960.

Porrit, S. W., "Commercial Storage of Fruits and Vegetables," Information Office, 930 Carlin Ave., Ottawa, Ont., Pub. 1532, 1976.

Redit, W. H., Heinze, P. H., and Hunter, J. H., "Storage and Transportation of Potatoes," Potato Assoc. *Amer. Potato Handbook,* 1963.

Sawyer, R. L., Boyd, L. L., Cetal, R. C., and Bennett, A. H., "Potato Storage Research on Long Island with Forced Air Ventilation Systems," N. Y. State Col. Agr., Cornell Exp. Sta. Bull. 1002, 1965.

Schales, F. D., and Isenberg, F. M., "The Effect of Curing and Storage on Taste Acceptability of Winter Squash," *Proc. Amer. Soc. Hort. Sci.* 83, 1963.

Showalter, R. K., Spurlock, A. H., Greig, W. S., *et al.,* "Long Distance Marketing of Fresh Sweet Corn," Fla. Agr. Exp. Sta. Bull. 638, 1961.

Smith, W. H., "Storage of Vegetables," *N. A. A. S. Quart. Rev.* 63, 1964.

Stewart, J. K., and Barger, W. R., "Effects of Cooling Method and Topicing on the Quality of Peas and Sweet Corn." *Proc. Amer. Soc. Hort. Sci.* 75, 1960.

Stewart, J. K., and Barger, W. R., "Effects of Cooling Method on the Quality of Asparagus and Cauliflower," *Proc. Amer. Soc. Hort. Sci.* 78, 1961.

Stewart, J. K., and Couey, H. M., "Hydrocooling Vegetables—A Practical Guide to Predicting Final Temperatures and Cooling Times," USDA Mkt. Res. Rep. 637, 1963.

Van Den Berg, L., and Lentz, C. P., "Effect of Temperature, Relative Humidity, and Atmospheric Composition on Changes in Quality of Carrots During Storage," *Food Technol.* 20, 1966.

Wager, H. G., "Physiological Studies of the Storage of Green Peas," *Jour. Sci. Food and Agr.* 15, 1964.

CHAPTER 13

Harvesting, Handling, and Marketing

The overall harvesting, handling, and marketing of vegetables are an involved series of procedures which tax the skills and ingenuity of people in the vegetable industry. Not only must a vegetable crop be well grown but also it must be harvested at the right stage of maturity, carefully handled and packed, and delivered to the market or to the processor in prime condition. After vegetables reach harvest maturity, speedy operations are required by growers, handlers, marketing specialists, wholesalers, and retailers to move produce from the farm to the consumer. The various procedures are discussed in this chapter in their sequence.

MAINTAINING QUALITY

The maintenance of quality from farm to consumer is perhaps the most important requisite in vegetable marketing. To begin with, it is usually necessary to have vegetables with good shipping and handling characteristics, which include harvesting at the proper stage of maturity. Tomatoes harvested when red ripe may be suitable for local market or processing but not for shipment.

Appearance

From the standpoint of sales, appearance is the most important factor in products that can be seen at the time of selection for purchase. Indeed, it may be the only basis that the buyer has for evaluation. Particular attention should be given to uniformity of size, shape, color, and freedom from blemishes, wilting, and dirt.

Texture

Although texture of produce may not be apparent at the time of purchase, the consumer may subsequently be impressed with its importance. Imagine the disappointment in buying a nice-appearing bunch of asparagus only to find it so fibrous as to be inedible. Equally undesirable is stringiness in celery and snap beans or toughness in corn and peas. A slice of red tomato should enhance the appearance of a salad but will not when it is so soft that it falls apart when sliced. It is amazing that so many consumers have never eaten garden-fresh sweet corn or vine-ripened tomatoes and melons. Proper texture in fresh vegetables depends upon cultivar, stage of maturity, cultural conditions, and handling. These factors are discussed in the corresponding crop chapters of Section Two.

Flavor

In spite of the desirability of good flavor, this factor of quality plays only a minor role in the marketing of vegetables. It is less apparent than either appearance or texture, and the consumer usually has no standard by which to judge flavor. People differ in their tastes and usually prefer flavors to which they are accustomed. In many cases the natural flavors of vegetables are masked by the additives used in their preparation for the table. Such undesirable characteristics as off-flavors, bitterness, astringency, and pungency in vegetable products are easily recognized and generally affect consumer demand.

HARVESTING

When to Harvest

Some crops such as beets and carrots may be harvested over a period of several weeks, depending upon market demand. Others like asparagus, sweet corn, peas, and okra quickly pass through the stage of optimum edible maturity. Frequent and timely harvests of these crops are necessary if the growers wish to supply a discriminating market with high quality produce. In crops such as pickling cucumbers and snap beans, high quality but not high yields result from early harvesting. The time of harvesting will depend upon the desired quality and the premium paid for it.

Harvesting a crop before it is of acceptable quality in order to take advantage of a good market may reduce the demand for a product later in the season. However, early harvesting of some crops may also decrease field and handling losses. High temperatures hasten maturity and necessitate more frequent and timely harvesting of some crops.

Those vegetables which lose quality rapidly at high temperatures should be harvested in the early morning and kept as cool as possible. While the quality of snap beans, for example, may be reduced by high temperatures, a small degree of wilting may prevent breakage in spinach and asparagus and actually be beneficial.

Preventing Injury

Vegetables are subject to harvesting and handling damages, which may result in substantial losses. Organisms enter broken areas and cause decay and spoilage. Even slight bruises may darken the produce and present an unsightly appearance. Injuries also increase respiration and loss of weight and constituents of quality.

PREPARING FOR MARKET

Trimming and Washing

The appearance of vegetables may be improved by removing damaged, diseased, dead, or discolored parts. In some cases, however, the outer leaves offer protection and may even enhance the appearance of the product. Some field trimming is desirable for most vegetables, but sufficient wrapper leaves should be left on such crops as lettuce, cabbage, and celery for protection. Damaged and discolored leaves can be removed in the market as desired.

The market demands clean produce, so most vegetables should be washed after harvesting. Washing removes dirt, freshens the produce, and may remove spray residues. After the produce is washed, it should be kept cool to prevent the development of rot organisms. Most of the root crops should not be washed until they are marketed. Muskmelons, cucumbers, and sweet potatoes are usually cleaned by brushing or wiping dry, rather than by washing.

Grading

Grading, the sorting of vegetables so that the contents of each package will be fairly uniform, makes produce more salable and is usually a paying operation. Even products of second quality will present a better appearance when packed by themselves, with no first-class products in the same package. Uniformity appeals to the eye and suggests that the vegetables have been carefully handled (Fig. 13.1).

Fig. 13.1—Packing trays of tomatoes at wholesale fruit and vegetable terminal.

USDA Photograph

Broadly speaking, the further the grower is from market or the greater his marketing costs, the more carefully he must grade and pack, and the less likely he is to be able to sell culls and overmatured products. The nearer the grower is to market and the smaller the market costs, the better are his chances to sell low grades for something more than the cost of handling.

The U.S. Department of Agriculture has established uniform grades for each important vegetable, as discussed under the "Standardization and Inspection" section of this chapter.

Packing

Although vegetables are packed in local or shipping-point packing sheds, field packing of some vegetables such as lettuce and celery is common. Increasing attention is being given to standard uniform packs in sufficient quantity to attract volume buyers. Many large central packing operations have increased their facilities and production to such volume and efficiency that numerous small packing sheds have been forced to close. Farmers have found that the most economical packing can be done by cooperatives or large private packing facilities. Table 13.1 lists the types and respective net weights of the most common containers for various vegetables.

Considerable packaging of some products is now being done in convenient-size consumer units, which are packed in larger containers for shipment. This type of operation is increasing rapidly, and consumers now are able to buy many products in a variety of small attractive packages of fiberboard, polyethylene, shrink-film overwrap, and other materials.

Prepackaging

The use of consumer packages is important in the marketing of fresh vegetables. Such packages increase the cost of retail merchandising in the self-service stores, through which most food is now sold, but reduce product loss. Packages protect the product against dust and dirt and reduce losses due to dehydration or bruising from handling by customers. Also, brand names and other information on quality and usage is shown on packages to assist the consumer. Prepackaging is a specialized business, usually requiring elaborate equipment and cold storage.

There has been a substantial increase in the quantity of fresh vegetables marketed in consumer-sized packages. The most recent estimates indicate that 40 percent of total volume is so packaged. Prepackaging is more common for the less perishable vegetables like potatoes, onions, and carrots. Tender vegetables usually are not prepackaged because consumers prefer to examine each item for quality before purchasing it. Although most of the warehouse prepackaging is automated and computerized, some retailers prepackage various bulk deliveries in their own stores before presenting the items for sale.

Table 13.1—Approximate Unit Weights and Specifications of Common Containers Used in Packaging Commercial Vegetables.*

Principal Vegetables	Common Units or Packs and Specifications	Approximate Net Weight in Pounds	Approximate No. of Containers (Units) per Railroad Car
Asparagus	Pyramid carton or crate	30	1,600
Beans, green	Bu. basket, carton, crate, or hamper	30	1,400
Beets (topped)	Sacks, as marked	25 & 50	2,880 & 1,440
Broccoli	Carton or crate, 14-18 bunches	23	1,600
Brussels sprouts	Carton	25	1,840
Cabbage	Carton, crate, or sack	50	1,000-1,120
Cantaloupes	Jumbo crate	80	850
Carrots (bunched)	Carton or crate, 24's	26	3,076-3,230
Carrots (topped)	48 1-lb. film bags in carton, crate, or sack	48	1,667-1,750
Cauliflower	Carton, 12 to 16 film-wrapped, trimmed heads	22	1,682
Celery (Calif. or Fla.)	Carton or crate	60	1,100
Corn, sweet	Wirebound crate, 4½ to 5 doz.	42	1,190
Cucumbers	Bu. basket, carton, or crate and 1-1/9 bu. carton or crate	55	1,200
Eggplant	Bu. basket, carton, or crate and 1-1/9 bu. carton or crate	33	1,758
Garlic	Carton or crate	30	1,867
Lettuce, iceberg	Carton, 24's	50	1,200
Okra	Bu. basket, crate, or hamper	30	1,500
Onions, dry	Sacks, loose	25 & 50	2,120 & 1,060
Onions, green	Carton, 24 bunches	10	3,900
Peas, green	Bu. basket, crate, or hamper and 1-1/9 bu. crate	30	1,030
Peppers, bell	Bu. basket, carton, or crate and 1-1/9 bu. carton or crate	25	1,920
Potatoes	50-lb. carton and various-sized bags		50,000-85,000 lb.
Radishes, (topped)	Basket or carton, 30 6-oz. bags	12	5,000
Spinach and greens	Bu. basket, carton or crate	25	1,360
Squash (summer)	½-bu. basket, carton, or wirebound crate	21	2,381
Squash and pumpkins	Crate	50	**
Sweet potatoes	Carton or crate	50	**
Tomatoes	Carton	30	1,667-1,800
Watermelons	Cartons, various counts	75	600
Vegetables, NOS	½-bu. basket, carton, film, or mesh bag	25	2,400

*The packages and net weights listed are commonly used in the important producing areas of the United States. Other packages of different types, materials, and volume are used under various circumstances in different parts of the country. Because of the variable size of railroad cars and prevailing regulations and loading incentives in different areas, the number of containers per car varies. Information adapted from "Table of Container Net Weights" and "Table of Net Weights of Rail Cars and Piggyback Vans," USDA, Agricultural Marketing Service, issued January 1, 1978.

**Unavailable.

Fig. 13.2—A U.S. Department of Agriculture inspector examining prepackaged spinach before package is heat sealed.

USDA Photograph

HARVESTING AND HANDLING EQUIPMENT

Harvesting Equipment

As in production, machinery is used extensively for harvesting vegetable crops, especially those for processing. Machines reduce costs, but may increase injury, which is disadvantageous for produce intended for fresh market. With improvements in harvesters and cultivars adapted to machine harvesting, most of the produce, even for fresh market, will eventually be harvested mechanically. Crops grown on a small scale or for home use will still be harvested by hand. Vegetables which cannot be harvested mechanically may gradually disappear from the markets or be produced in areas where hand labor is inexpensive and plentiful. Information on the increase of labor efficiency is provided in Table 1.6 and in the specific vegetable chapters of Section Two. It will be noted that the labor or man-hour requirements per unit of produce has been decreased several fold in the last 35 years, particularly during recent years.

Grading and Packing Equipment

Since most fresh produce is marketed through chain stores, uniformly graded products are demanded. These are best prepared by central packing sheds which are well equipped for all grading, packing, and other services. Produce harvested in the rough is conveyed, trimmed, washed, sometimes waxed, graded, and labeled in a production-line process. For the small grower with independent outlets, grading and packing equipment may be relatively simple.

A consolidated mobile-grading and packaging unit, referred to as the "mule train," has been commonly used in Florida and some other areas for crops such as celery and sweet corn (Fig. 13.3). This method is declining as most of the crop moves in bulk to central packing houses for sorting, grading, and packaging for market.

Cooling

Various methods are used to remove field heat from produce. Vegetables may be stored in refrigerator space, but this method is slow. Some products can be dipped in cold water and cooled rapidly, while others may decay when wet. Vacuum cooling is commonly used for such crops as lettuce or sweet corn if they are wetted before evacuating to supply water for evaporation and thus cooling. The produce is packed in fiberboard boxes, placed in a chamber, and cooled without serious wilting from rapid evaporation. Only vegetables subject to rapid water loss can be cooled in this manner.

Customer Harvesting

Customer or pick-your-own (PYO) harvesting is not new, but high cost of labor for harvesting is making it attractive. The grower gets his crop harvested with no grading and packing problems, and the customer gets very fresh vegetables at reasonable prices. The success of a PYO operation is dependent on a location near a population center. Sweet corn, staked tomatoes, and pole beans are especially well suited for PYO harvesting. The operation should be planned carefully. Crops must be planted in blocks according to expected dates of harvests. The check-

Fig. 13.3—Harvesting and field packing of celery.

USDA Photograph

in and check-out station should be located between a convenient park-
ing area and the picking plots. The grower usually furnishes picking
equipment, and the customer provides take-home packages. The grower
should also have packages available. It is generally more satisfactory
to sell by weight, and a rapid weighing scale is a necessity.

COOPERATIVE MARKETING ASSOCIATIONS

The Economics, Statistics, and Cooperatives Service of the U.S. Department of Agriculture reported in 1976 that fruit and vegetable growers marketed approximately $3 billion worth of produce annually
through 436 cooperative associations. These cooperatives accounted for
nearly 3 percent of all marketing cooperative memberships and about 10
percent of the value of all farm products marketed cooperatively.

Fig. 13.4—California lettuce being loaded for refrigerated shipment.

USDA Photograph

Organizations and Services Vary

Cooperatives vary considerably in organization, membership, and services, but basically all are designed to improve the farmers' incomes. This is done through the voluntary joining together of physical, financial, and human resources in associations which provide marketing services and production supplies at cost. The services of cooperative vegetable associations range from cleaning, grading, packing, and storing to more complete marketing services including processing, selling, and merchandising under cooperative labels. Some of the larger associations also engage in product research and handle production and marketing supplies for their members.

Location and Volume of Business

Cooperatives serve vegetable growers throughout the country but are concentrated in areas known for volume production of high quality vegetables. California and Florida lead in number of fresh vegetable marketing associations. California, Oregon, and New York are important for vegetable processing cooperatives.

The trend in recent years has been toward a reduction in the number of vegetable associations and an increase in the volume of business and number of services offered. Volume of produce handled varies from a few hundred truck or carlots to 6,000 or more carlots in some of the major areas of production.

Basic Cooperative Principles

Principles that distinguish farmer cooperatives from other types of free enterprise businesses are: (1) democratic control by producer-members; (2) limited returns on capital invested, usually not more than 8 percent; and (3) service provided at cost with any savings being distributed in direct proportion to the patronage of each member.

TRANSPORTING

Year-round availability of fresh vegetables has become an essential feature of the American life. Without the growth of a vast transportation system linking specialized growing areas with centers of population, this availability would be impossible. Production is concentrated in a few high-yield areas with suitable yearly climates. Today, California and Florida produce over half of the nation's commercial vegetables.

Transportation Requirements

The transportation of vegetables involves special considerations not required in the movement of nonperishable commodities. Shipments must be moved rapidly enough to preserve the natural freshness of the produce, a major factor affecting the market price. The cost of movement per pound must be commensurate with the relatively low-unit value of vegetables in comparison with finished goods and other commodities. Transportation facilities must be adequate and flexible enough to accommodate the highly seasonal and fluctuating demands. These special requirements continue to tax the ingenuity of growers, transportation companies, and dealers in determining the most desirable means of transport.

Motor Truck and Rail Transportation

Most vegetables move to market by motor trucks or rail. The railroads dominated volume transportation of vegetables for many years, but trucks have taken the lead and are increasing their percentage of haul.

With improvement in the size, speed, and mechanical refrigeration of trucks (Fig. 1.1) and the development of farm to market roads and trunk line highways, trucks are increasing in popularity. Trucks transport large amounts of produce long distances, most vegetables middistances, and practically all on short hauls to markets. Movements of vegetables by trucks from Texas to California and the reverse, from Florida to Texas and vice versa, and even between California and Florida are not unusual.

The annual share of California-Arizona fruits and vegetables moving to interstate markets by rail decreased from 70 percent in 1960 to 17 percent in 1977. During the same period the rail share of shipments of potatoes from the bi-state area to U.S. markets declined from 83 percent to 29 percent, tomatoes from 35 percent to 5 percent, and lettuce from 68 percent to 18 percent. The trend still continues. A major portion of vegetables shipped from California, Arizona, and other western or southwestern regions to points west of the Mississippi River are now hauled by trucks. Despite the increasing use of trucks, railroads still transport a relatively small portion of vegetables in the longest hauls.

The rail refrigerator fleet consisting of 130,300 refrigerator cars in 1949 declined to 93,800 cars in 1977. In 1973, the Interstate Commerce Commission permitted the railroads to remove all remaining ice-bunker cars from service. Thus, the only remaining cars that provide protective service against heat for shipment of perishables are mechanically refrigerated cars which totaled approximately 24,000 in 1977.

Some vegetables are still transported on flat cars in piggyback refrigerator units which are set off at specified places and trucked to their destinations (Fig. 13.5).

A major concern of producers and handlers is the lack of railroad refrigerator cars. This increases the transport burden of motor trucks which are exempt from economic regulations by the Interstate Commerce Commission. The limitations of rail transportation and the uncertain long-haul cost of truck transportation encourage air transportation both domestically and overseas.

Other Means of Transportation

Quantities of less perishable hardware-type vegetables have been transported by inland and ocean going ships for many years, but this mode of movement is generally not suitable for the more perishable vegetables. Refrigerated transports and the use of fishyback, self-refrigerated containers loaded on ships, provide low-cost coastal and overseas movement of perishable vegetables.

Fig. 13.5—Truck trailers ride piggyback on railroad cars to destination.

USDA Photograph

The increasing use of air transportation for "gourmet" and some high-value vegetables has focused attention on the maintenance of quality by high-speed transit. However, cargo planes are not all equipped with flexible refrigeration devices, thereby limiting their handling of certain vegetable types. Until refrigeration and other facilities are improved and costs are reduced, air movement of vegetables will be restricted to those high-priced items which are in short supply in discriminating markets.

Developments in Transportation

Experience and research are improving all types of transportation. For example, van containers are still being used somewhat. These large mobile trailer units equipped with self-contained refrigeration are loaded on railroad flatcars for long distance movement by rail, or placed aboard ships for movement by water transports. Upon arrival in market centers, the units are unloaded and usually trucked to terminal warehouses, distribution points, or retail outlets. This innovation, which developed in a small way in the Rio Grande Valley of Texas in 1957, has gradually declined, accounting for only 11 percent of the rail shipments in 1977.

Competition among the various means of transportation will force continuing improvements in the economical dispatch of commodities.

MARKETING

Marketing is the performance of services required to move commodities from farms into the possession of consumers—in the form, at the time, and to the places desired. Agricultural products move from many growers to a much smaller number of buyers, then through trade channels to retailers and on to millions of consumers.

Marketing Objectives

The objectives of a good marketing program are to: (1) move produce with the least loss of quality to consumers, (2) provide sales appeal by attractive and convenient packaging, (3) keep marketing cost at a minimum, and thereby, (4) provide both producers and consumers fair prices. In order to accomplish these objectives, careful and efficient handling, preparing, transportation, and the other marketing requirements discussed herein must necessarily be observed by all involved.

Marketing Services and Procedures

Agricultural marketing services may include assembling, grading and standardizing, storing, packaging, processing, transporting, financing, advertising, risk-sharing, and wholesaling and retailing. Some of these operations may be performed more than once in the marketing process; while others, such as storing, processing, and packaging, are not involved with certain vegetables.

Marketing procedures are expensive and technical and these functions are performed more and more by specialists and less and less by producers. Perishables, the stepchildren of food merchandising, belong in the most difficult category of commodities to market. Growers, who frequently complain of their small share of the consumer's dollar, have been generally willing to relinquish the complex marketing responsibility to a vast marketing industry, which employs millions of people and requires extensive technological and physical facilities. Continuing research and experience will no doubt improve the method and quality of this service.

RETAILING PRACTICES AND TRENDS

More and more sales in fewer and fewer stores is the trend of the nation's retail food business, according to a 1974 survey by the Ohio University Extension Service. This trend has continued, and the 1977 Annual Report of the Grocery Industry by *Progressive Grocer* magazine reveals that retail food stores in the United States realized sales of $163 billion in 1977. Fifteen years prior, total sales were $102 billion. During this period, food store sales increased nearly 60 percent, while food prices increased about 56 percent. Grocery stores captured 95 percent of the total food store sales, while specialty markets captured 10 percent of all food store sales. During this same 15-year period, the number of grocery stores in the United States decreased from 231,000 to 175,000—a reduction of 25 percent. This trend toward fewer but larger stores continues with one major exception: Since 1960, convenience stores have grown from 2,500 in number to 30,000, with sales of $7.4 billion.

Significant changes have also occurred in the structure of food retailing. Of all grocery stores, 19 percent were large enough to be classified as supermarkets (annual sales in excess of $1,000,000) in 1977, yet they made 76 percent of all grocery store sales. Approximately 56 percent of these supermarkets were operated by chain store companies (11 stores or more) and 44 percent by independents, continuing a long term of growth in chain store sales in 1977. Food distribution methods will change with the times.

Paralleling the growth of supermarkets and convenience stores is a trend toward complete self-service in food stores. Increased pre-packaging of produce is part of this trend (Fig. 13.2), as large-sized supermarkets unitize more produce so that it is sold by the package, price, or unit.

Few consumers are aware of the overall coordinated operations in supplying food stores with a wide variety of uniform quality, attractively packaged fruits and vegetables. This coordination attempts to schedule widely dispersed production (sometimes worldwide) and encourage harvesting, storage, transportation, advertising, and physical distribution to stores so that a satisfactory quality of many varieties of fresh produce is available to customers every day of the year. Little do consumers realize that many vegetables, fresh from the fields, ran the complicated gauntlet of marketing and were delivered to the grocery stores the night before they were retailed.

Fig. 13.6—A modern tomato grading and packing shed.

EXPORTING AND IMPORTING

Of the large volume of commercial vegetables produced in this country (Table 1.3), variable quantities of some fresh and processed items are exported to countries throughout the world. Conversely, slightly less quantities are imported, primarily from Mexico and Canada.

The United States exported a record of $23.7 billion worth of agricultural products in 1977, compared with $5.6 billion worth in 1963. Of this amount, vegetables, excluding dried beans and peas, accounted for approximately $479,035,000 as shown in Table 13.2. In 1977, U.S. imports of farm products totaled about $13.5 billion, of which about $502,522,000 were from fresh vegetables and their products.

By far the most important fresh-vegetable export market of the United States is Canada. For many years large quantities of potatoes, lettuce, fresh tomatoes, onions, celery, carrots, cabbage, peppers, asparagus, beans, cucumbers, and muskmelons have been shipped to Canada. The sum total amounted to about $163,685,200 in 1977, compared with $60,000,000 in 1963. Substantial quantities of fresh vegetables are also exported to Western Europe. Hong Kong, other Asian countries, and some Latin American countries.

About 90 percent of fresh vegetable imports to the United States came from Mexico in 1977. Large quantities of tomatoes, cucumbers, muskmelons or cantaloupes, watermelons, peppers, onions, and substantial amounts of eggplant, squash, garlic, and beans are imported annually. Canada is the second largest supplier, providing the United States with large quantities of table and seed potatoes, turnips, rutabagas, carrots, and variable amounts of cucumbers, lettuce, tomatoes, radishes, and some other vegetables.

Considerable quantities of canned whole tomatoes are imported from Italy and Spain, while limited amounts of mushrooms, asparagus, and other items come from Taiwan, Canada, Mexico, and other countries. International trade in vegetables, particularly exports from Mexico, will continue on a large scale.

The quantities of exported and imported vegetables and the principal countries involved are discussed separately by commodities under "Marketing" in Chapters 14 through 31 in Section Two.

Although the quantity and value of vegetable imports (Fig. 13.7) exceed exports (Fig. 13.8), the United States has the capability of increasing its exports substantially.

FEDERAL-STATE MARKETING SERVICES

The U.S. Department of Agriculture alone, or in cooperation with the state departments of agriculture, has provided research, reporting, news, inspection, standardization, and regulatory services on the major crops for many years. Such information and control services are tailored to the need and designed to protect both the growers and the consumers. Those services which deal with fruits and vegetables are discussed briefly in order for readers to make use of their provisions when desired. Detailed information on each of these services can be obtained from the Food, Safety, and Quality (FSQ) Service, U.S. Department of Agriculture, Washington, D.C., or from one of its state, regional, or field offices.

U.S. IMPORTS OF FRESH AND PROCESSED VEGETABLES

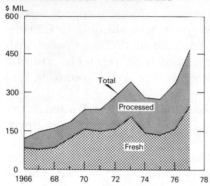

$ MIL.

U.S. Imports of Fresh and Processed Vegetables, by Origin[1]

	1974	1975	1976	1977
	Million dollars			
Imports	283.4	277.0	336.2	470.4
Fresh	145.6	137.0	159.0	260.0
Processed	137.8	140.0	177.2	210.4
Originating country:				
Canada	26.0	21.1	17.6	22.0
Italy	10.1	8.7	9.0	9.2
Mexico	118.3	115.4	136.9	252.3
Portugal	5.8	4.1	6.1	2.7
Spain	17.8	15.0	17.7	17.6
Taiwan	33.9	37.9	55.0	84.3
Other	71.5	74.8	93.9	82.8

[1] Excluding melons, dried beans, and dried peas.

Fig. 13.7—United States imports of fresh and processed vegetables.

USDA, ESCS

Market News Service

The Market News Service is simply an exchange of information on fruit and vegetable supplies, relating to the demand and prices between growers, shippers, wholesalers, and others in the produce industry. This information is gathered by skilled market reporters and flashed to all parts of the country over a nationwide teletype system provided by the U.S. Department of Agriculture and the state departments of agriculture. These market news reporters serve as the "eyes and ears" of the produce industry and provide valuable information on supply and demand, the basic factors in determining prices.

The Market News Service issues: (1) shipping point reports which show all rail movements, available truck shipments, and prices received by producers and shippers for various commodities; (2) terminal market reports which provide rail and truck receipts in the 25 largest cities of the country and prices received by wholesalers; and (3) Washington reports which show nationwide rail and available truck movements for all commodities, annual summaries of produce prices, and other special reports. Detailed market reports are mailed free upon request from shipping point and terminal market offices.

Many newspapers and trade journals such as *The Packer* and *The Produce News,* hundreds of radio stations, and many TV stations carry market news information from the Federal-State News Service. Instant market information is also available on up-to-date telephone recorders upon dialing designated telephone numbers.

U.S. VEGETABLE EXPORTS BY DESTINATION

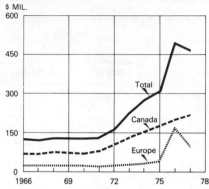

$ MIL.

U.S. Vegetable Exports by Destination[1]

	1974	1975	1976	1977
		Million dollars		
Exports	276.5	305.2	498.5	466.9
Fresh	132.9	158.0	247.4	213.9
Processed	143.6	147.2	251.1	253.0
Receiving country:				
Canada	154.7	175.1	201.4	219.1
Europe	33.4	43.7	174.2	106.3
Other	88.4	86.4	122.9	112.8

[1] Excluding melons, dried beans, and dried peas.

Fig. 13.8—Destination of United States vegetable exports.

USDA, ESCS

Standardization and Inspection Services

The packing of vegetables according to the requirements of official standards is the first step for orderly marketing and efficient buying and selling. Official standards provide a yardstick for measuring variations in quality and serve as a basis for dealing at long distance. Clear and definite standards are indispensable in the settlement of disputes between buyers and sellers.

The separation of products into standard grades makes equitable distribution according to demand possible. Separate grades also provide small and large growers an opportunity to pool their products in cooperative marketing associations, provide a continuity of supply, and attract volume buyers.

The number of grades and the grade names included in a standard vary depending upon the number of distinct quality gradations. Two or three distinct grades are usually enough to meet normal trading demands for most vegetables. Usual grades are designated as U.S. Fancy, U.S. No. 1, and U.S. No. 2. Some commodities, however, lend themselves to separation into several quality classes. For these, a greater number of grades and grade names are provided.

Standardization and inspection services are applicable to vegetables for processing as well as those for fresh market. United States standards for fresh market vegetables not only apply to quality and size but also provide standards for bunching in case of bunched vegetables, arrange-

**Table 13.2—U.S. Exports and Imports of Principal Fresh
and Processed Vegetables in 1977.**

Fresh and Processed Vegetables	Exports		Imports	
	Quantity, 1,000 lbs.	Value, $1,000	Quantity, 1,000 lbs.	Value, $1,000
Asparagus, canned	2,449	1,581	10,573	6,256
Asparagus, fresh	9,827	4,536	2,731	1,347
Beans (green), canned	25,220	4,666	1,063	567
Beans (green), fresh	17,584	2,537	17,486	3,374
Cabbage, fresh	72,798	8,430	39,878	2,542
Carrot, fresh	119,443	9,146	19,733	1,614
Celery, fresh	139,952	14,956	1,258	136
Corn, canned	68,917	17,673	NSC	NSC
Cucumber, pickled	7,852	2,205	NSC	NSC
Cucumber, fresh	25,457	2,860	250,957	18,760
Garlic, fresh	6,621	3,555	18,586	6,533
Lettuce	359,513	32,405	3,819	401
Muskmelon & others	57,647	8,670	218,894	24,758
Onion, fresh	189,195	20,589	33,017	2,685
Peas, canned	7,631	2,007	10,164	3,668
Peas, fresh & frozen	NSC	NSC	18,173	5,103
Pepper, fresh	41,962	6,407	121,485	22,945
Potato, fresh	693,379	46,217	106,447	5,219
Squash	NSC	NSC	67,786	6,133
Tomato, fresh	169,118	28,173	791,871	150,357
Tomato, canned	23,621	5,570	72,098	12,549
Tomato, concentrates	34,714	13,216	65,198	16,202
Turnip & Rutabaga	NSC	NSC	84,009	5,893
Watermelon, fresh	84,651	3,465	175,337	7,317
Other vegetables	729,875	240,171	437,855	198,163
Total all vegetables	2,887,426	479,035	2,568,418	502,522

NSC—not separately classified.

Export and import data from the USDA, Foreign Agricultural Service.

ment of items in containers, uniformity of size, and tightness of pack. In addition, they specify permissible tolerances which allow for variations incident to grading and packing. Thus, upon inspection, a product might meet the requirements of grade and fail to meet the standards of packing, or vice versa.

Generally speaking, U.S. standards are permissive, their use by producers and buyers being optional under the law authorizing such. Certain other Federal and state laws, however, grant authority for compulsory grading of produce under certain circumstances. The grading of some products is compulsory in those areas which have adopted marketing agreements and orders. Compulsory grading is also required by the provisions of many state laws; and a few states require compulsory inspection of some products, either by law or by regulations.

For established fees, trained inspectors at shipping points (Fig. 13.2) or in terminal markets inspect commodities and issue certificates stating their quality or condition and whether or not such comply with designated grades or specifications. The inspection certificate can be based on the official U.S. grade standards, a state grade, or on other written specifications designated by the buyer or seller. These certificates are accepted by law as *prima facie* evidence in all Federal courts and in nearly all state courts.

To provide inspection services nationwide, the U.S. Department of Agriculture has cooperative agreements with the state departments of agriculture or other cooperating state agencies in 49 states and Puerto Rico. Under these agreements, approximately 4,200 federally licensed inspectors perform the inspection work at points of origin. Inspectors are stationed throughout the country to provide fast, efficient service to growers, shippers, receivers, processors, repackers, and institutions, including government procurement agencies.

The inspection service performed under these cooperative agreements is operated jointly by the Food, Safety, and Quality Service of the U.S. Department of Agriculture and the cooperating state agencies and is known as the Federal-State Inspection Service. The Food, Safety, and Quality Service establishes basic inspection policies and procedures and furnishes overall direction.

Federal inspection services are provided in 75 of the largest terminal markets in the country. Assistance from cooperating state agencies is available at some of these markets.

Federal Marketing Orders

Produce growers face major marketing problems, often too great for each to solve individually. Many growers are now overcoming their big marketing problems by pooling their interests and working together through federal marketing orders.

The marketing-order program is simply a partnership between industry and government. If a two-thirds majority of the growers (either by number of growers voting in a referendum or by volume of production) favor a marketing order, the Secretary of Agriculture can issue an order binding on the whole industry in the producing area. The industry can then, through its administrative committee, tailor a marketing plan to fit its needs and initiate regulations under the authorized marketing order. The administrative committee is responsible for expenditures and must keep books, which are subject to annual audit.

The number of marketing orders and their volume of sales have increased somewhat in recent years. Details on the establishment, needs and advantages, and methods of operating and financing marketing-order programs are available upon request from the U.S. Department of Agriculture.

The Perishable Agricultural Commodities Act

The Perishable Agriculture Commodities Act (PACA) is designed to encourage fair trading practices in the marketing of fresh and frozen fruits and vegetables in interstate and foreign commerce. Certain unfair and fraudulent practices are prohibited and penalties are provided for violation. The act also provides for the award of damages against those who fail to live up to contract obligations.

The produce industry realized the importance of a code of fair trading standards and the PACA was passed by Congress in 1930 at the industry's request. It has been amended a number of times to keep it up-to-date with changing trade practices. The U.S. Department of Agriculture is responsible for administering this act.

The regulations under PACA include definitions of standard trade terms which have been used by the industry for many years. The PACA is primarily concerned in prohibiting (without reasonable cause) sellers from failing to deliver purchases, buyers from refusing to accept purchased produce, failures to make payments as agreed, the dumping or destroying of produce by consignees, failures to render correct accounting, and misrepresentations concerning the grade, brand, quality, weight, state of origin, and related violations.

Commission merchants, dealers, brokers, and others involved in handling fresh or frozen fruits or vegetables in interstate or foreign commerce are required to be licensed under this act. Farmers or growers selling only fruits and vegetables they grow are not subject to license. However, if they also sell in interstate or foreign commerce produce by other farmers, they are required to have a license. Truckers are not required to be licensed if they merely haul produce for freight charges, but if they buy and sell fruits and vegetables in interstate or foreign commerce, they must obtain a license.

A retailer is subject to licensing when the invoice cost of all his purchases of fresh and frozen fruits and vegetables during a calendar year exceeds $200,000. In computing this dollar volume, all purchases are to be counted regardless of the size of the lot involved or whether the transaction was in interstate, intrastate, or foreign commerce.

A frozen food broker who acts as an independent agent negotiating sales for the vendor and whose only sales of perishable commodities consist of frozen fruits and vegetables needs a license when the invoice cost of these sales is more than $200,000 in a calendar year.

All of the expenses of administering the act, except for the cost of legal services, are financed by the revenue from license fees. Annual license fees vary with the cost of operation up to a legal maximum of $1,000 per individual firm. The penalty for operating without a license when one is required is not more than $500 for each offense and not more than $25 for each day the offense continues. Other violations of the act can result in the suspension or revocation of a license issued under the act. Penalties up to $2,000 can be assessed for misrepresentation.

Inquiries on licensing and additional information on this and other acts designed to regulate fair trade practices should be directed to one of the PACA regional offices or to the Agricultural Marketing Service, U.S. Department of Agriculture, Washington, D.C.

Federal-State Marketing Improvement Program

Marketing service programs conducted by state departments of agriculture under the matching-fund authority of the Agricultural Marketing Act of 1946 were started in 1947 with 21 states participating. Programs on various farm products were carried on in 23 states in 1978. The office of this Federal-State Marketing Improvement Program, in the Agricultural Marketing Service, provides guidance and assistance to the states in conducting this work.

These programs are designed to: (1) help marketing agencies at the various levels of distribution adopt new techniques and methods for performing marketing operations discovered or developed through research, (2) show these marketing agencies and producers how to improve or maintain the quality of farm products during marketing, (3) provide producers and marketing agencies with new or more timely and complete marketing facts and information, and (4) expand markets for farm products.

General guidance to the Marketing Improvement Program is provided by the Advisory Committee on Cooperative Work under the Agricultural Marketing Act with state departments of agriculture. To improve the operation of their programs and prevent duplication of effort, the state departments of agriculture maintain close cooperation with industry and trade groups, state extension services, agricultural experiment stations, vocational education agencies, and the U.S. Department of Agriculture.

These programs are conducted under cooperative agreements between the state departments of agriculture or similar agencies responsible for marketing service work and the U.S. Department of Agriculture. Individual projects are initiated by the states and approved by the Agricultural and Marketing Service. The types of vegetable marketing services provided by this Federal-State Matching-Fund Program include: (1) projects on improving quality, (2) expanding export outlets, (3) improving marketing efficiency, and (4) providing basic data and marketing information. Presently 38 states are participating in most of these programs. Detailed information, including projects by states, is provided by the U.S. Department of Agriculture.

Research and Promotion Programs

There is increasing interest on the part of vegetable growers in self-financed research and promotion programs. For example, potato growers in all states work together to promote increased consumption of potatoes. Under the National Potato Research and Promotion Act, all potatoes sold for food or seed are assessed 1 cent per hundredweight. Assessment income is used by the potato board, an administrative group appointed by the USDA, to fund a nationwide education program which emphasizes the nutritional value of potatoes. (The potato is described to the public as the world's most versatile vegetable, high in complex carbohydrates, moderate in Vitamin C and other vitamins and minerals, and low in calories.)

SELECTED REFERENCES

Andrews, G. M., Leighton, N. C., and Lateremore, N. C., "Vegetable Marketing Structure and Expansion Potential," N. H. Exp. Sta. Res. Rep. 55 VII, 1977.
Anonymous, "Agricultural Marketing Service," USDA, AMS PA 1028, 1977.
Anonymous, "Developments in Marketing Spreads of Agricultural Products in 1976," USDA, ERS Rep. NC 367, 1977.
Anonymous, "Facts About Farmer to Consumer Direct Marketing," USDA, AMS 575, 1978.

Anonymous, "Facts About Federal Marketing Orders for Fruits and Vegetables," USDA, AMS 563, 1978.

Anonymous, "Farmers' Rights Under the Agricultural Fair Practices Act," USDA, AMS, Pamphlet 1005, 1972.

Anonymous, "Federal-State Market News Service," USDA, AMS Mktg. Bull. 40, 1977.

Anonymous, "The Fruit and Vegetable Grower and PACA," USDA, AMS 451, 1972.

Anonymous, "Harvesting Vegetables in Florida," Veg. Crops Ext. Rep. 10, 1976.

Anonymous, "Information Available from USDA's Food, Safety, and Quality Service," USDA, FSQS 6, 1977.

Anonymous, "Marketing Agreements and Orders," USDA, AMS, Pamphlet 1095, 1975.

Anonymous, "Marketing Information from USDA," USDA, AMS 574, 1978.

Anonymous, "The Market News Service of Fruits and Vegetables," USDA, Mktg. Bull. 61, 1977.

Anonymous, "Official Grade Standards and Inspection for Fresh Fruits and Vegetables," USDA, FSQS 520, 1963.

Anonymous, "The Perishable Agricultural Commodities Act," USDA, AMS Pamphlet 804, 1977.

Anonymous, "USDA Grade Standards for Food (How They Are Developed and Used)," USDA, FSQS Pamphlet 1027, 1977.

Anonymous, "U.S. Fresh Market Vegetable Statistics, 1949-75," USDA, ERS Stat. Bull. 558, 1976.

Antle, G. G., "Pick Your Own," Mich. State Univ. Ext. Bull. E-1246-SF-16, 1978.

Ashby, H. B., "Protecting Perishable Foods During Transport by Motor Truck," USDA Agriculture Handbook 105, 1970.

Bailes, J. P., and Anthony, J. P., "Problems in Palletized Transporting of Florida Fresh Vegetables," USDA, ARS 52-51, 1971.

Berberlich, R. S., "Effective Fruit and Vegetable Marketing," USDA Farmer Coop. Ser. Mkt. Res. Rep., 1974.

Boles, Patrick P., "Cost of Operating Refrigerated Trucks for Hauling Fruits and Vegetables," USDA, ERS 1977.

Click, J. H., "Statistics of Farmer Cooperatives," USDA, ESCS, 1975 (issued annually).

Fahey, James V., "How Fresh Tomatoes Are Marketed," USDA AMS M. Bull. 59, 1976.

Gould, W. A., "Food Processing and Technology 1978," Ohio Agr. Res. Center Circ. 240, 1978, Wooster.

Hinds, R. H., "Transporting Fresh Fruits and Vegetables Overseas," USDA, SEA 52-39, 1970.

Pullin, A. T., "Marketing Fruits and Vegetables," Miss. Ext. Ser. Pub. 570, 1975.

Ritter, C. J., and Thomas Ratcliff, Jr., "Fruit and Vegetable Shipment by Commodities, States, and Months," USDA, AMS, FVUS, 1977 (issued annually).

Ryall, A. L., and Lipton, W. J., "Handling, Transportation, and Storage of Fruits and Vegetables," Vegetables and Melons, Vol. 1, Westport, Conn.: Avi Publishing Company, 1972.

Schroeter, R. B., "U.S. Imports of Horticultural Products," USDA, FAS M 191, 1971.

Stewart, J. K., and Couey, M., "Hydrocooling Vegetables," USDA, ARS MRR
    637, 1963.
Stokes, D. R., and Woodley, G. W., "Standardization of Shipping Containers,"
    USDA, MRR 991, 1974.

Section Two

PRACTICES

INTRODUCTION TO SECTION TWO

Chapters 14 through 34 of Section Two deal with the economic importance and specific "practices" involved in the production, harvesting, handling, and marketing of the principal vegetable crops. These chapters contain the most applicable information on each vegetable crop.

In discussing the culture of different crops, it is assumed that the reader is familiar with the principles underlying the various operations as discussed in the first 13 chapters. An understanding of these principles will be a considerable aid in the application of the different operations.

In view of the fact that the botanical and horticultural relationships of the various vegetables were fully discussed in Chapter 2, "Classifying Vegetables," the arrangement of the crop production chapters is alphabetical by crops, rather than by botanical relationships. This arrangement provides for convenient reference and should not discourage the student from studying or comparing related vegetables.

Each chapter is complete in itself, but references are made to similar discussions elsewhere in order to supplement information or to conserve space. Pertinent facts on the crop under discussion, including botanical classification, history, production, economic importance, and climatic requirements, are systematically given at the beginning of the chapter.

The subject matter of the vegetable chapters is discussed by topics in the order of seasonal sequence. They are further subdivided into special operations.

A typical outline used in the chapter of each vegetable enterprise is given here.

SELECTING CULTIVARS AND SEED
Selecting Cultivars
Securing Seed

PREPARING THE SOIL
Soil Preference
Preparing the Seedbed

FERTILIZING, MANURING, AND LIMING
Fertilizing
Manuring
Liming

PLANTING AND PROTECTING
Starting Plants Under Protection
Seeding in the Field

CULTIVATING AND IRRIGATING
Cultivating
Irrigating
Thinning and Weeding
Training

CONTROLLING DISEASES AND INSECTS
Controlling Diseases
Controlling Insects

HARVESTING, HANDLING, AND MARKETING
Harvesting
Grading
Packing
Storing
Marketing
Exporting and Importing

SELECTED REFERENCES

The statistics on each crop, including acreage, acre yield, production, unit price, farm value, and comparative growing seasons by leading states, have not appeared in similar form elsewhere. The reader will find many interesting comparisons in these tables, which were prepared from reports supplied by the Crop Reporting Board of the Economics, Statistics, and Cooperative Service, U.S. Department of Agriculture. The dot maps, prepared by the U.S. Department of Commerce, are only approximate since production and related values are constantly shifting, as shown by data on the maps.

Readers should bear in mind that vegetable acreage, yields, production, and value vary considerably from year to year. Consequently, the 1977 data appearing in the vegetable chapters should be considered on an annual basis and not as an average or trend.

Diseases and insects have been discussed somewhat in detail, because they are of great economic importance; and because their control is closely associated with production, and, in many cases, with transportation and marketing.

For completeness and convenient reference, scientific names of plants, diseases, and insects appear in parentheses following the common names.

Another feature contained in the crop chapters is the parallel description of the outstanding characteristics of some of the principal cultivars.

CHAPTER 14

Asparagus

CLASSIFICATION, ORIGIN, AND HISTORY

Asparagus *(Asparagus officinalis)* is a member of the lily family and is indigenous to parts of Russia, the Mediterranean region, and the British Isles. It was used for food by the Romans and other ancient peoples and was also highly regarded for medicinal purposes. The plant was brought to America by the early colonists.

SCOPE AND IMPORTANCE

Commercial asparagus production is concentrated primarily along the west and east coasts and the Great Lakes region. It is a popular early spring crop for home use and local markets in many parts of the country. Of the 22 principal vegetable crops, asparagus ranked twelfth in acreage and eighteenth in value in 1977.

Asparagus acreage increased from 127,270 in 1949 to 161,150 in 1959, then declined to about 36,000 in 1977. During this 28-year period, production fluctuated slightly while total value more than doubled. California is by far the leading state, followed by Washington, Michigan, and Illinois. The distribution and 28-year acreage and value record of asparagus production are shown in Fig. 14.1, while the 1977 harvest season, acreage, production, and value by leading states are presented in Table 14.1.

TRENDS IN PRODUCTION EFFICIENCY

Asparagus is comparatively expensive to produce primarily because

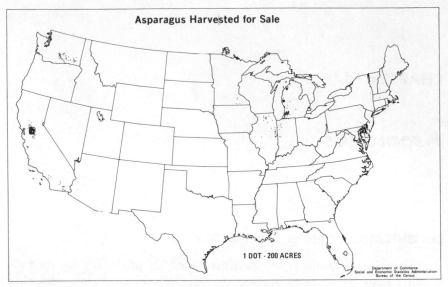

Fig. 14.1—Acreage distribution, production, and value of asparagus.

UNITED STATES TOTAL

Year	Acreage	Production 1,000 Cwt.	Value, $1,000
1949	127,290	3,277	33,137
1959	161,150	3,627	40,682
1969	115,350	2,815	55,249
1977	85,820	2,181	80,049

of high labor requirements in planting, fertilizing, cultivating, and harvesting. Fresh market asparagus required 190 man-hours per acre for growing and harvesting in 1939, 173 hours in 1959, and 71 hours in 1977. Processing asparagus required less labor per acre but unit output per man-hour actually decreased during the 1939-1959 period. Progress is being made in mechanical harvesting, and this crop should become more competitive with other vegetables.

CLIMATIC REQUIREMENTS

Asparagus grows best where cool temperatures prevail during the growing season and where adequate moisture is available. The high summer temperatures and mild winters occurring in the southern states do not favor maximum production of spears; but where there is sufficient cold in winter to render the plants dormant for a considerable period, profitable yields are possible if the crop is well fertilized and properly

Table 14.1—Asparagus for Fresh Market and Processing: Estimated Acreage, Yield, Production, and Value in Leading States, 1977.

State	Harvest Season	Harvested Acreage	Yield per Acre, Cwt.	Production per 1,000 Cwt.	Price per Cwt.	Value, $1,000
California	Spring	30,300	37	1,121	$38.20	42,775
Washington	Spring	20,200	33	667	32.70	21,815
Michigan	Spring	17,300	11	190	43.90	8,345
Illinois	Spring	4,500	11	50	34.50	1,725
New Jersey	Spring	2,300	14	32	55.10	1,763
Other States		11,220	11	121	31.60	3,826
United States		85,820	25	2,181	36.80	80,249
Fresh Market (42%)				714	46.90	33,458
Processing (58%)				3,667	31.90	46,791
Canning (67%)				969	32.50	31,503
Freezing (33%)				498	30.70	15,288

The above and similar data on the production and value of fresh market and processed vegetables in subsequent chapters were obtained from the 1977 "Annual Summary of Acreage, Yield, Production and Value of Principal Vegetable Crops," USDA, ESCS, Crop Reporting Board, 1978.

States in this and similar tables in subsequent chapters are ranked according to "Harvested Acreage."

cultivated. The crowns are very hardy and are seldom injured by the cold winters of the northern states. Winter injury is usually restricted to fields where the tops of the plants have been removed in the fall. In mild, dry regions, such as the Imperial Valley of California, a resting period is provided by withholding irrigation water.

SELECTING CULTIVARS AND SEED

Cultivars

Male and female flowers of asparagus are borne on different plants. This dioecious condition results in the cross pollination and mixing of strains in the field. Since the crowns are propagated almost wholly from seed, wide variability may appear in any lot of crowns unless seed-producing plants are selected and isolated. Because a planting will last for many years, special care should be exercised in securing good seed.

Mary Washington has been the leading cultivar of asparagus, and practically all of those presently used are either selections or crosses of this cultivar. It is tolerant of asparagus rust, is vigorous and productive, and has wide adaptability. Some of the selections include: California 500, Seneca Washington, Waltham Washington, and New Jersey Improved. U.C. 66 and U.C. 72 tolerate *Fusarium oxysporum* and for this reason are recommended for planting on old asparagus land. The latter is preferred for its larger-sized spears. U.C. 157, a new hybrid, is early, highly productive, and uniform in size and color of spears. Brock's Special was developed for adaptation to a hot desert area.

Securing Seed

Some asparagus seed is saved in most of the areas where the crop is grown commercially. California, New Jersey, and South Carolina are the sources of considerable quantities of seed. Prices of seed vary depending upon the source. Seed saved in the fall from a planting which produces good-quality asparagus is probably about as satisfactory as any.

GROWING AND SELECTING CROWNS

Asparagus plants are grown in a nursery for one season and then set in permanent fields. The grower may buy crowns or grow them at home. If home-grown crowns are used, production of a crop will be delayed one year; but the cost of establishing may be less, and the grower will have more opportunity to practice crown selection.

In growing crowns, the seed is usually planted on sandy loam soil as soon as the soil is warm in the spring, with the rows 24 to 30 inches apart. Garden seed drills or other planters provided with special plates are commonly used for planting. Preferably, seeds are dropped singly 2 or 3 inches apart and covered 1 to 1½ inches deep. Thinning is difficult, and the crowns are hard to separate after digging if they are grown so close together that the roots are interwoven. Since the seed is slow to germinate at low temperatures, it is difficult to get early uniform seedling development. This can best be done by germinating the seed at high temperatures (80° to 90° F.) and transplanting the seedlings. Such a practice would be expensive and therefore applicable only to a small-scale operation. The practice of soaking the seed is of doubtful value. Delayed plantings germinate promptly without treatment.

In growing crowns on a large scale, the seed is usually planted at the rate of four or five pounds per acre. This quantity of seed will, according to nurserymen, produce about 30,000 or more plants.

Ordinarily the soil used for growing asparagus crowns should be well fertilized at planting time. The plants are cultivated during the season as any other row crop. It is preferable to dig the crowns shortly before planting in the spring, and the digging should be done in such manner as to injure the storage roots as little as possible. Although the results of experiments are somewhat conflicting, it is probably advisable to use only the larger crowns for planting.

Crowns may be purchased from plant growers and the price is usually dependent upon size. The cheaper crowns should weigh 75 to 80 pounds per 1,000, while well grown ones may weigh as much as 150 pounds or more per 1,000. Male plants yield higher than female plants, but the crowns would have to grow two years to make a sex determination. Injury in digging and handling the two-year-old crowns would make the separation impractical.

PREPARING THE SOIL AND PLANTING THE CROWNS

Soil Preferences

Asparagus may be grown on a wide variety of soils, but, for best results, the soils should be well drained, deep, loose, and light. Mucks and light sandy loams favor the development of healthy root systems and unblemished spears. Light, sandy, or gravelly soils having porous subsoils should be avoided because of their low moisture-holding capacities.

Preparing the Soil for Planting

Preparation of the soil for planting asparagus is usually best done in early spring. Since asparagus occupies the land for 15 years or longer, the soil should be put in good condition at the start. It is desirable to plow under a green manure crop in the fall before planting. The land should be free from stumps and from coarse rubbish which might cause crooked spears. It should also be as free as possible of weeds, particularly perennial weeds. Since deep planting of the crowns is commonly practiced, the soil should be plowed rather deeply.

Planting the Crowns

Asparagus crowns are usually set in the field as soon as the soil can be worked in the spring, and before shoot development has begun.

In mild regions they may be planted in the late fall or winter after they have become dormant. Furrows should be plowed out to a depth of 8 or 10 inches with a turning or a double moldboard plow. In these furrows, the crowns are placed with buds 6 to 8 inches below the general ground level and covered about 2 inches deep. As the tops grow, the soil is gradually worked toward the plants until the furrows have been entirely filled. In some parts of the country shallow planting is recommended, especially on heavy soils. Better stands are obtained, but shallow crowns may be injured by discing and freezing so that they produce small spears.

The spacing of asparagus plants varies considerably in different sections of the country. Close planting may be practiced in home gardens, but plantings for commercial production usually consist of rows 4 to 6 feet apart with the plants 12 to 18 inches apart in the row. However, according to observations made by the South Carolina Experiment Station over a period of eight years, a spacing of 2 by 5 feet, or not more than 2 by 6 feet, gave better yields, quantity and quality considered, than either a 2- by 4-foot or a 2- by 8-foot spacing. These results are in line with similar data secured in Iowa and California. With a spacing of 2 by 5 feet, 4,356 crowns are required to plant an acre. A closer spacing may be necessary for mechanical harvesting. White or blanched asparagus is grown by ridging the soil over the rows during the cutting season. This method requires a spacing of 7 to 8 feet between rows.

When high populations are required, direct seeding may be more economical than using crowns. Seeds are precision-planted in furrows 6 to 8 inches deep. One row or two rows 8 to 12 inches apart can be used. The seedlings develop slowly, and consequently, weed control becomes an important problem, requiring herbicides for economical control. Consult latest recommendations.

FERTILIZING, LIMING, AND MANURING

Fertilizing

The cost of fertilizing asparagus is the largest single item of expense in its production. Fertilizer practices should therefore be carefully considered so that the outlay may be no more than is necessary. Because of the premium paid for the colossal grade, growers have a tendency to adjust fertilizer and other practices so as to secure as much of this grade as possible, without due regard for the economics involved. If the increased yields from excessive amounts of fertilizer are not enough to off-set the extra cost as compared with that of a moderate application, the use of the larger amount of fertilizer should be discontinued.

KIND AND AMOUNT OF FERTILIZER. It is important to have the soil well fertilized, especially with phosphorus and potassium, before setting the crowns. These elements do not move readily in the soil, and efforts to place them down to the feeding roots after the plants are established results in injury and reduced yields. Surface applications, on the other hand, are not very effective. If the soil is well supplied with phosphorus and potassium before planting, annual applications of fertilizer may be limited to nitrogen primarily. On soils where leaching is not an important factor, the young planting will respond to about 100 pounds of nitrogen applied annually. This amount may be gradually reduced to 50 pounds in an old field. Fertilizer mixture such as 10-5-5 is commonly used in asparagus growing. This may be applied at the rates of 1,000 to 2,000 pounds per acre, depending upon type of soil.

TIME OF APPLYING FERTILIZERS. Considerable difference of opinion prevails as to the proper time for applying fertilizers to asparagus. Much of the experimental data available indicate that the primary application of fertilizer should be made immediately after the cutting season. This tends to stimulate rapid and vigorous top growth necessary for a good crop the following year. The nitrogenous reserves are exhausted more readily than the carbohydrates of the crowns during harvesting. For this reason a response to readily available nitrogen applied early in the spring may also be expected.

METHOD OF APPLYING FERTILIZERS. Whether applied before or after harvesting, the fertilizer should be spread and disced into the soil. The early application and discing should be done before the spears begin growth, and should be shallow enough to prevent injury to the crowns.

LIMING AND MANURING. Asparagus does best on soils ranging from slightly acid to slightly alkaline (pH 6.5 to 7.5). If acid soils are used they should be limed to bring the reactions to pH 6.0 or 6.5.

Organic matter is important for improving the physical condition of the soil. Animal manure is a good source when it can be obtained. Even though manure may be used to supply fertility it should be supplemented with commercial fertilizers, especially in the early years of planting. At the Maryland Experiment Station, a comparison of manure and chemical fertilizer on a fairly fertile loam soil showed that yields over a nine-year period were larger from the latter and were also much more profitable.

CULTIVATING AND CARE

Cultivating

Asparagus should be cultivated to keep down weeds and grass and thus encourage good top growth. During the harvesting season, however, it is difficult to cultivate the beds without injuring the developing shoots. The spears are less brittle in the afternoon and cultivation is best done at this time. The weeding problem has been simplified by the use of chemicals. Recommendations are given in Chapter 9.

Disposing of Tops

The tops should be left standing in the field over winter and should be disced into the soil in early spring before any shoot development. The old tops protect the crowns over winter and add organic matter when incorporated into the soil.

Life of Asparagus Plantations

The life of an asparagus plantation depends upon natural conditions and upon the treatment received. Plantings are in existence which are said to have produced profitable yields for more than a hundred years. Commercial fields receiving average care remain profitable for 15 to 18 years and yield their best crops at 5 to 10 years of age. The crowns spread with age and cultivation without injury becomes difficult.

CONTROLLING DISEASES AND INSECTS

Asparagus Rust

This disease is caused by *Puccinia asparagi*. It injures the tops of the plant and limits the storage of reserve food in the crowns, thereby reducing the crop of the following season. Rust does not develop on the marketed product. It appears first as small reddish-yellow spots on the main stem and branches. The fungus produces spores in large numbers, and these are disseminated by wind. The spots enlarge and become darker as the season advances, and the foliage turns brown and drops off, giving the plants a naked appearance.

Spraying and dusting are not usually effective enough to warrant their use. However, spraying the unharvested plants in the spring with zineb or maneb may prevent the buildup of inoculum and thus reduce the severity of the disease. The use of a cultivar not highly susceptible to rust is recommended.

Asparagus Beetle

The common asparagus beetle (*Crioceris asparagi*) is the most destructive insect attacking asparagus. It injures the spears during the harvest season and the full-grown tops later. The adult beetle overwinters in rubbish surrounding cultivated fields and emerges in time to feed upon the developing spears, causing them to become crooked and unsightly. Eggs are deposited on the spears, and later, both adults and larvae attack the fully developed plants, defoliating them in some instances and giving them a setback which may be reflected in reduced yields the following season.

The beetle does not thrive in hot weather. Although it causes considerable damage in certain cases, it has not proven as troublesome in the South as elsewhere. The most serious damage is that done to the marketable spears, and no remedy has been devised for this. The insect may be kept in check by dusting the mature plants with rotenone at 0.3 pounds, carbaryl at 1.0 pound, or malathion at 1.25 pounds per acre. Where rust is not a serious disease, a few of the early spears may be left to develop into mature plants to attract the emerging beetles. As the insects collect on these, they may be destroyed by dusting with a carbaryl dust or spray.

HARVESTING, HANDLING, AND MARKETING

Harvesting

It is perhaps best to delay harvesting until the bed is two years old, and to limit the cutting to not more than three or four weeks the first season.

The spears are cut when they have grown 5 to 8 inches above the surface of the ground. When cut, the spears are severed just below the surface by means of an asparagus knife. They are collected in baskets and taken to the packing shed. Cutting is done preferably in the morning and as frequently as is necessary, which may be every day or only every two or three days, depending on the temperature and other growing conditions. Care should be exercised in cutting the asparagus in order to avoid injuring the younger spears. Tests in Massachusetts have shown that there is great variation in the quality and quantity of asparagus harvested from similar areas by different individuals, depending on the care used in cutting.

Grading, Bunching, and Packing

The returns from asparagus growing depend in a large measure upon proper grading, bunching, and packing. Usually No. 1 asparagus is shipped. The spears are first separated into three grades, Colossal, Fancy, and Choice, depending upon their diameter. The diameters of the spears included in each grade are as follows: Extra Colossal, $7/8$ inch and over; Colossal, $11/16$ to $7/8$ inch; Fancy, $1/2$ to $11/16$ inch (Fig. 14.2); and Choice, $1/4$ to $1/2$ inch. Bunches of asparagus are normally $8\frac{1}{2}$ inches long but in recent years 10-inch bunches also are shipped. Extra Colossal is always 10 inches long and the other grades may be of that length. All stalks should be straight, unblemished, and fresh.

When bunched, the required number of spears are placed with the tips even in a bunching machine. The bunch is then clamped and tied firmly near each end with red or blue tape or held together with colored rubber bands. The butts are then cut squarely with a large knife, leaving the bunch either $8\frac{1}{2}$ or 10 inches in length. Twelve of the 2- to $2\frac{1}{2}$-pound bunches are placed in a crate which has a pyramidal shape, assuring a tight pack. Before being packed, the bottom of the crate is lined with waxed paper and then with a layer of moist sphagnum moss on which the bunches of asparagus are set with the butts down.

Unless asparagus is kept at temperatures near the freezing point, the quality deteriorates rapidly, and the spears continue to grow, thus causing loose bunches of ragged appearance. The packed crates should therefore be put into iced cars as promptly as possible.

On local markets, 1-pound or smaller bunches may be preferred, or the asparagus may be sold without grading or bunching.

Marketing

Much of the commercial asparagus crop is marketed through growers' associations and farmers' markets at shipping points. Strict regulations have been established in grades and packages in order to market a standardized product. Fresh market asparagus is shipped in trucks and refrigerator cars, with trucks accounting for the largest portion of the total movement.

EXPORTS AND IMPORTS. The United States, once a major supplier of canned asparagus to the world, has experienced a steady drop in exports over the past 13 years. Shipments were only 2,449,000 pounds valued at $1,581,000 in 1977. Imports of canned asparagus have grown steadily, reaching 10,573,000 pounds, worth $6,256,000 in 1977. Taiwan and Mexico supplied virtually the entire amount. There is considerable trade in fresh asparagus, with most of the exports going to the United Kingdom and imports arriving from Taiwan (Table 13.2).

Fig. 14.2—Harvesting asparagus.

USDA Photograph

Fig. 14.3—Bunches of asparagus placed on damp peat moss in flat to keep them fresh.

USDA Photograph

SELECTED REFERENCES

Anonymous, "Commercial Growing of Asparagus," USDA Farmers' Bull. 2232, 1972.

Berry, J. W., et al., "Grower's Guide for Vegetable Crops," Wash. State Univ. Coop. Ext. Ser. Col. of Agr., E. M. 3513, 1978.

Bouwkamp, J. C., and McCully, J. E., "Competition and Survival in Female Plants of Asparagus officinalis L., J. Amer. Soc. Hort. Sci. Vol. 97 (1): 74-76 1972.

Bouwkamp, J. C., and McCully, J. E., "Effects of Simulated Non-Selective Mechanical Harvesting on Spear Emergence of Asparagus officinalis L.," Scientia Horticulturae, 3: 157-162, 1975.

Combs, O. B., et al., "Asparagus," Coop. Ext. Ser. Pub. A1622, 1978.

Fridley, R. B., and Adrian, P. A., Evaluating the Feasibility of Mechanizing Crop Harvest, Vol. II, Am. Soc. Agr. Eng., 1968.

Gorter, C. J., "Vegetative Propagation of Asparagus officinalis by Cuttings," Hort Sci. 40: 177-179, 1965.

Putnam, A. R., and Lacy, M. L., "Asparagus Management with No-Tillage," Mich. State Univ. Agr. Exp. Sta. Res. Rep. 339, 1977.

Putnam, A. R., et al., "Know Your Asparagus Pests," Mich. State Univ. Ext. Bull. E-959, 1976.

Sims, W. L., et al., "Direct Seeding of Asparagus," Univ. of Calif. Div. Agr. Sci., Leaflet 2776, 1976.

Takatori, F. H., "Asparagus Production in California," Univ. of Calif. Div. Agr. Sci. Bull. 1882, 1977.

CHAPTER 15

Beans (Snap and Lima)

CLASSIFICATION, ORIGIN, AND HISTORY

The snap or kidney bean (*Phaseolus vulgaris*) was grown by the Indians over a considerable part of both North and South America, and was introduced in Europe by early American settlers. The species includes field beans as well as cultivars used in the green or immature stage. Snap beans have thick-walled pods that are free from strings (bast fibers) in the early stages of development.

The lima bean (*Phaseolus limensis*) is a native of tropical America. It grows wild in Brazil, and its seeds have been found in Peruvian tombs at Pachacamac and Ancon. The name "lima" probably comes from Lima, Peru, where large lima beans were secured and imported to the United States.

SCOPE AND IMPORTANCE

Snap beans are extensively grown, both commercially and in home gardens. Beans for fresh market and processing comprise one of the most important vegetables, ranking fifth in acreage and seventh in value among the 22 principal vegetables in 1977.

Harvested acreage of snap beans for fresh market declined from 188,400 in 1949 to 78,250 in 1977. Total production also decreased but value increased from $41,447,000 in 1949 to $60,965,000 in 1977. Snap bean acreage for processing rose from 126,450 in 1949 to about 258,000 in 1977, while acre yields remained stable. Crop value rose phenomenally from $29,520,000 in 1949 to an estimated $96,128,000 in 1977. Florida is by far the leading state in snap beans for fresh market, while Wisconsin, New York, Oregon, and Michigan lead in the processing crop. (Tables 15.1 and 15.2)

Commercial lima beans for fresh market have almost disappeared and national production records are discontinued. Limas for processing remain important, but acreage and production have declined, while

Table 15.1—Snap Beans for Fresh Market: Harvest Season and Estimated Acreage, Yield, Production, and Value in Leading States, 1977.

State	Harvest Season	Harvested Acreage	Yield per Acre, Cwt.	Production per 1,000 Cwt.	Price per Cwt.	Value, $1,000
Florida	Spring	13,500	36	486	$18.60	9,040
Florida	Fall	12,000	37	444	21.00	9,324
New York	Summer	7,400	36	266	22.30	5,958
Florida	Winter	5,500	36	198	25.80	5,108
New Jersey	Summer	4,600	35	161	19.40	3,123
N. Carolina	Summer	3,700	36	133	25.60	3,405
Virginia	Summer	2,900	29	84	19.50	1,638
Michigan	Summer	2,700	34	92	20.20	1,858
N. Carolina	Spring	2,700	24	65	19.30	1,255
Tennessee	Summer	2,200	40	88	20.30	1,786
S. Carolina	Spring	2,000	33	66	16.50	1,089
Virginia	Fall	2,000	26	52	18.50	962
Maryland	Summer	1,800	23	41	12.90	529
California	Summer	1,700	90	153	20.20	3,091
California	Fall	1,200	70	84	24.60	2,066
Alabama	Summer	1,200	30	36	30.60	1,102
New Jersey	Spring	1,200	37	44	24.40	1,074
Georgia	Summer	1,200	26	31	20.60	639
Ohio	Summer	1,000	40	40	21.10	844
Other States	..	7,750	..	320	..	7,074
United States	..	78,250	37	2,884	21.10	60,965

values rose along with the increasing prices. California and Delaware lead in lima bean production (Table 15.3). The distribution and 28-year performance of snap and lima beans are shown in Figures 15.1, 15.2, and 15.3 respectively.

TRENDS IN PRODUCTION EFFICIENCY

Both snap and lima beans are comparatively inexpensive crops, as they are grown and harvested by efficient machines. In 1939 it required

Table 15.2—Snap Beans for Processing: Estimated Acreage, Yield, Production, and Value in Leading States, 1977.

State	Harvested Acreage	Yield per Acre, Tons	Production in Tons	Price per Ton	Value, $1,000
Wisconsin	67,200	2.76	185,450	$128.00	23,738
New York	43,000	2.23	96,100	149.00	14,320
Oregon	32,500	4.31	140,200	137.00	19,207
Michigan	16,800	2.46	41,300	125.00	5,163
Tennessee	13,700	1.91	26,100	166.00	4,340
Illinois	7,200	2.80	20,150	142.00	2,861
Maryland	6,800	1.90	12,900	171.00	2,206
California	6,000	2.62	15,700	186.00	2,925
Pennsylvania	5,000	2.07	10,350	162.00	1,681
Arkansas	4,700	1.80	8,450	120.00	1,014
Alabama	3,100	2.03	6,300	153.00	966
Virginia	3,000	1.82	5,450	179.00	975
Oklahoma	2,200	1.64	3,600	95.60	344
Colorado	1,700	3.56	6,050	126.00	762
Washington	1,700	2.68	4,550	136.00	619
N. Carolina	1,400	1.32	1,850	154.00	285
Ohio	200	2.25	450	100.00	45
Other States	41,540	2.19	90,950	161.00	14,677
United States	257,740	2.62	675,900	142.00	96,128
Canning (78%)	200,250	2.59	519,350	141.00	73,293
Freezing (22%)	57,490	2.72	156,550	146.00	22,835

132 man-hours to produce and harvest an acre of snap beans for fresh market compared with 15 hours in 1977. The man-hour output increased a phenomenal 1,123 percent during that 38-year period (Table 1.6). Also spectacular increases in man-hour production for both snap beans and limas for processing have resulted through improved mechanization, cultivars, fertilizers, and cultural practices.

The average acre yield of snap beans for fresh market increased from 29 to 36 hundredweight during the 1939-1959 period, during which time the output per man-hour rose 23 percent. The production of snap beans for processing rose from 36 to 45 hundredweight per acre as labor efficiency increased 79 percent. Labor efficiency for snap bean production increased phenomenally—1,123 percent between 1939 and 1977—more than for any other vegetable except spinach (Table 1.6).

The yield of lima beans for fresh market did not increase during the 1939-1959 period, while yields for processed limas almost doubled. Acre production, for both marketing and processing, rose somewhat be-

Table 15.3—Green Lima Beans for Processing: Estimated Acreage, Yield, Production, and Value in Leading States, 1977.

State	Harvested Acreage	Yield per Acre, tons	Production in Tons	Price per Ton	Value, $1,000
California	26,900	1.61	43,200	$384.00	16,627
Delaware	9,000	.57	5,100	248.00	1,265
Wisconsin	5,900	1.17	6,900	246.00	1,697
Maryland	2,800	.75	2,100	264.00	554
Other States	15,710	1.08	16,900	313.00	5,283
United States	60,310	1.23	74,200	343.00	25,426
Canning (37%)	22,090	.88	19,500	283.00	5,523
Freezing, Fordhook (16%)	9,750	1.61	15,700	365.00	5,733
Freezing, Baby (47%)	28,470	1.37	39,000	363.00	14,170

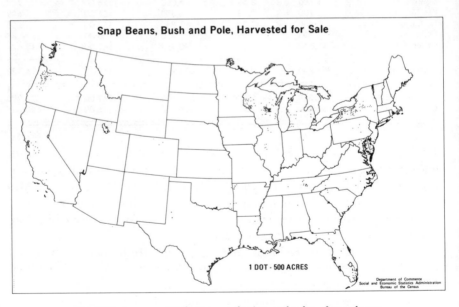

Snap Beans, Bush and Pole, Harvested for Sale

1 DOT - 500 ACRES

Department of Commerce
Social and Economic Statistics Administration
Bureau of the Census

Fig. 15.1—Acreage, distribution, production, and value of snap beans.

UNITED STATES TOTAL

Year	Acreage	Production 1,000 Cwt.	Value, $1,000
1949	314,850	11,072	70,967
1959	281,570	11,575	78,022
1969	326,890	14,644	99,219
1977	335,990	16,402	157,093

Fig. 15.2—Acreage, distribution, production, and value of green lima beans.

UNITED STATES TOTAL

Year	Acreage	Production 1,000 Cwt.	Value, $1,000
1949	141,450	2,568	19,125
1959	95,310	2,027	14,654
1969	83,180	1,974	17,659
1977	60,310	1,484	25,426

tween 1959 and 1965. The output per man-hour for fresh lima beans decreased slightly during the 1939-1959 period, while that for the processed crop increased by 210 percent. Man-hour output has increased substantially since 1959, due to improved machines.

CLIMATIC REQUIREMENTS

Beans require a warm, frost-free climate, but the plants may drop their blossoms or pods during excessively hot or rainy weather. Cultivars differ in sensitivity to weather conditions, and tests should be conducted to determine which ones are best suited for a given locality. Lima beans are especially sensitive to cold, water-soaked soil. When lima beans are grown in the northern border sections, it is especially important to select warm soils that will hasten maturity. Beans thrive best on a mildly acid soil (pH 5.5 to 6.5). Sandy to clay loam and muck soils are used for growing beans, but good yields are seldom produced on very heavy soils.

SELECTING CULTIVARS AND SEED

Cultivars

Both bush and pole cultivars of beans are grown. Because of the cost of materials and labor, the pole types are limited to the home gardens and also to the western United States, where high yields and prices offset the higher cost of production. The pole cultivars require some means of support and produce later harvests over longer periods

Fig. 15.3—Supergreen, a mosaic-resistant cultivar of snap beans.

USDA Photograph

than the bush cultivars. With the perfection of the mechanical bean harvester, the bush cultivars with concentrated maturity and erect plants should replace pole beans for canning and freezing and also for the fresh market. In addition to low-cost production, processors are demanding round-podded, dark green beans with a minimum of fiber in the pods. Wax-podded cultivars are discriminated against because they show mechanical injuries and disease spots very plainly. However, they do find a good market when they can be grown satisfactorily.

A wide choice of cultivars of snap beans is available to the grower. A selected list of these with a brief description and their principal use is shown in Table 15.4. Most of those listed are resistant to one or more diseases. The choice of cultivar for a particular locality may depend to a large extent upon its resistance to a disease prevalent in the area.

Lima bean cultivars may be grouped as to dwarf or pole types and as to thin- and thick-seeded types. The dwarf types are used for processing and make up most of the lima beans grown for market (Fig. 15.4). The climbing or pole cultivars are grown mostly in home gardens.

Henderson Bush (thin-seeded) and Ford Hook (thick-seeded or potato) and selections from these are used for most of the acreage planted to bush lima beans. Cangreen, Thaxter, and Early Thorogreen are similar to Henderson but have green cotyledons which are desired for processing. Ford Hook does not set pods well under unfavorable weather conditions and has been largely replaced by Ford Hook 242 and Concentrated Ford Hook. Nemagreen is a nematode-resistant baby lima which may be expected to outyield other cultivars in nematode-infested soil. Challenger is a thick-seeded type cultivar. King of the Garden, Florida Butter, and Carolina or Sieva are leading pole cultivars.

Securing Seed

A number of serious bean diseases, such as anthracnose, are carried in the seed, and for this reason it is a great advantage to secure seed from relatively disease-free fields or sections. Low humidity and limited rainfall are unfavorable to the development of bean blight, anthracnose, and mosaic.

Only seed grown in regions where seed-borne diseases do not exist or can be controlled should be used. Most of the seed is produced in the semi-arid regions of California and Idaho. Locally grown seed or seed from bypassed crops should never be used for growing a crop of snap beans. The use of resistant cultivars and treated seed is recommended. Bean seed should be handled carefully to prevent mechanical

Table 15.4—Brief Description of Selected Cultivars of Snap Beans.

Cultivar	Days to Maturity	Pod Cross Section	Pod Color	Seed Color	Principal Use	Resistance
Bush Green Pod						
Astro	52	Oval-round	Deep green	White	Processing, shipping	Common, N.Y. 15
Bush Blue Lake 274	58	Round	Dark green	White	Canning, home, freezing	Bean virus 1, N.Y. 15
Cascade	54	Round	Bright green	White	Processing	Common, N.Y. 15
Contender	55	Round	Dark green	Buff, light mottling	Home, market shipping	Common, powdery mildew
Early Gallatin	53	Round	Medium green	White	Canning	
Harvester	53	Round	Medium dark green	Pure white	Garden, market processing	Rust, N.Y. 15, common virus
Provider	53	Round	Medium green	Purple	Market	Common, N.Y. 15
Resistant Asgrow Valentine	52	Oval	Medium green	Black	Market	N.Y. 15, common virus
Slenderwhite	56	Round	Medium dark green	Pure white	Canning, freezing	Common
Spartan Arrow	55	Oval	Medium green	Light buff	Market	
Sprite	53	Round	Medium green	White	Canning	Common, N.Y. 15
Tendercrop	54	Round	Medium green	Purple-buff mottled	Garden, market, freezing	Pod mottle, common, N.Y. 15
Tenderette	52	Round	Deep green	White	Garden, canning, freezing	
Tendergreen	53	Round	Dark green	Brownish purple mottled	Canning	Common
Tenderwhite	58	Round	Medium dark green	Pure white	Garden, canning, freezing	Common

(Continued)

Table 15.4 (Continued).

Cultivar	Days to Maturity	Pod Cross Section	Pod Color	Seed Color	Principal Use	Resistance
Topcrop	52	Round	Medium green	Brown buff splashing	Canning, freezing	Common
Bush Wax Pod						
Brittle Wax	57	Round	Yellow	White, black eye	Garden, canning, freezing	
Earliwax	54	Round	Golden yellow	Pure white	Garden, canning, freezing	Mosaic
Kinghorn Wax (Resistant)	54	Round	Golden yellow	Pure white	Garden, canning, freezing	N.Y. 15, strains
Surecrop Wax	53	Oval	Yellow		Garden, Shipping	Common
Resistant Cherokee Wax	53	Oval	Bright yellow	Black	Garden, shipping	Common, N.Y. 15
Pole Green Pod						
Blue Lake types	63-66	Round	Dark green	Pure white	Garden, canning, freezing	Common
Kentucky Wonder 191	67	Round	Medium light green	Buff, brown stripes	Garden	Some traces of rust
McCaslan	64	Flattened oval	Medium green	Ivory white	Garden, market	
Romano	70	Flattened oval	Silvery	Tan	Market, garden, freezing	

Fig. 15.4—Triumph, a bush type of lima bean.

USDA Photograph

injury. Some cultivars are more susceptible than others. Very dry seed is more prone to injury in handling and to differential swelling of cotyledons during germination, which results in breakage and thus in poor and uneven germination. Seed from dry storage should be conditioned at a relative humidity of about 60 percent for 1 or 2 weeks before planting. The most severe injury occurs when beans are planted in cold wet soil.

PREPARING THE SOIL

Soil Preferences

The bean is a universal crop in the United States and can be grown on soils that range from sand to clay and peat. On sandy soils, beans mature in a shorter time than on the heavier soils. High-moisture content and high nitrogen delay maturity. Most growers prefer a well drained, fairly fertile loam containing considerable humus. Soils more acid than pH 5.5 should usually be limed, but overliming should be avoided.

Where soil-borne diseases are prevalent, beans should not be planted more than once or twice in a five-year rotation.

Preparing the Seed Bed

Bean cotyledons push up through the soil in germination and need a well prepared seedbed. A well prepared, firm seedbed also saves cultivation costs after the crop is planted. Beans thrive after a cultivated crop, partly because of freedom from weeds. Sod land to be planted to beans is best plowed in the fall.

FERTILIZING AND MANURING

Fertilizing

Beans may be placed in the group of vegetable crops least responsive to the application of fertilizers. However, the crop does well on fertile soils. The application of fertilizer should be based upon known requirements of the soil. When this information is not available, a moderate amount of a complete fertilizer high in phosphorus may be applied. Excessive nitrogen should be avoided, since this element may increase vine growth at the expense of pod production and may interfere with mechanical harvesting.

Manuring

Soils of low humus content need a green-manure crop in the rotation. This should be plowed under at least one month before the beans are to be planted. Stable manure is usually high in nitrogen and can be used to best advantage on other crops.

PLANTING, CULTIVATING, AND IRRIGATING

Planting

Most plantings of both lima and snap beans are best made after the soil is warm and the danger of frost is over. Earlier plantings are often made for early market and in home gardens. A fall crop is often grown in many sections of the South; and in Florida, most of the plantings are made during the fall and winter. Although beans quickly lose the ability to germinate under warm, humid conditions, they should not be removed from dry storage and planted immediately, especially in cold and wet soils.

Pole cultivars of snap beans and lima beans are commonly planted in hills 3 to 4 feet apart each way. Five or six seeds are planted in each hill, and the plants are later thinned to three or four. In California, unsupported pole limas are grown in drills. Garden cultivars of the bush type are commonly spaced 2 to 4 inches apart in drills, with the closer spacings usually producing larger yields, but requiring more seed per acre. Gillis found that at the rate of six seeds per foot and with rows 3 feet apart, it would require 90 pounds of Stringless Green Pod seed to plant an acre. Ordinarily, about 50 pounds of snap bean seed of average size are planted to the acre. Large-seeded cultivars would increase this amount, and small-seeded ones would decrease it.

A higher rate of seeding is recommended for mechanical harvesting. In New York, suggested planting rates range from 6 to 7 plants per foot for areas where moisture is a limiting factor to 10 plants per foot for areas with ample fertility and soil moisture. The average rate and method of planting different kinds of beans are given in Table 8.1.

Cultivating

It is not advisable to cultivate or to work among bean plants when the foliage is wet, because anthracnose and other fungus spores are easily disseminated in this way. Cultivation and hoeing, which are employed primarily to keep down and destroy weeds, should start when the bean plants first appear above ground, and should be shallow, especially as the plants approach maturity. Many of the feeding roots of beans are near the surface and are easily injured by deep cultivation. If beans are grown on a site relatively free of weeds, the number of cultivations for control may be reduced. The danger of injuring the roots and the cost of production will thus be decreased.

Beans are especially susceptible to injury by cultivation during the time of pod set. Hilling of the rows to control weeds is undesirable for mechanical harvesting. Herbicides may be economically substituted for some of the cultivation (Chapter 9).

Irrigating

A constant supply of moisture is one of the critical factors affecting yield, uniformity, and quality in snap beans. A shortage of moisture just before or during flowering can cause serious losses. Even in areas of relatively high average rainfall, irrigation is a necessity for beans on light, sandy soils and, even on heavier soils, it can often mean the difference between a good crop and a poor one.

Supporting Vines

The dry climate in certain sections of California enables farmers to grow both pole and bush cultivars without support. Staking or trellising is expensive, but necessary for pole cultivars in humid regions, since pods touching or near the surface of the ground are usually injured. The vines can be supported by placing 6-foot posts 20 feet apart in the row; connecting the posts with two wires, one at the top and the other a few inches above the ground; and running twine between the wires.

CONTROLLING DISEASES AND INSECTS

Diseases

Usually, lima beans are injured less by diseases than are snap beans. General control measures include using disease-free seed, rotating crops, disposing of diseased bean refuse, using resistant cultivars, and working the plants only when the foliage is dry.

ANTHRACNOSE. Anthracnose is caused by several strains of *Colletotrichum lindemuthianum* and is a destructive fungus disease of snap and field beans grown in humid regions. Hot and dry weather is unfavorable for the development of anthracnose. The fungus overwinters in the seed and in bean refuse. The somewhat circular, dark, sunken spots are easily recognized on the pods and stems. Affected areas on the leaves become discolored and die. Most snap cultivars show little resistance. The term "rust-proof," as used by seedsmen, refers to this disease, but anthracnose should not be confused with bean rust, which is caused by another organism discussed. Seed grown in regions where this disease does not occur should be used and plants sprayed or dusted weekly with zineb, ziram, or Bravo W-75.

BACTERIAL BLIGHT. Associated with *Xanthomonas phaseoli,* bacterial blight is common on snap beans in the central and eastern part of the United States. Diseased spots on the pods appear water-soaked, changing to a reddish brown, and infected seeds are yellowish or yellow-blotched. The common bacterial blight, as well as similar blights on beans, may be controlled by using disease-free seed, by rotating beans with other crops, and by not cultivating the plants while they are wet.

RUST. Rust, caused by *Uromyces phaseoli typica,* is widely distributed over the eastern United States; it also occurs in the coastal section along the Pacific coast and is especially destructive on Kentucky Wonder. Lesions may appear on all aerial parts of the plant, but rust is most destructive on the leaves. The growing of resistant cultivars such as Burpee's Stringless, Pencil Pod, Refugee, and Horticultural Pole and the use of maneb and zineb sprays are recommended as control measures.

DOWNY MILDEW. Downy mildew, *Phytophthora phaseoli,* is a serious fungus disease along the eastern coast, especially on lima beans. Control methods include crop rotation, use of well drained fields, and spraying weekly with maneb and zineb.

COMMON BEAN MOSAIC. Common bean mosaic causes mottling, curling, crinkling, and malformation of the leaves. Occasionally the pods are mottled, deformed, or rough. Diseased plants are often dwarfed and unproductive. The disease can be prevented by growing resistant cultivars.

Insects

Bean insects cause widespread destruction of this crop, especially in home gardens, where satisfactory control measures are difficult to carry out. The rapid spread of the Mexican bean beetles has greatly increased control problems.

MEXICAN BEAN BEETLE. The Mexican bean beetle (*Epilachna varivestis*), believed to be a native of Mexico, has been present in the western United States since 1850, and has now spread over the eastern states. It prefers to feed on snap beans, field beans, and lima beans, but beggarweed is also a common food plant. The beetles usually appear before the beans start to blossom, and after feeding for a week or 10 days, they start to deposit their eggs. Reproduction is rapid, since the average female lays more than 400 eggs. The insect passes the winter as an adult.

The young larvae are more easily killed than the adults. Turning under vines immediately after harvest removes the food supply and helps in control.

Control measures should begin as soon as the beetles appear, and the treatment should be repeated if control is not obtained. Malathion or carbaryl may be used (see Chapter 11).

BEAN LEAF BEETLE. The bean leaf beetle (*Cerotoma trifurcata*) is a small, dark yellow beetle with six black dots on the wing covers. It eats large holes in the leaves, feeding from the underside (Fig. 15.5). The eggs are laid at the bases of the plants, and the grubs feed on the roots. Control can be had with rotenone or carbaryl.

ADULT BEAN WEEVIL. The adult bean weevil (*Acanthoscelides obtectus*) is a small, dull-colored beetle, and the larva is white. The bean weevil

Fig. 15.5—Injury by the bean leaf beetle.

is chiefly a pest of dry beans, including bean seed. Infested seed should not be planted, as germination is poor, and adults emerging from such seed may infect the next crop. The seed should be fumigated or treated with pyrethrins or premium-grade malathion. Treatment should be given early in the storage period before much injury has occurred.

HARVESTING, HANDLING, AND MARKETING

Picking

Bush, as compared to pole cultivars, mature over a relatively short time and may be harvested in only a few pickings. A concentrated set on

Fig. 15.6—A fork-lift truck moving beans.

USDA Photograph

erect plants is required for machine harvest. This method is used for those grown for processing and for much of those grown for the fresh market crop. Snap beans are picked when the pods are nearly full size and the beans small, about one-fourth developed. Green-shell limas are picked when the seeds are nearly full size and the pods green. Less mature limas bring a slightly higher price but yield less. Lima beans for canning are cut by a mowing machine and shelled by machinery.

Grading and Packing

Snap beans should be carefully sorted and graded for market. Lima beans handle and ship best in pods, but are often marketed after being shelled. Both snap and green lima beans need prompt refrigeration after they are harvested; they also need refrigeration in transit all the way to retail stores in order to reduce the amount of soft rot. Hampers, bushel and half-bushel baskets, and crates are common packages.

Grade standards for green beans are sometimes revised, and the latest specifications can be obtained from the Agricultural Marketing Service of the U.S. Department of Agriculture.

Marketing

Immature beans wilt quickly after harvesting in hot weather and need cooling. Commercial production of lima beans is now very small. A large part of the snap bean crop is shipped to northern markets during winter and early spring in refrigerated trucks. In addition to Florida's heavy winter and spring shipments (Table 15.1), summer and fall production in northern states is an important source of fresh snap beans. Marketing practices are generally similar to those in the winter and early spring states. Volume buyers prefer fast, direct handling of beans from modern packing centers, which usually assure standard quality and established daily market prices for the various grades.

EXPORTS AND IMPORTS. In 1977 about 17,584,000 pounds of fresh beans valued at $2,537,000 were exported. In the same year, 17,486,000 pounds valued at $3,374,000 were imported (Table 13.2). The bulk of the imports were made during the winter and early spring and came almost entirely from Mexico, while exports were shipped primarily to Canada. (See Table 13.2 for canned exports and imports.)

SELECTED REFERENCES

Ammerman, G. R., and Campbell, G. M., "Mississippi Delta Snap Beans for Processing," Miss. State Univ. Agr. and For. Exp. Sta. Tech. Bull. 57, Mississippi State, 1970.

Anonymous, "Growing Snap Beans for Processing," Asgrow Seed Co., Orange, Conn., 1968.

Atkin, J. D., "Nature of the Stringy Pod Rogue of Snap Beans, *Phaseolus vulgaris*," N. Y. State Agr. Exp. Sta. *Search Agriculture*, Vol. 2 (9), 1972.

Brown, J. F., Coffey, D. L., and Swingle, H. D., "Plant Population Studies with Lima Beans," Univ. of Tenn. Agr. Exp. Sta., Tenn Farm and Home Science Pro. Rep. 104, 1977.

Cook, W. P., *et al.*, "Commercial Lima Bean Production," Clemson Univ. and USDA Ext. Ser., Veg. Leaflet 13, 1978.

Cook, W. P., *et al.*, "Commercial Pole Bean Production," Clemson Univ. and USDA Ext. Ser., Veg. Leaflet 12, 1978.

Cook, W. P., *et al.*, "Commercial Snapbean Production," Clemson Univ. and USDA Ext. Ser., Veg. Leaflet 1, 1978.

Curwen, D., and Schulte, E. E., "Snap Beans—Green and Wax," Univ. of Wisc. Coop. Ext. Prog., Commercial Vegetable Production A2328, 1978.

Fletcher, R. F., Tetrault, R., and MacNab, A. A., "Growing Snap Beans for Processing," Pa. State Univ. Agr. Ext. Ser. Circ. 564, 1976.

Ford, K. E., "Distribution of Green Beans on the Fresh Market," Univ. of Ga. Res. Dept. 116, 1972.

McMaster, G. M., *et al.*, "The Influence of Soil Moisture on Snap Bean Production," Ida. Agr. Exp. Sta. Bull. 435, 1965.

Morris, J. R., "Growing Snap Beans for Processing," Univ. of Ark. Ext. Ser., Leaflet 492, 1971.

Natti, J. J., "Control of Halo Blight of Bean by Foliage Sprays," N. Y. State Agr. Exp. Sta., *Search Agriculture*, Vol. 1 (11), 1971.

Patterson, D. R., *et al.*, "Effects of Nitrogen on Yield Quality and Mineral Uptake of Harvest Snap Beans," Tex. A & M Univ. Exp. Sta. MP-808, 1966.

Robins, J. S., and Howe, O. W., "Irrigating Dry Beans in the West, USDA Leaflet 499, Washington, D.C., 1961.

Rutledge, A. D., "Commercial Snapbean Production," Univ. of Tenn. Agr. Ext. Ser. Ext. Circ. 823, 1975.

Sandsted, R. F., *et al.*, "Growing Dry Beans in New York State," N. Y. State Col. Agr. Coop. Ext. Pub., *Plant Sciences Vegetable Crops 1*, Inf. Bull. 2, 1974.

Schales, F. D., and Watts, V., "Lima Beans and Snap Beans," Va. Poly. Inst. Ext. Dir. Pub. 239, 1968.

Sims, W. L., Harrington, J. F., and Tyler, K. B., "Growing Bush Snap Beans for Mechanical Harvest," Univ. of Calif., Div. Agr. Sci. Leaflet 2674, 1977.

Westerman, D. J., and Crothers, S. E., "Plant Population Effects on the Seed Yield Components of Beans," *Crop Sci.* 17 (4): 493-496, 1977.

CHAPTER 16

Cabbage

CLASSIFICATION, ORIGIN, AND HISTORY

Cabbage (*Brassica oleracea* var. *capitata*) is the most important member of the *Cruciferae* or mustard family. It is generally conceded that our present-day cultivars of cabbage originated from the wild cabbage which is found growing along the chalky coasts of England and along the western and southern coasts of Europe. Cabbage has been used as a food crop since earliest antiquity. The ancient Greeks held it in high esteem, and their fables claim its origin from the father of their gods. The Egyptians are said to have worshiped cabbage. Today it still remains one of the leading vegetable crops of the world.

SCOPE AND IMPORTANCE

Although the popularity of cabbage decreased somewhat in recent years, it ranked eleventh in acreage and sixth in value among the 22 principal vegetables in 1977. Cabbage acreage for fresh market and kraut decreased from 169,880 acres in 1949 to approximately 91,500 acres in 1977. During this period, total production decreased gradually, while value increased from $36,569,000 to about $172,860,000. Likewise, cabbage acreage for sauerkraut declined from 17,500 acres to 13,060 acres during the 1949 to 1973 period, and to 10,380 acres in 1977, while total value rose from $2,190,000 to approximately $7,022,000. Commercial cabbage is produced in numerous states as illustrated in Fig. 16.1, which also shows the 1949 to 1977 performance record of cabbage. Florida, Texas, California, North Carolina, and Georgia lead in production and value of fresh cabbage, while New York, Wisconsin, and Ohio lead in produc-

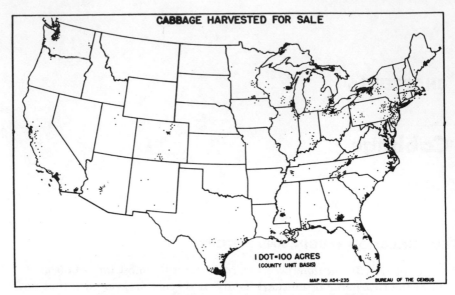

Fig. 16.1—Acreage, distribution, production, and value of cabbage.

UNITED STATES TOTAL

Year	Acreage	Production 1,000 Cwt.	Value, $1,000
1949	169,880	26,163	36,569
1959	122,880	21,076	48,709
1969	111,330	22,960	67,550
1977	101,920	28,366	119,388

tion and value of cabbage for kraut, as shown in Tables 16.1 and 16.2, respectively.

TRENDS IN PRODUCTION EFFICIENCY

Cabbage production is comparatively expensive because of the outlay for plants, fertilizers, pesticides, and labor. Acre yields of fresh cabbage increased from 124 to 167 hundredweight between 1939 and 1959 and rose to 259 by 1977 (Tables 1.6 and 16.1). Cabbage for sauerkraut yields rose from approximately 200 hundredweight in 1949 to 264 in 1959 and up to 444 in 1977.

In 1939, producing an acre of market and kraut cabbage required 108 and 94 man-hours respectively. These figures declined to 104 and 56 man-hours in 1959. However, efficiency for fresh market cabbage improved considerably in recent years, as the increase in output per man-hour rose 357 percent between 1939 and 1977 (Table 1.6).

Table 16.1—Cabbage for Fresh Market and Processing: Harvest Season, Estimated Acreage, Yield, Production, and Value in Leading States, 1977.

State	Harvested Season	Harvested Acreage	Yield per Acre, Cwt.	Production per 1,000 Cwt.	Price per Cwt.	Value, $1,000
New York	Fall	9,400	385	3,619	$ 5.69	17,156
Florida	Winter	9,000	215	1,935	15.20	29,412
Texas	Winter	6,200	280	1,736	17.70	30,727
Florida	Spring	5,600	285	1,596	9.46	15,098
Texas	Fall	5,500	200	1,100	7.47	8,217
New York	Summer	3,800	380	1,444	3.05	4,408
Texas	Spring	3,200	310	992	8.58	8,511
Wisconsin	Summer	3,000	425	1,275	2.51	3,205
N. Carolina	Summer	2,600	185	481	4.29	2,064
Georgia	Spring	2,600	83	216	7.37	1,592
New Jersey	Summer	2,400	185	444	5.31	2,358
California	Spring	2,300	225	518	5.56	2,880
Michigan	Summer	2,300	170	391	5.32	2,080
California	Winter	2,200	235	517	15.70	8,117
N. Carolina	Fall	2,200	110	242	6.10	1,476
N. Carolina	Spring	2,200	110	242	3.89	941
Wisconsin	Fall	2,000	425	850	3.64	3,097
Florida	Fall	1,800	215	387	7.91	3,061
California	Fall	1,600	270	432	6.35	2,743
Illinois	Summer	1,600	200	320	4.53	1,448
Michigan	Fall	1,600	195	312	4.72	1,474
Other States		18,444		3,760		19,556
United States		91,540	259	23,751	7.47	172,866

Table 16.2—Cabbage for Kraut: Estimated Acreage, Yield, Production, and Value in Leading States, 1977.

State	Harvested Acreage	Yield per Acre, Tons	Production in Tons	Price per Ton	Value, $1,000
New York	4,100	22.18	90,950	$29.90	2,719
Wisconsin	3,500	21.27	74,450	29.30	2,181
Ohio	950	25.26	24,000	30.50	732
Other States*	1,830	22.46	41,100	33.80	1,390
United States	10,380	22.21	230,500	30.50	7,022

*Mostly from Colorado, Illinois, Indiana, Michigan, N. Carolina, Oregon, Pennsylvania, Tennessee, Virginia, and Washington.

CLIMATIC REQUIREMENTS

Cabbage is a hardy cool-season crop and is at its best during a cool, moist period. It will, however, stand wide variations in temperature. Plantings of cabbage are made in the South from July to April, during a period of extremes in weather.

Young cabbage plants of the Wakefield group, if well hardened, will stand temperatures as low as 15° F. without serious damage. However, most cultivars, particularly those of the Copenhagen type, will not stand temperatures below 20° F., and even at 20° F., the plants must be well hardened.

SELECTING CULTIVARS AND SEED

In selecting a cultivar, one must consider such factors as market demand, cold and disease resistance, season of the year to be planted, and resistance to premature seeding.

Types and Cultivars

Small conical-headed cultivars are grown early in the season. The Jersey Wakefield and the Charleston Wakefield are similar, but the heads of the latter are slightly larger, later, and less pointed. The earliest of the globe-headed cultivars is Golden Acre, which belongs to the Copenhagen Market group. Midseason cultivars include Globe and Marion Market (round-head types) and Wisconsin All Seasons and Flat Dutch (flat-head types). The Hollander or Danish Ballhead type is grown in the North for winter storage. The outstanding characteristics of the principal cultivars of cabbage are given in Table 16.3, and some are shown in Figure 16.2.

Securing Seed

Up until about 1915, most of the cabbage seed was imported from Europe, chiefly from Denmark and Holland. Since then many American seedsmen have been growing their own seed in the Puget Sound district, centering around Mount Vernon, Washington. Long Island, New York, is the oldest cabbage seed-producing district in the United States; but production in that area was discontinued in favor of the Puget Sound region. The ease with which members of the cabbage family cross makes it a difficult problem to maintain pure stock. For this reason, it is well to

Fig. 16.2—Heads of yellow-resistant cabbage cultivars: (A) Jersey Queen; (B) Resistant Detroit; (C) Marion Market; (D) Globe; (E) All Head Select; (F) Improved Wisconsin All Seasons; (G) Improved Wisconsin Ballhead; (H) Wisconsin Hollander.

USDA Photograph

Table 16.3—Chief Characteristics of Selected Cultivars of Cabbage.

Cultivar	Chief Use	Season (Days)	Plant Size	Leaf Color	Wt. (lbs.)	Shape	Firmness
C. C. Cross	Early market	61	Small	Blue green	2	Round	Firm
Emerald Cross	Garden, market	63	Small	Blue green	3	Round	Firm
Greenback*	Market, shipping	74	Compact	Blue green	7-7½	Round	Firm
Hybrid H*	Shipping	85	Small	Blue green	2-3	Round	Compact
King Cole	Market, early kraut	66	Medium	Medium green	5	Flat globe	Firm
Market Topper	Shipping	73	Large	Blue green	5	Round	Firm
Red Acre (Red)	Market, garden	74	Small	Deep red	5	Round	Hard
Red Danish (Red)	Pickling, coleslaw	97	Medium	Purple red	7	Round	Solid
Resistant Danish*	Storage	75	Medium	Blue green	5	Round	Firm
Res. Golden Acre*	Market, shipping	64	Medium small	Medium green	3½-4	Round	Firm
Ruby Ball*	Coleslaw	72	Small	Red	2½	Round	Solid
Saf-gard*	Market, shipping	78	Medium	Green	4-6	Semi-flat	Medium
Savoy Ace*	Market	83	Medium	Green	4	Flat globe	Medium
Savoy King Hybrid	Market	90	Large	Deep green	5	Semi-flat	Medium
Stone Head	Market	63	Small	Blue green	3	Round	Hard
Wisc. All Seasons*	Kraut, storage	93	Large	Medium green	9	Flat globe	Solid

*Resistant to Fusarium wilt.

buy seed from seedsmen who are interested in cabbage seed production themselves and who maintain reliable stocks. In buying seed, a record should be kept of the stock number so the particular strain or stock can be duplicated another season if desired.

PREPARING THE SOIL

Soil Preferences

For fall, summer, and early winter plantings, cabbage does best on the heavier loams, while the spring crop does best on a sandier loam. The sandy soils drain better and naturally are warmer than the heavier soil types. While the cabbage crop requires an abundant supply of water, good drainage is very necessary. The soil should contain a liberal supply of organic matter.

Preparing the Seed Bed

A green-manure crop should be turned under at least a month in advance of planting. The land should be disced and the rows prepared a week or 10 days before planting. The disc cultivator is a good tool with which to prepare the rows as it pulverizes the soil thoroughly. Heavy soil should be sufficiently harrowed before planting.

FERTILIZING AND LIMING

Fertilizing

Cabbage belongs to the group of vegetable crops giving greatest response to soil fertility. Recommended amounts of nitrogen are given in Table 6.4, while phosphorus and potassium requirements are shown in Table 6.5. Part of the nitrogen on sandy soils may be applied as a side dressing, but phosphorus and potash are usually applied before or at the time of planting.

Liming

Cabbage grows best where the pH range is from 6.0 to 6.5. Where the soil is more acid than pH 5.5, an application of lime will be beneficial. Phosphorus, an important element, is most available between pH

5.5 and 6.5. The reaction should not be above this range except where clubroot is a serious problem. If crop rotation cannot be used to control the disease, soil reaction can be raised to neutral by applying hydrated lime. Lime requirement for different soils is given in Table 6.2.

PLANTING, CULTIVATING, AND IRRIGATING

Growing Plants

Three distinct methods of plant growing are used.

PLANTING DIRECTLY IN THE FIELD. This method is adapted to areas favorable to germination and early plant growth. On sandy soils, irrigation is necessary to insure stands. On heavier soils, a stand can be obtained when the rainfall is well distributed. Before planting, the land should be well settled by rains or irrigation. The seed is drilled at the rate of 3 pounds per acre and given shallow covering, especially on heavy soils, the soil being firmed with a roller after planting. When the plants have grown to the usual transplanting size, some thinning is usually necessary, the plants that are removed being either sold or transplanted to other fields. The plants seeded directly in the field usually mature two or three weeks before transplanted plants of the same age.

PLANTING ON OPEN FIELD BEDS. In practicing this method, land is prepared in beds of convenient width, usually 5 to 6 feet, and the seed is drilled in rows 4 to 6 inches apart. Sometimes the seeds are sown broadcast over the bed, but the row system is recommended as it is more convenient to care for the plants properly. This method is used extensively in plant-producing areas around Charleston, South Carolina, and for late cabbage in the North. Seeding in the beds for the early spring crop is usually done during fall—September and October—depending somewhat upon the locality.

PLANTING IN COLD FRAMES. This method of plant production is used extensively in the interior cabbage-producing areas such as the Crystal Springs area of Mississippi. Cautious growers along the Gulf and Atlantic coasts use this method along with the open field beds so that they will have reserve plants in case of a heavy freeze. The cold frames may be covered with glass sash, cloth, or transparent polyethylene. Additional cover is needed to protect the plants against heavy freezes, and on warm days careful ventilation is necessary to prevent overheating. The cold frame not only protects the plants against unfavorable weather but also enables them to develop in a shorter time. Plants to be transplanted where severe freezes may occur should be well hardened.

Setting Plants

Although transplanting is generally done with machinery, it may be done by hand where labor is not a problem or where only small plantings are made. When transplanting is done during late summer and early fall, only large, stocky plants should be used; and these should be watered and the soil firmed about the roots.

In the vegetable areas from Virginia to Georgia, many of the plantings for the spring crop are set in the field in late fall and early winter. The plants make very little top growth during the winter, but as spring opens, they begin to grow and usually mature earlier than spring-set plants. In Texas and Florida, commercial plantings are made during fall and winter. In Alabama, Louisiana, and Mississippi, plants are seldom set in the field before January for the spring shipments. Plants for the early crop in the North are transplanted to the field as soon as hard freezes are over, while late cabbage is set out the latter half of June and in July.

The planting distances in the row are usually 12 to 18 inches for the Jersey and Copenhagen types, and 18 to 20 inches for domestic cultivars such as the All Head Early and Flat Dutch. The width between the rows varies from 28 inches to 4 feet, depending upon the soil type and methods of irrigation and drainage used. Closer planting tends to produce smaller heads but larger yields per acre.

Cultivating

Cabbage has an extensive shallow root system. Deep cultivation should not be used except when the soil becomes very hard and then only when the plants are small. After that, shallow cultivation should be practiced (Fig. 16.3). Fall and spring crops usually need three cultivations, while the winter crop requires less attention. Only when weeds are present should large plants be cultivated. Cultivation should be discontinued when the plants start to head. Broken leaves may result if plants are cultivated too early in the morning when they are turgid.

Fig. 16.3—Well grown and cultivated field of cabbage.

USDA Photograph

Irrigating

Maintaining favorable moisture throughout development is necessary to produce a successful crop of cabbage. The consumptive use of moisture increases until the time of heading, and thus the need for more frequent irrigations. Water may be applied by either the furrow or the sprinkler system. Uneven moisture after the heads are formed may cause splitting.

Premature Seeding

Investigations have shown that the single factor most closely associated with premature seeding is the size of the plants when exposed to the low temperature. Small plants having leaves about 1 to 1½ inches wide can stand low temperatures for six months without going to seed. However, if the plants are large, having leaves 2 to 3 inches wide, many of them will shoot seed stalks if exposed to continuous cold weather, 40° to 50° F., for a period of 30 to 60 days. The longer the period of exposure, the higher will be the percentage of plants producing seed stalks. Some cultivars and strains are more subject to premature seeding than others. The Copenhagen Market cultivar is more subject to bolting than the Jersey cultivars. It is clearly evident that strains can be bred that are highly resistant to premature seeding. About the best control measures are to (1) use the best strains of seed available, (2) avoid setting plants too early in the field, and (3) prevent the stimulation of early plant growth. The plants should be relatively small during midwinter when there is a continuous low temperature. It is not the freezing temperature that causes premature seeding, but a very low growing temperature that initiates seed-stalk formation.

CONTROLLING DISEASES AND INSECTS

Diseases

The most important cabbage diseases the grower has to contend with are black rot, root knot, yellows, club root, and blackleg.

BLACK ROT. Black rot, caused by *Xanthomonas campestris,* appears at any stage of plant growth. The disease is first indicated by a yellowing of the leaves and a blackening of the veins. Later the plants show dwarfing and one sided heads. If the disease attacks the plants early no heads will be formed. The organism is carried over on the seed and residues of infected plants. Soaking seed in water at 122° F. for 25 to 30 minutes will destroy the organism in as well as on the seed. The use of clean seed, crop rotation, and sanitation is recommended. Cruciferous plants should not be allowed to grow in the soil for at least three years.

ROOT KNOT. Root knot (*Meloidogyne sp.*) is a disease caused by a parasite eelworm which attacks the roots of the plants, producing irregularly shaped galls. These are sometimes confused with the galls produced by club root, which are located nearer the stem of the plant. Rotation with small grains, corn, velvet beans, some cultivars of cowpeas, soybeans, and other crops immune to the nematodes is recommended. Soil fumigation is an effective but an expensive means of control, and may have to be limited to the seedbed. Methyl bromide, vapam, or chlorobromopropene may be used.

YELLOWS. Yellows, caused by *Fusarium oxysporum f. conglutinans,* while primarily a northern disease, does some damage to cabbage in the upper South. The plants turn yellow soon after they are transplanted, the leaves fall, and the plants die. If this trouble results, yellows-resistant cultivars which have been developed and are to be had on the market should be used.

CLUB ROOT. Club root (*Plasmodiophora brassicae* Wor.) attacks the roots of cruciferous plants, causing characteristic swellings. The malformed roots are club-like in appearance. The disease may be controlled by avoiding infested areas, using crop rotation, keeping the soil alkaline (pH 7.2), and using PCNB at the time of transplanting.

BLACKLEG. Blackleg is caused by the fungus *Phoma lingam* Desmax. It attacks the stems of young plants, causing dark sunken areas. The entire plant wilts and the dead leaves adhere to the stem. Control is similar to that for black rot.

Insects

The most destructive insects to cabbage are various kinds of cabbage worms, particularly the green worm, the larvae of the cabbage butterfly, the diamond back, and cabbage looper. Plant lice and the harlequin bug are also serious pests.

CABBAGE WORMS. Cabbage worms, including the cabbage looper, can be controlled with methomyl before the heads are formed and with rotenone afterwards (see Chapter 11). Control measures should begin as soon as evidence of feeding is observed.

CABBAGE APHID. The cabbage aphid (*Brevicoryne brassicae*) is a sucking insect. It has a waxy covering similar to the cabbage leaves. It is thereby protected from spray materials unless a detergent or sticker is used. Timeliness is very important in the control of aphids. The plants should be treated before the insect is established and before serious damage is done. Malathion, Diazinon, and nicotine sulphate are effective insecticides.

HARLEQUIN BUG. The harlequin bug (*Murgantia histrionica*) is mottled red, black, or yellow and about ⅗ inch long. Both the young and adult feed on cabbage, sucking juices and injecting poison into the plant. The adults can be controlled with malathion or naled.

HARVESTING, HANDLING, AND MARKETING

Harvesting

Since both Texas and Florida have been making heavy shipments, there is not the rush to ship immature heads as in former years. The plant should be allowed to mature into a firm white head before harvesting. From two to three green wrapper leaves, unless worm-eaten, should be left attached, as new cabbage is wanted green and fresh. As the heads are cut, they are usually tossed to a man in a wagon or truck and hauled to the packing shed. Care should be taken not to bruise the head as this makes it unattractive.

Grading and Packing

The tendency is for better grading of cabbage as the market wants a firm, uniform head of high quality. The most desirable heads weigh between two and five pounds, the smaller ones being preferred. Prevailing grade and size standards and regulations can be obtained from the U.S. Department of Agriculture upon request.

In most sections, the cabbage is hauled from the field to a central packing house, while in some areas the crates are filled in the field or on the headlands. The heads should be arranged in orderly layers in the crates, with the stem ends to the outside. They should be packed firmly, but not tightly enough to cause bruising. The mesh bag and 1¾ bushel carton are standard containers for cabbage. In warm weather it is desirable to place crushed ice in or around the containers while in transit to prevent deterioration. In cool weather, cabbage should be transported in containers with open vents.

Storing

With the increase in production of winter cabbage, the acreage grown for storage in the North has markedly decreased. There is a definite consumer preference for the fresh green cabbage even though it is higher in price than the stored heads. Successful storage requires: (1) a good storage variety, (2) freedom from disease or injuries, (3) a temperature near 32° F., and (4) relatively high humidity. Well grown, solid heads of the Danish Ballhead cultivar keep best in storage.

Very little cabbage is stored in the South. To store spring cabbage for any length of time, it is necessary to place it in cold storage; and since the crop is bulky and the cold-storage rates are usually high, storage usually does not pay. However, if prices are low and expected prices high, cabbage can sometimes be stored to advantage.

Marketing

In some leading cabbage-growing areas produce agencies arrange for their own production and marketing. In most cases, however, volume buyers have a local agent or send a representative to buy on location. Some cabbage is shipped on consignment, but this method of marketing is limited. In many areas a portion of the crop is marketed through various types of cooperatives. This latter method is recommended only when the organization is large enough to maintain efficient management.

EXPORTS AND IMPORTS. Exports of fresh cabbage were slightly below average in 1972, reaching 90,179,000 pounds, valued at $3,413,000. In 1977, 72,798,000 pounds, valued at $8,430,000 were exported (Table 13.2). Canada was the prime country of destination, with small quantities shipped to the Caribbean area and Western Europe. Moderate quantities of cabbage were imported in 1977 (Table 13.2).

SELECTED REFERENCES

Anonymous, "Market Diseases of Cabbage and Other Crops," USDA *Agriculture Handbook 184*, 1961.

Anonymous, "Pest and Disease Control Program for Cole Crops," Colo. Agr. Ext. Ser. Pub., 1975.

Becker, R. F., "Cabbage: Tipburn and Other Internal Disorders," N. Y. State Agr. Exp. Sta., *Food & Life Sci.* Bull. 7, 1971.

Binning, L. K., Libby, J. L., and Wade, E. K., "Cole Crops—Pest Control," Univ. of Wisc. Coop Ext. Prog. Commercial Veg. Production A2357, 1978.

Cook, W. P., *et al.*, "Commercial Cabbage Production," Clemson Univ. Coop. USDA Ext. Ser. Veg. Leaflet 6, 1978.

Cress, D., and Wells, A., "Cole Crops Insect Pests," Mich. State Univ. Coop. Ext. Ser. Ext. Bull. E-968, 1976.

Dodge, J. C., "Cabbage," Wash. State Univ. Coop. Ext. Ser., *Grower's Guide for Veg. Crops*, E. M. 2925, 1972.

Eckenrode, C. J., "A Continuing Search for Effective Maggot Control in New York," N. Y. State Agr. Exp. Sta., *Search Agriculture*, Vol. 2 (11), 1972.

Ford, K. E., "Distribution of Cabbage on the Fresh Market," Ga. Ext. Sta. Res. Rep. 117, 1972.

Guzman, V. L., "Comparison of Cabbage Breeding Lines for Bacterial Black Rot, Bacterial Black Spot, and Fresh Market Quality," Fla. Agr. Exp. Sta., 1974.

Kohn, H., and Levitt, J., "Frost Hardiness Studies on Cabbage Grown Under Controlled Conditions," *Plant Physiol.*, 40: 476-80, 1965.

Larsen, J., Cotner, S., and Longbrake, T., "Keys to Profitable Cabbage Production," Tex. A & M Univ. Agr. Ext. Ser. Fact Sheet L-918, 1971.

Marvel, M. E., and Montelaro, J., "Cabbage Production Guide," Fla. Agr. Ext. Ser. Circ. 117C, 1967.

Moreau, A. C., and Montelaro, J., "Growing Cabbage in Louisiana," Univ. of La. Coop. Ext. Ser. Pub. 1492, 1966.

Morrison, W. W., "Fresh Cabbage, from Grower to Retailer," USDA Mktg. Bull. 21, 1962.

Neild, R. E., "Cole Crop Varieties, Harvesting, Storage," Univ. of Neb. Coop. Ext. Ser. Neb. Guide G 75-251, 1975.

O'Dell, C. R., "Cabbage and Broccoli," Ext. Div. Va. Poly. Inst and State Univ., *Vegetable Production Series*, Pub. 162, 1971.

Oyer, E. B., "Growing Cabbage in New York," Cornell Univ. Agr. Ext. Bull. 1042, 1960.

Seelig, R. A., "Fruit and Vegetable Facts and Pointers: Cabbage," United Fresh Fruit and Veg. Assoc. Rep., Alexandria, Va., 1969.

Sherf, A. F., "Storage Diseases of Cabbage and Carrots," N. Y. State Col. Agr. Cornell Univ. Inf. Bull. 35, 1972.

Swan, D. G., "Weed Control in Cabbage, Carrots, Lettuce and Peas," Univ. of Alas. Coop. Ext. Ser. P-140, 1978.

Turner, D. O., Halvorson, A. R., and Jarmin, M. L., "Fertilizer Guide—Cabbage, Broccoli, Cauliflower, and Brussels Sprouts," Wash. State Univ. Coop. Ext. Ser. Pub. FG-47, 1974.

CHAPTER 17

Carrots

CLASSIFICATION, ORIGIN, AND HISTORY

The carrot (*Daucus carota* var. *sativa*) belongs to the *Umbelliferae* family which also includes celery, parsnips, and parsley. About 60 species of *Daucus* have been described. Historically, the carrot was used primarily for medicinal purposes, and was not generally used as a food plant until the beginning of the twentieth century. It has been reported that the carrot with purple roots was domesticated in Afghanistan and spread to the eastern Mediterranean area under Arab influence in the tenth to twelfth centuries and to western Europe in the fourteenth and fifteenth centuries. By the sixteenth century, roots which varied in size, color, and shape had been developed. In the New World, the carrot soon became popular among the Indians. In fact, the Flathead Indians of Oregon were so fond of them that they could not forbear stealing them from the fields. Carrots are an excellent source of vitamin A and a good source of vitamins B_1, C, and G (B_2) (see Table C in the appendix).

SCOPE AND IMPORTANCE

Carrots for home use and local markets are grown throughout the country, and those for use commercially are grown in a dozen states. Among the principal vegetable crops, carrots ranked fifteenth in acreage and eighth in value in 1977. Acreage decreased from 93,200 in 1949 to 80,750 in 1959 and down to approximately 70,000 acres in 1977. Acre yields rose from 156 to 276 hundredweight between 1949 and 1977. Production increased from 14,536,000 to about 19,200,000 hundredweight during the 1949 to 1973 period. The value of carrots rose from $39,523,-000 to about $141,432,000 during the same time. Leading states in acreage, production, and value in 1977 were California, Texas, Michigan, and Wisconsin, as shown in Table 17.1.

Table 17.1—Carrots for Fresh Market and Processing: Harvest Season, Estimated Acreage, Yield, Production, and Value in Leading States, 1977.

State	Harvest Season	Harvested Acreage	Yield per Acre, Cwt.	Production per 1,000 Cwt.	Price per Cwt.	Value, $1,000
Texas	Winter	8,000	140	1,120	$12.60	14,103
California (Other)	Fall	7,000	285	1,995	6.73	13,417
California (Other)	Summer	6,800	345	2,346	5.60	13,129
California (Desert)	Spring	5,700	190	1,083	8.79	9,518
California (Other)	Spring	4,900	320	1,568	9.12	14,304
California (Other)	Winter	4,100	270	1,107	11.30	12,459
California (Desert)	Winter	4,000	260	1,040	12.00	12,520
Washington	Fall	4,000	475	1,900	2.61	4,966
Texas	Spring	3,200	185	592	8.45	5,004
Michigan	Summer	3,000	230	690	9.57	6,601
Michigan	Fall	2,600	235	611	10.10	6,192
Texas	Fall	2,200	155	341	7.56	2,577
New York	Fall	1,900	310	589	13.10	7,696
Wisconsin	Fall	1,800	465	837	3.17	2,656
Wisconsin	Summer	1,700	470	799	3.33	2,664
Oregon	Fall	1,200	440	528	3.26	1,720
Arizona	Spring	1,200	150	180	9.01	1,622
Minnesota	Fall	1,100	485	534	3.57	1,909
Other States		4,120		5,105		8,375
United States		69,520	276	19,208	7.36	141,432
Total	Fall (33%)	23,270	333	7,756	5.11	42,700
Total	Winter (24%)	16,700	201	3,357	12.10	40,502
Total	Spring (22%)	15,000	228	3,423	8.90	30,448
Total	Summer (21%)	14,550	322	4,678	5.94	27,782

TRENDS IN PRODUCTION EFFICIENCY

The carrot is a comparatively expensive crop to grow. Improved herbicides now eliminate expensive, repetitive hand weeding and hoeing, and precision planters are especially helpful in reducing labor requirements of thinning—a practice which is eliminated on most farms. In 1939, about 284 man-hours were required to grow and harvest an acre, 105 man-hours were used on the average in 1959, and this was reduced to 77 man-hours per acre by 1977. The output per man-hour increased 663 percent during the 1939 to 1977 period (Table 1.6).

PLANT CHARACTERISTICS

A cross section of the root shows two distinct regions, an outer core and an inner core. The outer core consists of (1) a thin periderm, a layer of cork cells; and (2) a relatively wide band of secondary phloem, the region where sugars are mainly stored. The inner core consists of (1) secondary xylem and (2) pith. High-quality carrots are those which have a relatively large outer core. Carotene is highest in the older cells of the cortex. It increases with the age of the root and accumulates most rapidly at temperatures of 65° to 70° F. in well aerated soils.

Carrots develop a deep, extensive, absorbing root system. During the seedling stage, the absorbing roots develop rather slowly, but as the edible portion enlarges, it gives rise to a large number of fine absorbing roots. Investigations at the New York (Cornell) Agricultural Experiment Station have shown that carrots growing in gravelly sandy loam fill the soil with roots to depths of 25 to 30 inches.

The stem consists of a small plate-like crown which develops from the plumule. During the second year the plate-like stem elongates and forms branches 2 to 4 feet high which bear the flowers and seed. The leaves arise in the form of a rosette and are long-petioled and decompound. The seed is a very small, dry, indehiscent, one-seeded fruit. It germinates very slowly and requires a fine, friable seedbed and a uniform supply of moisture.

CLIMATIC REQUIREMENTS

Investigations at the New York (Cornell) Agricultural Experiment Station have shown that temperature has a marked effect on the growth and shape of the root of the Red Cored Chantenay cultivar. Total growth was greater and type of growth more normal at 60° to 70° F. than at 70° to 80° F., or 50° to 60° F., or 40° to 50° F. As the temperature was increased, roots of the Red Cored Chantenay became shortened like those of Oxheart. When the temperature was decreased, the roots became long and pointed, more like those of Long Orange.

Low temperature has been found to be the main factor responsible for poor color development of the carrot root, which is a problem with winter-grown carrots in certain areas of the South. The orange color is chiefly due to the presence of beta carotene, a precursor of vitamin A.

Exposure of the developing plants to relatively low temperatures is an important factor in causing premature seeding, which is sometimes a problem.

SELECTING CULTIVARS

Carrots are generally classified according to shape and length of the root. There are (1) cultivars which are blunt and (2) those which are pointed. Within the former class there are cultivars which are short (length exceeding two but not four times the diameter) as well as long. Within the latter class there are cultivars which are moderately short (length not exceeding four times the diameter) and those which are long (length exceeding four times the diameter).

Oxheart is a representative cultivar of the blunt-short type; Chantenay is representative of the blunt half-long type; Danvers Half Long is of the pointed half-long type; and Imperator is a representative cultivar of the pointed-long type. Cultivars such as Imperator, Goldpak, Hi-Pak Hybrid, Scarlet Nantes, Carousel, Trophy, and Spartan Sweet are used for the fresh market trade. The cultivars for processing include Red Cored Chantenay, Royal Chantenay, Danvers 126, and Spartan Bonus. Greater uniformity of color and shape can be expected from the hybrid cultivars. These characters are important for the fresh market, while good uniform color in the roots and high yields are required for processing. Nantes and Danvers Half Long are used as home garden and market cultivars.

PREPARING THE SOIL AND PLANTING

Soil Preference

For best development the carrot requires deep, loose, well drained sandy loams or loams with a slightly acid reaction. If carrots are grown on comparatively heavy soil, they are likely to produce abundant leaf growth and forked roots. Some carrots are grown on muck land, which is desirable because of its light texture, but the roots tend to be rougher than those grown on light mineral soils.

Fig. 17.1—Carrots used in cooking.

Since carrot seed is small, and since the seedling grows slowly, the seedbed should be in fine physical condition.

The edible roots of the carrot may become misshapen as a result of poor soil structure or obstructions such as stones or coarse trash in the soil. Therefore, it is especially important that the soil for carrots be prepared for planting in the most thorough and careful manner practicable.

Seedling establishment is a major problem in carrot production. Except where irrigation is available, the major objective is to produce a compact, well pulverized seedbed that will readily conduct soil moisture from the lower depths to the germinating seed, yet will not puddle and crust during heavy rains.

Tillage operations should be done only when soil moisture is favorable, and the number of operations should be held to a minimum. Working the soil when it is too wet impairs its structure. Working the soil when it is either too wet or too dry will greatly increase the number of tillage operations required to prepare a seedbed.

Excessive tillage not only is costly but, even more important, it impairs soil structure and causes crusting to be more serious. After being plowed, the soil should be worked no more than is required to produce a firm, well pulverized seedbed.

Planting

The seed is planted about ½ to ¾ inch deep. The rate of planting ranges from 2 to 4 pounds of seed per acre in rows 12 to 24 inches apart. The time of planting varies, but seed may be planted as soon as hard freezes are over in the spring. Fall and winter plantings are usually made in the South and West. In the West, carrots are frequently planted on raised beds, two rows on each. In some areas of the West, seed is scattered thinly in a row 3 to 4 inches wide to permit production without thinning. Seeds generally germinate rather slowly and irregularly, and seedling growth is quite weak. For this reason, soils that crust badly are poorly adapted for carrot production. Hand thinning of commercial plantings is seldom practiced as the cost is excessive. Therefore, seeding rates should be controlled as accurately as possible.

FERTILIZING

The kind and amount of fertilizer to apply varies with the locality and the time of year the crop is grown. Fresh manure should not be used, as investigations have shown that the liquid portion of the manure apparently stimulates branching of the roots. If manure is to be used, it should be well decomposed or composted before applying. On muck soils only small amounts of nitrogen are needed. Table 6.5 may be used as a guide to the application of phosphorus and potassium. On mineral soils in the West, nitrogen is applied at the rate of 60 to 100 pounds per acre, and about 25 pounds of phosphorus is applied as an average. Potassium is rarely used. A side dressing with nitrogen is a general practice, but care must be taken to avoid causing excessive top growth.

CULTIVATING AND CHEMICAL WEED CONTROL

Since the seedlings grow slowly, weed control, particularly during the early portion of the growing season, is necessary. Weeds are difficult to control by machine cultivation while the carrots are small. Hand weeding is too expensive in commercial plantings. Since 1945, the use of herbicidal oils, which give excellent control, has been developed. Carrot fields are sprayed with Stoddard solvent after the first true leaves have formed and preferably not later than the four-leaf stage. Spraying should be done when the weather is warm but not over 80° F. as injury may result. Beds should be sprayed with 50 to 60 gallons per acre. On level plantings, 75 to 85 gallons per acre are required. The chemical treatment will keep most weeds under control until the foliage is large enough to shade weed seedlings within the rows. See Chapter 9 for other herbicides for carrots. Conventional shallow cultivation will take care of those between the rows. At the last cultivation, a little soil should be moved to the rows to cover the tops of the roots and thus prevent greening.

IRRIGATING

Carrots require an abundant and well distributed water supply. Even in many humid areas where irrigation is not normally used, supplemental sprinkler irrigation has resulted in substantial increases in yield, especially on soils of low water-holding capacity. Three to six 1-inch applications over the season during short, dry spells have increased yields materially.

On muck lands that are kept moist by a high water table, the water table should be kept at 30 to 36 inches below the soil surface.

For crops grown during long, rainless periods, the amount of irrigation water required depends on such factors as soil character, rate of evaporation, and amount of water in the soil at planting time. The total amount of water needed, including both that in the soil at planting plus rainfall or irrigation after planting, ranges from about $1\frac{1}{2}$ to 3 acre-feet. In the less hot districts where the evaporation rate is moderate, the equivalent of about an inch of water per week is applied at intervals of 10 days to 2 weeks, amounting to $1\frac{1}{2}$ to 2 acre-feet. In the warmer and dryer districts, applications are heavier or more frequent or both—usually more than an inch every 7 to 10 days, amounting to $2\frac{1}{2}$ to 3 acre-feet of water.

CONTROLLING DISEASES AND INSECTS

A general discussion of vegetable insects and diseases, some of which attack carrots, is given in Chapter 11. The county extension adviser should be consulted before any insecticide or fungicide is applied.

CARROT YELLOWS. Carrot yellows is a virus disease that occasionally cause serious damage. It is transmitted by the six-spotted leaf hopper. A practical means of control is to spray or dust with malathion or carbaryl to control the leaf hopper.

Other diseases include bacterial blight, leaf spot, scab, and soft rot.

CARROT RUST FLY. The carrot rust fly (*Psila rosae*) causes serious damage in certain areas as the larvae burrow into the roots, often in large numbers. Satisfactory control has been achieved by soil applications of diazinon.

Other insects that may cause damage are the vegetable weevil, wireworm, and carrot beetle.

HARVESTING, GRADING, AND MARKETING

Carrots are harvested either with or without the tops. Those harvested with the tops are called bunch carrots, while those harvested without the tops are called bulk carrots. Most carrots for market are now topped, washed, graded, and packaged in transparent film bags. Topping greatly reduces weight loss of the roots and increases storage life. Washing and topping are usually done mechanically. Roots are sorted into various sizes for packaging. Processing carrots are harvested with beet harvesters in many areas.

Carrots store well under proper conditions. Cold storage at 32° F. with high humidity gives best results.

Carrots should be relatively mature when harvested for storage. They should be handled carefully to avoid bruising, which causes them to be very susceptible to storage diseases. Prompt removal of field heat and protection from freezing are important.

EXPORTS AND IMPORTS. In 1977, the United States exported 119,443,000 pounds of carrots worth $9,146,000, and 19,733,000 pounds valued at $1,614,000 were imported (Table 13.2). Canada is the principal supplier to the U.S. market as well as its major foreign customer. Exports take place primarily during the late winter through early summer months, while imports peak in the fall through winter months.

Fig. 17.2—Carrots being examined by federal-state inspector before packaging.

USDA Photograph

SELECTED REFERENCES

Becker, R. F., "The Influence of Environment on Carrot Quality," Cornell Univ. Agr. Exp. Sta. Misc. Bull. S85, 1970.

Boswell, V. R., "Commercial Growing of Carrots," USDA Leaflet 353, 1966.

Cotner, S., Longbrake, T., and Larsen, J., "Keys to Profitable Fresh Carrot Production," Texas A & M Univ. Coop. Ext. Ser. Fact Sheet L-889, 1972.

Crete, R., "Diseases of Carrots in Canada," Canada Dept. of Agr. Information Div. Pub. 1615, 1977.

Duncan, A. A., "Carrot and Parsnip Seed Production," Ore. Agr. Ext. Ser. FS-86, 1965.

Kyle, J. H., "Relationship of Seed Size to Seeding Rate in Carrot Production," Tex. A & M Univ. PR-2533, 1968.

Lipe, W. N., Martin, C., and Eddins, R., "Carrot Varietal and Breeding Line Evaluations in 1971 in the Texas High Plains," Tex. A & M Univ. PR-3078, 1972.

Murray, J., "Fruit and Vegetable Facts and Pointers: Carrots," United Fresh Fruit and Veg. Assoc. Pub., Alexandria, Va., 1976.

Nicklow, C. W., et al., "Carrots," Mich. State Univ. Coop. Ext. Ser. Ext. Bull. E-675, G Farm Sci. Series, 1970.

Schoenemann, J. A., et al., "Carrots," Univ. of Wisc. Coop. Ext. Ser. Pub. A2333, 1978.

Whitaker, T. W., et al., "Carrot Production in the United States," USDA Agriculture Handbook 375, 1970.

CHAPTER 18

Celery

CLASSIFICATION, ORIGIN, AND HISTORY

Celery (*Apium graveolens* var. *dulce*) belongs to the *Umbelliferae* family, which includes carrots, parsley, and parsnips. The native habitat of celery extends from Sweden to Egypt and Abyssinia, and in Asia from the Caucasus to India. It has also been found growing wild in California and New Zealand. Celery was first mentioned as a cultivated food plant in France in 1623.

The plant is normally a biennial, although under certain conditions it develops as an annual. During the vegetative stage a mass of roots are produced from a compacted stem, which forms a rosette of leaves with thick petioles, the edible portion. After exposure to low temperatures, the stem elongates and branches to produce the inflorescence.

SCOPE AND IMPORTANCE

Celery was once available for only a short period during the year and was considered a luxury item. It is now grown in many sections of the country and is popular year-round as a salad ingredient. Celery ranked nineteenth in acreage and ninth in value among the 22 principal vegetable crops in 1977.

Commercial celery acreage declined gradually from 38,310 acres in 1949 to approximately 33,800 acres in 1977. Acre yields rose and total production increased consistently from 12,678,000 hundredweight in 1949 to 16,561,000 hundredweight in 1977. The value of the celery crop fluctuated around $50,000,000 between 1949 and 1959, rose to $85,865,000 in

1969 and escalated to $140,576,000 in 1977. California and Florida are the predominant states in acreage, production, and value as shown in Table 18.1.

Table 18.1—Celery for Fresh Market and Processing: Harvest Season and Estimated Acreage, Yield, Production, and Value by Leading States, 1977.

State	Harvest Season	Harvested Acreage	Yield per Acre, Cwt.	Production per 1,000 Cwt.	Price per Cwt.	Value, $1,000
California (C. Coast)	Fall	4,900	885	2,867	$ 7.21	20,683
California (S. Coast)	Spring	4,800	285	2,808	7.39	20,763
California (S. Coast)	Winter	4,100	565	2,317	11.40	26,511
Florida	Winter	4,100	400	1,640	12.50	20,500
California (C. Coast)	Summer	4,000	585	2,340	6.50	15,208
Florida	Spring	4,000	290	1,160	10.60	12,296
California (S. Coast)	Fall	2,000	580	1,160	5.90	6,844
Michigan	Summer	1,900	445	846	8.39	7,096
Florida	Fall	1,800	235	423	7.66	3,240
California (C. Coast)	Spring	600	560	336	6.48	2,177
Michigan	Fall	500	455	228	7.71	1,758
New York	Summer	440	420	185	8.47	1,567
Washington	Fall	280	385	108	6.90	745
Ohio	Summer	230	420	97	8.12	788
New York	Fall	110	420	46	8.70	400
United States		33,760	491	16,561	8.49	140,576
Total	Fall (29%)	9,590	504	4,832	6.97	33,670
Total	Spring (28%)	9,400	458	4,304	8.19	35,236
Total	Winter (24%)	8,200	483	3,957	11.90	47,011
Total	Summer (19%)	6,570	528	3,468	7.11	24,659

TRENDS IN PRODUCTION EFFICIENCY

Celery is an expensive crop to produce, requiring considerable labor, heavy fertilization, and extensive cultural and harvesting operations. Its man-hour requirements to produce an acre was 371 in 1939, 335 in 1959, and 143 in 1977. Man-hour output increased 504 percent during this 38-year period. Average yield also increased from 251 to 491 hundred-weight per acre (Table 1.6). Increased production efficiency resulted from better cultivars, cultural methods, and pest control.

CLIMATIC REQUIREMENTS

Celery thrives best where the weather is relatively cool, especially at night, and where rainfall is well distributed or irrigation is used. Production is limited to the winter and spring in Florida, and to fall, winter, and early spring in the rest of the South, except for especially favored localities. In California, fall, winter, and spring crops are produced, while in the North only summer and fall crops are grown.

SELECTING CULTIVARS AND SEED

Cultivars

Cultivars of celery are generally classed as yellow or green. The former, which have been decreasing in importance, are earlier, less vig-

Fig. 18.1—Celery growing on muck soil with overhead irrigation.

USDA Photograph

orous with thinner petioles, easier bleached, and inferior in both eating
and keeping quality to the green cultivars. Crossing has resulted in intermediate types, and strains showing differences in resistance to diseases,
bolting to seed, and nutrient deficiencies are available. Important yellow
cultivars are Golden Spartan and Golden Self-blanching. The cultivar
Utah and its several strains are used for most of the green celery. Selected
green cultivars include: Tall Utah 52-70, Florida 683, Tendercrisp, Slow
Bolting No. 91, Tall Utah 52-70H, Tall Utah 52-70R, and Florimart.

Securing Seed

Celery seed is expensive, but its cost is only a minor item in the total
cost of production. The quality of seed, on the other hand, may be a
major factor affecting the value of the crop. The purchase of good seed
of a desirable strain is therefore good economy. Since celery seed retains
its viability for three or four years, it may be bought a year in advance
and tested.

PREPARING THE SOIL

Soil Preferences

Because of the high nutrient and water requirements of celery, soil
character is a determining factor in celery production. A fertile muck or
sandy loam soil, which is loose and friable and has high waterholding
capacity, is best. Celery prefers a moderately acid soil, approximating a
pH of 6.0.

In the Great Lakes area, celery is grown primarily on mucks. In
Florida, sandy loams as well as mucks are used. In California, celery is
grown in delta regions where the soils are alluvial in character. With
all types of soil, adequate drainage must be provided.

Preparing the Soil

One of the determining factors of successful celery production is the
preparation of the soil. The soil should be plowed deeply to increase its
water-holding capacity, since celery, because of its shallow root system,
suffers very readily from drouth. Deep plowing should be followed by
thorough pulverization. Usually numerous and thorough harrowings are
sufficient.

Plowing should be done long enough before setting the plants to allow ample time for pulverization, the exact time depending on the crop previously grown. If a cover crop is used, it should be turned under in time to allow sufficient decomposition before the plants are set out, and the soil should be harrowed, raked, and smoothed, either by a roller or by a drag implement.

FERTILIZING AND MANURING

Celery is a heavy feeder and a very poor forager. Therefore, large quantities of fertilizers are generally applied. When mineral soils are used for growing this crop, manure usually is applied in large quantities if available. In addition to the manure, it is advisable to supply some commercial fertilizer, especially some readily available nitrogen, such as ammonium nitrate, and also some phosphorus carrier, such as superphosphate. In Florida, dependence is placed on commercial fertilizer and soil-improving crops.

A crop of celery has been shown to remove 280 pounds of nitrogen, 72 pounds of phosphorus, 635 pounds of potassium, and 35 pounds of magnesium per acre. Over 45 percent of the mineral nutrients are absorbed during the month preceding harvest.

The kind, amount, and method of applying fertilizer vary considerably from section to section and within a single producing area. On sandy soils in Florida where no marketable celery was produced without fertilizer, best results were obtained with a mixture containing approximately 6 percent nitrogen, 2 to 4 percent phosphoric acid, and 8 percent potash, used at the rate of 8,000 pounds per acre. In some areas in California there has been no response to applied phosphorus or potash, but good response to nitrogen. Muck and peat soils are usually deficient in potash and often low in phosphorus. Nitrogen may be limiting in these soils when they are cold and wet. The fertilizer recommendation for a given soil should provide a high level of fertility throughout the growing season and a maintenance application of P and K, regardless of the response to these elements, should be administered.

PREPARING THE SEEDBED AND PLANTING

Celery seed is planted either in the open or under protection. It is seldom planted where the crop is to grow to maturity, except in California, because of the care necessary to get a stand of good plants.

Soaking seed prior to planting hastens germination and is practiced by growers in many sections, especially for the late crop. A common method is to moisten the seed in a receptacle and put it in a warm place for several days until the sprouts begin to appear. Another method used by some growers is to place the seed between folds of cloth, which are kept moist.

When the seed is sown in outdoor beds, and the plants are taken directly to the field, it is advisable to sow ½ pound for each acre to be planted. When the plants are grown in the greenhouse and transplanted prior to setting in the field, ¼ pound of seed is sufficient for 1 acre planted in rows 3 feet apart.

Celery seed is planted shallow, not deeper than ½ inch. It should be covered with pulverized soil and sufficiently wet down.

In Florida, open seedbeds are prepared in the early part of July. After the ground has been thoroughly conditioned, the beds are made by digging shallow trenches 2 feet wide and 6 feet apart, leaving 4 feet for the slightly raised beds (Fig. 18.2). Seed is sown in drills across the beds, which are covered with burlap bags until the seed sprouts. When the seedlings emerge, shade is provided by stretching light muslin over triangular supports placed on the beds 12 feet apart. These supports are held in place by three wires which also act as anchors for the muslin which is fastened to them with clothespins. On one side of the bed a fourth wire is stretched high enough that one side of the muslin may be raised to permit better aeration and hardening of the plants. Later, as the weather cools, these covers are removed entirely. Spraying begins as the leaves appear and continues at 7- to 10-day intervals until the plants mature, in order to control early and late blight. Maneb, thiram, Dyrene, and zineb may be used.

Plants seeded in the greenhouse or hotbed for the early crop are often transplanted after four or five weeks to flats or beds, spaced 1½ by 1½ or 2 by 2 inches. For a large portion of the acreage, however, the plants are transplanted from the seedbed directly to the field. In the coastal region of California where irrigation is available, some celery is seeded directly in the field.

SETTING AND IRRIGATING

Setting Plants

The plant bed should be watered a few hours before taking up the

Fig. 18.2—Celery plants grown for transplanting.

USDA Photograph

plants to set in the field. It is desirable to set the plants when the soil is moist and the air rather humid.

Plants are generally removed from the beds and set in the field when they have attained a height of 5 to 7 inches and a crown diameter of $\frac{1}{4}$ to $\frac{3}{8}$ inch. The plants should be set at the proper depth, not deep enough to cover the growing point, and the soil should be firmly pressed around the roots.

Planting distances and methods vary in different parts of the country. The distance between rows varies from 30 to 42 inches, and .he distance between plants in the row varies from 5 to 8 inches.

The rows should be straight to accommodate machine cultivation, dusting, or spraying. The use of gang transplanters insures a uniform distance between rows and reduces the cost of planting.

Irrigating

Celery is a moisture-loving plant, and unless the soil is naturally moist, the application of water is necessary. Three systems of irrigation are in general use: (1) the underground or subirrigation method, which is principally used in Florida; (2) the furrow or surface system, most common in California; and (3) the overhead-sprinkler system. The last mentioned is the most expensive to construct and operate, and it does not provide drainage during wet weather. The subirrigation system gives the grower almost complete control of the moisture supply, as it is used for both irrigation and drainage. Many muck soils and some sandy soils are ditched so the ditches can be filled for irrigation or used for drainage by reversing the pumps.

CULTIVATING AND BLANCHING

Cultivating

Good, clean cultivation throughout the growing season is important, since weeds are troublesome on most soils used for growing celery. The celery plant grows slowly and is easily injured by weeds. Celery responded more to cultivation for the purpose of maintaining a soil mulch than any of the other crops grown in the cultivation experiment at Ithaca, New York. Celery roots do not have as much spread as most other vegetable roots, and it is thought that because of this, less moisture is intercepted by celery roots than by roots of cabbage, for example. In all cultivation the surface soil should be left as level as possible. Therefore, it is desirable to use small-tooth cultivators. Shallow cultivation is desirable at all times, especially near the plants, as many of the roots grow near the surface and within 6 to 12 inches of the row.

Blanching

The demand for green celery has increased so that blanching is no longer a common practice. This change in consumer preference has been due to improved cultivars and the association of the green color with vitamin A content. The green celery is also cheaper to produce.

The blanching of celery results in the loss of green coloring, reduces the strong flavor, and makes the leaf stalks crisp and tender. Blanching is accomplished by excluding the light from the leaf stalks while the plants are still growing or are in storage.

CONTROLLING DISEASES AND INSECTS

Diseases

Celery is subject to many diseases which, if not controlled, may cause serious losses. Some of these can be avoided by cultural practices and field sanitation, while others are controlled by spraying.

PINK ROT. Pink rot is caused by the fungus *Sclerotinia sclerotiorum*. It is one of the most destructive diseases of celery, especially during years when climatic conditions are favorable for the development of the fungus. Pink rot causes a damping off of young plants in the seedbed, a light pinkish rot of stalks in the field, and a watery soft rot in transit. It is prevalent in Florida and in northern celery-growing areas. Pink rot can be controlled partially by spraying with either maneb or zineb. Field sanitation and careful washing and packing are effective in preventing the disease in transit.

EARLY BLIGHT. Early blight, caused by *Cercospora apii*. first occurs in the seedbed. It causes great damage there and is transmitted to the field by the young seedlings. It appears first as small, circular, yellowish-brown spots on the leaves; these spots enlarge and eventually assume a grayish appearance. Early spraying with maneb or zineb is usually sufficient to control early blight, but it is profitable to continue spraying, in order to catch the late blight.

LATE BLIGHT. Late blight, *Septoria petroselini* var. *apii,* attacks the plants only in the cooler part of the growing season. It is very similar to early blight, being distinguished only by the smaller, more oval spots speckled with black dots, which occur on the petioles. It attacks all parts of the plant above the ground. The control is the same as for early blight. Emerson Pascal is fairly resistant to both early and late blight and is also highly resistant to fusarium yellows.

ROOT KNOT. (See Nematodes, Chapter 11.)

CRACKED STEM. Cracked stem is a very destructive disease in Florida, due to a deficiency of boron, and has caused considerable loss to celery growers in other regions. This disease first manifests itself by a brownish mottling of the leaf, usually appearing first along the margins. This mottling is accompanied by a brittleness of the petiole and is soon followed by the appearance of crosswise cracks in the outer layers of the petiole. The tissues surrounding the cracks turn brown. The roots also turn brown and the laterals die.

Results of experiments conducted in Florida indicate that an application of 10 pounds of borax to the acre is effective in preventing the development of cracked stem and in increasing the yield and quality of celery. Larger quantities of borax—even as little as 30 pounds to the acre—were found to be distinctly harmful.

BLACK HEART. Black heart often causes greater losses than any other disease. It is non-parasitic, being caused by a deficiency of calcium. It is particularly serious in regions where the irrigation water has a high content of sodium salts. The disease can be controlled by spraying the foliage at intervals with calcium nitrate.

Insects

A large number of pests may attack celery. Among them are aphids, flea beetles, springtails, carrot rust flies, mole crickets, army worms, tarnish plant bugs, wireworms, celery worms, celery leaf tiers, celery loopers, thrips, and spider mites.

Although any of these may cause serious losses, most of them seldom do. In many of the celery-growing regions the tarnish plant bug and the carrot rust fly are injurious pests. See Chapter 11 for control methods.

Premature Seeding or Bolting

Premature seeding as plants reach full development results in the loss of a portion of the crop. In some seasons premature seeding is very serious in Florida and may result in almost total loss of a planting, but it seldom happens that all plantings are affected.

The temperature under which the plants are grown is a very important factor in premature seeding. If the temperature averages between 40° and 50° F. for two weeks or longer, or between 50° and 60° F. for a month or two while the plants are small, they are likely to develop seed stalks. After the plants have been subjected to the temperatures mentioned, any treatment that stimulates growth, such as applying nitrate of soda, tends to hasten seed stalk development. Contrary to a fairly common belief, freezing does not cause seeding, but rather tends to delay it. Likewise, checking growth by other means, such as withholding water, delays seeding and may prevent it entirely. Relatively high temperatures (averaging 70° F.) may prevent seeding even after the plants have been subjected to the relatively low growing temperatures mentioned above.

Heredity is important in premature seeding. Some strains are much more subject to bolting than others, and under conditions favoring premature seeding a slow bolting cultivar is recommended. In fact, at least one such strain has been developed. So-called nonbolting strains require a longer exposure to relatively cool temperatures for seed stalk development than do bolting strains. If conditions are likely to favor bolting, Slow Bolting Green or another resistant strain should be used.

HARVESTING, HANDLING, AND MARKETING

Harvesting

Celery may be harvested as soon as it attains proper size. Early celery often is harvested before the plants are full grown in order to take advantage of a high price. The celery plants are cut off below the surface of the ground with a sharp knife, with a spade, or with special large-scale implements. The trimmers follow the cutters, lift the stalk and strip off the outer leaves. During hot weather the celery should be taken from the field as soon as possible after it is removed from the row, as exposure to sun and wind causes plants to wilt. Harvesting machines are used in some localities. As the machine moves slowly through the field, the celery is harvested, trimmed, washed, and packed in crates. Figure 18.3 shows the "mule train" in operation.

Preparing for Market

After harvesting, celery stalks should be thoroughly cleaned by stripping off damaged and discolored leaves and then washing with fresh or chlorinated water to remove soil and trash. Washing may be done in the field when the stalks are packed, but in large operations it is done in packing sheds, where it is inspected for grade (Fig. 18.4).

Packed crates of celery are sprayed with water at 33° F. and precooled in tanks for about 30 minutes. The crates are then passed down chutes or conveyed mechanically from the precooling room to refriger-

Fig. 18.3—Harvesting, grading, and packing celery in the field with portable equipment.

USDA Photograph

Fig. 18.4—Federal-state inspector examines celery during harvesting and packing.

USDA Photograph

ator cars or trucks, which are usually "blower iced" in warm weather to prevent deterioration. Open ventilation is usually sufficient when transporting in cool weather.

If celery is shipped in the rough, leaves that are unwashed, discolored, and damaged should be removed. Packing is done in the field and the stalks are usually washed and repacked in terminal markets.

Although various types of crates are used in different areas, the 16-inch standard crate, containing 30 to 36 stalks and weighing 55 to 60 pounds, is common. Information on celery grades and packaging can be obtained from the Agricultural and Marketing Service, U.S. Department of Agriculture.

Storing

Celery may be stored for four or five weeks at 32° F. and at high relative humidity. Because the crop is available from producing areas most of the year, storage is seldom necessary. It can be used advantageously to prevent market gluts, and has to be done to prevent freezing during harvest. If the crop is to be shipped, the field heat should be removed as soon as feasible.

In the cooler sections, where celery is grown in late summer and fall, it may be kept for several weeks by trenching it in the field or garden.

Marketing

Celery marketing is very competitive, especially in California and Florida where large buyers vie for quality and price in order to meet the demands of retail stores, especially the supermarkets. A marketing agreement and order program (see Chapter 13 for information on "Federal-State Marketing Services") has been active in Florida since the 1965-66 season. A principal provision includes volume limitations on the total marketable quantity from Florida. Marketable allotments refer to the amount of celery which may be purchased from or handled on behalf of individual producers.

EXPORTS AND IMPORTS. Fresh celery exports reached a record of 139,753,000 pounds in 1977, valued at $14,956,000. As is the case with most U.S. shipments of fresh vegetables, Canada was the major foreign customer, with exports also being made to Hong Kong, Europe, and Mexico. Small quantities of celery are imported (Table 13.2).

SELECTED REFERENCES

Anonymous, "Mechanical Sizing of Celery Stalks by Weight," USDA, ARS MRR 822, 1968.

Broome, D. L., and Jung, G. H., "Market Organization and Operation of the Florida Celery Industry," Fla. Exp. Sta. Bull., 1966.

Burns, A. J., Podany, J. C., and Wynn, "California Celery Prices, Coast and Margins," USDA, ERS TVS 192, 1974.

Cress, D., and Wells, A., "Celery and Carrot Insect Pests," Mich. State Univ. Ext. Bull. Coop. Ext. Ser. 90, 1977.

Grizells, W. G., "A Central Packing-Precooling System for Celery," USDA, ARS MRR 869, 1971.

McCarver, O. W., "Suggested Vegetable Varieties," Montana State Univ. Ext. Circ. 1060, 1978.

Nicklow, C. W., et al., "Celery," Mich. State Univ. Coop. Ext. Ser. Ext. Bull. E–675–1, 1970.

Paulus, A. O., Hall, D. H., and Teviotdale, B., "Late Blight of Celery," Univ. of Calif., Div. of Agr. Sci. Leaflet 2982, 1977.

Paulus, A. O., Hall, D. H., and Teviotdale, B., "Pink Rot of Celery," Univ. of Calif., Div. of Agr. Sci. Leaflet 2929, 1976.

Sackett, C., and Murray, J., "Celery," United Fresh Fruit and Veg. Assoc., Alexandria, Va., 1977.

Schoenemann, J. A., et al., "Celery," Univ. of Wisc. Ext. Coop. Ext. Programs A2334, 1978.

Sims, W. L., Welch, J. E., and Rubatsky, V. E., "Celery Production in California," Univ. of Calif., Div. of Agr. Sci. Leaflet 2673, 1977.

CHAPTER 19

Corn (Sweet)

CLASSIFICATION, ORIGIN, AND HISTORY

Sweet corn (*Zea Mays* var. *saccharata*) is a member of the grass family and a native of America. It is a comparatively modern vegetable crop. History records that the colonists began to grow the plant about 1780.

SCOPE AND IMPORTANCE

Sweet corn has become one of the most important vegetable crops, ranking second in acreage and fourth in value among the 22 principal vegetables in 1977. This crop is grown commercially in about 25 states, and for local markets and in home gardens throughout the country.

Sweet corn acreage for fresh market fluctuated downward from 211,300 in 1949 to 169,700 in 1977. Acreage for the processed crop remained fairly constant around 450,000 for the same period. The value of fresh market corn increased from $30,923,000 in 1949 to $48,026,000 in 1959 and up to $107,052,000 in 1977. Concurrently, the value of sweet corn for processing increased from $28,554,000 to $114,286,000. Florida led in fresh market corn with about 30 percent of the acreage in 1977. Wisconsin and Minnesota had the largest acreage for processing.

The 1949 to 1977 performance record of fresh market and processing sweet corn combined and their approximate distribution are shown in Figure 19.1. The 1977 harvest season, acreage, production, and value for fresh market and processing corn are presented by leading states in Tables 19.1 and 19.2. Sweet corn has many table uses, and it excels as "corn on the cob" (Fig. 19.2).

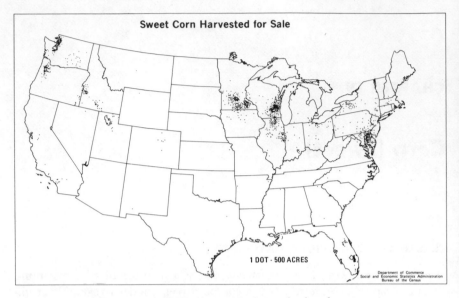

Fig. 19.1—Acreage, distribution, production, and value of sweet corn.

UNITED STATES TOTAL

Year	Acreage	Production 1,000 Cwt.	Value, $1,000
1949	672,180	13,358	59,477
1959	633,910	44,666	78,272
1969	637,800	55,183	117,044
1977	618,680	60,354	221,338

TRENDS IN PRODUCTION EFFICIENCY

The growing and harvesting of sweet corn is highly mechanized, requiring considerably less labor than most other vegetables. Between 1939 and 1959 the labor requirement for sweet corn remained constant, around 48 man-hours per acre, while that for the processed crop declined from 46 to 12 man-hours. Spectacular progress has been made in the unit output per man-hour in recent years—an 800 percent increase between 1939 and 1977 (Table 1.6). The acreage yield for sweet corn for fresh market rose from 50 hundredweight in 1949 to 78 hundredweight in 1977. During the same period the acre yield of processing corn increased from 3.0 to 5.24 tons as shown in Table 19.2.

Sweet corn differs from field corn by having a recessive modifying gene which alters the composition of the endosperm. The two modifying genes commonly used are designated as su and sh_2. The former is most frequently used and causes the endosperm to be high in water soluble

Table 19.1—Sweet Corn for Fresh Market: Harvest Season and Estimated Acreage, Yield, Production, and Value in Leading States, 1977.

State	Harvest Season	Harvested Acreage	Yield per Acre, Cwt.	Production per 1,000 Cwt.	Price per Cwt.	Value, $1,000
Florida	Spring	32,500	110	3,575	$ 8.89	31,782
New York	Summer	20,500	74	1,517	6.12	9,284
Florida	Fall	15,000	71	1,065	8.83	9,404
Ohio	Summer	14,500	75	1,088	8.11	8,824
Michigan	Summer	12,300	63	775	7.07	5,479
New Jersey	Summer	11,100	70	777	7.57	5,882
Pennsylvania	Summer	11,100	60	666	8.02	5,341
Massachusetts	Summer	7,200	60	432	8.90	3,845
California	Summer	6,800	60	408	7.82	3,191
California	Spring	6,600	95	627	9.74	6,107
N. Carolina	Summer	4,900	60	294	7.15	2,102
Connecticut	Summer	4,400	63	277	7.00	1,939
Illinois	Summer	4,000	86	344	4.27	1,469
Florida	Winter	3,800	75	285	11.30	3,221
Colorado	Summer	3,300	95	314	7.31	2,295
Texas	Spring	3,100	65	202	7.20	1,454
Oregon	Summer	1,900	90	171	9.90	1,693
Washington	Summer	1,900	90	171	9.32	1,594
Virginia	Summer	1,200	77	92	5.88	541
Alabama	Summer	1,200	50	60	8.80	528
Alabama	Spring	1,000	60	60	8.10	486
United States		169,700	78	13,270	8.07	107,052

Table 19.2—Sweet Corn for Processing: Estimated Acreage, Yield, Production, and Value in Leading States, 1977.

State	Harvested Acreage	Yield per Acre, Tons	Production per 1,000 Tons	Price per Ton	Value, $1,000
Wisconsin	130,700	4.56	596,000	$42.30	25,211
Minnesota	120,000	5.40	648,000	46.00	29,808
Illinois	45,900	4.91	225,350	52.80	11,898
Oregon	40,900	7.38	301,700	56.70	17,106
Washington	31,800	6.31	200,650	56.70	11,377
Idaho	24,500	5.77	141,300	48.70	6,882
New York	17,000	5.68	96,500	45.70	4,408
Maryland	12,900	3.53	45,550	57.90	2,637
Iowa	9,200	5.04	46,350	45.80	2,125
Pennsylvania	5,000	3.34	16,700	49.40	825
Other States	11,080	3.26	36,100	55.70	2,009
United States	448,980	5.24	2,354,200	48.60	114,286
Canning (72%)	321,330	4.92	1,580,250	45.80	72,403
Freezing (28%)	127,650	6.06	773,950	54.10	41,883

Fig. 19.2—Sweet corn for the table.

United Fresh Fruit and Vegetable Association Photograph

polysaccharides (WSP) but comparatively low in sugars and of good texture. The latter results in high sugar but low in WSP. The sugar is retained well during maturity and in storage, but the texture is watery. A new breeding line, IL677a, from the Illinois Agricultural Experiment Station has an additional modifier, *se,* which, in combination with *su,* produces kernels high in WSP as well as high in sugar and with good texture.

CLIMATIC REQUIREMENTS

Principal climatic factors are (1) temperature and (2) moisture supply. The temperature has a marked effect on the growth of sweet corn. In general, the higher the temperature, between 40° and 90° F., the greater is the rate of growth and the shorter is the time necessary for the plant to attain a particular stage of maturity. Data presented in

Table 19.3 obtained with Stowell's Evergreen grown at the Maryland Agricultural Experiment Station illustrate the effect of temperature.

Fairly uniform distribution of rainfall is necessary for good growth and high yields. If soil moisture is low when the weather is hot, the plant does not receive sufficient moisture for growth; the manufacture of food declines, and yields are low.

Table 19.3—Calculated Rate of Sweet Corn Ripening for Mean Temperatures, 60° to 80° F.

Average of Daily Mean (Degrees F.)	Time Required to Pass from Pre-milk to Best Canning Stage* (Days)	Time Remained in Canning State (Days)
60	14.5	5.0
65	12.0	4.0
70	10.0	3.0
75	8.0	3.0
80	7.0	2.0
85	5.5	1.5

*The juice of the kernel is clear and watery at the pre-milk stage and milky at the canning stage.
Data from Maryland Agricultural Experiment Station.

SELECTING CULTIVARS AND SEED

Cultivars

Most sweet corn cultivars now used are hybrids, each resulting from the cross of two inbreds. The preference for hybrids is due primarily to their vigor, high yields, and uniformity. A few cultivars in use are top crosses, with the seed parent an open-pollinated cultivar.

Cultivars may be classified as early, medium, and late, with the time required for maturity varying from about 65 days for early cultivars to 100 days for late ones. Among the popular early cultivars are Sprite, Sundance, Spring Gold, and Seneca 60; Duet, Gold Cup, Seneca Chief, and Wonderful are of medium maturity; and the late group includes cultivars such as Silver Queen, Golden Queen, NK 199, Merit, Jubilee, and Northern Belle. These are among cultivars described in Table 19.4.

The cultivar should be productive and should yield high-quality ears which are relatively free from damage by the corn earworm. In addition, the kernels should be tender and sweet. Although tenderness of the pericarp (skin of the kernel) is an important varietal characteristic, it may also be associated with seed injury.

Table 19.4—Brief Description of Selected Cultivars of Sweet Corn.

Cultivar	Chief Use*	Season (Days)	Stalk Height (In.)	Color	Ear Length (In.)	No. Rows	Quality
Bonanza	M	85	79	Yellow	8-8½	16-18	Good
Butter and Sugar	M	75		White & Gold	6½-7½	12-14	Excellent
Gold Cup	M,F	80	78	Bright Yellow	7½	14-16	Excellent
Gold Winner	M	79	80	Yellow	8	14-16	Good
Gold Beauty	M,H	75	64	Yellow	6-8	12-14	Very Good
Jubilee	P,M	87	90	Yellow	8½-9	18-20	Good
Merit	F,P,M	88	89	Yellow	8	16-20	Good
Northern Belle	M	74		Yellow	7½-8	14-18	Good
NK 199	P,H,M	84	93	Yellow	7½-8	18-20	Fine
Seneca Chief	H	81	67	Yellow	6-8	12	Excellent
Silver Queen	H,M	92	90	White	8-9	14-16	Good
Spring Gold	H,M	67		Yellow	7	12-16	Fine
Sprite	M	69	66	Bicolor	7	16	Good
Stylepak	P	84		Yellow	8	18-20	Excellent
Sundance	M	70	66	Yellow	7½	14-16	Superior
Wonderful	H,F	82		Yellow		12-16	Excellent

*F, freezing; H, home gardening; M, market; P, processing.

Securing Seed

If sweet corn is grown for either the fresh market or processing, it is desirable to harvest the entire crop at one picking. This requires uniform maturity, characteristic of good hybrids. Sizing of seed may also increase uniformity of maturity. In the home garden it is often desirable for the harvest to spread over a period of several days, and thus it may be advantageous to use an open-pollinated cultivar.

The production of sweet corn seed requires not only carefully controlled pollination but careful handling as well. The tender pericarp of sweet corn is easily injured, and the endosperm because of its high sugar content dries slowly and may readily absorb moisture during storage. It is therefore important to secure seed from a concern equipped to produce and handle it.

PREPARING SOIL, FERTILIZING, AND MANURING

Preparing the Soil

Sweet corn is grown on a wide variety of soil types. Growers for the early market usually plant on well-drained, sandy loams, while those for the late market or for the cannery usually select silt or clay loams or well-drained bottom land.

Soil preparation consists of plowing and harrowing as needed. Usually the rows are $2\frac{1}{2}$ to 4 feet apart. Fertilizer is applied in furrows and mixed with the soil or applied at the time of planting. If well-rotted manure is used, it should be applied broadcast on the plowed land and thoroughly disced into the soil. If coarse manure is used, it should be plowed under three or four weeks before planting time.

Fertilizing

Sweet corn is placed in Group II according to its nutrient requirements, and fertilizer recommendations are given in Tables 6.4 and 6.5. The kind and amount of fertilizer that should be applied depends on the fertility of soil used and how subject it is to leaching.

Tests with field corn have shown that commercial fertilizers applied in 1-inch bands slightly below and about 2 inches from the seed produce greater yields than fertilizer applied under the seed. Since the root system of sweet corn is similar to that of field corn, sweet corn should respond in much the same way as field corn. As is true of other vegetable crops, commercial fertilizer should never come in contact with the seed.

PLANTING

Treating Seed

Sweet corn seed is more susceptible than field corn seed to the rot-producing fungi in the soil. The tender pericarp of sweet corn is easily injured, allowing the entrance of decay organisms during germination. This is especially true if the seed is planted when the soil is cold and wet. Investigations have shown that treating the seed with thiram effectively protects it against rot-producing fungi. Thiram can be purchased at most seed stores, and the directions should be followed closely.

There is considerable variation in seedling vigor and time of maturity with different size seeds. Therefore, graded seed should be used if the crop is to be harvested mechanically. Some seedsmen grade their seed, specify the planter plate to be used with each size, and treat the seed with a fungicide and an insecticide before offering it for sale.

Planting Dates

The seed for the early crop is usually planted just before or immediately after the average date of the last killing frost. However, market and home gardeners frequently take a chance on the frost. In this case, usually two or three plantings at intervals of 5 to 10 days are made.

The time required between planting and maturity depends primarily upon temperature and cultivar. The effective temperature may be calculated as heat units or degree days, the daily average above a predetermined base temperature. With a base temperature of 45° F., a day averaging 70° F. would accumulate 25 degree days. The number of heat units required for the development of a cultivar may be determined. These data together with the average accumulation of heat units per day during the growing season can be used to predict time of maturity. Early plantings usually require more days to mature than later ones. By taking the expected accumulation of heat units between desired harvesting intervals at harvest time and allowing the same to accumulate between planting intervals, properly spaced harvests can be provided. These are essential for sweet corn grown for processing and may be important for supplying a particular market.

To secure a continuous supply of sweet corn throughout the growing season in the home garden, two systems may be used: (1) the same cultivar may be planted at intervals of 10 days or two weeks; or (2) early, midseason, and late cultivars may be planted at the same time. In the South, the latter method is probably more advantageous than the former.

Whether different cultivars or successive plantings are made, each should be planted in a block to insure pollination.

Planting Methods

Kernels of sweet corn are rough, wrinkled, and irregular in shape. Unlike smooth, uniform size seeds, they do not feed easily into a planter plate. Not only should the planter plate be specified for seed of a certain size but the speed of the tractor should also be regulated. The rate of planting is best controlled by adjusting the speed of the planter plate rather than changing the size of the plate. The soil should be firmed around the seed, which should be planted no deeper than necessary. More rapid and uniform emergence results from shallow planting in moist soil. About $1\frac{1}{2}$ inches is a good depth in sandy loams.

Planting Rates

Sweet corn is planted in rows varying from $2\frac{1}{2}$ to 4 feet apart, and spaced from 8 to 12 inches in the drill. The rate of seeding depends on (1) the time of planting, (2) the spacing, and (3) the cultivar. Ordinarily, the earlier the seed is planted or the colder the soil, the greater is the rate of seeding. As a rule, the true sweet corn cultivars require a higher rate of seeding than field corn cultivars. This is particularly true if the weather is cold and wet at the time seeding is made. Generally, 8 to 14 pounds of seed are required per acre.

CULTIVATING AND IRRIGATING

Cultivating

The primary purpose of cultivation is to control weeds, and a secondary purpose is to break the crust of self-crusting, usually heavy soils. In general, shallow cultivation should be practiced. To avoid the necessity of deep cultivation, weeds should be destroyed when they are small. When the weather is hot and dry, the moist soil should never be exposed to dry air, as the moisture evaporates and is lost to the plant.

Herbicides can be used to control weeds in sweet corn. Suggestions are made in Chapter 9, but before chemicals are used, the local extension adviser should be consulted for changes in regulations.

Under average conditions, cultivation may be outlined as follows: (1) The first cultivation should be relatively close to the plants to loosen the soil and to permit lateral root growth. (2) Succeeding cultivations should be relatively shallow and successively farther from the plants. Scraper types of cultivators should be used rather than the toothed types so the cultivations will not be deep enough to injure the feeding roots just beneath the surface. (3) Cultivation should stop when the main stem is about half grown, unless weeds are prevalent or the soil crusts badly after heavy rains.

Irrigating

Sweet corn requires from 12 to 25 acre-inches of water. The rate of use increases with the development of the plant until the time of pollination. Water stress resulting in serious wilting will reduce yields, but greatest damage by drouth occurs at the time of silking. Either furrow or sprinkler irrigation may be used. Thorough but infrequent watering is recommended.

CONTROLLING DISEASES AND INSECTS

Diseases

The principal diseases are bacterial wilt and corn smut.

BACTERIAL WILT. Bacterial wilt, caused by *Bacterium stewartii,* develops inside the water-conducting tubes and produces wilting about the time the plants silk. The bacteria are carried over in the bodies of the corn flea beetles and in the seed. Cucumber beetles and flea beetles are known to spread the parasite from infected stalks to healthy, noninfected stalks. The only reliable control measure is the use of resistant cultivars, a number of which are now on the market. They should be tested on a small scale before they are planted extensively.   •

CORN SMUT. Corn smut, caused by the fungus *Ustilago maydis,* produces puffed-out membranous growths on the ears and stems. Inside these membranes are compact masses of black spores, which are liberated when the membranes break open. Control measures consist of (1) rotating crops and (2) practicing field sanitation. Manure containing diseased stalks should not be used on land planted to sweet corn. The development of resistant cultivars appears to be a promising method of control.

HELMINTHOSPORIUM LEAF BLIGHT. Helminthosporium leaf blight is caused by a fungus, *Helminthosporium turcicum,* and results in large, linear water-soaked areas, which change to black or straw-yellow on drying. Control methods include a 3-year rotation, resistant cultivars, and spraying with maneb or zineb when heavy damage occurs.

Insects

The principal insects are corn earworm, the Southern corn stalk borer, and the European corn borer.

CORN EARWORM. The corn earworm *(Heliothis zea)* is destructive to a number of vegetable crops, but its damage is most severe on sweet corn and tomatoes. The corn earworm is the larva of a light grayish-brown moth. The front wings are marked with dark, irregular lines, and there is a dark area near the top of the wing. The back wings are light in color.

In the fall the larvae burrow 2 to 6 inches into the soil to pupate. When spring comes, the moths emerge from the pupal cells and crawl up the tunnels made by the larvae in the fall. The eggs are laid singly on the corn silks. (If tomatoes are attacked, the eggs are deposited on the underside of the leaves.) After the larvae reach maturity, they drop to the ground and burrow in the soil, completing the cycle. This is repeated for each generation.

To control corn earworms on sweet corn in the whorl stage, they should be treated with carbaryl (see Chapter 11). Some cultivars of sweet corn have been developed which are more resistant to the attacks of the corn earworm than other cultivars are.

SOUTHERN CORN STALK BORER. The Southern corn stalk borer *(Diatraea crambidoides)* is the larva of a night-flying moth. The adult lays eggs on all parts of the plant. After the eggs hatch, the larvae bore into the stem. No chemical control measures are used, but crop refuse destruction is recommended, along with crop rotation and late fall and winter plowing.

EUROPEAN CORN BORER. The European corn borer *(Pyrausta nubilalis)* is also the larva of a night-flying moth. Eggs are laid on the leaves and the larvae bore through the stems, thus entering the ear from within. Control measures include using carbaryl and methomyl.

HARVESTING AND GRADING

Harvesting

When the kernels are young and small, the juice is clear and watery, and the corn is said to be in the pre-milk stage. As the kernels become larger, plumper, and older, the juice becomes milky, and this is known as the milk stage. In a relatively short time the kernels pass from the milk stage to the dough stage. At the pre-milk stage, the kernels are fairly sweet, but they are small and generally lack plumpness. At the milk stage they are also sweet, but they have attained full size and plumpness, while at the dough stage, most of the sugars have changed to starch. Obviously, ears should be harvested when the kernels are in the milk stage.

Experienced growers do not press the juice from the kernels to determine when they are in the milk stage. This would require partial stripping of the husks, which is objectionable. With many cultivars, growers have found that when the silks first become brown and the ears feel plump they are ready to be picked.

After the ears are picked, the sugar decreases and the starch increases rapidly, and this change is directly proportional to the temperature. Table 19.5 presents data showing the effect of temperature on the loss

Table 19.5—Loss of Sugar from Stowell's Evergreen Sweet Corn Stored for 24 Hours.

Temperature (Degrees F.)	Percent Sugars		
	Start of Storage	End of Storage	Less
32	5.91	5.43	0.48
50	5.83	4.83	1.00
68	6.17	4.59	1.58
86	5.34	2.65	2.69
104	6.72	3.64	3.08

Data from Appleman, C. O., and Arthur, J. M.: "Carbohydrate Metabolism in Sweet Corn in Storage at Different Temperatures," **Jour. Agr. Res.** 17: 137-152.

of sugar from Stowell's Evergreen cultivar. The higher the temperature the more rapid was the decrease in sugar and hence the more rapid was the lowering in quality.

Corn should be picked in the early morning, and the ears should be kept in a cool place. Piling the ears or placing them in nonventilated crates increases the respiration rate and the loss of sugar. Because of the marked effect of temperature on the loss of sugar, sweet corn to be canned should be processed immediately after picking. Equipment for rapid handling is illustrated in Figures 19.3 and 19.4.

Fig. 19.3—A portable machine used in harvesting and packing sweet corn in the field.

USDA Photograph

Grading and Shipping

Well filled, uniform ears of optimum maturity should be selected for best results. Poorly-filled, worm-eaten, overripe, and undersized ears should be discarded. For long distance shipments, the ears are packed in boxes or crates. Much of the corn crop is shipped by trucks on both long and short hauls (Fig. 19.4).

General experiences indicate that the quality of sweet corn for market can be improved by (1) harvesting at optimum maturity, (2) picking after midnight or early in the morning and placing in ventilated crates, (3) cooling as soon as possible, (4) precooling to lower temperatures before shipping, (5) transporting under ideal refrigeration, (6) providing more adequate refrigeration facilities in the retail stores, and (7) shortening the marketing period in every practical way.

Sorting and packing are done by hand, usually in packing sheds, but any cool location may be used. On a large scale a well organized packing shed will save time and money.

Fig. 19.4—Sweet corn being unloaded at the processing plant.

Photograph by E. K. Alban

Because of the marked effect of temperature on the loss of sugar, sweet corn for canning should be handled quickly under cool conditions if possible and processed immediately after picking.

Marketing

It is evident from Table 19.5 that sweet corn must be marketed as soon after harvest as possible. Buyers insist on precooled corn regardless of distance to markets. Opportunities exist for growers near urban areas to develop profitable local markets for high quality corn if it is properly handled.

EXPORTS AND IMPORTS. In 1977 exports of canned corn totaled 68,917,000 pounds valued at $17,673,000 (Table 13.2). This was significantly above any previous year. Western Europe, Hong Kong, Japan, and Mexico are the principal markets for U.S. canned corn.

SELECTED REFERENCES

Andrew, R. H., *et al.*, "Sweet Corn," Univ. of Wisc. Coop. Ext. Programs Pub. A2343, 1976.

Anonymous, "Growing Sweet Corn for Processing," Asgrow Seed Co., Orange Conn., 1967.

Anonymous, "Pest and Disease Control Program for Sweetcorn," Colo. Agr. Ext. Ser. Pub., 1975.

Anonymous, "Sweet Corn," Fla. Coop. Ext. Ser. Circ. 99D, 1977.

Colditz, P., "Successful Gardening in Georgia: Corn," Ga. Coop. Ext. Ser. Univ. of Ga., SG–004.

Cook, W. P., "Commercial Sweet Corn Production," Clemson Univ. Coop. Ext. Ser. Veg. Leaflet 16, 1978.

Cress, D., and Wells, A., "Sweet Corn Insect Pests," Mich. State Univ. Ext. Bull. E–967, 1976.

Ells, J. E., "Sweet Corn for the Home Garden," Colo. State Univ. Coop. Ext. Ser. 7.607, 1977.

Hall, R. H., *Sweet Corn*, United Fresh Fruit and Vegetable Assoc., Alexandria, Va., 1968.

Hannah, L. C., and Basset, M. J., "Use of Brittle—A Gene in Sweet Corn Breeding," *Hort. Sci.* 12 (4): 313-314, 1977.

Heichel, G. H., and Washko, W. W., "Bird Damage to Connecticut Corn," Conn. Agr. Exp. Sta. Bull. 761, 1976.

Huffman, D. C., and Cravens, M. E., "Trends in Ohio Sweet Corn Industry 1918-1960," Ohio Agr. Exp. Sta. Res. Bull. 927, 1972.

Neild, R. E., *et al.*, "A Guide for Producing Top Quality Sweetcorn in Nebraska," Univ. of Neb. Coop. Ext. Ser. E.C. 71–1219 (current).

Nicklow, C. W., *et al.*, "Sweet Corn," Mich. State Univ. Coop. Ext. Ser. Ext. Bull. E–675–R, 1970.

Roberts, R., *et al.*, "Keys to Profitable Sweet Corn Production in Texas," Texas A & M Univ. Agr. Ext. Ser. L-1464, 1976.

Schales, F. D., "Sweet Corn," Va. Poly. Inst. Ext. Div. Pub. 240, 1968.

Showalter, R. K., *et al.*, "Long Distance Marketing of Fresh Sweet Corn," Fla. Agr. Exp. Sta. Bull. 638, 1961.

Sims, W. L., Kasmire, R. F., and Lorenz, O. A., "Quality Sweet Corn Production," Calif. Agr. Ext. Ser. Leaflet 2818, 1978.

Swan, J. B., and Hicks, D. R., "Irrigated Corn Production," Univ. of Minn. Agr. Ext. Ser. Ext. Folder 263, 1972.

Wann, E. V., and Yarnell, S. H., "Commercial Growing of Sweet Corn," USDA Farmers' Bull. 2042, 1966.

CHAPTER 20

Cucumbers

CLASSIFICATION, ORIGIN, AND HISTORY

The cucumber (*Cucumis sativus*) belongs to the same genus as the melon. It is probably a native of Asia and Africa, and there is evidence that it has been cultivated in western Asia for at least 3,000 years. Cucumbers were known to the ancient Greeks and Romans, who introduced them into Europe. They have been grown in America since the earliest settlements.

SCOPE AND IMPORTANCE

Cucumber production has increased over the years and ranked eighth in acreage and tenth in value among the 22 principal vegetables in 1977.

The acreage for fresh market cucumbers remained fairly stable, around 50,000 acres until 1969, but increased to 51,910 acres in 1977. Total value rose from $14,269,000 in 1949 to more than $55,400,000 in 1977. Acreage of pickling cucumbers decreased from 136,110 acres to 98,960 acres between 1949 and 1959, and rose to 124,000 acres in 1977. The value of pickling cucumbers rose precipitously from $16,955,000 in 1949 to $79,244,000 in 1977. Florida and the Carolinas are the leading fresh market cucumber states, while the Carolinas and Michigan led in the production and value for pickles. Tables 20.1 and 20.2 show the harvest season, acreage, production, and value by states, while Figure 20.1 presents the approximate distribution and the 1949-1977 performance record of all cucumbers.

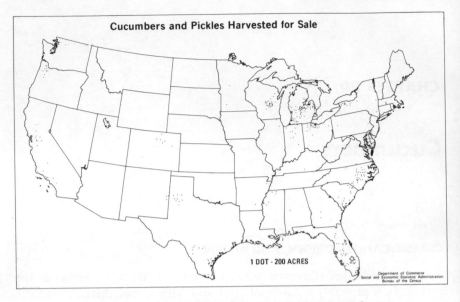

Fig. 20.1—Acreage, distribution, production, and value of cucumbers.

UNITED STATES TOTAL

Year	Acreage	Production 1,000 Cwt.	Value, $1,000
1949	187,860	9,042	31,224
1959	151,440	10,653	39,235
1969	183,600	14,762	79,395
1977	174,900	18,100	134,646

TRENDS IN PRODUCTION EFFICIENCY

The planting, fertilization, pest control, and harvesting of cucumbers require considerable labor. Between 1939 and 1959, acre man-hour requirements for fresh market cucumbers decreased slightly from 127 man-hours to 114 and dropped to 73 man-hours in 1977. During the 1939-1977 period, improved machines and cultural practices increased the output per man-hour 342 percent (Table 1.6). Mechanical harvesting should continue to increase labor output.

CLIMATIC REQUIREMENTS

The cucumber is a warm-season crop, and young plants are seriously injured by frost. However, cucumbers can be grown anywhere in the

Table 20.1—Cucumbers for Fresh Market: Harvest Season and Estimated Acreage, Yield, Production, and Value in Leading States, 1977.

State	Harvest Season	Harvested Acreage	Yield per Acre, Cwt.	Production per 1,000 Cwt.	Price per Cwt.	Value, $1,000
Florida	Spring	8,000	145	1,160	$ 9.38	10,881
Florida	Fall	7,800	110	858	9.35	8,022
Texas	Fall	4,300	71	305	9.70	2,959
S. Carolina	Spring	4,100	90	369	7.20	2,657
N. Carolina	Summer	3,800	58	220	8.61	1,894
Virginia	Summer	3,000	68	204	11.00	2,244
N. Carolina	Spring	3,000	70	210	7.02	1,474
Texas	Spring	2,900	100	290	11.90	3,451
New York	Summer	2,200	115	253	10.70	2,707
Michigan	Summer	2,100	80	168	9.28	1,559
Texas	Summer	1,800	120	216	11.90	2,570
Maryland	Summer	1,600	94	150	10.30	1,545
New Jersey	Summer	1,500	150	225	13.10	2,948
Virginia	Fall	1,500	56	84	6.07	510
S. Carolina	Fall	1,200	51	61	9.89	603
California	Spring	850	265	225	12.20	2,745
California	Fall	700	190	133	13.30	1,769
California	Summer	1,300	280	364	10.60	3,858
Hawaii	Fall	260	165	43	23.40	1,006
United States		51,910	107	5,538	10.00	55,402
Total	Spring (36%)	18,850	120	2,254	9.41	21,208
Total	Summer (34%)	17,350	104	1,800	10.70	19,325
Total	Fall (30%)	15,760	93	14,484	9.62	14,869

United States, because the crop matures in a relatively short season. Average daily temperatures of 65° to 75° F. are most favorable for growth, but heat is not so essential for cucumbers as it is for melons.

SELECTING CULTIVARS AND SEED

Cultivars

Cultivars should be selected which grow vigorously, yield well, resist disease, and have desirable market characteristics. The selection of cultivars will also depend upon the use for which the product is intended. Some cultivars are best suited for slicing purposes, and others are especially desirable for pickling. Table 20.3 gives a description of a selected list of the leading cultivars.

**Table 20.2—Cucumbers for (Pickles) Processing: Estimated
Acreage, Yield, Production, and Value
in Leading States, 1977.**

State	Harvested Acreage	Yield per Acre, Tons	Production, in Tons	Price per Ton	Value, $1,000
N. Carolina	28,000	2.60	72,900	$132	9,623
Michigan	24,500	4.65	114,000	109	12,426
Wisconsin	9,400	6.23	58,550	127	7,436
S. Carolina	8,700	2.87	24,950	141	3,510
Ohio	6,400	11.12	71,200	132	9,398
Texas	5,500	7.25	39,850	139	5,557
California	4,300	14.37	61,800	120	7,425
Alabama	3,800	1.75	6,650	163	1,084
Mississippi	3,600	2.40	8,650	143	1,237
Maryland	2,800	6.95	19,450	112	2,178
Virginia	2,800	3.07	8,600	119	1,023
Colorado	1,600	10.78	17,250	108	1,863
Indiana	1,400	6.96	9,750	108	1,053
New Jersey	1,400	9.43	13,200	132	1,742
Other States	19,790	5.12	101,300	135	13,689
United States	123,990	5.07	628,100	126	79,244

Gynoecious Hybrids

Hybrid cultivars have been developed, incorporating a genetic factor known as the gynoecious flowering habit. Normally, cucumber plants are monoecious, producing both male and female flowers separately on the same plant. Plants with the gynoecious flowering habit produce only female flowers. This genetic character has been incorporated into breeding lines, and can be retained in successive generations by treating plants with gibberellic acid to produce a few male flowers for self-pollination. In commercial seed lots, a small amount of seed of a standard cultivar is added to provide pollen for pollination. Gynoecious hybrids tend to be earlier, produce a concentrated set, and outyield standard cultivars. They are perhaps more subject to stress than other cultivars but are especially suited for mechanical harvesting.

Securing Seed

It is of the utmost importance to use good seed since the quality of the seed may be the margin of difference between success and failure of the crop. The difference in price between high- and low-quality seed is insignificant as compared with the difference in results. Seed should be purchased from seed houses which make a point of selling only the best.

Table 20.3—Selected Cultivars of Cucumbers.

Cultivars	Resistant to
Slicing Type:	
Open Pollinated	
Marketmore	3, 4
Meridian	3, 4
Poinsett	1, 2, 5, 6
F₁ Hybrid	
Burpee's M & M Hybrid	3, 5, 6
High Mark II	3, 4, 5
Triumph	3, 5
Victory	3, 5
Gynoecious Hybrid	
Cherokee 7	1, 2, 5, 6
Gemini 7	1, 3, 4
Meridian T	3, 4
Pickling Type:	
Open Pollinated	
Chipper	1, 2, 3, 5, 6
Pixie	1, 2, 5, 6
Wisconsin SMR 18	3, 4
Wisconsin SMR 58	3, 4
Gynoecious Hybrid	
Bounty	1, 2, 3, 4, 5, 6
Explorer	1, 2, 3, 5, 6
Greenpak	4
Pioneer	1, 2, 3, 4, 5
Premier	1, 2, 3, 4, 5, 6
Score	4

1—Angular Leaf Spot
2—Anthracnose
3—Cucumber Mosaic
4—Cucumber Scab
5—Downy Mildew
6—Powdery Mildew

Seed of F₁ hybrids usually costs several times as much as that of standard cultivars. The grower must decide if the added vigor and uniformity obtained is worth the extra seed cost. It is recommended that hybrids be tried on a small scale in comparison with standard cultivars to determine their value.

Most of the supply of cucumber seed is produced in California, Colorado, and Michigan, although some seed is produced locally in other cucumber-producing areas.

PREPARING THE SEEDBED

Soil Preferences

Cucumbers can be grown on almost any good soil. A light, loamy, well drained soil, which contains an abundance of organic matter and is fertile, is very desirable for early cucumbers. Although cucumbers are fairly tolerant to strongly acid soils, best results will be obtained if the soil reaction is kept between pH 5.5 and pH 6.8.

Preparing the Seedbed

The light soils used for cucumber production are relatively easy to prepare. However, the more thorough the preparation, the easier it will be to cultivate and work the crop. Plowing, discing, and harrowing are all necessary operations. The time of plowing and breaking will vary in the different regions according to the time of planting. For example, in North Carolina, where the planting dates are from March 25 to April 10, the land is broken during February or early March. In the South, cucumber land is frequently bedded up in order to facilitate drainage. The height of the beds will depend on the drainage situation. On the well drained soils, the land is broken flat and the row-beds made by throwing together two or four furrows with a turn-plow and dragging the ridge down almost level. The rows are bedded up usually when the fertilizer is applied. The final dragging and harrowing are done just ahead of the planter. In more poorly drained soils, high beds are thrown up when the land is first broken and these beds are reworked and dragged down just before planting time.

In other sections the land is plowed, disced, and harrowed, and the seed is planted on the level or in slight furrows.

FERTILIZING AND MANURING

Fertilizing

The cucumber is a quick-growing crop, and must be well supplied with nutrients and moisture to keep it growing vigorously. As seen in Table 6.4, the crop requires from 30 to 45 pounds of nitrogen per acre. If the soil is subject to leaching, more should be supplied, part before planting and the remainder as a side dressing. On soils of medium fertility cucumbers require about 70 pounds of phosphorus and about 116 pounds of potassium per acre (Table 6.5). These nutrients should be worked into the soil before planting.

Manuring

Animal manures are an excellent source of soil organic matter and fertility. However, manure is now rather expensive and not readily available, so a combination of green manure crops and commercial fertilizers is employed to meet the requirements of the crop. When a small amount of manure is available, it can be used to advantage by mixing with the soil under the row.

Summer soil-improvement crops of soybeans, cowpeas, or velvet beans are recommended. They should be turned under when they have reached full growth but before they mature and become woody. For an early cucumber crop, rye is a practicable winter cover crop, and it should be turned under three or four weeks before planting time.

PLANTING

Planting dates vary with climatic conditions. Cucumbers are easily injured by frost; consequently, field planting should be delayed until the soil temperature reaches 60° F. and the danger of frost is over. Some experienced growers make two or three different plantings, a week apart, the first about 10 days before the average date of the last killing frost. If the first planting is not killed by frost, it will give an extra early crop. If the first planting is killed, the grower still has one of the later plantings to fall back on.

Some cucumbers are still planted in hills but most commercial acreage is now planted in drill rows. When the hill method is used several seeds are planted in each hill and the plants are later thinned. The spacings vary from 4 by 5 feet up to 6 by 8 feet. In the row method the seeds are planted with a drill in a continuous row. The spacing between rows varies from 4 to 8 feet. Where the crop is grown in beds, the beds are usually 4 to 6 feet apart.

On land that has been previously bedded up, the beds are reworked at planting time, and the seed is planted in a row down the center of the bed. The depth of planting will vary with soil type and moisture conditions but will generally average about $\frac{1}{2}$ to 1 inch. From 2 to 4 pounds of seed are required to plant an acre, depending on the space between the rows and the method of planting used.

Pickling cucumbers have been found to give satisfactory yields with plant populations of from 25,000 to 30,000 per acre, using 42- to 60-inch row spacings and allowing 5 to 6 inches per plant. With precision planting, about 2 pounds of seed are required per acre.

Planting for Destructive Harvest

Populations of 80,000 to 100,000 plants per acre are necessary for optimum yields with a single destructive harvest. In some cases, 4-row beds, allowing somewhat wider space between beds to permit passage of equipment, have been found desirable. In California, where furrow irrigation is widely used, twin rows, spaced 12 to 14 inches apart on 40-inch beds, have been found satisfactory, with six plants per foot of row.

The heat unit system may be used to space plantings for successive harvests. By subtracting a base temperature (55° F. for cucumbers) from the daily mean temperature, the heat units (H. U.) can be determined. Investigations have indicated that an accumulation of 75 to 100 H. U. is required for germination and a total of 850 to 1,000 H. U. from planting to harvest. By taking the normal mean daily temperature during the expected time of harvest and the daily capacity of the harvesting machinery, the H. U. between plantings can be determined. As an example, if the average daily mean temperature at harvest time is 75° F., the crop will be accumulating 20 H. U. per day as it reaches maturity. This amount should be allowed to occur between planting dates. Cultivars differ in H. U. required to reach maturity, and some variation may be expected for both location and season.

CULTIVATING AND IRRIGATING

Cultivating

Cultivation should be started as soon as the plants are up and continued frequently enough to keep the weeds down and the soil loose. Early cultivations may be near the plants, but since the cucumber is shallow-rooted, all cultivations after the plants begin to run should be shallow and not too close to the plants. Sometimes the vines are turned to permit later cultivation, but hand hoeing may be necessary to destroy weeds close to the plants. Herbicides may be used to control weeds, especially for close planting (Chapter 9).

Pollinating

Cucumbers require insects, chiefly honey bees, either wild or domesticated, to transfer pollen from male to female flowers for the development of usable fruit. In the vicinity of large tracts of woodland or other uncultivated land, the wild bee population may be adequate for good pollination. In other areas, however, it will be necessary to place colonies of domesticated bees near cucumber plantings. One hive may pollinate an acre of cucumbers. The hives should be placed near the plantings after flowering begins.

Irrigating

Cucumber crops require a continuous supply of moisture during the growing season. The most critical need occurs at the time of fruiting. Moisture stress then can seriously reduce the yield of marketable fruit. Furrow irrigation is preferable where it can be used. When an overhead system is used, water should be applied early enough in the day so that the soil and leaves can dry before nightfall to reduce the spread of fruit-rotting and foliage diseases.

CONTROLLING DISEASES AND INSECTS

Diseases

Downy mildew, bacterial wilt, anthracnose, root knot, angular leaf spot, mosaic, and scab are important diseases of cucumbers. The first four of these are discussed in Chapter 22. Resistance to downy mildew has been found and transferred into such commercial cucumber cultivars as Palmetto, Santee, Ashley, Stono, Palomar, Chipper, Explorer, and Pixie.

ANGULAR LEAF SPOT. Angular leaf spot (*Pseudomonas lachrymans*) is a bacterial disease carried over winter on the seed and in the soil. It causes small, angular, water-soaked or tan-colored spots on the leaves and fruits. To control the disease, clean seed should be used and the plants sprayed with thiram or captan.

MOSAIC. Mosaic or "white pickle" is a virus disease found in many areas throughout the country and frequently causes heavy loss. It is characterized by a dwarfing of the plants; mottling, yellowing, and wrinkling of the leaves; and a warting and mottling of the fruits. Mosaic affects other cultivated plants such as muskmelons, squash, peppers, tomatoes, and celery. The organism also attacks several wild plants, including pokeweed, milkweed, catnip, and ground cherry. It overwinters on their roots or seeds, and is carried to cultivated crops in the spring by aphids and the striped cucumber beetle. It is also spread in the cucumber fields by pickers. Thorough eradication of wild host plants near the cucumber fields and strict control of insects are most important in the control of mosaic. Mosaic-resistant cultivars have been developed for both slicing and pickling cucumbers. The leading resistant cultivars are listed in Table 20.3.

SCAB. Scab is caused by a fungus (*Cladosporium cucumerinum*) which produces sunken, dark-brown spots on the fruits. In moist weather, the spots are covered with a greenish mold. A gummy substance oozes from the fruits. The leaves and stems may also be affected. The fungus also attacks muskmelons and pumpkins. The disease is found primarily in the north central and northeastern states and is most damaging in cool, moist weather. The organism overwinters in old refuse and on the seed. The best control measures are fixed coppers, ziram, maneb, rotation, and use of disease-resistant cultivars. In addition to the two resistant pickling cultivars listed in Table 20.3, the slicing cultivar Highmoor is resistant.

Insects

The principal cucumber insects include aphids, twelve-spotted cucumber beetles, striped cucumber beetles, and spider mites. These insects and methods of control are described in Chapter 11.

Another insect, the pickle worm, feeds on flowers and leaf buds. It tunnels into the flowers, terminal buds, vines, and fruits. It is found in the southeastern part of the country and may be destructive as far north as New York, Michigan, and parts of Canada. Spraying or dusting with rotenone, lindane, or cryolite is recommended. Worms must be killed before they enter the fruits.

HARVESTING, HANDLING, AND MARKETING

Harvesting

Slicing or fresh market cucumbers must be fresh and crisp when received by the consumer. The market desires a medium-sized, well-formed, dark green cucumber. This requires frequent picking and careful and prompt handling. They must be gathered often enough to prevent their becoming too large or overripe. No fruit should be allowed to ripen on the vines as further yield of the plant will be markedly decreased.

In normal seasons, the first picking can be made 60 to 65 days after planting. Normally, pickings may be made at two- to three-day intervals, but, during the height of the season, it may be necessary to harvest daily. Cucumbers usually are picked or cut from the vines, placed in baskets or hampers, and carried to the ends of the rows for packing, but labor-saving devices may also be used (Fig. 20.2).

Pickling cucumbers mature a few days earlier than slicing cucumbers. Frequency of picking will depend on the size desired by the pickling factory. Small-sized cucumbers are usually less profitable to the grower than larger ones. The increased price paid for the small sizes does not generally offset the lower yields obtained.

Fig. 20.2—Mechanical harvesting of cucumbers.

USDA—Soil Conservation Service Photograph

Machine harvesting works best on early cultivars with relatively small but vigorous vines, concentrated set, and uniform maturity. The fruit should be slow to develop color, have a uniform blocky shape and the ability to hold on the vines until harvested, be resistant to damage from handling, be small in the seed cavity, and be slow in seed development.

Grading and Waxing

Slicing cucumbers are usually sorted and graded by hand in the field or packing shed (Fig. 20.3). U.S. Fancy, U.S. No. 1, and U.S. No. 2 are the standard grades, but the U.S. Fancy grade is seldom used. Pickling cucumbers are sorted into various grades and sizes on belt grading machines at the pickling factory.

Slicing cucumbers are usually waxed after grading and washing or brushing. A number of different types of waxes with different methods

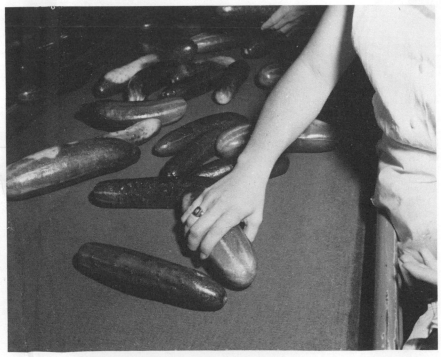

Fig. 20.3—Cucumbers sorted for size and grade on conveyer belt.

USDA Photograph

of application are available. Waxing adds slightly to the cost of production, but is quite effective in preventing shrinkage and loss of freshness during shipping and marketing.

Packing

Sometimes cucumbers are packed in the field, although larger growers use packing sheds. A variety of packages is used, including bushel baskets, hampers, crates, and many kinds of boxes. Lug boxes and 12-quart baskets with handles have been used considerably in recent years, especially for fancy packs. The fruits should be well placed to minimize shifting within the package while in transit.

Marketing

Cucumbers are commonly shipped to distant markets under refrigeration. Most of the crop is hauled to market by trucks, both with and without refrigeration, depending upon the distance and weather conditions. Competition among buyers and sellers is keen, especially when supplies are low.

EXPORTS AND IMPORTS. Fresh cucumbers have become a major import item totaling 250,957,000 pounds valued at $18,760,000 in 1977. Mexico has been supplying about 94 percent of the imports, and the Bahamas and Honduras have been supplying smaller quantities. These imports take place primarily during the five-month period, December through April. Small quantities of pickled cucumbers are also exported (Table 13.2).

SELECTED REFERENCES

Anonymous, "Growing Cucumbers for Processing," Asgrow Seed Co., Orange, Conn., 1968.

Anonymous, "Pest and Disease Control Program for Cucurbits," Calif. Agr. Ext. Ser. Pub., 1975 (issued annually).

Anonymous, "Pickle Research," Mich. State Univ. Farm Science 213, 1973.

Barnes, G., and McDaniel, M. C., "Control of Insects and Diseases on Cucumbers," Univ. of Ark, Agr. Ext. Ser. Leaflet 273, 1970.

Binning, L. K., Libby, J. L., and Wade, E. K., "Pickling Cucumbers—Pest Control," Univ. of Wisc. Coop. Ext. Programs A2358, 1977.

Curwen, D., and Schulte, E. E., "Pickling Cucumber Production," Univ. of Wisc. Fact Sheet A1587, 1978.

Hammett, H. L., "Production of Cucumbers for Pickles," Miss. Agr. and For. Exp. Sta. Bull. 801, 1974.

Johnson, W. A., "Soil Fertility Studies with Pickling Cucumbers in the Piedmont Area of Alabama," Auburn Univ. Coop. Ext. Ser. Circ. 211, 1973.

Marshall, D. E., et al., "Handling of Pickling Cucumbers," Amer. Soc. of Agr. Eng., St. Joseph, Mich., Paper 71–347, 1971.

McGregor, S. E., "Insect Pollination of Cultivated Crop Plants," USDA, ARS, Agr. HB 496, 1976.

Motes, J. E., "Pickling Cucumbers Production-Harvesting," Mich. State Univ. Coop. Ext. Ser. Ext. Bull. E-837, 1977.

Seelig, R. A., "Cucumbers," United Fresh Fruit and Vegetable Assoc., Alexandria, Va., 1972.

Sims, W. L., and Zahara, M. B., "Growing Pickling Cucumbers for Mechanical Harvesting," Univ. of Calif. Coop. Ext. Ser. Leaflet 2677, 1978.

Swingle, H. D., and Mullins, C. A., "Evaluation of Fresh Market Cucumber Varieties for Trellis Production," Univ. of Tenn. Agr. Exp. Sta. Farm and Home Sci. Progress Rep. 100, 1976.

Whitaker, T. W., and Davis, G. N., Cucurbits, New York: Interscience Pubs., Inc., 1962.

CHAPTER 21

Lettuce

CLASSIFICATION, ORIGIN, AND HISTORY

Lettuce (*Lactuca sativa*) belongs to the sunflower or *Compositae* family. It is closely related to the wild lettuce *L. serriola*—in fact, so closely related that the two species cross readily.

The three most commonly grown types in the United States are: (1) leaf or bunching type; (2) head lettuce, including both crisphead and butterhead varieties; and (3) cos or romaine type.

Lettuce is not new when compared with other vegetable crops. This is evident from historical references which relate that lettuce appeared at the royal tables of the Persian kings as long ago as 550 B.C.

SCOPE AND IMPORTANCE

Lettuce is the most important salad crop. It is grown commercially in at least 20 states and produced for local market and home use in areas throughout the country. Its production and consumption have increased markedly during the past 40 years. Lettuce ranked sixth in acreage and third in value among the 22 principal vegetables in 1977, and was exceeded in value only by potatoes and tomatoes.

Lettuce acreage ranged from 202,320 in 1949 to about 231,500 in 1977, while acre yields rose from 132 to 243 hundredweight. Production increased from 26,674,000 hundredweight in 1949 to approximately 56,233,000 in 1977; and values more than tripled from $125,981,000 to $424,496,000 during the 28-year period. California is by far the leading state with almost 70 percent of the acreage, production, and value.

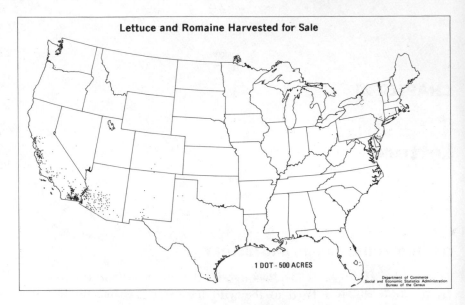

Fig. 21.1—Acreage, distribution, production, and value of lettuce.

UNITED STATES TOTAL

Year	Acreage	Production 1,000 Cwt.	Value, $1,000
1949	202,320	26,674	125,981
1959	221,610	35,182	134,482
1969	228,370	44,744	241,764
1977	231,480	56,233	424,496

Figure 21.1 shows the approximate acreage, distribution, production, and value trends between 1949 and 1977. Table 21.1 presents the season, acreage, production, and value by states.

TRENDS IN PRODUCTION EFFICIENCY

Special production and harvesting requirements categorize lettuce as a relatively expensive crop. Between 1939 and 1959, average labor requirements declined from 141 to 115 man-hours per acre and fell to 78 man-hours by 1977. Mechanical selective harvesting and other improvements increased the output per man-hour 433 percent between 1939 and 1977 (Table 1.6).

CLIMATIC REQUIREMENTS

Lettuce thrives best at a relatively cool temperature. For that reason, it is grown principally as an early spring, fall, and winter crop in the

South and Southwest. It is only in the most northern states, at high alti-
tudes in the West, and near the coast in California, Oregon, and Washington that it can be grown as a summer crop. Ample sunlight, uniformly
cool nights, and plenty of moisture in the soil are essential to well-
developed, solid heads.

Control of soil moisture is important. Even where irrigation is practiced, the eastern grower does not have the control of soil moisture that
western growers have. Sudden increases of soil moisture through heavy
rains may cause rapid changes in the plant's growth rate. If such changes
occur during heading, large, puffy heads may result.

High temperatures are conducive to early seedstalk development and
inferior quality. Slow-bolting types have been bred that will help prevent
premature seedstalk development.

Table 21.1—Lettuce for Fresh Market: Harvest Season and Estimated Acreage, Yield, Production, and Value in Leading States, 1977.

State	Harvest Season	Harvested Acreage	Yield per Acre, Cwt.	Production per 1,000 Cwt.	Price per Cwt.	Value, $1,000
California	Spring	41,800	280	11,704	$ 5.47	64,021
California	Summer	41,000	290	11,890	7.21	85,727
California	Winter	40,900	235	9,612	7.98	76,704
California	Fall	36,000	245	8,820	8.74	77,087
Arizona	Fall	16,500	210	3,465	8.15	28,240
Arizona	Winter	14,000	200	2,800	8.54	23,912
Arizona	Spring	7,400	240	1,776	5.15	9,146
Florida	Winter	4,300	160	688	13.30	9,150
Colorado	Summer	4,300	235	1,011	5.89	5,955
New Jersey	Summer	3,300	200	105	7.22	758
New Mexico	Fall	3,000	200	600	8.85	5,310
Florida	Spring	2,800	145	406	8.77	3,561
Texas	Winter	2,800	175	490	6.57	3,219
Florida	Fall	2,300	135	311	17.80	5,536
Texas	Fall	1,800	165	297	12.70	3,772
New Jersey	Spring	1,700	160	272	8.06	2,192
Wisconsin	Summer	1,400	250	322	9.65	3,107
Michigan	Summer	1,400	170	238	9.60	2,285
New Jersey	Fall	1,100	200	220	10.80	2,376
Washington	Summer	1,100	195	215	7.40	1,591
Other States		2,580		991		10,847
United States		231,480	243	56,233	7.55	424,496
Total	Winter (27%)	62,000	219	13,590	8.31	112,985
Total	Spring (24%)	54,450	262	14,286	5.58	79,752
Total	Fall (26%)	61,230	226	13,811	8.92	124,193
Total	Summer (23%)	53,800	270	14,546	7.39	107,566

SELECTING CULTIVARS AND SEED

Cultivars

Lettuce cultivars may be classified roughly into crisphead, butter-head, cos or romaine, and looseleaf or bunching types.

The crisphead cultivars are by far the most important commercially. Of these Great Lakes group because of their dark green color, vigorous growth, compact heads, and good shipping and handling qualities have replaced the Imperial cultivars. Since the crisphead cultivars can be delivered to the consumer in good condition after long-distance shipment, they can be grown in areas best suited for lettuce. Fulton, Empire, Mesa 659, Minneto, Great Lakes 659, Fairton, Climax, Ithaca, and New York 515 Improved are a few of the many cultivars of the crisphead type (Fig. 21.2).

Cultivars of the butterhead type have soft, pliable leaves, a delicate flavor, and smaller and less firm heads than those of the crisphead type.

Fig. 21.2—A Great Lakes cultivar of head lettuce.

Leaves bruise and tear easily and become discolored. Even for local market, butterhead lettuce should be handled carefully. Some of the commonly used cultivars include Dark Green Boston, Green Mignonette, Wayahead, Bibb, and Summer Bibb (Fig. 21.3).

Fig. 21.3—Planting of bibb lettuce.

Cos or romaine cultivars are easily recognized by their upright habit of growth, long heads, and long narrow leaves. Like the butterhead, they are best adapted for local market. Commonly used cultivars are Paris Island Cos., Dark Green Cos., and Valmaine.

Looseleaf or bunching cultivars do not form heads. They are early, easy to grow, and popular for the home garden. Leaf lettuce is not adapted for long distance shipment and its market life is short. Cultivars include Black Seeded Simpson, Grand Rapids (tip burn resistant), Prizehead, Domineer, Oak Leaf, Ruby, Salad Bowl, and Slo-Bolt (Fig. 21.4).

Securing Seed

The importance of securing good seed cannot be overemphasized. The success or failure of the crop is determined to a large extent by the

Fig. 21.4—Black seeded Simpson cultivar of leaf lettuce.

Ferry Morse Seed Co.

seed. Each grower, therefore, should be satisfied with none but the best. The seed supply should come only from a reliable seedsman, one who has established a reputation for his integrity and whose stocks have given good results in tests and in commercial plantings. The best seed may cost slightly more than an inferior grade, but this slight increase in cost is of minor importance when compared with the loss that may result from the use of inferior seed or a poorly adapted cultivar or strain.

PREPARING THE SOIL

Soil Preferences

Lettuce is grown on a wide variety of soil types. The largest commercial acreages are on muck, sandy loam, and silt loam soils. A fertile sandy loam is preferred for the early spring crop, while crops started in warm weather are grown most extensively on mucks and loams.

Preparing the Seedbed

The preparation of the soil for planting and growing lettuce is much the same as for growing other vegetables. The land should be thoroughly prepared, both to assure germination of the small-sized seed and to give the comparatively shallow roots of the lettuce plant a chance to develop to best advantage.

Kinds of soil and climatic conditions govern somewhat the time for plowing. The soil should be plowed as early as possible, but never when it is too wet. Plowing should be deep wherever practicable. Preparation of the bed depends on type of soil, time of year, and method of irrigation used. In areas where lettuce is grown commercially, it is best to consult a local agricultural extension publication for detailed procedures.

MANURING, FERTILIZING, AND LIMING

Since rapid growth is essential to crispness and high quality, there must be a liberal supply of readily available nutrients in the soil at all times.

Manuring

Where stable manure can be obtained at a reasonable price, heavy applications, 20 to 30 tons per acre, will give excellent results on mineral soils. It should be broadcast on the land at least four weeks before the time of planting and disced as soon as possible. If stable manure is not available, humus can be supplied by growing green manure crops such as cowpeas, soybeans, alfalfa, clover, and vetch. When these are turned under, an application of about 50 pounds of N per acre will hasten decomposition and prevent a temporary deficiency.

Fertilizing

Although the uptake of nutrients by lettuce is low compared to that of other crops, high fertility is required for good production. This is because of the plant's limited root system for absorbing nutrients and the necessity for rapid, continuous growth. Nitrogen is the most critical element in fertilizing lettuce. About 30 pounds of N should be applied before planting and about the same amount after thinning. Any additional N would depend upon nitrogen made available from organic matter in the soil and the amount of leaching. Loose heads may result from high nitrogen at the time of heading. If a soil test is available, Table 6.5 can be used to indicate amounts of phosphorus and potassium to use. These should be applied before planting. As an example, the table shows that a soil giving a medium test for both elements requires 18 pounds of phosphorus and 112 pounds of potassium per acre for a crop of lettuce. Some of the western soils are high in K and the application of this element may not be recommended.

Liming

Experimental results indicate that lettuce does not thrive on a highly acid soil. A soil reaction between pH 5.5 and pH 7.0 is satisfactory. If the soil is more acid than pH 5.5, lime should be applied. Muck soils should be limed if they are more acid than pH 5.2.

SEEDING AND TRANSPLANTING

Seeding and Growing Plants for Transplanting

A common practice for the extra early spring crops is to grow the plants under cloth or glass sash protection for transplanting to the field. The soil in the seedbed should be prepared carefully and should be made reasonably fertile by thoroughly mixing 2 to 4 pounds of a complete fertilizer per 100 square feet of soil.

One-fourth pound of good seed sown thinly on a well-prepared seedbed should produce enough strong, healthy plants to set an acre, but more seed is commonly used. Crowding the seedlings can be detrimental as it results in inferior plants and increases the danger from damping off and other diseases. The seed should be planted in an area covering at least 300 square feet. Very good results can be obtained by making the beds 12 feet wide and covering them with muslin or tobacco cloth stretched over a ridge pole supported on posts through the center of the bed. In the North most transplants are grown in sack-covered hotbeds or cold frames. For the winter or extra early spring crop it will take 8 to 10 weeks to produce plants large enough to be transplanted. Great care should be exercised in watering and ventilating the plant beds to prevent loss from damping off.

Planting in the Field

Early spring plants should be hardened and may be set as soon as hard freezes are over. When the plants are transplanted to the field, they should be lifted carefully from the soil and planted so that the tap roots are set straight in the soil. The plant should not be set deeper than it grew in the bed. All spindling and diseased plants should be discarded. The rows are spaced the same distance apart for plants as for seed sown directly in the field.

Commercially, most lettuce is grown from seed planted directly in the field with mechanical seeders. Seeding is usually at the rate of about 2 pounds per acre. Under good conditions adequate stands may be obtained with as little as 1 pound per acre. Lighter rates of seeding will save labor on thinning and blocking.

Systems of planting vary from one- to six-row beds. The most widely used method in the West is the two-row bed. The height of the bed varies with soil type, drainage, and season.

Planting distances between rows vary, depending upon the systems of cultivation and irrigation used and the cultivars grown. The smaller butterhead cultivars can be grown closer than the crisphead types. Distances between rows in single-row systems should not be greater than 18 inches. Much of the western lettuce is grown on 2-row beds with 40 to 42 inches from center to center. The beds are from 18 to 22 inches wide and rows 3 to 4 inches from each edge. Beds may be shaped, smoothed, and planted in one operation. Lettuce seed does not germinate well at high temperatures, and the soil should be kept moist until the seedlings emerge. A preplant application of benefin at the rate of 1.5 pounds per acre could aid in the control of annual weeds.

THINNING, CULTIVATING, AND IRRIGATING

Blocking and Thinning

When the seed is sown directly in the field or when the plants are too thick in the plant bed, it will be necessary to do some hand thinning. In the field, the plants should first be blocked—usually 10 to 14 days after planting. All plants are removed from the row except small clusters, 10 to 16 inches apart. A few days later, as soon as the first true leaves are formed, the clusters are thinned to one plant. Frequently the more vigorous plants removed can be transplanted in areas where the stand may be poor. It is important that only one plant be left in a place.

The distance between plants in a row is determined by the cultivar, fertility of the soil, and size of plant desired. Small cultivars should be spaced about 10 inches apart, while larger cultivars like New York need a 12- to 16-inch spacing.

Thinning is the most laborious and expensive operation in the production of lettuce. In the large western areas, the blocking and thinning operation is often done under contract on an acre basis.

Cultivating

Shallow cultivation frequent enough to keep down weeds and to provide a light mulch is recommended. Lettuce plants have comparatively small root systems and most of the small roots are near the surface. For that reason, cultivation deeper than 2 or 3 inches will break off many roots and cause serious injury to the plants. Cultivator attachments which cut the weeds off just below the surface and leave a shallow mulch are usually more satisfactory than cultivator teeth or narrow shovels. If the soil is free of weeds and a mulch is present, nothing will be gained by additional cultivation until more weeds appear. It will be necessary to do some weeding between the plants in the row. This may be done effectively with the hands in loose soil or with a hand hoe.

Irrigating

For optimum growth, lettuce requires a constant and relatively abundant supply of moisture throughout the growing period. Fluctuations in soil moisture, especially during the later stages of development, are severely detrimental to best growth. Too much water during this period with high temperatures may result in loose, puffy heads. In the western region, lettuce is irrigated by open furrows. In humid regions, supplemental water is usually applied through a sprinkler system.

CONTROLLING DISEASES AND INSECTS

General recommendations for both disease and insect control can be found in Chapter 11. The reader is also directed to his local agricultural experiment station or extension service for the latest recommendations for his area.

Diseases

TIP-BURN. One of the most prevalent and serious diseases of lettuce is tip-burn. The marginal tissues of the leaves turn brown and later die. The disease is nonparasitic and is most prevalent in hot weather. Plants making very rapid growth appear to be most susceptible to the disease. Factors which tend to check the rate of growth at maturity serve to reduce the amount of injury, but no satisfactory control has been found. Some progress has been made in breeding cultivars with resistance to tipburn.

LETTUCE DROP. Lettuce drop is the common name of a disease caused by *Sclerotinia libertiana* and *S. minor* fungi, which induce wilting and sudden collapse of the outer leaves. The organisms causing drop are widespread throughout the country and may attack many plants besides lettuce. Loss can occur in transit, in storage, and in the market, as well as in the field. Soil disinfection with formaldehyde solution is a satisfactory control on a small area. A gallon of formaldehyde solution (1 part of commercial formaldehyde in 100 parts of water) should be used to a square foot. Steam sterilizing or treating the soil with PCNB or captan is also effective. No resistant cultivars are available. Crop rotation is recommended.

BOTTOM ROT. A common fungus disease that is most prevalent during damp weather is bottom rot. It is caused by one of the organisms that commonly causes damping off (*Rhizoctonia solani*). The plants may be attacked at nearly all stages of growth, and the disease may be present throughout the growing season. Cultivars that have a spreading habit of growth are most commonly infected, since the organism enters the plant through the lower leaves that are in contact with the soil. Rotation with nonsusceptible crops such as sweet corn and onions is a practical means of control. Treating the soil beneath the plants with PCNB has also proved effective, since it is quite specific for *Rhizoctonia*.

MOSAIC. Mosaic is a widespread virus disease characterized by a mottling of the leaves and stunting of the plants. The disease is spread by sucking insects such as aphids; therefore, a special effort should be made to control these insects. The initial infection in a field usually comes from infected seed. Some control can be obtained by roguing the infected plants.

DOWNY MILDEW. Downy mildew (*Bremia lactucae*) is characterized by a distinctly visible downy or velvety growth upon the affected surface. The disease is widespread, but is more common in western areas than in the East. It is most likely to develop in damp, foggy, moderately warm weather. Wild lettuce is a host for the organisms that cause downy mildew. Eradication of this plant, therefore, is helpful in the control of the disease. Crop rotation also is recommended.

BIG VEIN. Big vein is a relatively new disease but is now known to be widespread in both eastern and western lettuce fields. It is a virus disease that is soil-borne. It is sometimes confused with mosaic, but the leaf symptoms are quite different. Rotation is partially effective as a control measure.

ASTER YELLOWS. A virus disease that has become very serious, especially in the northeastern states, is aster yellows. The virus is transferred from plant to plant by a species of leaf hoppers. Control of the insect vector is the only practical means of control.

Insects

Lettuce is frequently attacked by several kinds of insects. The main ones are cutworms, cabbage loopers, six-spotted leaf hoppers, wireworms, and aphids. Army worms and corn earworms will occasionally attack lettuce in its early stages of growth. Malathion as applied for cabbage loopers (see Chapter 11) is effective in control. Chlordane is recommended for wireworms. The six-spotted leaf hoppers are best controlled with malathion or carbaryl. Toxaphene is effective on cutworms, while aphids are best controlled with nicotine, malathion, or diazinon.

HARVESTING, HANDLING, AND MARKETING

Harvesting

Leaf lettuce is harvested for home use as soon as the leaves are large enough. For local market, the whole plant is harvested when it is well developed yet not so advanced that the leaves are tough and the flavor is bitter.

The home gardener sometimes harvests head lettuce before the heads become very firm. For market, however, the plants should be harvested when the heads become as hard as existing weather conditions will permit but before the seed stalk begins to develop. Immature heads are spongy and will not withstand the process of marketing.

Lettuce is usually cut with a sharp knife of convenient size. Head lettuce is commonly cut at or just below the surface of the ground, and all soiled and diseased leaves are removed before packing. Where lettuce drop is serious, the head should be cut above the leaves that come in contact with the soil. This will aid in preventing the spread of the disease spores throughout the package. The crop should never be cut when the heads are wet, as much breakage of the brittle leaves will occur in handling.

Grading and Packing

A marked change has taken place in the methods of harvesting and packing lettuce in the large producing areas of California, Arizona, and other sections. This change was brought about by the use of the vacuum cooling process. This process eliminated the need for direct icing and made it feasible to use corrugated paperboard cartons instead of wooden crates. This also moved the site for packing from the sheds to the field. Practically all of the lettuce crop from the Salinas, California, district is field-packed and vacuum-cooled. Figures 21.5 and 21.6 show lettuce being harvested and packed in the field. The new paperboard cartons hold two dozen heads drypacked (Fig. 21.7). The cartons are mechanically placed in the precooling chambers. As much as half a carload can be handled at one time, and the temperature at the center of each head of lettuce

Fig. 21.5—Machine to aid harvesting of lettuce in Arizona.

The Progressive Farmer Photograph

can be reduced to 34° F. in less than 30 minutes. The cooled cartons are placed in precooled refrigerator cars and trucks for shipment to market.

Packing and grading should be carefully done according to recognized standards. The U.S. Department of Agriculture has established specifications for standard grades, copies of which can be obtained from Washington or from state marketing agencies.

Storing

Lettuce may be kept in cold storage for a period of three to four weeks after harvest, if it is in good condition at the beginning of the storage period and is held at 32° F.

Marketing

Lettuce grown in the principal producing areas of California and

Fig. 21.6—Field packing van in operation.

USDA Photograph

Fig. 21.7—Carton of lettuce showing method of packing.

USDA Photograph

Arizona (Table 21.1) is shipped in refrigerator cars and trucks to market, with increasing quantities being moved by refrigerator trucks. Prior to being shipped under refrigeration (Arizona and California), the lettuce is normally vacuum cooled. The great year-round demand for lettuce requires expeditious handling under competitive conditions. Consumers demand good quality at reasonable prices.

EXPORTS AND IMPORTS. Exports of U.S. lettuce have been increasing, with total shipments in 1977 of 359,513,000 pounds valued at $32,405,000 (Table 13.2). Although Canada has dominated the market, receiving over 90 percent of the exports, some quantities are also shipped to Western Europe and Hong Kong. Imports are limited.

SELECTED REFERENCES

Barger, W. R., "Vacuum Precooling Lettuce in Commercial Plants," USDA, AMS 469, 1962.

Burns, A. J., and Podany, J. C., "Lettuce Prices, Costs, and Margins," USDA, ERS, TVS 209, 1978.

Cudney, D. W., et al., "Weed Control in Lettuce," Univ. of Calif. Div. of Agr. Sci. Coop. Ext. Leaflet 2987, 1977.

Gardner, B. R., and Pew, W. D., "Response of Spring Grown Head Lettuce to Nitrogen Fertilizer," Univ. of Ariz. Agr. Exp. Sta. Tech. Bull. 210, 1974.

Garnett, Ed., and Sprott, M., "An Overview of the Texas Fall Lettuce Industry," Tex. A & M Univ. Agr. Ext. Ser., 1971.

Lenker, D. H., and Adrian, P. A., "Use of X-rays for Selecting Mature Lettuce Heads," Am. Soc. Agr. Eng., Vol. 14, St. Joseph, Mo., 1971.

Longbrake, Tom, "Keys to Profitable Lettuce Production," Tex. A & M Univ., Coop. Ext. Ser. Fact Sheet L-949, 1976.

Montelaro, J., "Lettuce and Endive," Univ. of Fla. Coop. Ext. Ser. Circ. 123C, 1977.

Oebker, N. F., et al., "Lettuce Containers and Head Characteristics," reprint from Western Grower and Shipper magazine, Nov., 1965.

Pew, W. D., et al., "Growing Head Lettuce in Arizona," Univ. of Ariz. Coop. Ext. Ser. Bull. A87, 1977.

Ryder, E. J., "Evaluation of Lettuce Varieties (and Breeding Lines for Resistance to Common Lettuce Mosaic)," USDA Tech. Bull. 1391, 1968.

Schoenemann, J. A., et al., "Lettuce," Univ. of Wisc. Coop. Ext. Programs Pub. A2340, 1978.

Seelig, R. A., "Lettuce," United Fresh Fruit and Vegetable Assoc., Alexandria, Va., 1970.

CHAPTER 22

Muskmelons (Cantaloupes)

CLASSIFICATION, ORIGIN, AND HISTORY

The muskmelon (*Cucumis melo*) is frequently referred to as cantaloupe in the South and by the trade. It is believed to have originated in India, was mentioned as being grown in Central America in 1516, and was reported in Virginia and New York in 1609 and 1629, respectively. Some refer to the botanical variety *reticulatis* as muskmelon and to the variety *cantilupensis* as cantaloupe.

SCOPE AND IMPORTANCE

The muskmelon is a popular, relatively important crop. It ranked thirteenth in acreage and twelfth in value among the 22 principal vegetables in 1977.

Muskmelon acreage of 128,300 acres in 1949 fluctuated downwardly for many years to 79,500 acres in 1977. Acre yields increased substantially, and production rose slightly during the 28-year period. Total crop value increased from $35,443,000 in 1949 to $113,991,000 in 1977.

Figure 22.1 shows the approximate distribution of muskmelons and its 1949-1977 record of acreage, production, and value. The acreage, production, and value for 1977 are shown in Table 22.1. California was outstanding with about 51 percent of the acreage. Texas and Arizona are also important producing states.

In addition to cantaloupes, honeydew melons are increasingly important. Their harvested acreage has ranged from around 10,000 to 15,800 between 1949 and 1977. Since 1949, acre yields increased substantially from about 120 to 174 hundredweight during the 28-year period

Fig. 22.1—Acreage, distribution, production, and value of cantaloupes (muskmelons).

UNITED STATES TOTAL

Year	Acreage	Production 1,000 Cwt.	Value, $1,000
1949	128,300	10,913	35,443
1959	123,850	12,870	56,361
1969	124,300	13,697	76,850
1977	79,500	10,760	113,991

and the value of honeydews moved upward from $6,000,000 in 1949 to more than $25,560,000 in 1977. California, Texas, and Arizona are the principal producing states.

TRENDS IN PRODUCTION EFFICIENCY

The cost of producing muskmelons varies considerably in different sections, depending primarily upon natural fertility, labor, and general efficiency of operations. About 115 man-hours were required in 1939 to produce and harvest an acre of muskmelons compared with 109 man-hours in 1959. With increased yields, the man-hour output increased about 80 percent during the 1939-1959 period and has continued upward with improved mechanization and methods.

CLIMATIC REQUIREMENTS

An ideal muskmelon climate includes a fairly long frost-free season

Table 22.1—Muskmelons (Cantaloupes) for Fresh Market: Harvest Season and Estimated Acreage, Yield, Production, and Value in Leading States, 1977.

State	Harvest Season	Harvested Acreage	Yield per Acre, Cwt.	Production per 1,000 Cwt.	Price per Cwt.	Value, $1,000
California	Summer	27,200	165	4,488	$ 9.97	44,745
Texas	Spring	10,700	125	1,338	14.60	19,535
California	Spring	10,700	140	1,498	9.68	14,501
Texas	Summer	6,500	105	683	11.40	7,786
Arizona	Spring	5,300	150	795	10.90	8,666
Arizona	Summer	4,300	160	688	10.10	6,949
Georgia	Summer	3,700	63	233	6.20	1,445
S. Carolina	Summer	3,100	45	140	8.56	1,198
California	Fall	2,500	100	250	13.20	3,300
Michigan	Summer	2,000	80	160	11.10	1,776
Indiana	Summer	1,800	150	270	9.79	2,643
Colorado	Summer	850	135	115	4.50	518
Arizona	Fall	850	120	102	9.11	929
United States		79,500	135	10,760	10.60	113,991
Total	Summer (62%)	49,450	137	6,777	9.90	67,060
Total	Spring (34%)	26,700	136	3,631	11.80	42,702
Total	Fall (4%)	3,350	105	352	12.00	4,229

with plenty of sunshine and heat, a dry atmosphere, and sufficient soil moisture. The Southwest is particularly suited to melon culture, but favorable natural conditions prevail in many other sections of the country, making it possible for skilful farmers to grow the crop advantageously for local markets. Ordinarily, 80 to 110 days of favorable growing weather are required between planting and the first harvest.

SELECTING CULTIVARS AND SEED

In selecting muskmelon cultivars, the grower should consider market preference, earliness, yield, disease and insect resistance, shipping quality, and other factors which influence profits. Muskmelons grown for shipment are mainly heavily netted, medium-size, nearly round specimens of both the green and salmon-fleshed cultivars. This type is preferred because of its carrying quality, desirable size and shape, and superior quality when sufficiently matured on the vine.

Cultivars

Many cultivars are grown for commercial and home use. A brief description of some of them is given in Table 22.2. Cultivars used primarily for the home and local market are usually high in quality but are often not firm enough for shipment. Many of the older cultivars are being replaced by similar ones resistant to one or more diseases. These should be considered in a region where a particular disease is prevalent.

Table 22.2—Brief Description of Selected Cultivars of Muskmelons.

				Fruit			
Cultivar	Use	Season (Days)	Size (Lbs.)	Shape	Netting	Color (Flesh)	Resistant to*
Burpee Hybrid**	Market, home	82	4-4½	Oval	Heavy	Deep Orange	
Casaba (Golden Beauty)	Shipping	101	7	Oval	None	White	
Crenshaw	Shipping	110	9	Acorn	None	Light Orange	
Delicious 51	Market	86	3½	Round	Close	Bright Orange	FW
Edisto 47	Market	95	4½	Round	Heavy	Salmon	DM,PM,ALS
Goldstar**	Market	87	Medium	Oval	Thick	Dark Orange	FW
Gulf Stream	Shipping	90	2½	Oval	Heavy	Salmon	DM,PM
Harper Hybrid**	Market	86	Medium	Round	Fine	Salmon	FW
Harvest Queen	Market	95	3½	Oval, round	Coarse	Orange	FW
Honey Dew	Market	38	6	Oval	None	White	
PMR 45	Shipping	86	3-5	Oblong	Coarse	Salmon Orange	PM
Saticoy Hybrid**	Shipping, market	90	6½-5½	Oval	Fine	Orange	
Small Persian	Shipping	110	6	Round	Fine	Orange	
SR 91	Shipping	96	3½	Oval, round	Heavy	Salmon	SR FW,DM
Supermarket**	Local market	84	Medium	Oval	Coarse	Orange	
Top Mark	Shipping	90	4-6	Oval	Smooth	Salmon	

*FW—fusarium wilt; DM—downy mildew; PM—powder mildew; ALS—alternaria leaf spot; SR—sulfur res.
**Hybrid.

Securing Seed

Since the cost of seed is a small item in the production of muskmelons, it is important to obtain the very best quality available. Markets require melons of certain characteristics, and such fruit cannot be grown unless the seed planted came from melons having the desired qualities. Some commercial seed is produced in the areas of production, yet large quantities come from the central valley of California, where climatic conditions and production methods are especially favorable for seed production and the elimination of seed-born diseases. It is a good practice to secure seed only from a reliable distributor or producer.

PREPARING THE SOIL

Soil Preferences

Muskmelons are grown on a great variety of soil types, but they thrive best on a well-drained, sandy or silt loam soil. The soil should be fairly fertile, well supplied with organic matter, and free from nematodes and disease. A soil slightly acid or neutral is desirable. Sandy loams are often used for early plantings, but later crops are more productive on heavier soils.

Preparing the Seedbed

Seedbed preparation varies greatly in different regions. One essential everywhere, however, is thorough plowing, 5 to 9 inches deep, early enough in the spring to allow proper settling. It is very desirable to have the beds firm yet thoroughly broken.

In some sections, the beds are 5 to 8 feet wide with one row in a bed. In other areas, it is common practice to flat break the land and lay off narrow beds 18 to 24 inches wide and 5 to 7 feet apart. This elevates the plants for adequate drainage, and the interlying area can be worked toward the bed as the young plants develop. Where furrow irrigation is practiced, raised beds are essential. They are also used where heavy rains are expected and where drainage is inadequate.

FERTILIZING, MANURING, AND LIMING

Muskmelon plants grow rapidly and require an abundance of plant nutrients. Unless the soil is naturally fertile, commercial fertilizers or manure or both must be added for satisfactory production.

Fertilizing

Commercial fertilizers are almost indispensable in large producing areas because of the limited amount of animal manure. The amount, kind, time, and method of application vary considerably from region to region.

In several southern states, a complete fertilizer of a 1-1-1 ratio, analyzing approximately 10-10-10, is commonly applied a few days before planting. It is generally applied in a wide strip under the row, at the rate of about 500 pounds per acre, rather than broadcast. In addition, when blooming starts, many commercial growers apply a side dressing of approximately 100 pounds of quick-acting, nitrogen-carrying fertilizer a foot from the plants. Tables 6.4 and 6.5 can be used as guides for rates of applying N, P, and K.

Manuring

Green manures produced by turning under cover crops have been found to increase materially the yields of subsequent muskmelon crops. Legume covers are preferable for the purpose, as nitrogen is added in addition to organic matter. Where winter crops are used, they should be turned under early enough to decay thoroughly before planting time.

For best results, the organic content should be maintained by either barnyard manure or soil-improving crops.

Liming

Muskmelons do not thrive on the medium or strongly acid soils. Investigations in Rhode Island and Virginia place the muskmelon with that group of vegetables which prefer soils ranging from slightly acid to neutral (pH 6 to pH 7). Tests in Arkansas, North Carolina, and other states have confirmed this classification. On very acid soils the plants make poor growth and the foliage becomes yellowish-green in color.

Soil acidity is generally corrected by applying some form of lime to the soil, calcium carbonate (ground limestone) being the most practical form to use. Hydrated lime acts more quickly, but the cost is greater. The amounts of lime to apply on different types of soils are indicated in Table 6.2.

PLANTING

Starting Plants

Seeds of the muskmelon do not germinate well at low temperatures, and the seedlings are very susceptible to freezing injury. Planting in the open should, therefore, be delayed until the soil becomes warm and there is no danger of frost. If early maturity is desired, plants may be started in greenhouses, hotbeds, or sash covered frames and shifted to the field when weather conditions become favorable. This method is suitable for comparatively small acreages and may be necessary in regions where the frost-free season is too short for maturing the crop in the field. Melons are difficult to transplant except when young. When started inside, they should be seeded in plant-growing containers so the plants can be shifted to the field without disturbing their roots. Seeding is usually done about 10 to 20 days before the plants are to be moved to the field.

Seeding in the Field

Seed is most commonly drilled in rows 5, 6, or 7 feet apart. Later the plants are thinned so as to stand 2½ to 4 feet apart in the row. With this method an economical use of labor and a good distribution of plants may be obtained. Seed may be planted in hills 4 to 6 feet apart and check-rowed so the field can be cultivated in both directions early in the season. Eight or 10 seeds are planted by hand in each hill and covered from ½ to 1 inch deep. About 2 pounds of seed is required to plant an acre by drill or hill seeding.

Frost protectors are used in a limited way for starting muskmelons. The benefits resulting from desirable covers include (1) protection from unfavorable weather and pests, (2) higher germination and earlier emergence, (3) larger percentage of earlier melons, and (4) increase in total yield. The chief disadvantages of using protectors are (1) cost; (2) difficulty of properly applying, ventilating, and removing them; and (3) inability to forecast the weather, which determines their value.

CULTIVATING, THINNING, AND IRRIGATING

Cultivating

Cultivation of muskmelons should begin as soon as the young plants break ground. The muskmelon is a shallow-rooted plant, the roots often extending beyond the vines. Frequent shallow cultivations should be made until the vines interfere. In many sections where the muskmelons are drilled on narrow ridges, soil is worked toward the ridges at subsequent cultivations until the middle is finally broken out, thus leaving a wide, gently sloping bed. Where the hills are carefully checked, cultivation can be given in both directions by means of a weeder or any light cultivator. For the greater part, however, muskmelons are cultivated in one direction. Vine turning may be necessary during later cultivations. Cultivation after the vines cover a considerable portion of the ground is probably of little, if any, value, unless weed growth is heavy.

Weeding is one of the most essential and costly operations in the production of good quality muskmelons. The cost of controlling annual weeds may be reduced by the use of herbicides. A granular application of 3 to 6 pounds of Vegiben made immediately after seeding or transplanting, or another recommended herbicide may be used. Sandy soils require a lower rate than loams. The herbicide is most effective when moisture levels and temperatures promote rapid germination of weed seed.

Thinning

Two or more thinnings are necessary to reduce safely the final stand to the desired number of plants. To begin with, there are considerably more plants than needed. The first crowded plants are removed a few days after emergence, when the first true leaves develop. If the seed has been planted in hills, each hill is usually thinned to four or five well distributed plants the first time. Where striped cucumber beetles or other injurious insects are troublesome, the final thinning is delayed until the plants are well established and have formed three or four true leaves. The number of thinnings required to obtain a desirable final stand varies from year to year, depending on the original stand, presence of pests, weather conditions, and local practices. Where the hill method is practiced, two plants are usually left in each hill. When the seed is drilled, single plants are left at intervals varying from 1 to 2 feet, depending on the distance between rows, fertility, and other factors.

Irrigating

Muskmelon plants require an abundance of moisture during the period when the vines are developing most rapidly, and up to the time the melons are practically grown. Great care should be taken, however, to avoid overwatering just before and during the ripening period.

Where furrow irrigation is practiced, the melons are grown on beds and quick applications of water are applied in the furrows as needed. Careful study of soil conditions and weather prospects is necessary to irrigate successfully. This subject is discussed more fully in Chapter 10. Care

should be taken not to wet the foliage as this would increase susceptibility to leaf spot diseases.

Training and Removing

In most sections, vines are trained parallel with the rows to permit
closer cultivation. In addition, growers claim that increased shade protects the melons from extreme sunshine and heat.

Removing part of the melons from the vines will increase the size of
the remaining fruit. This practice is not commonly followed, however,
as melons will grow large enough without reducing their numbers.

CONTROLLING DISEASES AND INSECTS

Diseases

Both the plant and the fruit of the muskmelon are susceptible to
diseases, many of which can be prevented by planting on clean land, or
reduced by seed treatment, spraying, and dusting.

BACTERIAL WILT. Caused by *Erwinia tracheiphila,* bacterial wilt is
widely distributed, attacking muskmelons, cucumbers, squash, and pumpkins. The bacterial growth occupies some of the water vessels at the roots,
stems, and leaves and causes the plants to wilt and die. The bacteria
causing this disease do not live in the soil but are carried over by the
striped cucumber beetle, which spreads the disease from plant to plant.
The best control measure for wilt is to treat for the cucumber beetles (see
Chapter 11) as soon as the plants appear above the soil. On a small planting prompt removal and destruction of diseased plants are recommended
as an aid in controlling the disease.

FUSARIUM WILT. Fusarium wilt, caused by *Fusarium Oxysporium* f.
Niveum, turns vines yellow, resulting in wilt near fruiting time. A cross
section of the stem shows the usual dark ring, characteristic of Fusarium.
Control is accomplished with a three- to five-year rotation and planting of
resistant cultivars.

ANTHRACNOSE. Commonly called blight, anthracnose is caused by
Colletotrichum lagenarium and may appear in epidemic form. The disease is more common on watermelons and cucumbers than on musk-

melons. All parts of the plant above ground may be affected. Small yellowish or water-soaked areas develop on the leaves and fruit. The lesions on the fruit become dark, round, and sunken. This fungus is transmitted through the soil and by diseased plants and seed. It may be avoided or decreased by crop rotation, sanitation, and by planting treated seed. Field control can be achieved by spraying or dusting with ziram, maneb, or captan every seven days *after* runners have begun to form.

DOWNY MILDEW. Downy mildew, caused by *Pseudoperonospora cubensis,* attacks only the leaves during warm, damp weather. Thorough spraying with ziram or zineb at weekly or 10-day intervals is recommended.

ROOT KNOT (NEMATODES). Root knot, caused by the nematode *Meloidogyne* sp., attacks the roots. The galls produced on the roots by the eelworms check plant growth and prevent proper fruit maturity. Considerable damage is done by root knot on sandy soils, and the most practical control measure under field conditions consists of rotating with resistant plants. Nearly all cultivated grasses and cereals, such as corn, oats, wheat, rye, barley, and sorghum, are resistant, and if they are grown for approximately two seasons in heavily infested soil, the numbers of the parasite will be greatly reduced. Laredo soybeans, Brabham, Victor, and Monetta cowpeas, velvet beans, and peanuts also are resistant. When rotation is impractical, soil fumigants can be incorporated in the soil before planting with excellent results. However, soil fumigation is still quite costly.

Insects

Growers should be prepared to combat insects which attack all parts of the muskmelon at different stages of growth.

STRIPED AND SPOTTED CUCUMBER BEETLES. The striped and spotted cucumber beetles are very serious pests in many sections, destroying the young plants as soon as they come up. Methods for controlling these beetles are given in Chapter 11.

MELON APHID. The melon aphid *(Aphis gossypii)* or louse is a small, green, soft-bodied insect, which obtains its food by sucking plant juices. It can be controlled with malathion or diazinon.

It feeds on the underside of the leaf, causing it to curl, change color, and die. Muskmelon plants should be examined frequently so that an infestation of aphids can be detected early. If insecticides are applied promptly, they will be more effective and less damage will be done by the insect than if applications are delayed. Recommended control measures are given in Chapter 11.

PICKLE WORMS. Pickle worms (*Diaphania nitidalis*) frequently cause much damage in Georgia, the Carolinas, and other southern states. The adult is a large moth which emerges in the spring. It lays its eggs on the plant, and the young larvae bore into the fruit during the ripening season. Early planting and the use of bush squash, planted as a trap crop, are preventive measures. In areas of serious damage, weekly applications of carbaryl are recommended.

HARVESTING, PACKING, AND MARKETING

Good production practices alone do not insure financial success. Much depends on the care and judgment exercised in harvesting, handling, and marketing the cantaloupe crop (Fig. 22.2).

Fig. 22.2—Muskmelons packed for market.

Harvesting

The length of time required to reach market, the cultivar, temperature at harvest time, and the method of shipment determine the stage of maturity at which melons must be harvested. Since edible quality depends on texture, flavor, and sweetness, the stage of maturity is a very important factor. The muskmelon does not increase in sugar after harvest but may improve in flavor and texture.

Proper maturity is difficult to ascertain, as color of skin, stem abscission, netting, and other familiar indications of maturity are not infallible in determining the degree of ripeness. A common guide used in determining the time of picking melons is the ease by which they can be removed from the vines. As a rule, the "full-slip" melon is one which has reached advanced maturity and can be easily removed. The stem separates from the melon, leaving a clean stem cavity. Melons pulled at this stage must be carefully handled and promptly shipped, either under refrigeration or to nearby markets. The "half-slip" melon is one which is less mature, requiring more pressure to detach. Upon removal, about one-half of the stem next to the melon remains attached. Most muskmelons which are shipped to distant markets are firm-fleshed cultivars harvested at the "full-slip" stage. They should be ready for eating in 36 to 48 hours after reaching market, depending, of course, on shipping and weather conditions. Both the "full-slip" and "half-slip" melons are fully netted; and the background color has changed from a cucumber green to a mottled green and light yellow. In all cases, it is desirable for the melons to remain on the vines until they have reached the greatest degree of maturity which is consistent with the method of handling. Markets have made frequent complaints that many melons are picked too immature for best quality, thereby reducing the price and sale of the product.

Western growers now commonly ship the "cantaloupe" cultivars harvested at the early "full-slip" stage to eastern markets. These are quickly precooled and shipped under refrigeration.

The stem does not separate from the fruit of Honey Dew, Honey Ball, Crenshaw, Casaba, and Persian cultivars at maturity. Maturity in these is determined by yellowing of the skin and a slight yielding of the blossom end when slightly pressed.

Grading

Melons are graded for uniformity in size and maturity. Although standard grades have been devised by the U.S. Department of Agriculture, specifications have been altered from time to time. Supply and price determine shipping grades to a large extent. Cracked, bruised, diseased, misshaped, soft, ripe, immature, and slick melons are discarded as culls. It usually pays to ship only the best quality melons of uniform size and maturity.

Packing

Although types of containers and methods of packing vary considerably, practices have been fairly well standardized in most commercial sections of the West. Crates are primarily used for shipping long distances. The 12- by 12- by 22⅛-inch standard crate is popular, but conditions frequently require the jumbo crate (13 by 13 by 23⅛ inches) or the pony crate (11 by 11 by 22⅛ inches). In addition, two sizes of flat crates are rather extensively used—the standard flat (4½ by 13½ by 22⅛ inches) and the jumbo flat (5 by 14½ by 22⅛ inches). Two sizes of flat crates are used for Honey Dew melons: 6¾ by 16 by 22⅛ inches, and 7¾ by 16 by 22⅛ inches.

The large markets recognize a pack consisting of 45 melons to a standard-sized crate. In this pack, the melons are 4 to 4½ inches in diameter. The 45-pack consists of three layers, each containing three rows of five melons each. The melons are placed end to end and completely fill the crate. Slightly larger melons are packed 36 to the standard crate, each of the three layers consisting of three rows of four melons each. This size constitutes the bulk of the commercial crop in many sections. Melons exceeding 5 inches in diameter are usually packed 27 to a standard crate or 36 to a jumbo crate.

A large variety of crates are used in the East. A crate similar to the 32-quart berry crate is used to some extent in Virginia and other sections (Fig. 22.3). Hampers and baskets are used considerably for local markets and short hauls. In recent years, especially during periods of low prices, many muskmelons have been sold directly to truckers. The melons are loaded on the trucks in bulk or in various kinds of containers, both in the field and at packing sheds.

Marketing

Muskmelons and other melons are an important part of the American diet. The western melons are of good uniform quality and have contributed much to more orderly marketing (of cantaloupes). Consequently,

Fig. 22.3—Graded and sized muskmelons packed in crates for shipment.

USDA Photograph

melons of standard quality are generally available. Some melons are still marketed by hucksters, but most are handled through regular commercial channels.

EXPORTS AND IMPORTS. Imports of cantaloupes and other melons (excluding watermelons) were 181,256,000 pounds valued at $10,215,000 in 1972. This compared with 218,894,000 pounds worth $24,758,000 imported in 1977 (Table 13.2). Mexico was by far the largest supplier, with various Latin American countries supplying smaller quantities. Imports are at a peak during the four-month March through June period. Exports were 51,097,000 pounds valued at $4,694,000 in 1972 and 57,647,000 pounds worth $8,670,000 in 1977. Shipments went primarily to Canada (74 percent), with Hong Kong and Japan receiving smaller quantities. Although exports are made year-round, June, July, and August are the peak months.

SELECTED REFERENCES

Anonymous, "Muskmelons for the Garden," USDA Leaflet 509, 1968.

Barber, J. M., "Growing Cantaloupes," Univ. of Ga. Coop. Ext. Ser. Circ. 480, 1974.

Basham, C. W., "Cucumbers, Pumpkins, Squash, Muskmelons, Watermelons for the Home Garden," Colo. State Univ. Coop. Ext. Ser. 7.609, 1976.

Binning, L. K., Libby, J. L., and Wade, E. K., "Vine Crops—Pest Control," Univ. of Wisc. Coop. Ext. Pro. Pub. A2465, 1976.

Bohn, G. W., and Andrus, C. F., "Cantaloupe Breeding," USDA Tech. Bull. 1403, 1969.

Bouwkamp, J. C., Angell, F. F., and Schales, F. D., "Effects of Weather Conditions on Soluble Solids of Muskmelon," Scientia Horticulturae, 8:265-271, 1978.

Cook, W. P., et al., "Commercial Cantaloupe Production," Clemson Univ. Coop. Ext. Ser. Veg. Leaflet 11, 1978.

Davis, G. N., et al., "Fertilizer Experiments with Cantaloupes," Calif. Exp. Sta. Bull. C–536, 1965.

Davis, G. N., et al., "Muskmelon Production in California," Calif. Agr. Ext. Ser. Circ. 536, 1965.

Ferretti, P. A., and MacNab, A. A., "Growing Vine Crops," Pa. State Univ. Coop. Ext. Ser. Special Circ. 207, 1975.

Gilbert, D. A., and Dedolph, R. R., "Quality Evaluation of Muskmelon Fruits," Mich. Agr. Exp. Sta. Quart. Bull. 45: 589-594, 1963.

Halderman, A. D., "Cantaloupe Water Use," Univ. of Ariz. Coop. Ext. Ser. Q–195, 1973.

Halderman, A. D., et al., "Irrigation Schedule for Cantaloupe," Univ. of Ariz. Coop. Ext. Ser. Q–249.

Hoop, R. J., "Muskmelons in Vermont," Univ. of Vt. Exp. Sta. Bull. 653, 1968.

Lingle, J. C., and Wright, J. R., "Fertilizer Experiments with Cantaloupes," Calif. Agr. Exp. Sta. Bull. 807, 1964.

Longbrake, T., Cotner, S., and Larsen, J., "Keys to Profitable Production of Cantaloupes and Honeydew Melons," Tex. A & M Univ. Agr. Ext. Ser. L-903, 1977.

Loy, J. B., and Wells, O. S., "Response of Hybrid Muskmelons to Polyethylene Row Covers and Black Polyethylene Mulch," Scientia Horticulturae, 3:223-230, 1975.

Mansour, N. S., et al., "Growing Cantaloupes in Oregon," Ore. Agr. Ext. Ser. EC-622, 1971.

Neild, R. E., "Growing Muskmelon and Watermelon," Univ. of Neb. Agr. Exp. Sta. SB528, 1973.

Nicklow, C. W., et al., "Muskmelon and Watermelon," Mich. State Univ. Coop. Ext. Ser. Bull. E-675—L, 1970.

Pew, W. D., et al., "Growing Cantaloupes in Arizona," Univ. of Ariz. Coop. Ext. Ser. Bull. A86, 1976.

Seelig, R. A., "Cantaloupes," United Fresh Fruit and Veg. Assoc., Alexandria, Va., 1977.

Sullivan, G. H., and Shelley, V. W., "Costs and Returns for Melon Production in Southwestern Indiana," Purdue Univ. Agr. Exp. Sta. 909, 1974.

Thorp, R., and Mussen, Eric, "Cantaloupe, Cucumber, Watermelon Pollination," Univ. of Calif. Div. of Agr. Sci. Leaflet 2253, 1977.

CHAPTER 23

Onions

CLASSIFICATION, ORIGIN, AND HISTORY

The onion *(Allium cepa)* belongs to the *Liliaceae* or lily family. There are about 300 widely scattered species in the genus *Allium,* and many of them have the characteristic onion flavor and odor. The onion has been used by man as far back as history records. The cultivated species are probably native to the general area of southwestern Asia. Early settlers introduced the onion to North America.

SCOPE AND IMPORTANCE

The onion is used in many ways and represents a major vegetable in the American diet. Onions ranked tenth in acreage among the 22 principal vegetables in 1977, but attained fourth position in value.

Onion acreage declined gradually from 122,760 acres in 1949 to 113,530 acres in 1959, and down to an estimated 107,650 acres in 1977. Yields per acre rose from 160 hundredweight in 1949 to 226 hundredweight in 1959 and up to 319 hundredweight in 1977. Values declined from $57,600,000 in 1949 to $54,756,000 in 1959 and then rose sharply to $203,053,000 by 1977.

Onions are grown commercially in many states with California and Texas capturing about half of the market as shown in Table 23.1. The approximate distribution and a 28-year acreage, production, and value record of onions appears in Figure 23.1. Onions of various kinds are widely used in their fresh or prepared state (Fig. 23.2).

Fig. 23.1—Acreage, distribution, production, and value of onions.

UNITED STATES TOTAL

Year	Acreage	Production 1,000 Cwt.	Value, $1,000
1949	122,760	19,604	57,601
1959	113,530	25,609	54,756
1969	100,000	28,234	107,450
1977	107,650	34,305	203,053

TRENDS IN PRODUCTION EFFICIENCY

Onion production costs vary considerably, depending upon seed, fertilizers, irrigation, cultural practices, and extent of mechanization. The labor involved in producing and harvesting declined sharply over the years. In 1939, about 271 man-hours were required to grow and harvest an acre. This dropped to 139 man-hours by 1959 and decreased spectacularly to 86 man-hours by 1977. Acre yields rose sharply, making it possible to increase the man-hour output 742 percent between 1939 and 1977 (Table 1.6).

CLIMATIC REQUIREMENTS

The onion is a cool-season plant that will grow well over a wide

Fig. 23.2—Types of onions for many uses.

United Fresh Fruit and Vegetable Association Photograph

range of temperature. Onion seed will germinate best near 65° F., but will germinate satisfactorily between 45° to 85° F. The plant will grow best between 55° to 75° F. Best growth and quality are obtained if the temperature is cool during the early development and warm near ma-

Table 23.1—Onions for Fresh Market and Processing: Harvest Season and Estimated Acreage, Yield, Production, and Value in Leading States, 1977.

State	Harvest Season	Harvested Acreage	Yield per Acre, Cwt.	Production per 1,000 Cwt.	Price per Cwt.	Value, $1,000
California	Summer	24,500	345	8,453	$ 4.15	34,220
California	Spring	16,900	165	1,967	8.44	16,601
New York	Storage	13,300	305	4,057	7.81	25,367
Michigan	Storage	7,100	295	2,095	6.30	10,584
Texas	Summer	6,800	275	1,870	9.85	18,420
Colorado	Storage	6,800	300	2,040	5.53	8,793
Oregon—East	Storage	6,600	500	3,300	5.45	12,938
California	Storage	5,700	345	1,967	8.44	16,601
Idaho	Storage	5,300	455	2,412	5.45	9,461
New Mexico	Summer	3,200	325	1,040	7.70	8,008
Washington	Storage	2,700	410	1,107	5.94	4,075
Oregon—West	Storage	2,100	470	987	5.39	4,016
Arizona	Spring	1,400	440	616	7.54	4,644
Utah	Storage	1,400	335	469	4.63	1,783
Wisconsin	Storage	1,200	290	348	5.56	1,724
Minnesota	Storage	840	260	218	6.35	1,270
New Jersey	Summer	650	180	117	8.32	973
Washington	Summer	600	340	204	8.10	1,652
Ohio	Storage	560	385	216	6.12	1,151
United States		107,650	319	34,305	6.77	203,053
Total	Spring (22%)	24,000	224	5,372	10.90	58,618
Total	Summer (78%)*	83,650	346	28,933	5.87	144,435

*All storage onions included in the summer total.

turity. A dry atmosphere at harvest is desirable to obtain satisfactory curing of the bulbs. The onion is fairly resistant to frost injury, but not immune. The root system is shallow, and to thrive well, the onion must receive a fairly adequate water supply. The crop responds well to irrigation in many areas. The bulbing of the onion is affected by the length of day and not by the age of the plant. The length of day required for bulbing varies with cultivar and ranges from 12 hours for very early types to 15 hours for late types.

SELECTING CULTIVARS AND SEED

Rapid changes are being made in the cultivars of onions. The new F_1 hybrids are replacing many of the older standard cultivars throughout the country. Onion hybrids are being produced in all the major types; and the superior ones are more uniform and higher-yielding than the standard cultivars.

Two dry bulb groups of onions are generally recognized in the United States. One, the American or domestic, includes many cultivars; the other, referred to as the European or foreign, contains chiefly the Bermuda and Spanish types, all of which are grown more commonly in the South and in certain sections of the West and Southwest than in other regions. These two groups of onions are supplemented by the Egyptian, or top onions, and the multiplier, or potato onions, all of which are grown for green bunching. Onion cultivars and hybrids vary in color, shape, flavor, and keeping quality as well as in time of maturity.

In selecting a cultivar, consideration should be given to climate, market, and soil requirements, particularly to the first. Bermuda cultivars are naturally more adapted to the extreme South than to other sections because normally they will mature in a shorter day, before the hot weather sets in. All the American types, as well as the Spanish cultivars, will not mature in southwest Texas until late June, no matter how early the seed may have been sown the previous fall. Usually, only a small percentage of the crop will be marketable, since the atmospheric and soil temperatures during May and June are not conducive to normal growth.

Cultivars

Yellow cultivars of the American type make up about 75 percent of the bulb crop grown in the country. The most important cultivars of this type are Early Yellow Globe, Australian Brown, Empire, Fiesta, and Downing Yellow Globe. The most popular cultivar grown from sets in this class is Ebenezer. White sets are usually White Ebenezer, and red sets are usually Red Wethersfield. White Portugal is grown from sets to produce green onions and is also good for pickling. Southport White Globe is a popular storage and processing onion. In addition to Red Wethersfield, Southport Red Globe is also a well known red cultivar. Early Harvest and Empire are outstanding hybrids of the yellow globe class. Early Harvest is primarily for first-early harvest and direct shipping in main crop areas, where it matures from direct seeding at about the same time as standard cultivars grown from sets. It is not intended for storage. Empire is about five days later. Fiesta, which is about five days later than Empire, is a very heavy-yielding hybrid of the sweet Spanish type with good storage qualities.

The sweet Spanish types require a long day length to bulb, as do the American types. They are grown in Texas, California, and other areas of the West and Southwest. A number of strains and hybrids of the sweet Spanish type are available. Yellow Granex and white Granex are hybrids of the Bermuda type grown in the deep South. F_1M Hybrid is similar and grown primarily in California. (See Table 23.2 for characteristics of leading cultivars.)

Leading cultivars of green onions are Japanese Bunching and Evergreen. These are popular because they are hardy and overwinter in some areas. These types will not form bulbs. Any standard cultivar can be used as "green bunching" onions if harvested at the proper stage. White cultivars are most generally used.

Securing Seed

Over 90 percent of the onion seed used in the United States is produced in this country. Seed production is concentrated in the dry areas of the West. The leading states are Idaho, California, Oregon, and Colorado. The Canary Islands are heavy producers of Bermuda onion seed.

Regardless of the cultivar being grown, it pays to buy clean seed that has high germination and is true to type. Good seed is rarely cheap, but the product of good seed will usually repay the extra cost many times over.

PREPARING THE SOIL

Soil Preferences

Good onion land should be friable, fertile, well supplied with humus, and well drained. A heavy soil which will bake after rains or after irrigation is not desirable. Clay, alluvial, and sandy loams, as well as mucks, are often used for onions. Of the four types the last two are preferable, although they usually need more fertilizer. Muck soils are considered best for bulb onion production in the North.

Preparing the Land

The soil should be plowed to a depth of 6 to 8 inches, harrowed, and left in good tilth. The surface should be well worked and smooth; rough, lumpy ground is not suited to the planting of onion seeds, small plants or dry sets. In irrigated sections, the land must also be leveled in order to irrigate properly. Muck soils are easily prepared as they have very good texture. They should be disced and harrowed or dragged smooth before planting.

FERTILIZING, LIMING, AND MANURING

Fertilizing

The onion, with its limited root system, responds to good fertilizer practices on almost any soil. Most nutrients are applied in the form of commercial fertilizer. In most areas, on mineral soils receiving no manure, 75 pounds each of nitrogen and potassium and 70 pounds of phosphorus should be sufficient. No potassium is used in western areas and Texas under irrigation. From 40 to 60 pounds of N and P are used and supplemented with additional nitrogen as a side dress. California growers use from 60 to 100 pounds of nitrogen per acre on early and intermediate crops but cut down to about 40 pounds on late crops. Phosphorus is also needed in California at the rate of about 25 pounds per acre.

Fertilizer requirements for muck soils vary considerably. Potassium is usually the most limiting element, but good increases in yield can usually be had by applying only phosphorus. Even nitrogen under certain conditions will give a good response. This is especially true on poorly drained and strongly acid mucks. On old mucks in New York, the usual application is 1,000 pounds of a 5-5-12 fertilizer per acre. Michigan generally uses less nitrogen and more potassium at the usual rate of 1,000 pounds of 0-5-16. A deficiency of copper and manganese sometimes causes trouble with onions in certain muck areas. Copper deficiencies in New York have been corrected by making applications of 200 to 300 pounds of powdered copper sulfate per acre. As the treatment usually lasts several years, it may be reapplied only when needed. The application of 150 pounds per acre of manganese sulfate mixed with the fertilizer will be effective for the control of manganese deficiency in most areas.

Liming

The onion thrives best on slightly acid soils (pH 6.0 to pH 6.5), but it grows poorly on very acid soils. Very acid soils need a ton of hydrated lime or 1½ tons of finely ground limestone per acre per year until the acidity of the topsoil is sufficiently reduced. One-half ton of lime should

Table 23.2—Brief Description of Selected Cultivars of Onions

Cultivar	Season (Days)	Shape	Size	Color	Flesh	Remarks
Aristocrat*	110	Globe	Medium large	Yellow	Firm	Storage
Downing Yellow Globe	105	Globe	Medium	Deep amber	Firm	Storage, South
Early Harvest*	95	Globe	Medium	Yellow	Mild	Poor storage
Early Yellow Globe	100	Globe	Medium	Yellow	Medium soft	Early
Ebenezer (yellow)	105	Thick flat	Small	Yellow	Very firm	Sets
Ebenezer (white)	105	Thick flat	Small	White	Firm, mild	Sets, bunching
El Capitan*	110	Globe	Large	Yellow	Mild	High Yield
Epoch*	110	Globe	Medium	Dark yellow	Firm	Storage
Empire*	105	Tall globe	Medium	Yellow	Firm, pungent	Long day, storage
Evergreen	70	Nonbulbing	Long stem	White	Tender	Green, bunching
Fiesta*	110	Deep globe	Large	Yellow brown	Firm, pungent	Sweet Spanish type
Granex (Yellow)*	165	Flat	Large	Yellow	Mild	Deep South
Granex (White)*	175	Flat	Large	White	Mild	Deep South
Japanese Bunching		Nonbulbing	Long stem	White		Bunching, hardy
Ruby	105	Deep globe	Medium large	Red	Firm	Storage
Southport Red Globe	110	Tall globe	Medium	Red	Firm	Storage
Spartan Banner*	99	Globe	Medium	Yellow	Firm	Storage
Spartan Sleeper*	105	Globe	Medium	Brown	Firm	Storage
Sweet Spanish hybrids*	100-130	Globe	Large	White-brown	Mild	General purpose
Sweet Spanish strains	100-130	Globe	Medium large	White-brown	Mild	General purpose
White Portugal	100	Flat	Medium	White	Firm	Storage, sets

*Hybrid

suffice on moderately acid soils. After the soil has reached the desired state, only occasional liming is necessary. Few, if any, of the soils used for onions in Texas or the dry areas of the West require lime.

Manuring

Organic matter in the form of either barnyard or green manure should be added to the mineral soils at every opportunity, as it conserves soil moisture, improves the physical condition of the soil, and tends to retard the loss of available nutrients. If barnyard manures are available, they should be applied at the rate of 15 to 20 tons per acre. Even when well rotted, they should be added several weeks before planting. In Texas, growers are resorting more than formerly to green manures, such as cowpeas. Summer legumes alternate well with winter-grown onions and other vegetables. They shade the ground, reduce weed growth, and add an abundance of organic matter to the soil.

Manures are not needed on muck soils since they already have a high organic-matter content.

PLANTING

The most distinct methods of planting onions include (1) sowing seed directly in the field where the crop is to mature, (2) sowing in a seedbed from which the plants will be transplanted later to the field, and (3) planting sets. A grower may buy these sets, or grow them from seed himself. Most of the bulb onion crop, especially that for late market and storage, is direct-seeded. The transplanting method is used more commonly for early and intermediate cultivars, especially in the Texas and California areas.

Seeding

Seed is generally sown with drills for the commercial crop. On large acreages gangs of four or more planters are used. The rate of seeding depends upon the purpose for which planting is done, and the distance between the rows. Where the bulb crop is to mature, 4 to 6 pounds of seed per acre is a common rate for rows 12 to 18 inches apart. However, the rate may vary from 1 to 10 pounds; as in some sections very wide spacing is used, and in others, growers prefer to obtain a thick stand, so that there will be surplus plants to sell at thinning time. For the production of plants in southwest Texas, rates range from 20 to 30 pounds per acre, although experiments indicate 18 to 20 pounds as preferable. To produce dry sets, 60 to 80 or even 100 pounds of seed per acre are planted, depending on the soil fertility. The extremely crowded conditions cause the onions to mature when very small. Desirable sets are $\frac{1}{2}$ to $\frac{3}{4}$ inch in diameter.

Setting Plants

Only strong, healthy plants should be set. Medium or pencil-sized plants are the most dependable ones to use. The yield of small plants is undesirable, and when large plants are used there is more danger of splits, doubles, and seedstems in the mature crop, unless the plants are handled very carefully.

The practice of pruning the tops back to about half their length is not to be recommended, as experiments in Louisiana, California, and Texas have indicated that this reduces yields and delays maturity to a certain extent. However, the unpruned plants are more difficult to handle. Plants are usually spaced 2 to 3 inches apart in the row, with the rows 14 to 16 inches apart.

The recent trend is away from transplanting toward direct seeding, as the labor requirement for transplanting is nearly 20 times that of direct seeding.

Planting Dry Sets

The operation of planting sets is very similar to that of planting seedlings. The chief difference is that the sets are dropped into a shallow furrow about 3 inches apart in the row, and then covered, permitting only the tips to show. Machines are available for this job, but the sets should be graded as to size to make efficient use of the machine. The quantity of sets needed for an acre varies with the size of the sets and the planting distances. The amount usually ranges between 15 and 30 bushels per acre.

Planting Time and Method

The time of planting will vary with the locality, type of onion, and method of propagation in use. In general, in the North, seed planted in place is sown as early as possible after the danger of severe frosts is over. Sets for dry bulbs and green onions are also planted as early as the soil can be prepared. In the far South onions are grown in the winter so seed, sets, or seedlings are planted in the fall or winter. The time will vary with local conditions. Seed for producing transplants is usually sown from 6 to 10 weeks before the time of transplanting.

Close spacing of the rows, 12 to 18 inches, is common in most irrigated sections, as well as in sections where rainfall is abundant. In some nonirrigated sections of Texas, onions are planted in rows 3 feet apart; these are frequently interplanted with cotton shortly before harvest.

CULTIVATING AND IRRIGATING

Cultivating

Because of their slow growth, small stature, shallow roots, and lack of dense foliage, onions more than most vegetables cannot withstand the ill effects of weeds. In practically all sections, the onion crop is cultivated every week or two after the seedlings emerge or plants are set out. This operation is continued until several weeks before harvest. It not only helps to control weeds but also loosens the soil after irrigations and rains. All cultivations except the very first ones should be very shallow, as many of the onion roots are close to the soil surface. Cultivating too deeply or too closely to the plants after the crop is well advanced may do more harm than good.

In narrow-row seedbeds, wheel hoes and small garden tractors are commonly used for cultivation and weeding.

Thinning and Controlling Weeds

Thinning is practiced only when the seed has been sown in the location where the crop is to mature. This is expensive and is not resorted to if it can be avoided. It is usually cheaper to control the stand as much as possible by a lower rate of seeding. In certain sections of south Texas, however, the practice of thinning often pays for itself because of the market farther north for plants that are removed.

Onions frequently require at least one good hand weeding. Sometimes this can be combined with the thinning operation, but more often it is an entirely separate job.

Expensive hand weeding in large plantings of onions has been virtually eliminated through the advent of chemical weed control (Fig. 23.3). A number of herbicides can be used to control weeds in onions at different stages of development. These chemicals are listed in Table 9.2.

Irrigating

In irrigated sections, where the success of the crop depends on proper irrigation methods, the time to apply water is important. Soil, both surface and subsoil, current weather conditions, and age of the crop need to be considered in deciding when to irrigate and how much water to apply. A seedbed is usually irrigated immediately after planting, and then just as frequently as is necessary to maintain a moist condition until emergence occurs. Normally one to three irrigations are necessary after the seedlings have emerged to insure steady growth. Sufficient water should be applied to moisten the soil thoroughly. Irrigation of onions in Texas is either by the furrow or by the flooding system.

The seedlings should be irrigated as soon as possible after transplanting. Between this irrigation and harvest time, irrigated onions in south

Fig. 23.3—Good weed control is essential for high yields of onions.

Ohio Exp. Sta. Photograph

Texas usually receive five to seven additional applications of water. At first, irrigations may be spaced as much as four to six weeks apart. For two to three weeks before harvest, when the onions are bulbing, irrigations may be as often as every week or 10 days, in order to prevent the soil baking around the bulbs, which causes them to be misshapen. Experiments in Texas have shown that overirrigation of onions should be avoided, since it may seriously reduce yields. When plants have started to mature, irrigation should cease and the soil allowed to dry out as much as possible.

CONTROLLING DISEASES AND INSECTS

General recommendations for disease and insect control can be found in Chapter 11. Current recommendations should be obtained from the area agricultural experiment station and extension service.

Diseases

The onion is subject to a number of diseases, the most important of which are discussed here.

PINK ROOT. Pink root is caused by the soil-borne fungi, *Pyrenochaeta terrestis* and *Fusarium sp.*, that may infect onion plants of any age. Since the disease, especially in the early stages, is confined to the roots and bulb plate, it may go unnoticed for some time. Roots turn pinkish in color, then shrivel and die; yields are thereby considerably reduced. Every pre- caution should be taken to use disease-free land for the seedbed and the transplanted seedlings or to purchase plants free from the disease. If disease-free seedlings are grown on disease-free land, there is no danger of pink root. In addition to this precaution, it is well to combine rotation and proper fertilization and cultural practices in order to produce fairly rapid and steady growth. Cultivars and hybrids are being produced with resistance to pink root.

NECK ROT. Neck rot *(Botrytis sp.)* is a rather serious disease in all sections. Infection occurs at the neck or in the wounds on the bulbs during or following harvest. The disease can be recognized by the grayish mold on the surface of the infected area. Losses may occur in the field, and bulbs often decay while in storage or in transit. Stands in certain sections of Virginia were reduced as much as 80 percent on one occasion. Control measures for neck rot include proper curing and storing. Bulbs that are well dried, especially at the neck, are less likely to succumb to the disease than those that are not well cured. They should be dried at 90° to 120° F. for two to three days and then stored at 32° F. Temperatures in storage should be kept as near 32° F. as possible, and there should be adequate ventilation to maintain a dry atmosphere. The disease can be reduced in the field by planting only healthy sets.

ONION SMUT. Onion smut *(Urocytis cepulae)* is usually the most de- structive disease on northern-grown onions. High soil temperatures are unfavorable for its growth, hence it is not generally a problem in the

South on onions grown in warm weather. The disease is caused by a soil-borne fungus. Infection occurs only in seedlings before the first leaf has made full growth. Onion sets, being largely resistant, are used in some areas where smut is severe. Pelleting seed with a fungicide such as thiram and a methocel sticker is the most effective method of control. The Beltsville Bunching and Nebuka type bunching onions have good resistance to smut.

DOWNY MILDEW. Downy mildew *(Peronospora destructor)* is a common disease of onions and is especially destructive in onion seed crops. The disease is favored by cool, wet weather. Resistance to the disease is found in the Calred cultivar. Six to 10 applications of a zineb fungicide spray at approximately weekly intervals is recommended for control.

Other diseases of limited importance are black mold, leaf mold, smudge, yellow dwarf, and white rot.

Insects

Onion thrips and onion maggots are the only important widespread onion insect pests.

ONION THRIPS. Onion thrips are similar to other thrips such as the bean thrips and can be controlled by two or three applications of malathion or diazinon spray or dust. Rotenone can be used on dry onions only.

ONION MAGGOTS. The onion maggot is a larva of a small fly that lays its eggs near the base of the plant. The small maggots kill the plant by burrowing into the stem and bulb. Control is best obtained by spraying with malathion or diazinon.

Other insects that cause damage in certain areas are wireworms and leaf miners.

HARVESTING, HANDLING, AND MARKETING

Harvesting

Onions may be harvested either as green-bunch onions or as mature bulbs. An onion is suitable for green bunching from the time it has reached pencil size until it begins to bulb. Such immature onions are commonly harvested in home and market gardens. In the large onion-growing sections, the crop is harvested almost entirely at the mature stage. Harvesting may begin when the tops start to fall over (Fig. 23.4). The exact time of harvest varies with environmental conditions. In the West and South it should begin during warm weather when approximately 25 percent of the tops are down. Under cooler weather conditions, harvesting is usually delayed until over 50 percent of the tops are down. In the East it does not usually begin until most of the tops are down.

Fig. 23.4—Matured onions harvested and placed in windrows for drying.

USDA Photograph

A small onion plow is frequently used to loosen the bulbs. In muck soils bulbs are easily pulled by hand without lifting. In irrigated sections water may be used to soften the ground a day or two before harvesting. The pulled onions are thrown into windrows with the bulbs being shaded by the tops to minimize sunscald. In many cases harvesting is now done by machines that lift and top the bulbs and then sack or place the cleaned bulbs in crates. Some onions are also handled in bulk.

A period of curing usually follows the pulling (Fig. 23.5). In the South and West, curing is usually accomplished in a few days, but in the North the curing period may take three or four weeks depending upon climatic conditions. In Texas, onions are often pulled, clipped, and shipped the same day. Care should be taken to avoid sunscalding caused by curing too long in direct sunlight.

Tops are usually removed after they are well dried down. The tops may be cut by hand with shears, or by a topping machine. One-half to 1 inch of the top is usually left on the bulb to prevent entrance of disease organisms.

Fig. 23.5—Windrowed onions being cleaned, topped, and bagged.

Yields in all sections vary greatly depending on conditions, but in general range between 140 and 500 hundredweight per acre. The average yield in the United States is around 300 hundredweight per acre.

In the Chicago area onion sets that were planted in April are harvested in mid-July. Most sets are harvested when the tops are yellow and falling over unless a harvesting machine is used. The roots are cut with a blade attachment that runs beneath the row. The sets are then pulled by hand and the tops are removed by twisting them off. Preliminary screening is done in the field to remove soil. The sets are placed in shallow crates, which are stacked in the fields to permit curing. After six to eight weeks, when the tops are dry, they are nipped off, and the sets are placed in storage.

Grading and Packing

After the tops have been removed, the onions are cleaned and graded. Onion grades depend somewhat on the cultivar involved, Bermuda and domestic onions all being classified on slightly different bases. These grades change slightly from time to time, and it is well to obtain periodically the latest rulings direct from the U.S. Department of Agriculture or from local state marketing agencies.

In nearly all sections 50-pound open-mesh bags have practically replaced all other containers. Onions are also packed by some growers in smaller mesh bags of 3- to 10-pound sizes for direct use in the retail trade.

Storing

Cultivars vary considerably in their storage characteristics, Bermuda onions are notoriously poor keepers and are rarely stored for any length of time. The late maturing American or domestic types are generally much better adapted to storage. However, marked varietal differences do exist even within this group.

Unless the onions have been carefully handled and properly cured and are free from disease, storage is likely to lead to disappointment and loss instead of gain. Under any storage conditions handling, repacking, and shrinkage are unavoidable. Cold storage at slightly above 32° F. with a dry atmosphere and adequate ventilation is the only method which will normally give satisfaction. Even then bulbs must be cured properly and be free from disease. Actual freezing must be avoided.

The chemical maleic hydrazide has been found effective in the inhibition of sprouting. The most satisfactory treatment has been a spray application of two pounds of maleic hydrazide on the plants when 50 percent of the tops are down. Timing of the spray is very important, as an application too early may result in puffy bulbs while one that is too late will give little sprout inhibition.

Marketing

The problem of marketing onions is a very specialized one. In the West and South many growers dispose of their crop at or soon after harvest. Dealers, jobbers, shippers, supermarket buyers, and others are usually on hand at harvest time to buy onions for cash provided they meet the federal-state inspection satisfactorily. In the large onion-producing sections, federal or state agencies publish daily reports of the number of cars being sold, the range of prices, and the general conditions of the market. Such information is available on other major crops. Fresh market onions are distributed through broker-shippers, grower-shippers, and chain store buyers. In some areas, onions are commonly sold under marketing contracts between growers and shippers. In addition to delivery schedules, these contracts may involve arrangements in which the shipper finances all or part of a grower's production expenses.

Mention should be made of the important "storage onion crop" which accounts for about 70 percent of the total U.S. production. In addition to fresh market sales, a sizeable volume from the summer storage crop is processed. The California Extension Service indicated that approximately two-thirds of California's onion production is used for making dehydrated onion products. Onions are also used for canning and freezing.

EXPORTS AND IMPORTS. Considerable quantities of fresh onions are both exported and imported annually. In 1972, exports totaled 128,817,000 pounds valued at $7,837,000, while imports were 61,452,000 pounds valued at $5,309,000. These export figures were 189,195,000 pounds worth $20,589,000 in 1977, while imports amounted to 33,017,000 pounds valued at $2,685,000 (Table 13.2). U.S. exports are destined largely for Canada (63 percent), but Western Europe, Japan, Bermuda, the Caribbean, and Mexico also receive considerable quantities. Mexico supplies almost all of the total imports, with most entering the United States during the January-April period.

SELECTED REFERENCES

Ajakaiye, M. B., and Greig, J. K., "Response of 'Sweet Spanish' Onion to Soil-applied Zinc," Kan. State Univ., *J. Amer. Soc. Hort. Sci.* 101 (5): 592-596, 1976.

Duncan, A. A., "Onion Seed Production," Ore. Exp. Sta. FS–88, 1965.

Gomez, R. E., and Corgan, J. N., "Spring-Planted Onions in Southern New Mexico," N. Mex. State Univ. Coop. Ext. Ser. Guide 400 H-210, 1973.

Hopen, H. J., "Seeding Rates, Cultivars, and Planting Methods for Small Processing Onions," Univ. of Ill. Agr. Exp. Sta. Bull., 1974.

Kyle, J. H., "Fall Seeding of Onions on the High Plains of Texas," Tex. A & M Univ. PR-2540, 1968.

Lipton, W. J., and Harris, C. M., "Factors Influencing Translucent Scale of Stored Onion Bulbs," *Proc. Amer. Soc. Hort. Sci.* 87: 341-354, 1965.

Longbrake, T., *et al.*, "Keys to Profitable Onion Production in Texas," Tex. A & M Univ. Agr. Ext. Ser. MP–971, 1974.

Mansour, N. S., *et al.*, "Commercial Onion Production in Oregon," Ore. Exp. Sta. EC–817, 1970.

Marvel, M. E., and Montelaro, J., "Onion Production Guide," Fla. Ext. Ser. Circ. 176-A, 1965.

Montelaro, J., and Cannon, J. M., "Louisiana Onions," La. State Univ. Coop. Ext. Ser. Pub. 1194, 1975.

Neild, R. E., "Growing Onions from Sets or Slips," Univ. of Neb. Coop. Ext. Ser. G 74–97, 1974.

Nicklow, C. W., *et al.*, "Onions," Mich. State Univ. Coop. Ext. Ser. Bull. E–675–M, 1970.

Nour, M., "Onions in the Middle Rio Grande Valley—Varieties and Planting Dates," N. Mex. Agr. Exp. Sta. Res. Rep. 84, 1963.

O'Dell, C. R., "Onions," Va. Poly. Inst. Ext. Div. Pub. 376, 1970.

Rosberg, D. W., and Johnson, H. B., "Artificial Curing of Texas Onions," Tex. A & M Univ. MP–395, 1959.

Schoenemann, J. A., *et al.*, "Onions (Dry Bulb)," Univ. of Wisc. Coop. Ext. Pro. Pub. A2332, 1978.

Seelig, R. A., "Dry Onions," United Fresh Fruit and Vegetable Assoc., Alexandria,, Va., 1970.

Seelig, R. A., "Green Onions," United Fresh Fruit and Vegetable Assoc. Alexandria, Va., 1974.

Sullivan, G. H., "Onions: Production, Marketing and Economic Trends," Purdue Univ. Agr. Exp Sta. Res. Bull. 948, 1977.

Vaughan, E. K., *et al.*, "Effects of Field-Curing Practices, Artificial Drying, and Other Factors in the Control of Neck Rot in Stored Onions," Ore. Agr. Exp. Sta., Tech. Bull. 77, 1964.

Vest, G., and Peterson, C. E., "Spartan Sleeper—A New Hybrid Onion for Long Storage," Mich. State Univ. Agr. Exp. Sta. Res. Rep. 259, 1974.

Walker, J. C., and Larson, R. H., "Onion Diseases and Their Control," USDA *Agriculture Handbook 208*, 1961.

Williams, R. D., and Montelaro, J., "Onion," Univ. of Fla. Coop. Ext. Ser. Circ. 176D, 1977.

CHAPTER 24

Peas

CLASSIFICATION, ORIGIN, AND HISTORY

The garden pea (*Pisum sativum*) is a cool-season, hardy, annual, tendril-climbing plant, belonging to the *Leguminosae* family. It is grown primarily for edible green seeds, although one kind is grown in Europe for the edible pods, as are snap beans. In the South, peas are generally referred to as English peas. The pea originated in Europe and Asia, and the plant was commonly grown in the gardens of the ancient Romans and Greeks.

SCOPE AND IMPORTANCE

Once a popular vegetable, fresh green peas are produced commercially only in a few states and did not appear in 1977 U.S. crop reports. Processed green peas have largely replaced the fresh ones and enjoy a major position in the vegetable industry, ranking fourth in acreage and thirteenth in value among the 22 principal vegetables in 1977. Harvested acreage of processing peas dropped from about 400,000 acres in 1949 to 352,000 in 1977. Values, however, increased substantially from $30,672,000 to about $100,842,000 during the 1949 to 1977 period.

Wisconsin leads in acreage, production, and value, followed by Minnesota, Oregon, and Washington. About 37 percent of the total crop is frozen and 63 percent is canned.

Figure 24.1 shows the approximate acreage distribution and 1949 to 1977 performance of peas. Table 24.1 ranks processing peas by states, acreage, production, and value in 1977.

Green Peas Harvested for Sale

1 DOT - 500 ACRES

Department of Commerce
Social and Economic Statistics Administration
Bureau of the Census

Fig. 24.1—Acreage, distribution, production, and value of green peas.

UNITED STATES TOTAL

Year	Acreage	Production 1,000 Cwt.	Value, $1,000
1949	418,810	7,851	37,074
1959	354,080	9,737	44,368
1969	404,150	10,488	55,699
1977	352,180	9,832	100,842

Table 24.1—Green Peas for Processing: Estimated Acreage, Yield, Production, and Value in Leading States, 1977.

State	Harvested Acreage	Yield per Acre, in Tons	Production in Tons	Price per Ton	Value, $1,000
Wisconsin	107,500	1.36	146,200	$204	29,825
Washington	70,700	1.54	108,900	201	21,889
Minnesota	65,600	1.53	100,400	201	20,180
Oregon	27,700	.83	23,000	188	4,324
Delaware	8,700	1.37	11,950	231	2,760
Idaho	7,500	.77	5,750	236	1,357
California	7,100	1.63	11,600	179	2,076
Maryland	5,400	1.42	7,650	230	1,760
New York	5,200	1.38	7,200	248	1,786
Colorado	420	1.31	550	271	149
Other States	46,360	1.48	68,400	215	14,736
United States	352,180	1.40	491,600	205	100,842
Canning (63%)	220,830	1.35	297,200	208	61,812
Freezing (37%)	131,350	1.48	194,400	201	39,030

TRENDS IN PRODUCTION EFFICIENCY

Green peas for processing are comparatively inexpensive to produce. Seed, fertilizer, and labor are modest, and machines have greatly decreased production cost. Labor requirement for processing green peas is the lowest of any vegetable crop. In 1939 it required 25 man-hours to produce and harvest an acre of peas compared with 11 man-hours in 1959 and only 9 in 1977. With some increase in acre yields and spectacular gains in mechanization, man-hour output increased 486 percent between 1939 and 1977 (Table 1.6).

CLIMATIC REQUIREMENTS

The pea is a cool-season crop and thrives best when the weather is cool and when ample moisture is available. The young plants will tolerate considerable cold and light frosts, but the flowers and green pods are often injured by heavy frost. If the crop is planted late, maturity takes place when the temperatures are too high for optimum growth and yields. Therefore, it is important to plant late enough to avoid freezes, yet early enough to mature the crop before hot weather. Pea plants are very sensitive to drouth and grow best in regions of moderate rainfall or with irrigation.

SELECTING CULTIVARS AND SEED

Cultivars

Cultivars of garden peas may be divided into two types, smooth-seeded and wrinkled-seeded. The former are hardy but low in quality. Seeds of cultivars also vary in size, skin toughness, and color. The smaller-seeded cultivars have been preferred for canning because the small seeds were associated with sweetness and tenderness. A pea with a tough skin will hold its shape during processing. A dark green color and wrinkled type are essential for freezing. Cultivars range in size from small dwarf to tall climbing plants. The dwarf types tend to be earlier and produce pods over a shorter period of time. This is desirable when the plants are harvested at one time for processing, but would not be advantageous for the home gardener desiring a succession of harvests.

A brief description and the chief use of some of the leading cultivars

Fig. 24.2—The Little Marvel cultivar of peas approaching maturity.

of peas are given in Table 24.2. The list includes cultivars suitable for the home and market gardens, for canning, and for freezing. Although the time required for maturity varies primarily with temperature, relative values are given. For example, under the same weather conditions, Sparkle would require 60 days to edible maturity, while Giant Stride would require 75 days.

Securing Seed

Since it is impossible to definitely identify cultivars of peas by the seed alone, growers should procure their seed from reliable sources. The seed should be from the crop of the previous year. Most seed-producing areas are in the semi-arid West and on the Pacific Coast, where diseases are less of a problem than elsewhere. Experiences of growers indicate that it is essential to secure seed from such sections.

Table 24.2—Characteristics of Selected Cultivars of Peas.

Cultivar	Chief Use	Days to Maturity	Plant Height in Inches	Pod Color	Pea Size	Resistant to Wilt
Alderman	Garden, freezing	75	60	Dark green	Large	+
Dark Seeded Perfection	Garden, freezing	67	30	Dark green	Medium	+
Dark Skin Perfection	Processing	64	26	Dark green	Medium	+
Early Perfection	Canning	65	30	Med. green	Small	+
Freezer 69	Processing	62	36	Dark green	Medium	+
Freezonian	Freezing	63	35	Dark green	Small	+
Frosty	Market, freezing	64	26	Dark green	Medium	+
Giant Stride	Market	75	30	Dark green	Large	+
Greater Progress	Market	62	18	Dark green	Large	
Green Arrow	Market	68	26	Dark green	Small	+
Lincoln	Market, freezing	67	28	Dark green	Medium	+
Little Marvel	Home garden	64	18	Dark green	Medium	+
Perfected Freezer 60	Freezing, market	69	30	Med. green	Medium	+
Progress Strains	Home garden	60	20	Dark green	Large	
Sparkle	Garden	60	15	Dark green	Small	+
Wando	General purpose	66	26	Dark green	Small	+

PREPARING THE SEEDBED

Soil Preferences

Peas are grown on a variety of soils. The sandy loams with clay sub-soil are generally preferred for earliness. Ample drainage is essential, especially in sections where heavy rainfall occurs during the early part of the growing season. If well drained, some of the heavier soils, such as the clays and loams, produce higher yields than do the more porous, sandy soils, but maturity is later.

Regardless of the soil type, humus or organic matter is very essential in the satisfactory production of peas. Experiences indicate that soils which have previously been improved by applications of barnyard manure or by growing and turning under cover crops are best for grow-ing fine crops of peas. Studies at the Maryland Agricultural Experiment Station indicate that soil organic matter was the factor most positively correlated with plant growth, yield, and nodule formulation.

The garden pea, like most legumes, prefers a slightly acid soil, but will not tolerate excess soil acidity. The crop should be grown in a soil with a pH range of 5.5 to 6.5. While lime is very desirable for strongly acid soils, it should be remembered that liming will not solve other production problems, and that the use of excess quantities of lime would be very undesirable. On some soils that are limed too heavily, peas and other vegetable crops fail to grow and become chlorotic because of the lack of available manganese. Some of the southeastern sandy soils are deficient in magnesium, and, on such soils, a magnesium limestone should be used.

Preparing the Soil

Very close attention should be given to the matter of soil preparation, because poor growth and low yields often are traceable to the lack of thorough soil preparation. During the fall months, the soil should be thoroughly disced to cut up and incorporate any cover crop or other plant residues and hasten their decomposition. The land should later be plowed deeply; and just before preparing the beds for planting, further discing or harrowing should be done. Poor soil preparation results in uneven germination, and the peas do not mature uniformly. This is particularly disadvantageous for processing.

FERTILIZING

Peas are less responsive to fertility than are most of the other vegetable crops. Even so, in most sections some commercial fertilizer is essential. On some very rich, fertile virgin soils, only a maintenance application of fertilizer may be needed, while in some of the less fertile sections, growers use 400 to 500 pounds per acre of a high-grade fertilizer. Not over 200 pounds per acre should be applied by a grain drill at the time of planting. The fertilizer is usually applied to the side and slightly below the seed or thoroughly mixed with the soil before planting in order to prevent the fertilizer from seriously interfering with germination.

Certain coastal plains soils of the Atlantic seaboard are quite generally deficient in magnesium and manganese. Where these elements are deficient and the soil also needs liming, basic slag is an excellent material to use, because it contains these two minor elements in addition to calcium. It also contains iron oxide, which is helpful on some of the very light sandy soils of the area. A very cheap source of magnesium is dolomitic (or magnesium) limestone. Unless deficiencies in magnesium and manganese have been corrected with basic slag or magnesium limestone, a special fertilizer containing the necessary minor elements should be applied.

Inoculating

The garden pea, as other legumes, requires inoculation with specific legume bacteria. The nodule-forming bacterium is the same for garden peas, vetch, and Austrian peas. Where the soil has not been inoculated in previous years by growing one or more of these crops, the seed should be artificially inoculated. In some demonstrations, yields have been increased 50 to 100 percent by inoculation, while in others on soils containing the inoculum no increase in yields was obtained.

PLANTING AND CULTIVATING

All cultivars should be planted as early as the season will permit. Planting made later than the earliest practicable dates usually mature in less time but invariably produce lower yields, apparently on account of high temperatures.

Most of the peas for processing are planted with grain drills in rows 7 inches apart. From $3\frac{1}{2}$ to 5 bushels of seed are required per acre, depending upon the size of seed planted. For the home and most market gardens, peas are planted in rows. When they are planted in single rows, the distance between rows varies from 2 to 3 feet; when double rows are used the beds are about 4 feet apart, the two rows on each bed being 8 to 12 inches apart. About 2 bushels of seed are required per acre. The usual depth of planting is 1 to 2 inches depending upon earliness of season, the type of soil, and moisture content.

Plantings of peas have to be carefully scheduled to provide a processing plant steady work during the season, without jams or shut-downs. Since temperature is the most important factor affecting the time required for maturity of a cultivar, a "heat unit" system may be used. Heat units (H. U.) may be determined by subtracting a base temperature (40° F. for peas) from the daily average. With temperature records during the season, the H. U. accumulating during the development of a cultivar can be calculated. With this information, the expected time of maturity of a cultivar can be determined from mean temperatures. By allowing the number of H. U. per day during harvest to accumulate between the plantings of enough acreage for one day's operation, spacing of harvests may be achieved. Cultivars vary widely in their H. U. requirements, and a cultivar may vary from season to season and area to area. However, the difference between two cultivars remains rather constant.

Cultivating

Peas are cultivated only where the rows are far enough apart for cultivation. Since the pea develops rapidly, no great amount of cultivation is necessary. The cultivations should be shallow to avoid destroying too many of the fibrous roots and only frequent enough to destroy weeds. The plant is a poor weed competitor, so in commercial production, herbicides are often used for weed control (Chapter 9).

Staking

With few exceptions, no support is given the vines in the commercial pea sections. Cane or small stakes, set at intervals in the row and overlapping near the top, are generally used by home gardeners. Wire netting supported by stakes between double rows or to the side of single rows is sometimes employed. Inexpensive twine also is used, three to five parallel lines being fastened to laths or small stakes spaced 6 to 10 feet apart along the rows.

CONTROLLING DISEASES AND INSECTS

Diseases

The most important pea diseases found are: (1) root rot, (2) Fusarium wilt, (3) Aschochyta blight, (4) mosaic, (5) bacterial blight, (6) downy mildew, and (7) powdery mildew. From a practical standpoint, the only feasible control measures are: (1) use of disease-free seed, (2) seed treatment, (3) use of resistant cultivars, and (4) crop rotation. Bacterial blight and Aschochyta blight are seed-borne diseases; the wilts also are seed-borne to a slight extent. For the control of these seed-borne diseases, disease-free seed should be obtained from the semi-arid West and Pacific Coast states when available. The wilt organisms are reported to live almost indefinitely in the soil, and the only satisfactory control, therefore, is the use of resistant cultivars. There is no definite control for the root rots, but good soil drainage, crop rotation, and seed treatment with thiram is recommended.

Insects

The following insects attack peas: (1) pea aphid, (2) thrips, (3) spider mite, (4) seed corn maggot, and (5) pea weevil. The pea aphid (*Macro-siphum pisi*) is the worst pest in some sections. It can be controlled with malathion or nicotine sulphate (see Chapter 11). Treatments should be applied when the aphids are first observed and before serious damage is done. Except where the pea aphid is bad, insect control in peas has not generally been found economical.

The only control for nematodes is to practice a rotation and to avoid growing susceptible crops on the land.

Fig. 24.3—Harvesting peas for processing.

USDA Photograph

HARVESTING, HANDLING, AND MARKETING

Harvesting

Peas for processing are harvested with a mowing machine. The plants are usually hauled to a vining station where the peas are shelled by machinery. Some viners are self-propelled and harvest or pick up the plants from windrows in the field. Rapid handling is essential to prevent loss of quality after harvesting, especially during high temperatures. Yields of shelled peas increase with maturity, while quality decreases. Sieve size thus becomes an important factor determining price.

Green peas for the fresh market are harvested entirely by hand. Two or three pickings are usually necessary. The vines should be handled carefully if the yield and quality of the later pickings are not to be impaired. In some sections the peas are picked and placed directly into the container in which they are to be shipped, while in other sections field crates or picking containers are used. Common labor is employed to do the harvesting, but it is desirable to have a competent foreman or supervisor in charge.

Often too little attention is given to harvesting peas at the proper stage of growth for a product of highest quality. The pods should be picked when fully green and well developed, and before the peas start hardening. It has been shown that quality depends primarily upon tenderness and sugar content. As the peas increase in size during maturity the percent of sugar decreases while starch and proteins increase. The seed coats as well as the cotyledons become tougher. Maturity is measured by the sizes of peas in a sample and by tenderness determined with a tenderometer.

Packing and Loading

Since peas are very perishable and heat easily, a shallow or flat container is desirable. The container should be well filled, since a slack pack detracts materially from the package and is often the cause of poor sales. The field heat should be removed from fresh peas as soon as possible after harvest. This can be done by immersing them in cold water. After wetting, however, the pods must be kept refrigerated and shipped to market in a refrigerated car or truck. Salability can be maintained for about two weeks at 32° F. and a relative humidity of 90 to 95 percent.

Marketing

The method of marketing the small volume of green peas for fresh market depends upon the prevailing practice in the particular section. Where production is controlled by an organization, it is desirable to use central packing houses not only to standardize the product but also to aid in marketing. Because of the limited volume, the USDA Crop Reporting Board discontinued reports on green peas for fresh market in 1968.

The high percentage of green peas produced for canning and freezing are grown under contracts between growers and processors. Contract terms range widely but generally include price schedules, agreements on planting dates, charges for seed and pest control, cultural practices, and arrangements for harvesting and delivery schedules.

EXPORTS AND IMPORTS. The United States exported declining quantities of peas in recent years. However, imports of fresh and frozen peas totaled 9,251,000 pounds valued at $2,324,000 in 1972. Imports of canned peas totaled 16,471,000 pounds valued at $3,910,000. In 1977, about 7,631,000 pounds of canned peas valued at $2,007,000 were exported, and 10,164,000 pounds worth $3,668,000 were imported (Table 13.2). Most of the imports of green peas originate in Mexico, Canada, Taiwan, and the Dominican Republic.

SELECTED REFERENCES

Anonymous, "Development of Irrigation and Specialty Crops," Univ. of Minn. Agr. Exp. Sta. Misc. Rep. 145, 1977.

Anonymous, "Growing Peas for Processing," Asgrow Seed Co., New Haven, Conn., 1966.

Anonymous, "Pest and Disease Control Program for Beans and Peas," Colo. Agr. Exp. Ser. Pub., 1975.

Baker, A. S., Mortenson, W. P., and Dudley, R. F., "Fertilizer Placement for Processor Peas," Wash. State Univ. Agr. Exp. Sta. Bull. 721, 1970.

Doersch, R. E., and Harvey, R. G., "Peas—Weed Control," Univ. of Wisc. Coop. Ext. Pro. A2355, 1978.

Gritton, E. T., Oplinger, E. S., and Schulte, E. E., "Peas," Univ. of Wisc. Coop. Ext. Pro. A2346, 1978.

Gritton, E. T., et al., "Peas," Univ. of Wisc. Coop. Ext. Pro. A2346, 1978.

Meiners, J. P., and Kraft, J. M., "Beans and Pears Are Easy to Grow," USDA Agr. Inf. Bull. 409: 171-180, 1977.

Neild, R. E., and Whitney, W. C., "Growing Garden Peas," Univ. of Neb. Coop. Ext. Ser., EC 71–1220 (current).

Nicklow, C. W., et al., "Green Peas," Mich. State Univ. Coop. Ext. Ser. Bull. E–675–N, 1970.

Sandsted, R., Becker, R., and Ackerman, R., "Production of Processing Peas," N. Y. State Col. of Agr. Cornell Univ. Ext. Pub. Inf. Bull. 118, 1977.

Shehata, M. W., Davis, D. W., and Bissonnette, H. L., "A New Testing Approach for Breeding Peas Resistant to Common Root Rot Caused by *Aphanomyces euteiches* Drechs," *J. Amer. Soc. Hort. Sci.* 101 (3):257–261, 1976.

Wade, E. K., and Libby, J. L., "Peas—Insect and Disease Control," Univ. of Wisc. Coop. Ext. Pro. A2354, 1978.

Watts, A. V., et al., "Green Peas," Va. Poly. Inst. Ext. Ser. Circ. 681, 1966.

CHAPTER 25

Peppers

CLASSIFICATION, ORIGIN, AND HISTORY

The peppers (*Capsicum annuum* and *C. frutescens*) belong to the *Solanaceae* or nightshade family, and are therefore closely related to eggplant, potato, tomato, and tobacco. Virtually all cultivars of the commonly cultivated pepper belong to the species, *C. annuum*. Tabasco is the only cultivar of *C. frutescens* grown commercially in the United States.

The native home of the peppers is thought to be tropical America, where they have always been very popular. After the discovery of America, peppers were rapidly disseminated over Europe. The garden pepper is unrelated to the vine that produces black pepper, *Piper nigrum*.

SCOPE AND IMPORTANCE

Green peppers have increased in popularity over a long period and ranked seventeenth in acreage and sixteenth in value among the 22 principal vegetables in 1977. They are grown commercially in more than a dozen states and for local market and home use throughout the country.

Pimento peppers are produced primarily in Georgia, paprikas are grown principally in small areas of California and Arizona, and chili peppers come mainly from southern California and New Mexico. The main crop, sweet peppers for fresh market, are grown over a wide area, primarily in the eastern half of the United States.

The acreage of peppers for fresh market and processing rose from 41,190 acres in 1949 to 46,590 acres in 1959 and then increased to about 56,000 acres in 1977. Yields increased from 57 to 94 hundred-weight per acre during this 28-year period and production more than doubled from 2,368,000 hundredweight in 1949 to 5,255,000 hundred-weight in 1977. Concurrently, total value rose from $17,551,000 in 1949 to $30,116,000 in 1959 and up to an estimated $87,294,000 in 1977. Table 25.1 shows pepper acreage, yield, production, and value by leading states in 1977.

Table 25.1—Green Peppers for Fresh Market and Processing: Harvest Season and Estimated Acreage, Yield, Production, and Value in Leading States, 1977.

State	Harvest Season*	Harvested Acreage	Yield per Acre, Cwt.	Production per 1,000 Cwt.	Price per Cwt.	Value, $1,000
Florida	Spring	7,800	125	975	$21.20	20,670
New Jersey	Summer	7,100	65	462	17.40	8,039
N. Carolina	Summer	7,000	37	259	12.10	3,134
Florida	Fall	5,200	100	520	18.20	9,464
Florida	Winter	4,800	55	264	29.10	7,682
California	Summer	3,700	210	777	12.20	9,457
Kentucky	Summer	3,000	76	228	7.71	1,759
Texas	Summer	2,000	85	170	18.00	3,060
Texas	Spring	2,000	80	160	15.80	2,528
Michigan	Summer	1,400	75	105	17.50	1,838
Louisiana	Spring	1,300	45	59	14.30	844
New Jersey	Fall	1,100	70	77	13.80	1,065
Ohio	Summer	900	100	90	19.20	1,728
California	Spring	400	180	72	22.00	1,584
California	Fall	3,700	200	740	13.10	9,720
Texas	Fall	4,500	66	297	15.90	4,722
United States		55,900	94	5,255	16.60	87,294

*Summer Acreage (45%), Fall (26%), Spring (20%), and Winter (9%).

TRENDS IN PRODUCTION EFFICIENCY

Green peppers are comparatively expensive to produce because of plants, fertilizer, cultural, and labor requirements. Hand work from seed-ing through harvest involved approximately 200 man-hours per acre dur-ing the 1939 to 1959 period and to 160 in 1977. Man-hour output in-creased slowly compared with that of most other vegetable crops; 174 percent between 1939 and 1977.

CLIMATIC REQUIREMENTS

Peppers have very much the same climatic requirements as the egg-plant and tomato, although pepper plants may withstand lower temperatures. They thrive best in a relatively warm climate where the growing season is long and where there is little danger of frosts. The pepper is apparently more drouth-resistant than either the tomato or eggplant; nevertheless, best yields are contingent upon an ample supply of well-distributed rainfall and a mean temperature at blossom-setting time ranging from 65° to 80° F.

Irrigation is necessary in some pepper-growing sections of the West and Southwest, and it is used to some extent in other areas. Water should be applied frequently enough to maintain a steady rate of growth.

SELECTING CULTIVARS AND SEED

Cultivars

Of the several groups of peppers grown, there are two general classes: (1) those which produce mild or sweet fruits called sweet peppers and (2) those which bear pungent or hot fruits better known as hot peppers. Generally the sweet cultivars are harvested at the mature green stage, while the hot cultivars are harvested when at the mature red stage, except for the wax types which are picked when yellow. Table 25.2 gives the important characteristics of a selected list of the leading cultivars.

Securing Seed

Growers should make a special effort to obtain the best seed available of cultivars that are well adapted to their particular region. Proper seed production is a specialized business, and, as a rule, growers should not attempt to raise their own seed.

PREPARING THE SOIL

Soil Preferences

A sandy loam which holds moisture fairly well and which has a liberal supply of organic matter is the ideal soil for the growing of bell peppers. For canning peppers, a soil with some clay is preferable, as the

Table 25.2—Important Characteristics of a Selected List of Leading Cultivars of Peppers.

Cultivar	Use	Season* (Days)	Flavor	Fruit Shape Length (Inches)	Diameter
Anaheim M	Home, canning, market, drying	110	Hot	6-8	1½
Bellboy Hybrid	Market	70	Sweet	3	3½
California Wonder 300	Home, shipping, market, canning	74	Sweet	4½	3½-4
Canape	Market	62	Sweet	3½	3
Cubanelle	Home, market	62	Sweet	6	2
Emerald Giant	Market	74	Sweet	4½	3¾
Florida Giant	Market, shipping, home	75	Sweet	4½	3½-4
Goldspike	Market, pickling	75	Hot	1½	2½
Hungarian Yellow Wax	Home, market, canning	65	Hot	6	1½
Jalapeno M	Market, canning	75	Pungent	2½	2¾
Keystone Res. Giant	Home, market	75	Sweet	4	3½
Midway Hybrid	Home, market	74	Sweet	4	3½
Pennbell	Home, market	72	Sweet	3½	3½
Pimiento	Canning	80	Sweet	3	4
Tabasco	Canning, drying	95	Hot	1	¾
World Beater	Home, market, shipping	70	Sweet	4-4½	3-3½
Yolo Wonder B	Market, shipping	78	Sweet	4	3¾
Yolo Wonder L	Market, shipping	78	Sweet	4	3¾

*Days from transplanting until marketing stage.

color of the fruits seems to develop better than on lighter soils. Soils conducive to earliness are especially desirable in regions where the growing season is limited by killing frosts. The pepper is not especially sensitive to soil acidity, having an optimum pH range between 5.5 and 7.0. Strongly acid soils should be limed to bring the pH within this range.

Breaking and Conditioning

Land to be planted to peppers in the spring should be broken deeply during the previous late fall or early winter. If green-manure or cover crops are used, they may be plowed under in the early winter or early spring. In the spring the surface should be disced and well harrowed.

FERTILIZING

To produce high yields of peppers on soils low in fertility, manures and commercial fertilizer will be needed. Barnyard manure, compost, or green manure at the rate of 10 to 15 tons per acre should be applied annually.

The fertilization of peppers is similar to that of tomatoes. However, peppers seem to require a little more nitrogen and potassium. On light sandy soils, 750 to 1,000 pounds per acre of a 5-8-8 or 5-10-10 fertilizer should be worked into the soil before transplanting. A top dressing of nitrogen fertilizer is needed at the time of fruit setting to prevent a check in the growth of the plants. About 100 pounds of ammonium nitrate or its equivalent should be used. For sandy soils an additional 50 pounds of muriate or sulfate of potash should be added to the nitrogen top dress.

On heavier soils of fair to good fertility, less fertilizer is required. Five hundred to 600 pounds per acre of a fertilizer containing 4 to 5 percent nitrogen, 6 to 8 percent phosphorus, and 6 to 8 percent potassium should be applied before transplanting. A nitrogen top dressing should be used at about the same rate as listed above, after first fruit set.

PLANTING AND CULTIVATING

Growing the Plants

Seed should be treated with a protective fungicide before planting. If hotbeds are employed, the seed should be sown six to eight weeks before the plants are to be set in the field. In most areas, the seed is planted about a month before the average date of the last spring frost. A soil temperature of 70° to 75° F. before emergence of the seedlings, and a soil temperature between 65° and 70° F. after emergence should be maintained. After emergence, the plants should be kept at about 75° F. during the day and 65° F. during the night. Watering should be carefully done during bright, warm mornings if possible. Excessive moisture lowers soil temperature and encourages damping off. To encourage moderate hardening, increased ventilation should be given as the plants approach the transplanting stage.

Large acreages of peppers for shipping, canning, or drying are grown with plants produced in open beds. The seed is sown thinly and the plants are undisturbed until they are ready to be pulled for transplanting in the field. Seed is sown at the rate of about 20 seeds per foot in rows 6 inches apart. Plants are generally thinned to a spacing of about 12 to 15 plants per foot.

Setting the Plants in the Field

It is the usual practice to set plants, 4 to 8 inches tall, in rows 3 to 3½ feet apart with the plants spaced 1½ to 2½ feet apart in the row. Good yields, however, are obtained in some sections with closer spacings. The plants are set either by transplanting machines or by hand, the former method being much faster and just as efficient. In either case, care must be taken to see that the plants are properly placed and that the soil is firmed about the roots. Plants set by machine are usually smaller in size than those set by hand (Fig. 25.1).

Transplanting machines should be equipped with a watering device that will supply about a cup of water or starter solution per plant. A starter is frequently dissolved in the transplanting water. A mixture of 1½ pounds of monopotassium phosphate and 1½ pounds of diammonium phosphate in 50 gallons of water is recommended. Commercial preparations of these soluble chemicals are available under various trade names.

Fig. 25.1—Transplanting pepper plants in the field.

Photograph by E. C. Wittmeyer

A homemade mixture of 5 pounds of commercial fertilizer analyzing about 5 percent nitrogen, 8 to 10 percent phosphorus, and 5 percent potassium in 50 gallons of water is also effective when plants are set by hand. This mixture would contain an insoluble residue not suitable for a transplanter.

Cultivating

As soon as the young plants have become established in the soil, they should receive shallow cultivation only often enough to control the weeds. Deep cultivation invariably results in root pruning as well as a drying out of the soil, both of which cause a severe check in plant growth. Continued rapid growth is essential for best yields, and this is usually not possible without irrigation.

CONTROLLING DISEASES AND INSECTS

Diseases

The pepper is subject to diseases which may become very destructive under certain conditions, especially where a large acreage is grown without proper rotation. Seed treatment, crop rotation, and seedbed sterilization are general control measures that should be followed in the production of peppers. Many of the diseases that attack peppers are the same as those which attack the tomatoes, and the control methods are similar. For specific control measures, refer to Chapter 11. For methods applicable under local conditions, help may be obtained from agricultural experiment stations and extension services.

Very often damping off is destructive to young seedlings, causing the stems to decay near the soil line. Usually it can be kept under control by planting treated seeds in rows 4 to 6 inches apart and stirring the surface soil soon after each rain in order to keep it loose and dry. In rainy weather, other means of control, such as maneb, thiram, and captan sprays, are sometimes necessary.

BACTERIAL SPOT. Associated with *Xanthomonas vesicatoria*, bacterial spot causes small, dark-brown, wart-like spots on the leaves and fruits. During damp weather the disease spreads rapidly and may cause almost complete defoliation of the plants. The spots in the fruits allow the entrance of molds and other decay organisms. The same disease is common on the tomato. Seed treatment, seedbed sanitation, and crop rotation are the recommended control methods. Fixed copper sprays also aid in control.

SOUTHERN BLIGHT. Southern blight, associated with *Sclerotium rolfsii*, is often one of the most destructive pepper diseases in the South. The plants are attacked near the soil line, and during dry periods the roots are destroyed. The plants turn yellow and wilt gradually. A carefully planned rotation is the only means of control which can be recommended. Peppers should never be planted after soybeans or cowpeas, but cotton, corn, and small grains are almost immune and are good crops to precede peppers.

BLOSSOM-END ROT. Blossom-end rot (physiological) causes spots to appear near the tips of the fruits during dry periods before the plants have established a large root system. The early crop is most seriously affected. The spots usually become infected with *Alternaria* and other fungi which may decay the entire fruit. The plants should be set deeply in well-prepared soil. The roots should not be disturbed after fruiting begins.

ANTHRACNOSE. Caused by *Gloeosporium piperatum*, anthracnose frequently causes serious spotting of both green and ripe peppers. The fungus lives on and within the seed coat, and that within the seed coat cannot be killed by seed treatment. Seeds should be saved from disease-free fruits and treated to destroy any spores that may adhere to them. Spraying in the field and seedbed with captan, zineb, or maneb also helps hold down this disease.

RIPE ROT. Associated with *Colletotrichum capsici*, ripe rot is one of the most serious diseases of the pimiento pepper, destroying the fruit after it has ripened. Like the anthracnose fungus, it penetrates the seed coat and is not controlled by seed treatment. It also lives from season to season in the field. Careful seed selection from disease-free fields and crop rotation are necessary for control.

Other diseases causing economic loss are blue mold or downy mildew, *cercospora* leaf spot, *phytophthora* blight, fusarium wilt, bacterial soft rot, and virus diseases. Cultivars such as Yolo Wonder, Rutgers World Beater No. 13, and Burlington have high resistance to tobacco mosaic virus, but are susceptible to cucumber mosaic and tobacco etch virus. Curly top, another virus disease, causes damage in the West and Southwest. The root knot nematode also causes losses, chiefly in southern re-

gions. Pepper fruits are susceptible to sunscald when exposed to direct
sunlight. Partial defoliation of plants by bacterial spot or *cercospora* leaf
spot increases the danger of sunscald to the fruit.

Insects

There are a number of important insect pests of peppers in the
United States.

PEPPER WEEVIL. The pepper weevil (*Anthonomus eugenii*) is closely
related to the cotton boll weevil but is much smaller. Grubs feed in blossoms and in the core of young pods, causing the fruits to drop prema-
turely. This pest is established in most pepper growing regions. In the
western states, it breeds during the winter on black nightshade, *Solanum
nigrum,* and it is essential that this weed be eradicated around pepper
fields. The remains of the pepper crop should also be disposed of after
harvest. Treating with carbaryl on a 10-day schedule is usually an effective control.

PEPPER MAGGOT. The pepper maggot (*Zonosemata electa*) is the larva
of a species of fruit fly. Eggs are laid through the wall of the pod and
the maggots feed on the core, causing it to rot. The maggot is very injurious in New Jersey, and it is known to occur in northern Florida and
also may appear in other pepper-growing sections. Horse nettle is a native host plant, and the eggplant also is sometimes infested. Picking of
peppers while they are green prevents great injury by the pepper maggot,
though the cores may already be infested. Dusting or spraying with malathion has been proven effective. The dusts should be applied two days
after flies appear in the field, and the treatment should be repeated
at five-day intervals as long as any flies can be found.

Aphids, cutworms, flea beetles, hornworms, and leaf miners may
also cause economic loss. The methods of control for these insects on
peppers are generally the same as for their treatment on other crops.

HARVESTING, HANDLING, AND MARKETING

Harvesting

The time to harvest bell peppers should be determined largely by
the size of the fruit and its stage of maturity. For market, they are picked

as soon as they reach approximately full size and become firm, but before they begin to turn red or yellow, as the respective colors may be when ripe (Fig. 25.2). Green peppers are picked in baskets and hauled to central packing sheds for grading. Yields ranging from 3 to 8 tons per acre may be expected on the most fertile soils, though greater yields have been reported. Mechanized harvesting of green peppers is shown in Figure 25.3.

Practically all of the pimientos grown are canned in the red or ripe stage. They are harvested either in cotton-picking sacks or in baskets and are hauled in bags to the cannery, where they are run through grading machines and then processed. Yields of 3 to 5 tons of pimientos per acre are considered average.

A machine designed for the single destructive harvesting of pimiento and bell peppers has been built. Its success will depend on the availability of cultivars with concentrated set and other characteristics necessary for mechanical harvesting.

Pepper yields are at times unusually low because of the dropping of the young buds, blossoms, and immature fruits. Growers have attributed this almost complete shedding to various conditions, but results of controlled experiments at Ithaca, New York, justify the conclusion that hot

Fig. 25.2—Liberty Bell cultivar of green pepper.

USDA Photograph

Fig. 25.3—Green peppers conveyed to bags in the field.

Photograph by E. C. Wittmeyer

dry weather is the condition that causes most of the difficulty. The soil fertility also is important.

Sweet or bell peppers are subject to chilling injury at temperatures below 45° F. Storage above 50° F. encourages ripening and bacterial soft rot. At 45° to 50° F. and relative humidity of 90 to 95 percent, peppers can be stored as long as three weeks. Prepackaging in polyethylene film and light waxing reduces shrinkage and improves storage life.

Grading and Packing

Bell peppers, after reaching the packing shed, are graded either by hand or by machinery. Various kinds of containers are used for shipment to market. In some sections of the South, the crop is packed for shipment in specially constructed 1- and ½-bushel crates, which are easier to handle and ship than the standard 1-bushel hamper, which is still used to some extent, along with cartons and crates.

Peppers are sold commercially in four grades: U.S. Fancy, U.S. No. 1, U.S. No. 2, and Unclassified. The current grade specifications may be secured from the U.S. Department of Agriculture.

Marketing

The green bell pepper is perishable and should be sold as soon after picking as possible. The crop is moved short distances from the packing plant by unrefrigerated trucks but is shipped to large terminal markets in refrigerated trucks and freight cars. Buyers for large produce companies or dealers customarily visit the intensive vegetable-growing sections of the South and West and purchase most of the peppers in season, f.o.b., at the growers' shipping points. Some of the growers, however, sell their crop through certain local vegetable associations and a few sell on consignment, the latter method usually being the last resort.

EXPORTS AND IMPORTS. Imports of fresh peppers have increased substantially over the past 15 years, totaling $11,446,000 (64,888,000 pounds) in 1972. This rose to $22,945,000 (121,485,000 pounds) in 1977 (Table 13.2). Exports increased but not to the same degree as imports. Mexico is by far the major foreign supplier on the U.S. market, with the Dominican Republic a distant second.

SELECTED REFERENCES

Boswell, V. R., et al., "Pepper Production," USDA Agr. Res. Ser. Agr. Inf. Bull. 276, 1964.

Combs, O. B., et al., "Peppers," Univ. of Wisc. Coop. Ext. Pro. A2339, 1978.

Fullilove, H. M., and Futral, J. G., "A Mechanical Harvester for Pimento Peppers," Ga. Agr. Exp. Sta. Res. Rep. 142, 1972.

Longbrake, T., et al., "Keys to Profitable Pepper Production," Texas A & M Univ. Coop. Ext. Ser. Fact Sheet L–966, 1976.

McColloch, L. P., "Chilling Injury and Alternaria Rot of Bell Peppers," USDA Mkt. Res. Rep. 536, 1962.

McColloch, L. P., and Wright, W. R., "Botrytis Rot of Bell Peppers," USDA Mkt. Res. Rep. 754, 1966.

Montelaro, J., and Kostewicz, S. R., "Pepper Production Guide," Univ. of Fla. Coop. Ext. Ser. Circ. 102D, 1974.

Rutledge, A. D., "Pepper Production in Tennessee," Univ. of Tenn. Agr. Ext. Ser. Pub. 363, 1975.

Sims, W. L., and Smith, P. G., "Growing Peppers in California," Univ. of Calif. Div. of Agr. Sci. Leaflet 2676, 1976.

CHAPTER 26

Potatoes

CLASSIFICATION, ORIGIN, AND HISTORY

The potato (*Solanum tuberosum*) belongs to the family *Solanaceae* and is a close relative of the tomato, eggplant, pepper, tobacco, and the wild nightshade. The potato and Indian corn are the New World's greatest contributions to the food supply of mankind. Peru is thought to be the place of origin of the potato; some authorities, however, believe that it was also native to parts of Mexico. When and how it reached the United States is not known.

Potatoes had little significance as a food crop in this country prior to the influx of Presbyterian immigrants from Ireland in 1718. The crop gained its greatest impetus in America, however, immediately after 1846, the year that blight destroyed the potato crop in Ireland and caused a famine.

The reliance of the Irish people on the potato as a food crop and their influence on its extended culture and use in this country were no doubt responsible for this product's being called the Irish potato rather than the Peru or South American potato. The word *Irish* as a prefix to the word *potato* has a very definite meaning in the rural South, where the single word *potato* is often understood to mean sweet potato. In the North, the reverse is true.

SCOPE AND IMPORTANCE

Three centuries ago the potato was scarcely known as a food crop in either Europe or America. Today, however, its culture encircles the globe in both temperate zones, and it stands out as the most important food crop in the world. In the United States potatoes are by far the most important of the vegetables in terms of quantities produced and consumed. They are grown commercially and for home use throughout the United States and lead all vegetables in acreage and value. The importance of this basic food crop may have declined slightly over the years, but it remains the principal vegetable and is undergoing rapid changes. Americans are eating more potatoes but fewer fresh ones. During the 1970 to 1977 period, fresh potato consumption declined from 58.3 to 57.7 pounds. Per capita consumption of potatoes rose from 117.5 pounds in 1970 to about 123 pounds in 1977. Per capita consumption of frozen potatoes increased from 27.7 pounds in 1970 to 37.9 in 1977.

These figures indicate a new trend in the potato industry. Sparked by rising labor and capital costs, consumer preference for convenience foods, the fast-food-chain boom, and recent record-high potato prices, 60 percent of the 1977 potato crop earmarked for human consumption went to the processing market, which includes frozen, canned, and dehydrated potatoes.

While frozen potatoes (especially French fries) still dominate the processing sector, dehydrated flakes and granules are picking up a sizeable share of the market. Dehydrating manufacturers had boom years in 1972 and 1976. In 1977, flakes and granules accounted for almost 19 percent of all processed potatoes; and the U.S. Department of Agriculture believes that this category will remain fairly stable. Consumers may expect even newer processes and potato products in the future. (See last paragraph page 220 for further importance of potatoes.)

Potato acreage decreased steadily from around 3,000,000 acres in the 1930's to 1,755,000 in 1959, then to 1,358,700 acres in 1977. Total production increased to 240,950,000 hundredweight by 1949, up to 245,272,000 in 1959, and 312,418,000 by 1969, and then up to approximately 354,-576,000 hundredweight by 1977. The crop value of $236,839,000 in 1939 rose to $512,393,000 in 1949, then to $555,889,000 in 1959 and fluctuated upwardly to $1,126,033,000 in 1977.

Figure 26.1 shows the 1949 to 1977 trends in acreage, value, production, and the approximate distribution of potatoes. Table 26.1 presents leading states by acreage, production, and value in 1977. Idaho leads, followed by North Dakota, Maine, Washington, Minnesota, California, and Oregon. The late main crop, which comprises a bulk of the total, is produced primarily in the northern tier of states from Maine to North Dakota, Idaho, and Washington.

Fig. 26.1—Acreage, distribution, production, and value of potatoes.

UNITED STATES TOTAL

Year	Acreage	Production 1,000 Cwt.	Value, $1,000
1949	1,755,000	240,950	512,393
1959	1,331,000	245,272	555,889
1969	1,415,500	312,418	697,104
1977	1,358,700	354,576	1,126,033

TRENDS IN PRODUCTION EFFICIENCY

The potato is an expensive crop to produce. Seed, fertilizers, cultural and pest control practices, and labor vary considerably in different regions, but average costs are high. With improved mechanism, fertilization, and other practices, potato yields have increased rapidly during the last 40 years. Acreage man-hour requirements decreased from 69 man-hours in 1939 to 50 in 1959, and down to 26 man-hours in 1977. With phenomenal increases in yields and labor-saving equipment, the man-hour output increased 350 percent between 1939 and 1959 and spectacularly to 956 percent between 1939 and 1977 (Table 1.6).

CLIMATIC REQUIREMENTS

The potato requires a cool growing season with an abundant and

Table 26.1—Potatoes for Fresh Market: Estimated Acreage, Yield,
Production, and Value of Sales in Leading States, 1977.

State	Harvested Acreage	Yield per Acre, Cwt.	Production per 1,000 Cwt.	Price per Cwt.	Value, $1,000
Idaho	360,000	245	88,200	$2.95	233,130
North Dakota	135,000	160	21,600	2.70	48,697
Maine	118,000	240	28,320	3.36	77,636
Washington	110,000	460	50,600	2.80	131,046
Minnesota	79,500	189	15,023	2.77	37,294
California	60,700	361	21,890	5.77	120,470
Oregon	60,000	426	25,550	2.89	68,144
Wisconsin	55,500	325	18,038	3.95	63,666
New York	43,400	289	12,538	3.94	43,347
Colorado	43,300	261	11,292	2.88	28,520
Michigan	39,800	257	10,243	4.14	35,596
Florida	30,100	206	6,207	6.71	41,447
Virginia	27,700	125	3,463	4.99	16,113
Pennsylvania	25,500	250	6,375	4.70	26,217
Other States	170,200	207	35,231	4.83	154,709
United States	1,358,700	261	354,576	3.55	1,126,033

well distributed rainfall. Since the seed pieces will usually sprout at temperatures ranging from 40° to 50° F., it is the common practice to plant early potatoes five or six weeks before the last spring frost is expected. It requires about this length of time for the eyes to sprout and the young plants to push through about 2 to 3 inches of soil, the usual depth of planting. There is, of course, some risk of the young plant's being injured by frost, although the increased yields and prices obtained from early planting warrant taking this risk. The late or main crop is generally grown in regions with mild summers. Planting is done in May and June, and maturity occurs during the cool fall weather, which is favorable for tuber development.

SELECTING CULTIVARS AND SEED

Cultivars

A large number of cultivars of potatoes are available. These differ in time of maturity, yield, appearance, cooking and marketing qualities, and resistance to various insects and diseases. If other characteristics are equal, a resistant cultivar should be chosen. A cultivar may be well adapted to one region but not to another. For this reason a new cultivar should be first tried on a small scale only. A number of cultivars and their characteristics are given in Table 26.2. It includes some that have been in use for many years and shows characteristics that might be considered in choosing a cultivar.

Securing Seed

It is desirable to purchase certified seed when possible. Most states growing seed potatoes commercially have associations which send out inspectors to inspect both field and storage bins of potatoes before giving a certificate of inspection to show that the seed stock is standard in type and free of serious diseases. Field inspection of the plants is the only way known to identify some of the virus diseases, such as mosaic, which are carried in the tubers. This is discussed under the disease section of this chapter.

Tubers are dormant for about three months after maturity, and normally they will not sprout. If used for seed during this time, a treatment to break dormancy should be used. The cut seed pieces can be dipped in potassium gibberelate (1 to 2 ppm). If seed tubers have been held in storage too long, they may produce too many sprouts of weakened vigor. These tend to produce more tubers of smaller size per hill. Tubers removed from cold storage will not sprout immediately, nor will cut surfaces heal properly. The seed should be conditioned for about two weeks at 65° F. before planting.

PREPARING THE SOIL

The potato must have a fertile soil for even moderate yields. If drainage is good, heavy clay soils can be made to produce potatoes by adding large quantities of organic matter, or very porous sandy soils can be used by adding heavy applications of commercial fertilizers.

The land should be broken deeply and then harrowed just before planting in the early spring. Where the land is very flat, it should be thrown up into high beds and a ditch provided along the ends of the rows for taking off the drainage water.

Table 26.2—Brief Description of Selected Potato Cultivars.

Variety	Season	Flower Color	Resistant to	Shape	Tubers		
					Color	Eyes	
Chippewa	Midseason	Lavender	Mild mosaic	Long-oval flat	White	Shallow	
Irish Cobbler	Early	Lilac	Wart, mild mosaic	Roundish	Creamy	Medium	
Katahdin	Late	Lavender	Mild mosaic, brown rot, net necrosis, wart	Oval	White	Shallow	
Kennebec	Late	White	Mild mosaic, late blight, net necrosis	Elliptical	Creamy buff	Shallow	
Norchief	Medium Late		Common Scab	Round	Red	Shallow	
Norchip	Midseason		Common Scab	Round	White	Shallow	
Norgold Russet	M. Early		Common Scab	Oblong	Russet	Shallow	
Norland	105 days	Purple		Oblong, thick	Red	Shallow	
Red Lasoda	Early	Lavender	Comman scab	Long-elliptical	Red	Medium	
Red Pontiac	Late	Lavender		Oval-round	Dark red	Medium	
Russet Burbank	Late	White	Comman scab	Long, roundish	Russet	Shallow	
Russet Sebago	Late	Lavender, dark	Common scab	Oval-round	Russet	Shallow	
Sebago	Late	Lavender, dark	Yellow dwarf	Oval-round	White	Shallow	
Superior	Med. early		Comman scab	Round	White	Shallow	
White Rose	Midseason	White		Long, flattened	White, smooth	Medium	

FERTILIZING AND MANURING

Fertilizing

Nitrogen, phosphorus, and potassium are required in a fertilizer mixture for practically all the soil types used for growing potatoes. There may be exceptions in the case of some of the muck soils containing a high percentage of available nitrogen and some western soils high in potassium.

The potato belongs to the group of vegetable crops having the highest fertilizer requirement. The amount of fertilizer that can be applied profitably depends not only upon soil type and fertility but also upon environmental conditions affecting yields. Tables 6.4 and 6.5 can be used as guides for fertilizer recommendations. It may be noted that more nitrogen is recommended for the early crop than for the late crop. This element is usually less available early in the season, and potatoes need to develop rapidly. For this reason fertilizer placement often gives increased yields, especially if less than optimum amounts are applied. Best results are obtained when the fertilizer is applied about 2 inches to the side and slightly below the seed piece. Injury and reduced yields result when the fertilizer and seed piece are placed together.

Manuring

Animal manures should be used where available. Summer cover crops turned under in the fall are good soil-improvement crops for potatoes to follow in the spring. Winter cover crops are not well suited because the potatoes are planted before the crop has time to make any appreciable amount of spring growth.

PLANTING

Treating Seed

Whether certified or common seed stock is used, the potatoes should be disinfected before planting. Captan, maneb, Polyram, zineb, or maneb plus zinc ion may be used. The fungicide may be applied as a dust or a dip to the cut or uncut tubers. The manufacturer's directions should be followed.

Planting Rate

From 9 to 20 bushels of seed potatoes are required to plant an acre.

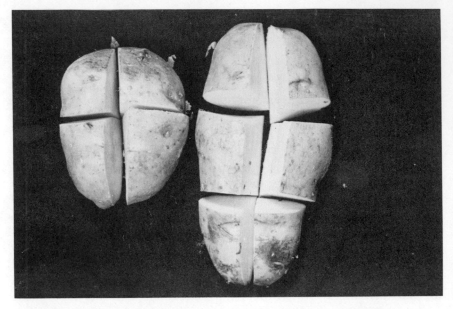

Fig. 26.2—Blocky seed pieces with one or more well placed eyes are desirable.

The heavier rate of seeding should be employed on the most fertile soils under ideal climatic conditions.

A medium-sized tuber is cut into four to six pieces, each piece containing one or more eyes (Fig. 26.2). Very small pieces containing only one eye frequently produce weak plants. If the pieces are cut too large, a large amount will be required to plant a given area, thus increasing the cost of seed.

There are mechanical devices for cutting potatoes for planting, but if the work can be done by hand, there will be a greater certainty of each piece containing one or more eyes. Potatoes should be planted soon after cutting, or the cut pieces should be cured by keeping them in an atmosphere of high humidity (85 percent or higher) and at a temperature of 60° to 65° F. If the cut seed is to be kept more than a week, curing is desirable. The tubers should not be cut immediately after removal from low-temperature storage.

Planting Time

In most sections early potatoes should be planted about five or six weeks before the last spring frost is expected or when the soil temperature reaches 40° F. In the milder sections of the South, as in Florida and in the Gulf Coast sections of Texas, the main planting of early potatoes is done in late fall or early winter. The date of a late planting depends upon the length of the growing season. However, plantings on muck soils should be made early enough that the plants will shade the soil before hot weather. High temperatures prevent tuber set as shown in Figure 26.3.

Planting Methods

The grower has a choice of one- or two-row planters, which will enable him to plant rather large areas in a comparatively short time. The usual custom is to space the rows from 32 to 36 inches apart and drop the seed pieces from 12 to 15 inches apart in the row. Close spacing on good land well supplied with moisture tends to increase yields.

The seed pieces should usually be planted 2 to 3 inches deep. On the flat lands where drainage is difficult, the potatoes are planted only about 2 inches below the general level of the land, and ridges are thrown up over the rows, covering the seed pieces about 2 inches more. Since the tubers are formed on the plant above the planted seed piece, it is well to plant deeply on lands where the crop is subject to dry weather. Some growers follow the plan of throwing up high ridges over the rows after planting, covering the seed pieces 5 to 6 inches deep. Then just before the young plants emerge a spike-tooth harrow is run over the land, killing the first crop of small weeds and breaking the crust of the soil to assist the plants in coming through.

CULTIVATING, SPRAYING, AND IRRIGATING

Cultivating

If the land has been deeply broken and well harrowed before the potatoes are planted, the cultivation of the crop is a rather simple task. Sufficient shallow cultivations should be given to keep down weeds. At the same time, the soil should be gradually worked to the plants as they increase in height. If the soil becomes compact after planting, it may be necessary to give one deep cultivation soon after the plants come up. Following this, however, deep cultivation should be avoided to prevent serious injury to the roots.

By the time the plants bloom freely and begin to form tubers, beds

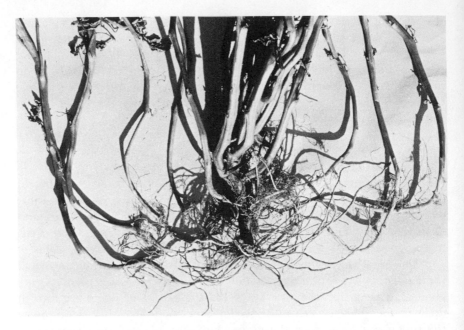

Fig. 26.3—The potato may fail to produce tubers at high soil temperatures.

or ridges in which the potatoes form should be completed and the crop no longer cultivated.

Spraying and Dusting

Foliage diseases of the potato are most effectively controlled by keeping the plants covered with a fungicide. Spraying or dusting should begin when the plants are 4 to 6 inches tall and should be repeated at regular intervals throughout the growing season. Bordeaux mixture was formerly used almost exclusively, but it is now being replaced by newer fungicides such as maneb, defolatan, or Polyram. These give effective control of the early and late blights and are less toxic to the plants.

In the spray schedule an insecticide should be included to control insects prevalent at the time of application. See Chapter 11 for specific recommendations for controlling insects and diseases.

Irrigating

Growers prepared to irrigate are most certain of success. Irrigation is decidedly important for growing late potatoes, and it helps to assure the early crops, which mature during periods of uncertain rainfall. In dry areas irrigation is absolutely essential.

For good growth and development, the potato has a high water requirement. The available soil moisture should be maintained between 45 and 65 percent. The time of stolonization and tuberization constitutes the period of most critical need for soil moisture. A temporary deficiency during the time of tuber formation may result in growth crack or knobby tubers. Both furrow and sprinkler irrigation are used for applying water in the production of potatoes. Excessive irrigation or rainfall may increase the need for nitrogen.

Fig. 26.4—Furrow irrigation of potatoes in Idaho.

USDA Photograph

CONTROLLING DISEASES AND INSECTS

Diseases

The potato is subject to a great variety of fungus, bacterial, and virus diseases requiring a variety of control methods. Some of these diseases cause serious losses wherever the potato is grown, while others are more localized. Many of the most important diseases are seed-borne. Therefore, the importance of disease-free seed and seed treatment is being recognized by growers everywhere. Crop rotation is necessary to prevent increasing destructiveness of organisms that live over in soil and on old decaying vines and tubers, and spraying or dusting is necessary for control of insects and leaf diseases.

EARLY BLIGHT. Caused by *Alternaria solani,* early blight appears as large grayish-brown spots, usually showing concentric light and darker markings on the leaves. As the spots enlarge, they coalesce and finally involve the entire leaf.

This disease is most common in the South when a rainy period occurs during May or June. It is often confused with tip-burn, which becomes serious during dry, hot weather immediately following a period of excessive moisture. Together they cause heavy reduction of the crop nearly every year, sometimes as much as 50 percent. Loss from early blight can be reduced by spraying or dusting with zineb or maneb to kill this fungus.

LATE BLIGHT. Associated with *Phytophthora infestans,* late blight is usually considered the most serious leaf disease of the potato. Ordinarily it is not important in the South, but flourishes in the cool, wet weather common in the North. Control is accomplished by planting disease-free tubers, partly-resistant cultivars, and spraying with fixed copper, maneb, or zineb.

MOSAIC. *Mosaic* is a virus disease, appearing as a mottling of the leaves with paler areas interspersed between darker ones and accompanied by more or less crinkling. The loss of chlorophyll causes reduced elaboration of starch and consequent reduction of the tuber yield. The disease is carried from year to year in seed tubers. In the field, it is spread by insects, principally the potato aphid, which carries the juice from infected to healthy plants. Control consists in the use of properly certified seed.

LEAF ROLL. Leaf roll is a virus disease in which the affected plants are of a paler green color, more upright in habit, with the lower leaflets rolled upward. The yield is more seriously reduced than by mosaic. The means of transmission and methods of control are the same as for mosaic.

SCAB. Scab, resulting from attacks of *Streptomyces scabies,* is recognized by most potato growers by the characteristic pitting of the tubers. Badly pitted tubers are unsalable. The fungus lives in the diseased spots on the surface of healthy tubers, and in the soil. It grows best in slightly alkaline, neutral, and slightly acid soil and may survive for several seasons unless the soil reaction is below pH 5.2. Cultivars with resistance include Menominee, Ontario, Cayuga, Seneca, and Cherokee.

RING ROT. Ring rot is caused by the bacterium (*Corynebacterium sepedonicum*) and is extremely infectious. It affects the plants as well as the tubers. The lower leaves of an infected stem first turn yellow. Other leaves begin to roll and wilt, and the stem soon dies. Tubers are infected at the stem end, and the organism follows the vascular area.

The bacteria causing ring rot are spread by diseased seed, handling, and storage equipment. Only disease-free seed should be used, and anything used in handling diseased tubers should be thoroughly disinfected.

BLACKLEG. Blackleg is a bacterial disease caused by *Erwina astroseptica*. Diseased plants assume a yellowish-green color, the stem is blackened below the soil line, the soft parts and the old seed piece decay, and with continued moist conditions the new tubers may decay in place. Tubers may also rot in storage or in transit. The bacteria may be carried either within or on the surface of the potato. When infected tubers are planted, the bacteria may enter the sprouts. The bacteria also live in the soil. Control methods include the use of disease-free seed stock, seed treatment, and crop rotation.

BLACK SCURF. Caused by *Pellicularia filamentosa,* black scurf consists of irregular, scurfy, blackish patches (sclerotia) on the surface of the potato. When such infected tubers are planted, the fungus often attacks the sprouts, killing them before they emerge from the soil or causing wilting and death at a later date. Infected tubers should not be used for seed. Large sclerotia are difficult to kill by the most thorough seed treatment, and thus it is not too satisfactory. PCNB disced into the top 4 to 6 inches of severely infected soils has given some control. Disease-free seed is still the most effective method.

Insects

More than 25 species of insects have been found injurious to the potato, but most of these are seldom seriously destructive over any great area (Fig. 26.5).

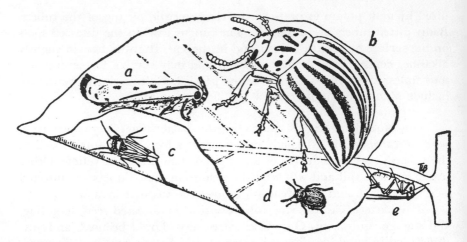

Fig. 26.5—Important potato insects: (a) tuber moth; (b) Colorado potato beetle; (c) potato leaf hopper; (d) potato flea beetle; (e) potato aphid.

COLORADO POTATO BEETLES. Colorado potato beetles (*Leptinotarsa 10-lineata*) are thick-bodied yellow beetles about ⅜ inch long, with dark-brown stripes on the wing covers. The young are red and soft-bodied and cling to the edges of the leaves. Yellow eggs stand in close groups on the under sides of the leaves. Adults and young eat irregular holes in the leaves and branches, beginning to feed as soon as plants are up.

The beetle is the best-known and most destructive enemy of potatoes in the United States. Since its spread eastward from its native home in the Rocky Mountains, it now occupies all the potato-growing regions. The potato is its favorite food plant; it also feeds freely on tomato, eggplant, and horse nettle.

POTATO FLEA BEETLES. Potato flea beetles in the adult stage are about ¹⁄₁₆ inch long, black, and oval in outline. They jump quickly when disturbed and disappear from sight. The adults chew the leaves, causing shot-holes, while the larvae feed on the roots and tubers. The overwintering adults will attack young potato plants early in the spring. If control measures are used at this time, later damage may be reduced.

POTATO LEAF HOPPERS. Potato leaf hoppers (*Empoasca fabae*) are small, green, active-jumping, streamlined insects which suck juice from the under side of the leaves, causing the tips to turn brown and the edges to curl upward.

The leaf hopper is the worst pest of potatoes in the north central states, and it occurs over the East and South, except in the southern parts of Florida and Texas. Its feeding brings about the condition called hopper-burn. Beans, alfalfa, and apple trees also suffer from this insect, and many other herbaceous and woody plants serve as hosts.

POTATO APHIDS. Potato aphids or plant lice of four different kinds feed on the potato plant. They cause damage by sucking juices from the foliage and by spreading virus diseases.

POTATO TUBERWORMS. Potato tuberworms (*Gnorimoschema opercuella*) are pinkish-white caterpillars, approximately ¼ inch long. They mine the leaves and stems and burrow into the tubers. Late potatoes and those in storage are more frequently attacked than the early crop. The tuberworm has been of importance in practically every state. Hot, dry weather in the field and the accumulation of potatoes in storage encourage this pest.

In Maryland, infestation of potatoes by the tuberworm was prevented by hilling the tubers 6 to 8 inches deep about 40 days after planting. Tubers, after being dug, should not be left on the ground overnight and should not be covered with potato vines. Eggs are laid by moths on exposed tubers during the late afternoon and night.

OTHER PESTS. In addition to these specific pests, several general feeders sometimes become destructive to potatoes. They include blister beetles, white grubs, wireworms, plant bugs, nematodes, and vegetable weevils. The general treatment of these is discussed in Chapter 11.

HARVESTING, GRADING, STORING, AND MARKETING

Potatoes of the early crop seldom reach full maturity on account of dry, warm weather, early blight, tip-burn, and other conditions which interfere with their normal growth. Consequently, the plants usually begin to die down before the crop is mature, even though good culture has been given and a spray schedule followed. As this stage approaches, harvesting is in order. Some growers harvest even earlier if the price for early or new potatoes is high. On the other hand, harvesting is delayed when prices are low.

Although the harvesting time for late potatoes is determined primarily by maturity of the crop, other considerations such as market prospects, availability of help, and weather conditions may be influencing factors. The vines should mature and die before harvest so the skins of the tubers will set and thus decrease the likelihood of skinning and bruising. Also, if the vines are not dead, there is a chance spores of late blight will be transferred from the vines to the tubers, where they may later produce rot in storage. Especially now, with more effective methods of pest control, the vines live longer, and it is often necessary to kill them before harvesting. This can be done by machines that have a beating action on the plants, but this is costly. DNBP used at 2 pounds per acre of active ingredient in 30 gallons of solution can be applied with regular spray equipment, and a good kill can be obtained in 4 to 10 days.

Harvesting and Grading

Potatoes should be handled as gently as practicable from the harvesting machine to the retail store. They are dug by a variety of machines ranging from one-row potato diggers to elaborate two-row mechanical harvesters (Fig. 26.6). In any case, the potatoes should be removed from the soil economically with the least possible movements and injury to the tubers. Modern potato harvesters convey potatoes to low-level trailers in order to minimize movement and bruising. To decrease handling, supplemental grading and bagging equipment are attached to or operate in conjunction with mechanical harvesters in many instances.

Early potatoes are sensitive to the sun and wind and may be easily damaged by handling in the field and packing shed. They are frequently washed in chlorinated water for cleaning and disinfecting. Early potatoes should be harvested, graded and packed as expeditiously as feasible, and shipped under refrigeration when the weather is warm.

The U.S. Department of Agriculture has developed detailed specifications and tolerances which are generally understood by growers and packers and demanded by the trade.

Storing

Most of the main crop of potatoes cannot be marketed immediately after harvesting and must be placed in storage. At first the tubers should be held at 55° to 60° F. with high relative humidity and good ventilation for two to three weeks. These conditions favor the healing of cuts and bruises. The temperature may then be lowered to 38° to 40° F. At this range the tubers will not sprout in storage. Where low temperatures are not available, sprouting of table stock may be reduced by the use

Fig. 26.6—Two-row harvester delivering potatoes to truck.

Photograph by E. C. Wittmeyer

of a sprout inhibitor. Maleic hydrazide at the rate of 3 pounds per acre applied to the plants a few weeks before harvesting is effective. Temperatures below this range, to some extent, favor the accumulation of sugars, making potatoes unsuitable for chips. This condition can be overcome by storing the tubers for about two weeks at 60° to 70° F.

Marketing

Potato growers usually sell through cooperatives or central packing sheds as volume buyers want a uniform quality pack in dependable quantities. Most of the larger producing districts attract buyers from large markets who purchase potatoes at the assembling and shipping points. Attractive packaging promotes sales. Potatoes are sold in 50-pound fiberboard boxes or paper or mesh bags, 3-, 5-, 10-, and 15-pound plastic film or mesh consumer bags, and more infrequently in 100-pound burlap bags.

The shift from fresh market potatoes to the processed product has drastically changed the structure of the potato market. Sizeable quantities are now grown under contractual arrangements between growers and processors. In some instances, these pre-season agreements on prices have obscured the response in potato prices to changes in seasonal supply. Also inventories of frozen and dehydrated potatoes have had an impact on prices received for fresh potatoes.

EXPORTS AND IMPORTS. In 1972, about 383,774,000 pounds of fresh potatoes valued at $12,445,000 were exported primarily to Canada (60 percent), with various quantities going to Western Europe and Latin America. In 1977, potato exports of 693,379,000 pounds were valued at $46,217,000. About 60 percent went to Canada, with various quantities going to Western Europe and Latin America. Imports, mostly from Canada, totaled 106,447,000 pounds valued at $5,219,000 (Table 13.2).

SELECTED REFERENCES

Anonymous, "Pest and Disease Control Programs for Potatoes," Calif. Agr. Ext. Ser. Pub., 1975.

Binning, L. K., et al., "Potatoes: Chemical Recommendations," Univ. of Wisc. Coop. Ext. Pro. A2352, 1978.

Chase, R. W., and Thompson, N. R., "Potato Production in Michigan," Ext. Bull. 546, 1967.

Chen, P., Li, P. H., and Cunningham, W. P., "Ultrastructural Differences in Leaf Cells of Some Solanum Species in Relation to Their Frost Resistance," Bot. Gaz. 138(3):276-285, 1977.

Dallyn, S. L., "The Use of Minimum Tillage Plus Herbicides in Potato Production," Amer. Pot. J. 51:278, 1975.

Heinze, P. H., et al., "Storage and Transportation of Potatoes," Potato Assoc., Amer. Potato Handbook, 30-34, 1964.

Ide, L. E., "How to Buy Potatoes," USDA H & G Bull. 198, 1972.

Krofta, R. N., and Harlan, R. K., "Costs, Returns and Capital Requirements for Producing Potatoes in Maine," Univ. of Me. Agr. Exp. Sta. Bull. 730, 1976.

Lana, E. P., "Potato Production in North Dakota," N. Dak. State Univ. Ext. Bull. 26, 1976.

Mondy, N. I., Sieczka, J. B., and Dallyn, S. L., "The Effect of Sprouting and Sprout Inhibition on the Chemical Composition of Potatoes," Amer. Pot. J. 51:278, 1975.

Orr, P. H., "Handling Potatoes from Storage to Packing Line," USDA, MRR Rep. 890, 1971.

Parfit, D. E., and Peloquin, S. J., "Variation of Potato Vine and Tuber Yield as a Function of Harvest Date and Cultivar," Am. Potato J. 54 (9): 411-417, 1977.

Pew, W. D., et al., "Growing Potatoes in Arizona," Univ. of Ariz. Coop. Ext. Ser. Bull. A83 (current).

Schippers, P. A., "The Rate of Respiration of Potato Tubers During Storage," Pot. Res. 20:321-329, 1977.

CHAPTER 27

Root Crops

Root crops include the beet, horseradish, parsnip, radish, rutabaga, and turnip. These crops are grown for an enlarged fleshy structure called the root. This enlarged root consists of both root and stem tissue. From the lower part arises the absorbing roots and from the upper part arises the stems and leaves. All root crops thrive best in relatively cool weather and have similar cultural requirements; and all are biennials except the radish, which is either annual or biennial and horseradish, which is a perennial. In a particular area, these crops should be planted so as to develop during a relatively cool part of the growing season. Carrots and sweet potatoes are discussed under separate chapters.

BEET

Classification and History

The beet (*Beta vulgaris*) is a native of Europe, North Africa, and West Asia. Swiss chard, sugar beets, and stock beets or mangel-wurzels all belong to the same species as the garden beet. De Candolle states that though the ancients knew about the beet, they did not cultivate it until the third century A.D. The Germans and the French became interested in beets about the year 1800. Since that time, many improved types have been developed.

Scope and Importance

Beets ranked twenty-second in both acreage and value among the 22 principal vegetables in 1977 and are relatively unimportant economically. They are grown commercially in limited sections of the country but are produced for local market and home use in many areas.

The acreage of fresh beets declined from 10,170 acres in 1949 to 1,800 acres in 1968—the last report year. Beets for canning declined from 18,860 acres in 1949 to 14,120 acres in 1977. Value for the fresh market crop decreased from $2,015,000 to $1,260,000 between 1949 and 1968, while that for canned beets increased from $3,176,000 to $7,981,000 during the 1949 to 1977 period. The acreage, production, and value of beets for canning are shown in Table 27.1.

Table 27.1—Beets for Canning: Estimated Acreage, Yield, Production, and Value in Leading States, 1977.

State	Harvested Acreage	Yield per Acre, Tons	Production in Tons	Price per Ton	Value, $1,000
Wisconsin	6,900	13.77	95,000	$36.60	3,477
New York	3,600	14.33	51,600	35.00	1,806
Other States*	3,620	16.46	59,600	45.30	2,698
United States	14,120	14.60	206,200	38.70	7,981

*In 1977, California, Indiana, Michigan, Ohio, Oregon, and Texas were prominent.

Trends in Production Efficiency

Efficiency in beet production has increased considerably in recent years. Between 1939 and 1959, labor required to grow and harvest the fresh market crop decreased from 201 to 94 man-hours per acre, while man-hour unit production increased 176 percent. Beets for processing experienced a more spectacular decrease from 146 to 58 man-hours per acre for the same period, while labor-unit output rose 381 percent. Average yields of fresh market beets increased from 93 to 119 hundredweight in the 1939 to 1959 period while those for processing rose from 108 to 292 hundredweight per acre between 1939 and 1977.

Plant Characteristics

The edible portion of the root consists of alternating circular bands of conducting and storage tissues. The bands of storage tissues are relatively broad and dark; those of conducting tissues, relatively narrow and light. The contrast in color between these alternating bands is known as zoning, which varies greatly between cultivars and within a cultivar. High temperatures will usually result in poor color development of the root.

The beet has a relatively large absorbing system. Studies at the New York (Cornell) Agricultural Experiment Station have shown that the roots extend downward $2\frac{1}{2}$ to 3 feet, and that numerous branches arise in close proximity to the enlarged roots.

The stem is short and platelike; the leaves are simple and arranged in a closed spiral on a short stem called the crown. They vary from dark red to light green. Stomata occur on both the upper and lower surfaces. The so-called seed is really a fruit which contains from two to five or six seeds.

Selecting Cultivars

In general, beet cultivars are classified according to the shape and the time of maturity of the root. There are (1) flat or globular, early-maturing cultivars; (2) globular, second-early-maturing cultivars; and (3) long, late-maturing cultivars. Representative cultivars of the flat or globular, early-maturing sorts are Crosby's Egyptian, Green Top Bunching, Ruby Queen, and Early Wonder. Representative cultivars of the globular, second-early sorts are Detroit Dark Red and Perfected Detroit. A representative cultivar of long, late-maturing sorts is Long Dark Blood or Long Smooth Blood. The Crosby's Egyptian, Ruby Queen, and Early Wonder are early market garden cultivars. Detroit Dark Red is a second-early market garden beet and is used for canning and for general purposes in the home garden. It remains tender and edible over a long season, which is desirable for home use. Perfected Detroit is a very good processing beet due to its superior interior color and globular shape at an early age. Figures 27.1 and 27.2 represent flat and globular types respectively. Monoking Explorer has a monogerm seed desired for precision planting.

Preparing the Seedbed

Beets thrive best in well-drained, slightly acid soils including sandy loams, loams, silt loams, and high-lime mucks. Beets will do well over a fairly wide range of pH, but they are quite sensitive to soils of high acidity. The optimum pH range is from 6.0 to 7.0.

Soil preparation should be thorough. Deep plowing, immediately followed by discing, pulverizes the surface, promotes the formation of a fine seedbed, and conserves moisture.

Fig. 27.1—Acceptable range in type of Crosby Egyptian beet (flat type).

USDA Photograph

For highest quality, beets must make rapid and uninterrupted growth. Well-rotted stable manure, where available, is recommended at the rate of 10 to 15 tons per acre. As with other crops, the kind and amount of commercial fertilizer required varies with the soil type, soil fertility, previous fertilization, and the rotation. Commercial fertilizers containing 6 to 7 percent nitrogen, 5 to 6 percent phosphorus, and 5 to 6 percent potassium should be used at a rate of not less than 1,000 pounds per acre. Side dressing with a nitrate form of nitrogen fertilizer when the plants are 4 to 6 inches high is a recommended practice. On muck soils less nitrogen is needed and usually more potassium is applied. In certain areas of New York, Wisconsin, and Oregon, deficiencies of boron have to be corrected to prevent internal black spot. Applications of borax or boric acid in amounts varying from 10 to 40 pounds per acre will correct the deficiency. Too much boron is toxic, so care must be exercised in its application. Recommendations from local agricultural experiment stations and extension services should be closely followed.

Fig. 27.2—Acceptable range in type of Early Wonder beet (globular type).

USDA Photograph

Planting and Thinning

The seed balls are usually planted with a seed drill at rates varying from 4 to 6 pounds per acre, in rows 18 to 24 inches apart. Thinning is usually necessary for market crops, as each seed ball may produce from one to five or six plants. In market gardens and in home gardens thinning is frequently delayed until the plants are sufficiently large for use. In general, plants are thinned 3 to 4 inches apart. In fields of beets grown for processing, thinning is seldom practiced since labor costs are too high. Processors usually pay a premium for small-sized beets, so close spacing is desirable.

Cultivating

Cultivation is necessary to keep down weeds; investigations have shown that weeds markedly decrease the yields of beets. Continuous cultivation of a sandy loam in the absence of weeds slightly increased yields in some years, but decreased them in other years.

In general, the cultivation program will depend on the type of soil, the season in which the crop is grown, the character of the rainfall, and the prevalence of weeds. On light soils it is less necessary than on heavy soils. Seasons of heavy rainfall require more cultivation than seasons of light rainfall. Deep cultivation should not be practiced, because many of the roots are found near the surface of the soil.

Controlling Pests

Principal pests are leaf spot and scab, both fungus diseases; and insects, especially the webworm and the leaf miner, which is a white maggot. Cutworms and wireworms sometimes cause damage. All of these pests are controlled largely by practicing sanitation and rotation. Leaf miners can be controlled with malathion if applications are properly timed; webworms are best controlled with carbaryl.

Harvesting

Beets for market are harvested and bunched when they reach a diameter of from $1\frac{1}{4}$ to $1\frac{1}{2}$ inches. Many beets are now mechanically harvested and topped. The washed beets are prepackaged in transparent film bags for sale in retail stores. Such a practice extends the shelf life over that of beets with tops. Nearly all of the beets for processing are mechanically harvested with a machine that lifts, tops, and conveys the topped beets into trucks. Beets can be stored under proper conditions for relatively long periods of time, as can most of the root crops. Beets are also satisfactorily dehydrated.

HORSERADISH

Classification and Importance

Horseradish (*Armoracia rusticana*) is a well-known garden perennial in many long-established vegetable gardens. It is a near relative of cabbage, turnips, and mustard, belonging to the *Cruciferae* family. Horseradish is highly prized as an appetizing condiment with oysters and cold meats.

As a commercial crop, horseradish is grown in but few places. An area about St. Louis, Missouri, has long enjoyed distinction as the chief horseradish-growing district of the United States.

Soil and Cultural Requirements

The plant will survive in most soils except deep sterile sands and shallow heavy clays with a hardpan subsoil. Best crops are grown on rich, moist, deeply-tilled, friable loams of river bottoms.

Although a crop of horseradish will remove large amounts of nutrients from the soil, it does not require highly fertile soil. The plant has a long growing season and an extensive root system for absorbing nutrients. It is important, however, to have a continuous supply of nutrients and moisture during the summer months. A plant that has survived the summer in good shape will produce large roots in the fall.

Horseradish is grown from root crowns and root cuttings. Most commercial crops are grown from sets or root cuttings. As the crop is prepared for market (Fig. 27.3) during the autumn and winter, all branch roots as large as or larger than a lead pencil are saved as cuttings. Good cuttings are 6 or more inches long and fairly straight. The bottoms of the roots are given a slanting cut and the top ends a square cut, which facilitates the work of planting.

Commercial practices have been highly developed. The land for horseradish is deeply tilled and plots of uniform length and width are laid off side by side. Furrows 4 or 5 inches deep and 30 inches apart are laid off the long way of the plots. The sets are usually spaced about 1½ to 2 feet apart in the furrows. Experience has demonstrated that the sets are best planted with the tops all sloping in the direction that cultivation is to proceed. By slanting the plants opposite ways in adjoining plots, cultivation can proceed in one direction in one plot and in the opposite direction in the neighboring plot. The idea is to keep the cultivator from dragging out the sets.

In order to obtain straight merchantable roots, some growers remove the side roots early in the season. This is done by removing the soil and stripping off the side roots from the upper part of the main root. The soil is then replaced. This is usually done twice during the growing season.

Harvesting, Storing, and Marketing

Horseradish makes its best growth during the cool weather of autumn. Harvesting should not be started until such growth has taken place.

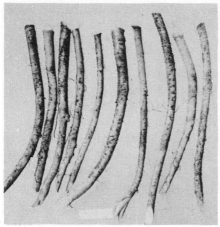

Fig. 27.3—(Above) Branch roots of horse-radish properly cut for propagation. (Right) A marketable root.

USDA Photograph

Digging is accomplished with a heavy plow. A furrow is run along the outside row of roots in the opposite direction from that used in cultivation. A second furrow in the same direction as the first turns the roots out with the furrow slice. The roots are then gathered and placed in pits or storage cellars, to be prepared for market. Pits, cool cellars, or barns will answer for holding the crop over winter, but roots to be held for summer use should be placed in cold storage.

Preparation for market may be done at any time during the winter when weather permits. The merchantable roots are tied in bundles after all lateral and bottom roots have been removed. The lateral roots suitable for sets are prepared as described above. Yields range from 3,000 to 6,000 pounds of salable roots per acre.

PARSNIP

Classification and History

The parsnip *(Pastinaca sativa)* is a native of Europe and Asia. It was brought to America by the early colonists. It is a member of the *Umbelliferae* family, which also includes carrots, celery, and parsley. The parsnip is a long-season crop that will withstand freezing weather if left in the field. The crop is not grown extensively. Pennsylvania, Illinois, California, and New York lead in its production.

Selecting Cultivars

Very few cultivars are listed in seed catalogues. The most popular are Hollow Crown and All American. Parsnip seed does not retain its viability for very long, so freshly grown seed should always be obtained.

Preparing the Soil

A deep, fertile soil is essential for successful production of this crop. Smooth roots and good stands are difficult to obtain on heavy soils. In general, the methods of soil preparation are similar to those for carrots or beets.

Planting

Parsnip seed is usually planted in rows ranging from 15 to 18 inches apart for hand cultivation or from 24 to 30 inches apart for tractor cultivation. A half ounce of seed is usually sufficient for a 100-foot row and 3 to 4 pounds is sufficient to plant an acre with rows 15 inches apart. Seed is covered ½ to ¾ inch deep. Plants are usually thinned to a stand of three to six per foot in the row. Parsnips grow during a long season and for this reason have a low fertilizer requirement.

Fertilizing

Commercial fertilizers should be applied at a rate slightly lower than is required for carrots under comparable conditions.

Cultivating

Cultivation for control of weeds should begin as early as possible. Parsnip plants develop slowly and are poor competitors with weeds. Weeding as well as cultivation is usually necessary. Much of the early cultivation is usually done with wheel hoes or small tractors. Shallow cultivation for control of weeds should continue until the leaves practically cover the ground.

Harvesting

The roots are usually left in the ground until late fall and sometimes throughout the winter. Where severe freezing occurs, it is not practical to leave the roots in the ground because of the difficulty in digging them when needed.

The roots attain a length of 10 to 12 inches and care must be exercised in digging so as not to break them. At the time of harvest the roots are high in starch which changes to sugar upon storage at low temperatures. Storage of the roots is a common practice; methods similar to those for other root crops are used.

RADISH

History and Classification

The writings of ancient naturalists indicate that the radish (*Raphanus sativus*) has been cultivated for a long time. Pliny records that it was extensively cultivated in Egypt at the time of the Pharaohs. The Greeks were especially fond of radishes and always served them on dishes of gold in their sacrificial offerings to Apollo. The radish was introduced into England and France about the beginning of the sixteenth century. In 1806, eleven sorts were known in America.

Plant Characteristics

The edible portion consists of both root and stem tissue, which varies greatly in color, size, shape, and texture of the flesh. Color varies from white to black. Size and shape are the most distinguishing characteristics.

According to investigations at the Nebraska Agricultural Experiment Station, the absorbing system is not very extensive. Though certain absorbing roots had a lateral spread of 12 to 16 inches, most of the roots were 2 to 8 inches long. Radishes can be cultivated 2 inches deep with little damage to the root system.

The stem is a short crown, and when the plant produces seed, the stem elongates and bears perfect, insect-pollinated flowers and podded fruits. Some cultivars bear flowers and seed the first year, while others bear seed the second year; hence the radish is either an annual or a biennial. With the annual cultivars, flowering is apparently controlled by the length of the day. The Scarlet Globe, an important commercial cultivar, was grown under a 7-hour day at Washington, D.C., in the spring; other lots were grown under a 12-hour day. The plants subjected to the 7-hour day produced a large, overgrown root, while those subjected to a 12-hour day produced flowers and seeds. The leaves, which arise in a rosette, are simple and lobed and vary in size according to the cultivar.

Temperature Requirements

The radish is a hardy, cool-season crop which withstands subfreezing temperatures. Certain cultivars, particularly the spring cultivars, become pithy and pungent in hot weather.

Selecting Cultivars

Cultivars are classified according to the length of time needed for the roots to attain maturity and the shape of the root. There are (1) the spring cultivars, (2) the summer cultivars, and (3) the winter cultivars. Within each of the three maturity groups, long and globe-shaped cultivars are to be had. The spring cultivars grow quickly, mature in a relatively short time (20 to 30 days), and the root remains in an edible condition for a short time only. The summer cultivars grow less quickly, mature in a relatively longer time (35 to 40 days), and the roots remain in an edible condition longer. The winter cultivars grow slowly (50 to 60 days), attain a larger size, and can be stored readily.

The most popular spring cultivars are globe-shaped and bright red in color. Some of the best are Early Scarlet Globe, Cherry Belle, and Comet Cavalier. Long-rooted spring types include White Icicle, Cincinnati Market, and Long Scarlet Short Top. Typical summer cultivars are White Strasburg and White Vienna, which are long types. Summer cultivars are not grown to any extent in this country. The most popular winter cultivars are Chinese White Winter (Celestial, California Mammoth White), Chinese Rose Winter (Scarlet China), Round Black Spanish, and Long Black Spanish. Commercial varietal types are shown in Fig. 27.4.

Selecting and Preparing Soils

In general, radishes produce satisfactory crops on well-drained, moderately to slightly acid sandy loams, loams, and clay loams, the type of loam depending on the type of radish grown. Muck soils are used in some areas. Sandy loams are preferred for spring market crops, while well-drained silt and clay loams are preferred for the summer and winter sorts. The soil must be thoroughly prepared and the surface smooth in order to obtain uniform depth of planting.

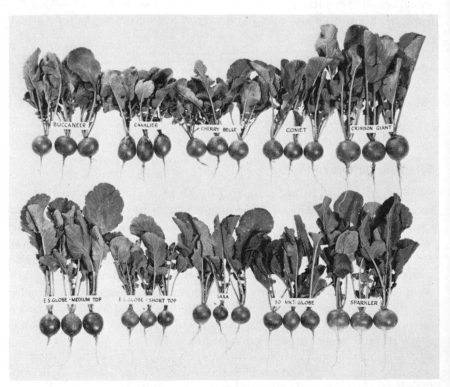

Fig. 27.4—Common cultivars of radish.

Associated Seed Growers

Fertilizing

A rich fertile soil is necessary for rapid growth. Usually 1,000 pounds of 5-10-10 or a similar fertilizer is applied broadcast before seeding. Less fertilizer is needed if the crop follows one that has been heavily fertilized.

Planting

Plantings in the North are started very early in the spring. Winter plantings are common in the South. To obtain successive harvests, seed usually is planted at about 10-day intervals. Spacing of harvests can also be obtained by careful selection of cultivars. Seed is drilled from ½ to ¾ inch in rows 12 to 18 inches apart at the rate of 10 to 12 pounds per acre to obtain a stand of about 12 to 18 plants per foot. In the West two rows are planted per bed with seeding at the rate of three to four seeds per inch. Some seed is also sown broadcast. The larger-growing winter types are usually thinned to a stand of four to six plants per foot. Grading seed to a uniform size is a good commercial practice to obtain a uniform seeding rate.

Harvesting and Marketing

Harvesting operations consist of pulling, topping, washing, grading, bunching, and packing. All small, diseased, and cracked roots are discarded. Bunching is frequently done in the field but the practice is seldom practiced except for local market. Long-rooted cultivars are bunched in fours and fives, while round and globular-rooted cultivars are tied in bunches of 6 to 12. Baskets, hampers, and crates are the principal containers. For long-distance shipment, cracked ice is placed in the middle and top of the containers, and the radishes are shipped under refrigeration. Winter radishes are handled and stored in much the same way as are turnips. A large portion of the commercial acreage is now harvested by machine. Several types of machines are used. One lifts, tops, and drops the radishes in containers. Others only lift the radishes, and the topping is done in a packing shed. The topped radishes are washed and packaged in transparent film bags. Nearly all radishes are prepackaged for the retail trade.

RUTABAGA

The rutabaga (*Brassica campestris* var. *napobrassica*), sometimes called Swede turnip, closely resembles the turnip. Distinguishing characteristics between the two crops are given in Table 27.2.

Table 27.2—Rutabaga and Turnip Characteristics.

Parts Compared	Turnip Characteristics	Rutabaga Characteristics
Leaves	Green and hairy	Grayish green and nonhairy
Crown	Indistinct	Distinct
Root	Small	Large

The cultural requirements of the rutabaga are similar to those of the turnip. The crop is widely grown in Canada and is grown commercially in Minnesota, Wisconsin, and Washington. It is generally planted in June and harvested in October and November. The roots are trimmed, washed, and waxed for market. The American Purple Top cultivar is most commonly grown.

TURNIP

Classification and History

The turnip (*Brassica rapa*) is a native of Siberia. It was grown in olden times and introduced into England about 1550. It was brought to America by the early colonists. Turnips are grown both for greens and for the fleshy roots. The turnip is most extensively grown in the South.

Plant Characteristics

The turnip develops an extensive and finely branched root system. Studies at the Nebraska Agricultural Experiment Station have shown that plants three weeks old have deep roots 2 feet long. Plants 41 days old have roots which extend to the 3-foot level. The leaves, which arise in the form of a rosette, are simple, grass-green, and hairy. Seed is small, reddish black, and germinates quickly. The turnip is primarily a cool-season crop, hence it is grown in the fall, winter, and early spring in the South, and in the spring or fall in the North.

Selecting Cultivars

Two groups exist, the white-fleshed group and the yellow-fleshed group. The white-fleshed group is more extensively grown. Within this group there are (1) cultivars grown primarily for the top and (2) those grown primarily for the root. Japanese Shogoin is the most important cultivar grown for greens. Seven Top, an old cultivar, is still grown, but the roots are woody and of poor quality. The principal white cultivars grown for the root are Purple Top White Globe, White Flat Dutch, White Milan, and Crawford. Some yellow-fleshed cultivars are Yellow Globe, Golden Ball, and Yellow Aberdeen.

Preparing the Soil

Turnips thrive well on moist well-drained, moderately to slightly acid sandy loams and loams. Preparation of the soil in the manner recommended for beets will give satisfactory results with turnips. Actually, however, turnips are not as exacting as either beets or carrots. Both germination and seedling growth are rapid. Heavy fertilization to stimulate rapid development is essential for the spring crop, but not so important in the fall.

Planting

Seed is planted either by hand or by machine, at the rate of 2 or 3 pounds per acre. Rows are spaced from 12 to 15 inches apart for hand cultivation and about 24 inches apart for tractor cultivation. Seed is covered about ½ inch deep.

Cultivation

The cultivation program is similar to that of other root crops. The first or second cultivation may be relatively deep, but succeeding cultivations should be shallow.

Controlling Pests

The diseases and insects that attack turnips are usually the same as or very similar to those on cabbage, and these are discussed in Chapters 11 and 16.

Harvesting, Packing, and Marketing

Preparing turnip roots for market consists of (1) pulling, (2) grading, (3) bunching or topping, and (4) washing. Pulling is done by hand, and yellow, diseased, or injured leaves are removed. If bunched, four to six plants are tied together and washed to remove adhering soil. Most of the roots are now topped and packed for retail sale in transparent film bags. Beet harvesters are frequently used for the purpose of lifting and topping.

When the tops of turnips are harvested as greens, they are either picked or cut by hand or cut by improvised machines. Turnip greens may be graded and packed or sold in bulk. The root crops are marketed much the same as other vegetables. Quality and uniformity of cultivar, grade, color, and size are important in the market and consumers' acceptance of these vegetables.

Volume buyers prefer to purchase from areas which can provide standard grades in sufficient quantities for economical transportation.

SELECTED REFERENCES

Anonymous, "Commercial Growing of Horseradish," USDA Leaflet 547, 1970.

Anonymous, "Growing Parsnips," USDA Leaflet 545, 1967.

Anonymous, "Growing Root Crops for Processing," Asgrow Seed Co., Orange, Conn., 1967.

Anonymous, "Growing Table Beets," USDA L 360, 1976.

Anonymous, "Pest and Control Program for Vegetable Root Crops," Calif. Agr. Ext. Ser. Pub., 1975 (issued annually).

Anonymous, "Yam Production Methods," USDA, PRR 147, 1973.

Bohnenblust, K. E., and McAnelly, C. W., "Potatoes for the Home Garden," Univ. of Wyo. Agr. Exp. Sta. Bull. B–631, 1975.

Duncan, A. A., "Spinach, Beet, Swiss Chard and Mangel Production," Ore. Exp. Ext. Scr. FS–87, 1965.

Hall, Harwood, Wada, Susan, and Voss, R. E., "Growing Root Crops," Univ. of Calif. Agr. Sci. Leaflet 2928, 1976.

Merkley, D. R., "New Gardening Varieties," (Including Root Crops), Mont. Agr. Exp. Sta. Pub. 16, 1978.

Murray, Judy, "Radishes," United Fresh Fruit and Vegetable Assoc., Alexandria, Va., 1977.

Neild, R. E., "Growing Table Beets," Univ. of Neb. Ext. Ser. Leaflet G–15–250, 1975.

Neild, R. E., "Radishes," Univ. of Neb. Ext. Ser. Leaflet G–74–85, 1974.

Seelig, R. A., "Turnips," United Fresh Fruit and Vegetable Assoc., Alexandria, Va., 1973.

CHAPTER 28

Spinach

CLASSIFICATION, ORIGIN, AND HISTORY

Spinach (*Spinacia oleracea*) belongs to the *Chenopodiaceae* family which includes the beet and chard. Spinach was first introduced into Europe in the thirteenth or fourteenth century, coming from Asia, where it originated, by way of Africa. The date of its introduction to the United States is unknown, but records indicate it was commonly grown in the early nineteenth century.

SCOPE AND IMPORTANCE

Although cultivated for generations, spinach attained commercial importance relatively late. It is highly recommended in the diet and remains an important but declining vegetable crop as greens. Spinach ranked twentieth in acreage and twenty-first in value among the 22 principal vegetables in 1977.

Fresh market spinach acreage declined from 60,010 acres in 1949 to 26,500 acres in 1959 and down to 9,920 acres in 1977. Although acre yields increased substantially between 1949 and 1977, production declined from 2,667,000 hundredweight to 812,000 hundredweight, and value increased from $13,050,000 to $13,746,000 during the 28-year 1949 to 1977 period.

Spinach harvested for processing also decreased from 40,140 acres in 1949, to 32,330 acres in 1959, and then to about 20,600 acres in 1977. Concurrently, acre yield almost doubled and total production increased from 117,100 tons in 1949 to 147,820 tons in 1959 and 153,700 tons in 1977. In those same years values rose from $4,850,000 to $5,531,000 and $10,600,000.

Tables 28.1 and 28.2 present the relative importance of the different states in fresh and processing spinach acreage, production, and value in 1977. Table 28.2 also shows the relative percentage of frozen and canned processed spinach. Both fresh and processing spinach totaled 30,520 acres in 1977, with a combined production of 3,886,000 hundredweight valued at $24,346,000. Although the consumption of spinach is declining, it is still an important vegetable on most tables (Fig. 28.1).

Table 28.1—Spinach for Fresh Market: Harvest Season and Estimated Acreage, Yield, Production, and Value in Leading States, 1977.

State	Harvest Season	Harvested Acreage	Yield per Acre, Cwt.	Production per 1,000 Cwt.	Price per Cwt.	Value, $1,000
Texas	Winter	2,200	58	128	$21.70	2,778
Maryland and Virginia	Spring	1,880	39	73	20.00	1,459
Texas	Fall	1,200	39	47	16.80	790
Colorado	Summer	860	70	60	22.60	1,356
California	Winter	800	165	132	14.20	1,874
California	Spring	700	160	112	10.90	1,221
California	Fall	700	150	105	12.80	1,344
California	Summer	600	145	87	15.90	1,383
New Jersey	Spring	560	73	41	17.70	726
New Jersey	Fall	420	65	27	30.20	815
United States		9,920	82	812	16.90	13,746
Total	Spring (32%)	3,140	72	226	15.10	3,406
Total	Winter (30%)	3,000	87	260	17.90	4,652
Total	Fall (23%)	2,320	77	179	16.50	2,949
Total	Summer (15%)	1,460	101	147	18.60	2,739

TRENDS IN PRODUCTION EFFICIENCY

Production and harvest costs per acre of spinach are low, primarily because of highly mechanized practices. Spinach requires less labor than any crop except green peas and sweet corn for processing. From 1939 to 1959, labor requirements decreased from 124 to 32 man-hours per acre and to 18 by 1977 for the fresh market crop. During the 1939 to 1954 period, labor output per acre dropped from 83 to 22 man-hours per acre for processed spinach, which is harvested entirely by machines and hauled in bulk to processing plants.

Table 28.2—Spinach for Processing: Harvest Season and Estimated Acreage, Yield, Production, and Value in Leading States, 1977.

State	Harvest Season	Harvested Acreage	Yield per Acre, Tons	Production in Tons	Price per Cwt.	Value, $1,000
California	Winter	9,000	10.21	91,900	$63.90	5,872
Arkansas	Spring	2,100	4.67	9,800	80.70	791
Oklahoma	Spring	1,800	4.50	8,100	80.00	648
Arkansas	Fall	240	4.58	1,100	90.00	99
Oklahoma	Fall	180	4.17	750	90.70	68
Other States	Winter	4,000	5.11	20,450	98.00	1,596
Other States	Spring	2,260	6.44	14,550	69.60	1,013
Other States	Fall	1,020	6.91	7,050	72.80	513
United States		20,600	7.46	153,700	69.00	10,600
Freezing	Winter (35%)	7,150	9.93	71,000	62.50	4,441
Freezing	Spring (10%)	2,160	6.00	12,950	71.80	930
Freezing	Fall (4%)	910	6.32	5,750	80.30	462
Canning	Winter (28%)	5,850	7.07	41,350	73.20	3,027
Canning	Spring (20%)	4,000	4.88	19,500	78.10	1,522
Canning	Fall (3%)	530	5.94	3,150	69.20	218

Between 1939 and 1977, average acre yields of spinach for fresh market almost doubled from 46 to 82 hundredweight while the unit output per man-hour enjoyed a spectacular increase of 1,232 percent. Correspondingly, spinach for processing increased from 54 to 373 hundredweight per acre, and the unit increase per man-hour exceeded that of any other vegetable crop. Man output per hour may continue to increase with improved machines and cultural practices.

CLIMATIC REQUIREMENTS

Spinach is essentially a hardy, cool-season crop. When fairly well hardened, it has survived temperatures of 20° F. or lower without suffering injury. High temperatures and especially long days cause spinach to bolt to seed, thus destroying its market value. In general, it is a short-season crop, maturing in 6 to 10 weeks, depending on climatic conditions.

SELECTING CULTIVARS AND SEED

Market demand, earliness, disease resistance, tendency to bolt to seed,

Fig. 28.1—Spinach can add zest to many dishes.

United Fresh Fruit and Vegetable Association Photograph

and time of the year to be planted are factors which need to be considered in selecting a cultivar.

Cultivars

Cultivars have been classified into either prickly-seeded or smooth-seeded groups, and also into savoy-leaf (wrinkled) or flat-leaf groups. Most commercial cultivars are now smooth-seeded, which are much easier to handle and to plant accurately. Cultivars with savoyed leaves are usu-ally preferred for market, while flat-leaved types are preferred for processing, primarily because the leaves are easier to wash. Recently, semi-savoyed types have been used for both processing and market.

Some cultivars are more resistant to bolting to seed than others, and are called "long standing." These should be used for plants maturing during long days. High yielding F_1 hybrids are now in production. These hybrids and those soon to be released are expected to replace cultivars now used in many areas of commercial production. The important characteristics of a selected list of important cultivars are found in Table 28.3.

Securing Seed

Most of the seed used by American growers comes from Europe (chiefly Holland). Relatively small amounts are also grown in California and in the Puget Sound district. Lower production costs favor the European grower. It pays to buy seed from a reliable seedsman who makes it a practice to supply high-quality seed.

PREPARING THE SEEDBED AND FERTILIZING

Soil Preferences

Spinach grows well on a wide range of soils, but it yields best on a heavy loam. In southwest Texas, much of the spinach is grown on well-drained alluvial soils, silt and clay loams, but sandy loams also are used fairly widely. In Virginia, there are large acreages of spinach on sandy and gravelly loams. Sandy soils are desired for winter and early spring crops. Muck soils are used in the North for main crop and processing spinach. A soil should have good drainage and if possible be well supplied with organic matter.

Breaking and Conditioning

Land to be planted to spinach should be put in a condition of good tilth, which requires that it be plowed at least 8 inches deep and harrowed thoroughly. In irrigated sections, it may be necessary to level the seedbed so that the water will flow evenly.

Fertilizing

General recommendations for fertilization are difficult to make be-

Table 28.3—Important Characteristics of a Selected List of Important Cultivars of Spinach.

Cultivar	Chief Use*	Season (Days)	Long-standing	Leaf Type	Resistance to			
					Heat	Cold	Mosaic	Mildew
Bloomsdale Dark Green	H, M, S, C, F	40	Med.	Savoy	No	Med.	No	No
Bloomsdale Long Standing	H, M, S, C, F	42	Yes	Heavy Savoy	Fair	Med.	No	No
Bounty	M	42	Yes	Semi-Savoy	No	Good	Yes	Yes
Chesapeake Hybrid	F	40	No	Semi-Savoy	No	Med.	Yes	No
Dixie Market	M, C, F	37	Med.	Savoy	—	Med.	Yes	Yes
Hybrid 7	H, M, S, C, F	39	No	Semi-Savoy	No	Med.	Yes	Yes
Hybrid 424	H	38	Med.	Smooth	—	Med.	—	Yes
Hybrid 612	M	43	No	Savoy	—	Med.	Yes	Yes
Packer	M, C	39	Yes	Savoy	—	Good	—	Yes
Seven R Hybrid	C, F	37	No	Semi-Savoy	No	Exc.	Yes	Yes
Viking	S, C, F	45	Yes	Smooth	Fair	Med.	No	Yes
Virginia Savoy	M, S, C, F	39	No	Savoy	No	Med.	Yes	Yes
Viroflay	C	45	No	Smooth	No	Med.	No	No

*—Home; M—Market; S—Shipping; C—Canning; F—Freezing.

cause spinach is grown on widely varying types and fertility of soils. In the West profitable returns have been given by nitrogen applications alone. In eastern areas, relatively heavy applications of 1,200 to 1,500 pounds per acre of a mixture containing 7 to 10 percent nitrogen, 14 to 16 percent phosphorus, and 3 to 5 percent potassium have given good results. Higher proportions of potassium are recommended for the eastern peat and muck areas. Methods of applying fertilizer vary. Often fertilizers are broadcast and worked into the soil before planting. More frequently on lighter soils split applications are made.

On boron-deficient soils increased yields may be obtained by applying commercial borax at the rate of 10 pounds per acre. Broadcast applications should be worked into the soil before the seed is sown. Boron should not be used as a general practice, but only where a known need for the material has been demonstrated.

Liming

Experimental results indicate that spinach is very sensitive to acid conditions and will not thrive on soils more acid than pH 5.5. Plants grown on soils with reactions below pH 5.0 usually show severe injury. Normally, for spinach to make optimum growth, a soil should range between pH 6.0 and pH 7.0. Unfavorable acid conditions can be corrected successfully by liming the soil. Applications of 1 ton per acre of hydrated lime on two sandy loams, one with pH 4.6, the other with pH 4.7, greatly increased the yield of spinach. Where the soil was strongly acid, heavier applications increased yields still further. In spite of the response to liming, the practice can be overdone.

The spinach soils in Texas have a reaction of about pH 7.0 (neutral) with a tendency towards higher pH, rather than lower. Liming is unnecessary under average conditions in the Southwest.

Manuring

The relative scarcity and the high cost of barnyard manure make its use prohibitive to the average spinach grower, even though its addition is beneficial. Green manuring is becoming more common among Texas spinach growers. However, preliminary experiments at the Texas Agricultural Experiment Station indicate that such manures plowed under a short time ahead of spinach will not increase yields materially, if at all. A legume green-manure crop incorporated in the soil fully a year ahead of the spinach crops seems most feasible.

PLANTING, CULTIVATING, AND IRRIGATING

Planting

In the extreme South, and in areas of California and Arizona, spinach is planted at any time from September until early February. In more northerly sections very early plantings are made for spring harvests, or the crop may be wintered over after being planted in the fall. Spinach planted in late summer is harvested in the fall. In certain areas of the North as well as in some of the Pacific Coast, the crop is grown throughout the summer.

The rate of seeding varies greatly, depending somewhat on the spacing but to a greater extent on the section of the country and local experience. In the northerly sections of the South, seed is drilled at rates ranging from 12 to 20 pounds per acre, 15 pounds being an average rate. This could perhaps be reduced by seed treatment. In Texas, when the seed is broadcast, 8 to 10 pounds per acre is more normal, and even 8 pounds may give too thick a stand.

Row planting has long been an established practice in most sections. Rows in Texas are usually either 14 or 16 inches apart and may be flat or raised on low ridges according to the method of irrigation. In Virginia, spinach is planted on broad, slightly raised beds on which there are usually five to six rows 8 to 10 inches apart. Spinach is usually planted about ½ to ¾ inch deep, depending on the method of planting and soil conditions. The furrow between the beds provides ideal drainage.

Thinning and Cultivating

In most areas, commercial crops are not thinned. A correct stand is best obtained by using good, fresh, viable, treated seed and accurate seeding rates. The plants should be spaced 3 to 6 inches apart in the row.

Spinach does not compete well with weeds, and the harvesting operations are complicated by them. Whenever spinach is planted in rows, shallow cultivation is usually practiced. Frequent cultivation in the absence of weeds is unnecessary. Herbicides, such as Furloe and vegedex, have been used successfully with spinach in certain areas. It may be used alone or in combination with cultivation.

Irrigating

The spinach plant has a relatively shallow root system and thrives best in a uniformly moist soil. In the irrigated sections of the Southwest, irrigation is one of the major concerns of the spinach grower. The first irrigation immediately follows planting. This irrigation will frequently bring up the crop, but sometimes a second application is necessary within three or four days if the soil dries too quickly. Between emergence and harvesting, one to three irrigations are usually required, depending on soil and climatic conditions. Experiments at the Texas Experiment Station show that overirrigation of spinach will definitely reduce yields.

Fields are irrigated either by flooding (border method) or by the furrow method. In the former method the rows are flat, while in the latter they are on low, raised ridges. Spinach can also be irrigated by the sprinkler method.

CONTROLLING DISEASES AND INSECTS

Diseases

Spinach is subject to a number of diseases, including damping off, mosaic, downy mildew, and fusarium wilt. It is seldom that all of these are injurious in any given region on the same crop.

DAMPING OFF. Damping off and closely related rots of germinating seeds are largely responsible for poor stands and for the necessity in the past of high rates of seeding.

The disease can be controlled by seed treatment. To get rapid germination with a minimum of decay, the seed should be soaked for 24 hours, dried, and dusted with thiram (0.75 percent) or captan (1 percent). Planting should then be done without delay.

MOSAIC. Mosaic, commonly known as blight, or yellows, is caused by the cucumber mosaic virus. It is widespread and sometimes causes serious losses. In the early stages of the disease, the young center leaves turn yellow and cease to grow. Later, all growth stops and the larger leaves become mottled and even turn brown and die. It has been shown that insects, especially aphids, carry the disease from plant to plant. The most practical method of control is to grow resistant cultivars (see Table 28.3).

DOWNY MILDEW. Downy mildew, caused by *Peronospora effusa* and known as blue mold, may cause serious losses in foggy or rainy weather.

The disease first appears on the underside of the leaves, where irregular patches of grayish mycelia will be found. Later the upper surface of the leaves turns yellowish. Under favorable conditions, the disease spreads rapidly, and whole fields of spinach are quickly ruined. Resistant cultivars and hybrids are now available that effectively control the disease (see Table 28.3). When the disease does appear, it can be held down with zineb or maneb sprays.

FUSARIUM WILT. Fusarium wilt, caused by *Fusarium solani,* may be troublesome either in early fall or in late spring plantings. The fungus can live for several years in the soil. Young plants, if attacked, remain stunted, and old plants wilt and rarely recover. Air temperatures above 72° F. or soil temperatures above 70° F. at the depth of 2 inches favor spread of the disease. Growing spinach during cool weather and crop rotation are the only known means of practical control.

CURLY-TOP. Curly-top, a virus carried by the beet leaf hopper, causes the young leaves to become crinkled, deformed, and reduced in size. The plants usually turn yellow and die. Control can only be effected by controlling the insect vector, since nothing can be done after the plant is infected.

HETEROSPORIUM LEAF SPOT. Heterosporium leaf spot, a widely distributed fungus disease, may injure the crop severely. The disease first appears as small brown spots that increase in size and number on both sides of the leaf. It is most severe on winter crops grown under cold, wet conditions. No definite control measures are recommended.

Insects

Any blemishes such as those of insect damage on spinach leaves would make the crop unsalable. Furthermore, aphids spread diseases. Consequently, insects should be controlled before any damage has been done.

APHIDS. Aphids *(Myzus persicae)* or plant lice sometimes cause serious damage to spinach by sucking the juice from the foliage and by transmitting the mosaic disease from infected plants to healthy ones. Because the spinach plants grow close to the ground in a more or less compact rosette, control by dusting or spraying is not easy. Success in aphid control is dependent upon dusting or spraying when the infestation is small. Malathion is currently in use.

SPINACH LEAF MINERS. Spinach leaf miners (*Pegomyia hyoseyami*) damage spinach by feeding inside the leaves between the two leaf surfaces. The entire leaf may be destroyed or otherwise rendered unfit for marketing. Diazinon has been proved effective in certain areas if applied when the first miners' tunnels are seen. Crop rotation and destruction of crop residue will aid in their control.

OTHER INSECTS. Insects such as seed corn maggots, grasshoppers, and flea beetles may occasionally cause damage. Leaf hoppers may carry the curly-top virus and can be controlled with applications of carbaryl.

HARVESTING, GRADING, AND MARKETING

Harvesting

The time of harvesting depends on the market as well as the size of the plant. When the price is high, growers may harvest medium-sized plants having only five to seven fully matured leaves, but if the price is low, the plants will probably be allowed to continue growing. After a seed stalk begins to form, a spinach plant is no longer marketable; hence, high value is attached to long-standing cultivars.

The harvesting period in the extreme South extends from early November to April of the following year; in more northerly sections, it occurs only during the fall, spring, and early summer. More than one cutting can be made in the same field, if only the large plants are taken.

Spinach plants are harvested for market by cutting the tap root at the soil surface, with various kinds of knives, hoes, or cutting implements. Unsightly and dead leaves should be removed. Trimming may be done in the field as the plants are cut, or in packing sheds. Spinach sometimes has to be washed, but before long-distance shipping such a practice should be avoided, if possible, as it hastens decay. Plants harvested for market are usually allowed to wilt slightly before hauling, in order to minimize the breakage of the leaves.

Spinach for processing should be cut about an inch above the surface of the soil. Mechanical harvesters have been developed for this operation. More than one harvest can be made from plants that have been cut above

Fig. 28.2—Spinach treated with gibberellic acid to increase height for mechanical harvesting. (Top left) 20 ppm. (Top right) 10 ppm. (Bottom) Control.

the growing point under short-day conditions. Spinach grown for manufacture is trimmed at the processing plant.

Grading

Spinach is commonly graded in accordance with the standards set up by the federal-state inspection service. A certificate signed by an official inspector assures both the seller and the buyer that the product at the time of shipment was a certain grade. The grades applying to spinach change slightly from time to time, and it is well to obtain periodically the latest rulings direct from the U.S. Department of Agriculture. Because of the nature of a spinach plant, all grading has to be done by hand, and hence it is often done as the plants are harvested.

Packing

Spinach for market is packed in bushel baskets, hampers, and crates. For long-distance shipping, a shovelful of ice (approximately 10 pounds) is packed in the upper portion of each basket just before it is put in the car or refrigerated truck. The car is also iced or refrigerated.

Marketing

Spinach is marketed in much the same manner as other vegetables. Volume buyers prefer to purchase from standard packing sheds or assembly points. That portion of the crop which is stored usually is not held in cold storage for more than 10 days. This commodity is moved to market under cool or refrigerated conditions, principally by trucks.

Consumers prefer clean, stem-trimmed spinach in standard-sized cellophane bags so they can inspect the product. The sealed transparent packages help to prevent the spinach from wilting and allow gaseous exchange for the maintenance of quality.

EXPORTS AND IMPORTS. Since spinach exports are included in "other vegetables" in Table 13.2, the amount of exports which formerly went to Canada, Kuwait, and various other countries was not determined.

SELECTED REFERENCES

Anonymous, "Pest and Disease Control Program for Lettuce, Spinach and Celery," Calif. Agr. Ext. Ser. Pub., 1975 (issued annually).

Anonymous, "Spinach, Beet, Swiss Chard, and Mangel Seed Production," Ore. Exp. Sta. FS-87.

Bowers, J. L., Vose, H. H., and McFerran, J., "Turnip Greens and Spinach: Cultural and Fertilizer Studies," Ark. Agr. Exp. Sta. Bull. 654, 1962.

Longbrake, T., et al., "Keys to Profitable Spinach Production," Texas A & M Univ. Coop. Ext. Ser. Fact Sheet L–1076, 1973.

Neild, R. E., "Spinach and Swiss Chard," Univ. of Neb. Coop. Ext. Ser. G 74–84, 1974.

O'Brien, M. J., and Winters, H. F., "Evaluation of Selected Spinach Accessions for Resistance to Fusarium oxysporum F.," Plant Dis. Rep. 62(5): 427-429, 1978.

Sackett, C., "Spinach," United Fresh Fruit and Veg. Assoc., Alexandria, Va.

Schales, F. D., "Collards, Kale and Spinach," Va. Poly. Inst. VPS Pub. 153, 1968.

Wiggins, S. C., Marshall, C. E., and Odell, G. V., "Cultural Studies with Spinach," Okla. Agr. Exp. Sta. Bull. B–606, 1963.

Yao, Benita C., and Geisman, J. R., "Removal of Malathion from Spinach by Commercial and Home Preparation Procedures," Ohio Agr. Res. Circ. 188., 1972.

CHAPTER 29

Sweet Potatoes

CLASSIFICATION, ORIGIN, AND HISTORY

The sweet potato (*Ipomoea Batatas*) is a native of Central and South America and belongs to the morning-glory family, *Convolvulaceae*. Early explorers carried it to Spain and other subtropical and tropical countries, and the earliest writers mentioned different cultivars and colors. The sweet potato has been grown in Virginia for nearly 300 years. The name "batatas" was used by the Indians in referring to this vegetable. The term "yam," as commonly used in the South, usually refers to the more moist-fleshed varieties, although there is a different group of plants known as yams.

SCOPE AND IMPORTANCE

The sweet potato is grown extensively in the South. It is the great carbohydrate food crop of the southern states, corresponding to the Irish or white potato in more northern sections. Unlike the Irish potato it was not extensively shipped until the development of proper storage.

Although the sweet potato has declined in popularity over the years, it ranked ninth in acreage and eleventh in value of the 22 principal vegetable crops in 1977. Sweet potato acreage declined from 472,000 acres in 1949 to 256,600 acres in 1959 and 112,400 acres in 1977. Acre yields almost doubled between 1949 and 1977. Production decreased from 24,804,000 to 12,395,000 hundredweight for the corresponding period. Farm value increased from $96,377,000 in 1949 to $110,142,000 in 1977.

The approximate geographical acreage distribution and the 1949 to

Fig. 29.1—Acreage, distribution, production, and value of sweet potatoes.

UNITED STATES TOTAL

Year	Acreage	Production 1,000 Cwt.	Value, $1,000
1949	472,000	24,804	96,377
1959	256,600	18,865	62,253
1969	136,900	14,370	60,642
1977	112,400	12,395	110,142

1977 performance of sweet potatoes are shown in Figure 29.1. Acreage, production, and value in 1977 are presented by states in Table 29.1. North Carolina excelled in acreage, production, and value, followed by Louisiana.

TRENDS IN PRODUCTION EFFICIENCY

Sweet potatoes are comparatively expensive to produce. Costs for sets, fertilizer, and cultural and harvesting practices are considerable. Labor saving machines have increased the efficiency of production and harvesting appreciably. Man-hour requirements were reduced from 118 to 96 man-hours per acre between 1939 and 1959 and lowered to 55 man-hours by 1977. Acre yields more than doubled during this period and the output per man-hour rose more than 518 percent between 1939 and 1977

Table 29.1—Sweet Potatoes for Fresh Market: Estimated Acreage, Yield, Production, and Value of Sales in Leading States, 1977.

State	Harvested Acreage	Yield per Acre, Cwt.	Production per 1,000 Cwt.	Price per Cwt.	Value, $1,000
N. Carolina	33,000	135	4,455	$ 9.20	34,086
Louisiana	27,000	90	2,430	7.27	15,558
Texas	9,500	95	903	14.80	11,470
Mississippi	8,000	85	680	9.20	5,078
California	7,800	150	1,170	16.90	18,066
Virginia	5,600	125	700	8.65	5,233
Georgia	5,500	90	495	14.10	5,753
Alabama	5,300	85	451	12.90	4,347
Tennessee	2,800	100	280	9.70	2,037
New Jersey	2,400	105	252	14.60	3,227
S. Carolina	2,300	91	209	12.10	2,057
Maryland	1,600	155	248	10.60	2,417
Arkansas	1,600	76	122	9.35	813
United States	112,400	110	12,395	10.50	110,142

(Table 1.6). Increasing efficiency is anticipated with improved machines and methods of production.

CLIMATIC REQUIREMENTS

The sweet potato thrives in the warmer portions of the United States from New Jersey to Texas. It can be grown under irrigation, although it is considered a drouth-resistant plant. Irrigation water is best applied before the vines cover the ground, as late applications may result in excessive vine growth. The leaves, vines, and the entire plant are easily injured by frost.

Sweet potato production is best in areas with 175 frost-free days, although the more northern producing centers have as little as four months. Warm nights and plenty of sunshine increase growth, which continues to increase with temperatures up to 95° F.

SELECTING CULTIVARS AND SEED

Cultivars

Sweet potatoes that are used for human consumption have been referred to as "food types." These may be divided into soft-fleshed and firm-fleshed cultivars. The former are sweeter and softer when cooked.

Important attributes for food types are attractiveness of skin and flesh colors, uniformity of root shape, pleasing flavor and texture of flesh, high vitamin and nutritional value, and productiveness. High-yielding capacity, high-percent solids and carbohydrates, including starch content and recovery, and superior propagative and storage properties are important in cultivars for feed and industrial uses.

Some of the soft-fleshed cultivars include Centennial, Georgia Red, Goldrush, Jasper, Nemagold, Porto Rico (Fig. 29.2), Rose Centennial, Jewel, and N. C. Porto Rico 198. Suggested firm-fleshed cultivars include Big Stem Jersey, Little Stem Jersey, Orlis, Nugget, and Yellow Jersey. Leading nonfood cultivars are Pelican Processor and Whitestar.

Securing Seed

If high yields of uniform, marketable potatoes are desired, only well-selected seed should be used, as unselected seed is often mixed in cultivar if not in type. Unless the local supply is known to be free from diseases and insects, certified seed should be purchased. Sporting or mutation is not very common, but may cause considerable variation. Hill selections can be used in maintaining type and to secure seed free from disease.

PREPARING THE SOIL

Soil Preferences

It is generally agreed that a sandy-loam soil with a clay subsoil is best for sweet potatoes. Roots from such a soil tend to be smooth and not too large. Silt loams usually give good results, but heavy clay loams do not. Roots grown in such soils are usually rough and irregular in shape. Very light deep soils tend to produce long slender roots. Good drainage is essential for growing sweet potatoes. A soil more acid than pH 5.0 should be limed to bring the reaction within the desirable range of pH 5.2 to pH 6.7.

Preparing the Soil

A fair crop of sweet potatoes can be grown on carelessly prepared soil, but thorough preparation will usually give larger yields and reduce labor later. The soil should be plowed and worked down about the same

Fig. 29.2—A hill of Porto Rico sweet potatoes.

USDA Photograph

as for corn and similar crops. Then the land is generally allowed to lie several days before being put into condition for planting. A large part of the crop is planted on ridges made up several days before planting. The tops of the ridges are rolled or dragged off at planting time. A low flat ridge is more desirable than a narrow high one, as the latter dries out badly. Level culture has some advantages on sandy, well-drained soils.

FERTILIZING AND MANURING

Fertilizing

The New Jersey station found that potassium had a striking influence on the shape of the Jersey type of sweet potato when grown on sandy soil. In similar experiments at the Tennessee station on clay loam soils, potassium had no appreciable effect on shape except where the soil was of very low fertility. In general, late planting and an excess of nitrogen tend to produce long slender roots that mature late. Early planting and an abundance of potassium tend to produce early-maturing chunky potatoes.

According to Table 6.4, the sweet potato can be expected to respond to 30 to 45 pounds of nitrogen (N) per acre, depending on soil type. In Table 6.5, the sweet potato is placed in Group II according to its requirements for phosphorus (P) and potassium (K). The table indicates that the sweet potato should be supplied about 18 pounds of P and 112 pounds of K per acre on a soil giving a medium test for these elements. They could be supplied by 500 pounds of a 6-4-20 fertilizer.

Heavy applications of mineral fertilizers in the drill often cause injury to newly transplanted plants. Several plans are followed to avoid this injury, such as (1) broadcasting before making up the ridges, (2) mixing with the soil in the drill, and (3) applying as a side dressing after the plants have become established. The first may result in leaching on light soils. Side dressing costs somewhat more but on sandy soils should enable the plants to make good use of the fertilizer applied.

Manuring

Stable manure is usually scarce, expensive, and less profitable when used for potatoes than for other crops. It is common practice for those who use manure to apply it in a furrow under the ridge and at the rate of 2 to 5 tons per acre. Fresh stable manure on fertile loams often results in oversize and irregularly shaped roots. Sandy soils often need a green-manure crop, such as crimson clover, soybeans, or cowpeas, to increase their water-holding capacity. These legumes should be disced and plowed under at least a month before the plants are set.

GROWING AND CARING FOR SLIPS

Size of Seed

It is standard practice to use small- or medium-sized roots for seed. Roots from ¾ to 1½ inches in diameter (strings) will produce more plants per bushel of seed and per square yard of seedbed than will larger potatoes. Such seed should be free from disease, clean, vigorous, and true to the type desired for the cultivar.

Seed potatoes should be removed from 55° to 60° F. storage and held at 80° to 90° F. with high humidity for about two weeks or until sprouts appear. When these are bedded, plants will reach transplanting size in approximately six weeks.

Treating Seed

Even seed which is apparently healthy should be treated as a precaution against scurf, stem rot, black rot, and root rot before it is bedded. The disease-free roots should be dipped in a solution of thiram (1½ oz./gal.) or into another registered, effective disinfectant to eliminate any surface contamination by disease organisms. Those underneath the skin of the roots will not be controlled by the dipping treatment. Previously used plant hotbeds and coldframes should be cleaned out and disinfected before use.

Bedding

Clean, fresh sand on which sweet potatoes have not been grown for a number of years is preferred as a bedding medium. This is often hauled from woodlands to avoid all chance of contamination. Plant beds should be located on a sheltered slope where sweet potatoes have not been grown recently. About 25 square feet of bed are required for 1 bushel of so-called strings or 15 square feet for 1 bushel of No. 1's. About 6 to 7 bushels of the small roots are allowed for each acre where one pulling is made and only the slips are planted. If the larger roots (over 1½ inches in diameter) are used, 5 or 6 bushels will produce enough plants in three pullings for an acre.

In the warmer sections, unheated open beds or cold frames commonly are used (Fig. 29.3). The former are usually 5 to 6 feet wide and as long as necessary. A pit may be dug about 6 inches deep and the bedding medium filled in or the potatoes bedded in the soil without excavating. In either case, the roots are covered about 1 inch deep and additional sand is applied when the sprouts appear. A deep layer of soil delays sprouting of newly bedded potatoes. There should be 3 to 4 inches of soil over the mother potatoes at pulling time to insure long, stocky, well-rooted slips. Canvas and sash covers produce somewhat earlier plants.

In the more northern sections, plants are grown in heated beds to secure as long a growing season as possible. Such beds are started about six weeks before the plants are to be set in the field. The beds may be heated by manure, hot air, steam, hot water, or electricity, as described in Chapter 7.

Caring for the Beds

High temperatures increase the rate of growth, but produce soft, weak plants. An air temperature of 70° to 80° F. is considered best for most of the growing period. Covered beds will need ventilation on bright days to control the temperature. Beds with dry heat require more water than those heated by manure. Unheated beds often need covering on very cold nights, as the plants are easily injured by frost. It is well to harden off the plants by increasing the ventilation just before planting time.

PULLING AND SETTING SLIPS

Pulling Slips

In drawing the slips, the seed potato is held down with one hand while the plants are removed with the thumb and finger of the other. Only plants that have formed good roots are taken, and the others are left to grow (Fig. 29.4). Plants to be set with a transplanting machine must be arranged in the best possible way, which includes trimming the tops and placing all of the roots in one direction in such manner as to avoid sticking. Some growers puddle the roots in mud, while others only cover the plants with wet burlap. Water is usually applied with the transplanter but may be omitted if planting is done on cloudy days following a rain.

Fig. 29.3—Cold frames used for growing sweet potato slips.

USDA Photograph

Setting Slips

Sweet potato slips are set in the northern section as soon as danger of frost is over. Where only a few hundred plants are to be set, hand planting with a dibble or a trowel is the common method. It is usually convenient to water such plants, if they are not puddled in a paste of clay and water before setting. For larger areas, the shovel and tongs method is fairly rapid and less tiresome than hand planting with a dibble. The shovel, a sharpened piece of lath, is used to open the soil and is managed in the right hand. Tongs made of wood are used to pick up the slip by the roots and to thrust it into the ground. The soil may be firmed about the roots with the foot or by a second thrust of the shovel. The larger commercial areas use planting machines which can plant 3 to 4 acres a day under favorable conditions.

In Louisiana it was found that early-planted Porto Rico sweet potatoes produced more chunky roots than late-planted ones. However, the soil should be warm and all danger of late frosts over before the plants are set in the field.

Fig. 29.4—Sweet potato plants for transplanting. Plant on left is too short for easy handling.
USDA Photograph

Planting Rates

The distance between rows and spacing within the row depend on such factors as time of setting, cultivar, and soil type and fertility. Large-growing cultivars such as Porto Rico and Southern Queen need more space than do those with shorter vines. Close spacing, 9 to 12 inches in the row, is desirable on rich fertile soils, as it reduces the number of jumbos, and experiments indicate it may increase the yield.

Setting Vines

A large part of the sweet potatoes in the lower South are grown from vine cuttings, the vines being secured from an early planting of slips. Such cuttings are usually about 15 inches long and should include two joints. The Georgia Agricultural Experiment Station found little difference between cuttings taken from various parts of the same vine. Such pieces of vines may be planted by pushing the middle portion into the soil with a notched stick or by inserting the butt end 6 to 8 inches into the soil. Vine cuttings are fairly resistant to adverse conditions. This method of propagation is relatively inexpensive and involves less danger of diseases than does growing the crop from slips. However, delayed plantings result in decreased yields.

CULTIVATING AND IRRIGATING

Cultivating

Sweet potatoes are given the usual row cultivations practiced with other crops, mainly for the purpose of controlling weeds. Several cultivations are usually made before the vines seriously interfere with the cultivators. The sweet potato vine takes root at various places if left undisturbed. Moving the vines to permit late cultivations may slightly increase yields, but it is not likely to be profitable. Vine pruning to stimulate development of roots has, instead, retarded root development in several experiments and is of questionable value.

In the production of sweet potatoes, herbicides are generally used to control weeds early in the season, to reduce the amount of cultivation needed, and to maintain weed control after lay-by without the use of hand labor. Effective herbicides include Dacthal and Amiben (Chapter 9).

Irrigating

The sweet potato is considered to be a moderately drouth-tolerant crop. After the plants are established, they can withstand severe drouth, but a deficiency of moisture during storage root formation may reduce yields. In Louisiana the average daily water requirement for sweet potatoes early in the season is about $\frac{1}{10}$ acre-inch per day. This increases to $\frac{1}{4}$ acre-inch in midsummer. Water may be supplied by either surface or overhead irrigation. Noncontaminated water should be used.

CONTROLLING DISEASES AND INSECTS

Diseases

A number of serious diseases attack the sweet potato. The more important ones, including control measures, are discussed briefly.

BLACK ROT. Black rot, caused by the fungus *Ceratocystis fimbriata,* is generally considered to be the most destructive field disease of the sweet potato. It attacks all parts of the plant below the ground. This fungus lives from one year to another on the dead vines or other decayed vegetable matter in the soil and infects sweet potatoes by contact. Slips from diseased seed are usually infected.

Precautions necessary to avoid this disease include selecting disease-free seed, disinfecting as described under seed treatment, and avoiding all contaminated material in manure or about the plant beds. Crop rotation tends to prevent an accumulation of diseased material in the soil. Spring selection as well as fall selection helps to eliminate diseased roots.

STEM ROT. Stem rot, caused by *Fusarium oxysporium f. batatas,* is about second in destructiveness in most sections. This fungus, like the preceding one, can live for several years on decaying vegetation in the soil. They usually enter a plant through the roots, and the foliage of infected plants turns yellow. The vascular system is usually invaded by the fungus, and dark-colored lesions are found on the stem. The discoloration disclosed by splitting the stems is used to identify infected seed. Spores of the stem-rot fungi are developed on dead vines and are readily carried by wind and other agencies.

Cultivars show a marked difference in susceptibility to this disease. Nancy Hall and Porto Rico are moderately susceptible, while Goldrush is fairly resistant. The same sanitary measures described for black rot apply to this disease. Infected soil should not be planted to sweet potatoes for at least five years.

SCURF. Caused by *Monilochaetes infuscans,* scurf is one of the secondary sweet potato diseases, although it is widely disseminated. The fungus lives in the soil, can be carried on slips, and causes no apparent injury above ground. Diseased areas on the sweet potatoes are brown and are likely to continue to develop in storage. Discolored roots lose water and are likely to shrivel even in fairly humid storage houses. The use of disease-free seed and treatment with thiram are important preventive measures. Infected soil should not be planted to sweet potatoes for at least three years.

FOOT ROT. Foot rot is caused by a soil fungus, *Plenodomus destruens.* Late-infected sweet potatoes develop a firm brown rot. Early-infected plants are attacked near the surface of the ground and are usually girdled. Control measures are the same as for black rot.

ROOT ROT. Root rot, caused by *Phymatotrichum omnivorum,* is often called Texas root rot and is induced by the same organism that causes root rot on cotton and alfalfa. Its distribution is limited to the southwestern United States. No satisfactory control is known; however, hard freezing is likely to kill the organism. Corn and cereals may be grown in an effort to starve out the fungus.

ROOT KNOT. Root knot, caused by the common garden nematode (*meloidogyne sp.*), may result in a superficial decay in sweet potatoes, which are likely to spread this pest. Nemagold is resistant, and Porto Rico and Jersey cultivars are claimed to be fairly resistant. Good crops of sweet potatoes have been grown on badly infested soil. No method of seed treatment is effective.

SOFT ROT. Soft rot, including ring rot, is usually caused by the common breadmold fungus, *Rhizopus stolonifer.* Ring rot develops in storage from a side infection and the diseased tissue forms a ring about the sweet potato. Soft rot under favorable conditions may start in the field. The middle cell wall is dissolved during the spread of this rot, which at first renders the potato soft and mushy. Loss of water later produces a dry, mummy-like condition often called a dry rot. Entrance starts at wounds, although a rotting sweet potato often infects surrounding ones. A relatively low humidity during the curing process decreases infections. As this fungus lives on a wide range of decaying vegetable matter, it cannot be excluded from storage houses. Proper curing and handling are the best preventive measures.

DRY ROT. Dry rot, caused by the fungus *Diaporthe batatatis,* like soft rot is widely distributed. It probably starts in the field and develops slowly from the stem end. Small domelike fruiting structures can often be seen with the naked eye. The tissue under the skin is coal-black in appearance.

STORAGE DISEASES. These include soft rot, dry rot, Java black rot, charcoal rot, black rot, internal cork, and field diseases that continue to develop in storage.

Their control starts with the development of a clean healthy crop in the field, and continues with careful handling during harvesting and storage. Injury resulting from careless handling favors the entrance of the rot-causing organisms. Proper curing and favorable storage conditions will keep the diseases from getting a start. Storage houses should be thoroughly cleaned and disinfected with formaldehyde.

Insects

The sweet potato is usually free from very serious insect attacks.

SWEET POTATO WEEVIL. The sweet potato weevil (*Cylas formicarius elegantulus*) is of Asiatic origin and is the most destructive insect pest of this crop, causing serious damage from Texas to Florida. Other host plants include members of the morning-glory family. The adult of this insect is a slender snout beetle about $\frac{1}{4}$ inch long. The larvae tunnel through the vines to the roots and often riddle the sweet potatoes. The weevil overwinters in sweet potatoes in storage and in roots left in the ground. A dieldrin dust applied to the soil gives good control with this contact insecticide.

Other suggested control measures include: (1) cleaning up sweet potato fields after harvest, (2) disposing of the crop as soon as possible after digging, (3) selecting only clean seed at bedding time, and (4) growing plants as far away from infested fields as possible. Another precaution is to disinfect the storage.

OTHER INSECTS. Other insects which occasionally attack this crop include the cutworm, sweet potato flea beetle, striped blister beetle, and sweet potato whitefly. The injury resulting from these insects is usually slight.

HARVESTING, HANDLING, AND MARKETING

Harvesting

Mature sweet potatoes are characterized by high starch content, the cut surfaces drying on exposure to air. The crop may be dug at any time when the roots reach marketable size. Table 29.2 shows the influence of time of digging on total yield and grade of sweet potatoes. While these figures are for only one year, they indicate that very early digging must be accompanied by increased price to offset the reduction in grade and yield.

The sweet potato has a thin, delicate skin that is easily broken and flesh that is readily cut or bruised. Injuries provide opportunity for entrance of decay organisms and may constitute grade defects. The methods used in digging and handling during harvest greatly influence subsequent storage and market quality. While mechanical harvesters are commonly used for digging stocks for processing or industrial uses, they have been successfully modified for fresh market stock.

Producers in the northern part of the sweet potato-producing area usually allow the frost to injure the vines slightly before digging. Frosted vines should be cut from the sweet potatoes to prevent decay from starting in the dead vines and passing to the roots. Sweet potatoes are injured at temperatures below 50° F. So whether the plants are frosted or not, the roots should be harvested before the soil gets cold. Most growers try to dig sweet potatoes when the soil is dry, as the crop comes out clean and is easier to handle. A plow with a sharp rolling colter and an 8-inch shielded moldboard with rods attached is a popular implement for digging. The roots are usually permitted to dry slightly after they have been freed from the soil.

Grading

Since sweet potatoes require care in harvesting and marketing, and field grading reduces the amount of handling, the marketable potatoes are picked up first, the culls and strings being gathered later. If the crop is

Table 29.2—Effect of Dates of Harvesting Sweet Potatoes on Grade and Yield.

Date Dug	Grades	Cultivar Yields				
		Triumph	Nancy Hall	Yellow Jersey*	Southern Queen	Porto Rico
August 15	Marketable	41.2	89.5	55.6	41.1	48.4
	Strings	26.6	72.6	91.9	44.8	46.0
	Total	67.8	162.1	147.5	85.9	94.4
September 1	Marketable	111.3	179.1	96.8	85.3	111.3
	Strings	38.7	116.1	87.1	55.6	50.8
	Total	150.0	295.2	183.9	140.9	162.1
September 15	Marketable	248.3	280.7	137.9	179.1	227.9
	Strings	99.2	41.1	94.4	32.7	81.1
	Total	347.5	321.8	232.3	211.8	309.0
October 30	Marketable	309.8	559.8	293.3	309.8	200.0
	Strings	96.8	77.4	116.1	71.0	100.0
	Total	406.6	637.2	409.4	380.8	300.0

*Yields and grades seriously affected by vines from larger cultivars.
Data from Tennessee Agricultural Experiment Station.

to be stored, it is best to pack the sweet potatoes on padded tables in a shed. The U.S. Department of Agriculture will supply standard grades for this crop. This is a general standard and a minimum, but many growers prefer to put up a pack that is more than this minimum.

Fig. 29.5—Federal-state inspector examining sweet potatoes for shipping.

Packing

Hampers, bushel baskets, and boxes are popular commercial packages, while baskets are in common use on local markets. Regardless of the container, it should be clean and neatly packed, and the product should be free from bruises when displayed for sale. The shape of the sweet potato makes it somewhat hard to handle in a jumble pack. Hand placing is justified on some markets. If the pack is only faced, it should be representative of the remaining contents.

Curing

Successful storage of sweet potatoes depends to a large extent on curing. When sweet potatoes are harvested in the lower South in early October, they may be cured by placing a large quantity in a fairly tight building. The heat of respiration, together with fairly high outside temperatures, is often sufficient for curing. In more northern districts, artificial heat is used to bring temperatures to 80° to 90° F. This treatment with a relative humidity of about 85 percent causes wounds to heal rapidly and brings about some drying of the roots. The U.S. Department of Agriculture, *Agriculture Handbook 358* gives plans for storage-house construction, as does Miscellaneous Publication 822.

Storing

The sweet potato should be stored in a warm building where the air is dry and the temperature uniform. Bins, crates, boxes, or baskets may be used as containers, and these should be arranged to provide ventilation. Heat may be necessary to keep the air dry and warm. Injury occurs considerably above freezing.

Heat when the temperature drops to 48° F., ventilate at 60° F., and close ventilators at 55° F. Outdoor cellar houses often are used, but they should have provision for ventilation. Pits and banks lack provision for curing and ventilating, and storage in them often results in heavy loss.

Sweet potatoes should be disturbed as little as possible after they have been cured and stored, as rot is spread rapidly by handling. It is usually necessary to sort stored roots again before selling.

Marketing

Sweet potato production and consumption have been declining for many years. Competitive vegetables and other food items may continue to decrease the demand of this important crop. The volume being canned has increased, some are frozen, and an instant, mashed, dehydrated sweet potato is being considered for market. However, consumption will likely continue downward unless new ways are found to use this commodity for food or industrial purposes.

A large part of the sweet potato crop is consumed in the areas of production. Northern markets have long been supplied with dry-fleshed potatoes such as Yellow Jersey, establishing a demand for this type. Porto Rico and other soft-fleshed varieties are being shipped to these markets from Louisiana and North Carolina.

Improvements in cultivars, harvesting, curing, processing, storing, packaging, transporting, and merchandizing may increase demand and slow the downward trend in consumption. No exports or imports were reported in 1977.

SELECTED REFERENCES

Bouwkamp, J. C., and Scott, L. E., "Production of Sweet Potatoes from Root Pieces," *HortScience* 7 (3), 1972.

Charney, Patricia, and Seelig, R. A., "Sweet Potatoes," United Fresh Fruit and Veg. Assoc., Alexandria, Va., 1967.

Clark, John C., "Quality Sweet Potato Production," Univ. of Tenn. Coop. Ext. Ser. Pub. 420, 1976.

Hammett, H. L., and Ammerman, G. R., "The Technology of Production and Processing Sweet Potatoes in Mississippi," Miss. Agr. Exp. Sta. Bull. 795, 1973.

Harris, W. L., Scott, L. E., and Bouwkamp, J. C., "Harvesting Sweet Potatoes for the Fresh Market," *Transactions of the ASAE* 16(4): 627-631, 1973.

Hernandez, Teme P., Ed., "Thirty Years of Cooperative Sweet Potato Research, 1939-1969," Southern Coop. Series Bull. 159, 1970.

Jones, L. G., *et al.*, "Effects of Soil Amendment and Fertilizer Applications on Sweet Potato Growth, Production, and Quality," La. State Univ. Agr. Exp. Sta. Bull. 704, 1977.

Kostewicz, S. R., and Montelaro, J., "Sweet Potato Production Guide," Univ. of Fla. Coop. Ext. Ser. Circ. 97C, 1975.

Larsen, J. E., and Patterson, D. R., "Storage and Handling of Sweet Potatoes," Tex. A & M Univ. Coop. Ext. Ser. L709, 1974.

Montelaro, J., and Martin, W. J., "Sweet Potatoes in Louisiana," La. State Univ. Coop. Ext. Ser. Pub. 1450, 1977.

Scott, L. E., and Bouwkamp, J. C., "Effect of Chronological Age on Composition and Firmness of Raw and Processed Sweet Potatoes," *HortSci.* 10 (2), 1975.

Steinbauer, C. E., and Kushman, L. J., "Sweet Potato Culture and Diseases," USDA *Agriculture Handbook 388*, 1971.

CHAPTER 30

Tomatoes

CLASSIFICATION, ORIGIN, AND HISTORY

The tomato (*Lycopersicon esculentum*), a member of the nightshade family, is a native of tropical America.

The large-fruited forms of tomato are reported to have been taken from Peru to Italy, thence to Northern Europe, and finally to the United States by 1781. In 1812, tomatoes were commonly on the market at New Orleans. In 1817, tomato seed was first offered for sale in a seed catalogue in the United States, but it was not until about 1835 that the tomato became quite generally cultivated for culinary purposes in this country. Even at that time, there was considerable prejudice against its use. The first tomato fruits grown in the United States were large, oblate, and ribbed. Since 1895, the important developments include: (1) improvement of extra-early cultivars, (2) development of disease-resistant strains, and (3) improvement of plant type and fruit quality.

SCOPE AND IMPORTANCE

The popularity of the tomato and its products continues to rise. Tomatoes ranked third in acreage and second in value, next to potatoes, among the 22 principal crops in 1977. The acreage for fresh market tomatoes declined from 241,290 acres in 1949 to 193,170 acres in 1959 and down to 124,080 acres in 1977. During this 1949 to 1977 period, acre yields increased from 73 to 159 hundredweight, total production rose from 17,700,000 to 19,779,000 hundredweight, and values escalated from $98,233,000 to about $405,163,000.

Acreage of tomatoes for processing declined from 324,500 acres in

1949 to 296,930 acres in 1959, then rose to 346,360 acres in 1977. Yields per acre almost doubled between 1959 and 1977, while values increased spectacularly from $58,985,000 to $497,976,000. The estimated acreage for both fresh and processing tomatoes totaled 470,650 acres in 1977 and was valued at $904,987,000.

California and Florida, combined, produced 60 percent of the volume and 48 percent of the fresh market value in 1977. California also produced more than 85 percent of the volume and value of processing tomatoes. The approximate acreage distribution and the 1949 to 1977 record of tomatoes are depicted in Figure 30.1. Tables 30.1 and 30.2 show the comparative acreage, production, and value of fresh and processed tomatoes by states.

TRENDS IN PRODUCTION EFFICIENCY

Acrewise, the tomato is one of the most expensive crops to produce.

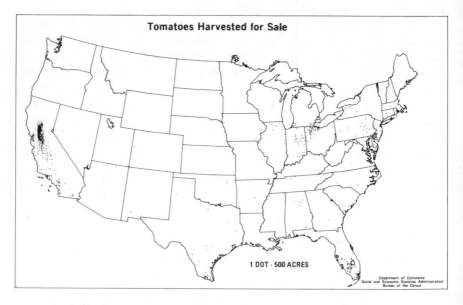

Fig. 30.1—Acreage, distribution, production, and value of tomatoes.

UNITED STATES TOTAL

Year	Acreage	Production 1,000 Cwt.	Value, $1,000
1949	565,790	67,082	157,218
1959	490,100	90,267	236,757
1969	414,170	117,282	393,253
1977	470,680	175,242	904,987

Table 30.1—Tomatoes for Fresh Market: Harvest Season and
Estimated Acreage, Yield, Production, and
Value in Leading States, 1977.

State	Harvest Season	Harvested Acreage	Yield per Acre, Cwt.	Production per 1,000 Cwt.	Price per Cwt.	Value, $1,000
Florida	Spring	16,400	215	3,526	$19.10	67,347
California	Summer	14,700	275	4,043	21.60	87,329
California	Fall	10,700	230	2,461	22.70	55,865
Florida	Fall	10,300	200	2,400	20.60	49,440
Florida	Winter	7,300	145	1,059	25.70	27,216
S. Carolina	Spring	7,000	100	700	12.00	8,400
New Jersey	Summer	6,500	85	553	22.70	12,553
Alabama	Summer	5,000	70	350	29.30	10,255
California	Spring	4,200	164	688	18.79	12,929
Michigan	Summer	4,100	95	390	22.90	8,931
Arkansas	Spring	3,400	90	306	17.50	5,355
Georgia	Summer	3,100	60	186	17.20	3,199
New York	Summer	3,000	93	279	21.20	5,915
Tennessee	Summer	2,600	120	312	23.60	8,299
Texas	Spring	2,600	77	200	21.80	4,360
Virginia	Summer	2,400	130	312	14.40	4,493
Pennsylvania	Summer	2,300	130	299	10.50	3,140
Maryland	Summer	2,300	92	212	13.20	2,798
N. Carolina	Summer	2,000	140	280	17.00	4,760
Other States		14,180	—	1,163	—	222,584
United States		124,320	159	19,779	20.60	407,011
Total	Spring (6%)	36,470	154	5,622	18.30	103,041
Total	Summer (29%)	56,910	143	8,126	20.70	168,261
Total	Fall (46%)	23,400	210	4,912	21.70	106,645
Total	Winter (19%)	7,300	145	1,059	25.70	27,216

The 189 man-hours required to grow and harvest an acre of fresh market tomatoes in 1939 dropped slightly to 186 man-hours in 1959, to 118 in 1964 to 1968, and down to 86 man-hours by 1977. As acre yields more than doubled, the output per man-hour increased 529 percent between 1939 and 1977, as shown by stages in Table 1.6. The acre production and man-hour output for processing tomatoes have likewise increased substantially with promises for further improvements.

By 1965, the mechanical tomato harvester performed admirably in California. Some 262 machines harvested nearly one-third of the acreage for processing and did it considerably cheaper than by hand (an estimated $8 to $10 per ton less). By 1967, this crop was harvested primarily by machine. The 1965 California employment of seasoned workers in tomatoes amounted to 29,600 workers as compared with 44,400 workers

Table 30.2—Tomatoes for Processing: Estimated Commercial Acreage, Yield, Production, and Value in Leading States, 1977.

State	Harvested Acreage	Yield per Acre, Tons	Production in Tons	Price per Ton	Value, $1,000
California	276,400	24.13	6,669,550	$63.90	426,184
Ohio	20,900	19.94	416,750	66.00	27,506
Indiana	12,500	13.85	173,100	66.70	11,546
New Jersey	8,000	15.15	121,200	63.00	7,636
Pennsylvania	5,800	19.70	114,250	62.00	7,084
Michigan	4,100	15.49	63,500	65.80	4,178
Maryland	4,000	11.49	45,950	64.30	2,955
Virginia	3,600	8.07	29,050	70.60	2,051
Texas	2,000	10.20	20,400	64.60	1,318
New Mexico	900	11.00	9,900	75.00	743
Colorado	640	10.94	7,000	63.70	446
Other States*	7,520	13.63	102,500	61.70	6,329
United States	346,360	22.44	7,773,150	64.10	497,976

*Delaware, Florida, Illinois, Iowa, Kentucky, Louisiana, New York, North Carolina, Utah, and West Virginia excluded.

in 1964; a drop of one-third.[1] Now, practically all the tomatoes grown for processing in California and some other areas are direct seeded and mechanically harvested. The mechanical harvesting of tomatoes for the fresh market has not been generally successful.

CLIMATIC REQUIREMENTS

The tomato is a warm-season plant which requires three to four months from the time of seeding to produce the first ripe fruit. It thrives best when the weather is clear and rather dry and temperatures are uniformly moderate—65° to 85° F. Plants are usually frozen at temperatures below 32° F., and they do not increase in size at temperatures above 95° F. High temperatures accompanied by high humidity favor the development of foliage disease. If the night temperature stays above 85° F., the fruit does not become red enough for the U.S. No. 1 grade for canning.

Hot, drying winds cause the flowers to drop. In the Southwest, where such winds prevail, the tomato field should be protected from the prevailing wind by a stream, woods, or hill. Cultivars with pistils shorter than the staminal cone have less blossom drop than others. Irrigation will low-

[1]*Farm Labor Developments*, USDA, p. 16, Oct., 1965.

er the temperature, raise the humidity, and prevent much of the blossom drop.

SELECTING CULTIVARS AND SEED

Cultivars

The importance of good seed of the right cultivar or strain suitable for the locality cannot be overemphasized. Some tomato cultivars produce exceptionally well under one set of conditions but may be poorly adapted to others. Great effort has been made to produce new tomato cultivars, and a large number is available to the grower. Cultivars with disease resistance, earliness, concentrated fruit set, good fruit color, firmness, resistance to cracking, and other desirable characters have been developed. Thus the choice of cultivars may be important in minimizing some of the problems of production.

Where most of the tomatoes are grown for shipment, the fruits should be smooth, fleshy, medium-sized, highly colored, and solid enough to withstand transportation. A cultivar for processing should have well-colored, solid fruits and plants with enough foliage to shade the fruits. A concentrated fruit set is required for mechanical harvesting.

A selected list of cultivars is briefly described in Table 30.3 and the chief use of each is given.

Securing Seed

The quality, strain, and trueness of varietal type of seed have such an important bearing upon the yield, earliness, and uniformity of the crop that no pains should be spared in getting the best seed. Some seed firms specialize in producing tomato seed of the highest quality and have their product certified for purity and freedom from disease. In view of the fact that only 2 ounces of seed will produce sufficient plants for an acre, seed cost should be of secondary importance, and only seed of the best quality should be used.

PREPARING THE SOIL

Soil Preferences

The tomato will grow on nearly all types of soils. A light or warm,

Table 30.3—Brief Description of Selected Cultivars of Tomatoes.

Cultivar	Chief Use	Season	Plant Type*	Resistant to**	Color	Size	Shape
						Fruits	
Better Boy	Home	Medium	I	FW, VW, N	Red	Medium large	Globe
Burpee's VF	Market	Medium	I	VF	Red	Medium	Round
Campbell 28	Market, processing	Med. early	I	FW, cracking	Red	Medium large	Flat globe
Campbell 1327, 37	Market	Medium	D	VW, FW, cracking	Red	Large	Flat globe
Chico III	Processing	Med. early	D	FW	Red	Large	Pear
Earlypak 707	Shipping, canning	Med. early	D	VW, FW	Red	Medium	Globe
Fantastic	Greenhouse	Med. early	I		Red	Large	Globe
Glamour	Market, home	Med. early	SI	Cracking	Red	Medium	Flat globe
Heinz, 1350, 1409, 1439	Market, home	Early	D	Cracking, VW, FW	Red	Medium	Flat globe
Knox	Processing	Early	P	VF, cracking	Red	Small	Round
Manapal	Market, home	Medium	I	FW	Red	Medium large	Globe
VF 134-1-2	Processing	Early	D	FW, VW	Red	Small	Long globe
Moreton Hybrid	Market	Early	I		Red	Medium	Flat globe
Red Cherry	Home	Early	I		Red	Small	Globe
Red Rock	Processing	Medium	I	VF	Red	Small	Round
Roma VF	Processing	Early	I	FW, VW	Red	Small	Pear
Spring Set	Market	Early	D	VF	Red	Large	Round
Traveler 76	Shipping	Med. early	I	FW	Pink	Large	Flat globe

*D—determinate; I—indeterminate; SI—semideterminate.

**FW—Fusarium Wilt; VW—Verticillium Wilt.

well-drained, and fertile soil is best suited to produce early fruit of high quality. The loams and clay loams have a greater water-holding capacity and are better suited to a longer season of production when large yield and not earliness is of prime importance.

If any soil is to give the best results, it should contain a good supply of organic matter and mineral nutrients. The degree of acidity which tomatoes will withstand is increased considerably by a plentiful supply of organic matter. Soils ranging from medium acid (pH 5.5) to neutral (pH 7.0) are best for tomato production.

Preparing the Soil

It is important to plow the soil for tomatoes some time in advance of planting so it will have time to settle. Fall plowing is preferable except on sandy soil. Any undecomposed organic matter should be well covered to prevent interference with transplanting or seeding.

FERTILIZING

The amount and kinds of fertilizers and manure to apply economically for the tomato crop depend not only upon the available fertility of the soil but also upon the organic content, moisture supply, season, cropping system, cultivar, and the expected returns from the crop. However, in order to produce high yields of good-quality tomatoes a well-fertilized soil must be used. The tomato is listed with those vegetable crops giving highest response to fertility (Table 6.5).

With few exceptions, experiments have shown the following results: (1) applications of quickly available superphosphate results in earlier and increased yields, (2) rapid early growth is essential, (3) liming the soil is seldom beneficial, (4) the content of sulfur and its distribution in the tomato plant give evidence that this element is quite important, (5) soils high in humus are better for main-crop production, and (6) legume crops are desirable in the rotation.

As a rule, where it is necessary to add nitrogen, phosphorus, and potash, a complete fertilizer containing part of the nitrogen and all of the phosphorus and potash needed for the crop should be applied before planting. Where the plants are to be set close together or where large quantities of fertilizer are used, broadcasting is desirable, but where the rows are to be wide apart or where moderate amounts of fertilizer are used, the fertilizer is best distributed in the rows or in bands near the row.

At the setting of the first fruit cluster, a side dressing of 100 pounds of sulfate of ammonia per acre may be desirable. Should the plant show signs of nitrogen deficiency later in the season, additional nitrogen side dressings should be applied, provided that climatic conditions are favorable.

On heavily watered sandy or porous soils, as much as 90 percent of the soluble fertilizer may be leached so that side applications of fertilizer during the growing season are necessary for continued growth. In Florida, polyethylene mulched tomatoes on highly unfertile soil are given a total of 350 to 450 pounds of nitrogen, 300 to 500 pounds of phosphorus, and 500 to 600 pounds of potassium, in addition to minor elements and lime to bring the soil reaction to pH 6.5. Any fertilizer recommendation should be based on local experience.

GROWING AND SETTING PLANTS

Early tomato plants produce larger and more profitable yields than late ones. To secure the early and greater yields it is essential to have large, stocky, disease-free plants with a well-developed root system. For maximum production, the plants should be 6 to 10 inches tall in soil blocks, pots, or other containers at the time of the frost-free date when they can safely be set in the field. The least desirable plants are grown 200 to 300 plants per square foot in the hotbed and then pulled for setting and those started too early and then overhardened.

Direct Seeding

Tomatoes to be harvested mechanically are generally direct seeded. High plant populations necessary for good yields with a single destructive harvest make it uneconomical to transplant tomatoes. When 5-foot rows are used, seed is planted to give a spacing of 8 to 12 inches or 12 to 16 inches if double rows are used.

"Plug mix seeding" is used for much of the acreage of tomatoes in Southeastern Florida. A machine prepares beds, applies fertilizer, fumigates with methyl bromide, and lays polyethylene mulch. After about five days a seeder burns holes in the mulch through which a seed mix is placed and covered with vermiculite or perlite to prevent drying. The mix contains a slow release fertilizer, sphagnum peat moss, water, and seed. About five seeds in 2 ounces of the mix are used in each hill. Plants are thinned to one and spaced 5 feet by 12 to 18 inches.

Seeding and Growing Plants

Plants are either produced by the grower or bought from commercial plant producers as explained fully in Chapter 7.

Many growers produce their own plants, for either small or large plantings. In such cases, 2 ounces of seed will produce enough selected plants for planting 1 acre. Because of the prevalence of seed-borne diseases, which are at times quite serious, it is a good policy to treat the seed with a fungicide before it is sown. Two of the better treatments are captan and thiram, thoroughly dusted on the seed at the rate of 1 level teaspoonful per pound of seed.

The seedbed soil should be friable, so that it will (1) drain well, (2) not crust, and (3) crumble easily from the seedling roots when plants are removed from the seedbed for transplanting. The addition of sand usually improves the texture. The soil should be free from tomato diseases. Soil not previously used for tomatoes is preferable, but, when it is necessary to use soil more than once, it should be sterilized with steam or treated with formaldehyde.

Early plants can be started in the greenhouse or hotbed and then transplanted to the hotbed or cold frame, depending upon seasonal conditions. Six to eight weeks are required to produce large plants. Where the seedlings are to be transplanted to produce early plants, the seed is sown in flats or hotbeds at the rate of 8 to 12 seeds per inch in rows $1\frac{1}{2}$ to 3 inches apart and covered $\frac{1}{4}$ to $\frac{1}{2}$ inch.

For later plants, which are to be transplanted directly from the seedbed to the field, the seed is sown in the hotbed or cold frame so that the thinned plants will stand $\frac{1}{2}$ to 2 inches apart in rows 4 to 6 inches apart. Watering should be thorough and preferably limited to mornings of bright, clear days.

Transplanting

The potting or growing soil differs from the seedbed soil in that it must be fertile to supply nutrients to the growing plants and must be less friable, so that the soil will adhere to the roots in transplanting to the field. A good soil may be made by mixing four parts of loam, two parts of rotted manure, and one part of sand. It is usually well to add $\frac{1}{2}$ pound of a complete fertilizer to each bushel of potting soil.

When the first pair of true leaves appear, 10 to 20 days after seeding, the seedlings are at the best stage for transplanting into beds or containers (Fig. 30.2). Plants grown in pots or bands have the advantage of re-

Fig. 30.2—Early tomato plants started in a flat. The plants are transplanted at this stage to other plant-growing structures.

Okla. Exp. Sta.

taining most of their roots when set in the field, but are more expensive than those set 3 or 4 inches apart and grown in cold frame beds, being moved later to the field in soil cubes. Potted plants are plunged into the soil to prevent excessive drying. It is often necessary to shade the transplanted seedlings for a day or two until they are re-established, regardless of how and where they are transplanted.

To produce medium-sized plants in flats, the seedlings are set not to exceed 40 per square foot. For large early plants in the hotbed or cold frame, the plants are usually set 4 by 4 inches or 5 by 5 inches. The minimum spacing should be 3 by 3 inches.

Regardless of how the plants are grown, they should be hardened to the extent that they will withstand the transfer to outdoor conditions with as little shock as possible. The hardening may be accomplished by lowering the temperature, giving more ventilation, and lessening the water supply. The process may require from 3 to 10 days, depending upon the original conditions of the plants. Over-hardening, causing the plants to yellow, produces later and lower yields.

Transplants are often grown in the field without protection from cold for shipment to regions farther north. They can be grown on a large scale and handled efficiently by machinery. This method is used almost exclusively when transplants are employed to produce tomatoes for processing. When the plants are large enough to be set in the field, the soil is loosened and the plants pulled and hauled to the packing shed. Here they are sorted and bunched in sizes convenient for transplanting machines. The roots of each bunch are dabbed with wet peat moss and wrapped with paper to prevent drying. The bunches are then packed in hampers or other containers for shipping. This is the least expensive method of growing plants and can be quite satisfactory when early yields are not important.

Setting Plants in the Field

A few days previous to setting the large plants in the field from the cold frames, they are blocked by cutting the soil in squares with a square spade. Blocking lessens the shock at transplanting. At setting time, each plant is lifted and set out with a 3- to 5-inch cube of soil on its roots.

Plants should be watered moderately a few hours before setting, so as to prevent wilting during transplanting. Watering also makes it easier to remove plants from pots and prevents crumbling of the soil from the roots of either potted or blocked plants.

After the field is thoroughly prepared, rows may be marked off and a lister or small plow used to open the furrows in which the plants are to be set. Small potted plants are often set with planting trowels. Transplanting machines may be used for setting plants without a ball of soil on the roots.

The planting distances vary with the locality and the methods of cultivation from 1½ to 4 feet apart in rows that are from 3½ to 6 feet apart. In setting the plants, it is essential to pack the soil around the roots or root ball. If the soil is not moist, water should be applied. After the water has soaked in, loose soil should be raked or cultivated in to level the soil about the plants.

Occasionally the plants become leggy in the plant bed. When such plants have to be used for the spring crop, it is best to put the roots not more than 6 inches below the soil surface, then lay the long stem down in the furrow, allowing just enough of the top above ground to bear the first fruit cluster safely above the soil. At this season, the upper 6 inches of soil is warm and contains available nutrients. The buried long stem will take root, resulting in a vigorously growing, productive plant. For the fall crop, which, particularly in the Southwest, must make the early part of its growth during a relatively hot, dry season, a tall plant with a woody stem is often desirable. In setting this crop, the root ball is set as low as 8 to 10 inches in order to reach cooler soil and more abundant moisture. The plant grows slowly at first; then, as temperatures moderate, it produces roots on the covered part of the stem and grows rapidly.

CULTIVATING, PRUNING, TRAINING, AND IRRIGATING

Cultivating and Controlling Weeds

Unless there is a danger of frost, tomatoes should be cultivated soon after they are set, to stir the soil which has been packed in setting the plants. Early cultivation should be fairly close to the plant, but the succeeding ones should be more shallow and farther away, the main object being to eliminate weeds. Cultivating equipment should be adjusted so that large plants will not be injured. The cost of cultivation can often be reduced by the use of herbicides. This is especially true with direct-seeded tomatoes because of their slow early growth. At this time cultivation is difficult and weeds may become a problem. Consult your local cooperative extension service for latest recommendations. If weeds are permitted to grow, they not only rob the tomatoes of moisture and plant nutrients but also become hosts for diseases and insects that attack tomatoes.

Pruning and Training

The value of pruning and training tomatoes varies considerably with different localities, seasons, and cultivars. Under humid conditions, training reduces losses from soft rot, but in the drier areas of the Southwest, the trained crop exposed to drying winds is less productive than the untrained plants (Fig. 30.3).

The most common method of pruning and training tomatoes is to prune them to one-, two-, or three-stemmed plants by pinching out the lateral branches as they appear in the axis of each leaf, and then to tie the plant to a 5-foot stake driven a foot into the ground about 3 inches from the plant. The pruning should be done shortly after the branches appear. When more than one stem is desired, the larger lower branches are selected and all other branches are then removed. Strong, soft string is used to tie the plants. It is first tied tightly around the stake, and then a loose tie is made around the stem or stems of the plant. Plants can also be supported by strings running on each side of the stakes from one to the other. Plants are then held between the strings.

Fig. 30.3—Plants pruned and trained to stakes on left, not pruned or trained on right.

Plant Appearance as a Guide to Cultural Practices

In order to produce good yields of high-quality fruit, a high level of soil fertility must be maintained. Deficiency symptoms do not have to be apparent before yields are reduced. When they do appear, however, some correction can often be made.

An acute deficiency of some of the soil nutrients can be detected by certain plant characteristics. A white margin on the leaves of a vigorously growing young tomato plant may indicate potash deficiency. A purple under-color on the leaves of the young plant indicates insufficient available phosphorus. The more intense the purple under-color and the slower the plant growth, the greater the phosphorus deficiency. When there is ample phosphorus and potash and the plant is growing slowly with slender stems, the indications are that the nitrogen supply is low. Lack of nitrogen is characterized also by the lessening of the number of buds in the newly formed clusters and by the dropping of the unfertilized flowers. In the more severe stages, the terminal vegetative growth ceases and the plants become hardened and yellow-green in color. Lack of water may be the cause of lack of nitrogen in the plant.

It should be remembered that the growing green fruit consumes large quantities of nitrogen. Therefore, as the number and size of tomatoes increase, the nitrogen supply must be increased. To provide for this need, many growers start side dressing with nitrogen as soon as the first cluster of fruit is set. An oversupply of nitrogen is characterized by difficulty in setting the first cluster, rough, fasciated fruits, large succulent stems, and leaves of a light green color, especially at the top of the stem. This is usually a very temporary condition.

Irrigating

Sufficient moisture should be present for germination or quick recovery of transplants. Rapid early growth is essential for good yields, so during this period optimum moisture is essential. The use of water by the tomato increases until the fruit crop is developed. Water should be withheld during the harvest season depending upon the type of soil, rain, and method of harvesting. Machines do not work on fine-textured, wet soils. Sprinkler irrigation should be used in the morning so the plants will dry before night.

CONTROLLING DISEASES AND INSECTS

Diseases

Tomato diseases that are of importance are fusarium wilt, bacterial wilt, early blight, nailhead spot, leaf spot, root knot, gray leaf spot, damping off, bacterial canker, anthracnose, blossom-end rot, sunscald, and viruses.

FUSARIUM WILT. Fusarium wilt, caused by the fungus *Fusarium oxysporium f. lycopersici,* is one of the most prevalent of the tomato diseases. The disease is characterized by a yellowing and dying of the tomato leaves progressively from the base upward, and by the discoloration of the vascular tissue.

The disease is controlled by use of disease-resistant cultivars and disease-free seed, seed treatment, use of disease-free soil in seedbeds, disposal of diseased plants, and rotation. A number of cultivars have a high degree of resistance to fusarium wilt and one of these should be planted on soils known to be infested with the disease.

BACTERIAL WILT. Bacterial wilt is caused by *Pseudomonas solanacearum,* a soil parasite which enters the roots through wounds. Insects spread it from one plant to another. The diseased plants wilt during the day and partially recover at night. Freshly cut stems exude a gummy, yellow mass of bacteria.

Control is effected by planting disease-free plants, by removing the diseased plants, and by rotation.

EARLY BLIGHT. Early blight is produced by *Alternaria solani,* the same fungus that causes early blight of potatoes. The spores of the fungus may be in or on the seed or may live over in the soil, attacking the plants at any stage of their development.

To control, (1) sow only treated seed from disease-free plants; (2) practice sanitation by deep fall plowing, after burning all plant refuse; (3) set stocky, well-hardened plants early in the season; and (4) spray plants with Maneb or Zineb.

NAILHEAD SPOT. Caused by *Alternaria tomato,* nailhead spot is a disease characterized by grayish-brown spots on the fruit, and is controlled by using resistant cultivars, such as Marglobe, and by spraying with Maneb or Zineb.

SEPTORIA LEAF SPOT. Septoria leaf spot, associated with *Septoria lycopersici,* appears first as small water-soaked spots on the underside of the older leaves. The older spots have brownish borders with grayish centers. Small, elongated, brownish lesions occur on the stem.

Control methods are the same as for early blight.

ROOT KNOT. Root knot is an enlarged malformation of the roots caused by very tiny nematodes. The nematodes can be starved out by rotating for two or three years with such crops as iron cowpeas, corn, oats, velvet beans, and peanuts. Care should be taken to use nematode-free soil in the plant bed.

GRAY LEAF SPOT. Gray leaf spot (*Stemphylium solani*) is a fungus disease receiving considerable attention recently. Small black specks appear on older leaves, causing them to drop after becoming glazed. Control is accomplished by using disease-free seedlings and spraying weekly with Maneb or Zineb.

DAMPING OFF. Caused by several organisms, *Pythium, Phytophthora,* and *Botrytis,* damping off attacks the small seedlings at the surface of the soil, causing the stems to shrivel and the plants to topple over.

The control consists of using fresh or sterilized sandy soil, treating

Fig. 30.4—Tomato plant showing good set of fruit.

the seeds with thiram or captan, and keeping the small plants and the surface of the soil dry.

BACTERIAL CANKER. Associated with the bacterium *Corynebacterium michiganense,* bacterial canker is one of the most serious diseases of tomatoes. It is carried on and in the seed.

The first signs are a curling downward of the lower leaves, which begin to wilt and die. Pale streaks appearing on the stems and veins of the leaves crack open and form cankers. A diseased stem lesion shows a mealy-looking layer of bacteria-filled tissue.

Diseased fruits are spotted first with small white specks, and later have brown spots encircled with a white ring.

The control is the same as that for early blight, except for application of fungicides.

BLOSSOM-END ROT. Blossom-end rot is a physiological disease of the fruit, caused by severe changes in moisture conditions, which bring about a physiological drouth in the fruit, causing the breakdown. The disease appears as a dark brown, leathery rot on the blossom end of the fruit. Under some conditions, the rot can be held in check by cultural practices which help to conserve the soil moisture and by spraying plants with calcium nitrate.

SUNSCALD. Sunscald is caused by sudden exposure of tender green fruits to the sun. Any measure which encourages foliar growth will tend to reduce this malady.

VIRUS DISEASES. There are several virus diseases of tomatoes including tobacco mosaic, cucumber mosaic, double virus streak, single virus streak, spotted wilt, and curly top. The virus diseases of tomatoes are important because of the large number of perennial weeds which are host plants. The diseases are highly infectious and readily spread by insects and cultural operations. Sanitation and the control of vectors will reduce the spread of viruses.

GROWTH CRACKS. Fruit cracking results in one of the most serious problems of tomato production, especially for processing. Decay organisms and fruit flies gain entrance through the cracked area. This part of the fruit must be cut away, adding to the waste and cost of trimming.

If conditions are favorable, cracking may begin from the mature-green through the turning stage. The ripe fruit are not susceptible, but cracks already started may grow during ripening.

Cultivars with partial resistance are being developed, and these should be used where cracking is prevalent.

Insects

Several insects attack tomatoes and these are listed in Chapter 11. The two discussed below are particularly devastating in certain areas.

HORNWORM. Hornworms, of which two species *(Protoparce quinque, Maculata* and *P. sexta)* feed on tomatoes, are large, green larvae. They are ravenous feeders and quickly damage the plants if not controlled. Spraying or dusting with carbaryl is recommended.

TOMATO FRUITWORM. The tomato fruitworm *(Heliothis zea)* is also known as cotton boll worm and corn earworm. It eats into the fruit from the stem end, and thereafter feeds from the inside. Thorough, persistent spraying with carbaryl or toxaphene reduces the losses. See Chapter 11.

HARVESTING, HANDLING, STORING, AND MARKETING

Harvesting

Practically all the tomatoes grown for processing in California and increasing amounts in other regions are harvested mechanically (Fig. 30.6). Machines for harvesting fresh market tomatoes have also been successfully used. However, much greater care must be exercised to prevent bruising the fruits for the fresh market.

The picking basket should be rigid, smooth, not over $\frac{1}{2}$ bushel in capacity, and preferably lined for protection against bruising.

The degree of ripeness at which the tomatoes are harvested depends upon the purpose for which they are grown and the time and method of shipping.

For canning and for manufacturing of tomato products, the fruit is fully ripened on the vine (Figs. 30.5 and 30.6). For local markets, it is harvested in the hard ripe and pink stages. For the bulk of the distant shipments to the northern markets, the fruit is picked in the mature-green stage. However, a considerable portion of the crop picked for shipment is in the turning and pink condition. The mature-green fruits are termed "green stock" and the turning and pink fruits called "pink stock" by the trade.

The green stock is shipped either without refrigeration on short hauls or with refrigeration on the last part of long hauls exceeding 8 to 10 days. Pink stock requiring over 24 hours to reach the market is shipped under refrigeration. Prolonged exposures to low temperatures interfere with coloring.

For home use tomatoes may be left on the plants until they are fully colored, if the average daily temperatures are 75° F. or below. At higher temperatures the rate of softening is increased and coloring is delayed. The fruits should be harvested at the turning stage and ripened at 60° to 70° F.

Fig. 30.5—Tomatoes for processing harvested by hand.

Photograph by E. C. Wittmeyer

Fig. 30.6—Tomatoes harvested by machine for processing.

Univ. of Ill. Photograph

Distinguishing Mature Fruits

The future of the fresh-tomato industry depends largely upon supplying the trade with tomatoes of high quality. The longer the tomato can be left on the vine before picking for market, the higher will be the quality of the fruit when ripe. The grower should train and supervise his pickers to recognize and pick only the mature fruits. A practical test is to cut a few average tomatoes crosswise with a sharp knife. If the pulp surrounding the seeds is slightly jellylike, permitting the seeds to give way before the edge of the knife without being cut, the fruit is then mature.

Following are definitions of terms in describing the degrees of tomato maturity:

IMMATURE. Before the seeds have fully developed and before the jellylike cells surrounding the seeds have developed.

MATURE-GREEN. The fruit is fully grown and shows a brownish ring at the stem scar after removal of the calyx; the light green color at the blossom end has changed to a yellow-green cast, and the seeds are surrounded with jellylike cells filling the seed cavity.

TURNING. About one-fourth of the surface, at the blossom end, shows pink ("breaker" stage).

PINK. About three-fourths of the surface is pink.

HARD RIPE. The fruit is nearly all red or pink, but the flesh is firm.

OVER RIPE. The fruit is fully colored and soft.

Ripening

Mature-green tomatoes require from 6 to 20 days to ripen in air at 68° to 70° F. and will not color faster at higher temperatures. When either storage or field temperatures remain continuously above 80° to 85° F., the fruit does not develop a red color.

Oxygen is essential for the coloring of tomatoes. Therefore, ventilation is beneficial, and wrapping in paper is detrimental to the development of the best quality when transporting and ripening tomatoes.

Grading and Packing

Different systems of grading are followed in different parts of the country. The U.S. Department of Agriculture has established U.S. grades, Numbers 1, 2, and 3, which have been adopted in many localities. The essentials of grading are to eliminate all injured fruits and to separate the sound fruits according to their grade, maturity, and size. When tomatoes are sold on grade, the careful grower is repaid for his production and careful handling of a high-quality product. Methods of packing vary in different parts of the country. Regardless of the pack, uniformity always makes it more attractive and commands a better price (Fig. 30.7).

Fig. 30.7—Fruits harvested at the "breaker" stage packed for market.

Storing

Tomatoes can be kept in storage for only a comparatively short time. The best storage temperature at which breakdown is not likely to occur and ripening will take place is between 54° and 59° F. Fruit picked when three-fourths ripe and placed in well-ventilated storage with low humidity and at 34° to 36° F. will keep for about three weeks.

For home use, picking green-mature fruit just befort frost, storing it in the most desirable place about the premises, and sorting it every two or three days will give a gradual supply of ripening fruit for about a month. Most rapid coloring occurs at about 68° F.

Marketing

Most of the tomatoes for processing are grown under contract with prices based on grades determined by federal-state graders at the time of delivery.

If fresh market tomatoes are to be sold directly to local retail stores, they may be harvested at the firm-ripe stage. When the channel from grower to retailer is not so direct, turning or pink fruit may be harvested.

It is questionable whether the quality of pink tomatoes is superior to mature-green fruit at the retail level. Mature-green tomatoes are ripened in ripening rooms at major shipping points as well as in terminal markets. The shipment of tomatoes harvested at the "breaker" stage is increasing.

Tomatoes shipped long distances to market are harvested at the mature-green and breaker stages. Some begin ripening in transit, while the remainder are held in ripening rooms at the terminal markets. As the fruits ripen, they are sorted and packed in retail containers. The average repacker prefers to handle mature-green rather than pink tomatoes.

Tomatoes go to the packing house from the field partially culled or straight field run. They are usually handled in boxes that can be lifted and emptied readily. Packing house operations may include unloading, weighing, checking, cleaning, drying, waxing, sorting, grading, sizing, wrapping, packing, lidding, and loading into cars or trucks. Many shippers have ripening rooms where the tomatoes are exposed to ethylene gas. The operations may depend on how and where the tomatoes are to be marketed.

The packing house may buy the tomatoes outright; pack them for a fee; handle them on consignment; or in the case of a co-operative, act for the grower-members as their sales agent. Small growers may grade and pack their tomatoes on the farm. This type of operation is not likely to attract buyers for chain stores that demand a large volume of a uniform pack.

EXPORTS AND IMPORTS. Fresh tomatoes are both imported and exported in substantial volume. Imports have grown steadily, totaling 586,844,000 pounds valued at $88,745,000 in 1972 compared with $20,926,000 in 1963. Mexico supplies virtually all the imported fresh tomatoes. Exports were 136,751,000 pounds in 1972, valued at $17,480,000 and were shipped almost entirely to Canada. In 1972 about 158,600,000 pounds of canned tomatoes were imported valued at $16,059,000, compared with 72,098,000 pounds valued at $12,549,000 in 1977 (see Table 13.2 for 1977 figures). Italy and Spain supplied most of the canned tomatoes, while Mexico and Israel were the major suppliers of tomato concentrates. Imports of the latter, mostly tomato paste, totaled 126,-241,000 pounds valued at $18,483,000 in 1972, compared with 65,198,000 pounds and $16,202,000 in 1977. Exports of tomato paste in 1977 were 34,714,000 pounds valued at $13,216,000. Other significant foreign sources of these tomato products include Israel, Mexico, Portugal, and Spain, while Canada, Europe, the Caribbean area, and Japan were the principal markets for these products. Exports of canned tomatoes in 1972 were 19,230,000 pounds valued at $2,778,000, compared with 23,621,000 pounds valued at $5,570,000 in 1977 (see Table 13.2 for 1977 figures).

SELECTED REFERENCES

Allen, E. J., and Fudge, T. G., "Producing Early Tomato Plants," Univ. of Ark. Agr. Ext. Ser. MP 119, 1969.

Anonymous, "Commercial Production of Greenhouse Tomatoes," USDA *Agriculture Handbook* 328, 1971.

Anonymous, "Controlling Tomato Diseases," USDA Farmers' Bull. 2200, 1972.

Coffey, D. L., *et al.*, "Tomato Production in Tennessee," Univ. of Tenn. Agr. Exp. Sta. Bull. 546, 1975.

Courter, J. W., and Vandemark, J. S, "Growing Tomatoes at Home," Ill. Agr. Ext. Circ. 981, 1973.

Fletcher, R. F., and MacNab, A. A., "Growing Tomatoes at Home," Pa. State Univ. Coop. Ext. Ser. Circ. 558, 1975.

Gould, W. A., "Mass Sorting of Mechanically Harvested Tomatoes," Ohio Agr. Exp. Sta. Res. Circ. 209, 1975.

Johnson, H., Jr., *et al.*, "Greenhouse Tomato Production," Univ. of Calif. Coop. Ext. Leaflet 2806, 1975.

Johnson, P. E., *et al.*, "Tomato Production and Mechanization in Indiana," Purdue Univ. Coop. Ext. Ser. ID 95, 1978.

Magoon, C. E., "Tomatoes," United Fresh Fruit and Vegetable Assoc., Alexandria, Va., 1969.

Marlowe, G. A., Jr., and Montelaro, J., "Tomato," Univ. of Fla. Coop. Ext. Ser. Circ. 98D, 1977.

McCarver, O. W., "Tomatoes," Mont. State Univ. Coop. Ext. Ser. Circ. 297, 1978.

O'Dell, C. R., and McCart, G. D., "Fertilization of Fresh Market Tomatoes Grown Under Trellis and Cage Culture," Va. Poly. Inst. Res. Div. Rep. 157, 1974.

Precheur, R., Greig, J. K., and Armbrust, D. V., "The Effects of Wind and Wind-Plus-Sand on Tomato Plants," *J. Amer. Soc. Hort. Sci.* 103(3):351-355, 1978.

Schoenemann, J., "Growing Tomatoes in Wisconsin—For Home and Market," Univ. of Wisc. Coop. Ext. Pro. A1691, 1975.

Shannon, D. J., and Cotter, D. J., "Tomato Disease Control," N. Mex. Ext. Ser. Circ. 437, 1971.

Sims, W. L., *et al.*, "Mechanized Growing and Harvesting of Fresh Market Tomatoes," Univ. of Calif. Coop. Ext. Leaflet 2815, 1976.

Sims, W. L., Zobel, M. P., and King, R. C., "Mechanized Growing and Harvesting of Processing Tomatoes," Univ. of Calif. Agr. Ext. Ser. AXT—232, 1968.

Stoner, A. K., "Commercial Production of Greenhouse Tomatoes," USDA *Agriculture Handbook 382*, 1971.

Rutledge, A. D., "Growing Staked Tomatoes in Tennessee," Univ. of Tenn. Coop. Ext. Ser. Pub. 737, 1977.

CHAPTER 31

Watermelons

CLASSIFICATION, ORIGIN, AND HISTORY

The watermelon *(Citrullus lunatus)* is thought to be native to Africa, although evidence of possible American origin has been reported. Early French explorers found Indians growing melons in the Mississippi Valley. Melons are also reported as having been cultivated in New England in 1629, and in Florida prior to 1664. However, descriptions indicate that the early American melon was of the citron type and that the true watermelon came originally from Africa. Its culture was unknown in Europe until the sixteenth century.

SCOPE AND IMPORTANCE

Since the days of early American settlers, the watermelon has increased in importance commercially. Watermelons ranked seventh in acreage and fifteenth in value among the 22 principal vegetables in 1977. Acreage has fluctuated gradually downward from 383,800 acres in 1949 to 327,990 acres in 1959 and down to 227,400 acres in 1977. Like most crops, acre yields increased from 67 hundredweight in 1949 to 82 in 1959 and to a record 116 hundredweight in 1977. Concurrently, crop value rose from $29,450,000 to $46,708,000 and to $89,414,000 between 1949 and 1977.

The approximate geographical distribution and 1949 to 1977 performance of watermelons are shown in Fig. 31.1 Texas, Florida, Georgia, South Carolina, and Mississippi led in production and value in 1977 as presented in Table 31.1.

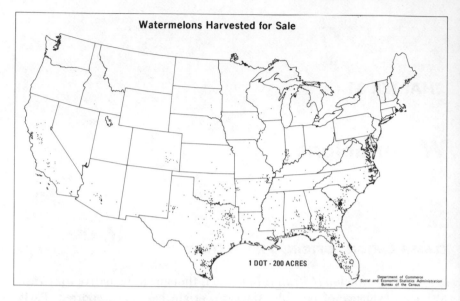

Fig. 31.1—Acreage, distribution, production, and value of watermelons.

UNITED STATES TOTAL

Year	Acreage	Production 1,000 Cwt.	Value, $1,000
1949	383,800	25,692	29,450
1959	327,990	26,995	46,798
1969	272,400	25,950	53,267
1977	227,400	26,371	89,414

TRENDS IN PRODUCTION EFFICIENCY

Watermelons are a relatively extensive, inexpensive crop to produce, and less labor is required to produce and harvest an acre than for most vegetables. Between 1939 and 1977 the production-harvest labor input decreased from 60 to 35 man-hours per acre during a substantial increase in acre yields. The man-hour output increased 338 percent during this period. With improved cultivars, cultural practices, and machines, labor efficiency continues to rise.

CLIMATIC REQUIREMENTS

The watermelon requires a long, frost-free growing season with relatively high temperatures. It is not highly sensitive to extremes in humid-

Table 31.1—Watermelons for Fresh Market: Harvest Season and Estimated Acreage, Yield, Production, and Value in Leading States, 1977.

State*	Harvest Season	Harvested Acreage	Yield per Acre, Cwt.	Production per 1,000 Cwt.	Price per Cwt.	Value, $1,000
Florida	Spring	51,000	175	8,925	$2.97	26,507
Texas	Summer	30,000	125	3,750	3.26	12,225
Texas	Spring	28,000	99	2,772	4.52	12,259
S. Carolina	Summer	18,000	65	1,170	2.50	2,925
Georgia	Summer	14,400	74	1,066	2.40	2,558
Georgia	Spring	14,200	85	1,207	2.80	3,380
Mississippi	Summer	12,000	67	804	2.12	1,704
Alabama	Summer	11,000	65	715	3.35	2,395
N. Carolina	Summer	7,000	55	385	3.34	1,286
Oklahoma	Summer	7,000	110	770	2.60	2,002
California	Summer	6,600	159	1,048	5.22	5,477
California	Fall	5,900	155	915	5.23	4,785
Missouri	Summer	4,200	125	525	3.00	1,575
Arkansas	Summer	3,600	11	256	3.70	947
California	Spring	3,500	195	683	5.30	3,620
Maryland	Summer	2,700	155	419	3.59	1,504
Arizona	Summer	2,600	160	416	4.90	2,038
Delaware	Summer	1,900	150	285	3.59	1,023
Arizona	Spring	1,200	150	180	5.70	1,026
United States		227,400	116	26,371	3.39	89,414
Total	Spring (54%)	101,400	138	14,012	3.42	48,005
Total	Summer (46%)	126,000	98	12,359	3.35	41,409

*Commercial quantities of watermelons are grown in some other states.

ity, and therefore, it can be grown over a wide range of varying climatic conditions extending from the humid regions of the Southeast to the arid sections of the Southwest. However, leaf diseases are more destructive in humid climates. Normally, the watermelon requires 80 to 120 days to mature fruit, the time varying with the date of planting and the locality in which melons are grown.

SELECTING CULTIVARS AND SEED

Commercial cultivars of watermelons may vary in color from gray to dark green; and in shape, from round to long and cylindrical. Cultivars having deep red flesh and dark-colored seed are preferred because of popular association of those characters with proper maturity and desirable eating quality. The market demand in the past has been for medium to large melons. There are indications that the greater demand in the future will be for medium to small fruit. Toughness of rind and solidity of flesh, combined with excellent eating quality, are essential factors in a desirable shipping melon, while for home use, quality only is of prime consideration.

Cultivars

There are many well-known market cultivars; however, some of them are being replaced by disease-resistant types. A tabular description of some of these and other cultivars is given in Table 31.2.

Securing Seed

Purchasing seed from reputable seedsmen should be a universal practice among melon growers. Knowledge of the origin of seed is preferable, so that repeated orders of desirable cultivars or strains may be obtained from year to year. Good seed should be viable, true to name, and free from seed-borne diseases and insects. Commercial seed production is confined largely to the vicinities of Leesburg, Florida, and Rocky Ford, Colorado; however, it is not uncommon for melon growers in the various commercial sections to produce seed in limited quantities. Since watermelons are pollinated by insects, the seed fields must be isolated to maintain purity.

PREPARING THE SOIL

Soil Preferences

Watermelons thrive best on newly cleared, sandy-loam soils that are rich in humus, fertile, well drained, and slightly acid. There should be enough litter to provide anchorage for the vines, thus preventing them from being rolled by high winds. It is a common practice in commercial sections to grow watermelons on almost any type of soil that is well drained, warm, fairly productive, and free from injurious insects and diseases. However, it has been observed that, when planted on heavy soils, the plants develop slowly, and the size and quality of the fruit are usually inferior.

Table 31.2—Brief Description of Selected Cultivars of Watermelons.

Cultivar	Chief Use	Season (Days)	Resistance	Size (Lbs.), Shape	Fruit Ext. Color	Fruit Flesh	Fruit Seed Color
All Sweet	Market	90	Anthracnose F Wilt	25 & oblong	Green stripe	Red	Small, brown
Charleston Gray 133	Shipping	85	Anthracnose F Wilt	30 & oblong	Pale green	Red, sweet	Brown, dark veins
Congo	Shipping	95	Anthracnose	25 & oblong	Med. green dark stripe	Red, firm, sweet	Light tan
Crimson Sweet	Market	85	Anthracnose F Wilt	25 & oval	Striped	Red, sweet	Small, brown
Garrisonian	Trucking	85	Anthracnose	35 & oblong	Striped	Bright red, very sweet	Marked, dark white
Jubilee	Shipping	95	Anthracnose F Wilt	40 & oblong	Striped	Red, good flavor	Large, brown
Klondike 155	Shipping	85	F Wilt	25 & oblong	Dark green	Dark pink	Black
Klondike R-7	Shipping	85	F Wilt	25 & oblong	Green	Red	Black tips
Peacock Improved	Shipping	90		20-25, oblong	Striped	Blood red, crisp	Brown, small
Petite Sweet	"Ice Box"	75	Anthracnose F Wilt	8 & round	Dark green striped	Red	Brown, small
Smokylee	Market	85	Anthracnose F Wilt	23 & oblong	Green	Red	
Sugar Baby	"Ice Box"	75		8 & round	Dark green	Red, good flavor	Dark tan, small
Tri-X 313	Market	90		Medium & oval	Striped	Red, sweet	Seedless

Preparing the Seedbed

Preparation of the watermelon seedbed should begin well in advance of the planting season. The land should be turned to a depth of 7 or 8 inches during the late fall or early winter to allow ample time for vegetable matter to decay. Just before planting, the land should be thoroughly harrowed. The field should then be marked off in rows varying from 8 to 12 feet apart, the distance being determined by the capacity of the land to produce light or rank vine growth. In the southeastern states, a 10- by 10-foot spacing is generally used. In Texas and some southwestern sections, spacing approximates or exceeds 10 by 10 feet. After fertilizer has been applied in the row that designates the direction in which the melons are to be cultivated, two furrows are thrown together with a turning plow, thus providing a slight ridge on which to plant. Seeding on this ridge elevates the plants and affords better drainage. Some very early plantings in California are made on the south sides of sloping beds.

FERTILIZING, MANURING, AND LIMING

Since watermelons normally are grown on the lighter soil types, fertilization is practically indispensable in the commercial production of this crop.

Fertilizing

All available data indicate that a complete fertilizer is essential for successful watermelon production. The most generally used analysis contains about 5 percent nitrogen, 8 percent phosphorus, and 8 percent potassium. The rate of application normally ranges from 400 to 800 pounds per acre. Fertilizer may be applied continuously along the row, or it may be placed in a more concentrated position around the plant by extending the application 2 or 3 feet on each side of the hill. If applied directly under the seed, it should be thoroughly mixed with the soil, although there is likely to be less injury to germination if it is placed in furrows 2 or 3 inches on either side of the seed. A supplemental side dressing of a nitrogen fertilizer may be applied at the time vine growth begins. This is considered an excellent practice among leading commercial growers in some sections.

Manuring

Barnyard and stable manures are common spreaders of *Fusarium* wilt. Such manure, if used for watermelons, is likely to introduce diseases early in the growing season that will result in serious loss. However, if manure is known to be free of harmful diseases, it is an excellent source of nutrients and humus and may be used to advantage in supplementing commercial fertilizer. The usual rate of application is 2 to 4 tons per acre, applied in the drill in advance of the planting season. There are no data showing the value of green manure in watermelon production, although it is general knowledge that the lighter soils in the South are low in humus content and that increased yields almost invariably result from the use of cover crops. Green cover crops should be turned under about one month in advance of the planting season.

Liming

Since the watermelon is tolerant of the degree of acidity normally contained in the soils, liming has not been proved essential in the culture of this crop. Only when the pH is below 5 should liming be considered.

PLANTING

Starting Plants in Bands

Maturity may be hastened a few days and production slightly increased in the South by starting plants in bands or peat pots in greenhouses or hotbeds and then transplanting them to the field after the danger of frost has passed. It is doubtful, however, whether the narrow margin of profit justifies the practice, and most growers in the South have not adopted it. In areas with a relatively short growing season, transplanting may be profitable. Seed should be planted in containers not more than three weeks before the plants are to be shifted to the field.

Seeding in the Field

Practically all watermelons grown in the South are seeded in the open field. The date of planting in the various sections should be such that the seedlings will appear above ground just after the danger of frost has passed. This may be brought about by planting the seed approximately 10 days to 2 weeks in advance of the average date of the last killing frost. To compensate for any frost injury that may occur to this planting, growers frequently make one or two additional seedings at seven-day intervals.

The watermelon hill usually is indicated by intersecting furrows marked off at 10-foot intervals in the field. After the fertilizer has been applied and a ridge has been established, eight to ten seeds are planted in each hill at a depth of ¾ to 1 inch. Planting normally is done by hand. Approximately 1 pound of seed is required to plant an acre. The date of planting varies from early January in Florida and southern California to the first part of June in the late-growing areas.

CULTIVATING AND WEEDING

Cultivating

The watermelon is a shallow-rooted plant; consequently, shallow tillage should be practiced. Cultivation should begin soon after the young plants emerge and should continue as long as vine length will permit. Usually not more than three or four thorough workings are necessary in producing a crop of melons. However, the crop should be cultivated often enough to prevent weed growth. In cultivating, care should be taken that the vines are not bruised as they are highly susceptible to mechanical injury. It is advisable to turn vines only at the tip as excessive turning is likely to roll the vines and thus cause shedding of the young fruit.

Where the hills have been carefully checked, watermelons may be cultivated in both directions with a harrow or weeder until vine-growth interferes. These implements, supplemented with a cultivator for close work, will reduce the necessity for hand weeding. After the vines have grown to considerable length, they should be turned into a clearly defined row. This will leave an open space in the middle which will facilitate late cultivation.

Thinning and Weeding

Where there is no indication of disease or insect injury, thinning of the young plants should begin soon after they appear above the ground. It is advisable to reduce the plants gradually to the desired number. At the first thinning four or five of the most vigorous seedlings should be left. These plants should be well distributed in order that proper development may take place. The last thinning should be deferred until the plants are well established and several true leaves have developed. In the final stand, it is a general practice to leave two plants to each hill, but some growers leave only one.

Often it is necessary when the plants are small, to supplement cultivation with hand weeding and hoeing near the hills. This can be done
while thinning. Cost of weeding can be reduced by applying Alanap-3 at
the rate of 3 to 6 pounds per acre at the time of planting (Table 9.2).

Pruning

It is customary among producers of high-grade watermelons to prune
or thin the fruit in order to obtain a larger, more uniformly shaped
melon. Pruning does not mean cutting away the vine but rather reducing
the number of melons on the vine. It is generally recommended that two
melons be left to each plant or hill. However, in the light of data resulting from a pruning test at the Georgia Coastal Plain Experiment Station,
it seems that better practice, in early-season pruning, would be to remove
only melons that are illshaped or that have no potential market value.
After the early crop is set, subsequent pruning of the late-set fruit should
increase the size of marketable melons. Four to six fruits may be left on
small-fruited cultivars.

The theory involved in pruning is that when the number of melons
per vine is reduced, the plant's producing power will be concentrated in a
smaller number of fruits, thereby increasing size and perhaps quality.

Setting Fruit

The watermelon, like other cucurbits, is monoecious, both male and
female flowers being produced separately on the same plant. Pollen must
be transferred from one flower to another by insects. Poor fruit set and
misshapen melons can result from an insufficient population of bees.

CONTROLLING DISEASES AND INSECTS

Diseases

The leaf, stem, and fruit of the watermelon are attacked by diseases,
among the most destructive of which are wilt, anthracnose, root knot, and
stem-end rot.

WILT. Wilt, caused by *Fusarium oxysporium niveum,* is widely distributed in commercial producing areas and is perhaps the greatest men-
ace to watermelon production in the South. The organism lives in the soil
and penetrates the roots, growing up through the water-conducting channels of the stems. The symptoms are a dark brown discoloration in the

woody portion of the stem and sudden wilting of the individual branches, which soon results in the death of the plant.

The disease can be controlled by using wilt-resistant cultivars, some of which are grown commercially. Losses from the disease can be reduced by using long-time rotations with nonsusceptible crops, preventing drainage water from flowing in from infested fields, and avoiding the use of stable manure that is likely to carry infestation. After land has once become infested with the wilt organism, it is practically unfit for future use in production of susceptible watermelon cultivars, as the disease has been known to survive from 10 to 15 years in the soil.

ANTHRACNOSE. (See Chapter 22.)

ROOT KNOT (NEMATODES). (See Chapter 22.)

STEM-END ROT. Caused by a species of *Diplodia,* stem-end rot is primarily a transit disease and is common and destructive in all sections of the South. Uninjured fruits on the vine are entirely resistant to the disease. Any abrasion on the melon becomes a suitable entry place for the spores, thus causing infection of the fruit. However, the disease normally enters through the stem. It is effectively controlled by careful handling of the fruit to prevent bruises or scratches and by treating the stem with a fixed copper paste as the melons are loaded in the car.

Insects

The principal insects attacking watermelons are melon aphids, cucumber beetles, leaf hoppers, and pickleworms. Controls for these insects are given in Chapter 11.

HARVESTING AND MARKETING

Harvesting

Watermelons should not be harvested until they are ripe, as melons do not develop the desired internal color or sugar content if taken from the vines while immature. There is no marked difference in the appearance of green and ripe melons; consequently, only experienced pickers should be used in harvesting. The sound method, which consists of thumping, is generally used. Other indications of maturity are (1) dying of the tendril accompanying the fruit, although this is not a true indication for all cultivars; and (2) change in color of the portion of the melon resting on the ground, from a pale white to a creamy yellow.

Melons should be cut from the vines rather than pulled or broken off, and the stems should be left as long as possible in order that they may be reclipped and treated for stem-end rot as they are loaded in the car.

Handling

In handling melons, care should be exercised to avoid bruising and scratching, as the stem-end rot fungus enters the fruit through abrasions. When being carried to heap rows in the field, melons should be placed carefully on the ground, and the trucks or wagons in which they are hauled should be well padded.

Grading

Uniformity is an essential factor in marketing watermelons. Consequently, grades have been established which group melons according to weight. Most wholesaling of watermelons is conducted on the basis of U.S. standards. Copies of these standards can be obtained from the Fruit and Vegetable Division of the Agricultural Marketing Service, U.S. Department of Agriculture, Washington, D.C. Most shipments by rail are inspected at shipping points and certified as to quality, condition, grade, and size by federal-state inspectors. Truck shipments are seldom inspected.

Loading

Proper loading is highly important in the successful transportation of watermelons to distant markets. Only sound melons with fresh green stems should be loaded. Cars should be clean, ventilated on sides and ends, with walls amply covered with paper and the floor with dry bedding. It is preferable to haul to concentration points where several cars may be loaded during the same day, thereby making it possible to segregate grades. All stems should be recut and treated with bluestone paste as melons are placed in the car. In placing melons in the car, sizes should be selected that will give a smooth, tight pack (Fig. 31.2) as melons that are held firmly in place while in transit reach the consumer in better condition than those that are loosely packed. Watermelons that weigh over 20 pounds each should not be loaded more than four layers deep if long, or three deep if round. Lighter melons may be packed one layer

Fig. 31.2—(Top) Doorway view of Congo watermelons loaded lengthwise in railway car. (Bottom) Melons loaded crosswise. This method results in less bruising in shipment.

Photograph by R. K. Showalter

higher. Over 80 percent of the shipped watermelons are moved by truck. Rail shipment is used primarily for long distances.

Marketing

Volume buyers prefer to purchase watermelons in production areas where dependable supply, quality, and prices are established. Growers in many sections have established cooperatives or selling agencies to supply this demand.

The principal crop of watermelons is still produced in the South, but substantial areas have developed in the Middle West and in California.

Southern grown watermelons generally are shipped north, while those from other producing areas move in various directions to accommodate demand. Early melons bring higher prices, which generally decline as the peak of production is reached in hot weather.

Large quantities of watermelons are shipped from the areas of production in refrigerated or vent-cooled trucks or railroad cars. Considerable amounts are transported in open trucks to local markets, and a large volume is sold at roadside and drive-in markets and by hucksters.

EXPORTS AND IMPORTS. U.S. exports of watermelons, which in 1972 totaled 102,979,000 pounds valued at $3,276,000, were destined almost exclusively for Canada. Very small quantities were also shipped to the United Kingdom and Bermuda in 1972. Exports traditionally take place largely during the months of May through August. Imports of watermelons in 1972 totaled 159,090,000 pounds valued at $3,439,000. They originated almost entirely from Mexico and entered largely during the March through June period.

In 1977, the export of 84,651,000 pounds of watermelons was valued at $3,465,000 and went principally to Sweden and Bermuda. In 1977, watermelon imports of 175,337,000 pounds amounted to $7,317,000 (Table 13.2).

SELECTED REFERENCES

Andrus, C. F., et al., "Production of Seedless Watermelons," USDA Tech. Bull. 1425, 1971.
Anonymous, "Watermelons for the Garden," USDA Leaflet 528, 1966.
Brown, J. D., and Elrod, J. D., "Competitive Position of the Georgia Watermelon," Ga. Agr. Exp. Sta. Res. Bull. 28, 1968.
Close, E. G., and Varick, J., "Comparative Methods of Handling Watermelons—Bulk and Cartons," USDA, ARS Series MA–1–71, 1971.
Cook, W. P., Smith, F. H., and Thomas, C. A., "Growing Watermelons in South Carolina," Clemson Univ. Coop. Ext. Ser. Bull. 121, 1974.
Curwen, D., and Schulte, E., "Vine Crops," Univ. of Wisc., Coop. Ext. Pro., A2419, 1978.
Doolittle, S. P., et al., "Commercial Watermelon Growing," USDA, ARS Agr. Inf. Bull. 259, 1962.
Ford, K. E., "Distribution of Watermelons on the Fresh Market," Ga. Exp. Sta. Res. Rep. 126, 1972.
Hall, C. V., "Producing Watermelons in Kansas," Kansas State Univ., Agr. Exp. Sta. Bull. 532, 1970.
Kucharek, T., "Disease Control Program for Watermelons," Univ. of Fla. Coop. Ext. Ser. Rep. No. 15, 1975.
Montelaro, J., and Marvel, M. E., "Watermelon Production Guide," Fla. Agr. Ext. Ser. Circ. 96B, 1965.

Montelaro, J., *et al.*, "Grow Watermelons More Profitably," La. State Univ. Coop. Ext. Ser. Pub. 1146, 1977.

Schweers, V. H., and Sims, W. L., "Watermelon Production," Univ. of Calif. Div. of Agr. Sci. Leaflet 2672, 1977.

CHAPTER 32

Other Vegetables

A number of vegetables which are either grown in restricted areas or are of less general economic importance are discussed in this chapter. Special information on the most important phases of culture is included; but the more general practices are omitted, since they are treated in Section One. For example, Chapters 9 and 11 discuss cultivation and pest control, respectively, and Tables 8.1, 8.2, and 8.3 give information on planting dates, rates, depths, and methods. Since the vegetables are conveniently grouped according to botanical families or growing seasons in Chapter 2, complete information may be found on a related crop in one of the special crop chapters in Section Two. For example, Chapter 16 on cabbage contains considerable information which is applicable to collards, Brussels sprouts, and cauliflower.

For convenient reference, the vegetables in this chapter are arranged alphabetically by their common names. The principal ones are listed in Table 32.1 by acreage, production, and value in leading states.

BROCCOLI (SPROUTING)

Classification and Importance

Broccoli (*Brassica oleracea* var. *italica*) belongs to the Brassica group, and, in recent years, it has become an important addition to the seasonal supply of our cabbagelike vegetables. Broccoli is becoming increasingly important, ranking fourteenth in acreage and fourteenth in value among the 22 principal vegetables in 1977. From 9,000 acres in 1939, an estimated 37,670 hundredweight valued at about $18,500,000 was harvested in 1965. By 1977, acreage had increased to 70,890 acres, and value to $92,748,000 (Table 32.1). California produced about 96 percent of the commercial crop in 1977, followed by Oregon, Texas, and Arizona.

While the labor required to produce and harvest broccoli is relatively high, it decreased more than 25 percent between 1939 and 1959, and substantially more recently because of improved practices and mechanization.

Table 32.1—Miscellaneous Vegetables for Fresh Market and Processing: Principal States by Estimated Acreage, Yield, Production, and Value in 1977.*

Vegetable	Principal States	Hervested Acreage	Yield per Acre, Cwt.	Production per 1,000 Cwt.	Price per Cwt.	Value, $1,000
Broccoli	California, Texas Oregon, Arizona	70,890	80	5,694	$16.30	92,748
Cauliflower	California, New York, Arizona, Michigan	37,360	99	3,707	19.80	73,387
Artichoke	California	10,800	66	713	19.30	13,775
Garlic	California	10,400	110	1,144	14.30	16,336
Escarole (Endive)	Florida, New Jersey, Ohio	7,750	130	1,008	15.60	15,729
Brussels Sprouts	California	5,400	120	648	19.70	12,765
Eggplant	Florida, New Jersey	3,150	203	641	11.40	7,297

*These seven miscellaneous vegetables represent only 3.1 percent of the harvested acreage and 5.0 percent of the total value of the 22 principal commercial vegetables produced in the United States in 1977 (see Table 1.3).

Cultivars

Cultivars of broccoli may be classed as early, medium, or late according to their response to time of planting. When seeded or transplanted in the early spring, early cultivars will mature rapidly enough to produce crops before the onset of hot weather. They may also be seeded in summer to be harvested in early fall. Early DeCicco and Early Spartan are included in this group. Cultivars of medium maturity are seeded in late spring or summer and would include Calabrese, Waltham 29, Atlantic, Coastal, and Medium 90. Late cultivars are adapted only to areas where broccoli can be grown throughout the winter. These are planted in fall for spring harvest. Medium Late and Neptune (F_1 hybrid) are late maturing cultivars.

Production

Climatic requirements, culture and fertilizer practices, diseases, and insects are similar to those for cabbage (Chapter 16).

Fig. 32.1—A good head of green sprouting broccoli.

BRUSSELS SPROUTS

Classification, Habit, and Culture

Brussels sprouts (*Brassica oleracea* var. *gemmifera*) is one of the numerous cultivated forms derived from the wild cabbage. The plant is a nonheading cabbage which develops miniature heads (sprouts) in the axils of the leaves. It requires a somewhat longer growing season than late cabbage and must, therefore, be planted in the seedbed and in the field earlier than late cabbage. In other respects, its culture up to harvest is the same as that for autumn or late cabbage. The Brussels sprouts plant is as hardy as kale and can be planted in any area where this crop is grown during winter. Like all other cabbages, it is a gross feeder and does best on fertile soil.

Scope and Importance

Acre yields and total production have edged upward since 1949.

California produced practically all of the commercial Brussels sprouts in 1977. About 5,400 acres produced 648,000 hundredweight valued at $12,765,000 (Table 32.1).

Cultivars

There are two general forms of Brussels sprouts, tall growing and dwarf. The dwarf cultivars, Jade Cross and Long Island Improved, are grown in New York. A taller growing cultivar, Half Dwarf Improved, is commonly used in California.

Controlling Diseases and Insects

Brussels sprouts is susceptible to all insects and diseases which attack other cabbages. Among insects, the most troublesome during the warm weather are aphids, caterpillars, and harlequin bugs, all of which should be treated the same as when they attack cabbage. Among diseases, club root is the most troublesome. To control these pests, the seedbed should be on sterile soil, and the field for growing the crop should not have been in cabbage, turnips, or other cabbagelike crops for at least three years previous to the planting of Brussels sprouts.

Harvesting and Packing

The sprouts are produced earliest in the axils of the lower leaves of the plant (Fig. 32.2). When they have attained market size (1 to $1\frac{1}{4}$ inch in diameter), the lower leaves are broken away and the sprouts are cut off close to the stem with a sharp knife. They are carried in baskets or trays to a packing house and are conditioned for packing. Usually they are packed in quart berry boxes, which in turn are packed in 24- or 32-quart crates for shipment. In California, where 90 percent of the commercial crop is grown, plastic film bags are used for packing the sprouts. An increasing amount of the crop is processed by freezing, and is being well accepted by the public.

From the manner of the growth of the plant, it is evident that there will be several successive harvests from the same plant during the season. However, by treating the plants with succinic acid-2,2-dimethylhydrazide (SADH), the set of sprouts can be concentrated so the crop can be harvested mechanically (Fig. 3.2).

Fig. 32.2—Brussels sprouts plants showing leaves removed and lower sprouts harvested.

Ferry Morse Seed Co.

CAULIFLOWER AND HEADING BROCCOLI
OR HARDY CAULIFLOWER

Classification and Importance

Cauliflower (*Brassica oleracea* var. *botrytis*) is the aristocrat of the cultivated cabbages. It is more exacting as to climatic and other environmental conditions than any of its relatives. For these reasons, cauliflower culture is carried on only in relatively few favored localities. California outstands in its production, with New York second. It is also produced commercially in Texas, Michigan, Arizona, Oregon, Colorado, and Washington. A portion of the crop, primarily on the West Coast, is processed by freezing. Most of the cauliflower in California is harvested from November to the first of April, while in New York, it is harvested from August to November. Cauliflower ranked eighteenth in acreage and sixteenth in value among the 22 principal vegetables in 1977, when the estimated 37,360 acres had a farm value of approximately $73,400,000 (Table 32.1).

Cauliflower acreage has fluctuated from 26,000 acres to 30,000 acres during the past 24 years, and acre yields rose slightly. The man-hour requirements to grow and harvest an acre have decreased sharply in recent years because of improved cultural practices and harvesting machines.

Cultivars

The number of actual cultivars is rather small, but a large number of strains are available. These differ mainly in their season of maturity. Cultivars can be grouped into two classes: early cauliflower, of which Snowball and its various strains are the most popular, and the late cauliflower. The late cauliflower is generally grown in the West, and cultivars used are Snowball 421, Helios, and Mayflower.

Soil and Cultural Requirements

The culture of cauliflower should be undertaken only upon very fertile, moist, but well-drained soils. It is essentially a cool-weather crop and should not be planted at a time which will mature the crop in very hot weather.

The production of the plants, the transplanting to the field, and the subsequent handling of the crop up to the time of curd formation is the same as for cabbage. As soon as the heads or buttons appear, care should be exercised to protect them from full sunshine and injury from insects or dirt. Early-maturing cultivars are protected from sun injury by tying the long outside leaves loosely over the forming heads. Late-maturing cultivars are usually self-blanched by the incurving inner leaves.

Harvesting and Packing

The growing heads should be inspected frequently, so that they may be cut as soon as they have attained marketable size and before the curds become discolored, loose, or ricy. All off-type or soiled curds should be kept out of the commercial pack. Marketable heads should be cut with three or four whorls of leaves. These should be trimmed so as to leave a circle of leaf petioles about the head long enough to protect it (Fig. 32.3). The pack presents a better appearance if heads of uniform size are placed in the same receptacle. The style of package varies with the region and the distance to market, but most commercial growers use crates of some kind.

Fig. 32.3—A cauliflower head ready for harvest.

USDA Photograph

CHIVES

Classification and Habit

Chives (*Allium schoenoprasum*) belong to the onion family. In form and habits of growth they closely resemble the wild onion or garlic of the southern states. The plant is supposed to be of European origin. It is a perennial and is propagated both by planting seed and by subdividing the clumps which it forms by natural multiplication (Fig. 32.4). This plant is not grown to any large extent in America, although it is listed in seed catalogues.

Cultural Requirements

Chives should be planted in rows where they may remain for several seasons. In practice, this plant is found to do best if reset every two or three years. In resetting, the compact clumps are lifted and broken into sections of about 25 bulbs each, and these are placed in the new locations. The culture and fertilization is very similar to that of onions.

Harvesting and Use

The leaves are the part of the plant used, principally for flavoring soups, stews, omelets, cottage cheese, and cream cheese. Cutting off the leaves appears to stimulate multiplication of the plants. Small clumps may be placed in flower pots, forced to produce new growth, and marketed as potted plants.

COLLARDS

Classification and Habit

Collards (*Brassica oleracea* var. *virdis*) belong to the cabbage family, and are grown extensively for winter greens from Virginia southward throughout the Cotton Belt. In these regions the plants are winter hardy.

The collard is a nonheading type of cabbage (Fig. 32.5). The plant is a gross feeder and frequently attains the height of 3 or 4 feet. Collards, besides being winter hardy, will stand more heat than cabbages and provide a supply of cabbage greens long into the hot weather.

Fig. 32.4—The leaves of the chives plant are used for flavoring.

USDA Photograph

Cultivars

The Georgia or Southern, Green Glaze, Morris Heading, and the Vates are the important cultivars. Some seed companies list a cabbage collard, which is a cross between a Georgia collard and the Charleston Wakefield cabbage. Claims indicate that it has the hardiness of the collard and forms loose heads with the quality and flavor of the cabbage. It is also claimed that heads can be left on the plants all winter and used as needed.

Fig. 32.5—Georgia collards are nonheading but otherwise similar to cabbage.

Cultural Requirements

Seeds may be sown in the spring or in the fall where the plants are to stand, or they may be sown in seedbeds and transplanted to the field. They are spaced further apart than cabbage in rows 3 to 4 feet apart. The subsequent cultivation is the same as that for kale or cabbage. The leaves are gathered for food as they approach full size, but before they become tough or woody. This process produces a tall bare stalk with a tuft of succulent leaves at its top. Staking is frequently necessary to hold plants upright.

DASHEEN OR TARO

Classification and Importance

The dasheen (*Colocasia esculenta*) is a caladiumlike plant. The starchy corms are the edible portion of this widely grown tropical arum. It is closely related to and resembles the common, ornamental elephant's-ear.

The starch content of the dasheen is greater than that of either the potato or the sweet potato. Its protein content is about double and its sugar content about one-half that of the sweet potato. The sugar gives the cooked corm a sweet, nutty flavor, while the large percentage of highly digestible starch, in addition to the protein, renders it a more nutritious food than either the potato or the sweet potato.

This plant is capable, when forced, of providing succulent shoots that may be prepared in the same manner and used in the same way as asparagus, but with a flavor similar to that of the mushroom.

The dasheen is not a common vegetable in the United States, but is cultivated extensively in tropical America, South China, Japan, and the tropical islands of the world. The use and culture of the plant are probably more highly developed in the Hawaiian Islands than elsewhere.

Cultivars

The Trinidad dasheen is considered the best of the large number of cultivars collected and tested.

Soil and Cultural Requirements

The best environment for the dasheen is a rich, moist, but well-drained alluvial, silty soil of creek or river bottom. On hammock soils of North Florida a fertilizer carrying 4 percent nitrogen, 6 percent acid phosphate, and 10 percent potash (as sulfate) at the rate of 700 pounds per acre gave satisfactory results. The dasheen is a long-season crop and for that reason is best adapted to the South Atlantic and Gulf Coast states.

Planting should be done as early as conditions will permit, two to three weeks before the date of the last killing frost. Where the growing season does not exceed six months, it is best to start the tubers or cormels in a greenhouse, hotbed, or cold frame, at least a month in advance of the safe season for planting in the open.

Tubers weighing two to five ounces each are best for seed; they should be planted 2 to 3 inches deep, 2 to 2½ feet apart, with 3½ to 4 feet between rows. Such spacing will permit cultivation early in the season and complete shading of the ground later on. The dasheen is a shallow-rooted plant; therefore, deep cultivation should cease before the roots are injured by the practice.

Harvesting and Storing

A plow may be run under the hills in such a way as to turn the corms out of the ground after the tops have been removed. With small lots that must be harvested by hand, two men with long-handled, round-pointed shovels, one on each side of the plant to be lifted, can usually do the work satisfactorily. After the plants are lifted, the corms must be divided, cleaned, and the so-called tubers or cormels separated from the parent corm.

Dasheens keep satisfactorily at about the same temperature as sweet potatoes, as far as known; however, they do not require the high temperatures necessary for drying and curing sweet potatoes. As large corms do not keep so well as the cormels or tubers, the marketable or edible portion of the crop should be sold without holding too long.

EGGPLANTS

Classification, Origin, and History

The eggplant (*Solanum melongena* var. *esculentum*), often referred to as the "Guinea squash," is a native of the tropics. It has been cultivated for many centuries in India, China, and Arabia and was probably introduced into Europe during the Moorish invasion of Spain.

Scope and Importance

The eggplant is grown commercially in only a few states, but it is produced for local markets and in home gardens in many areas. It is considered a minor vegetable commercially, being the least important of the vegetable crops for market. It ranked last both in acreage and value among the 22 principal vegetables in 1977 (Table 32.1).

Climatic Requirements

The eggplant is a warm-season crop and thrives best at relatively high temperatures. Day temperatures of 80° to 90° F. and night temperatures of 70° to 80° F. are considered optimum. It is more susceptible to injury by low temperature than are tomatoes or peppers. It also has a high-moisture requirement and responds well to irrigation during the periods of drouth and high temperature. A growing season of from 100 to 140 days with high average day and night temperatures is desired for this crop.

Cultivars

The principal cultivars grown are Black Beauty and Fort Myers Market. Florida Market has resistance to Phomopsis fruit rot. The early hybrid cultivar, Black Magic, is adapted to regions with shorter growing seasons. Two other cultivars used to a limited extent are Improved Long Purple and Burpee Hybrid. Most cultivars reach maturity 85 to 90 days after transplanting, but Black Magic will mature in 72 days. A good plant type is shown in Fig. 32.6.

Fig. 32.6—Eggplant showing good set of fruit.

Soil Preferences

For best development, the eggplant requires a well-drained, fertile, sandy-loam soil with a high organic content. In Florida, well-drained hammock lands are preferable because of their fertility and moisture-holding capacity. In northern areas, a location with woods or windbreaks on the north and west sides is desirable because the young plants are susceptible to wind injury soon after being set in the field. The same care is needed in preparing the soil for eggplants as is required for other vegetable crops.

Fertilizing and Manuring

Soils low in humus should be planted to a green-manure crop the previous year, or if barnyard manure is available, it should be used at the rate of 15 to 20 tons per acre or as much as 30 tons on less fertile soils. Commercial fertilizer mixtures containing 5 to 6 percent nitrogen, 8 to 10 percent phosphorus, and 5 to 7 percent potassium are commonly used. They may be applied at the rate of 750 to 1,000 pounds per acre broadcast before working the soil for planting, plus an equal amount as a side dress three to four weeks after planting. The plant is a heavy feeder and occupies the ground for a long season, so one or two side dressings of nitrogen may be necessary. Applications of 20 to 25 pounds per acre should be used.

Growing Plants

This is probably the most important and most difficult job in the whole procedure of eggplant culture. Temperature and moisture requirements are very exacting, and insect and disease control is also a problem. Eggplants are not readily transplanted to the field, particularly in periods of dry weather, unless the plants are stocky and a fair-sized clump of soil is attached to the roots when the plant is removed from the bed (Fig. 32.7).

It is usually desirable to transplant the seedlings, when about 4 to 5 inches high, into veneer bands or pots, or to space them at least 4 inches apart in the plant bed, so that the soil can be cut out in squares with a knife and a block of soil be lifted with the plant when it is transferred to the field.

In the far South, seeds are planted from June to August for the fall and early winter crop and in February and March for the spring crop. In more northern regions plants are started in greenhouses or hotbeds about 8 to 10 weeks before they are to be transplanted in the field. Care must be given not to check the growth of the seedlings.

Planting and Setting

Plants are usually set 2 to 3 feet apart in 3- to 4-foot rows. Small-growing cultivars such as the New Hampshire can be set in 2½-foot rows and spaced from 1½ to 2 feet apart in the row. In general, eggplant should be transplanted into the field about 10 days later than the usual date for tomatoes. If plant protectors such as "hotcaps" are used the plants may be set about two weeks earlier than otherwise.

Fig. 32.7—The stocky plant on right is preferable to the spindling plants grown in smaller containers.

Cultivating

Frequent shallow cultivations should be given to eradicate weeds, and some hand hoeing may be necessary in weedy soil. Since the eggplant is a long-season crop, careful weed control before the plants become large is important.

Harvesting

The fruits when of marketable size are clipped from the plant, leaving the calyx or cap attached to the fruit. Very careful handling is essential, because even slight bruising will disfigure the fruit. Higher yields will be produced if fruits are harvested before they reach full size, provided they are well-colored and of good size. The fruits are edible from the time they are one-third grown until they are fully ripe.

Grading and Marketing

If the fruits are harvested regularly at a definite size, there will be no need for grading except to discard all diseased, misshapen, or bruised fruit. The individual fruits are sometimes wrapped in paper or placed in small paper sacks before being packed in crates, bags, or baskets for shipment. The type and size of container varies from bushel and ⅝-bushel baskets to pepper and berry crates, but the 30-pound bushel basket, hamper, and crate are standard containers.

Eggplants are sold for distant as well as for local markets. Attractive packaging and proper handling are necessary for maximum returns. Retail preference appears to be for small, uniform-sized fruits.

ESCAROLE OR ENDIVE

Classification and Importance

Endive (*Cichorium endivia*) is probably of East Indian origin and belongs to the *Compositae* family. It was used as a food plant by the early Egyptians and later by the Greeks and Romans. It was eaten as a salad and potherb, but is now used mainly as a salad. Although endive has been grown by market gardeners on a small scale for many years, production did not show a marked increase until after 1940. In 1939, statistics were available only for Florida, where 1,000 acres were produced. By 1949, about 3,400 acres valued at $1,870,000 were produced, compared with 8,000 acres worth $4,460,000 in 1959 and 7,750 acres valued at $15,729,000 in 1977. Florida produces more than 70 percent, followed by New Jersey and Ohio (Table 32.1).

Cultivars

There are two types of endive: the curled or fringed, and the broad-leaved, known on the market as *escarole*. Because of its attractiveness in tossed salads and for garnishing, the fringed-leaved type is more widely grown. Cultivars of this type are: Green Curled, Green Curled Pancalier, and Salad King. The broad-leaved cultivars include Full Heart Batavian and Florida Deep Heart.

Culture

Endive grows best in a mild climate. In the deep South, it may be grown as a winter crop. In most regions it can be grown as a spring or early summer crop. In the North, endive can be grown throughout the summer where irrigation is available. The plants flower in response to low temperatures (vernalization) and long photoperiods. The early spring crop should be grown from transplants produced at temperatures above 60° F. to avoid premature flowering.

Soil and fertility requirements for endive are similar to those for lettuce. Well fertilized soil and irrigation, where water may be limiting, are important for rapid, continuous growth. This is essential for good yields and high quality.

Plants may be spaced 12 inches apart in 18-inch rows or set in beds 12 inches apart. Crowding of the plants with the latter spacing will cause some blanching of the center leaves (Fig. 32.8). This may be desired to reduce bitterness associated with the green leaves. Blanching can be done by tying the leaves of a plant together loosely over the top, but this practice has been largely discontinued.

Harvesting and Marketing

Plants are harvested by cutting them off at the soil surface. Diseased,

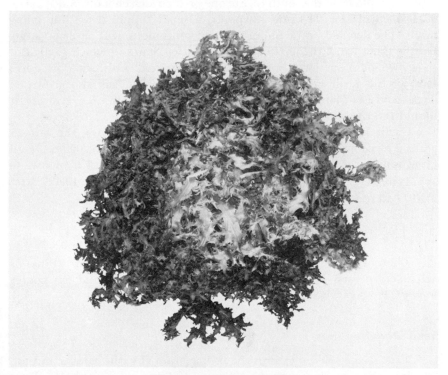

Fig. 32.8—Curled leaved endive.

USDA Photograph

discolored, or blemished leaves are removed. Outer leaves are folded over the centers of plants before packing in crates or baskets. Refrigeration is used for distant shipments. Methods used for precooling and icing lettuce may be used for endive.

GARLIC

Classification and Importance

Garlic (*Allium sativum*) is a member of the onion group, but it differs from the onion in that it consists of a multiple bulb composed of small bulblets called cloves. Nature packs these cloves together in a rough bulblike mass and covers them with a parchmentlike membrane. This package of cloves makes up the garlic bulb of commerce.

Garlic is offered in every market catering to any considerable population of people from the south of Europe or their descendants. Since garlic is used chiefly for flavoring purposes, a small supply serves for many meals. The demand, while important and continuous, will never be large. On the other hand, the territory of the United States in which garlic can be grown most successfully is decidedly restricted. California produces most of the garlic grown in the United States. Some is also grown in Texas and Louisiana. As a special crop in the hands of a few growers, it should return a reasonable profit.

Garlic acreage and production have fluctuated during the last 25 years. The commercial planting of 4,300 acres valued at $563,000 declined to around 2,500 acres during the 1951 to 1957 period and then rose to approximately 4,600 acres valued at $4,295,000 in 1965. The 10,400 acres in 1977 were valued at $16,336,000 (Table 32.1).

Cultivars

There are the early (White or Mexican) and the late (Pink or Italian) cultivars. The early cultivar does not store well and has poorer quality. However, it will outyield the late type.

Seed Requirements

True seed is seldom used in the propagation of garlic. Cloves and top sets are used, but cloves are more common. Since the size of the cloves determines the number of planting units per pound, a sample of the stock to be used for seed should be taken and the average number of cloves per pound determined. From this, one can compute the number of pounds of seed required to plant a given area when the rows are set with plants at a given distance in the row. Usually 800 to 1,000 pounds of cloves are needed to plant an acre.

Soil and Cultural Requirements

Garlic thrives best on a friable sandy loam well supplied with organic matter. The culture and fertilization of garlic is essentially the same as for set onions. Seed is prepared by breaking the mother bulbs apart, so that the cloves of which they are composed become individual units (Fig. 32.9). These units are planted singly, 3 to 6 inches apart, according to cultivar, in rows 12 to 16 inches apart.

In California, plantings are usually made between October and January. Early planting is desirable because the plant remains vegetative dur-

Fig. 32.9—Garlic bunched for market.

USDA Photograph

ing the short days and grows larger before bulbing. The larger plants produce larger bulbs.

Harvesting and Handling

If the soil is very rich, it may be necessary to break over the tops to prevent too much top growth, and to make the bulbs better, as is sometimes done with onions. As soon as the crop is mature, as indicated by the discoloring and wilting of the leaves, the plants should be pulled and placed in windrows, with the tops covering the bulbs to prevent sunscald. After curing for several days, the tops and roots are trimmed. The bulbs are then graded and bagged for market. Garlic will endure a wide range of temperatures, but must be kept dry to prevent sprouting.

No one kind of package is widely used for shipping garlic. A mesh bag or a well-ventilated slat crate may be used, but the volume in each crate should not be large because there is a tendency to heat when garlic is packaged in any considerable mass. Garlic is usually retailed in small film bags. See Table 13.2 for exports and imports.

GLOBE ARTICHOKES

Classification and Importance

The globe artichoke *(Cynara scolymus)* is a robust, perennial, thistle-like plant, grown chiefly for the edible receptacles and scales of the blossom bud (Fig. 32.10). It is not hardy to cold, so its culture is chiefly confined to the South Atlantic and Gulf Coast regions and to the Pacific Coast in California, south from San Francisco to Los Angeles. Only in California has the crop gained commercial rank, and most of the market supply comes from that state. Production in other areas is confined to local market and home gardens.

The production of artichokes has fluctuated slightly downward during the past 28 years. The commercial acreage of 10,400 acres valued at $1,762,000 in 1939 decreased to an estimated acreage of 9,200 acres valued at $5,761,000 in 1965, then rose to about 10,800 acres valued at $13,-775,000 in 1977. California produces most of this crop (Table 32.1).

Soil and Cultural Requirements

Best conditions for the globe artichoke are obtained on rich friable lands under irrigation. Outside of the irrigated area rich, well-drained soil

Fig. 32.10—Globe artichoke showing edible scales of blossom bud.

USDA Photograph

is best. The plant is a gross feeder and should have from 800 to 1,000 pounds per acre of a high-grade vegetable fertilizer in the form of a side dressing.

Globe artichokes grow readily from seed, but the seedlings are highly variable; hence, vegetative propagation by means of offshoots or suckers is recommended. These spring up from the base of the original plant after the blossom stalk has died down. Several sucker plants usually develop about the original crown. The most recent and preferred method of propagation is by division of the old crown so that each section includes a piece of stem from a sucker plant. The plants are usually spaced 6 feet apart in rows 8 feet apart, and set at a depth of 6 to 8 inches. The crop is usually planted in February and March, and renewed every four to seven years.

Controlling Insects

The insect enemies are chiefly two, the artichoke aphid, which may be controlled by dusting with nicotine or malathion, and the plume moth, the larvae of which bore into the blossom buds, causing considerable loss of the crop in California. Thistles are an alternate host of the plume moth, and they should be kept down in the vicinity of artichoke fields. Field sanitation and dusting with parathion or lindane have given control.

Harvesting and Handling

As soon as the blossom buds have attained maximum growth, but before signs of flower opening appear, the crop is ready to harvest. There is considerable variation in time of maturity among plants as well as among the buds on an individual plant; consequently, the harvest season is prolonged and is usually terminated by weather conditions rather than by the exhaustion of the crop.

The mature buds are cut with 1 to 1½ inches of the stem attached. They are graded for size and quality, and packed in large paperlined boxes carrying 48 to 125 buds. Lug boxes are usually used for local markets.

KALE

Classification and Importance

Kale *(Brassica oleracea* var. *virdis)* is a winter-hardy, nonheading, cabbagelike plant grown for its much-curled and succulent leaves. It was known to the Greeks and was mentioned by Cato in 200 B.C. This potherb is extensively grown in the Norfolk area of Virginia. The plant is bulky and can be grown profitably only in localities enjoying cheap transportation over a short haul.

The commercial acreage of kale has fluctuated downward from 2,900 acres worth $268,000 in 1939 to approximately 1,000 acres valued at $638,000 in 1968, when estimates were discontinued. Virginia is the leading state in the production of this crop.

It is essentially a cool-season crop and does best when planted in late summer for autumn and early winter use.

Types

Two types of kale are grown in the United States. One, known as Scotch, has much-curled and crumpled foliage of a grayish-green color; the other, called Siberian, is less crinkled and is bluish-green. Both dwarf and tall forms are grown, with the dwarf forms being most popular. Kale and the closely related collards are favorite plants for the production of winter greens throughout the South.

Cultural Requirements

Quickly grown plants are less fibrous and more tender than slowly grown ones. The soil best suited for good production is friable loam well stocked with organic matter through the use of manure or cover crops. These should be supplemented by the application of a 5-10-5 fertilizer at the rate of about 1 ton per acre. For hand cultivation, kale is usually planted with a seed drill in rows 18 inches apart, but for tractor cultivation the rows are 24 to 30 inches apart. When the plants are well established, they should be thinned to stand about 6 inches apart in the row. Kale is subject to all the pests that affect cabbage and the same remedial measures should be employed.

Harvesting and Marketing

For home use, kale is best if harvested before the plants are large and tough; otherwise only the young leaves should be gathered. For market, quickly grown plants are cut at the surface of the ground and packed in tall hampers or bushel baskets. Some kale is now prepackaged in transparent film bags for retail trade. With an excess of more refined vegetables available at all seasons, kale has strong competition, but it is still extensively planted in the maritime section of Virginia.

KOHLRABI

Classification and Use

Kohlrabi *(Brassica oleracea* var. *gongylodes)* is grown for the turnip-like enlargement of the stem above ground (Fig. 32.11). It is little known and is not appreciated in the United States, although it is an excellent vegetable if used before it becomes tough and stringy. For good quality, growth must be rapid and unchecked. The plants may be started in the greenhouse or hotbed for an early crop, but the more common practice is to plant the seed where the crop is to mature.

Cultivars

The most popular cultivars are White Vienna, Green Vienna, Purple

Fig. 32.11—Kohlrabi plants ready for harvest.

USDA Photograph

Vienna, and the Earliest Erfurt. The White Vienna is probably grown to a greater extent than all of the others combined.

Cultural Requirements

The seed is sown in rows 18 inches apart for hand cultivation, or 24 to 30 inches for tractor cultivation. The plants are thinned to stand 6 to 8 inches apart in the row. Planting intervals of two to three weeks will secure the proper sequence and insure a continuous supply of tender kohlrabi.

A rich garden soil will produce excellent kohlrabi. If the soil is not already rich, a liberal dressing of manure is desirable. If manure is not available, green-manure crops and commercial fertilizer may be used as substitutes. A fertilizer similar to that suggested for cabbage would be satisfactory for this crop.

Cultivation similar to that given cabbage or cauliflower is satisfactory for kohlrabi, but when it is planted in rows less than 24 inches apart, garden tractors or hand cultivators are used.

Harvesting

Kohlrabi should be harvested when the swollen stem is 2 to 3 inches in diameter and before it becomes tough and woody. When prepared for market, the root is cut off and the plants are tied together in bunches like beets, or sold in bulk.

MUSTARD

Classification and Cultivars

White mustard *(Brassica hirta)* is grown for salad and greens to some extent, but has been replaced largely by spinach and kale. This plant is a hardy annual of the *Cruciferae* family. The White London is one of the well-known cultivars of this species. Black mustard *(Brassica nigra)* is grown largely for its seed, which is made into the mustard of commerce. This type is grown to a great extent on the adobe soils in Santa Barbara County, California.

Giant Curled and Tendergreen are cultivars of *Brassica júncea* var. *crispifolia* grown to some extent in the South. Chinese Broad Leaf and Florida Broad Leaf are also extensively planted.

Soil and Cultural Requirements

Mustard is generally sown for greens very early in the spring for spring use, and in the fall for the winter crop. To provide a season's supply, successive plantings should be made at intervals of 10 days or two weeks. Seed is sown in drills 12 to 18 inches apart and the plants thinned as they become crowded in the row (Fig. 32.12).

Fig. 32.12—A plant of curled leaf mustard.

USDA Photograph

On a good sandy-loam soil, 50 to 75 pounds of nitrogen, 100 to 150 pounds of acid phosphate, and 50 to 75 pounds of potash per acre should give good results, even without manure, provided the humus supply is maintained by turning under soil-improving crops. Where manure is used, an application of 25 to 30 pounds of nitrogen and 80 pounds of phosphoric acid should be sufficient.

NEW ZEALAND SPINACH

Classification and Habit

New Zealand spinach (*Tetragonia expansa*) differs from the true spinach in being a much-branched plant 4 to 5 feet across and 1 to 2 feet tall. It belongs to the family *Aizoaceae*. Its leaves resemble somewhat those of the true spinach, but the chief similarity between the two plants is in the flavor. New Zealand spinach lacks commercial importance as compared with true spinach, but it can be a valuable addition to the home garden. Unlike ordinary spinach, it does not withstand low temperatures, but thrives in warm weather, thus extending the spinach season. However, it will not survive the hot summers of the extreme South unless given protection.

Cultural Requirements

Seeds can be planted in warm, protected seedbeds in late winters to be later transplanted, or they may be planted directly in the field when the season permits. Whatever the procedure, plants need to be finally spaced 2 to 3 feet in rows 3 to 4 feet apart. Aside from the difference in time and method of planting, the general culture closely follows that for ordinary spinach.

Harvesting and Grading

As soon as the plants are large enough, the tender tips, 3 to 4 inches long, can be cut off. This stimulates the growth of more branches, and so harvesting continues until some unfavorable condition terminates the life of the plant.

OKRA

Classification and Importance

Okra, or gumbo (*Hibiscus esculentus*), is a popular home garden vegetable in the South. It is thought to be of Asiatic origin and is reported to have been used by the Egyptians in the twelfth century. Production has nearly doubled since 1939, with practically all of the commercial production for market and processing being in the southern states.

Cultivars

Cultivars of okra may be classified as dwarf, intermediate, or tall according to the height of the plant. Most commonly used cultivars have spineless pods ranging in color from creamy white to dark green. Some of the popular cultivars are Perkins Spineless, Dwarf Long Pod, Clemson Spineless, Louisiana Green Velvet, and Emerald.

Soil and Cultural Requirements

Any good garden soil will produce a satisfactory crop of okra if other conditions are favorable. Barnyard manure is desirable for poor soils and

Fig. 32.13—Okra plant showing pods.

USDA Photograph

a supplementary application of 500 to 1,000 pounds of a 5-10-5 fertilizer per acre will pay under many conditions.

Okra is a tender plant and should not be planted until the danger of frost is over. Seed is drilled thickly on slightly bedded rows 2½ to 4 feet apart. When the plants are established, they are thinned so that the plants of dwarf cultivars are 12 inches apart, and those of larger cultivars 18 to 24 inches apart. The cultivation of okra should be about the same as for any other cultivated crop. Weeds should not be permitted to become established.

Harvesting and Use

Okra yields over a long period of time, usually from June to October. Only the young, tender pods are desired, and pods should be picked daily to secure a product of best quality (Fig. 32.13). All pods should be removed to keep the plants producing. Okra deteriorates rapidly, and consequently does not ship well.

Okra is used principally in soups and stews. The pods are sometimes stewed and eaten as a vegetable. A large portion of the crop is processed by canning, freezing, or preserving in brine for future use in canned soups.

PARSLEY

Classification and Importance

Parsley (*Petroselinum crispum*), a native of Europe, is a near relative of celery and parsnips. It is the universal favorite for garnishes and is used also for flavoring salads, soups, and stews. There are two types of parsley, one with fibrous roots and finely divided, much curled or crinkled leaves; the other with plain leaves and fleshy roots which are used for flavoring soups and stews. The leafy type is chiefly grown in the United States, while the fleshy-rooted sorts are largely grown in Europe.

Cultivars

Parsley has been developed with three types of foliage: (1) the plain leaf, (2) the double-curled, and (3) the moss or triple-curled (Fig. 32.14). The fleshy-rooted parsley has plain celerylike leaves.

Soil and Cultural Requirements

The seed of parsley is small and slow to germinate. Soaking the seed overnight induces quicker germination. Young plants are small and quite delicate and require protection and frequent watering to prevent loss from drying. When established, the plants are more resistant to cold than to heat.

Because of their tender nature while young, the plants are frequently

Fig. 32.14—Parsley leaves bunched for market.

USDA Photograph

started in cold frames or hotbeds. Parsley, however, does well under favorable conditions in the open. Rich, fine, moisture-retentive soil is best. In the South, the crop is grown mostly in the autumn, winter, and spring, the summer heat being too severe.

In the North, parsley is grown in greenhouses, cold frames, and hotbeds during the winter months. The Norfolk, Virginia, area grows parsley in sash-and-muslin-covered frames as a winter crop. The plants can be set about 6 inches apart each way, kept free of weeds, and the entire top clipped off to thicken the crown of leaves on well-established plants.

RHUBARB

Classification and Culture

Rhubarb *(Rheum rhaponticum)* is a member of the buckwheat family. It thrives best in regions having cool moist summers and winters cold enough to freeze the ground to a depth of several inches. It is not adapted to most parts of the South, but in certain areas of higher elevation it does fairly well. A few hills along the garden fence will supply all that a family can use.

Any deep, well-drained, fertile soil is suitable for rhubarb. Spade the soil or plow it to a depth of 12 to 16 inches and mix in rotted manure, leafmold, decayed hardwood leaves, sods, or other form of organic matter. The methods of soil preparation suggested for asparagus are suitable for rhubarb. As rhubarb is planted in hills 3 to 4 feet apart, however, it is usually sufficient to prepare each hill separately.

Planting and Fertilizing

Rhubarb plants may be started from seed and transplanted, but seedlings vary from the parent plant. The usual method of starting the plants is to obtain pieces of crowns from established hills and set them in prepared hills. Top-dress the planting with a heavy application of organic matter in either early spring or late fall. Organic matter applied over the hills during early spring greatly hastens growth, or forces the plant. A pound of complete commercial fertilizer high in nitrogen applied around each hill every year insures an abundant supply of plant food. The plants can be mulched with green grass or weeds.

Crimson, Red Valentine, MacDonald, Canada Red, and Victoria are standard cultivars.

Harvesting and Utilizing

Seedstalks should be removed as soon as they form. No leaf stems should be harvested before the second year and but few until the third. Moreover, the harvest season must be largely confined to early spring. The hills should be divided and reset every seven or eight years. Otherwise, they become too thick and produce only slender stems.

Only the leafstalk is used as a food. (Rhubarb leaves contain injurious substances, including oxalic acid. They should never be used for food.)

Rhubarb can be used as a forcing crop. Two-year-old vigorous crowns can be dug after they become dormant and placed in forcing structures. Low temperature is used to break dormancy, but it can be replaced in part or totally by gibberellic acid (Fig. 3.3). A temperature of 56° F. will produce stalks of good color and a moderate rate of growth.

SALSIFY

Classification and Importance

Salsify *(Tragapogon porrifolius)* is commonly known as the "oyster plant" or "vegetable oyster" because of its flavor when made into soups and cooked in other ways. The edible part is the long, fleshy white tap root. As a vegetable in this country, it is relatively unknown, but it is fully deserving of greater appreciation. It is a member of the *Compositae* family and is a native of the Mediterranean area. Only one cultivar, Mammoth Sandwich Island, is grown in this country. Salsify is distinct from black salsify *(Scorzonera hispanica)* and Spanish salsify *(Scolymus hispanicus)*. The latter two are grown in Europe, but are practically unknown in the United States.

Cultural Requirements

The culture is practically the same as for parsnips. A long growing season is required for full development. Salsify is winter hardy in most regions and can be harvested throughout the winter. It can also be stored, using the same methods employed for other root crops.

SHALLOTS

Classification and Importance

The shallot *(Allium ascalonicum)* is an ancient, universally distributed, onionlike plant. It is believed to have come from western Asia. Nearly all of the commercial crop in the United States is produced in southern Louisiana.

Shallots have declined in importance from 5,400 acres valued at $317,000 in 1939 to about 1,000 acres with a farm value of about $444,000 in 1968, when estimates were discontinued.

Plant Habit

The plant is a perennial that seldom produces seeds and therefore must be increased by division of its compound bulbs, which are made up of several bulblets, or cloves, held together at the base. The bulbs are not encased by a sheath as is garlic. The bulblets are planted in the same manner and at the same season as are onion sets, each set developing into a compound bulb. The mature bulbs are harvested, cured, and stored in the same manner as onions. In suitable storage, the bulbs will keep from one season to the next.

Use

The flavor of shallots is somewhat milder than that of onions. The chief use is for flavoring, both leaves and cloves being used. Most of the crop is produced for sale in the green state, but some dry bulbs are also sold.

SOUTHERN PEA (COWPEA)

Classification and Importance

The southern pea (Cowpea) *(Vigna sinensis)* is an important forage and soil-improving crop, extensively grown in the South. It is a member of the great group of legumes of the bean type, and is used for human food both in the green-shelled and dry state. Its ease of culture and ability to grow on poor land makes it an important food crop in the South.

Cultivars

There are a number of different kinds of southern peas, which may be distinguished mainly by the pod type and color and pattern of seed coat. Within each color group is what is known as the crowder type, in which the seeds are tightly crowded in the pod. Each group is represented by a large number of cultivars and strains. Some of the different types are the purple-hull, the cream, and the black-eyed. The black-eyed group is extensively used as a culinary vegetable. Throughout the South and especially in parts of Texas and California, black-eyed peas are grown as a field crop to supply the marked demand for the dry shelled product. The Yardlong or Asparagus bean, one of the southern peas with seed pods of extraordinary length, is sometimes included in the southern vegetable garden for its edible pod, which is used as a substitute for snap beans. Commonly grown cultivars include California Black-eye, Purple Hull Bush Pinkeye, Crimson, Mekan, Dixielee, Bush Purple Hull, and Mississippi Silver.

Soil and Cultural Requirements

Although southern peas can be grown on poor soil under adverse conditions, an application of 200 to 300 pounds of 5-10-5 or some similar complete fertilizer will materially increase production.

As a field crop, southern peas are frequently sown broadcast, or they are sown in drills 6 to 8 inches apart. Approximately 1 to 1½ bushels of seed are required to plant an acre. The pods are gathered when in condition for green or dry shelling. The vines are either cut for hay or turned under as a soil-improvement crop.

Southern peas are sometimes sown in rows 2½ to 3 feet apart in the same manner as garden peas or beans, using about a peck of seed per acre. The rows are cultivated until the vines overlap. Weeding and thinning are seldom necessary.

SOYBEANS

Classification and Importance

The soybean (*Glycine max*) is a close relative of the southern pea. As a garden crop, it has not been generally cultivated in England or in the United States. In Japan and in Manchuria, it is a food crop of prime importance.

Cultivars

The cultivars of soybeans are exceedingly numerous, many of them having been developed by the Japanese. They vary from 75 to 170 days for maturity, and they also vary greatly in soil and climatic adaptation, color, quality, flavor, and ease of cooking. For garden purposes the Hahto, Disoy, Zogun, Green Giant, and Favorite are commonly used. Kim and Kanrich are two promising cultivars recently introduced.

Soil and Cultural Requirements

Soybeans do well under the conditions suitable for ordinary garden beans. They should be planted in rows 24 to 30 inches apart and the seed distributed so as to insure a stand of plants 3 to 4 inches apart.

The time of planting in the North is immediately after corn planting, and in the Gulf states the best time is from April 15 to June 1. Soybeans are not as sensitive to frost as are garden beans and may be planted somewhat earlier.

Harvesting and Use

Soybeans as a green vegetable should be harvested when the seeds are fully grown, but before they have hardened, as the pods are then rough, hairy, and hard to shell. The young beans resemble young lima beans, but have a richer, nutlike flavor. Tough pods, if boiled for about three minutes, may be shelled with comparative ease. Cooked immature soybeans are a rich source of protein, fat, calcium, phosphorus, and iron, and are also good sources of vitamins A and B, but are a poor source of vitamin C.

Soybeans are not a favorite food of the Mexican bean beetle, and can be grown in localities where this insect prevents the culture of bush beans. Japanese beetles and rabbits are fond of soybeans, however.

Soybean flour has long been used in making bread and cakes for diabetics, because of its low starch content. Soybean milk is extensively used as infant food and as a means of restoring normal flora in the digestive tract. As a food, it is non-acid forming.

SQUASHES AND PUMPKINS

Origin and Classification

For generations, the place of origin of pumpkins and squashes has been a matter of doubt. Archeological investigations conclusively prove that pumpkins, squashes, and gourds were widely distributed in both South America and North America, and were extensively used by the people of the Americas for receptacles, utensils, and food, long before these continents were discovered by Columbus. Overwhelming evidence is in favor of an American origin for all the species mentioned above.

The plants spoken of as squashes and pumpkins comprise no less than four species of the genus *Cucurbita,* namely *C. pepo, C. maxima, C. moschata,* and *C. mixta.* The nomenclature of this group of plants is greatly confused because of culinary terminology. The species characteristics have not been followed in distinguishing squashes and pumpkins.

SUMMER SQUASHES. Summer squashes, commonly *C. pepo,* are eaten in the immature stages when the rind is very soft. White Bush Scallop, Early Prolific Straightneck, Seneca Butterbar Hybrid, Seneca Prolific, Zucchini Hybrid, Striata, Cazerta, Cocozelle, and Zucchini are popular cultivars. All these are of the bush type.

WINTER SQUASHES. Winter squashes, utilized when the fruits are mature, have hard rinds and store well. The members of this group usually have flesh of mild flavor and fine texture, and are suitable for baking. Cultivars of winter squash are included in all the species of *Cucurbita.* They include Table Queen, Butternut, Buttercup, Green Hubbard, Blue Hubbard, Golden Hubbard, Warted Hubbard, Gold Nugget (bush type), Kinred, Sweet Meat, Delicious, and Banana.

PUMPKINS. Pumpkins are also used when the fruit is mature. The flesh is often coarse or strong and hence not generally served as a baked vegetable. The rind of most cultivars of pumpkins is not hard even at full maturity and in this respect they may be distinguished from winter squashes. The name pumpkin is applied to cultivars in all species of cucurbita. Some of the important cultivars are Connecticut Field, Small Sugar, Cinderella (bush type), Jack O'Lantern, Spookie, Young's Beauty, and the Cushaws.

Scope and Importance

The members of the genus *Cucurbita* are considered minor crops and consequently statistics of their production are meager. One or more cultivars, though, are found in most home and market gardens; they are ever present in the markets; and pumpkins and squashes are extensively canned and used for stock feed. It is readily apparent that the group as a whole is very important in our agricultural economy.

The states most important in the production of pumpkins are Illinois, New Jersey, California, Indiana, New York, Ohio, Michigan, and Pennsylvania. Largest acreages of squashes are grown in Florida, California, Texas, New York, Georgia, New Jersey, Massachusetts, Michigan, North Carolina, and South Carolina. The relative positions of these states may vary from year to year because these crops can be grown almost anywhere and with only a small investment of capital.

Soil and Climatic Requirements

Almost any good, well-drained soil will grow pumpkins and squashes. It should be well supplied with organic matter and provided with a uniform supply of moisture. Soil type is not critical if each is properly handled and fertilized. A light, fertile soil that warms up quickly is desired for summer cultivars for the early market. Heavy soils are best for cultivars grown during late summer and fall. Soils slightly acid to slightly alkaline (pH 5.5 to pH 7.5) are satisfactory. Extremely acid soils should be avoided or limed.

Squashes and pumpkins are warm-season plants and are easily injured by frost. Nevertheless, they will succeed in cooler climates than will melons or even cucumbers. Cloudless weather is especially important in the development of mature fruits.

Culture

Like other cucurbits, squashes and pumpkins are somewhat difficult to transplant, and the practice has proven profitable only with the summer squashes. When transplanting is to be practiced, the seeds are usually planted in individual containers, and the seedlings are shifted to the field without disturbing the root systems.

Field plantings are made after the danger of frost is over. The bush and small-vine cultivars are planted in hills as close as 4 by 5 feet apart, while cultivars having long vines should be spaced 8 to 12 feet apart each way. Clean culture and protection from insects are essential to success (see Chapter 11). Hives of bees are often placed near fields to insure pollination, since the plants are monoecious and the flowers must be insect-pollinated (Fig. 32.15).

Fig. 32.15—Squash stem showing both male and female flowers.

Harvesting, Storage, and Shipment

The summer squashes are all harvested while immature and while the shell is soft and easily cut with the thumbnail (Fig. 32.16). If the fruits reach full size and the shell begins to harden, they are of no culinary value. The winter squashes, as well as the pie and stock pumpkins, should be well matured before harvest, but should not be exposed to frosts if they are to be stored for winter use.

Hard-shelled cultivars, like Hubbard and Vegetable Marrow, keep best in storage. They should be well matured when harvested and cured at a temperature of 80° to 85° F., and with a relative humidity of about 80 to 85 percent for 10 days. After curing, the squash can be stored for several months on shelves in a dry, frost-free room at a temperature of 50° to 55° F. Fruit intended for storage should be handled with great care, so as to avoid bruises and wounds that break or scratch the skin and to avoid breaking off the stems of the fruit.

Summer squashes are often shipped in bushel baskets, lug boxes, or crates of various kinds. The fruit should be packed tightly to avoid jos-

Fig. 32.16—Planting of Cocozelle squash showing harvested fruit.

S. C. Exp. Sta.

tling and bruising in transit. The hard-shelled winter cultivars are usually handled in bulk, but some of the smaller cultivars, such as Butternut, Buttercup, and Table Queen, are marketed in baskets, boxes, crates, and occasionally in bags.

MISCELLANEOUS VEGETABLES

To round out the array of vegetables in the text, brief discussions follow on some of the uncommon ones which are comparatively unimportant. Despite their limited status, these minor vegetables are most important to some growers and to those consumers who desire them. Although most of these vegetables are sold by market gardeners and commercial growers in some areas, they are grown primarily in home gardens for family consumption.

Information on these vegetables was obtained primarily from the USDA Home and Garden Bulletin No. 202, 1972. Additional information on culture can be obtained from similar practices of related vegetables discussed herein. Suitable cultivars are available from most seed stores which strive to provide tested cultivars of good quality. For convenient reference, these minor vegetables are discussed in alphabetical order.

Celeriac

Celeriac *(Apium graveolens* var. *rapaceum)* is developed for the root instead of the top. Its culture is the same as that of celery, and the enlarged roots can be used at any time after they are big enough. The late-summer crop of celeriac may be stored for winter use. In mild winter areas, the roots may be left in the ground and mulched with several inches of straw or leaves, or they may be lifted, packed in moist sand, and stored in a cool cellar.

Chard

Chard, or Swiss chard *(Beta vulgaris* var. *Cicla),* is a type of beet that has been developed for its tops instead of its roots. Crop after crop of the outer leaves may be harvested without injuring the plant. Only one planting is necessary, and a row 30 to 40 feet long will supply a family for the entire summer. Each seed cluster contains several seeds, and fairly wide spacing of the seed facilitates thinning. The culture of chard is practically the same as that of beets, but the plants grow larger and need to be thinned to at least 6 inches apart in the row. Chard needs a rich, mellow soil, and it is sensitive to soil acidity.

Chervil

Chervil *(Anthriscus cerefolium)* comes in two distinct types, salad chervil and turnip-rooted chervil. Salad chervil is grown about like parsley. The seeds must be bedded in damp sand for a few weeks before being sown; otherwise, their germination is very slow.

Turnip-rooted chervil thrives in practically all parts of the country where the soil is fertile and the moisture sufficient. In the South, the seeds are usually sown in the fall, but they may not germinate until spring. In the North, the seeds may be sown in the autumn to germinate in the spring; or the plants may be started indoors in late winter and transplanted to open ground later on. The spacing and culture of chervil are about the same as for beets and carrots.

Chicory

Chicory *(Cichorium intybus),* also known as French endive, witloof and succory, is grown for both roots and tops. It is a hardy plant, not especially sensitive to heat or cold. It does, however, need a deep, rich, loamy soil without too much organic matter. The tops are sometimes harvested while young. The roots are lifted in autumn and placed in a box or bed of moist soil in a warm cellar for forcing. They must be covered with a few inches of sand. Under this covering the leaves form in a solid head, known on the market as witloof.

The culture of chicory is simple. The seeds are sown in spring or early summer in drills about 18 inches apart. Later, the plants are thinned to 6 or 8 inches apart in the rows. If sown too early, the plants shoot to seed and are worthless for forcing. The kind known as witloof is most generally used.

Chinese Cabbage

Chinese cabbage *(Brassica chinensis or pekinensis)* is more closely related to mustard than to cabbage. It is variously called Crispy Choy, Chihili, Michili, and Wong Bok. Also, it is popularly known as celery cabbage, although it is unrelated to celery. The nonheading types deserve greater attention.

Chinese cabbage seems to do best as an autumn crop in the northern tier of states. When full grown, it is an attractive vegetable. It is not especially successful as a spring crop, and gardeners are advised not to try to grow it at any season other than fall in the North or in winter in the South.

The plant demands a very rich, well-drained but moist soil. The seeds may be sown and the plants transplanted to the garden, or the seed may be drilled in the garden rows and the plants thinned to the desired stand.

Corn Salad

Corn salad (*Valerianella oliteria*) is also known as lamb's-lettuce and fetticus. The seed are sown in early spring in drills and the plants are cultivated the same as lettuce or mustard. For an extra early crop, the seed can be planted in the autumn and covered lightly through the winter. In the southern states, the covering is not necessary, and the plants are ready for use in February and March. The leaves are frequently used in their natural green state, but they may be blanched by covering the rows with anything that will exclude light.

Dandelion

The dandelion (*Taraxacum officinalis*) is a member of the sunflower family. It is favored as spring greens in either its wild or cultivated state. Although plants may be started indoors and transplanted to the garden, seed are usually sown outside in 12- to 15-inch rows and thinned to 10 to 12 inches apart. Dandelions prefer light sandy soil, and are grown and harvested like spinach.

Florence Fennel

Florence fennel (*Foeniculum vulgare*) is related to celery and celeriac. Its enlarged, flattened leafstalk is the portion used. For a summer crop, the seeds are sown in the rows in spring; for an autumn and winter crop in the South, they are sown toward the end of the summer. The plants are thinned to stand about 6 inches apart. When the leafstalks have grown to about 2 inches in diameter, the plants may be slightly mounded up and partially blanched. They should be harvested and used before they become tough and stringy.

Leek

Leek *(Allium porrum)* resembles the onion in its adaptability and cultural requirements. Instead of forming a bulb it produces a thick, fleshy cylinder like a large green onion. Leeks are started from seeds, like onions. Usually the seeds are sown in a shallow trench, so that the plants can be more easily hilled up as growth proceeds. Leeks are ready for use any time after they reach the right size. Under favorable conditions they grow to 1-½ inches or more in diameter, with white parts 6 to 8 inches long. They may be lifted in the autumn and stored like celery in a cold-frame or a cellar.

Orach

Orach *(Atriplex hortensis)*, called mountain spinach, is grown in some intermountain regions of the United States as a substitute for spinach. Under favorable conditions, orach has some advantages over spinach in that it provides early greens and may develop large tender leaves on the upper portion of its tall stalks throughout the growing season. Orach is drouth resistant and easily grown. Seed are planted in early spring in 18- to 24-inch rows and thinned to 10 to 12 inches apart. In general, its culture is similar to that of spinach.

Sorrel

Sorrel *(Rumex acetosa)* is a perennial that is usually started from seeds. It requires a rich, mellow, well-drained soil. Rows may be of any convenient distance apart. The plants should be thinned to about 8 inches apart in the rows. If the leaves alone are gathered and the plants are cultivated to prevent the growth of weeds, a planting should last 3 or 4 years. French Broad Leaf is a well-known cultivar.

Upland Cress

Upland cress *(Lepidium sativum)*, sometimes erroneously called peppergrass, is a hardy plant. It may be sown in all the milder parts of the country in autumn. In the colder sections it is sown in early spring as soon as the ground can be worked. The seeds are small and must not be covered deeply. After the plants are well established, they should be thinned to 4 to 6 inches apart in the rows. This is a short-season crop that should be planted in quick succession to insure a steady supply.

Watercress

Watercress *(Rorippa nasturtium-aquaticum)* is a joint-rooted perennial which can be propagated either by seed or by pieces of stem. Although grown in various places, it is commercially produced in Alabama, Virginia, West Virginia, Maryland, and Pennsylvania. It thrives in wet places and running water. Watercress is generally grown in carefully graded wide beds which permit slowly running water to flood them properly.

SELECTED REFERENCES

Anonymous, "Commercial Squash Production," S. C. Clemson Univ. Ext. Leaflet 14, 1978.

Anonymous, "Growing Cauliflower and Broccoli," USDA Farmers' Bull. 2239, 1971.

Anonymous, "Growing Pumpkins and Squashes," USDA Farmers' Bull. 2086, 1968.

Anonymous, "Growing Table Beets," USDA, ARS Leaflet 360, 1976.

Anonymous, "Louisiana Okra," La. State Univ. Ext. Pub. 1141, 1972.

Anonymous, "Rhubarb Production," USDA Leaflet 555, 1972.

Averre, C. W., "Bell Pepper Production," N. C. State Univ. Est. Leaflet 21, 1975.

Cannon, J. M., and Brown, R. T., "Production of Cauliflower, Broccoli, and Brussels Sprouts," La. Est. Pub. 1169, 1976.

Combs, O. B., Wade, E. K., and Libby, J. L., "Eggplant," Univ. Wisc. Ext. Ser. Pub. A2360, 1978.

Duncan, A. A., "Garlic for the Garden," Ore. Agr. Ext. Ser. FS–138, 1970.

Duncan, A. A., "Kohlrabi, Mustard, Radish, Rutabaga and Turnip Seed Production," Ore. Exp. Sta. FS–90, 1965.

Dunn, C. M., "Squash," Wisc. Agr. Ext. Ser. Leaflet B2546, 1973.

Johnson, W. A., *et al.*, "Production Practices for Pimiento Pepper," Ala. Auburn Univ. State Bull. 444, 1973.

Marr, Charles, and Greig, J. K., "Rhubarb," Kansas Sta. Univ. Ext. Ser. Pub., 1973.

Martin, F. W., "Yam Production Methods," USDA Prod. Res. Rep. 147, 1973.

Shear, G. M., "Commercial Growing of Watercress," USDA Farmers' Bull. 2233, 1968.

Sims, W. L., and Little, T. M., "Growing Garlic in California," Calif. Agr. Ext. Ser. AXT–28, 1970.

Yamaguchi, M., "Production of Oriental Vegetables in the United States," *HortSci.* 8 (5), 1973.

CHAPTER 33

Controlled-Environment Agriculture[1]

Controlled-environment agriculture is a total concept of modifying the natural environment for optimum plant growth. Historically, this began by the production of seedlings in protective hotbeds for setting into the field when the last threat of frost had passed. Today, this concept has been carried forward to the extent of supplying the optimum aerial and root environment to optimize plant growth. Control of temperature, humidity, and composition of the atmosphere and protection from rain, insects, and salt water mist can be functions of controlled environments, along with the supplying of optimum levels of moisture, air, and nutrients to the root zone.

The subject of "controlled-environment agriculture" encompasses the various systems or practices of controlled plant growth. For example, the operation referred to as "nutriculture" involves the production of plants in the greenhouse or laboratory in a soilless culture. There are several types of soilless culture, a common one being "hydroponics" which is defined as the science of growing plants in solutions containing the necessary minerals instead of soil. And there are "trough culture" and "sand culture" systems which are discussed later.

HISTORY, SCOPE, AND IMPORTANCE

The very primitive stages of controlled-environment agriculture originated in Rome between 14 and 37 A.D. The development in Europe

1. This chapter was prepared by Dr. M. R. Fontes, Research Horticulturist, Environmental Research Laboratory, University of Arizona.

between the fifteenth and seventeenth centuries was mainly confined to the production of out-of-season produce by the wealthy. It was not until the middle 1800's that commercial production of vegetables started, and during this period the development began in the United States where hotbeds were used for seedling production. By the late 1800's, structures for production of several crops began. In the early 1900's, it was estimated that 100 acres of protective coverings were used to produce winter vegetables. However, the area in the United States devoted to greenhouse vegetables has decreased from 1,029 acres in 1969 to 855 in 1974 (Table 33.1). Although there was some acreage increase by 1977, the overall trend in declining acreage can be attributed to the rising cost of energy and to capital cost.

The greenhouse-vegetable industry is still growing in Europe, especially in Spain, Bulgaria, Italy, and Portugal. The growth will, no doubt, continue to meet the demands of the increasing population. The use of plastic greenhouses is an important factor in this growth (Fig. 33.1).

In recent years, the concept of controlled-environment agriculture was employed in desert coastal regions to supply fresh vegetables where outdoor production is impossible. One such project was conducted by the Environmental Research Laboratory of the University of Arizona in the Arabian Gulf. This project involved the use of desalted seawater for the production of 10 different types of vegetable crops in 5 acres of greenhouses.

The dollar value of greenhouse vegetable production increased from $9.6 million in 1929 to $37.1 million in 1974 (Table 33.1). When inflation is considered, the actual growth during this period is not very significant. The slow development in the United States can be attributed to the large number of favorable climates within the country and the large winter importation of vegetables from nearby southern countries.

PRINCIPAL CROPS GROWN

The high capital costs of controlled-environment agriculture dictates that the crops produced must be of high value. Vegetables grown must have a high yield and demand a premium price. The principal crops produced under controlled-environments are lettuce, tomatoes, and cucumbers. As can be seen in Table 33.1, tomatoes are the leading crop, followed by lettuce and cucumbers. Cucumbers of the European type (*gynoecious* and *parthenocarpic*) are becoming of increasing importance (Fig. 33.2). The fruit of these cucumbers has an edible skin, are seedless,

Fig. 33.1—Modern controlled-environment complex with inflated plastic roof.

Photograph by Robert Townsend

Table 33.1—Area and Value of Leading Greenhouse Vegetable Crops in the United States, 1974.*

Crop	Total Acreage**	Value per Acre, $	Total Value, $
Tomatoes	542.4	40,009	21,701,000
Lettuce	167.0	20,245	3,381,000
Cucumbers	73.9	28,291	2,090,000
Other	71.7	63,054	4,521,000
All Vegetables	855.0	37,067	31,693,000

*Includes Alaska and Hawaii.

**Area harvested.

Data obtained from "1974 Census of Agriculture" Vol. II, Part 6.

Data involves greenhouse crops grown on farms with an annual income of $2,500 or more.

Fig. 33.2—Gynoecious and parthenocarpic type of cucumbers.

Manley Commercial Photograph

and reportedly do not cause gaseous discomforts. With increasing popularity of cucumbers, they are expected to move up in importance. The lettuce grown is of the loose leaf and Bibb types which have shorter growing cycles than head lettuce.

PRODUCTION COSTS, TRENDS, AND OUTLOOK

Information on the economics of controlled-environment agriculture in the United States is rather sparse. This is because of considerable variation in different facilities, capital costs, type of cropping patterns, and marketing systems. In general, capital costs are high, running from $2.50 to $6.00 per square foot or $109,000 to $350,000 per acre. The cost varies with the type of cover (fiberglass, plastic, or glass), type of structure (metal or wood), amount of heating and cooling required, and sophistication of electrical control systems.

A cost study reported in 1977 showed labor still to be the largest single item. The cost of producing 1 acre of tomatoes has increased steadily, generally reaching $89,637—$118,620 in Ohio, $56,494 in California, and $69,200 in New Jersey. The cost to produce a pound of tomatoes varies from 35 to 50 cents. The difference can be attributed to depreciation, interest charges, and cost of heating fuel. The increasing price of energy has been the most recent development which threatens the future of controlled-environment agriculture. It now costs $25,000 to heat an acre of greenhouse in northern locations, and this is increasing. The energy requirements for heating are less in southern locations, but utility costs for cooling are higher.

High capital cost and labor inputs are offset by greater yields which can be obtained from controlled-environment conditions. Tomatoes range from 70 to 130 tons per acre annually on a double-crop system, compared to the U.S. average of 8 tons for fresh market field-grown tomatoes in 1977. Fresh market cucumber yields range from 100 to 200 tons per acre, compared with the 1977 national field-grown average of 5.4 tons per acre. Since the environment for optimum growth is provided, crops can be produced throughout the year if light is not a limiting factor.

The ability to produce out of season when prices are higher is another distinct advantage. Higher prices are usually obtained because of superior quality and a limited supply on the market.

In California there has been a definite movement from tomato production to the production of the European cucumber. This cucumber has unique fruit characteristics which identifies it from field-grown cucumbers. It is being widely accepted in the marketplace and appears to have a bright future.

Controlled-environment agriculture allows the growing of crops in areas where the natural environment limits production. The higher-production-per-unit area will become increasingly important in the future as the population increases and agricultural land decreases. Research and development of structures, coverings, control systems, and the parallel developments in horticulture of new cultivars, innovative cultural practices, and improved nutritional regimes should lead to future increases in the production of food from controlled-environment systems. However, the future of controlled-environment agriculture will hinge on the cost of energy, where more research is needed.

CONTROLLING THE ENVIRONMENT

Controlling Temperature

Temperature control is important for the optimum growth and quality of produce. Night and day temperatures are regulated by heating and cooling, depending upon outside temperatures. Optimum temperatures are shown in Table 33.2.

Table 33.2—Optimum Growing Temperatures for Most Popular Greenhouse Crops.

Crop	Day Temperature	Night Temperature
Tomatoes	65° to 75° F.	60° to 65° F.
Cucumbers	70° to 80° F.	70° F.
Lettuce	60° to 70° F.	50° to 55° F.

Heating is accomplished by burning fuels and transferring the heat to air or water inside the growing area. Fan-coil space heaters attached to polyethylene ducts, which distribute the heat evenly in the house, are becoming popular.

Cooling is accomplished by convection or evaporative cooling. Convective cooling is adequate only in cool climates where investments in evaporative cooling systems cannot be justified economically. Usually this consists of a roof-top ventilator which opens when the house temperature rises above the desired level. The hot air rises to the roof and escapes.

Evaporative cooling systems are designed to move air through a wetted pad area into the house and cooling it by evaporation. Forced ventilation is required to pull air through the pads into the house. The amount of cooling depends on the water content of the ambient air—the lower level, the greater the cooling.

Heating and cooling can be regulated automatically by a centralized control system. Sensors for regulation are usually placed in the growing area.

Adjusting Humidity

Plants seem to do well under a wide range of humidity. Although low humidity can cause plant drying or wilting, this is usually not a problem in controlled environments which usually have a higher degree of humidity inside than outside. This is because of plant transpiration and evaporation within the enclosure. High humidity, however, is a disease threat. Humidity is controlled by proper ventilation and adequate air distribution within the system.

Controlling Carbon Dioxide

The enrichment of the air with carbon dioxide (CO_2) above ambient levels has been shown to have beneficial effects on the growth of several different kinds of plants. Carbon dioxide is required for photosynthesis, and most plant species have a higher photosynthetic rate under the increased CO_2 levels, if no other factors are limiting.

CO_2 enrichment has been found to be beneficial to lettuce and tomatoes under low-light conditions. Cucumbers also respond favorably to carbon dioxide under high-light conditions.

Sources of carbon dioxide are compressed gas, dry ice, and combustion products of burned fuel. The cheapest source is from the burning of fuel. Care must be taken in the selection of fuel sources so that no contaminants are present to hamper growth.

Controlling Light

Artificial light appears to have limited application because of cost. It has been used for seedling production in some areas and also for supplemental lighting under low-light winter conditions. Unless some drastic economic change occurs, the use of artificial lighting will remain very limited.

Under high-light conditions, light entering the greenhouse can be limited by applying shading-roof materials. This decreases the solar load on both the plants and the inside air and helps control temperature.

PROVIDING GROWING MEDIA, WATER, AND NUTRIENTS

Determining Growing Media

The types of media for soilless culture are quite varied and usually depend on their availability in a given area. Sand, gravel, sawdust, bark, and peat mixes have all been used. Because of bulkiness and high shipping costs, local media are usually preferred. Soilless media have the initial advantage of being disease free in areas where soils are unsuitable or have been cropped for several years. Use of these media results in significant yield increases. The following are popular cultural methods:

HYDROPONIC CULTURE. Hydroponic culture consists of a trough filled with pea-size gravel which is flooded with a complete nutrient solution and drained several times daily. Hydroponic beds are formed by excavating the soil and lining the troughs with film or fiber. These beds must be piped to a water sump to allow flooding and draining of nutrient solutions. This type of system is expensive because beds, sumps, pumps, and pH control of solution are required.

TROUGH CULTURE. Trough culture, using organic peatlike mixes, sawdust, vermiculite, perlite, and peat moss or mixes of these, is another popular method. The trough can be constructed of plastic supported by wire or wooden frames. The trough depth is usually between 8 to 12 inches. The plastic membrane isolates the rooting medium from the native soil. Draining holes can be placed in the bed sides or a drain tile can be set in the bottom of the trough, the bottom being sloped to facilitate drainage.

SAND CULTURE. Sand culture is another system which is becoming more popular in areas where mixes and hydroponic systems seem to be too expensive. In sand culture, the floor of the greenhouse is first leveled to the desired grade, and a plastic membrane is spread over the entire floor. Drainage tiles are placed on the membrane and the entire floor is covered with a foot of sand. No beds are required, and this low-cost medium provides a practicable system in the Southwest (Fig. 33.3).

Regulating Water Applications

Water is metered through a drip irrigation system or a polyethylene

Fig. 33.3—Sand culture system used for tomato production.

Manley Commercial Photograph

hose to allow uniform distribution in the beds. In a hydroponic system water is applied by flooding the beds. Frequency of the application depends on the plant size, environmental conditions, and type of medium. Normally, water is applied from one to nine times daily. Naturally, the more frequently watered, the smaller the application rates.

Controlling Nutrients

Nutrients are applied in the form of water soluble fertilizers. The basic solutions used, in general, are a modified type of Hoagland's solution. Solutions usually contain all elements required for plant growth. The concentration of the elements are varied with the type of crop and medium used. Commercial mixes are available but usually are more expensive than homemade ones. However, the convenience factor for small growers and hobbyists makes ready-mixes desirable.

In hydroponic systems, nutrients are dissolved in the water sumps.

The freshly made solutions are used to flood beds for a period of two to three weeks and then discarded, and a new solution is prepared. In the trough and sand culture systems, nutrients usually are mixed in a concentrated form and diluted into the water stream by proportioning units. Proportioners dilute the nutrient into the water at a constant rate.

PLANTING AND TENDING

Essentially all greenhouse crops are started in a nursery where they can be confined to small areas. As the plants develop in size, increased area is needed for growth so they must be spaced to permit normal development. When plants attain suitable size they are moved into the greenhouse to mature. By confining the seedling to a small area in the early stages of growth, the greenhouses can either be utilized more efficiently for production or left empty for economy.

Tending Tomatoes

Depending on the area of production, various-sized transplants are used. During winter months under low-light conditions, large transplants are usually grown in pots. They are allowed to develop flowers and possibly set fruit before being transplanted to the greenhouse.

Tomatoes of the indeterminate type are used in greenhouse culture. They are trained to a single stem and up a string by pruning out the lateral shoots and wrapping the stems around the string hanging from the overhead wire support system. Pruning and training are high-labor operations in tomato culture.

Tomatoes have a perfect flower, and pollination can be obtained by shaking the blossoms. Because of lack of wind and insects, compared to outdoor conditions, some form of pollination has to be provided. The one which is the most laborious is a mechanical vibrator which is placed on the base of each flower cluster to shake out the pollen. In areas where pollen shed is more profuse and light conditions are good, air-blast blowers can shake the plants to facilitate pollination. (Fig. 33.4).

Growing Cucumbers

Cucumbers are also trained up a single string, the main stem being wrapped around it. All lateral shoots and female flowers are removed on the first 18 inches, since fruit developing on the lower part of the plant

Fig. 33.4—Pollination of tomatoes using an airblast blower.

will usually touch the ground, causing an undesirable color or rough skin. Lateral shoots are then allowed to develop and are pruned at two nodes until the plant reaches the overhead wire support. At this time, the main growing point is removed, and the top two to three lateral shoots are allowed to develop. The shoots are wrapped in opposite directions over the wire and allowed to grow downward without slippage on the strings. At this stage, growth becomes so dense that all pruning can be stopped. Some of the seed companies are presently working on self-pruning types of cucumbers, and their specific recommendations for pruning should be followed.

Growing Lettuce

Lettuce is transplanted into the greenhouse and spaced 8 to 12 inches apart, resulting in an extremely high-plant population per acre. Except for transplanting, no additional plant care is required until harvest.

CONTROLLING DISEASES AND INSECTS[2]

Diseases

GRAY MOLD. Gray Mold (*Botrytis*) is primarily a problem with tomatoes, but can also cause either drop or bottom rot of lettuce. Usually this problem begins during cool conditions and high humidity. Botrytis can cause both a stem rot and a fruit rot on tomatoes. The easiest control is to reduce the humidity by bringing in drier outside air, provide good air circulation, and apply fungicides labeled for this use.

LEAF MOLD. Leaf mold (*Cladosporium*) attacks tomato foliage when the relative humidity rises above 95 percent. The first symptoms appear on the upper leaf surfaces as a light green or yellowish area. The fungus grows on the lower side of the leaf which becomes covered with a purple mold. The best control is proper air circulation and heating to hold the relative humidity below 90 percent. Cultivars resistant to several races are commercially available. Certain fungicides are effective in the control of this disease.

TOBACCO MOSAIC VIRUS. Tobacco mosaic (*Mamortabaci*) is caused by a virus and is present in almost all areas of greenhouse tomato production. The symptoms initially are mottling on new growth, malformation of the leaves and flowers, and wilt. Damage varies with the virulence of the strain. The best control is the use of resistant cultivars. Inoculation of seedlings with a mild virus strain to cross-protect against virulent strains is a common practice in Europe. Increasing interest in this procedure is developing in the United States.

CUCUMBER MOSAIC VIRUS. Cucumber mosaic virus (*Marmorcucumeris*) is a disease to which cucumbers are more susceptible than tomatoes, mainly because it does not spread so fast in tomatoes. The virus is disseminated

---

2. See Chapter 11 for general control measures and Chapters 20, 21, and 30 for specific control for cucumbers, lettuce, and tomatoes respectively.

by aphids, but can be spread mechanically by handling infected plants. Resistant cultivars are not available, so the best measure is to control the aphids.

NEMATODES. Root knot nematodes *(Meloidogyne)* can be a problem in the production of lettuce, tomatoes, and cucumbers. The first major symptom is plant stunting and wilting. Upon inspection, gall formations on the roots are usually visible. For control, the soil must be either sterilized by steam or fumigated by chemicals. Resistant cultivars of tomatoes suitable for greenhouse production are presently becoming available.

Insects

WHITE FLIES. White flies *(Trialeurodes vaporariorum)* are common pests on cucumbers, lettuce, and tomatoes. These minute insects are found on both upper and lower leaf surfaces and feed by sucking juices. Under greenhouse conditions, the life cycle can be repeated quickly and a high population may occur in a short time. Yield reductions do not occur usually until high populations are reached. Control is by spraying, by fogging insecticides, or by biological control with a small wasp—*Encarsia formosa.*

APHIDS. Aphids (several species) are small, sluggish, soft bodied insects which feed on leaves by sucking. These insects can multiply rapidly and attack most greenhouse crops. They also transmit several types of virus diseases. Control should begin when aphids are first noticed, to reduce losses and minimize chances of virus transmission. Several insecticides, such as malathion, are effective in controlling aphids.

TOMATO PINWORM. The tomato pinworm *(Keiferia lycopersicella)* is one of the most difficult insects to control. The adults, $1/4$ inch in length, are gray moths that deposit eggs on the foliage. After hatching, the larvae feed under the surface of the tissues and create clear areas on the leaf surfaces. As the population increases, fruits are attacked by the larvae, usually under the calyx. The damaged fruit area is hard to spot as only a small entrance hole is evident. Fruits must be culled, and close inspection is required to detect damage.

Control of the adults is obtained by fogging or spraying insecticides, which should be applied at dusk when the moths are active. Larvae are harder to control because of their protection by the leaf surface. Thus, repeated applications of the insecticides are needed to break the life cycle of this insect.

LEAF MINERS. Leaf miners *(Liriomyza)*, larvae of a small fly, attack cucumbers, lettuce, and tomatoes. The larvae feed between the leaf surfaces forming a light colored, narrow, winding trail. When abundant, fruit production can be reduced, and leafy vegetable yields can be severely reduced by cullage. Spray applications or fogging with an insecticide provide proper control.

THRIPS. Several species of thrips occur in the greenhouse. These small, slender insects (½₅ inch long) feed on leaf surfaces by rasping them and lapping up the exuding juices. This type of feeding results in the silvering of leaf surfaces. Thrips can be a problem on tomatoes and are capable of transmitting spotted wilt. Control is by spraying or fogging insecticides.

HARVESTING, HANDLING, AND MARKETING

Harvesting

The harvesting of greenhouse tomatoes, lettuce, and cucumbers is similar to harvesting similar crops in the field as explained in prior chapters. Tomatoes are usually harvested with more color than those from the field. Fruits are usually harvested from the time color begins to develop until it reaches the full pink stage. The later the stage of color at harvest, the more care must be taken in the handling to avoid fruit bruising and damage.

Cucumbers of the seedless types are harvested when they reach the proper length and fullness. Once into harvest, most crops are harvested daily.

Packing

Tomatoes of uniform size and color are usually packed in boxes with two layers per box. Cellpacks are common in some areas. In northern areas, an 8-pound basket is still being used.

In many sections, fruits are individually stickered with the grower's name and some form of advertisement. This project identification is felt to be important to many producers.

Cucumbers of European seedless type desiccate rapidly once harvested. Care must be taken to move them rapidly after harvesting to the packing area. Shrink film wrapping of these cucumbers prevents rapid desiccation and greatly extends shelf life. Shrink film is necessary if the cucumber is being stored or shipped any distance.

Marketing

Since the products grown under controlled environments are of high cost and quality, special consideration should be exercised in marketing. High quality demands premium prices. The products usually move through normal produce marketing channels, but some deserve special attention. See Chapter 13 for details on harvesting, handling, and marketing.

SELECTED REFERENCES

Anonymous, "Growing Crops Without Soil," USDA, ARS Bull. CA 34–125, Beltsville, Md. (current).

Anonymous, "1979 Insect Pest Management Guide for Commercial and Vegetable Crops and Greenhouse Vegetables," Univ. of Ill. Agr. Ext. Circ. 897 (revised annually).

Berry, W. L., "Hydroponics—Principles and Guidelines. Lasca Leaves," Arcadia, Calif., Los Angeles State and County Arboretum, 1974.

Brooks, W. M., "Growing Greenhouse Tomatoes in Ohio," Ohio State Univ. Coop. Ext. Ser. Ext. Circ. SB–19, 1974.

Cooper, A. J., "Nutrient Film Technique—Early Fears About Nutrition Unfounded," *The Grower*, 326-327, Aug., 1975.

Corgan, J. N., *et al.*, "Greenhouse Tomatoes: Structures, Production, Marketing," N. Mex. State Univ. Coop. Ext. Ser. Circ. 387, 1967.

Dalrymple, D. G., "Controlled-Environment Agriculture: A Global Review of Greenhouse Food Production," USDA Foreign Agr. Econ. Rep. 89, 1973.

de Bivort, L. H., Taylor, T. B., and Fontes, M., "An Assessment of Controlled-Environment Agriculture Technology," The National Science Foundation under Contract C–1026, 1978.

Ellis, N. K., Jensen, M., Larsen, J., and Oebker, N. F., "Nutriculture Systems," Purdue Agr. Bull. 44, 1974.

Fontes, M. R., "Controlled-Environment Horticulture in the Arabian Desert at Abu Dhabi," *HortSci.* 8 (1), 1973.

Jensen, M. H., "Proceedings on an International Symposium on Controlled-Environment Agriculture," April 7 and 8, 1978, Tucson, Ariz.

Jensen, M. H., and Hicks, N. C., "Exciting Future for Sand Culture," *American Vegetable Grower*, 33-34, 72, 74, Nov., 1973.

Loughton, A, "Growing Greenhouse Crops on Straw Bales," Fact sheet 75–078, AGDEX 250/24, Ministry of Agriculture and Food, Parliament Buildings, Toronto, Ont., Can., 1975.

Sheldrake, Raymond, Jr., "Planning Construction and Operating Plastic Covered Greenhouses," N. Y. Cornell Univ. Misc. Bull. 72, 1972.

Stuart, N. W., and Krizek, D. T., "Growing Crops Without Soil," USDA, ARS CA–34–125, 1970.

Sullivan, G. H., and Robertson, J. L., "Production, Marketing and Economic Trends in the Greenhouse Industry," Purdue Univ. Agr. Exp. Sta. Bull. 908, 1974.

Swartz, M., "Guide to Commercial Hydroponics," Daniel Davey & Co., Inc., Hartford, Conn., 1968.

Wittwer, S. H., and Honma, S., "Greenhouse Tomatoes, Guidelines for Successful Production," Mich. State Univ. Press, 1969.

Wittwer, S. H., Honma, S., and Robb, Wm., "Practices for Increasing Yields of Greenhouse Lettuce," Mich. State Univ. Agr. Res. Rep. 22, 1964.

CHAPTER 34

Home Vegetable Garden

A number of developments in the vegetable industry and in our overall economy, resulting from the high cost of energy and labor, have contributed to an increased interest in the home garden. Many vegetables are becoming unavailable or too expensive to the consumer because their production cannot be readily mechanized. With the high cost of food and a shrinking dollar, the home garden can supply an important part of the family diet and provide additional tax-free income. Gardening can be an interesting, rewarding, healthful, and remunerating hobby.

Fresh, home-grown vegetables are superior in quality to those generally sold on the market and are readily available when needed. Home gardens can be managed to provide an ample supply of fresh vegetables throughout the growing season. As large numbers of gardeners now use lockers and home freezers, even more vegetables can be utilized than when canning and fall storage were the only means of preservation.

PLANNING AND ARRANGING

Choosing a Location

Very little can be said in regard to location of the garden, as the location of the house and various other permanent structures, to a degree, determines the garden site. However, where possible, the garden should have a location that is convenient to the kitchen and that affords the maximum amount of sunlight. Also, frost is less likely to injure vegetables on high ground than on low ground or in valleys, and a southern exposure and sandy loam will produce earlier vegetables than a northern exposure and a heavy soil. It should be remembered, also, that a fairly level place, if properly drained, is desirable.

Selecting Soils

A good garden soil is one that carries an abundance of nutrients, is of open texture, is well supplied with humus, and is properly drained. It is necessary on most soils to add fertilizers, animal or green manures, and in some cases, lime and water. A large quantity of well-decayed vegetable matter adds nutrients to the soil, improves the texture, aids in the growth of beneficial bacteria, holds moisture, and helps to set free nutrients which are already in the soil but not available.

Determining Size

On the farm, it has long been the practice to grow melons, canning tomatoes, and other large and bulky vegetables in locations other than in the vegetable garden. In this case, the garden nearest the house is a kitchen garden, and the field garden may be in some well-chosen fertile location on the farm where the necessary care may be given with the tractor and field-cultivating tools, while the farmer is in the field for the general crop work. As a convenience to the housewife, however, crops which need frequent harvesting, such as tomatoes and beans for immediate use, should be in the kitchen garden or nearby.

A garden 100 by 150 feet containing approximately ⅓ acre of land will furnish enough vegetables for a family of five. Since the discussion in previous chapters covers, in the main, the problems encountered in field production, this chapter deals with the kitchen or city garden located at or near the house (Fig. 34.1).

Planning and Arranging

A planting plan of the garden furnishes the grower with a record of the cultivar and amount he wishes to plant, the succession of crops, and other worthwhile information necessary for proper management of the garden. In order to plan definitely, the length and breadth of the garden should be determined or measured and drawn to scale on a piece of white paper. A convenient scale is 1.8 inch to a foot. Accordingly, a garden measuring 100 by 150 feet would require a drawing 12½ by 18¾ inches. The kinds of vegetables and dates of planting can then be placed in the proper position on the plan. The plants should be grouped so that those

Fig. 34.1—Weeding the home garden.

USDA Photograph

needing the same cultural treatment may be together in the same section of the garden (Table 34.1).

The garden will have in general three main divisions, namely: (1) perennial section, (2) all-season section, and (3) part-season section. The last two divisions may be subdivided into cool- and warm-season crops. The perennial crops should, of course, be located at one side of the garden where they will not interfere with other garden practices. The all-season crops, such as parsnips, cucumbers, and tomatoes, should be located so as not to interfere with the successive or succession planting as indicated in the plot. The part-season crops, such as beans, beets, peas, and lettuce, should be grouped together to allow a large section of the garden to be vacated as the crops mature. This permits the preparation of the land and the planting of succession crops. The plan (Table 34.1) includes only suggestions for a home garden. Many other plans might be drawn which would serve the individual taste and desire of the grower, especially as to quantities to plant.

Table 34.1—Suggested Plan of a 100- by 150-Foot Home Garden.

Distance Between Rows	Kind, Amount and Succession of Crops		Distance Between Rows
	Spring Planting	**Summer or Fall Planting**	
6 ft. cold ...	Asparagus		4 ft.
3 ft. frames .	Parsley, horseradish, rhubarb	(Adapted only to the mountain regions of the South)	4 ft.
3 ft.	Radishes, 50 ft.—early lettuce, 50 ft.—beets, 50 ft.	Followed by fall cabbage	3 ft.
3 ft.	Early peas	Followed by fall cabbage	3 ft.
3 ft.	Late peas	Followed by fall broccoli	3 ft.
3 ft.	Onion, sets	Followed by radishes and lettuce	3 ft.
3 ft.	Beets, 100 ft.—early turnips, 50 ft.	Followed by spinach	3 ft.
3 ft.	Early cabbage, 100 ft.—cauliflower, 50 ft.	Followed by bush beans	3 ft.
3 ft.	Early broccoli	Followed by bush beans	3 ft.
3 ft.	Early potatoes	Followed by radishes	3 ft.
3 ft.	Early potatoes	Followed by turnips	3 ft.
3 ft.	Early potatoes	Followed by turnips	3 ft.
3 ft.	Onion, seeded		3 ft.
3 ft.	Swiss chard, 50 ft.—salsify (oyster plant), 100 ft.		3 ft.
3 ft.	Parsnips		3 ft.
3 ft.	Carrots		3 ft.
3 ft.	Late beets for winter ...		3 ft.
3 ft.	Bush beans		3 ft.
3 ft.	Bush beans		3 ft.
3 ft.	Lima beans		3 ft.
4 ft.	Tomatoes		4 ft.
4 ft.	Tomatoes, peppers, eggplants		4 ft.
4 ft.	Potatoes or sweet corn .		4 ft.
4 ft.	Sweet potatoes or sweet corn		4 ft.
4 ft.	Sweet potatoes or sweet corn		4 ft.
4 ft.	Cucumbers		4 ft.
4 ft.	Squash (summer and winter)		4 ft.

CULTURAL PRACTICES

Since the preparation of seedbed, plant growing, fertilization, cultivation, disease and insect control, and other necessary operations are discussed fully in preceding chapters, they will not be reviewed here. The home garden, like a commercial crop, should receive every necessary attention to make it productive and profitable. Vigilance and careful planning are necessary for success. Proper working facilities such as accessi-

Fig. 34.2—Harvesting vegetables from home garden.

USDA Photograph

bility, protection, moisture regulation, adequate tools, and simple storage space are well worth providing.

Some vegetables mature in a short time, while others need the entire season to reach maturity. A good plan aids the gardener in grouping such plants for the convenience of planting, cultivating, and disposal. Table

Fig. 34.3—Canned and stored vegetables from the home garden.

2.1 lists the relative hardiness and may indicate approximate time to plant and harvest.

Valuable planting information is given in Chapter 8. Table 8.1 gives full information on the quantity of different seed needed and method and depth of planting. Figures 8.1 and 8.2 show average dates for the latest killing frost in the spring and the first killing frost in the fall, respectively; while corresponding Tables 8.2 and 8.3 provide spring and fall planting dates for different sections of the country.

CHOOSING THE KINDS AND CULTIVAR
OF VEGETABLES TO GROW

The kind and cultivar of vegetables to grow will, of course, depend on the individual tastes of the family. Cultivars should be chosen to meet special requirements, such as earliness, succession, adaptability, disease resistance, and productivity. The experiment stations of the state colleges of agriculture will supply lists of the cultivars best suited to the states. Cultivars are also discussed in the chapters on particular crops.

ORGANIC GARDENING

Successful organic gardening is dependent upon good soil fertility; control of weeds, insects, and diseases; and adherence to other established gardening practices.

Providing Nutrients

Nutrients for growing plants can be supplied from organic materials such as leaves, grass clippings, peat moss, straw, or hay. These materials must be decomposed by microorganisms before their nutrients become available. More readily available nutrients may be obtained from compost, manure, sewage sludge, steamed bonemeal, rock phosphate, and hardwood ashes. Since organic matter will tend to make the soil slightly acid, ground limestone or marl may be needed.

Controlling Weeds and Pests

Since weeds compete with plants for nutrients, water, and sunlight, they should be removed as soon as they appear. By filling the space between the rows with straw or other undecomposed material, weed growth can be discouraged. The mulch will keep tomato fruits from contact with the soil and thus avoid fruit rots. It will also hold and conserve moisture.

Some crops can be grown with little or no danger from insects or disease pests. These include radishes, lettuce, onions, leeks, shallots, chives, beets, chard, mustard, Chinese cabbage, parsnips, salsify, peas, spinach, sweet potatoes, turnips, and most herbs. Tomatoes can usually be grown without pesticides if the tomato hornworms are hand-harvested.

Biological control is effective against some insects. *Bacillus thuringiensis* will control tomato hornworms, fruit worms, webworms, bagworms, and cabbageworms. Lady beetles may be effective against aphids. Other harmful insects such as striped cucumber beetles and flea beetles are difficult to control without the use of effective insecticides. Some insecticides such as pyrethrins, rotenone, and nicotine are of vegetable origin. These can be used when pest epidemics threaten, but many manufactured insecticides are both safer to use and more effective than the botanical insecticides.

CHOOSING THE KIND OF HERBS TO GROW

Every home garden should contain some of the herbs used for their flavor and fragrance in cooking. Herbs are annual, biennial, or perennial. Most of them should be planted in the perennial section of the garden.

A good discussion of the culture and uses of savory herbs can be found in the USDA Farmers' Bulletin No. 1977.

A few plants of the following herbs will supply the average family:

ANISE *(Pimpinella anisum)*. Seed used in medicine, cooking, and for flavoring liquors (annual).

BALM *(Melissa officinalis)*. Leaves used for their lemonlike flavor in liquors and medicine (perennial).

BASIL *(Ocimum basilicum)*. Clove-flavored foliage used in flavoring meats, soups, and salads (annual).

BORAGE *(Borage officinalis)*. Coarse leaves sometimes used as potherbs and for seasoning salads (annual).

CARAWAY *(Carum carvi)*. Seeds used in making bread, also cheese, salads, sauces, soups, and cakes (biennial).

CATNIP *(Nepeta cataria)*. Leaves used in making sauces and teas; a mild condiment (perennial).

CHIVES *(Allium schoenoprasum)*. Leaves used for flavoring; belongs to the onion family (perennial).

CORIANDER *(Coriandrum sativum)*. Seed used in making confections and bread (annual).

DILL *(Anethum graveolens)*. Stems and blossom heads used for making dill pickles and flavoring soups (biennial).

FENNEL *(Foeniculum vulgare)*. Used in French or Italian cookery; stems sometimes used raw (biennial or perennial).

HOREHOUND *(Marribium vulgare)*. Used in tea and for flavoring sugar candy; supposed to be good for colds (perennial).

LAVENDER *(Lavandula officinalis)*. Used for pleasant fragrance; also used in medicine (perennial).

PEPPERMINT *(Mentha piperita)*. Green or dried leaves used in soups, sauces, and for meats; also for flavoring puddings and gelatin desserts (perennial).

ROSEMARY *(Rosmarinus officinalis)*. Aromatic leaves used for seasoning (perennial).

SAGE *(Salvia officinalis)*. Used for seasoning dressings and strong meats (perennial).

SPEARMINT *(Mentha spicata)*. Green or dried leaves used in soups, sauces, and for meats; also for flavoring puddings and gelatin desserts (perennial).

SUMMER SAVORY *(Satureia hortensis)*. Green parts used in flavoring meats and dressings (annual).

SWEET MARJORAM *(Marjorana hortensis)*. Leaves used in seasoning soups, meats, and dressings (annual or perennial).

THYME *(Thymus vulgaris)*. Used for flavoring soups, gravies, stews, sauces, and meats (perennial).

SELECTED REFERENCES

Anonymous, "Growing Vegetables in the Home Garden," USDA H & G Bull. 202, 1978.
Anonymous, Growing Your Own Vegetables," USDA Inv. Bull. 409, 1977.
Anonymous, "The Guide for Home Vegetable Gardeners," N. Mex. State Univ. Ext. Pub. 400 H–15, 1977.
Anonymous, "Insects and Diseases in the Home Garden," AB 380 USDA, 1975.
Anonymous, "Kentucky Home Fruit and Vegetable Gardening," Univ. of Ky. Ag. Rep. 2, 1978.
Anonymous, "Let's Take a Look at Organic Gardening," Ohio Agr. Ext. Ser. Bull. 555, 1973.
Anonymous, "Mulches for Your Garden," USDA H & G Bull. 185, 1971.
Anonymous, "Savory Herbs: Culture and Use," Farmers' Bull. 1977, 1958.
Anonymous, "Successful Gardening in Georgia," Univ. of Ga. Ext. Ser. SGP (current).

Anonymous, "The Wyoming Vegetable Garden," Univ. of Wyo. Ext. Circ. B–651R (current).

Askew, R. G., and Mills, S. R., "Everybody's Garden Guide," N. Dak. State Univ. Circ. H–618, 1977.

Boys, F. E., Carroll, R. B., and Orzolek, M. D., "Home Vegetable Gardening in Delaware," Univ. of Del. Ext. Bull. 55, 1977.

Brooks, W. M., Utzinger, J. D., and Wittmeyer, E. C., "Vegetable Varieties for Home Gardens," Ohio Ext. Leaflet 100, 1970.

Fletcher, R. F., et al., "Extension Agents' Guide to Organic Gardening, Culture, and Soil Management," Pa. State Col. of Agr. Ext. Ser., 1972.

Gomez, Ricardo, "Home Vegetable Gardening," N. Mex. Univ. Ext. Ser. Circ., 1978.

Griffits, A. E., "Vegetable Varieties for the Rhode Island Gardener," Univ. of R. I. Ext. Circ. 69, 1976.

Hamson, A. R., "Growing Vegetables," Utah State Univ. Ext. Circ. EC–313, 1978.

Hill, D. E., "Leaf-Mold for Soil Improvement," Conn. Agr. Exp. Sta. Bull. 774, 1978.

Hopp, R. J., Way, Winston A., Wiggins, S. C., and Flanagan, T. R., "The Home Vegetable Garden," Univ. of Vt. Ext. Circ. 138 (current).

MacDaniels, L. H., "Facts About Organic Gardening," Cornell Univ. Ext. Ser. Bull. 36, 1972.

Marr, Charles, "Vegetable Garden Planting Guide," Kan. State Univ. Agr. Ext. Ser. MF–315, 1974.

Neild, R. E., "Herbs for the Home Garden," Univ. of Neb. Agr. Ext. Ser. Circ. G 74-88, 1974.

Oebker, N. F., "Ten Steps to a Successful Vegetable Garden," Univ. of Ariz. Garden Guide Q–95, 1972.

Reed, L. B., and Webb, R. E., "Insects and Diseases in the Home Garden," USDA Agr. Inf. Bull. 380, 1975.

Stoner, A. K., "Growing Tomatocs in the Home Garden," USDA H & G Bull. 180, 1972.

Vandemark, J. S, and Courter, J. W., "Vegetable Gardening for Illinois," Univ. of Ill. Col. of Agr. Coop. Ext. Ser. Circ. 1150, 1978.

Webster, R. E., "Minigardens for Vegetables," USDA H & G Bull. 163, 1974.

Webster, R., and Kehr, A., "Growing Vegetables in the Home Garden," USDA H & G Bull. 202, 1978.

Wolf, Isabel, and Zottola, Edmund, "Home Canning Fruits and Vegetables," Univ. of Minn. Ext. Ser. Folder 100, 1977.

Yamaguchi, M., "Production of Ornamental Vegetables in the United States," Univ. of Calif., Davis, Oct., 1973.

APPENDIX

SOURCES OF INFORMATION

While this text covers a wide range of information on vegetable production, many problems are discussed only briefly and others not at all. Also, new developments in the industry, results of current investigations, and new cultivars are continually being made available. The reader may, therefore, want to consult other texts and sources of information on particular subjects.

Additional information can be obtained on vegetables as well as other subjects in mimeograph, circular, or bulletin form. Requests for a list of available publications of the U.S. Department of Agriculture should be addressed to the Office of Information, U.S. Department of Agriculture, Washington, D.C. 20250.

The state experiment stations, which are listed in Table A, can supply many valuable publications on agricultural subjects, upon requests to directors or mailing rooms.

VITAMINS IN VEGETABLES

Vegetables have long been valued for their health-giving qualities. Certain vegetables are rich sources of minerals needed for body building and body regulating; some are good sources of fats, proteins, and carbohydrates; certain ones possess laxative qualities; and certain others are rich sources of vitamins. These are accessory substances occurring in foods and are essential for growth, for reproduction, and for the maintenance of health.

It was in the effort to find the cause of the disease beriberi that the vitamin B_1 was discovered. In 1912 Funk named this class of essential dietary factors vitamins. Today many vitamins are known, including A, B_1, B_2 (G), C, D, K, niacin, and other growth factors. Each vitamin is specific and cannot be replaced by another or a combination of others.

Vitamin A is essential for integrity of epithelial cells and is a stimulus for new cell growth. It aids in maintaining resistance to infections, increases longevity, and decreases senility.

Thiamine (vitamin B_1) is essential for maintenance of good appetite, normal digestion, and gastro-intestinal tonus. It is necessary for growth, fertility, and lactation and is needed for normal functioning of nervous tissue.

Riboflavin (vitamin B_2 or G) has far-reaching biological significance. It functions in cellular metabolism and is believed to be especially important for respiration in poorly vascularized tissues such as the cornea. It is present in the retinal pigment of the eye, where it plays an important part in light adaptation.

Ascorbic acid (vitamin C) is essential for healthy gums and for the prevention of the disease scurvy.

Vitamin D is essential for the correct utilization of calcium salts and phosphates in the nutrition of the growing and adult skeleton, and for the prevention of rickets, osteomalacia, and dental diseases.

Vitamin E functions as an anti-oxidant, which preserves easily oxidizable

Table A—State Agricultural Experiment Stations.

State	Address	State	Address
Alabama	Auburn 36830	Missouri	Columbia 65211
Alaska	Fairbanks 99701	Montana	Bozeman 59715
Arizona	Tucson 85721	Nebraska	Lincoln 68503
Arkansas	Fayetteville 72701	Nevada	Reno 89507
California		New Hampshire	Durham 03824
Berkeley Station	Berkeley 94720	New Jersey	New Brunswick 08900
Davis Station	Davis 95616	New Mexico	Las Cruces 88003
Riverside Station	Riverside 92521	New York	
Colorado	Fort Collins 80523	State Station	Geneva 14456
Connecticut		Cornell Station	Ithaca 14853
State Station	New Haven 06504	North Carolina	Raleigh 27650
Ag. College and		North Dakota	Fargo 58103
Storrs Station	Storrs 06268	Ohio	
Delaware	Newark 19711	University Station	Columbus 43201
Florida	Gainesville 32611	Ag. Research	
Georgia		Station	Wooster 44691
University Station	Athens 30602	Oklahoma	Stillwater 74075
Main Station	Experiment 30212	Oregon	Corvallis 97331
Coastal Plain		Pennsylvania	University Park 16802
Station	Tifton 31794	Rhode Island	Kingston 02881
Hawaii	Honolulu 96822	South Carolina	Clemson 29631
Idaho	Moscow 83843	South Dakota	Brookings 57007
Illinois	Urbana 61801	Tennessee	Knoxville 37901
Indiana	West Lafayette 47907	Texas	College Station 77843
		Utah	Logan 84322
Iowa	Ames 50011	Vermont	Burlington 05405
Kansas	Manhattan 66506	Virginia	
Kentucky	Lexington 40506	Main Station	Blacksburg 24061
Louisiana	Baton Rouge 70893	Truck Station	Virginia Beach 23455
Maine	Orono 04469	Washington	Pullman 99164
Maryland	College Park 20742	West Virginia	Morgantown 26506
Massachusetts	Amherst 01002	Wisconsin	Madison 53706
Michigan	East Lansing 48824	Wyoming	Laramie 82071
Minnesota	St. Paul 55108		
Mississippi	Mississippi State 39762		

Source: USDA Agriculture Handbook No. 305, 1979.

vitamins and unsaturated fatty acids. It is necessary for normal reproduction in many animal species. It may act as a regulator of the metabolism of the cell nucleus, especially during maturation and differentiation.

Vitamin K is essential for synthesis of prothrombin and normal blood clotting.

Niacin is the anti-pellagra and anti-black tongue factor.

CONVERSION OF U.S. MEASUREMENTS TO THE METRIC SYSTEM

The metric system originated in France in 1790 and spread throughout Europe, Latin America, and the East during the nineteenth century. With the exception of the United States (now considering the system seriously) and a few former British associated areas, the metric system is the official language of measurements.

Simply described, the metric system is a decimal system of weights and measures in which the gram (.0022046 pound), the meter (39.37 inches) and the liter (61.025 cubic inches) are the basic units of weight, length, and volume respectively. Most names of the various other units are formed by the addition of the following prefixes to these three terms, namely:

milli—(one thousandth), as 1 millimeter (mm) = 1/1000 meter (m)

centi—(one hundredth), as, 1 centimeter (cm) = 1/100 m

deci—(one tenth), as, 1 decimeter (dm) = 1/10 m

deca or *deka*—(ten), as, 1 decameter (dkm) = 10 m

hecto—(one hundred), as, 1 hectometer (hm) = 100 m

kilo—(one thousand), as, 1 kilometer (km) = 1,000 m

Distance

1 in. = 2.54 cm; 12 in. = 1 ft.; 3 ft. = 1 yd.; 1 yd. = .91 (m.)
1,760 yd. (5,280 ft.) = 1 mi.; 1 mi. = 1,619 m.
Therefore, 1 km = .62 mi. or 1 mi. = 1.62 km.
Accordingly, for example, 50 km = 31 mi.

Area

1 a. (43,560 sq. ft.) = 4.047 sq. m = 0.405 (hectare) ha.
1 sq. mi. (a section of land) = 640 a. or 259 ha.
1 ha = 2.47 a. To convert a. into ha, simply multiply a. by 0.405.
Accordingly, for example, 200 a. = 81 ha.

Table B—Composition of Vegetables
(Constituents of 100 g of Edible Portion).

Name	APPROXIMATE COMPOSITION						MINERALS		
	Calories	Protein (g)	Fat (g)	Ash (g)	Total Carbohy-drates (g)	Crude Fibre (g)	Calcium (mg)	Phos-phorus (mg)	Iron (mg)
Roots and Tubers:									
Beet, red, raw	42	1.6	.1	1.1	9.6	.9	27	43	1.0
Carrots, raw	42	1.2	.3	1.0	9.3	1.1	39	37	.8
Parsnip, raw	78	1.5	.5	1.2	18.2	2.2	57	80	.7
Potatoes, sweet, raw ...	123	1.8	.7	1.1	27.9	1.0	30	49	.7
Potatoes, white, raw ...	83	2.0	.1	1.0	19.1	.4	11	56	.7
Radishes, raw	20	1.2	.1	1.0	4.2	.7	37	31	1.0
Rutabagas, raw	38	1.1	.1	.8	8.9	1.3	55	41	.4
Turnips, raw	32	1.1	.2	.7	7.1	1.1	40	34	.5
Leaf and Stem Vegetables:									
Asparagus, raw	21	2.2	.2	.7	3.9	.7	21	62	.9
Beet greens, raw	27	2.0	.3	1.7	5.6	1.4	118	45	3.2
Brussels sprouts, raw ...	47	4.4	.5	1.3	8.9	1.3	34	78	1.3
Cabbage, raw	24	1.4	.2	.8	5.3	1.0	46	31	.5
Celery, raw	18	1.3	.2	1.1	3.7	.7	50	40	.5
Chard, leaves, raw	27	2.6	.4	1.2	4.8	.8	105	36	2.5
Chicory, French endive ...	21	1.6	.3	1.0	2.9	.8	18	21	.7
Chives	52	3.8	.6	1.8	7.8	2.0	48	57	8.4
Cress, water	18	1.7	.3	1.1	3.3	.5	195	46	2.0
Endive, raw	20	1.6	.2	.9	4.0	.8	79	56	1.7
Kale, raw	40	3.9	.6	1.7	7.2	1.2	225	62	2.2
Kohlrabi, raw	30	2.1	.1	1.0	6.7	1.1	46	50	.6
Lettuce, headed	15	1.2	.2	.9	2.9	.6	22	25	.5
Onions, mature, raw ...	45	1.4	.2	.6	10.3	.1	32	44	.5
Onions, young green ...	45	1.0	.2	.6	10.6	1.8	135	24	.9
Parsley	50	3.7	1.0	2.4	9.0	1.8	193	84	4.3
Spinach, raw	20	2.3	.3	1.5	3.2	.6	81	55	3.0
Turnip greens, raw ...	30	2.9	.4	1.8	5.4	1.2	259	50	2.4

(Continued)

Table B (Continued).

Name	Calories	APPROXIMATE COMPOSITION					MINERALS		
		Protein (g)	Fat (g)	Ash (g)	Total Carbohydrates (g)	Crude Fibre (g)	Calcium (mg)	Phosphorus (mg)	Iron (mg)
Flower, Fruit and Seed Vegetables:									
Artichoke	63	2.9	.4	1.1	11.9	3.2	47	94	1.9
Beans									
Red kidney, raw	336	23.1	1.7	3.6	59.4	3.5	163	437	6.9
Lima, green, raw	128	7.5	.8	1.7	23.5	1.5	63	158	2.3
Lima, dry	333	20.7	1.3	3.8	61.6	4.3	68	381	7.5
Snap, green, raw	35	2.4	.2	.8	7.7	1.4	65	44	1.1
Broccoli, raw	29	3.3	.2	1.1	5.5	1.3	130	76	1.3
Cauliflower, raw	25	2.4	.2	.8	4.9	.9	22	72	1.1
Corn, sweet, raw	92	3.7	1.2	.7	20.5	.8	9	120	.5
Cucumbers, raw	12	.7	.1	.4	2.7	.5	10	21	.3
Eggplant, raw	24	1.1	.2	.5	5.5	.9	15	37	.4
Mushrooms, raw	16	2.4	.3	1.1	4.0	.9	9	115	1.0
Peas, green, raw	98	6.7	.4	.9	17.7	2.2	22	122	1.9
Peas, dry, split	344	34.5	1.0	2.8	61.7	1.2	33	268	5.1
Peppers, green, raw	25	1.2	.2	.5	5.7	1.4	11	25	.4
Pumpkin, raw	31	1.2	.2	.8	7.3	1.3	21	44	.8
Soybeans, dry	331	34.9	18.1	4.7	34.8	5.0	227	586	8.0
Soybean sprouts, raw	46	6.2	1.4	.8	5.3	.8	48	67	1.0
Squash, summer, raw	16	.6	.1	.4	3.9	.5	15	15	.4
Squash, winter, raw	38	1.5	.3	.8	8.8	1.4	19	28	.6
Tomatoes, raw	20	1.0	.3	.6	4.0	.6	11	27	.6

From **Nutritional Data** (second edition), H. J. Heinz Co., Pittsburgh, Pa.

Table C—Vitamin Content of Vegetables
(Constituents of 100 g of Edible Portion).

Name	A (IU)	B₁ (mg)	B₂ (mg)	Niacin (mg)	C (mg)
Roots and Tubers:					
Beet, red, raw	20	.02	.05	.4	10
Carrots, raw	12,000	.06	.06	.5	4
Parsnip, raw	0	.08	.12	.2	18
Potatoes, sweet, raw	7,700	.09	.05	.6	22
Potatoes, white, raw	20	.11	.04	1.2	17
Radishes, raw	30	.03	.02	.3	24
Rutabagas, raw	330	.07	.08	.9	36
Turnips, raw	Tr.	.05	.07	.5	28
Leaf and Stem Vegetables:					
Asparagus, raw	1,000	.16	.19	1.4	33
Beet greens, raw	6,700	.08	.18	.4	34
Brussels sprouts, raw	400	.08	.16	.7	94
Cabbage, raw	80	.06	.05	.3	50
Celery, raw	0	.05	.04	.4	7
Chard, leaves, raw	8,720	.06	.18	.4	38
Chicory, French endive	10,000	.05	.20	—	15
Chives	500	.12	—	—	70
Cress, water	4,720	.08	.16	.8	77
Endive, raw	3,000	.07	.12	.4	11
Kale, raw	7,540	.10	.26	2.0	115
Kohlrabi, raw	Tr.	.06	.05	.2	61
Lettuce, headed	540	.04	.08	.2	8
Onions, mature, raw	50	.03	.04	.2	9
Onions, young green	50	.03	.04	.2	24
Parsley	8,230	.11	.28	1.4	193
Spinach, raw	9,420	.11	.20	.6	59
Turnip, greens, raw	9,540	.09	.46	.8	136
Flower, Fruit and Seed Vegetables:					
Artichoke	390	.15	.03	—	11
Beans					
Red kidney, raw	0	.57	.22	2.5	2
Lima, green raw	280	.21	.11	1.4	32
Lima, dry	0	.48	.18	2.0	2
Snap, green raw	630	.08	.11	.5	19
Broccoli, raw	3,500	.10	.21	1.1	118
Cauliflower, raw	90	.11	.10	.6	69
Corn, sweet, raw	390	.15	.12	1.7	12
Cucumbers, raw	0	.03	.04	.2	8
Eggplant, raw	30	.04	.05	.6	5
Mushrooms, raw	0	.10	.44	4.9	5
Peas, green, raw	680	.34	.16	2.7	26
Peas, dry, split	370	.77	.28	3.1	2
Peppers, green, raw	630	.04	.07	.4	120
Pumpkin, raw	3,400	.05	.08	.6	8
Soybeans, dry	110	1.07	.31	2.3	Tr.
Soybean sprouts, raw	180	.23	.20	.8	13
Squash, summer, raw	260	.05	.09	.8	17
Squash, winter, raw	4,950	.05	.12	.5	8
Tomatoes, raw	1,100	.06	.04	.5	23

From **Nutritional Data** (second edition), H. J. Heinz Co., Pittsburgh, Pa.

Volume

1 qt. (58 cu. in.) = .9463 liter (l). One l = 1.0567 qt.
4 qt. = a liquid gal. = 231 cu. in. or 3.78 l.
1 cu. yd. (36 × 36 × 36 in.) = .76 (cu. m) m³.
1 bu. (dry measure) = 2,150 cu. in. = 35.2 l.

Weight and Yield of Commodities

1 oz. = 28.35 g; 16 oz. = 1 lb.; 100 lb. = 45.35 kg; 2,000 lb. = 1 short ton;
   1 short ton = .907 metric ton.
1 kg = 22.05 lb.; 1,000 kg = 2,204.6 lb. or metric ton; 1 cwt. (Br.) = 112 lb.;
   20 cwt. = 2240 lb. = long ton.
1 bu. of wheat weighs 60 lb. or 27.2 kg.
Therefore, 20 bu. wheat per a. gives 544 kg per a. (20 bu. × 27.2 kg = 544
   kg).
Accordingly, for example, 20 bu. of wheat per a. produces 1,344 kg per ha (20
   bu. a. × 27.2 kg per bu. × 2.47 a. per ha = 1,344 kg).
Bushel weight of other commodities are: Soybeans and dried peas 60 lb.; rye,
   corn and grain sorghums 56 lb.; millet 48-50 lb.; rice 45 lb.; oats 32 lb.; potatoes 60 lb.; sweet potatoes 55 lb.; tomatoes 53 lb.; prunes 56 lb.; peaches
   and apples 48 lb., etc.

Temperature

Temperature in the United States is measured in Fahrenheit (F.), while under the
   metric system in Celsius (C.). Freezing is 32° F. and boiling 212° F.—a
   difference of 180° F., compared with freezing at 0° C. and boiling at 100°
   C.—a difference of 100° C.
To convert degrees F. to degrees C., subtract 32, then multiply by 5/9.
Approximate F. and C. comparisons are: 50° F. = 10° C.; 60° F. = 16° C.;
   70° F. = 21° C.; 80° F. = 27° C.; 90° F. = 32° C.; 100° F. = 38° C.,
   etc.
To convert degrees C. to degrees F., multiply by 9/5 and add 32.
Approximate C. and F. comparisons are: 10° C. = 50° F.; 20° C. = 68° F.;
   30° C. = 86° F.; 40° C. = 104° F., etc.

RELEVANT NATIONAL SOCIETIES AND JOURNALS

American Horticultural Society, Mt. Vernon, Va. 22121. (Publishes the *American
   Horticulturist* bi-monthly.)

The American Phytopathology Society, 3340 Pilot Knob Rd., St. Paul, Minn. 55121. (Publishes *Phytopathology* [technical] and *Plant Diseases* [general] monthly.)

American Society for Horticultural Science, Alexandria, Va. 22314. (Publishes *HortScience* and the *Journal of the American Society for Horticultural Science* monthly.)

Entomological Society of America, Box 4603, Calvert Rd., College Park, Md. 20740. (Publishes the *Annals of the Entomological Society of America, The Journal of Economic Entomology,* and *Environmental Entomology* quarterly.)

Journal of the Weed Science Society of America, Charlotte, N. C. 28230. (Edited by the Univ. of N. C. at Charlotte and published bi-monthly.)

National Academy of Sciences, 2101 Constitution Ave., N.W., Washington, D. C. 20418. (Publishes the *Proceedings of the National Academy of Sciences of the United States of America* monthly.)

The Potato Association of America, Univ. of Me., Orono, Me. 04469. (Publishes *The American Potato Journal* monthly.)

The Society of Economic Botany, Bronx, N. Y. 10455. (Various publications.)

Soil Science Society of America, 677 S. Segoe Rd., Madison, Wisc. 53711. (Publishes the *Soil Science Society of America Journal* bi-monthly.)

SELECTED REFERENCES

Anonymous, "Crop Production: Annual Report of the National Research Programs 20020, 1980," USDA, SEA (issued annually).

Anonymous, "Directors of State Agricultural Experiment Stations, Institutes and Centers in the United States, and Regional Contacts," USDA, SEA-OD-1020, 1980 (issued annually).

Anonymous, "Fact Book of U. S. Agriculture," USDA Misc. Pub. No. M-1063, 1980 (issued annually).

Anonymous, "List of Available Publications of the USDA," 1979 (issued annually).

Anonymous, "The 1978 Handbook of Agricultural Charts," USDA, ESCS, *Agriculture Handbook 551,* 1979 (issued annually).

Anonymous, "Nutritive Value of Foods," USDA H & G Bull. 72, 1971.

Anonymous, "Professional Workers in State Experiment Stations and Other State Cooperative Institutions, 1978-79," USDA, CSRS, *Agriculture Handbook 306,* 1979 (issued as needed).

Anonymous, "U. S. Fresh Market Vegetable Statistics, 1949-75," USDA, ERS Stat. Bull. 558, 1976.

Anonymous, "The Vegetable Situation," USDA, ESCS, 1980 (issued quarterly).

Murphy, E. W., Watt, B. K., and Rizek, R. L., "Tables of Food Composition: Availability, Uses and Limitations," USDA reprint from *Food Technol.,* Vol. 27, 1973.

White, P. L., and Selvey, N., *Nutritional Qualities of Fresh Fruits and Vegetables,* Mount Kisko, N. Y., Futura Publishing Co., Inc., 1974.

GLOSSARY

Allelomorph. One of a pair of contrasting unit characters.

Alluvial. A stream-laid deposit.

Anaerobic. Pertaining to bacteria or other organisms which flourish without free oxygen.

Angiosperm. Any plant of the class having the seed in a closed ovary.

Anther. The pollen-bearing part of a stamen.

Anthesis. The time or process of expansion in a flower.

Axil. The angle formed by a leaf or branch with the stem.

Axis. The central line of any organ or support of a group of organs; a stem, etc.

Biennial. Living for two years under normal, outdoor conditions, usually producing seed the second year.

Buffer. Any material which prevents sudden changes in acidity.

Bulb. A subterranean leaf-bud with fleshy scales or coats.

Calyx. The outer perianth of the flower.

Cankers. Localized lesions on stems which generally result in the corrosion and sloughing away of tissues with the final production of an open wound, exposing or penetrating the wood.

Carbamates. Substituted organic nitrogen derivatives of carbamic acid, which may contain sulfur, used as insecticides, fungicides, and herbicides.

Carbohydrate. Any of certain organic compounds composed of carbon, hydrogen, and oxygen.

Catalytic. Pertaining to chemical action in which the speed of the reaction is hastened or retarded by a substance which does not enter into the end products.

Cellulose. A shapeless white compound, insoluble in all ordinary solvents, forming the fundamental material of the structure of the plants.

Chlorinated organic insecticide. Also referred to as chlorinated hydrocarbons or chlorinateds, basically the DDT or chlordane group of insecticides which contain chlorine, carbon, and sometimes hydrogen and oxygen.

Chlorophyll. The green coloring matter of plants.

Chloroplast. A plastid containing chlorophyll, developed in cells exposed to light.

Chlorotic. Lacking chlorophyll, giving the plants a blanched appearance.

Chromosomes. A number of well-individualized units, in the nucleus, which transmit hereditary characteristics.

Clove. One of a group of small bulbs produced by the garlic plant.

Colloids. Uncrystalline materials, often gelatinous, which diffuse slowly or not at all.

Connate. Being born or originating together; agreeing in nature.

Corm. The enlarged fleshy base of a stem, bulblike but solid.

Corolla. The inner perianth of distinct or connate petals.

Cotyledon. A seed leaf or first leaf of an embryo.

Cultivar. A horticultural variety.

Cuticle. A continuous layer of structureless, waxy substance which covers the aerial parts of vascular plants except the growing points.

Cutin. A waxy substance which covers most of the aerial parts of vascular plants.

Cytoplasm. A more or less transparent, viscous fluid constituting all of the protoplasm except the nucleus.

Decompound. More than once compounded or divided.

Dextrin. A shapeless, brownish-white carbohydrate substance.

Dibble. An instrument for making holes in which to insert plants or bulbs.

Dicotyledonous. Having two cotyledons.

Diffusion. The passage of molecules or ions in solution from one part of the solution to another, especially through a membrane.

Dihybrid. A cross which involves two character differences.

Dioecious. Unisexual, with the male and female flowers on separate plants.

Dominant. A parental character which has the ability to express itself in the resulting hybrid offspring.

Emasculation. The removal of the stamens.

Embryo. An organism in the early stages of development, as before hatching from an egg, or sprouting from a seed.

Emulsifiable concentrate. A liquid formation of pesticide which contains an emulsifier so that water may be added to form an emulsion.

Endodermis. A sheath, composed of one or more layers of modified parenchymatous cells, which encloses certain fibrovascular bundles.

Endosperm. The stored food supply in a seed.

Exosmosis. The diffusion of solvent or solute outward from the cell vacuole.

Family. A division of an order. Usually a family comprises two or more genera, but one genus possessing sufficiently distinctive characters may form a family.

Fixed copper. Any one of several complex copper compounds, only slightly soluble in water, which do not burn plants as do the soluble copper materials.

Flora. The aggregate of plants growing without cultivation in a country or district, or indigenous to a particular geological formation; as, a desert flora.

Floret. A small flower, usually one of a dense cluster.

Foliar. Of, pertaining to, consisting of, or resembling leaves.

Formalin. An aqueous solution of formaldehyde; a trade name.

Formulation. The form or concentration of a pesticide usually as purchased.

Fungicide. Anything that kills fungi or destroys their germs.

Gene. That portion of the chromosome which serves to transmit a character from parents to progeny.

Genotype. The constitution of an organism with respect to factors of which it is made up; the sum of all genes.

Genus. A classificatory group of animals or plants embracing one or more species.

Granular pesticide. A small clay pellet which is evenly impregnated with the pesticide, conveniently applied from aircraft and fertilizer and seeding equipment.

Gynoecious. Producing only female flowers.

Herb. A plant with no persistent woody stem above the ground.

Herbicide. A phytotoxic chemical used for killing or inhibiting the growth of plants.

Hermaphroditic. Being of both sexes.

Homologous. Alike, similar, or same.

Hybrid. The offspring of plants or animals of different genotypes, cultivars, species, or genera.

Hybridization. The practice of crossing between genotypes.

Hydrocooling. The removal of field heat by cold water.

Indehiscent. Not opening by valves, etc.; remaining persistently closed.

Inert ingredient. A substance, specifically in a pesticide formulation, which is not active.

Inflorescence. General arrangement and disposition of flowers on an axis; flower cluster.

Inoculation. The process of improving soils by the introduction of special microorganisms.

Inorganic pesticide. A compound which does not contain carbon as a part of the molecule.

Insecticide. A substance used to destroy or to repel insects.

Internode. The portion of a stem between two nodes or joints.

Keel. The two anterior united petals of a butterflylike flower, such as a bean flower.

Lignin. A substance related to cellulose, which, with it, constitutes the essential part of woody tissue.

Longevity. The length or duration of life.

Miticide. Any substance used to kill mites.

Molecule. A unit of matter, the smallest portion of an element or compound which retains identity in character with the substance in mass.

Monocotyledon. Having only one cotyledon.

Monoecious. Having both sexes on the same plant.

Mosaic. A disease characterized by mottling of the plant due to spots of light green or yellow on dark green.

Mulch. Any substance, as straw, used to protect roots of plants from heat, cold, or drouth, or to keep fruit clean.

Mutation. A hereditary change in the character of an organism.

Mycelium. The vegetative body of a fungus composed of threads.

Necrosis. A disease causing plant tissue to turn black and decay.

Nematocide. A material that kills nematodes.

Nematode. An eelworm (an unsegmented round worm) not usually visible to the naked eye, inhabiting soil, water, and plants.

Nucleus. The more or less centrally situated organ of the cell containing the chromatin, known as the hereditary substance.

Organic pesticide. A pesticidal compound containing carbon in addition to the other elements.

Organic phosphate insecticide or *Organophosphate.* Any of several derivatives of phosphoric acid which include the materials related to parathion, malathion, diazinon, TEPP, etc.

Osmosis. The passage of the solvent from one side of a membrane to another where the escaping tendency of the solvent on the two sides is unequal.

Ovary. In angiosperms, an enlarged portion of the pistil containing ovules.

Ovicide. A chemical compound specifically toxic to the egg stage of arthropods. Truly effective ovicides prevent the full development of embryos.

Panicle. A loose, irregular compound inflorescence with pedicellate flowers.

Parenchyma. The fundamental tissue, usually composed of thin-walled cells, making up the bulk of the substance of the leaves, the pulp of fruit, the pith of stems, etc.

Pectin. A neutral substance occurring in many vegetable tissues as part of the sap or cell wall.

Peduncle. A flower stalk.

Perianth. The floral envelope, consisting of the calyx and corolla (when present) whatever their form.

Pericycle. A thin cylinder of tissue sheathing the vascular tissues.

Periderm. The cortical tissue derived from the phellogen (cork cambium).

Pesticide. A material that kills pests such as insects, fungi, nematodes, weeds, rodents, etc.

Petiole. The stalk or stem of a leaf.

Phenotype. A type or strain of organisms distinguishable from others by some character, whether this character be due to heredity or environment.

Phloem. A part of the conducting tissue of plants, usually thought to be instrumental in the conduction of elaborated food.

Photosynthesis. The process of manufacturing food.

Pigment. A coloring matter, especially in the cell or tissue.

Pistil. The seed-bearing organ of a flower, consisting of the ovary, stigma, and style when present.

Pith. A roughly cylindrical body of undifferentiated tissue in the center of the axis, enclosed by the vascular tissues.

Plastid. A unit of protoplasm.

Plumule. The bud or growing point of the embryo.

Pollen. Dustlike male bodies capable of fertilization of ovules.

Pollinate. To transfer the pollen from the stamens to the pistils.

Ppb. Parts per billion.

Ppm. Parts per million.

Precooling. Lowering temperatures before shipping.

Progeny. The descendants of a single plant or pair of plants.

Propagate. To cause to multiply.

Protein. Any of several organic, nitrogenous compounds.

Protoplasm. The living substance within a cell.

Receptacle. The more or less expanded or produced portions of an axis which bears the organs of a flower or the collected flowers of a head.

Recessive. Pertaining to a character which is subordinate to or masked by an allelomorphic character.

Residue. That part of a pesticide which remains after application.

Rhizosphere. The immediate zone around the roots of plants.

Root crown. The region in a plant where root and stem join—usually the location of dormant buds.

Rouge (noun). An off-type plant or a diseased plant.

Rouge (verb). To remove off-type or diseased plants.

Sclerotium. A compact, waxy or horny mass of hyphal tissue found in certain higher fungi.

Seed. An embryonic plant with its surrounding integuments or coats.

Sepal. A leaf or division of the calyx.

Sheath. A tubular envelope, as in the lower part of the leaf in grasses.

Species. A classificatory group of plants or animals, subordinate to a genus, and having members that differ only slightly among themselves.

Sperm. A motile ciliated male reproductive cell.

Spreader. Wetting agent that causes the spray to spread over the leaf surfaces.

Stamen. A pollen-bearing organ of a flower.

Sticker. A material added to a spray or dust to improve adherence to the plant surfaces.

Stigma. The part of the pistil which receives the pollen in pollination.

Stipule. An appendage at the base of the petiole of a leaf.

Style. The extended portion of a pistil connecting stigma and ovary.

Suberin. A fatty or waxy substance characteristic of cork tissue.

Sucrose. A non-reducing sugar, the most common commercial form of which is cane or beet sugar, having the empirical formula $C_{12}H_{22}O_{11}$.

Systematic insecticide. A substance which, when absorbed by plants, renders them toxic to insects feeding on them.

Tendril. A slender clasping outgrowth, such as found on cucurbit or grape plants.

Tolerance. The amount of pesticide residue that is permitted by federal regulation to remain on or in a crop.

Toxicity. The capacity of a substance to produce injury; the measure of damage resulting from exposure to a substance.

Translocation. The movement of food or other materials from one part of a plant to another.

Transpiration. The movement of water from the inside of plants out into the atmosphere by evaporation.

Tuber. A short thickened underground stem having numerous buds or eyes.

Umbel. A flower cluster in which the flower stalks spring from the same point, as in a wild carrot.

Unisexual. Of one sex; either male or female; not hermaphroditic.

Vacuum Precooling. Cooling by evaporation of water from plants under reduced pressure.

Viability. Alive or ability to remain alive.

Virus. A group of materials acting poisonously, produced and increased within the plant.

Vitamins. A group of food substances other than fats, proteins, carbohydrates, and salts which are essential to normal nutrition and serve to prevent various diseases.

Volatile. Capable of rapid evaporation in air at ordinary temperatures.

Weed. A plant growing where it is not desired.

Wettable powder. A powder form of an insoluble material so treated that it will readily become suspended in water.

Wetting agent. A compound which when added to a spray solution causes it to contact plant surfaces more thoroughly.

Whorl. A group of organs arranged about a stem; arising from the same node.

Xylem. A part of the vascular bundle or conducting tissue.

Zero tolerance. No amount of the pesticide chemical may remain on the raw agricultural commodity when it is offered for shipment.

AUTHOR INDEX

A

Ackerman, R., 389
Adrian, P. A., 238, 342
Afanasiev, M. M., 184
Ajakaiye, M. B., 376
Alban, E. K., 154
Allard, R. W., 65
Allen, E. J., 492
Ammerman, G. R., 256, 468
Andrew, R. H., 311
Andrews, G. M., 220
Andrus, C. F., 65, 357, 505
Ang, J. K., 195
Angell, F. F., 357
Anthony, J. P., 221
Antle, G. G., 221
Apeland, J., 194
Armbrust, D. V., 492
Arnold, C. Y., 98, 116
Arraud, J. C., 184
Ashby, H. B., 221
Askew, R. G., 576
Atkin, J. D., 256
Audus, L. J., 154
Averre, C. W., 550

B

Bailes, J. P., 221
Bailey, L. H., 36
Bainer, R., 154
Baker, A. S., 389
Banham, T. L., 184
Banks, Vera J., 29
Barber, J. M., 357
Barger, W. R., 194, 196, 342
Barnes, G., 325
Base, L. N., 82
Basham, C. W., 357
Basset, M. J., 311
Becker, R. F., 270, 282, 389
Bell, R. S., 154

Benjamin, L. R., 44
Bennett, A. H., 194, 196
Benson, L., 36
Benton, J. D., 98
Berberlich, R. S., 221
Berry, J. W., 238
Berry, W. L., 565
Binning, L. K., 270, 325, 357, 420
Bird, G., 184
Bissonnette, H. L., 389
Black, Evelyn T., 29
Black, Michael, 44
Bogardus, R. K., 194
Bohn, G. W., 65, 357
Bohnenblust, K. E., 436
Boles, Patrick P., 221
Boodley, J. W., 117
Borthwick, H. A., 44
Boswell, V. R., 282, 402
Bottoms, Gene, vi
Bourdette, V. R., 65
Bouwkamp, J. C., 238, 357, 468
Bowers, J. L., 449
Bowes, A., 584
Boyd, L. L., 196
Boys, F. E., 576
Brooks, W. M., 154, 565, 576
Broome, D. L., 296
Brown, J. D., 505
Brown, J. F., 256
Brown, R. T., 550
Bryan, B. B., 163
Buelow, F. H., 194
Burgess, E. E., 184
Burns, A. J., 296, 342

C

Campbell, G. M., 256
Candolle, A., 36
Cannon, J. M., 136, 377, 550
Cargill, B. F., 29
Carolus, R. L., 44

SUBJECT INDEX